DATE DUE

FEB 13 2012

Developments in Music Therapy Practice:
Case Study Perspectives

Developments in Music Therapy Practice:
Case Study Perspectives

Edited by
Anthony Meadows

Developments in Music Therapy Practice:
Case Study Perspectives

Copyright © 2011 by Barcelona Publishers

*All rights reserved. No part of this book
may be reproduced in any form whatsoever
without prior written permission from Barcelona Publishers.*

ISBN: 978-1-891278-75-4
EISBN: 978-1-891278-76-2

Distributed throughout the world by:
Barcelona Publishers
4 White Brook Road
Gilsum NH 03448
Tel: 603-357-0236 Fax: 603-357-2073
Website: www.barcelonapublishers.com
SAN 298-6299

Cover design: © 2011 Frank McShane
Image taken from an unknown source

*In honor of my wife Kim Sajet
and sons James and Joshua*

ACKNOWLEDGEMENTS

I am indebted to a number of people for making this book possible. To Ken Bruscia, for his years of mentorship, wisdom, teaching and intellectual challenges, I am extremely grateful. To Dr Denise Grocke and Dr Lisa Summer I am grateful for the many ways they have helped me grow as a music therapist.

To my colleagues, I am especially grateful to Dr Lillian Eyre, Dr Debra Burns, Dr Mark Moore, Mary Pat Lynch, Marylou Osterman and Katie Opher for their support, camerarderie and opportunities they have given me. At Immaculata University, I'm especially grateful for the support of Sr Ann Heath, Deans Janet Kane and Sr Elaine Glanz, and my colleagues in the department of music. I would also like to thank Heather Wright to her patience and expertise in formatting this book.

To my friends, I am especially grateful for the kindness, support and caring of Dr Bryan Muller, Greg Hunt, Sue DeBono and Naomi James.

To my family, I thank Kim Sajet, my parents Carol and Graeme Meadows, Nelleke and Peter Sajet, my sister Janette, and my extended family for the many ways they have supported, encouraged, cajoled, challenged and watched me grow and change.

I thank each of the authors for their dedication to their chapters, for the thoughtful ways they undertook the project, their wisdom, and for their willingness to work with me through the writing and editing process. I also thank their clients for allowing their lives and experiences to be shared with others.

CONTENTS

Acknowledgments   vi
Contributors   xiii

Developments in Music Therapy Practice: A Reading Guide   1
Anthony Meadows (USA)

Part I: Children

Chapter 1   30
When Life Begins Too Early: Music Therapy in a Newborn Intensive Care Unit
Monika Nöcker-Ribaupierre (Germany)

Chapter 2   49
Medical Music Therapy with Premature Infants: Family-Centered Services
Miriam Hillmer, Olivia Swedberg and Jayne M. Standley (USA)

Chapter 3   70
Growing Up in Music: A Journey through Early Childhood Music Development in Music Therapy
Elizabeth K. Schwartz (USA)

Chapter 4   86
Unraveling Hidden Resources of a Girl with Rett Syndrome
Cochavit Elefant (Israel and Norway)

Chapter 5 104
Exploring Issues of Control through Interactive, Improvised Music Making: Music Therapy Diagnostic Assessment and Short-Term Treatment with a Mother and Daughter in a Psychiatric Unit
Amelia Oldfield (United Kingdom)

Chapter 6 119
Establishing Communication with a Boy with Autism Utilizing Recorded Music
Barbara J. Crowe (USA)

Chapter 7 134
Addressing Core Features of Autism: Integrating Nordoff-Robbins Music Therapy within the Developmental, Individual-Difference, Relationship-Based (DIR®)/Floortime™ Model
John A. Carpente (USA)

Chapter 8 150
Music Therapy for Children in Hospital Care: A Stress and Coping Framework for Practice
Jane Edwards and Jeanette Kennelly (Republic of Ireland and Australia)

Chapter 9 166
Developing Speech with Music: A Neurodevelopmental Approach
A. Blythe LaGasse (USA)

Chapter 10 182
From Violent Rap to Lovely Blues: The Transformation of Aggressive Behavior through Vocal Music Therapy
Sylka Uhlig (The Netherlands)

Part II: Adolescents

Chapter 11 198
Punker, Bassgirl and Dingo-man: Perspectives on Adolescents' Music Therapy
Jaakko Erkkilä (Finland)

Chapter 12 215
Crossing the Divide: Exploring Identities within Communities Fragmented by Gang Violence
Sunelle Fouche and Kerryn Torrance (South Africa)

Chapter 13 230
Our Path to Peace: Songwriting-Based Brief Music Therapy with Bereaved Adolescents
Robert E. Krout (USA)

Chapter 14 248
Moving Out of Your Comfort Zone: Group Music Therapy with Adolescents who have Misused Drugs
Katrina McFerran (Australia)

Chapter 15 268
Just Don't Do It: A Group's Micro Journey into Music and Life
Mercédès Pavlicevic (United Kingdom and South Africa)

Part III: Adults

Chapter 16 280
Facilitating Neurological Reorganization through Music Therapy: A Case of Modified Melodic Intonation Therapy in the Treatment of a Person with Aphasia
Felicity Baker (Australia)

Chapter 17   297
The Case of Paula: Music Psychotherapy with a Musician
Joanne Loewy and Stephan Quentzel (USA)

Chapter 18   313
From the Highest Height to the Lowest Depth: Music Therapy with a Paraplegic Soldier
Chava Sekeles (Israel)

Chapter 19   334
Music Therapy and Addiction: Addressing Essential Components of the Recovery Process
Jim Borling (USA)

Chapter 20   350
Making my Body a Safe Place to Stay: A Psychotherapeutically Oriented Approach to Vibroacoustic Therapy in Drug Rehabilitation
Marko Punkanen and Esa Ala-Ruona (Finland)

Chapter 21   368
A Flash of the Obvious: Music Therapy and Trauma
Julie Sutton (UK Northern Ireland)

Chapter 22   385
From Ego Disintegration to Recovery of Self: The Contribution of Lacan's Theories in Understanding the Role of Music Therapy in the Treatment of a Woman with Psychosis
Lillian Eyre (USA)

Chapter 23 400
Singing in the Recovery Model with a Chronic Mentally Ill Offender
Vaughn Kaser (USA)

Chapter 24 416
The Doors and Windows of the Dressing Room:
Culture-Centered Music Therapy in a Mental Health Setting
Brynjulf Stige (Norway)

Chapter 25 434
Music Is About Feelings: Music Therapy with a Young
Man Suffering From Anorexia Nervosa
Gro Trondalen (Norway)

Chapter 26 453
"Taking a Close Look": Emotional Awareness as a Core
Principle in the Music Therapy Treatment of a Patient with
an Anxious-Avoidant Personality Disorder
Ulrike Haase and Axel Reinhardt (Germany)

Chapter 27 470
The Use of Elemental Music Alignment in the Journey from
Singer to Healer/Therapist
Frank Bosco (USA)

Chapter 28 486
Music Therapy and Depression: Uncovering Resources in Music
and Imagery
Lisa Summer (USA)

Chapter 29   501
Bringing Light into Darkness: Guided Imagery and Music, Bereavement, Loss and Working Through Trauma
Leslie Bunt (United Kingdom)

Chapter 30   518
The Meta-Musical Experiences of a Professional String Quartet in Music-Centered Psychotherapy
Heidi Ahonen and Colin Andrew Lee (Canada)

Part IV: Older Adults and End of Life

Chapter 31   542
Music Therapy and Dementia: A Cognitive-Behavioral Approach
Melissa Mercadal-Brotons (Spain)

Chapter 32   556
Music as Life and Lifeguard: Music Therapy for an Older Adult with Depression
Ineke van Hest-de Witte, Jack Verburgt and Henk Smeijsters (The Netherlands)

Chapter 33   569
Home is Where the Heart Is
Monique van Bruggen-Rufi and Annemiek Vink (The Netherlands)

Chapter 34   582
Songs of Faith in End of Life Care
Russell Hilliard and Jenna Justice (USA)

CONTRIBUTORS

Heidi Ahonen (Canada) Ph.D., AMT, psychotherapist and group analyst, is a Professor of Music Therapy at Wilfrid Laurier University and the Director of the Manfred and Penny Conrad Institute for Music Therapy Research. She has extensive clinical and supervisory experience and has published widely on various therapeutic methodologies and qualitative research. Heidi has trained music therapists and psychotherapists and conducted workshops for healthcare professionals since 1991. As a clinician, Heidi practices music psychotherapy, having developed group analytic music therapy methods, a group analytic music therapy supervision model, integrated art and music therapy methods and music listening, imagination and improvisation methods. She specializes in adult clients with childhood traumas, PTSD, burn-out, vicarious trauma and depression.

Esa Ala-Ruona (Finland) Ph.D., is a music therapist, psychotherapist and university researcher working at the Music Therapy Clinic for Research and Training at the Finnish Centre of Excellence in Interdisciplinary Music Research, University of Jyväskylä. He has been a clinician for over 20 years, working with people with a wide variety of psychiatric and neurological problems. His primary interest is in studying clinical processes in music psychotherapy, and the effects of active music therapy on post-stroke recovery. Esa is a past Chair of the Finnish Society for Music Therapy, and past Chair of the Association of Professional Music Therapists in Finland. He is Editor-in-Chief of the *Finnish Journal of Music Therapy*, and co-editor of a number of publications.

Felicity Baker (Australia) Ph.D., RMT, is Program Convenor for the Master of Music Therapy program and Director of Research at the School of Music, The University of Queensland, Australia. She is internationally recognized for her research and clinical expertise in the areas of neurorehabilitation and therapeutic songwriting. She has an extensive list of publications in music therapy and interdisciplinary journals. She is editor-in-chief of *The Australian Journal of Music Therapy* and is a regular reviewer of more than ten interdisciplinary journals. In 2008, she was awarded the prestigious Foundation Research Excellence Award and in 2009 a National University Teaching Award. In September 2011, Felicity will take up the role of President for the Australian Music Therapy Association.

Jim Borling (USA) MM, MT-BC, FAMI, is Director of Graduate and Undergraduate Music Therapy Studies at Radford University. He has over 30 years of clinical experience, working with adult and adolescent addiction, adolescent emotional disorders, men's issues, and adults/adolescents in private practice. In addition to traditional group music therapy process, Jim's private practice makes use of the Bonny Method of Guided Imagery and Music (GIM). Jim is widely published and has been professionally active with the American Music Therapy Association and the Certification Board for Music Therapists throughout his professional career. His clinical work has taken him to Korea, Germany, and Mexico as both teacher and trainer of GIM.

Frank Bosco (USA) MA, MT-BC, LCAT, LMT, RPP, SEP, is the founder/director of Sound Health Studio, a body/mind/music therapy center in New York City. He has been in private practice since 1980, integrating a wide range of somatic and psychotherapy practices with a focus on the use of music in trauma resolution. Frank is an adjunct faculty member at New York University, where he has led music therapy group process classes for over 20 years as well as offering an elective course called "Energy Concepts in Music Therapy." He continues to write and present his work, contributing chapters to several books.

Leslie Bunt (United Kingdom) LGSM (MT), Ph.D., FAMI, MBE, is Professor in Music Therapy at the University of the West of England, Bristol, UK. He trained in music therapy with Juliette Alvin, in the Bonny Method of GIM with Kenneth Bruscia and has over 30 years of experience working with children and adults with wide-ranging healthcare needs, currently specializing in cancer care. As a BMGIM Primary Trainer Leslie works with groups in the UK, Italy and Ireland. He is published widely. In 1991 he founded the community-based charity MusicSpace and in 2009 was awarded an MBE in the Queen's Birthday Honors for his services to music therapy. Leslie is a Fellow of the Royal Society of Arts and a freelance conductor.

John A. Carpente (USA) Ph.D., LCAT, MT-BC, NRMT, Assistant Professor of Music Therapy at Molloy College, is the Founder and Director of The Rebecca Center for Music Therapy. He is also the Founding Clinical Director of the Center for Autism and Child Development at Molloy College, and the creator of the *Individual Music-Centered Assessment Profile for Neurodevelopmental Disorders of Relating and Communicating*. John has over 15 years of clinical and supervisory experience. His primary focus is on the use of clinical improvisation within a relationship-based developmental framework with children who have neurodevelopmental disorders.

Barbara J. Crowe (USA) MMT, MT-BC, has been Director of Music Therapy at Arizona State University since 1981. She is the author *Music and Soulmaking: Toward a New Theory of Music Therapy, Music Therapy for Children, Adolescents, and Adults with Mental Disorders,* and *Group Rhythm and Drumming with Older Adults,* along with other publications. She has completed over 90 conference presentations world-wide on various topics in music therapy. She is a past-president of the National Association for Music Therapy and served as Chair of the Unification Education and Clinical Training Committee. She is an Honorary Life Member of AMTA.

Jane Edwards (Republic of Ireland) Ph.D., PMT, is Course Director for the Main Music Therapy at the University of Limerick, Ireland. She is an experienced clinician with expertise in mental health, hospitalized children and their families, and in the use of music to promote parent-infant bonding. Jane is widely published in music therapy and serves on the editorial board of the *Arts in Psychotherapy* and *Voices* (www.voices.no). She is the inaugural President of the International Association for Music and Medicine.

Cochavit Elefant (Norway and Israel) Ph.D., is Associate Professor of Music Therapy at the Grieg Academy, University of Bergen, and a researcher at GAMUT (Grieg Academy Music Therapy Research Centre) in Bergen, Norway. She has worked for almost 30 years as a music therapist with children in the USA and Israel. She is the co-founder of the Israeli National Rett Syndrome Assessment and Evaluation team, in which she still practices. She also supervises music therapists and studies Lacanian psychoanalysis in Israel. She has published several articles, book chapters and co-authored *Where Music Helps*. She serves as an Associate Editor for the *Nordic Journal of Music Therapy*.

Jaakko Erkkilä (Finland) Ph.D., music therapist and psychotherapist, is Director of Graduate Music Therapy at the University of Jyväskylä, Finland, and Head of Music Therapy Clinical Training at Eino Roiha Institute, Jyväskylä, Finland. He has over 20 years of clinical experience, working with adolescents and adults with psychiatric disorders, children with neurological disorders and people with developmental disorders. His primary focus is music psychotherapy in a psychiatric setting, with a particular emphasis on clinical improvisation. Jaakko is a member of the Finnish Centre of Excellence in Interdisciplinary Music Research, where he directs music therapy research. He serves on the editorial boards of *Nordic Journal of Music Therapy*, *Musiikkiterapia* (Finnish music therapy journal), and is a founding member of Music and Medicine. He has published several book chapters and journal articles.

Lillian Eyre (USA) Ph.D., MT-BC, MTA, LPC, is Assistant Professor of Music at Immaculata University. She has worked extensively in psychiatry and community mental health, and with adults in private practice. Her research interests include applications of narrative therapy practices to music therapy and clinical improvisation. She serves on the editorial review boards of the *Canadian Journal of Music Therapy* and *The Arts in Psychotherapy*, and is a member of the Professional Supervision Training Committee for the Canadian Music Therapy Association.

Sunelle Fouché (South Africa) MA, is a graduate of the *University of Pretoria*'s Music Therapy Masters Program. In 2002 she co-founded (with Kerryn Torrance) the *Music Therapy Community Clinic,* a non-profit organization with the aim of providing music therapy services to marginalized communities in Cape Town. Her primary focus is music therapy with children who have been traumatized by ongoing gang violence and children and adults dealing with the psycho-social effects of HIV/AIDS. She currently serves as Executive Director of the *Music Therapy Community Clinic*.

Ulrike Haase (Germany) MSc (Dipl.-Phys.), is Director of the Academy for Applied Music Therapy, Crossen, Germany where she also works as a music therapy lecturer and supervisor. A physicist by training, she conducted polymer research before entering music therapy. She has over 15 years of experience in music therapy training, research and education. Her primary foci are conceptual and methodological questions regarding the use of music therapy and music education in clinical and social settings. She has authored numerous books, book chapters, and journal articles on music therapy. She is also a concert musician and plays the organ, piano and cembalo.

Russell Hilliard (USA) Ph.D., LCSW, LCAT, MT-BC, is the National Director of Supportive Care at Seasons Hospice and Palliative Care in Chicago, and the Founder of the Centers for Music Therapy in End of Life Care. His research, advocacy, and consultation have resulted in the development of first-time music therapy programs in hospices throughout the nation, thereby creating many new music therapy positions. He is the author of the text, *Hospice and Palliative Care Music Therapy: A Guide to Program Development and Clinical Care*, and his research has been published in a wide variety of scholarly journals. Dr. Hilliard has provided keynote addresses for healthcare conferences and is a frequent presenter at professional conferences worldwide.

Miriam Hillmer (USA) MME, MT-BC, NICU-MT, is the Internship Director and Coordinator of the Medical Music Therapy program at Tallahassee Memorial HealthCare. She regularly assists in the training of clinicians worldwide in researched NICU music therapy techniques through the National Institute for Infant and Child Medical Music Therapy. Her primary clinical and research focus is medical music therapy, including procedural support, NICU, and current perceptions of music therapy in the hospital setting.

Jenna Justice (USA) MM, HPMT, MT-BC, is the Agency Director for Addus Healthcare, Inc. in Montana. She was formerly Director of Supportive Care for Seasons Hospice and Palliative Care in Chicago, IL overseeing social workers, bereavement counselors, music therapists, chaplains, and volunteers. Additionally, she served as the Music Therapy Manager at Hospice of Palm Beach County and the Music Therapy Coordinator at Big Bend Hospice in Tallahassee, Florida. She has a wide range of experience providing presentations and clinical services, and serves as a clinical supervisor for music therapists nationwide.

Vaughn Kaser (USA) MCAT, MT-BC, has over 25 years clinical experience in Forensic Mental Health, with an emphasis on clinical improvisation and music therapy performance groups. He has also published in these areas. Vaughn is a former AMTA Western Region Internship Director and recipient of the WRAMTA Professional Practice Award (2005). He remains an active musician, performing professionally as a percussionist.

Jeanette Kennelly (Australia) BMusEd, PGDipMT, is currently completing her PhD in the School of Music, University of Queensland, Australia. Her contribution to this book took place during her time as Senior Music Therapist at the Royal Children's Hospital, Queensland. Jeanette has over 15 years of clinical experience, working mainly with children with burns, cancer and head injuries. She has also published a number of journal articles and book chapters which focus on these pediatric areas. Jeanette is currently a member of the Ethics Committee and Education Committee of the Australian Music Therapy Association.

Robert E. Krout (USA) Ed.D., MT-BC, is Professor and Director of Music Therapy in the Meadows School of the Arts at Southern Methodist University (SMU) in Dallas, Texas. Prior to joining SMU in 2004, Robert was Director of Music Therapy at Massey University in Wellington, New Zealand; Music Therapy Manager and AMTA Internship Director at Hospice of Palm Beach County, Florida; and Associate Professor at the State University of New York at New Paltz. In 2005, he received the Research and Publication Award of the American Music Therapy Association, and was named the SMU Meadows School of the Arts Distinguished Teaching Professor for 2010-2011. He has published and presented widely, and remains actively involved in a number of music therapy clinical, educational, and research areas. Robert was recently appointed as an Honorary Professor in the School of Music at The University of Queensland, Australia.

A. Blythe LaGasse (USA) Ph.D., MT-BC, NMT, is Assistant Professor of Music Therapy at Colorado State University where she teaches both undergraduate and graduate courses, and is Director of Music Therapy Clinical Practicum. Her clinical background includes work with persons with autism and developmental disabilities, with an emphasis on speech and language communication. She has contributed to several music therapy texts including *An Introduction to Music Therapy: Theory and Practice* (3rd ed.) and *Introduction to Approaches in Music Therapy* (2nd ed.). She serves as president-elect for the Midwestern Region of the American Music Therapy Association and on the Midwestern Region Assembly of Delegates.

Colin Andrew Lee (Canada) Ph.D., NRMT, is Director of Music Therapy at Wilfrid Laurier University, Canada. Following piano studies at the Nordwestdeutsche Musikakademie, Germany, he earned a Postgraduate Diploma in music therapy from the Nordoff-Robbins Music Therapy Center, London, England. He has extensive clinical and supervisory experience and has specialized in the areas of autism, developmental delay, HIV/AIDS and palliative care. His research has focused on the musicological potential for music therapy, looking at links between the micro/musical analysis of improvization and its potential understanding for therapeutic outcome. Colin's publications include *Music at the Edge: The Music Therapy Experiences of a Musician with AIDS* (1996), *The Architecture of Aesthetic Music Therapy* (2005) and *Improvising in Styles: A Workbook for Music Therapists, Educators and Musicians* (Lee & Houde, 2010).

Joanne Loewy (USA) DA, LCAT, MT-BC, is the Director of the Louis Armstrong Center for Music and Medicine. She is the co-Editor in Chief of the journal *Music and Medicine* and serves on several music and medicine editorial boards including the *Cochran Palliative Care Review* and the *Journal for Complementary and Alternative Medicine*. Dr. Loewy has edited several books, including *Music Therapy in Pediatric Pain*, *Music Therapy in the NICU,* and *Integrative Music Therapy: Music, the Breath and Health.* Joanne is a Founding Member of the International Association for Music and Medicine and guest lectures at the Albert Einstein College of Medicine, Molloy College and in the Hahnemann Creative Arts Therapy graduate music therapy program. She recently received the American Music Therapy Association's Outstanding Clinical Practice Award and the Society for the Arts in Healthcare team leadership and education award.

Katrina McFerran (Australia) Ph.D., RMT, is senior lecturer in music therapy at The University of Melbourne, Australia. She has worked with adolescents in a range of institutional and community settings as they face challenges related to loss and grief, eating disorders, learning and intellectual disabilities, chronic and terminal illness. She has published extensively on this topic in music therapy and interdisciplinary forums, including her first book *Adolescents, Music and Music Therapy: Methods and Techniques for Clinicians, Educators and Students*. Katrina continues to conduct mixed methods research investigations of music therapy with young people using contemporary frameworks such as community music therapy and other collaborative approaches.

Anthony Meadows (USA), Ph.D., MT-BC, FAMI, LPC, is Director of Music Therapy and Chair of the Graduate Music Therapy Program at Immaculata University. He has over 20 years of clinical experience, working with multiply disabled children, adults with cancer, and adults in private practice. His primary focus is music and imagery, with an emphasis on BMGIM. Anthony has edited two volumes of the *Qualitative Inquires in Music Therapy* series. He is Editor of *Music Therapy Perspectives*, and Chair of the Research Committee for the Mid-Atlantic Region of the American Music Therapy Association. He has published a number of book chapters and journal articles.

Melissa Mercadal-Brotons, Ph.D. MT-BC, is Director of the Interuniversity Music Therapy Masters Program (Universitat Pompeu Fabra-Universitat Ramon Llull) in Barcelona, Spain, and Professor of ESMuC (Escola Superior de Música de Barcelona). She has over 20 years of clinical experience, working with older adults with Alzheimer's disease and other types of dementia. Melissa has published extensively and is co-author of the book *Manual de Musicoterapia en Geriatría y Demencias: Teoría y Práctica* [Manual of Music Therapy in Gerontology and Dementias: Theory and Practice (2008)], and *Musicoterapia en Medicina: Aplicaciones Prácticas* [Music Therapy in Medicine: Practical Applications (2010)]. Melissa also serves on the editorial review board of the *Journal of Music Therapy*.

Monika Nöcker-Ribaupierre (Germany) Dr.sc.mus., has over 30 years of clinical experience, working in NICU, and with developmentally delayed and multiply disabled children. Currently, her primary focus is auditory stimulation after premature birth. Prior to this, Monika was chair of the postgraduate music therapy training program at Freies Musikzentrum Munich e.V. and Vice President of the European Music Therapy Confederation. She is Vice-President of the International Society of Music in Medicine and serves on the scientific board of "Musiktherapeutische Umschau," Bundesverband, "das frühgeborene Kind" e.V. and the Editorial Board of the interdisciplinary journal *Music and Medicine*. She has published a number of books, book chapters and articles.

Amelia Oldfield (United Kingdom) PhD, MPhil, LGSM(mt), has worked as a music therapist for over thirty years. She currently works part-time at a child development center and at a unit for child and family psychiatry. Since 1994, she has also been a part-time lecturer on the MA music therapy training course at Anglia Ruskin University, which she helped to create. She has completed four music therapy research investigations in the areas of learning disabilities, family work, children with autism and diagnostic music therapy. She has written two books on Interactive Music Therapy and co-edited a book on music therapy with families. She has published many book chapters and journal articles, and has produced six music therapy training videos.

Mercedes Pavlicevic (United Kingdom and South Africa) Ph.D. is Director of Research at Nordoff Robbins UK, and Associate Professor at the University of Pretoria in South Africa. She is a Nordoff Robbins trained music therapist, and completed her PhD with Colwyn Trevarthen at the University of Edinburgh in the early 1990s. Although now based in London, she continues to mentor music therapy training in South Africa and is also connected to the Music Therapy Community Clinic in Cape Town. Her practice interests and experience focus on community music therapy and community arts work. She has authored, co-authored and edited numerous books and papers on music therapy.

Marko Punkanen (Finland) M.Phil, is a social educator, music therapist, dance/movement therapist and trauma psychotherapist working in private practice in Lahti, Finland. He works mainly with children, adolescents and young adults with traumatic backgrounds and psychiatric problems. His special interest is in how a client's traumatic background affects and is related to addictive behaviour. Currently, Marko also works as a researcher at the Finnish Centre of Excellence in Interdisciplinary Music Research, University of Jyväskylä.

Stephan Quentzel (USA) MD, is board certified in psychiatry, family medicine and holistic medicine to support his roles as the Medical Director of the Louis Armstrong Center for Music and Medicine and Medical Director of Psychiatry for the Institute for Urban Family Health, both in New York City. He is a founding member of the International Association for Music and Medicine. Dr. Quentzel helps residents and faculty members in family practice, internal medicine, OB-GYN, pain medicine and palliative care, to better integrate psychiatry in their medical settings. Dr. Quentzel is also an assistant professor at the Albert Einstein College of Medicine and a senior clinician at the Continuum Center for Health and Healing.

Axel Reinhardt (Germany) MA (Dipl.Mus.), is a research associate and music therapist at the Department of Psychiatry and Psychotherapy at University Hospital, Dresden, Germany. He is also a music therapy lecturer and supervisor at the Academy for Applied Music Therapy, Crossen, Germany. Axel has over 30 years of clinical and supervisory experience in music therapy, working with adults with mental disorders. His primary focus is on the use of active and regulatory group music therapy in individual and group settings for patients with affective, personality, and psychosomatic disorders. He has authored numerous book chapters and journal articles in music therapy.

Elizabeth K. Schwartz MA, LCAT, MT-BC, is the senior music therapist at Alternatives for Children in Suffolk County, New York where she specializes in Early Intervention and preschool treatment. She is also an adjunct instructor in Music Therapy at Molloy College. Beth presents at national and regional conferences and is the author of *Music, Therapy, and Early Childhood: A Developmental Approach* and a contributing author for the AMTA publication *Effective Clinical Practice in Music Therapy: Early Childhood and School Age Educational Settings.* She was Chair of the Government Relations Committee for the Mid-Atlantic Region of the American Music Therapy Association and has been active in legislative and regulatory issues affecting Music Therapy. Beth is currently an extended member of the New York State Mental Health Practitioners Board which oversees licensure of Creative Arts Therapists, and served on the AMTA Task Force on Advanced Competencies.

Chava Sekeles (Israel) Ph.D., music therapist and certified supervisor, originated and managed the music therapy program at the David Yellin Academic College, and served as its director until her retirement (1980-2002). She is a trained musician, occupational therapist, and music therapist. As a therapist, she is interested in music therapy for patients affected by neuro-psychiatric problems and as a researcher, in the healing rituals of traditional societies. In her clinic in Nataf, Chava practices therapy and teaches music using the Developmental-Integrative approach. In 1981, Chava received the Arthur Rubinstein award for the first music therapy initiative in the state of Israel, and in 2010 the EMTC award for 15 years of volunteer contributions as the Israeli representative. She is author of numerous articles and two books: *Music: Motion and Emotion* (1996) and *Music Therapy: Death and Grief* (2007).

Henk Smeijsters (The Netherlands) Ph.D. is Professor of Arts Therapies, and Director of KenVaK, a Dutch Research Centre for the Arts Therapies. KenVaK is a joint venture of the Universities of Applied Sciences Zuyd, Utrecht, ArtEZ and Stenden. He is Head of Studies of the Master of Arts Therapies at Zuyd University and supervisor of Ph.D. studies at KenVaK. His primary focus is research and theory development in music therapy and other arts therapies. In The Netherlands, he has a leading position in the development of practice-based research in the field of mental health. He has published articles in international journals and is the author of many books that have been published in The Netherlands, Germany, USA and Japan.

Brynjulf Stige (Norway) Ph.D., Music Therapist, is Professor in Music Therapy, University of Bergen, and Head of Research in GAMUT – The Grieg Academy Music Therapy Research Centre, Uni Health, Norway. Stige has worked with children, adolescents, adults, and older adults in a number of different settings, including mental health care and community music therapy practices. He has researched and written on topics such as music therapy improvization, music therapy theory, and community music therapy. Stige has published a number of articles and books, including *Culture-Centered Music Therapy* (2002) and *Where Music*

Helps (with Ansdell, Elefant and Pavlicevic) (2010). He is founding co-editor (with Carolyn Kenny) of Voices: A World Forum for Music Therapy.

Jayne M. Standley (USA) Ph.D., MT-BC, is a Robert O. Lawton Distinguished Professor at Florida State University. Her research emphases are medical music therapy and music therapy in the Neonatal Intensive Care Unit. Standley is Director of the National Institute for Infant and Child Medical Music Therapy, and she is widely published, including seven books. She was editor of the *Journal of Music Therapy,* published by the American Music Therapy Association, and received a Lifetime Service Award for her editorial work.

Lisa Summer (USA) Ph.D., LMHC, MT-BC, FAMI, is Professor and Director of Music Therapy at Anna Maria College. Her clinical specialty is using music and imagery with adults with anxiety, mood, and addiction disorders. She conducts GIM trainings and seminars throughout the world, including Korea, China, Spain, Sweden, Denmark, Norway, Germany, Japan, Taiwan, and Canada. Lisa edited Helen Bonny's collected works – *Music and Consciousness,* published a critique of spurious music healing techniques – *Music: The New Age Elixir,* and chronicled her use of music and imagery in many book chapters and articles. She has served on the American Music Therapy Association Ethics Review Board and the National Assembly of Delegates. She has received two regional AMTA awards for Service and for Outstanding Research Achievements.

Julie Sutton (UK Northern Ireland) Ph.D., MPhil, BMus (hons), PGCE, DipMT (NR), is a Head Music Therapist employed by both the UK NHS and Nordoff-Robbins Centre, and with a private clinical and research supervision practice. She works at the Centre for Psychotherapy Belfast, is an executive member of the UK BAMT, a past Vice President of the EMTC, and Chair of the UK Training and Education Committee. She has worked for over 25 years with a wide range of children and adults, with post-doctoral research specializations (improvization, trauma, and silence), and is an examiner and guest lecturer on a number of training programs. Her stance is musical and psychoanalytic. She has published nationally and internationally, and is Editor-in-Chief of the *British Journal of Music Therapy.*

Olivia Swedberg (USA) MME, MT-BC, NICU-MT, is a doctoral student in music therapy at Florida State University. She has clinical experience with children with special needs, teens and adults with mental illness, and older adults with dementia. She previously coordinated the Tallahassee Memorial HealthCare/Florida State University music therapy partnership. Olivia is a Fellow of the National Institute for Infant and Child Medical Music Therapy. Her primary research focus is the use of music therapy with individuals who have Parkinson's disease. Since 2007, she has served as the coordinator of the Florida State Task Force for Government Relations for the American Music Therapy Association.

Kerryn Torrance (South Africa) MA, is a graduate of the *University of Pretoria*'s Music Therapy Masters Program. In 2002 she co-founded (with Sunelle Fouché) the *Music Therapy Community Clinic,* a Non-Profit organization with the aim of providing music therapy services to marginalized communities in Cape Town. Her primary focus is music therapy with children who have been traumatized by gang violence and children and adults dealing with the psycho-social effects of HIV/AIDS. She currently serves as Project Director for the *Music Therapy Community Clinic.*

Gro Trondalen (Norway) Ph.D., FAMI, Music Therapist, is Associate Professor in Music Therapy and Head of the Centre for Music and Health at the Norwegian Academy of Music in Oslo, Norway. She is an experienced clinician in the field of child welfare and adult mental health, and maintains a private practice in GIM. Her research focus has been on clinical work linked to philosophical and theoretical perspectives. Trondalen has published a number of articles and book chapters in music therapy, including the edited book *Musikk og helse [Music and Health]* (2008) with Even Ruud. Trondalen presents her work frequently at international conferences. She is a member of the Advisory Editorial Board of the *Nordic Journal of Music Therapy* and serves on the Board at the Doctoral Program in Music Therapy at Aalborg University, Denmark.

Sylka Uhlig (The Netherlands) MA, RMTh, is a doctoral student at Aalborg University (Denmark), and teaches music therapy methods and voice at HAN University for Professional Education, Nijmegen. She has practiced music therapy since 1991 in Europe and the USA in psychiatric hospitals, neurological rehabilitation, special education, and in private practice. She has specialized her practice in vocal music therapy, offering workshops, presentations and publications in this area. She is co-editor of the forthcoming book *Voicework in Music Therapy* and published *Authentic Voices, Authentic Singing: A Multicultural Approach to Vocal Music Therapy* (1996).

Monique van Bruggen-Rufi (The Netherlands) MAT, NMT, is a doctoral candidate at Leiden University, The Netherlands, and works as a music therapist with patients who suffer from Huntington's Disease, Korsakov Syndrome, psychiatric disorders and dementia. She also works as a music therapy teacher at the ArtEZ School of Music in Enschede. Monique recently finished her Master of Arts Therapies degree with Henk Smeijsters at Heerlen University.

Ineke van Hest-de Witte (The Netherlands) BMTh, RMTh, is a music therapist at Pro Persona (former Gelderse Roos), a music therapy clinic she founded 35 years ago. She supervises music therapy students from music therapy training programs at several Universities of Applied Sciences in The Netherlands. For several years she acted as a member of the Board of the Dutch Association for Creative Therapy. She was co-author of several publications about music therapy in psychiatric treatment for the elderly.

Jack Verburgt (The Netherlands) MA, BMTh, SRMTh, is a pedagogue and senior music therapist at Pro Persona (former Gelderse Roos), specializing in practice with adults who have personality disorders. He is also a lecturer in music therapy at ArtEZ University of Applied Sciences. Jack has published ten articles and was co-author of chapters in several books on refugees, system therapy and the method of music therapy.

Annemiek Vink (The Netherlands) MSc, is a doctoral candidate at Groningen University, and works as a music therapy educator in the Master of Arts Therapies program at the ArtEZ School of Music in Enschede. Additionally, she works as a researcher in dementia care for KenVaK, a research centre for the art therapies. She is a board member of the Dutch Foundation for Music Therapy (Stichting Muziektherapie).

DEVELOPMENTS IN MUSIC THERAPY PRACTICE: A READING GUIDE

Anthony Meadows

INTRODUCTION

There are many ways to understand music therapy practice. One way is to focus on the methods used (e.g., music listening), the clients served (e.g., recovering addicts), and the goals addressed (e.g., developing speech and language). *Developments in Music Therapy Practice* takes these dimensions as a starting point. Throughout these chapters are examples of improvisational (therapist and/or client improvise music), recreative (therapist and client sing songs), receptive (therapist and client listen to music), compositional (therapist and client write music) and multi-arts (client draws while listening to music with therapist) interventions (Bruscia, 1998). These interventions can be seen across age and client groups (children in hospitals; adults in drug rehabilitation; adults in hospice), and according to diverse therapeutic goals (skills development; behavior change; insight; emotional expression and release). As such, it is possible to understand ways in which these music therapists practice across the life span, from birth through death. It is also possible to understand how practices in one area (e.g., music listening) change by age, goal and setting. For example, music listening experiences with premature infants (see Chapter 1: Nöcker-Ribaupierre and Chapter 2: Hillmer, Swedberg and Standley) are used quite differently from those with adolescents (see Chapter 14: McFerran) and adults (see Chapter 20: Punkanen and Ala-Ruona, Chapter 21: Sutton, Chapter 22: Eyre, Chapter 27 Bosco, Chapter 28: Summer, Chapter 29: Bunt, Chapter 32: van Hest-de Witte, Verburgt and Smeijsters). Seeing these changes in practice according to client age also helps us to understand the importance of context. The time (client's age, stage of therapy), place (hospital, school, psychiatric facility, community, nursing home), therapeutic framework of the setting (educational, rehabilitation, recovery, psychoanalytic) and theoretical orientation of the therapist (neuro-developmental, behavioral, humanistic, psychodynamic) all converge into a guiding framework that helps us to understand the complexities of clinical practice. Such convergence helps us to see as the therapist sees, feel as the therapist feels, and respond with the therapist, living in their world with them.

This chapter begins with an overview of music therapy practices by population (children, adolescents and adults), goals and therapist orientation. In the latter part of the chapter, various models of practice are identified and discussed in terms of the Wilber Four-Quadrant Model (Wilber, 1995; 2000), which provides a framework through which to understand clinical practice.

Practices with Children

In this volume, practices with children tend to focus on developmental issues, in which the therapist addresses deficits that prevent his/her client(s) from reaching developmental milestones. In some cases, development is understood from a musical perspective (Schwartz), from others a neuro-developmental perspective (LaGasse), while others focus on skill development and behavior change within a broader developmental context (Carpente, Elefant, Uhlig). While all of these therapists address, to varying degrees, the children's emotional world, some place a particular emphasis on this. Elefant, Oldfield, Carpente, Crowe, Edwards and Kennelly, Schwartz, and Uhlig see the child's emotional world as central to overcoming limitations in development and adaptation. Further, Nöcker-Ribaupierre, Hillmer, Swedberg and Standley, Oldfield and Edwards and Kennelly all work with a parent-child dyad, addressing the parent's and child's therapeutic needs simultaneously. Table 1 provides a summary of these practices.

Table 1. Music Therapy Practices with Children

Author	Client(s)	Approach to Music Therapy	Type(s) of Experiences	Theoretical Foundation(s)
Nöcker-Ribaupierre	Premature infants and their parents	Auditive Stimulation	Receptive	Psychotherapeutic (Bowlby, 1969; Stern, 1985; Winnicott, 1965)

Hillmer, Swedberg & Standley	Premature infants and their parents	Medical Music Therapy	Receptive	Family centered (Henneman & Cardin, 2002; Standley, 2003)
Schwartz	Pre-school age children with developmental delays	Five level developmental continuum	Recreative; improvisational; movement	Developmental (Schwartz, 2008; Briggs, 1991; Kegan, 1982)
Elefant	Child with Rett Syndrome		Improvisational; recreative	Developmental (Stern 2000; Malloch & Trevarthen, 2009)
Oldfield	Child with psychiatric diagnoses	Interactive Music Therapy	Improvisational; recreative;	Developmental (Oldfield, 2006)
Crowe	Child with autism	Eclectic	Receptive; Recreative; improvisational; movement	Heimlich, 1980; Behavioral Music Therapy
Carpente	Child with autism	Nordoff-Robbins and DIR/Floortime	Improvisational; recreative	Developmental (Nordoff & Robbins, 2007; Greenspan & Weider, 2006)
Edwards & Kennelly	Child in hospital		Recreative; creative; improvisational	Stress and coping (Lazarus & Folkman, 1984)
LaGasse	Child with Down Syndrome	Neurologic Music Therapy	Recreative	Neurodevelopmental (Thaut, 2005)
Uhlig	Child with developmental delay	Vocal Music Therapy	Improvisation; recreative	Neurodevelopmental (Uhlig, 2006; Schneck & Berger, 2006)

Practices with Adolescents

Practices with adolescents (Table 2) tend to focus on addressing limitations in these clients' functional independence and emotional well-being: for example, attending school, and living in the community. As such, therapy tends to focus on working through problems, verbal processing, and insight. In focusing on these goals, therapists address personality structure (Erkkilä), violence (Fouche and Torrance, Pavlicevic), the impact of addiction (McFerran) and grief and loss (Krout). Of particular interest is the clinical context of this work. While Erkkilä worked in an inpatient psychiatric facility, Fouche and Torrance, Krout, McFerran and Pavlicevic all worked in community settings. Further, while all addressed skill development and behavior change, the central focus of work was the adolescent's emotional world, contextualized within the clinical setting, and understood from a variety of theoretical perspectives – psychodynamic, humanistic, behavioral and cognitive.

Table 2. Music Therapy Practices with Adolescents

Author	Clients	Approach to Music Therapy	Types of Experiences	Foundations
Erkkilä	Inpatient Psychiatry	Four-phase process	Recreative; creative	Eclectic (Erkkilä, 2004)
Fouche & Torrance	Vulnerable youth in the community	Eclectic	Improvisational; creative	Community Music Therapy (Stige, 2002; Ansdell, 2002)
Krout	Grieving Adolescents	Brief	Creative	Brief Therapy (Krout, 2005; 2006)
McFerran	Recovering addicts	Eclectic	Creative; Recreative; improvisational	Humanism (Maslow, 1968)
Pavlicevic	Vulnerable youth in the community	Nordoff-Robbins Music Therapy	Creative	Community Music Therapy (Pavlicevic & Ansdell, 2004)

Practices with Adults

Practices with adults have been divided into several sub-sections: medical (including rehabilitation), addictions, psychiatry and well adults. Each of these are introduced separately, along with an accompanying table.

Medical Settings

Table 3 provides an overview of work in medical settings. Baker's discussion of rehabilitation after brain injury is primarily focused on skill development, whereas Loewy and Quentzel and Sekeles focus primarily on addressing their clients' emotional struggles within the context of their medical problems. Further, while Baker's adaptation of Melodic Intonation Therapy, consistent with a rehabilitation focus, has a behavioral flavor, Loewy and Quentzel and Sekeles take bio-psycho-social and psychoanalytic perspectives, suggesting that music therapy can be practiced from quite diverse perspectives in medical settings.

Table 3. Music Therapy Practices with Adults in a Medical Setting

Author	Client	Approach to Music Therapy	Types of Experiences	Foundations
Baker	Adult with a brain injury	Modified Melodic Intonation Therapy	Recreative	Neuroplasticity (Patel, 2008); Melodic Intonation Therapy (Sparks & Deck, 1986)
Loewy & Quentzel	Adult Musician with medical problems	Eclectic	Recreative; improvisational	Bio-psycho-social (Quentzel & Loewy, 2010)
Sekeles	Traumatized Adult	Developmental-integrative Model in Music Therapy	Recreative; improvisational; receptive; creative	Sekeles, 2006

Addictions

Table 4 provides an overview of work with adults recovering from addictions. Both Borling and Punkanen and Ala-Ruona contextualize their practices around a stage-like recovery process specific to addictions treatment. Borling frames his practice around a three-stage process that incorporates the 12 steps developed by Alcoholics Anonymous (1952), integrating a range of music therapy interventions. Punkanen and Ala-Ruona frame recovery around a two-stage process, conceptually similar to Borling's three-stage process, focusing their work on the second of these stages, outpatient recovery. Although quite distinct in theoretical orientation, both place a value on the relationship between past and present, understanding addiction through a physiological and psychological lens. While addressing work with adolescents, McFerran's work (chapter 14) with recovering addicts could also be considered a practice in this area.

Table 4. Music Therapy Practices with Adults Recovering from Addictions

Author	Client(s)	Approach to Music Therapy	Types of Experiences	Foundations
Borling	Adults recovering from addictions	Three-stage model	Recreative, receptive, creative, improvisational	Eclectic (biophysical, psychodynamic, spiritual)
Ala-Ruona & Punkanen	Adult recovering from addictions	Physioacoustic therapy	receptive	Lehikoinen, 1997; Ala-Ruona & Punkanen, 2007

Psychiatry

Table 5 provides an overview of music therapy practices with adults in psychiatric settings. This includes both inpatient (Eyre, Kaser, Haase and Reinhardt) and outpatient (Stige, Sutton, Trondalen) work. Practices in this area are characterized by both uncovering and ego-strength-building processes. All take a dynamic perspective of the psyche, including relational, psychodynamic and psychoanalytic perspectives.

Sutton and Eyre orient the reader to the importance of making and maintaining contact with patients who are severely regressed and traumatized, describing the importance of listening and therapeutic presence, giving insight into the place of sound and silence in the fragmented world of psychosis and severe withdrawal. Kaser reflects on the importance of providing a musical space for prisoners who struggle with 'traditional' forms of therapy, emphasizing the importance of song communication. Trondalen focuses on the intra and interpersonal dimensions of improvisational therapy through her work with a young man with anorexia nervosa. Stige and Haase and Reinhardt describe the benefits of long-term therapy from two different perspectives. Stige's perspective is culture-centered, and as such is not a particular model of therapy per se, rather a meta-perspective that re-orients practice in relational and contextual directions. Haase and Reinhardt draw upon Schwabe's model of music therapy (Schwabe, 2005, 2007; Schwabe & Haase, 2008; Schwabe & Reinhardt, 2006), one based upon an integrative psychotherapeutic concept rooted in a biopsychosocial disorder and treatment model.

Table 5. Music Therapy Practices with Adults in Psychiatric Settings

Author	Client(s)	Approach to Music Therapy	Types of Experiences	Foundations
Sutton	Adult who has experienced trauma	Music-centered; psychoanalytic	Improvisational	Psychoanalytic (Bion, 1984; De Backer, 2008)
Eyre	Adult with psychosis	Psychoanalytic: Lacan's three orders	Improvisational; recreative; receptive	Psychoanalytic (Lacan, 1988; 1993)
Kaser	Prisoner with a psychiatric diagnosis	Eclectic	Recreative	Recovery Model (Anthony, 1993; Mahler, Tavano, Gerard & Baber, 2001)

Stige	Adult in a Mental health clinic	Culture-centered Music Therapy	Recreative, improvisational	Stige, 2002; Rogers, 1951; Goffman (1959/1990)
Trondalen	Adult with Anorexia Nervosa	Humanistic; developmental; relational	Improvisational	Ruud, 2010; Stern, 2000; Yalom, 2002
Haase & Reinhardt	Adult with anxious-avoidant personality disorder	Schwabe's biopsychosocial disorder and treatment model	Improvisational; recreative; receptive	Schwabe, 2005, 2007; Schwabe & Haase, 2008; Schwabe & Reinhardt, 2006

Well Adults

Table 6 provides an overview of music therapy practices with well adults.[1] Clinical practice in this area is characterized by an exploration of conscious and unconscious processes of clients, and ways in which past experiences, including trauma, are linked to current problems. Summer and Bunt describe their work in Guided Imagery and Music (Bonny, 2002). While Bunt describes the ways in which GIM addresses life traumas, grief and loss, Summer describes the ways she adapted the GIM model into a three-level practice of music and imagery based upon her client's needs and abilities. Bosco integrates bodywork into music therapy practice, combining music listening experiences with Polarity Therapy and verbal processing using a Gestalt framework. Ahonen and Lee combine two models of music therapy – Group Analytical Music Therapy and Aesthetic Music Therapy – to address the specific needs of musicians in a string quartet. Both Ahonen and Lee and Bosco address therapeutic problems of musicians, each with distinct purposes and outcomes. The reader is encouraged to consider the work of Loewy and Quentzel (chapter 17) as an additional case study focused on musicians, to gain further perspective on music therapy practices in this area.

---

[1] Well adults are a heterogeneous group often characterized by their physical, cognitive, emotional and spiritual well-being, independence, resilience to life's challenges, and ability to develop and maintain healthy interpersonal relationships.

Table 6. Music Therapy Practices with Well Adults

Author	Clients	Approach to Music Therapy	Types of Experiences	Foundations
Bosco	Adult musician	Elemental Music Alignment	Receptive; bodywork	Polarity therapy (Stone, 1986); Gestalt therapy (Perls et al., 1994)
Summer	Adult with depression and obsessive-compulsive behavior	Music and Imagery	Receptive	Bonny, 2002
Bunt	Adult recovering from trauma and loss	Guided Imagery and Music	Receptive	Bonny, 2002
Ahonen & Lee	Musicians	Group Analytic Music Therapy and Aesthetic Music Therapy	Improvisational	Lee, 2003; Ahonen-Eerikainen, 2007

Older Adults

Table 7 provides an overview of practices with older adults, including end of life care. Therapists practice from a broad range of theoretical perspectives, including behavioral (Mercadal-Brotons), cognitive (van Hest, Verburgt and Smeijsters) cognitive-behavioral (Hilliard and Justice), humanistic (Hilliard and Justice), analogy and insight oriented (Van Hest, Verburgt and Smeijsters) orientations. Goals also vary considerably, including skill maintenance, communication, emotional expression, the resolution of past conflicts, and preparation for death. Van Bruggen-Rufi and Vink discuss the importance of the client's cultural background in formulating and structuring therapy, while van Hest, Verburgt and Smeijsters show how group music experiences for older adults provide a supportive environment in which to work through grief, loss and depression. Mercadal-Brotons and Hilliard and Justice show how structured interventions support and contextualize their client's wellbeing, especially in the slow deterioration of awareness and skills associated with dementia and end of life care.

Table 7. Music Therapy Practices with Older Adults

Author	Clients	Approach to Music Therapy	Types of Experiences	Foundations
Mercadal-Brotons	Adult with dementia	Behavioral Music Therapy	Recreative	Madsen, 1999; Skinner, 1953
van Hest-de Witte, Verburgt & Smeijsters	Adult with depression	Eclectic (rooted in improvisation)	Receptive	Analogy, cognitive and insight therapies (Smeijsters, 2005, 2006)
van Bruggen-Rufi & Vink	Adult with dementia		Recreative, improvisational	Multi-cultural
Hilliard & Justice	Adult with end stage cancer	Cognitive Behavioral Music Therapy	Compositional	Cognitive behavioral (Simos, 2002); humanistic (Rogers, 1961)

A Four-Quadrant View

While focusing on clients, goals and methods provides us with one way in which to understand clinical practice, a second way of understanding these practices is through the model of, or approach to, music therapy developed and/or embraced by the therapist, and the underlying theory/theories that supports it. Bruscia (1998) defines a model as a comprehensive system of practice that includes theoretical principles, goals, indications and contraindications, methodological procedures and techniques, guidelines for relationships within the practice, expectations for the process of development and competency or training requirements (Bruscia, 2002 p. 40). Guided Imagery and Music (Bruscia & Erdonmez, 2002; Bonny, 2002) and Nordoff-Robbins Music Therapy (Nordoff & Robbins, 2007) are examples of models of music therapy. Muller (2008) defines an approach as "a way of applying a given perspective to a subject, object or thought; a general way of addressing a clinical concern or problem, along with a pathway through which a solution can be found" (n.p.). Auditive Stimulation (Nöcker-Ribaupierre, 2007) and Elemental Music Alignment (Bosco, 1992) are examples of approaches. Table 8 provides an overview of various models of, and approaches to, music therapy represented in this book. When examined as a whole, these models and approaches reflect differences in the ways the role of the therapist, music, therapeutic process and health can be understood.

Table 8. Models and Approaches to Music Therapy

Model or Approach	Primary Source(s):	Principle Applications:	Case Example(s):
Aesthetic Music Therapy	Lee (2003)	Various adult client groups	Chapter 29: Adult musicians
Auditive Stimulation	Nöcker-Ribaupierre (2004; 2007)	Premature infants	Chapter 1: Infant born prematurely
Behavioral and Cognitive-Behavioral Music Therapy	Madsen (1999); Hilliard, (2005)	Various populations and settings	Chapter 30: Adult with dementia Chapter 33: Adult with cancer
Culture-centered Music Therapy Community Music Therapy	Stige (2002); Pavlicevic and Ansdell (2004)	Various populations and settings	Chapters 12 and 15: Vulnerable Adolescents Chapter 24: Adult with psychiatric diagnosis
Group Analytic Music Therapy	Ahonen-Eerikainen (2007)	Adults in various settings	Chapter 29: Adult musicians
Interactive Music Therapy	Oldfield (2006)	Children with developmental delays/disorders	Chapter 5: Children with behavioral concerns

Guided Imagery and Music	Bonny (2002)	Adults in various settings	Chapter 28: Adult with depression; Chapter 29: Grieving adult
Medical Music Therapy	Standley and Walworth (2005)	Hospitals, focused on pediatrics	Chapter 1: premature infants in the NICU
Neurologic Music Therapy	Thaut (2005)	Rehabilitation	Chapter 9: Developmentally delayed Children
Nordoff-Robbins Music Therapy	Nordoff and Robbins (1983)	Children with neuro-developmental delays and disorders	Chapter 7: Children with autism Chapter 15: Vulnerable adolescents
Schwabe's biopsychosocial disorder and treatment model	Schwabe (2005; 2007)	Various populations and settings	Chapter 25: Adults in a psychiatric facility
Vocal Music Therapy	Uhlig (2006)	Various populations and settings	Chapter 10: Children with behavioral problems
Physioacoustic Therapy	Lehikoinen (1997)	Various adult client groups	Chapter 20: Adults recovering from drug addiction
Elemental Music Alignment	Bosco (1992)	Various adult client groups	Chapter 26: Adult musician

Wilber (1995, 2000) provides a guiding framework in which to further contextualize these models and approaches (Bruscia, 1998). According to Wilber, human experiences can be understood according to four basic dimensions: "I," "We," "It" and "They." These are outlined in Figure 1. The upper dimensions are "I" experiences. This includes internal (upper left – feelings, images, consciousness) and external experiences (upper right – skills, behavior, physiological measures) that can be reported by, or observed in, individuals. For example, when you take an upper right perspective ("It") in music therapy, you are primarily concerned with a client's skills and behavior, and how therapy supports changes in these areas (e.g., Behavioral Music Therapy). When you take an upper left perspective ("I"), you are primarily concerned with a person's inner experiences, such as his/her feelings and memories, and how therapy brings about changes in consciousness (e.g., insight and life meaning) (e.g., Guided Imagery and Music).

Figure 1. Wilber's Four-Quadrant Model

"I"	"It"
Personal, inner experiences, attitudes, meaning, emotions, consciousness	Externally observable behavior, skills, and physiological measures
"We"	"They"
Culturally shared experiences, values, ethics, language	Systems, laws, elemental properties of music and sound

The lower two quadrants are concerned with collective experiences. The lower left quadrant is concerned with "We" experiences – that is, all those inner experiences shared by our culture(s) (e.g., values, ethics and language). This includes shared meanings of events such as community drum circles and performance as therapy (see Fouche and Torrance, this volume). Therapy from this perspective is concerned with the ways in which culturally informed music experiences bring about therapeutic change in groups of clients, and may even include the community as client (e.g., Community Music Therapy). The lower right ("They") quadrant is concerned with outer collective experiences: the laws, rules and external structures that shape group/social behavior. In music therapy, this refers to all those practices that are concerned with the universal healing properties of music, such as sound healing (see Bosco, this volume) and vibroacoustic therapy (Skille & Wigram, 1995).

When the models of music therapy reflected in this volume are examined in relationship to Wilber's Four-Quadrant Model, we can see examples of practices in all four quadrants. These will be discussed in the forthcoming section.

Models and Approaches focused on "It" (upper right) and "I" (upper left)

Upper Right Models and Approaches

Cognitive-Behavioral Music Therapy (Mercadal-Brotons), modified Melodic Intonation Therapy (Baker), Medical Music Therapy (Hillmer, Swedberg & Standley), Neurologic Music Therapy (LaGasse) and strategic songwriting-based music therapy (Krout) are all examples of upper right approaches in music therapy. In these approaches, an emphasis is placed on developing skills (improved speech and language, active participation and/or attention) and behaviors (respiratory regulation and oxygen saturation, alertness and decreased negative behaviors) that meet neuro-developmental or adaptive goals. For example, LaGasse describes how her practice in Neurologic Music Therapy (NMT) addresses speech and language goals in a child with Down syndrome through a two-stage process that examines how music influences non-musical functioning. The Rational-Scientific Mediating Model (R-SMM) guides the development of evidence-based therapeutic interventions using standardized terminology and application to address functional speech goals. The five-step Transformational Design Model (TDM) aids in translating the R-SMM into functional, creative, age-appropriate therapeutic interventions that logically maintain treatment focus.

In these approaches, the therapist often draws upon his/her knowledge of the research literature, identifying best practices to inform clinical decisions. In this way, an emphasis may be placed on protocols and groups of interventions that address specific adaptive goals, which can then be applied clinically when the goals suggest such intervention(s). As such, an emphasis may be placed on generalizing goals and interventions across client groups, with a focus on replication and validation.

Theoretically, these upper right approaches are influenced by behavioral therapy (Skinner, 1953; Standley, et al., 2004), brief therapy (Krout, 2005; 2006), cognitive therapy (Krout, 2005; 2006) and neuroscience models (Thaut, 2005).

Upper Left Models and Approaches

Models and approaches that fall into the Upper left "I" quadrant have been divided into sections with children, adolescents and adults.

CHILDREN – Nordoff-Robbins Music Therapy (Carpente), Auditive Stimulation (Nöcker-Ribaupierre), Interactive Music Therapy (Oldfield), Vocal Music Therapy (Uhlig) and the approaches of Schwartz, Elefant, Edwards and Kennelly, and Crowe are all examples of upper left models and approaches in music therapy. In these practices, an emphasis is placed upon the client's internal world, and how skill development and adaptation interact with emotional experience(s). For example, Edwards and Kennelly discuss the importance of facilitating emotional expression in a young boy hospitalized with serious burns. By providing supportive music during debridement, along with opportunities to interact musically with family members while hospitalized, Edwards and Kennelly supported the adaptive needs of their client, easing the isolation of hospitalization, decreasing stress and anxiety, and facilitating positive mood.

In these approaches, the therapist draws upon his/her relationship with the client, shaping the music therapy experience according to the moment-to-moment needs of the client. An emphasis is placed upon subjective experiences, in which each client's therapy unfolds according to the unique circumstances of the client-therapist relationship, setting, goals, and health-related needs.

Theoretically, these upper left models and approaches are influenced by neuro-developmental (Uhlig) and developmental theory (Schwartz; Carpente), stress and coping models (Edwards & Kennelly), and theories of personality development (Elefant). An emphasis can also be placed on musical development, which is linked to non-musical development (e.g., motor and communication) and discussed in terms of musical communication (see, for example, Uhlig), and/or understood as the therapeutic process – that is, the therapeutic process is a musical process (see, for example, Carpente).

Additionally, some upper left models and approaches also have components of upper right thinking, thereby moving between these two quadrants. For example, Crowe begins her work with Mark by taking a behavioral approach (upper right), but then adopts practices based upon Heimlich's Paraverbal Therapy (Heimlich, 1980), an approach that uses multi-sensory stimulation, reciprocal interactions as a basis for relationship development, and the free expression of emotions through improvisations (upper left). Similarly, Schwartz takes a primarily upper left stance in her work with young children who have developmental delays, but the outcomes of her work are often discussed in terms of skill development (e.g., increased speech and language skills and/or behavior change). Similarly, while upper right approaches focus primarily on skills and behavior, they also consider the child's emotional world. For example, LaGasse adapted her interventions to the emotional state of her client, changing the session structure and activities accordingly.

ADOLESCENTS – Community Music Therapy (Fouche and Torrance), Nordoff-Robbins Music Therapy (Pavlicevic) and the approaches of McFerran and Erkkilä are all examples of upper left practices with adolescents. In these approaches, an emphasis is placed on the client's emotional world, whereby linking emotional expression and insight to problems through musical and verbal interventions is central to therapy. Therein, an emphasis is also placed on the dynamic interactions between client(s), music and therapist, in which past experiences are linked to present problems, and psychological theories of therapy become more prominent in the therapist's thinking (Erkkilä; McFerran). For example, Erkkilä describes a four-phase therapeutic process — creating contact, searching for creativity, working and closing — in which music therapy is understood as a dynamic unfolding experience. The client's problems can be seen in the music, the relationship with the therapist, and in the ways in which therapy develops. Health-related outcomes can be understood in terms of changes in behavior (no longer withdrawing from contact with others), skill development (increased verbal communication), music (increased musical engagement and sophistication) and the client-therapist relationship (a working relationship in which the client develops trust, increases interpersonal awareness, and autonomy).

Theoretically, these upper left models and practices are influenced by humanism (McFerran), psychodynamic (Erkkilä) and relational (Fouche and Torrance) thinking. An emphasis is placed on dynamic processes, in which the client's and therapist's music is a metaphor for therapy itself. As such, in many of these approaches, the musical process is the therapeutic process (Pavlicevic; Fouche and Torrance).

ADULTS – The Developmental-Integrative Model in Music Therapy (Sekeles), physioacoustic therapy (Punkanen and Ala-Ruona), Culture-centered Music Therapy (Stige), Schwabe's (Schwabe & Haase, 2008) biopsychosocial disorder and treatment model (Haase and Reinhardt), Guided Imagery and Music (Bunt), Group Analytic Music Therapy (Ahonen), and the approaches of Borling, Sutton, Eyre, Kaser, Trondalen, Bosco and Summer are all examples of upper left models and approaches with adults. In these practices, an emphasis is placed on the client's inner world, whereby past and present life experiences and conscious and unconscious processes are linked to current problems in living and adaptation. As such, therapeutic concepts such as transference, countertransference, projection and projective identification are used by therapists to understand the therapeutic process (see Bruscia, 1998). The therapist helps the client to work through life problems, including past traumas, drug addiction, depression, psychiatric problems, and body issues. Within this framework, health can be understood as resolving conflicts, developing greater expressive freedom, building core self, overcoming trauma, moving through grief, and reducing problematic symptoms associated with addiction and psychosis. For example, Sekeles integrated music listening, improvisational, and song writing experiences into a therapeutic process that helped an injured soldier address serious problems related to an accident in which he lost both his legs. As she developed a relationship with Dor, Sekeles helped him to express his withdrawal, depression and anger, and in so doing, began the long process of recovery and healing. Using a psychoanalytic frame, Sekeles couched Dor's early responses in therapy as resistance, in which he refused to allow thoughts and feelings associated with the events surrounding his injury to be expressed and worked through. It was only through slow and careful work that Sekeles was able to engage Dor in a music-centered process that allowed him to begin to re-build a core self.

Theoretically, these upper left models and practices are influenced by humanism (Stige; Trondalen), relational (Stige; Trondalen), developmental (Trondalen), biopsychosocial (Loewy and Quentzel), psychodynamic (Punkanen and Ala-Ruona; Haase and Reinhardt; Summer; Bunt), psychoanalytic (Sutton, Eyre, Sekeles, Ahonen), eclectic[2] (Borling; Stige) and Gestalt (Bosco) thinking.

OLDER ADULTS – The approaches of van Bruggen-Rufi and Vink, Hilliard and Justice, and van Hest, Verburgt and Smeijsters are all examples of upper left practices with older adults. In these practices, an emphasis is placed on the client's inner world, whereby past and present life experiences are linked to current problems in living and adaptation. Hilliard and Justice place further emphasis on the importance of addressing unresolved issues from the past in order to prepare for death in a

---

[2] Defined as multiple theoretical orientations used in an integrated way by the therapist

healthy way. As such, health outcomes in these practices focus on improved quality of life, emotional expression, social integration, and reduced symptoms (e.g., pain experience, depression, isolation). For example, van Hest, Verburgt and Smeijsters address the unresolved grief, depression and isolation of an older man who had recently lost his wife. They focused on the importance of increasing self-expression, connecting with positive inner resources, and working through blocked feelings using both receptive and improvisational experiences.

Theoretically, these upper left practices are influenced by humanism (Hilliard and Justice), analogy (van Hest, Verburgt and Smeijsters), cognitive and insight-oriented (van Hest, Verburgt and Smeijsters) thinking. Interestingly, in each of these chapters, authors take multiple theoretical perspectives. Hilliard and Justice combine humanism with cognitive-behavioral constructs (upper right and upper left), van Hest, Verburgt and Smeijsters combine Smeijster's (2005, 2006) theory of analogy with cognitive and insight-oriented theories (upper left and upper right), while van Bruggen-Rufi and Vink's approach is framed within a broad cultural context while the practice has many qualities of humanism (upper left and lower left).

Models and Practices focused on "We" (lower left) and "They" (lower right)

Lower Left Models and Practices

While none of the models or practices represented in these chapters reflects lower left "We" models and practices in their entirety, many authors adopt concepts that reflect a lower left way of thinking. Of these, Culture-centered Music Therapy (Stige), Community Music Therapy (Pavlicevic; Fouche and Torrance) and the practice of van Bruggen-Rufi and Vink are examples.

Fouche and Torrance address the therapeutic needs of a group of teenagers in a poor community outside Cape Town, South Africa. In their approach, which they describe as being influenced by Culture-centered (Stige, 2002) and Community Music Therapy (Pavlicevic & Ansdell, 2004) concepts, they see their clients as both the group of twelve boys they work with weekly, and the community from which these teens live. Sessions include community musicians and music therapists, who focus on music from the cultural heritage of the boys' communities. In addressing both the individual boy's needs, their needs as a group, and the problems of the community in which they live, Fouche and Torrance are concerned with individual and community health. This appears to be consistent with Stige's (2003, cited this volume) notion of health, which he defines in relation to Culture-centered Music Therapy as:

> ... a quality of mutual care in human co-existence and a set of developing personal qualifications for participation. As such, health is the process of building resources for the individual, the community, and the relationship between individual and community (Stige, 2003 p. 207).

Theoretically, these lower left practices are influenced by Stige (2002), Pavlicevic and Ansdell (2004), Nordoff and Robbins (1977), and the humanistic tradition (May, 1969/1977; Rogers, 1951/1999).

Lower Right Models and Practices

Elemental Music Alignment (EMA) (Bosco) and physioacoustic therapy (Punkanen and Ala-Ruona) are examples of lower right practices. In these practices, an emphasis is placed on the ways in which the client's psychological and physiological processes interact. As such, the goals of therapy include facilitating emotional expression, resolving past and present conflicts, releasing thoughts, memories, images, sensations and emotions held in the body, and creating calm within the body through direct vibrational intervention. Both EMA and physioacoustic therapy used a combination of music, sound treatment and verbal processing. EMA combines music and sound with bodywork, in which the therapist works directly with the client's body to activate, release and calm, working with specific parts of the body (such as chakras) to facilitate change in the client. Physioacoustic therapy uses low frequency sound vibration and music listening to calm or activate the body, stimulating a range of experiences therein. Because both approaches integrate sound, vibration, music and verbal processing, both belong in the upper left and lower right quadrants.

When considered from the lower right quadrant, these practices are theoretically influenced by Polarity therapy theory (Stone, 1986), the oriental five-element system (Lad, 1984), vibrational healing (Beaulieu,

1987), and Vibroacoustic therapy theory (Skille & Wigram, 1995; Lehikoinen, 1997).

Aesthetic and Transpersonal Models and Practices

In addition to the four quadrants defined by Wilber (1995; 2000), Bruscia (1998) identifies two additional dimensions of music that are related to clinical practice: the aesthetic and transpersonal. According to Aigen (1995, cited in Bruscia, 1998), "the aesthetic properties of music — incorporating the inherent dynamics of melodic, harmonic, and rhythmic structures — have the ability to frame raw experiences into a whole experience" (pp. 240–241) thereby creating meaning in the felt experience of the music. It is in these moments of aesthetic beauty that clients find/experience meaning in their lives. Thus, aesthetic experiences in music are meaning-making experiences, in which the aesthetic beauty of the music is transcendence, allowing clients to temporarily or permanently overcome impediments to their lives. In Aesthetic Music Therapy (AeMT) (Lee) aesthetic experiences in music are central to the therapeutic process. Lee defines AeMT as a primarily improvisational approach that views musical dialogue as its core. For Lee, musical processes *are* clinical processes; the working through of problems takes place within the music itself, without the need for verbal processing.

Although not specifically discussed in terms of aesthetic experience, numerous authors describe processes or experiences in which the beauty of the music is a force in the therapeutic process. For example, Summer and Bunt discuss the transcendent potential of music listening, in which the client can experience and work through their problems in music-imagery experiences inherent in GIM (Bonny, 2002) and adaptations. Further, Pavlicevic describes the moment at which her clients formed and performed an improvised rap as transcendent:

> The group now shifts into a different musical gear. The song is 'performed' with no more interruptions or hesitation. As one unified organism, they clap, tap their feet, and move their bodies, while Jabu [a group member] seamlessly signals as to who recites each verse.

These moments of aesthetic beauty, in which the client(s) transcends their current problems, lead to new experiences, insights, and potentials.

It is in these moments that clients experience themselves in new ways, or as renewed.

Theoretically, aesthetic experiences in music are influenced by Aigen (1995), Lee (2003), and Bonny (2002).

Transpersonal experiences in music are only briefly discussed in this volume. Drawing upon a transpersonal framework (Firman & Gila, 1997), Borling identifies psycho-spiritual experiences as important to recovery from addiction. He describes music's ability to "touch us very deeply and call forth those aspects of our being that are ready for growth and healing." As such, music can be a conduit to the spiritual, or a spiritual experience in itself. Borling describes a way he uses music-imagery experiences focused on connecting to a higher power (Alcoholics Anonymous, step 11) to bring his clients closer to their spiritual core. Using the phrase "let go, let god" his client Shirley connected to her higher power, and in so doing, experienced a kind of spiritual awakening.

Transpersonal experiences draw upon diverse theoretical foundations, including the work of Jung (1969), Grof (1988), May (1988) and Firman and Gila (1997).

Models, Approaches and Theories in Context

When examined as a whole, these authors discuss the ways in which they have linked theory and practice, describing how goals, methods and techniques form a coherent therapeutic whole. In some cases a theory of therapy is integrated into practice (e.g., Eyre's integration of Lacan), while in others it is a guiding idea placed within a larger theoretical framework (e.g., Sutton's concept of *listening*). Further, Wilber's Four-quadrant Model (1995; 2000) and Bruscia's six dynamic models of music therapy (1998) provide an additional lens through which to contextualize each chapter, presenting six distinct ways through which human experiences, and thereby therapy, can be understood.

In music therapy, our theories are both inductive and deductive. Sometimes we take a particular approach to music therapy (e.g., Neurologic Music Therapy or Behavioral Music Therapy) and when doing so, use a framework for thinking about the client, the music, the role of the therapist, and even how health outcomes are understood. At other times, clinicians use inductive processes, in which they build a theory of therapy from the particular circumstances of the client (e.g., Erkkilä and Stige). In reality, these chapters speak to the ways in which these clinicians do both of these things. Their foundations provide a lens(es) through which to see the client. In so doing, each clinician uses this lens in a different way. Sometimes, when we see clients do the same kinds of things over and over again, we can "confirm" parts of how we think about the therapeutic process, thereby developing a model of practice while doing so. For example, Hiller, Swedberg and Standley (chapter 2) use a kind of confirmatory approach to their clinical work. Based upon their integration of research and their own clinical practice, they have developed clear guidelines for practice with premature infants and their families. This focus is grounded in evidence-based practice, with a desire to develop protocols for their clients. In contrast, Sutton (chapter 26) meditates on the experiences of listening to her clients, and the "unknowns" of doing so. Sutton is focused on the ways she can apprehend[3] her clients, the intra-personal experiences of the therapist, and how these inform her clinical practice with trauma patients.

In these ways we can begin to see the complexities of clinical practice reflected in these chapters. Practices are built upon foundations. Foundations serve as lenses, scaffolding, and frameworks. They help us see our clients, understand their struggles, be with them, and find a way through to something that is healthier and more adaptive.

Each music experience helps us to understand these frameworks in different ways. When we sing a song with our clients, we use the framework of the song to structure the client's experience. The song, in itself, is a therapeutic experience, following a contour that is shaped by the music and lyrics. The ways in which the client and therapist sing this song gives meaning to the framework. When we improvise with a client, we create the therapeutic contour in-vivo. The music expresses the client's inner world, and thus the client hears him/herself, in sound.

How we then understand and use these experiences is further shaped by our theoretical foundations. Whether we have the client talk about the song, and the ways in which we interpret the client's responses (spoken and unspoken), are all built upon the foundations of our thinking about the nature of music, therapy, and health.

---

[3] "When the therapist apprehends the client, the therapist senses, becomes aware of, perceives, or intuits something about the client, the client's ongoing experience or state, or the client's needs" (Muller, 2008a p. 95).

Developmental Frameworks

Thus, as therapists, we live within our own developing theoretical framework(s). When we begin training, we learn about the frameworks of others, both within the field of music therapy (e.g., Nordoff and Robbins, Priestley, Bonny) and outside the field (e.g., Stern, Kegan). As we learn about the ways others approach their work with clients, we also begin to work with clients, thereby testing out these theories, and developing an understanding of what does, and does not work, within the context of the clinical setting.

When we begin working professionally, we deepen into our own understanding of the framework(s) we have developed in our training. This often involves learning how to "do" therapy within the particular dimensions of our training. For example, practicing music therapy with adolescents can be very different from practicing with adults (compare, for example, McFerran and Summer). Similarly, practicing in a hospital (see for example, Nöcker-Ribaupierre) can be very different from an outpatient drug and alcohol program (see, for example, Borling).

But sooner or later, we also begin to question what we have learned, and how we are practicing. Sometimes we feel dissatisfied with what we are doing clinically, and other times we look for new challenges — something "more," sometimes "richer," "deeper" or simply "different." As we grow and change, we want to find ways of growing and changing our clinical practice as well.

These junctures in our lives, of which there are many, present us with choices — sometimes we respond by changing who we work with, at other times, we go back to school. Always a search for more.

But, if we give up that search, slowly, sometimes imperceptibly, something within us withers. We become dissatisfied — with how we practice, with being a music therapist, with where we work — and that dissatisfaction gnaws at us. Our growth as therapists parallels the growth we seek in our own lives, as people, and the growth we hope to support in our clients.

So, *Developments in Music Therapy Practice* invites you, as reader, to question, using the frameworks of these authors, all of whom continue to re-question.

REFERENCES

Ahonen-Eerikainen, H. (2007). *Group Analytic Music Therapy.* Gilsum, NH: Barcelona Publishers.

Aigen, K. (1995). An aesthetic foundation of clinical theory: An underlying basis of Creative Music Therapy. In C. Kenny (Ed.), *Listening Creating Playing: Essays on the Power of Sound.* (pp. 233–257). Albany, NY: State University of New York.

Ala-Ruona, E. & Punkanen, M. (2007). *The Physioacoustic Treatment: The Training Manual.* Jyväskylä: Eino Roiha Institute.

Alcoholics Anonymous World Services, Inc. (1952). *Twelve Steps and Twelve Traditions.* New York: Alcoholics Anonymous World Services, Inc.

Ansdell, G. (2002). Community Music Therapy and the winds of change. *Voices: A World Forum for Music Therapy,* 2(2).

Anthony, W. (1993). Recovery from mental illness: The guiding vision of the mental health service system in the 1990s. *Psychological Rehabilitation Journal,* 16(4), 11–24.

Beaulieu, J. (1987). *Music and Sound in the Healing Arts.* New York: Station Hill Press.

Bion, W. R. (1984). *Attention and Interpretation.* London: Karnac Books Ltd.

Bonny, H. L. (2002*). Music and Consciousness: The Evolution of Guided Imagery and music* (L. Summer, Ed.). Gilsum, NH: Barcelona Publishers.

Bosco, F. (1992). Elemental Music Alignment. Unpublished master's thesis. New York University. New York, NY.

Bowlby, J (1969). *Attachment and Loss.* New York: Basic Books.

Briggs, C. A. (1991). A model for understanding musical development. *Music Therapy,* 10 (1), 1–21.

Bruscia, K. E. (2002). The boundaries of Guided Imagery and Music (GIM) and the Bonny Method. In K. Bruscia & D. Grocke (Eds.), *Guided Imagery and Music: The Bonny Method and Beyond* (pp. 37–61). Gilsum, NH: Barcelona Publishers.

Bruscia, K. E. (1998). *Defining Music Therapy* (second edition). Gilsum, NH: Barcelona Publishers.

Bruscia, K. E. & Grocke, D. E. (2002). *Guided Imagery and Music: The Bonny Method and Beyond.* Gilsum, NH: Barcelona Publishers.

De Backer, J. (2008). Music and psychosis: A research report detailing the transition from sensorial play to musical form by psychotic patients. *Nordic Journal of Music Therapy*, 17(2), 89–104.

Erkkilä, J. (2004). From signs to symbols, from symbols to words: About the relationship between music and language, music therapy and psychotherapy. *Voices: A World Forum for Music Therapy*, 4(2).

Firman, J. & Gila, A. (1997). *The Primal Wound: A Transpersonal View of Trauma, Addiction, and Growth*. Albany, NY: State University of New York.

Greenspan, S. I. & Weider, S. (2006). *Engaging Autism: Using the Floortime Approach to Help Children Relate, Communicate, and Think*. Cambridge, MA: Da Capo Press.

Grof, S. (1988). *The Adventure of Self-Discovery: Dimensions of Consciousness and New Perspectives in Psychotherapy and Inner Exploration*. Albany, NY: State University of New York.

Heimlich, E. P. (1980). Paraverbal techniques: A new approach for communication with children having learning difficulties. *Journal of Learning Disabilities*, 13(9), 16–18.

Henneman, E. & Cardin, S. (2002). Family-centered critical care: A practical approach to making it happen. *Critical Care Nurse*, 22(6), 12–19.

Hilliard, R. E. (2005). *Hospice and Palliative Care Music Therapy: A Guide to Program Development and Clinical Care*. Cherry Hill, NJ: Jeffrey Books.

Jung, C. (1969). *The Archetypes and the Collective Unconscious*. Collected Works, Vol. 9. NJ: Princeton University Press.

Kegan, R. (1982). *The Evolving Self*. Cambridge, MA: Harvard University Press.

Krout, R. (2005). Applications of music therapist-composed songs in creating participant connections and facilitating goals and rituals during one-time bereavement support groups and programs. *Music Therapy Perspectives, 23* (2), 118–128.

Krout, R. E. (2006). Following the death of a child: Music therapy helping to heal the family heart. *New Zealand Journal of Music Therapy. 4,* 6–22.

Lacan, J. (1988). *The Seminar of Jacques Lacan: Book I. Freud's Papers on Technique* 1953-1954. (J. Forrester, Trans.). Cambridge, MA: Cambridge University Press.

Lacan, J. (1993). *The Seminar of Jacques Lacan: Book III. The Psychoses* 1981. J. Miller (Ed.). (R. Grigg, Trans.). New York: Norton.

Lad, V. (1984). *Ayurveda: The Science of Self-Healing*. Santa Fe: Lotus Press.

Lazarus, R. & Folkman, S. (1984). *Stress, Appraisal and Coping*. NY: Springer Publications.

Lee, C. A. (2003). *The Architecture of Aesthetic Music Therapy*. Gilsum, NH: Barcelona Publishers.

Lehikoinen, P. (1997). The Physioacoustic Method. In T. Wigram & C. Dileo (Eds.), *Music, Vibration and Health*. Cherry Hill, NJ: Jeffrey Books.

Madsen, C. K. (1999, November). A behavioral approach to music therapy. Founding Model Address to the General Assembly, 9th World Congress of Music Therapy, Washington, DC.

Mahler, D., Tavano, P., Gerard T. & Baber, D. (2001). *The Recovery Model: A Conceptual Implementation Plan*. Contra Costa County Mental Health Recovery Task Force, October 1–8.

Malloch, S. & Trevarthen, C. (2009). *Communicative Musicality: Exploring the Basis of Human Companionship*. Oxford: Oxford University Press.

Maslow, A. (1968). *Toward a Psychology of Being* (3rd ed.). New York: John Wiley and Sons.

May, G. (1988). *Addiction and Grace: Love and Spirituality in the Healing of Addictions*. New York: HarperSanFrancisco.

May, R. (1969/1977). *Kjærlighet og vilje* [Love and will (Translated to Norwegian by Daisy Schjelderup and Hilde Andresen)]. Oslo: Dreyers Forlag.

Muller, B. (2008a). A phenomenological investigation of the music therapist's experience of being present to clients. In S. Hadley (Ed.), *Qualitative inquiries in music therapy*, volume 4 (pp. 69–111). Gilsum, NH: Barcelona Publishers.

Muller, B. (2008b). personal communication. May 27th.

Nöcker-Ribaupierre, M. (Ed.) (2004). *Music Therapy for Premature and Newborn Infants*. Gilsum NH: Barcelona Publishers.

Nöcker-Ribaupierre, M. (2007). The therapeutic use of sound at the beginning of life. In I. Frohne-Hagemann (Ed.), *Receptive Music Therapy* (pp. 267–276). Wiesbaden: Reichert.

Nordoff, P. & Robbins, C. (2007). *Creative Music Therapy: A Guide to Fostering Clinical Musicianship*. Gilsum, NH: Barcelona Publishers.
Nordoff, P. & Robbins, C. (1983). *Music Therapy in Special Education* (2nd ed.). St Louis, MO: Magnamusic-Baton.
Nordoff , P. & Robbins, C. (1977). *Creative Music Therapy.* New York: John Day.
Oldfield, A. (2006) *Interactive Music Therapy: A Positive Approach. Music Therapy at a Child Development Centre*. London: Jessica Kingsley Publishers.
Patel, A. D. (2008). *Music, Language, and the Brain*. NY: Oxford University Press.
Pavlicevic, M. & Andsell, G. (2004). *Community Music Therapy*. London: Jessica Kingsley Publishers.
Perls, F., Hefferline, R. & Goodman, P. (1994) *Gestalt Therapy: Excitement and Growth in the Human Personality*. Highland, NY: The Gestalt Journal Press, Inc.
Quentzel, S. & Loewy, J. (2010). An integrative bio-psycho-musical assessment model for the treatment of musicians: Part II — intake and assessment, *Music and Medicine*, 2(2), 121–125.
Rogers, C. (1961). *On Becoming a Person: A Therapist's View of Psychotherapy*. London: Constable.
Rogers, C. (1951/1999). *Client-Centered Therapy*. London: Constable.
Ruud, E. (2010). *Music Therapy: A Perspective from the Humanities*. Gilsum, NH: Barcelona Publishers.
Schneck, D. J. & Berger, D. (2006). *The Music Effect: Music Physiology and Clinical Applications*. Philadelphia, PA: Jessica Kingsley Publishers.
Schwabe, C. (2005). Resource-oriented music therapy. *Nordic Journal of Music Therapy,* 14, 49–57.
Schwabe, C. (2007). Regulatory Music Therapy (RMT) — Milestones of a conceptual development. In I. Frohne-Hagemann (Ed.), *Receptive Music Therapy* (pp. 203–210). Wiesbaden, Germany: Reichert-Verlag.
Schwabe, C. & Haase, U. (2008). *Die Sozialmusiktherapie (SMT). Das musiktherapeutische Konzept nach Christoph Schwabe* [Social music therapy (SMT). Christoph Schwabe's music therapeutic approach] (3rd ed.). Bad Klosterlausnitz, Germany: Akademie für angewandte Musiktherapie Crossen.

Schwabe, C. & Reinhardt, A. (2006). *Das Kausalitätsprinzip musiktherapeutischen Handelns* [The causality principle in music therapeutic action]. Bad Klosterlausnitz, Germany: Akademie für angewandte Musiktherapie Crossen.

Schwartz, E. K. (2008). *Music, Therapy, and Early Childhood: A Developmental Approach.* Gilsum, NH: Barcelona Publishers.

Sekeles, C. (2006). The Developmental-Integrative Model in music therapy. *Nordic Journal of Music Therapy*, 15 (1): 58–82.

Simos, G. (Ed.) (2002). *Cognitive Behaviour Therapy.* Hove: Brunner-Routledge.

Skille, O. & Wigram, T. (1995). Vibroacoustic Therapy. In T. Wigram, B. Saperston, & R. West (Eds.), *The Art & Science of Music Therapy: A Handbook.* Amsterdam: Harwood Academic Publishers.

Skinner, B. F. (1953). *Science and Human Behavior.* New York: Macmillan.

Smeijsters, H. (2005). *Sounding the Self. Analogy in Improvisational Music Therapy.* Gilsum, NH: Barcelona Publishers.

Smeijsters, H. (2006). *Handboek muziektherapie. Evidence-Based Practice Voor de behandeling van Psychische Stoornissen, Problemen en Beper-kingen.* [Music therapy handbook. Evidence based practice for the treatment of psychic disturbances, problems and limitations]. Houten: Bohn Stafleu Van Loghum.

Sparks, R.W. & Deck, J.W. (1986). Melodic intonation therapy. In R. Chipley (Ed.), *Language Intervention Strategies in Adult Aphasia* (pp. 320–332). Baltimore: Williams & Wilkins.

Standley, J. (2003). *Music Therapy with Premature Infants: Research and Developmental Interventions.* Silver Springs, MD: American Music Therapy Association, Inc.

Standley, J. M., Johnson, C. M., Robb, S. L., Brownell, M. D. & Kim, S. (2004). Behavioral approach to music therapy. In A. Darrow (Ed.), *Introduction to Approaches in Music Therapy* (pp. 103–124). Silver Spring, MD: The American Music Therapy Association, Inc.

Standley, J. & Walworth, D. (2005). Chapter 1: Overview. In J. Standley, D. Gregory, J. Whipple, D. Walworth, J. Nguyen, J. Jarred, et al. (Eds.), *Medical Music Therapy: A Model Program for Clinical Practice, Education, Training, and Research* (pp. 5–10). Silver Spring: American Music Therapy Association, Inc.

Stern, D. N. (2000). *The Interpersonal World of the Infant* (2nd ed.). New York: Basic Books.
Stern, D. (1985). *The Interpersonal World of the Infant.* New York: Basic Books.
Stige, B. (2003). *Elaborations Toward a Notion of Community Music Therapy.* Doctoral thesis, University of Oslo, published by: Unipub.
Stige, B. (2002). *Culture-Centered Music Therapy.* Gilsum, NH: Barcelona Publishers.
Stone, R. (1986). *Polarity Therapy: The Complete Collected Works (Vol. I & II).* Sebastopol, Calif.: CRCS Publications. (Reprint of works originally published 1954-1957).
Thaut, M.H. (2005). *Rhythm, Music, and the Brain.* London: Taylor & Francis.
Uhlig, S. (2006) *Authentic Voices – Authentic Singing: A Multicultural Approach to Vocal Music Therapy.* Gilsum, NH: Barcelona Publishers.
Wilber, K. (2000). *Integral Psychology: Consciousness, Spirit, Psychology, Therapy.* Boston MA: Shambhala Publications.
Wilber, K. (1995). *Sex, Ecology, Spirituality: The Spirit of Evolution.* Boston MA: Shambhala Publications.
Winnicott, D. J. (1965). *The Maturational Process and Facilitating Environment.* New York: International Universities Press.
Yalom, I. D. (2002). *The Gift of Therapy: Reflections on Being a Therapist.* London: Judy Piatkus Ltd.

Chapter One

WHEN LIFE BEGINS TOO EARLY: MUSIC THERAPY IN A NEWBORN INTENSIVE CARE UNIT

Monika Nöcker-Ribaupierre

INTRODUCTION

For the past 20 years, music therapists have been developing different approaches to providing recorded music for premature infants, the results of which have been significant (Loewy, 2000; Schwartz, 2004; Standley, 2004; Hanson-Abromeit et al., 2008). This type of *medical music therapy* focuses on the impact of selected music programs on infant development and behavior. However, clinical experience also suggests that, in many cases, music listening experiences may not provide optimal developmental support for the infant. As such, new approaches in music therapy are continually being included in the individualized care of premature infants. These may include singing, humming, and the use of gentle sounding instruments (Loewy, 2004; Haslbeck, 2004; Arnon et al., 2006; Gilad & Arnon, 2010). Music therapists initiate these interventions and often encourage parents to join in (Shoemark, 1999; Abromeit, 2003; O'Gorman, 2006). This chapter deals with yet another music therapy approach, called *Auditive Stimulation*. Auditive Stimulation is based on research (Nocker-Ribaupierre, 2004; 2007) focusing on relationships and bonding. Bonding begins in the mother's womb and is fundamental for life and development. The overall goal of Auditive Stimulation is to re-establish the interrupted mother-infant bonding process, providing a basis for its development, and preventing later relationship conflicts.

Orienting Vignette

Jane was born at 26 weeks of gestation and immediately brought to the newborn intensive care unit (NICU). She was placed in an incubator and hooked up to machines measuring heartbeat, oxygen, nutritional intake, and alarm signals in case of emergency. The oxygen mask was fixed to her small face, making it difficult for anyone to see her face. Her acoustical environment was dominated by technology — noisy and chaotic, interrupted by telephones, alarms, and conversations. Suddenly an alarm signaled — Jane's breathing had stopped. A nurse came running, shook her and observed the monitor. As her vital signs stabilized, the alarm stopped. The nurse waited a few seconds, then left for her next task. This happened several times a day.

Jane's mother often stood in front of her baby in the incubator. She didn't dare touch her — uncertain and not really understanding what the doctor and nurses had told her. The baby didn't meet her expectations of a normal, healthy baby. She was looking at a tiny little red being, so covered with technical equipment that she could hardly see her face or take her in her arms. Her infant was in the middle of a surrealist environment: lying in a glass box, cut off from her by walls. Was this really her baby? It was all so different, strange, and unknown. Her abdomen was empty and so were her arms.

This is a typical experience for many mothers of very premature babies. The situation within an intensive care unit (ICU), the combination of highly technical surroundings, and the state of her baby are enormously stressful — right from the beginning. On the one hand, mothers and fathers have to learn to accept and understand what is happening with their infant, especially since this intensive care may ensure the child's survival. On the other hand, they have to cope with their inner turmoil and completely changed life. The mother is in a particularly difficult situation. She has not succeeded where other mothers have done so — apparently effortlessly, and feels alone and isolated.

While it is often considered best for any affected person to avoid the scene of trauma after the event, it is not possible when a premature delivery occurs. Most mothers and fathers do what parents usually do and are present to their child immediately after birth and throughout their time in the ICU. They are encouraged to do so, although it may reinforce the trauma. This is a place to offer musical-psychotherapeutic support.

FOUNDATIONAL CONCEPTS

The foundational concepts of Auditive Stimulation are based on infant research and observation, psychotherapy, bonding and neuro-biological research (Winnicott, 1965; Bowbly, 1969; Klaus & Kennell, 1976; Eagle, 1984; Stern, 1985). Beyond the evaluated supportive impact of music and singing provided by a music therapist (e.g., Haslbeck, 2004; Loewy, 2004; Shoemark, 2004; Gilad & Arnon 2010), the effect of the mother's voice is something special and irreplaceable — it is fundamental to the developing bonding and relationship process.

It is well known that due to extensive improvement in medical technology over the last few decades, more and younger premature infants are surviving. However, several long-term studies have shown these infants to have a significantly higher risk of later neuro-developmental problems than their full-term peers (Crearsey et al., 1993; Hack et al., 1995). According to these findings, the goal of neonatal care has shifted from mere survival to the prevention of major disabilities (Linderkamp & Skuroppa, 2010). Accompanying studies have shown that structural and electro-physiological differences and their corollary psychological findings continue into childhood and adolescence (Als, 1995). These neurological findings indicate that brain development in pre-term infants is different rather than delayed. This explains why intervention programs starting after discharge from the NICU focused on ameliorating deficits in brain development, are less effective than interventions during intensive care (Fischer & Als, 2004).

There is abundant evidence (Klaus & Kennell, 1976; Brazelton, 1981) that the emotional state of the mother plays an important role in the infant's pre- and postnatal development. Other developmental studies focusing on the importance of the mother-infant relationship indicate that the infant's developmental outcomes correlate even more with socio-economic factors than with biological prenatal and postnatal risk factors (Riegel et al., 1985; Achenbach et al., 1993).

Besides individualized intervention and providing balanced sound/sensory stimulation in the NICU, developmental care, the therapeutic support of the mother, and hopefully the father, is also a goal. Among the different therapeutic approaches for parents, music therapy provides an important tool in supporting both infant and parents. The music therapy application of Auditive Stimulation, with the mother's voice, is a receptive form of music therapy. It also offers a form of crisis intervention for the mother, supporting the psychosocial and emotional importance of the bonding process.

Importance of the Mother's Voice

The fetus' ability to perceive acoustical perceptions has been definitively and empirically established as early as 18 weeks gestational age (Rubel, 1984). After birth, the baby immediately recognizes the mother's voice, not only when alone with her, but is also able to pick it out of a group. In addition, the baby also favors complex auditory stimulation in connection with its mother, which it has experienced during gestation. For example, infants show a special preference for their mothers' speech or for the music that she sang or listened to while pregnant. This same music can also quiet the infant after birth. He/she also has a noticeable interest in certain stories it recognizes from the pregnancy. After birth, it can differentiate one text from the other when read by the mother (De Casper & Fifer, 1980; Fernald, 1982; De Casper & Spence, 1986; Standley & Moore, 1995; Righetti, 1996; Nöcker-Ribaupierre, 2007).

The impact of the mother's voice is created not so much by its discursive content, but by the presentative content of the voice and its emotional message. This leads us to assume that the mother's voice is of unique importance during prenatal and early postnatal life. It is a sound, melody, rhythm and emotional carrier — representing the mother as a whole being. The mother's voice conveys security, closeness, and warmth. She represents the emotional home, unmistakable for the premature infant, distinctive in sound, melody and rhythm, and unique in its affective content (Stern, 1995). The mother's voice, singing or speaking, builds a bridge, creating the relationship between mother and infant.

During the prenatal period, from a psychoanalytical point of view, this voice is also important in the development of intra-psychological exponents (Maiello, 2004), provided the neuro-physiological prerequisites exist. The mother's voice is not physical. This means the fetus, in-utero, or in an incubator, cannot control it. Therefore, it may "challenge the primary sensation of fusional at-one-ness and stimulate... proto-forms of introjective mental processes" (Maiello, 2004 p. 59). The voice imparts emotions, a proto-feeling of presence and separation — the basic feeling of "I and not-I" as a requisite for mental and psychological development. It is a bonding element, for it secures continuity from pre- to postnatal life — physically near and simultaneously containing the entire blueprint for later verbal communication.

Fortunately, the developmental and psychodynamic theories (Bowlby, 1969; Winnicott, 1965; Eagle, 1984; Stern, 1985; Maiello, 2004) meet their counterpart in different neurobiological findings. Several neurobiologists (Duffy et al., 1990; Lickliter, 2000; Hüther, 2005) have found that human brain development not only follows genetic prerequisites, but is vitally influenced and formed by outside experiences. Outside experiences mean outside influences such as hormonal, biological, emotional, and sensorial inputs and changes; they influence proliferation, migration, sprouting of nerve cells in addition to the genetically determined growth, elimination and connections of synaptic neurons. The immature cortical system in pre-term infants is extremely vulnerable to all kinds of non-physiological, differently timed and unexpected stressors in a NICU. All these stimuli influencing brain development lead to less differentiated and modulated physiological functioning connected with affect regulation and mental processing (Duffy et al., 1990; Als, 1995). There is vital evidence that these problems are linked to microstructural changes in brain development, which definitely cannot be made up later (Hüppi et al., 1998, Linderkamp & Skuroppa, 2010).

As the mother's womb assures the most efficient environment, it is necessary to try to provide the premature infant with sound components that are as natural as possible. This includes decreasing the technological noises and providing harmonious sounds; for example using the mother's voice. Her voice can be seen as connecting the intrauterine world to the time spent in the NICU and subsequent world at home after discharge. During the duration of the infant's stay in the NICU, the mother's voice offers an opportunity for beginning their bonding process and relationship. After birth, the voice changes from just sound to a carrier of meaning, analogous to brain development, where the cognitive and contextual capacity now develops in the cerebral cortex. This is necessary for the infant to experience safety and security through continuous sensorial experience.

THE CLIENTS

The Infant

For a baby, very premature birth means early physical and mental trauma (Fischer & Als, 2004; Linderkamp & Skuroppa, 2010). This is an unusually stressful life event, which causes an acute bio-psycho-social stress reaction. Premature infants are not ill, but physically and emotionally vulnerable, needing enormous attention and care. In order to survive and grow after a very early premature delivery, they must remain in a NICU for several weeks or months — a totally unfamiliar, non-physiological, highly technical environment. This results in a necessary but chaotic and painfully intensive routine of treatment, with continuous bright lights and excessive noise (a constant noise level between 50–85 dB and unpredictable alarms up to 110 dB). These cause stress, anxiety, and agitation (Schwartz et al., 1998). The infant must often be sedated in order to handle and reduce the stress-induced physiological effects. In dealing with these stressful experiences, the infant uses an enormous amount of energy, which it would normally invest in its growth and development (Schwartz, 2004). As mentioned before, stress exposure has a lasting effect on brain development and places the infant in a vulnerable situation. In this technical environment, the baby has to live and grow, deprived of all the normal sensory experiences s/he had in her/his mother's womb.

The Mother

Mothers of premature infants experience a similar and profound range of stressors that are akin to trauma (Caplan et al., 1965; Klaus & Kennell, 1976). For her, it is a situation of acute separation. The mother of a premature baby is also in an extremely difficult and desperate situation, often suffering from guilt and depression, along with feelings of inadequacy and fear related to the survival and development of her baby (Vonderlin 1999; Jotzo, 2001; Jotzko & Poets, 2005).

Stern's concept of the motherhood constellation (1995) helps us understand the situation of a "premature" mother compared to a mother after a full term pregnancy. Pregnancy is a normal process involving psychological and physical changes. Coping with these changes is fundamental for the mother in order to develop basic mother-infant bonding. Stern (1995) has formulated four prerequisites: 1) the mother has to be able to assist her baby to stay alive, 2) the mother has to develop an emotional relationship, 3) the mother has to establish a reliable and protecting environment ("to build a nest"), and 4) the mother has to develop a feeling of identity as a *mother*.

A mother who gives birth to her child at half the gestation period is not able to hold her infant. She cannot help her baby stay alive. She has been replaced by doctors, nurses, and a technical environment. Her baby is in an incubator. She cannot communicate with her/him, nor convey her love. She cannot see that her baby loves her. She cannot build a protective environment. This is now the responsibility of the clinic staff. Last but not least, she has not had time to grow into her maternal identity.

The experience of premature delivery causes a definite change in her life, often compounded by her own personal vulnerability. If she experiences the situation as an actual burden, long-lasting disturbances may result. The inner symptoms can be as diverse as fear, insecurity, not being aware of or withdrawing from the actual situation at one end of the spectrum, to restlessness at the other end. Initially, each mother copes with feelings of guilt and mourning (Cramer, 1976; Jotzo, 2001). The overwhelming high-tech environment also increases this feeling of helplessness (Vonderlin, 1999).

THE THERAPEUTIC PROCESS

This therapeutic process of Auditive Stimulation is based upon recordings of the mother's voice and psychotherapeutic crisis intervention. The doctor or nurse suggests the infants they consider appropriate for therapy. Then the music therapist establishes contact with the mother, either in the maternity ward or at the infant's incubator. Premature birth requires crisis intervention and stabilizing resources for both mother and child. Due to bio-psycho-social stress states, it is absolutely necessary to immediately assist the mother in the NICU. After the trauma of a premature birth, this crisis intervention focuses on the mourning process. Success depends on how capable the mother is of dealing with this new life and finding her way back to her inner and outer resources (Nöcker-Ribaupierre & Zimmer, 2004).

After a premature birth, the father's problems are different from those of the mother. They are concerned with the survival of both mother and child. At the same time, fathers must also continue to support their families and possibly take care of other siblings. Despite these demands, they need to be included in this kind of therapeutic support whenever possible

As the purpose of the music therapy intervention during the NICU period is to support the mother-child relationship, this eliminates composed music or the use of other sounds in favor of the mother's voice. Consistent with Stern's (1985) concept of motherhood constellation, focus is given to the ways in which the mother and her child are linked together through the mother's voice.

Initially, the mother may be anxious, sometimes appearing to be in shock. It is helpful to offer her several options. She can sing lullabies or children's songs, she can write something at home (e.g., a letter to her baby) and read it, read something from a book, or she can just talk or sing. In this new situation, overwhelmed mothers often cannot sing. They are scared and normally prefer to read. The recording should last about 30 minutes. The therapist may remind the mother that the baby cannot understand the meaning, but always responds to the emotional content. So it is important that the mother feels comfortable with everything she wants to tell her/him. Is there, for example, anything she remembers from the pregnancy? Because of the early development of the human auditory system, the baby is already familiar with the sound of her voice (DeCasper & Fifer, 1980; Maiello, 2004; Nöcker-Ribaupierre, 2007). As babies recognize their mother's voice after birth and are able to distinguish it even while she is reading, it is important for the mother to understand that only she can give this to her child. "No one can replace her voice — no doctor, no nurse, no medicine, not even Mozart or Brahms" (Zimmer, 2004 p. 122). Before the recording, the therapist needs to carefully explain the whole procedure and its meaning. Sometimes it is necessary to wait a week or more until the mother is more prepared.

After this type of trauma, being active is a key experience in her ability to bond, and will help her regain her feelings of competence. During the recording, the therapist should leave the mother alone with a picture of her baby in order to respect her shyness and her privacy. The mother often seems relieved and quieter after this opportunity to convey her feelings, through stories, to her infant. While the mother is recording, the music therapist may install the audio equipment and loudspeaker in the incubator. Then they can listen to the beginning of the recording to assure that everything is in order, play the recording for the baby, and wait for and watch the baby's reaction. The therapist stays with the mother, supporting her emotionally. This is normally a very moving moment for the mother as she watches her baby recognize her voice. This recording does not and cannot replace the mother's physical presence, and it should not be turned on while she is with her/him. The recording has to be turned off when any nursing or invasive treatment is necessary, because the baby should not learn to associate painful or stressful procedures with her/his mother's voice.

Crisis Intervention

Based on Auditive Stimulation, Zimmer (2004) formulated the theoretical foundation for working with mothers after the premature birth of their infants. In order to address crisis intervention and the mourning process, primary contact should occur as soon as possible after delivery. This establishes a quiet and trusting foundation, and offers emotional relief from stress. In order to analyze the problem, the therapist listens to the mother's story, anamnesis, and asks about her social situation. Accompanying and repetitive questions focus on her actual experiences in the ward, any previous crises, and possible resources. Overall, the main focus is on her baby and on their relationship.

The explanation of Auditive Stimulation, and focusing on the recording of her voice,[1] will help her learn how to be competent in this situation. Feelings and conflicts not related to this situation may occur.

---

[1] A brief comment on the recording process: it is necessary to carefully select good technical equipment in advance. A recorder, microphone, sound transmission equipment (minidisk, walkman, iPod, etc., and loudspeakers), children's story, picture and song books should be prepared for the mother to read – culturally and linguistically appropriate for the family.

But as a whole, this intervention is intended to solve problems, not reveal them. This includes focusing on different aspects of the situation at hand — either just on the infant, or accompanying the mother, the father, and sometimes the whole family. It may also include the mourning process, crisis intervention, and/or working on re-discovering reliable skills or outside resources that help to manage the difficulties currently experienced (Zimmer, 2004, Nöcker-Ribaupierre & Zimmer, 2004).

As a whole, this music therapy process consists of:
- Providing the infant with the most natural and human acoustical stimulus possible by recreating those previously experienced in-utero
- Helping the mother to overcome the trauma of the premature birth
- Developing and stabilizing the mother's own resources
- Re-establishing the interrupted mother-child bonding process

Case Vignettes

Alice

Alice was born at 28 weeks gestation with life threatening medical problems. She was immediately placed on a ventilator and in the NICU. Her mother came to visit her the next day. She sat silently in front of the incubator, fearful and with little hope that her child would survive. However, she gladly accepted the offer of recording her voice. But her voice was flat and toneless. Her speech was slow and soft, interrupted by sobbing. After installing the recording and waiting for what seemed forever, she realized her baby was reacting. She began to visit Alice daily and spoke with her more and more. She didn't seem to need any other therapeutic support, although the therapist contacted her frequently. With time, the music therapist and especially the nurses saw the mother stabilizing psychologically. She cautiously began to help with Alice's care, was more interested in her surroundings, the other babies and mothers, and was happy about her daughter's development. When Alice was 32 weeks old, a nurse reported Alice began to cry when she heard her mother's voice via the loudspeaker. We didn't observe this when her mother was speaking directly to her. We could hear that her mother's voice had become stronger and positive, expressing a more positive emotional state. The music therapist contacted her again and suggested she make a new recording. From then on, Alice turned her head toward the loud speaker whenever she heard the new recording.

Mothers often don't seem to be interested in more support than just an opening conversation with the music therapist, an explanation of the method, and speaking or reading onto tape about their feelings, expectations, hopes, wishes or some family stories or fairy tales. Recording her own voice and observing her infant's reactions can be a door opener. The mother regains her ability to *mother* and starts to be actively involved in caring for her baby. The role of the music therapist is to assist her at the beginning – and then step back, ready to intervene if and when necessary.

Natalie

Rebecca, a well-adjusted middle-aged woman, had to stay in bed during the last two months of her pregnancy. Her daughter, Natalie, was then born at 24 weeks. This was her fifth pregnancy. The other infants had not survived because all were born premature. Three had died after 20 weeks. The last one, born after 22 weeks, died one week later. Natalie was a caesarian section and was immediately incubated and brought to the NICU. The next day Rebecca was pushed in a wheelchair to see her daughter, the tiniest baby on the ward, red, with cables taped to her. She seemed to be prepared for all of this, but didn't dare touch her baby. Her anxiety was noticeable. Would this baby survive? Would she begin to bond with another baby "which presumably will also die?" The music therapist was there each day to support her, sometimes in her office, or later by the incubator. Rebecca began speaking about her dead babies, her desires, expectations and hopes, interrupted again and again by tears. Many meetings were necessary until she was psychologically ready to record her voice, and with this to accept Natalie. She was so happy when she realized that Natalie became calmer (also observable via oxygen saturation and heartbeat) by listening to her voice and that she smiled when she heard it. From then on, Rebecca stayed with Natalie most of the day. Natalie's father joined her every evening. Her primary anxiety had changed into an impressive loving power.

Natalie then developed severe kidney problems. After several weeks, it was clear she wouldn't survive. Her parents decided to end the intensive treatment and to allow her to die in peace. For three days and nights, they alternated sitting beside the incubator with Natalie carefully and lovingly in their laps. The atmosphere in the whole ward changed to respectful silence. Every single member of the staff was touched by this strong and spiritual attitude. After Natalie's passing, Rebecca asked if she could take her recordings home.

Two years later, the music therapist met her again by chance. She was radiant and happy, with a healthy little boy – born after her first completed pregnancy.

The music therapist was present four times a week, during the afternoons when Rebecca came to the unit to sit beside the incubator, and was always ready for a talk. Rebecca, by profession a homeopathic therapist, was very pleased with the opportunity to reflect on her situation, her interrupted pregnancies, the death of her last baby, and her anxiety, fears and ambivalence about developing a relationship with this little girl. During the first weeks, they often went into the therapist's office in order to prevent her grief from affecting Natalie, and to allow her to express her feelings and fears, working through her previous traumatic experiences. The therapist's intention was to accompany Rebecca's mourning process in order to allow her to re-discover her resources and strengths. These talks, along with Natalie's obvious positive reactions, helped her to re-discover her ability to become a mother and to bond with her daughter. The therapist observed how consciously and lovingly experiencing their daughter's death allowed the parents closure with their other premature infants, and an opportunity to begin anew.

Ruth

Besides the trauma of premature birth, there are often severe unspoken problems that affect the mother-infant relationship. These can be unconscious or conscious partner conflicts, previous premature births, the infant seen as rescuing the partnership, a substitute for a dead child, or an unwanted pregnancy. These are separate from the mother's personal problems, such as her own adverse childhood experiences, drug abuse, or difficult social situations. These problems, conscious or unconscious, need to be revealed and brought into connection with this premature birth situation. To emphasize and clarify how necessary it is for a music therapist in the NICU to be trained psychotherapeutically, I want to describe a case example of work by my colleague Marie-Louise Zimmer (2004)[2].

Helen gave birth to twins, a boy and a girl, in the 29th week of gestation – not so unexpectedly, as a multiple birth is often a premature one. Her other son was 17 years old. She appeared to handle this situation very matter-of-factly, and did not appear too anxious. What attracted the attention of the nurses and music therapist was that she only paid attention to her son, Andreas. She left the care of her daughter, Ruth, to the nurses. All attempts to bring her closer to Ruth seemed futile. The music therapist proposed Auditive Stimulation and explained the procedure. Helen agreed immediately, happy to be able to do something for her infants. But she didn't want to make two separate recordings, one for each child, and commented, "This is not necessary, one will do."

During the preliminary conversation, the therapist noticed that Helen repeatedly named her daughter Eva instead of Ruth. Helen didn't notice her mistake. The therapist called her attention to the fact that she was constantly using another name for Ruth. Deeply shocked, she admitted she had had another daughter, Eva – who would now have been 10 years old. But at the age of three, she was overcome by an infection and died. Helen said that she hadn't said anything because she didn't want to think about her. Helen had never talked about her or worked through her grief. Her new daughter was overwhelmingly reactivating this suppressed grief. When she saw Ruth, Helen immediately remembered her dead daughter, and all the painful past memories surfaced. From the beginning, she felt uncomfortable and guilty because she had absolutely no idea how to enter into an emotional relationship with Ruth.

---

[2] I choose this case because it is an excellent illustration of this complex psychological network.

After this talk with the therapist, Helen agreed to make a recording for Ruth. Following this new recording, she was able to turn her interest towards her daughter and to increasingly care for her, now calling her by her own name.

The beauty of this method is that through the contact made to facilitate a supportive recording, the music therapist can learn about the mother's unconscious conflicts without asking her. Most mothers experience this as being relieved of a burden. Of course, there are also mothers and/or whole families with such severe problems that they have to be referred to other therapists for continuing support or therapy after discharge. Still, in Rebecca's case, this gentle intervention opened a healing door for her and allowed her to bond with her daughter while grieving the loss of her other child.

SUMMARY

As more and more infants who are born premature survive due to advances in medical technology, the need for supportive, psychotherapeutically oriented interventions increases. Auditive Stimulation is a method that provides the infant with the most natural and human acoustical stimulus possible by recreating what the infant experienced in-utero – thus supporting its neuro-biological and social development. For the mother, this helps her to overcome the trauma of the premature birth by developing and stabilizing her own resources. It also helps to re-establish the interrupted mother-child bonding process, which is decisive for development, interaction and communication.

Sometimes the opportunity to talk or sing for her child acts like a door-opener to re-activate healthy maternal feelings – but there are times, too, when the trauma of birth opens up past traumas and hurts that need to be addressed in order for a healthy bond to develop. In this case, the accompanying psychotherapeutic work takes the form of crisis intervention and provides support for the mother (and wherever possible, both parents) in order to cope with her infant's traumatic situation in a positive, healthy way.

In our daily music therapy practice, we often meet infants with bonding and attachment disorders. We find they were born too early, born at risk, or with early hospital experiences. Auditive Stimulation may be seen as an important early intervention to help these infants, and their parents, find a better start for their lives.

REFERENCES

Abromeit, D. H. (2003). The Newborn Individualized Developmental Care and Assessment Program (NIDCAP) as model for clinical music therapy interventions with premature infants. *Music Therapy Perspectives,* 21(2), 60-68.

Achenbach, T. M., Howell, M. S., Aoki, M. F. & Rauh, V. A. (1993). Nine-year outcome of the Vermont intervention program for low birth weight infants. *Pediatrics,* 91(1), 45-55.

Als, H. (1995). The preterm infant: A model for the study of fetal brain expectation. In J. Lecanuet, W. Fifer, W. Smotherman & N. Krasnegor (Eds.) *Fetal Development: A Psychobiological Perspective* (pp. 439-471). Hillsdale, N.J.: Erlbaum.

Arnon, S., Shapsa, A., Forman, L., Regev, R., Bauer, S. & Litmanovitz, I. (2006). Live music is beneficial to preterm infants in the neonatal intensive care environment. *Birth: Issues in Perinatal Care,* 33, 131-136.

Bowlby, J (1969). *Attachment and Loss.* New York: Basic Books.

Brazelton, T. B. (1981). A new model of assessing the behavioral organization in preterm and fullterm infants: Two case studies. *Journal of the American Academy of Child Psychiatry,* 20, 239.

Caplan, G., Manson, E., Kalpan, D. M. (1963). Four studies of crisis in parents of prematures. *Community Mental Health Journal, 1,* 149-161.

Cramer, B. (1976). A mother's reaction to premature birth. In M.K. Klaus & J.H. Kennell (Eds.), *Mother-Infant Bonding.* St. Louis: C.V. Mosby.

Crearsey, G., Jarvis, P., Myers, B., Markowitz, P. & Kerkering, K. (1993). Mental and motor development for three groups of premature infants. *Infant Behavior and Development,* 16, 365-372.

DeCasper, A. F. & Fifer, W. P. (1980). Of human bonding: Newborns prefer their mother's voices. *Science,* 208, 1174-1176.

DeCasper, A. J. & Spence, M. J. (1986). Prenatal maternal speech influences newborns' perception of speech sound. Infant Behavior and Development, 9, 133-150.

Duffy, F., Als, H. & McAnulty, G. (1990). Behavioral and electrophysiological evidence for gestational age effects in healthy preterm and full term infants studied 2 weeks after expected due date. *Child Development,* 61, 1271–1286.

Eagle, M. N. (1984). *Recent Development in Psychoanalysis. A Critical Evaluation.* New York: McGraw-Hill.Inc..

Fernald, A. (1982). Acoustic determinants of infant preferences for "motherese". Unpublished doctoral dissertation, University of Oregon.

Fischer, C. B. & Als, H. (2004). Trusting behavioral communication. In M. Nöcker-Ribaupierre (Ed.), Music Therapy for Premature and Newborn Infants (pp. 1-20). Gilsum, NH: Barcelona Publishers.

Gilad, E. & Arnon , S. (2010). The role of live music and singing as a stress-reducing modality in the Neonatal Intensive Care Unit. *Music and Medicine Journal,* 2(1), 18-22.

Hack, M., Klein, N. & Taylor, H. (1995). Long-term development outcomes of low birth weight infants. *The Future of Children,* 5, 171-196. www.futureofchildren.org/LBW/12LBWHAC.htm.

Hanson-Abromeit, D. & Colwell, C. (Eds.). (2008). *Medical Music Therapy for Pediatrics in Hospital Settings: Using Music to Support Medical Interventions.* Silver Spring, MD: American Music Therapy Association.

Hartling, L., Shaik, M., Tjolsvold, L., Leicht, R., Liang, Y. & Kumar, M. (2009). Music for medical indications in the neonatal period: A systematic review of randomised control trials. *Archives of Disease in Childhood: Fetal and Neonatal Edition,* 94, 349-354.

Haslbeck, F. (2004). Music Therapy with preterm infants – Theoretical approach and first practical experience. *Music Therapy Today,* 5, 4(Aug). Retrieved from http://musictherapyworld.net/modules/mmmagazine/issues/20040727092613/20040727094302/MTT5_4_Haslbeck.pdf.

Hüppi, P., Maier, S., Peled, S., Zientara, G., Barnes, P., Jolesz, F. & Volpe, J. (1998). Microstructural development of human newborn cerebral white matter assessed in vivo by diffusion tensor imaging. *Pediatric Research,* 44, 584–590.

Hüther, G. (2005). Pränatale Einflüsse auf die Hirnentwicklung. In I. Krens & H. Krens (Hg), *Grundlagen Einer Vorgeburtlichen Psychologie* (pp. 49–62). Göttingen: Vandenhoeck & Ruprecht

Jotzko, M. (2001). Elterliche traumatisierung durch die frühgeburt des kindes. *Pschotraumatologie,* 21(1), 34.

Jotzo, M. & Poets, C.F. (2005). Helping parents cope with the trauma of premature birth. An evaluation of a trauma preventive psychological intervention. *Pediatrics,* 115, 915-919.

Klaus, M. H. & Kennell, J. H. (1976): *Maternal-Infant Bonding.* St. Louis.

Lickliter, R. (2000). Atypical perinatal sensory stimulation and early perceptual development: Insights from developmental psychobiology. *Journal of Perinatology*, 20, 45–54.

Linderkamp, O. & Skuroppa, D. (in press). The Fetal Brain and Sensory Deprivation.

Loewy, J. V., (Ed). (2000). *Music Therapy in the Neonatal Intensive-Care Unit.* Boston, MA: The Louis & Lucille Armstrong Music Therapy Program, Beth Israel Medical Center.

Loewy, J. (2004). A clinical model of music therapy in the NICU. In M. Nöcker-Ribaupierre (Ed.), *Music Therapy for Premature and Newborn Infants*: (pp. 159-176). Gilsum NH: Barcelona Publishers.

Maiello, S. (2004). On the meaning of prenatal auditory perception and memory for the development of the mind: A psychoanalytic perspective. In M. Nöcker-Ribaupierre (Ed.), *Music Therapy for Premature and Newborn Infants* (pp. 51-66). Gilsum NH: Barcelona Publishers.

Nöcker-Ribaupierre, M. (1995). *Auditive Stimulation nach Frühgeburt. Ein Beitrag zur Musiktherapie.* G. Fischer, Stuttgart.

Nöcker-Ribaupierre, M. (1999): Premature birth and music therapy. In. T. Wigram & J. De Backer (Eds.), *Clinical Applications of Music Therapy in Developmental Disability, Pediatrics and Neurology* (pp.47-68). London: Jessica Kingsley Publishers.

Nöcker-Ribaupierre, M. (2004). The mother's voice – a bridge between two worlds. In M. Nöcker-Ribaupierre (Ed.), *Music Therapy for Premature and Newborn Infants* (pp. 97-112). Gilsum NH: Barcelona Publishers.

Nöcker-Ribaupierre, M. (Ed.) (2004). *Music Therapy for Premature and Newborn Infants.* Gilsum NH: Barcelona Publishers.
Nöcker-Ribaupierre, M. & Zimmer M.L. (2004). *Förderung Frühgeborener Kinder mit Stimme und Musik.* München: Reinhardt.
Nöcker-Ribaupierre, M. (2007). The therapeutic use of sound at the beginning of life. In I. Frohne-Hagemann (Ed.), *Receptive Music Therapy* (pp. 267-276). Wiesbaden: Reichert.
O'Gorman, S. (2006). The infant's mother: Facilitating an experience of Infant-Directed Singing with the mother in mind. *British Journal of Music Therapy* 20(1), 22-30.
Riegel, K., Ohrt, B. & Wolke, D. (1985). *Die Entwicklung Gefährdet Geborener Kinder bis zum Fünften Lebensjahr.* Stuttgart: Enke.
Righetti, P. L. (1996). The emotional experience of the fetus: A preliminary report. *Pre- and Perinatal Psychology Journal,* 11(1), 55-65.
Rubel, E. (1984): Ontogeny of auditory system function. *Annual Review Physiology,* 46, 213.
Schwartz, F.J. (2004). Medical music therapy for the premature baby: Research review. In M. Nöcker-Ribaupierre (Ed.), *Music Therapy for Premature and Newborn Infants* (pp. 85-96). Gilsum NH: Barcelona Publishers.
Schwartz, F., Ritchie, R. & Sacks, L. (1998). Music, stress reduction, and medical cost savings in the neonatal intensive care unit. In R. Rebollo-Pratt & D. Erdonmez-Grocke (Eds.), *MusicMedicine 3: MusicMedicine and Music Therapy: Expanding Horizons* (pp. 120- 130). Melbourne, Australia: University of Melbourne Press.
Shoemark, H. (2004). Family centered music therapy for infants with complex medical and surgical needs. In M. Nöcker-Ribaupierre (Ed.), *Music Therapy for Premature and Newborn Infants* (pp. 141-158). Gilsum NH: Barcelona Publishers.
Shoemark, H. (1999). Singing as the foundation for multi-modal stimulation of the older preterm infant. In R. Rebollo-Pratt & D. Erdonmez Grocke (Eds.), *MusicMedicine 3: MusicMedicine and Music Therapy: Expanding Horizons* (pp. 140-152). Melbourne, Australia: University of Melbourne Press.
Shoemark, H. (1994). The process of music therapy as it relates to the

development of children with multiple disabilities. In A. Lem (Ed.), *Music Therapy Collection* (pp. 45-49). Canberra, Australia: Ausdance.

Standley, J. M. & Moore, R. (1995). Therapeutic effects of music and mother's voice on premature infants. *Pediatric Nursing* 1, 90-95.

Standley, J. (1998). Music therapy research with premature infants: Clinical implications. In R. Pratt and D. Erdonmez Grocke (Eds.), *MusicMedicine 3: MusicMedicine and Music Therapy: Expanding horizons* (pp. 131-139). Melbourne, Australia: University of Melbourne Press.

Standley, J. M. (2004). Music Therapy with Premature Infants: Research and Developmental Interventions. Silver Spring, MD: AMTA.

Stern, D. (1985). The Interpersonal World of the Infant. New York: Basic Books.

Stern, D. (1995). *The Motherhood Constellation.* New York: Basic Books.

Vonderlin, E. (1999). *Frühgeburt: Elterliche Belastung und Bewältigung.* Heidelberg: Universitätsverlag C.Winter

Winnicott, D. W. (1965). *The Maturational Processes and the Facilitating Environment: Studies in the Theory of Emotional Development.* New York: International Universities Press.

Zimmer, M.L. (2004). Premature babies have premature mothers: Practical experiences with premature infants and their mothers using auditive stimulation with the mother's voice. In M. Nöcker-Ribaupierre (Ed.), *Music Therapy for Premature and Newborn Infants* (pp. 113-128). Gilsum NH: Barcelona Publishers.

Chapter Two

MEDICAL MUSIC THERAPY WITH PREMATURE INFANTS: FAMILY-CENTERED SERVICES

Miriam Hillmer, Olivia Swedberg and Jayne M. Standley

INTRODUCTION

Research on the effects of music listening with neonates has shown numerous benefits, including increased weight gain, decreased length of hospital stay, and improved oxygen saturation levels (Caine, 1991; Collins & Kuck, 1991; Standley & Moore, 1995). Training parents of premature infants in the use of music therapy techniques with their child has shown benefits for both infants and parents (Cevasco, 2006; Whipple, 2000). A family-centered approach to medical music therapy was used in this case study, wherein music listening was used to enhance parent-infant bonding and promote infant development. This clinical work took place in the Neonatal Intensive Care Unit (NICU) at a regional medical center in the Southeastern United States. Parents of an infant born prematurely were trained to use recorded music in their infant's isolette while the infant was an inpatient in the NICU. The parents indicated strengthened perceptions of bonding with their child and increased understanding of their infant's responses. The infant showed positive responses to the music intervention, including improved vital signs, as reported by parent feedback.

FOUNDATIONAL CONCEPTS

Medical music therapy involves the use of evidence-based music therapy practices to help meet the physical and/or psychosocial needs of patients receiving medical treatment (Gfeller, 1999). Physical needs may include pain reduction, sensory integration, and muscular functioning. Psychosocial needs may include normalization of the environment, anxiety reduction, and provision of emotional support that assists an individual in coping with their current situation (Gfeller, 1999). Protocols for medical music therapy treatment are based on findings from this growing body of medical music therapy research. Just as medical treatment is based on evidence-based standards of care with predictable outcomes for specific diagnoses, medical music therapy is grounded in research (Standley & Walworth, 2005).

Results from music therapy research in the Neonatal Intensive Care Unit (NICU) have shown positive benefits of medical music therapy with premature infants. A meta-analysis (Standley, 2002) showed an overall effect size of .83 for music interventions with premature infants. Standley (2003) describes five music therapy interventions that research shows are beneficial for premature infants:

i. *Sustained music, live or recorded, provided individually* - increases respiratory regularity and oxygen saturation (Collins & Kuck, 1991; Standley & Moore, 1995; Cassidy & Standley, 1995) and decreases distressed behaviors (Coleman, Pratt, Stoddard, Gerstmann, & Abel, 1997; Flowers, McCain, & Hilker, 1999).

ii. *Music to reinforce non-nutritive sucking using the Pacifier Activated Lullaby device* - increases sucking endurance (Standley, 2000; Standley, 2003) and reduces pain perception (Whipple, 2004).

iii. *Music and multimodal stimulation* - increases tolerance to stimulation and decreases length of stay (Standley, 1998).

iv. *Infant stimulation* - facilitates alertness and responses to others in infants close to discharge (Ilari, 2003; Standley, Walworth, & Nguyen, 2009; Tims, 1978; Trehub & Trainor, 1993).

v. *Parent counseling* - promotes parent/infant bonding and trains parents in the use of music with their child (Whipple, 2000; Cevasco, 2006).

Music therapists working in the NICU must be familiar with best-practices in NICU music therapy so they can convey these practices to the parents. Because of the fragility of premature infants, specialized training in NICU music therapy is recommended for qualified music therapists seeking to practice in the NICU. Standley (2003) provides a summary, based on the results of numerous studies, of guidelines for music use in the NICU:

- less than 70 dB on a C scale
- maximum of four hours per day
- music sung by the mother, another female, or children is preferable
- singing should be a cappella or with a single accompanying instrument
- the character of the music should be soothing, constant, and relatively unchanging
- light rhythmic emphasis, constant rhythm
- constant volume
- melodies in the higher vocal ranges, which are heard best by infants
- a variety of musical selections should be used so as not to cause habituation or fatigue
- most lullabies meet the above criteria and are thus appropriate for premature infants (Standley, 2003).

While music therapy has long been used in medical treatment and is becoming part of standard care in many NICUs, it has evolved as the practice of medicine has grown and changed. Recent studies promote a family-centered approach to medical care, which has shown beneficial outcomes for patients and their families (Henneman & Cardin, 2002; Kardia, et al., 2003). While traditional medical care has focused on the diagnosis and treatment of illness, family-centered care takes into account not only how the patient's psychosocial state impacts their physical health, but also the needs of the family who form the patient's support system. Because medical music therapy addresses psychosocial needs in addition to physical needs, this focus on family-centered care is not a new phenomenon for music therapists working in medical settings; indeed, the family-centered approach is easily incorporated in the medical music therapy model, in which the music therapist works with the patient and his/her family to help strengthen the patient's support system.

The benefits of using a family-centered approach to medical treatment have been documented in the NICU (Harrison, 1993; Cisneros Moore, et al., 2003). Having a pre-term infant can be stressful for parents, more so than having a full-term infant (Bremond et al., 1993). This early stressful experience can be detrimental to the formation of parent-infant attachment (Feldman & Eidelman, 2006; Forcada-Geux et al., 2006; Minde, et al., 1983). Parent-infant attachment has a great impact on child development (Crawford, 1982). Receiving appropriate support can help mediate the effects of a stressful experience on parents of pre-term infants (Lawhon, 2002; Brisch, et al., 2003). Training in uses of music with premature infants is a successful form of support for parents (Whipple, 2000; Lai, et al., 2006; Maguire, et al., 2007).

Henneman and Cardin (2002) recently published guidelines for family-centered critical care, broken into ten steps, which can provide foundation for the provision of family-centered care in the NICU. Step one is to understand the meaning of family-centered care, defined by the authors as "a philosophical approach to care that recognizes the needs of patients' family members as well as the important role that family members play during a patient's illness" (p. 12). Step two is to know the needs of the family. Step three involves integrating family-centered values into hospital standards and policies, leading to step four, using hospital resources to provide family-centered care, and step five, creating tools to help families. Step six cautions healthcare professionals not to confuse family issues with security and confidentiality issues and step seven reminds them to be consistent with patients' families. Step eight, making family-centered care a multidisciplinary group endeavor, will help with the implementation of step nine, which recognizes the need for ongoing attention and support for a family-centered approach. The authors' final advice in step ten is to be patient and recognize that implementing a new approach successfully will take time. When utilizing a family-centered approach to medical music therapy in the NICU, it is also important that the music therapist provide nonjudgmental understanding and acceptance of decisions made by parents regarding treatment or the withholding of treatment (Standley, 2003).

This case study utilized two of the NICU music therapy interventions described by Standley (2003): 1) individually provided periods of sustained music, and 2) parent counseling. These interventions were implemented by a NICU-MT using a family-centered approach. The protocols that were followed were based on the body of music therapy research with premature infants.

THE CLIENTS

This case example focuses on the use of parent training in the use of recorded music placed in the isolette/crib. Of particular importance were parent perceptions of their child's progress and feelings of bonding with their infant. The clients were parents of an infant in the High-Risk NICU. As is often found in parents with infants in the NICU, these clients experienced a high level of stress related to the condition of their child. The baby was born at 26 gestational weeks and had a birth weight of around 1.5 pounds. The young gestational age and small size of the infant initially restricted the amount of contact the parents were able to have with their baby. For several weeks they were limited to interacting with their infant through an isolette and were not able to hold their little one. The baby was born at such a young age that the mother commented during the first meeting with the music therapist that the infant had not yet developed the ability to cry. With conditions this serious, care was out of the parent's hands and, as a result, they missed out on an essential bonding period. The opportunity for the clients to provide music for their infant was seen as a possible way to promote bonding between parent and child.

The clients were offered parent training in playing recorded music for their baby once the infant was identified, in a weekly interdisciplinary meeting, as a possible candidate for services. This music therapy referral was based on gestational age and medical stability of the infant. Per hospital protocol for sound stimulation and current research literature (Standley, 2000; Standley, 2002; Standley, 2003), music therapy was not offered to the parents until the infant was 30 weeks corrected gestational age.

Assessment

In the NICU setting, it is important for both the infant and family needs to be assessed and addressed. The infant requires medical attention with the music intervention serving as an adjunct to treatment. The music therapist assesses the infant's appropriateness for music interventions on an ongoing basis. This includes understanding the infant's current medical condition, ability to tolerate auditory, tactile, visual, and vestibular stimulation, and positive reactions to music interventions. Families often require emotional support, and music-based interventions provide this. The music therapist assesses family needs through conversation with medical staff and the family as well as through observation of family interactions with both the infant and medical staff.

In this case study, the clients' needs were assessed during the music therapist's initial phone conversation and subsequent meeting in which training on playing recorded music took place. The family had heard about music therapy services prior to being contacted and had inquired about receiving these services for their child. They were pleased to find out that receiving training from a music therapist enabled them to have a more active role with their infant and that the benefits of music listening for neonates were supported by research. In assessing the clients, the music therapist paid particular attention to how both parents interacted with their infant, any concerns verbalized, their level of involvement with the standard care of their infant, and their level of passiveness or aggressiveness in interacting with the music therapist. The infant's ability to tolerate the auditory stimulation as well as positive signs was also assessed throughout the training session.

Upon our first meeting, the clients appeared anxious about the condition of their child as evidenced by their frequent questions and uncertainty of how to respond to statements relating to their baby's current condition. For instance, prior to training, the parents were asked to fill out a form assessing their feelings of closeness and bonding with their infant. For many of the statements on the questionnaire, parents asked for clarification, wrote explanations to their answers, or left the statement blank. The music therapist attempted to ease the client's concerns by assuring them there was no 'right' answer to the questionnaire, no 'wrong' questions to ask, and that they would receive further information on how to read their child's response to the music. It was determined that family centered music therapy, in the form of parent training, would be beneficial for the client and support a more active parenting role.

THE THERAPEUTIC PROCESS

The therapeutic process in the NICU is different with each individual client, depending on the level of family involvement and the overall family dynamics. It begins while the therapist is assessing the infant and family needs and continues once an appropriate course of action is determined. The music therapist has many researched treatment options at their disposal including multimodal stimulation, music listening, the Pacifier Activated Lullaby device, and parent training in therapeutic music techniques (Caine, 1991; Cassidy & Standley, 1995; Cevasco, 2006; Standley, 1998; Standley, 2000; Whipple, 2000). It is important that therapeutic interventions utilize a family centered approach whenever possible. As was mentioned earlier, Henneman & Cardin (2002) outline several steps to successfully implementing family centered care. Steps that are applicable for the music therapist in the NICU setting include:

- Step One – *Understanding what family centered care is*: The music therapist must understand that this approach to treatment recognizes the needs of the family, that these needs affect the patient, and understand this interplay. Specifically in the NICU, this includes understanding that the use of music strategies promoting parent education or bonding can have a direct impact on the infant.
- Step Two – *Knowing the needs of the family:* The family typically has three needs: 1) for information, 2) for reassurance, and 3) to be with the patient. NICU music therapy interventions can address all three needs if the music therapist communicates with the family about treatment and facilitates interaction between parent and infant.
- Step Three – *Integrating into standards and policies*: The music therapist must make it standard practice to contact the family of infants in the NICU when services have been referred. This provides the opportunity for the therapist to provide information, address parental concerns/assess parental needs, and offer family

centered services as appropriate. This practice should also be written into departmental policies.
- Step Four – *Creating tools to help*: The music therapist can offer information and packets to families to use as resources. Handouts highlighting the benefits of music, listing appropriate types of music, outlining steps to treatment, and listing music therapy contact information.
- Step Five – *Making family centered care a multidisciplinary group endeavor*: As a part of the clinical team in the NICU, the music therapist should be in close contact with staff from other disciplines (i.e., speech and/or occupational therapy, patient education, and nursing) who are providing treatment and/or are in contact with the patient and family. There should be open communication regarding family and patient needs between the music therapist and these individuals. This can take place in the form of interdisciplinary meetings, one on one interactions between the music therapist and specific staff members, or both.

When implemented correctly, these steps to family centered care aid parents in coping with their infant's hospitalization by addressing their concerns and needs. This, in turn, facilitates a healthier emotional state, creating a better environment for parents to make critical decisions regarding their child. However, even with family centered care, whatever the needs of the family, the needs of the patient come first. Medical staff must always be consulted before implementing any music therapy intervention with neonates.

Throughout the therapeutic process and regardless of the type of intervention, the music therapist is constantly monitoring three things: 1) the infant's response to music interventions; 2) the infant's medical progress and; 3) the changing needs of the parents. The infant constantly provides feedback as to how the intervention is being tolerated. Medical staff and therapists continually keep a watchful eye on vital signs (heart rate, respiratory rate, and oxygen saturation level), subtle distress signs, and signs of pleasure. Some of this feedback is obvious to the observer, such as crying, smiling, or a large change in the infant's vital signs. Conversely, some infant responses are more subtle and require careful observation, such as thrusting of the tongue or orienting toward a stimulus. For the music therapist, these signs, whether positive or negative, guide the therapeutic process. A sign of distress causes the therapist to pull back and allow the infant to return to its previous state. A positive sign indicates tolerance of the stimuli, is noted by the therapist, and as appropriate, further stimuli is introduced.

The current medical state of the infant is extremely important when providing any type of therapy. Placement of tubes, time of last feeding, and recent procedures are just a few of the issues the therapist should be aware of before starting a therapeutic intervention. Answers to these questions will determine whether music therapy is appropriate at the current time and, if appropriate, whether adaptations need to be made due to the infant's medical condition.

The parent's needs may change over time and the needs of one parent may be different from his/her partner/spouse. For instance, some parents are overwhelmed initially and cannot process all of the information they receive about their infant. They may initially reject attempts from medical staff to provide help and support, whereas later they may become empowered at the thought of caring for their infant and may seek as much information and support as possible. The infant's current condition and various other factors such as individual coping styles and support from extended family and community are variables that may affect the needs of the parents. The music therapist must be sensitive to this and offer information, reassurance, and facilitate opportunities for bonding, where appropriate.

The therapeutic process in this case example illustrates how music therapists provided family centered care while constantly monitoring infant responses, infant medical condition, and parental needs. The music therapist began treatment once parent training in recorded music was determined to be the appropriate therapeutic intervention for the clients. The parent training consisted of several steps:

1. *Parents selected a CD from the 'approved music' list to be placed in a provided CD player.* This was a list of approved CDs available for the clients to use while the infant was in the hospital and was categorized depending on the age of the baby. The music therapist explained what was taken into consideration when compiling the list, including limited instrumentation, slow, even tempo, few voices, and lack of sudden musical changes. It

was explained that the benefits of these musical qualities fostered soothing, predictable stimulation for infants. The clients were given a copy of this list to use as a future reference in selecting appropriate music for their infant (see Appendix 1 for a list of appropriate CDs).
2. *The importance of obtaining nurse permission prior to playing music was stressed.* The nurse in charge of the infant at the time of each intervention was the authority on his/her current medical condition and appropriateness for music listening at the time. Especially earlier on, as the infant's medical condition was more severe, the clients understood that the nurse had the child's best interest in mind in approving or declining the playing of recorded music on a particular day. As the infant aged, graduated to the intermediate nursery, and became more medically stable, the medical staff granted the clients a larger role in determining the appropriate time to play music. This was evidenced in feedback forms filled out by the clients, indicating a more independent role as the infant grew and developed.
3. *Equipment was cleaned in accordance with hospital infection control procedures and the importance of such procedures was explained.* Such precautions included cleaning with hospital-grade cleaners prior to each use and dedicating equipment to the individual patient. With antibiotic-resistant strands of viruses and bacteria fast becoming a problem in communities and hospitals, precautions to reduce the spread of germs are extremely important. This is especially true for a susceptible population such as premature infants. The parents were receptive and appreciative of the precautions taken to protect their loved one.
4. *The music therapist explained the set-up and position of the equipment in the infant's bed.* Correct placement included the speakers at the foot of the bed facing the infant. One speaker was placed by each foot to allow for equal stimulation across both hemispheres of the brain (Standley, 2003).
5. *Appropriate volume level was discussed to avoid levels exceeding 70 db (scale C).* All CD players were marked by the music therapist with an appropriate maximum volume level (less than 70db on scale C). This marking was based on tests with a decibel

meter in an empty isolette. Because different recordings produce different decibel blends, clients were informed that volume levels may need to be lowered, but should never be increased above the marked level.

6. *Music was started by the music therapist and continued through the rest of the training session.*
7. *Positive signs and ways to identify these signs were discussed.* These included, but were not limited to: smiling, cooing, stable vital signs or positive change in vital signs, head orientation toward the music and opening eyes.
8. *Subtle signs of overstimulation, ways to identify these signs and appropriate parental response were discussed.* These included, but were not limited to: crying, halt hand, finger splay, tongue protrusion, hiccup, grimace, spitting/vomiting and struggling movement. Clients were taught that if these signs continued for more then 15 seconds, the music should be stopped until the behavior ceases and the patient returns to his/her baseline behavior. The music therapist demonstrated this during the training session.
9. *Other distress signs, ways to identify these and appropriate parental response were discussed.* These included oxygen saturation level below 86%, heart rate less than 100 beats per minute, or heart rate greater then 200 beats per minute. Clients were told to halt the music immediately if these physiological changes occurred and to wait until the infant returned to baseline. The music therapist demonstrated this during the training session. Clients were given an information sheet listing all distress signs and ways to respond to these. This allowed for independence by reassuring them that they did not have to memorize everything discussed but would have the information in writing to which they could refer.
10. *The music therapist walked parents through completion of the 'Music Form' and where to place this when completed.* This form was completed by the clients every time music was played. It asked for clients to rate their perceptions of the music's effect on their infant. Completed forms provided feedback to the music therapist regarding the parent's and infant's changing needs, along with the effectiveness of the training intervention.

11. *Instructions were given regarding maximum duration and frequency of music playing*: 30 minutes at a time was recommended for each child, not exceeding three times per day. Music listening should be alternated with at least 30 minutes of silence. These guidelines were included in the previously mentioned information sheet. Research in the use of recorded music with premature infants shows benefits from listening to music for up to four hours a day, but adverse effects exceeding this amount (Baily, et al., 2005). Therefore, a conservative time limit was given in order to avoid the possibility of exceeding four hours of sound stimulation in a 24-hour period.
12. *The music therapist remained with the clients to answer any questions and contact information was provided for any future questions.*

As the training took place the music therapist made note of the client's reaction to the information provided. This involved paying attention to how they were able to identify positive signs from their infant or signs of overstimulation, types of questions asked, whether they seemed more or less anxious as a result of parent training, and the overall comfort level in administering the recorded music. By the end of the training, the clients appeared more relaxed and assured of themselves as they started to take over the role of music provider with a better understanding of how to interpret their infant's responses. From this one-time meeting, the parents were given a positive means of interacting with their child. The music therapist determined that the clients were ready to provide music for their infant independently with the music therapist available for any questions or concerns. The frequency of music, infant responses, and parent perceptions were monitored through the use of 'music record forms' (Appendix 2) that the clients filled out during each music session.

Throughout their time in the NICU, the clients rated their perceptions of bonding with their infant utilizing a 5-point Likert scale. This helped assess the effectiveness of family-centered music therapy interventions on the clients' feelings of involvement and comfort in caring for their loved one. The first assessment was taken prior to any intervention from the music therapist. Responses indicated overall uncertainty on the part of the clients. They rated their *feelings of anxiety* and fear that their *interactions may harm the infant* as 'high.' They gave a rating of 'low' to their feelings of being *able to calm* their loved one and *understanding the infant responses*. They were neutral about their *perceptions of bonding* with their child. Finally, they were unable to answer questions relating to *feeling helpful* to their baby, *understanding their parenting role*, perceptions of whether their *infant was jittery*, and *knowing how to nurture their infant*. Each follow-up assessment, taken throughout the infant's time in the NICU and post discharge, indicated that the clients gained more confidence in interacting with their child and feelings of bonding. Specifically, the clients demonstrated a positive change in response to the question *'I feel bonding with my infant'* and *'I know how to calm my baby.'* In fact, responses to the question about calming the infant changed from 'strongly disagree' prior to music therapy intervention to 'strongly agree' by the time the infant was discharged. The clients also demonstrated a positive change in their response to the question *'I feel my interactions may harm my baby'* moving from 'agree' initially to 'strongly disagree.'

The music record form also offered insight into the clients' perception of the effectiveness of the music intervention. The clients filled out ten separate forms indicating that they provided nine independent music listening sessions for their infant following the parent training session with the music therapist. Responses during the first and second sessions indicated a neutral response by the clients regarding their perceptions of the music's benefits for their infant. These questions specifically asked about the music's effect in calming and nurturing the infant, as well as improving vital signs, environment, and quality of life. Following the first two sessions, the clients always marked a positive response to these questions, suggesting a shift in perception and an increase in confidence. However, the one question that asked about the music's benefits on the infant's development was left blank on every form. This suggests that the parents lacked knowledge regarding music's researched benefits on infant development.

As the infant moved from the high risk NICU to the intermediate NICU and became more medically stable, the parents became even more independent in their administration of music. With medical staff permission, they brought their own CD player and made decisions regarding music's appropriateness at the time. This suggests an understanding of their child's current state, responses, and a confidence in providing the stimulus. This was a far cry from the music therapist's initial meeting with the clients where uncertainty prevailed. Through the information and support provided by the music therapist and medical staff, the clients were given an opportunity to take on a pro-active parenting role, have meaningful interactions with their child and bond during a critical period.

The baby was discharged at approximately 39 weeks corrected gestational age. The music therapist followed up with the clients one week post discharge to address any further needs and assess continued perceptions of bonding.

SUMMARY

When working in the NICU, the music therapist fulfills several roles. The most important is as an advocate for the patient in offering complimentary therapeutic interventions to soothe and promote optimal development in a stressful environment. This involves close contact and a healthy working relationship with various medical staff. Also important is for the music therapist to address family needs because this will have a direct impact on the long-term health of the patient. Family-centered care supports all of these roles and fosters an environment of healing.

All music therapy interventions, from multimodal stimulation (Standley, 1998) to parent training (Cevasco, 2006; Whipple, 2000), to the use of the Pacifier Activated Lullaby device (Standley, 2000), work with the family-centered model of care by focusing treatment on the specific needs of the patient, involving family, and engaging in constant consultations with medical staff. This case example is one illustration of the success of family-centered care through the use of parent training in playing recorded music. First, the infant's specific needs were identified at a multidisciplinary meeting. Next, the clients were consulted regarding possible music therapy interventions and an assessment of the client's needs was conducted by the music therapist. Given the infant's age and medical needs, as well as the client's desire for an increased role in care, reservation in interactions, and uncertainty in understanding their child's responses, parent training in playing recorded music was deemed the most appropriate intervention.

The clients were presented with information regarding the benefits of music for their child, signs of pleasure or overstimulation, and steps for offering music stimulation. The music therapist monitored the client's feelings of bonding with their infant as well as their perceptions of the music's benefit. Overall, the results suggest the effectiveness of the music therapy parent training intervention and continued follow-up. The clients' confidence in their role as parents, feelings of bonding, and understanding of their child's responses grew throughout the process. In addition, the feeling that the music was a positive intervention that benefited the infant, strengthened. However, the clients remained unsure about the music's benefits on their child's development. While they could physically see if the music positively affected the infant's current state, they did not show an understanding of its potential long-term benefit. This highlights an area to be stressed both in initial training with the clients as well as in follow-up interactions. The music therapist should stress research supporting the effectiveness of music interventions on child development, putting this information into terms that are easy for parents to understand. There is a rich amount of this type of literature both in the NICU setting and beyond (Tims, 1978; Ilari, 2003; Standley, et al., 2009). Articles or information sheets can be provided to the clients for continued reference, as well as more discussion of how the music may directly benefit their child (i.e. weight gain, neural development, etc.). This addition would further support family centered care, augment the therapeutic experience, and make a stressful situation for parents and infants in the NICU more manageable.

REFERENCES

Baily, L.A., Kantak, A., Jarjoura, D., Reuman, P. & Kantak, S. (2005). Music therapy and sound reduction in the Neonatal Intensive Care Unit. Unpublished paper presented at Music Therapy in the NICU: A Symposium, Cleveland, OH.

Bremond, M., Gold, F., Suc, A., Chamboux, C., Saliba, E., Guerois, M. & Laugier, J. (1993). The birth and subsequent hospitalization of premature infants born before 32 weeks of gestation: What do parents remember after one year? Survey on 94 cases. *Pediatrie, 48*(4), 275-281.

Brisch, K.H., Bechinger, D., Betzler, S. & Heinemann, H. (2003). Early preventive attachment oriented psychotherapeutic intervention program with parents of a very low birthweight premature infant:

Results of attachment and neurological development. *Attachment and Human Development, 5*(2), 120-135.

Caine, J. (1991). The effects of music on the selected stress behaviors, weight, caloric and formula intake, and length of hospital stay of premature and low birth weight neonates in a newborn intensive care unit. *Journal of Music Therapy, 28*(4), 180-192.

Cassidy, J. & Standley, J. (1995). The effect of music listening on physiological responses of premature infants in the NICU. *Journal of Music Therapy, 32*(4), 208-227.

Cevasco, A. (2006). The effects of mothers' singing on full-term and preterm infants and maternal emotional responses. Doctoral Dissertation, The Florida State University.

Cisneros Moore, K., Coker, K., DuBuisson, A., Swett, B. & Edwards, W. (2003). Implementing potentially better practices for improving family-centered care in Neonatal Intensive Care Units: Successes and challenges. *Pediatrics, 111*(4), 450-460.

Coleman, J., Pratt, R., Stoddard, R., Gerstmann, D. & Abel, H. (1999). The effects of the male and female singing and speaking voices on selected physiological and behavioral measures of premature infants in the intensive care unit. *International Journal of Arts Medicine, 5*(2), 4-11.

Collins, S. & Kuck, K. (1991). Music therapy in the neonatal intensive care unit. *Neonatal Network, 9*(6), 23-26.

Crawford, J.W. (1982). Mother-infant interaction in premature and full-term infants. *Child Development, 53*(4), 957-962.

Feldman, R. & Eidelman, A. (2006). Neonatal state organization, neuromaturation, mother-infant interaction, and cognitive development in small-for-gestational-age premature infants. *Pediatrics, 118*(3), 869-878.

Flowers, A., McCain, A. & Hilker, K. (1999). The effects of music listening on premature infants. Paper presented at the Biennial Meeting, Society for Research in Child Development, Albuquerque, NM.

Forcada-Geux, M., Pierrehumbert, B., Borghini, A., Moessinger, A. & Muller-Nix, C. (2006). Early dyadic patterns of mother-infant interactions and outcomes of prematurity at 18 months. *Pediatrics, 118*(1), 107-114.

Gfeller, K. (1999). Music therapy in the treatment of medical conditions. In W.B. Davis, K.E. Gfeller and M.H. Thaut (Eds.), *An Introduction to Music Therapy* (pp. 204-220). Boston: McGraw Hill.

Harrison, H. (1993). The principles of family-centered neonatal care. *Pediatrics, 92*(5), 643-650.

Henneman, E. & Cardin, S. (2002). Family-centered critical care: A practical approach to making it happen. *Critical Care Nurse, 22*(6), 12-19.

Ilari, B. (2003). Music and babies: A review of research with implications for music educators. *Update: Applications of Research in Music Education* (Online), 21(2), 1.

Kardia, S., Modell, S. & Peyser, P. (2003). Family-centered approaches to understanding and preventing coronary heart disease. *American Journal of Preventative Medicine, 24*(2), 143-151.

Lai, H., Chen, C., Peng, T., Chang, F., Hsieh, M., Huang, H. & Chang, S. (2006). Randomized controlled trial of music during kangaroo care on maternal state anxiety and preterm infants' responses. *International Journal of Nursing Studies, 43*(2), 139-146.

Lawhon, G. (2002). Facilitation of parenting the premature infant within the Newborn Intensive Care Unit. *Journal of Perinatal and Neonatal Nursing, 16*(1), 71-82.

Maguire, C., Bruil, J., Wit, J. & Walther, E. (2007). Reading preterm infants' behavioral cues: An intervention study with parents of premature infants born <32 weeks. *Early Human Development, 83*(7), 419-424.

Minde, K., Whitelaw, A., Brown, J. & Fitzhardinge, P. (1983). Effect of neonatal complications in premature infants on early parent-infant interactions. *Developmental Medicine and Child Neurology, 25*(6), 763-777.

Standley, J. (1998). The effect of music and multimodal stimulation on physiologic and developmental responses of premature infants in neonatal intensive care. *Pediatric Nursing, 24*(6), 532-538.

Standley, J. (2000). *Music Recommended for Soothing Premature Infants in the NICU and TMH NICU Policy on Sound Stimulation*. Tallahassee, FL: Author.

Standley, J. (2000). The effect of contingent music to increase non-nutritive sucking of premature infants. *Pediatric Nursing, 26*(5), 493-495, 498-499.

Standley, J. (2002). A meta-analysis of the efficacy of music therapy for premature infants. *Journal of Pediatric Nursing, 17*(2), 107-113.

Standley, J. (2003). *Music Therapy with Premature Infants: Research and Developmental Interventions.* Silver Springs, MD: American Music Therapy Association.

Standley, J. & Moore, R. (1995). Therapeutic effects of music and mother's voice on premature infants. *Pediatric Nursing, 21*(6), 509-512, 574.

Standley, J. & Walworth, D. (2005). Chapter 1: Overview. In J. Standley, D. Gregory, J. Whipple, D. Walworth, J. Nguyen, J. Jarred, et al. *Medical Music Therapy: A Model Program for Clinical Practice, Education, Training, and Research* (pp. 5-10). Silver Spring: American Music Therapy Association.

Standley, J., Walworth, D. & Nguyen, J. (2009). Effect of parent /child group music activities on toddler development: A pilot study. *Music Therapy Perspectives, 27*(1), 11-15.

Tims, F. (1978). Contrasting music conditions, visual attending behavior, and state in eight week-old infants. Doctoral Dissertation, The University of Kansas.

Trehub, S. & Trainor, L. (1993). Listening strategies in infancy: The roots of music and language development. In S. McAdams & E. Bigand (Eds.) *Thinking in Sound: The Cognitive Psychology of Human Audition* (pp. 278-320). Oxford: Clarendon Press.

Whipple, J. (2000). The effect of parent training in music and multimodal stimulation on parent-neonate interactions in the Neonatal Intensive Care Unit. *Journal of Music Therapy, 37*(4), 250–268.

Whipple, J. (2004). The effect of music-reinforced nonnutritive sucking on state of preterm, low birthweight infants experiencing heelstick. Doctoral Dissertation, The Florida State University.

APPENDIX 1: CD Master List

CDs for All Babies

No.	Artist	Album	Year	Company
1.	Various artists	*Baby's Best Sleepy Time Songs*	2004	Madacy Entertainment Group
2.	Various artists	*Baby's Best Bedtime Favorites*	2004	Madacy Entertainment Group
3.	Various artists	*The World Sings Goodnight*	1997	Silver Wave Records
4.	Anne Meeker Miller	*Clap Your Hands*	2004	Love Language
5.	Nina Gerber	*Sweet Dreams: Lullabies for Guitar*	2003	Goatscape Music
6.	Various artists	*Disney's Lullaby Album*	2000	Walt Disney Records
7.	Raffi	*Quiet Time: Raffi*	2006	Troubadour Records
8.	Carnie Wilson	*A Mother's Gift: Lullabies from the Heart*	2006	Big3 Records
9.	Various Artists	*Mama's Lullaby: Lullabies Sung by Women Around the World*	2001	Ellipsis Arts
10.	Various Artists	*Lullaby*	2005	Music for Little People

CDs for Older Babies

11.	Various Artists	*Song Kids Love to Sing*	1997	Straightway Music
12.	Various artists	*A Child's Gift of Lullabies*	2002	New Haven Kids
13.	Twin Sisters	*Baby Dreams*	2006	Twin Sisters
14.	Twin Sisters	*Good Night, Angel*	2006	Twin Sisters
15.	Various Artists	*I Can Only Imagine*	2003	Simpleville Music
16.	Lucas Richman	*Day is Done: An Album of Lullabies*	2001	LeDor Music Publishing

APPENDIX 2: MUSIC RECORD FORM

Name: _____ Date: _____ CD Used _____

Was nurse's approval obtained today? _____ yes _____ no

Music START time _____ AM PM **Warning: No more than 30 minutes 3 times/day, music alternated with silence**

Music STOP time _____ AM   PM

Was music used with kangaroo care? _____ yes _____ no

Place a mark on the line which best represents your child's state BEFORE MUSIC

_____

Asleep   Awake/Calm   Awake/Restless   Crying/Very Agitated

Place a mark on the line which best represents your child's RESPONSE to music

_____

Asleep   Awake/Calm   Awake/Restless   Crying/Very Agitated

                                                     Disagree   Agree

Music calmed my baby	1	2	3	4	5
Music nurtured my baby	1	2	3	4	5
Music improved my baby's monitor readings	1	2	3	4	5
Music benefited my child's development	1	2	3	4	5
Music improved the environment for my child	1	2	3	4	5
Music improved the quality of life of my child	1	2	3	4	5

Distress signs: Discontinue music immediately if any of these physiologic changes occur:

>   Oxygen saturation drops below 86% for more than 5 seconds
>   Heartrate is less than 100 or greater than 200 for more than 5 seconds
>   Infant has episode of Apnea or bradycardia

Subtle distress signs: Discontinue music if you observe these infants responses for more than 15 seconds:

>   Hiccoughs, grimace, clinched eyes, eyes averted, tongue protrusion, finger splay, struggling movement, crying, whining, fussing, cry face, spitting/vomiting, halt hand.

Chapter Three

GROWING UP IN MUSIC: A JOURNEY THROUGH EARLY CHILDHOOD MUSIC DEVELOPMENT IN MUSIC THERAPY

Elizabeth K. Schwartz

INTRODUCTION

Growing up happens so naturally for most children that parents, siblings, family and friends take for granted the complex experiences and responses necessary for growth. The first few years are crucial to this developmental process. Children embrace language, early friendships, physical coordination and control, and a fundamental sense of themselves in the world. The amount of change during these critical first years is commonly viewed as being greater than at any other time in their lives (Bredekamp & Copple, 2009).

Sometimes, though, development does not occur as expected, or when expected. Parents or others close to the child notice that s/he is not speaking or making sounds; s/he does not move as other children her/his age move; or that s/he does not smile or play. For these parents and children, the journey to adulthood will be challenging and frequently filled with uncertainty, fear and sadness.

In 1986, Early Intervention (EI) was formally instituted in the United States through the passage of Public Law 99-457, now known as the Individuals with Disabilities Education Act (Humpal & Colwell, 2006). As such, it formalized a process of support for children with special developmental or learning needs and their families. This chapter describes one such program, called My Grownup and Me, in which music therapy experiences provided support to several young children and their families. Music became a core experience through which these little ones, all under three years old, had the opportunity to develop and grow.

In the cases presented, children were able to access music therapy through the Early Intervention system. The therapist's task was to empower the family as they sought to give their child experiences that ameliorated disabling conditions and allowed for developmental growth. This was accomplished through the modeling of interventions, information sharing and supportive relationships. As part of the emphasis on family, the Early Intervention System, as regulated through the Individual with Disabilities Act, requires that any services be provided in 'naturalistic' or 'community' environments to the greatest extent possible (Schwartz, 2009). In the cases to follow, music therapy sessions were held as a group experience at the childrens' room of a local library. The name of the program – My Grownup and Me – spells out the importance of family as a focal point of the therapy.

FOUNDATIONAL CONCEPTS

Music and Child Development

Young children have a simple trajectory – to grow up. Expectations that they will grow in a certain way are commonly referred to as normal development (Kegan, 1982). This growth occurs simultaneously across cognitive, motor, language, social and behavioral domains, and is usually understood to occur in stages or levels. For example, Kegan (1982) and Piaget (Ginsberg & Opper, 1969) developed models of cognitive development using a stage-like framework, while Mahler, Pine and Bergman (1975), Erikson (1963) and Stern (1985) focused on identity development within a broader developmental framework during the first six years of life.

Music develops in young children just as movement, language, thoughts and feelings develop (Briggs, 1991; Gordon, 2003; McDonald & Simons, 1989). From coo to cry, the musical sounds made by young children are one of the foundations of communication that form a child's sense of self and connection to others (De L'Etoile, 2006). The elements of music, such as pitch, melody, rhythm and musical form are naturally absorbed, integrated and engaged by all children (Gordon, 2003). Furthermore, the way in which children begin to sing, move or play an instrument happens in a developmental sequence that parallels speech, cognition or physical development (Briggs, 1991).

Schwartz (2008) built upon these frameworks to articulate a five-level continuum of development central to her music therapy practice: Awareness, Trust, Independence, Control and Responsibility. *Awareness* is "an awakening of the senses, of physical and sensual being. It is the beginning of thoughts and feelings. Awareness is reflexive and instinctual" (Schwartz, 2008 p.49). Within the level of *Trust*, "the young child reaches out and finds a response that helps to form a perception of the world as a place that has meaning, reliability and safety. Trust also means looking inward and finding constancy and stability" (Schwartz, 2008 p. 59). The child gaining *Independence* "can have experiences separate from another person. He or she can create the opportunity for experience in response to his or her own internal motivation" (Schwartz, 2008 p. 69). As children move into the level of *Control,* "They can use their cognitive abilities and communication skill to make choices. These choices become integrated into the 'self' "(Schwartz, 2008 p. 79). *Responsibility* "implies the recognition of the interdependency of the self with the external world while preserving the cability to maintain the "self" (Schwartz, 2008 p. 91).

Movement from one level to the next is dependent on mastery of the prior level. Components of each level include all the areas that humans are made up of – physical, cognitive, emotional, social, sensory and of course, musical dimensions. In the three cases presented, the children are in the first three developmental levels: Awareness, Trust and Independence.

Music Therapy within a Developmental Framework

Music therapy within this early childhood framework seeks to promote and expand development in as healthy a manner as possible. This therapy focuses on dynamic growth from Awareness to Trust; from Trust to Independence to Control; and from Control to Responsibility. In partnership with the parent or caregiver, the therapist crafts interventions and experiences that allow the child the opportunity to fully explore and integrate oneself within each level. The therapeutic work described supports both expansion of self within a level, as well as movement toward the next level. Language in these levels is still rudimentary, and cognition is just beginning to emerge. Insight and self-awareness, or meta-cognition, are a long way off. What is left is music and relationships. The therapeutic process, by necessity in very early childhood, is all about the music and the music makers.

The music interventions used in the My Grownup and Me follow this developmental design. Pitch and rhythm are the earliest elements used, as they are the earliest elements developed (Schwartz, 2008). The unaccompanied voice is the primary tool in the beginning. The immediacy and spontaneity afforded by singing is modeled after the 'motherese' and 'sing-song' vocal quality used in early parent/child dyads (De L'Etoile, 2006). The singing voice also provides a musical format that can be adopted by any adult and emphasizes the shared nature of music experienced by children in these early years.

Singing simple songs, vocalizing freely, and moving to rhythms are all musical experiences in which any child can learn to participate. The role of the music therapist in this type of program is to create interventions that the parent[1] can learn, remember and recreate within and outside the music therapy session. In this way, the therapist gives the music to the child and parent so that the activity/experience can be owned by the duo. This kind of giving/letting go imitates, in many ways, the process of parent/child individuation that is necessary for growth.

In My Grownup and Me, the child becomes part of a larger community represented by the other children and parents who join the group. Again, the emphasis is on supporting the child as he or she connects with other children and to their caregivers. This web of relationships becomes a social community though the shared experience of music making. Rather than the commonly used therapeutic triangle of therapist, client and music, early childhood music therapy can be pictured as a circle of music surrounding, encouraging, supporting and fostering all of these complex relationships.

The early childhood music therapist, then, engages the child and family in music that promotes healthy, normal development. Therapy is considered from a strength-based point of view intended to reposition the

---

1 or caregiver

child away from particular deficits and toward increasing positive, functional and dynamic growth. The therapy happens at the moment in which the child's drive to develop and the barrier of the disability collide. The music therapist uses music interventions to propel the child toward healthy development and away from this restraint of the disability.

THE CLIENTS

Concern for their child's development is only one challenge faced by parents who access Early Intervention. Emotional upheaval swings from hope to despair, frustration to longing and love. These myriad, complex and contradictory emotions all surface as the family comes to terms with the idea that their child may be disabled. Many families are uninformed about child development. And for many, the true nature of their child's difficulties are only unveiled over time. Early Intervention regulations speak of challenges and needs rather than diagnosis; hence the majority of young children only receive a formal diagnosis much later.

Michael[2] was 21 months when he began My Grownup and Me. He was a substantial little fellow who still had his chubby "baby cheeks." He wore glasses, even at his young age. Michael was initially referred to Early Intervention with concerns of developmental delay. He was slow to sit up and turn over. At 21 months he had only a few word approximations. He was just beginning to stand and was not yet walking. Michael came to group most often with his mother, but was frequently joined by his extended family.

Peter had just turned two when he started in My Grownup and Me. He was an active boy whose handsome face and compact frame looked like the epitome of the word "toddler." Peter had begun to receive speech therapy as part of Early Intervention, and his family was most concerned about his developing language. Peter came to group with his

---

[2] The children whose stories are told below have been created from real life events, but are not specific, actual children. Unlike therapy with many adults, children are unable to consent to their own therapy. While parents must agree to therapy, the fragile nature of this time of life makes it extremely difficult to expose parents to the possible pain an examination of their child might pose through publication. However, the details of the music, the therapy and the responses in these case studies reflect children I have encountered in my many years of clinical experience.

mother, who struggled to keep up with him as he darted about the room. She also shared that he had difficulties in other structured activities such as parent/child groups or library programs. Peter had two older siblings who shared in the responsibility of looking after Peter.

Emma was 26 months old and one of the few girls receiving services in My Grownup and Me. She was slight and quick to show intense determination in everything she did. Emma's family had her evaluated through Early Intervention primarily because of difficulty understanding her speech. As there was a history of special needs in the family, they were concerned that her language difficulties might speak to more significant developmental problems. Emma's mother was committed to bringing Emma to the group even though she was extremely busy juggling family responsibilities.

Assessment

Children within Early Intervention receive a professional, comprehensive assessment in order to determine eligibility, necessary services, and outcomes expected from interventions. The parent/child group does not have a separate assessment process for eligibility, but it is generally provided when the treatment team feels that the child and caregiver would benefit from greater exposure to the experiences that come from participating in a community group. Since My Grownup and Me is centered in music therapy interventions, the recommending team recognizes that the child responds well to music and thereby suggests placement in the program.

Assessing the child's needs through musical play happens naturally within the first few group sessions, and is accomplished through observation. Musical responses are used, in addition to non-musical information, as an indication of developmental maturity. My Grownup and Me also makes use of a more formal assessment tool, the MIECD – Music Indicators of Early Childhood Development (Schwartz, 2008).

During his first session, Michael maintained a pleasant affect as he sat in his mother's lap. He did not focus his gaze, but scanned from side to side, most often turning towards his mother's face. He briefly grasped toys placed in his hands but did not hold them for long. He needed support to sit independently. When greeted by the music therapist with a vocalized ascending octave followed by a descending minor third (Good Morning!), Michael swung his head to search for the source of the sound. As the group began to join in the gathering song, Michael moved his entire body in a steady rhythmic bounce. The end of each song phrase was followed by a defined silence. Michael filled in with a non-specific short vocalization each time, combined with a gestural approximation of the sign for 'more.' With these responses as the basis, Michael was assessed to be in the developmental level of Awareness.

Peter's first session was distressing and chaotic. He resisted coming into the room and had to be carried by his mother. The greeting music, based on pitch and melody, did nothing to soothe or attract him. It wasn't until movement and rhythm became prominent that Peter lessened his crying and looked toward the face of the therapist. The music had a very clear structure with a sixteen bar format, 2/4 meter and consistent tempo sung by the therapist with accompanying drum beat. Peter let his mother put him down, and he began to move around the room in a rhythmic march. When the music stopped, Peter stopped and glanced at the therapist. Although it first appeared that Peter was unaware of his surroundings, his subsequent musical responses made it clear that he was hyper aware of the musical environment but was not able to accept and integrate these experiences. Peter was assessed to be in the developmental level of Trust.

Emma immediately moved close to the music therapist as she began to sing a melody built around notes of the triad. Emma repeated back the simple intervals with pitch accuracy but had difficulty pronouncing the words of the lyrics. She would dance up to the therapist, bring her face close, but as soon as the melody ended, would take off. When presented with a maraca, Emma's shaking was fast and active. While she gazed intently at the music therapist, Emma did not look at either her mother or the other children in the group for any length of time. Emma was assessed to be beginning the developmental level of Independence.

THE THERAPEUTIC PROCESS

Michael: Becoming Aware

In Michael's first two sessions of My Grownup and Me, he was literally and figuratively surrounded by the love of his family. He had great difficulty maintaining an erect posture and needed his mother's support to remain upright. Michael's hands would flex open and closed, and he would sporadically bring them together in a clap. His legs and lower body needed positioning in order to move.

Despite this obvious physical weakness, Michael had a bright affect and an animated face. He would swivel to put his face up against his mother's chest and tip his head back to focus on her. He would smile, and his pudgy cheeks would crinkle up delightfully. Sometimes, however, this look of adoration would morph into an open-mouthed bite. Equally unexpectedly, Michael would roughly bang his head on mom's chest or knee. Mom appeared to be confused and dismayed by these behaviors.

As the pair sat on the floor, I moved closer and sang a "Good Morning" greeting utilizing an octave leap followed by a descending minor third (sol, Sol, Mi). Michael shifted his upper body toward me and the source of the sound. His eyes opened wide. I moved to his other side and repeated the musical phrase. Michael followed me with his eyes, face and upper body. The improvised song continued as I changed my position throughout all the planes surrounding Michael - up, down, in and out. Each time he made attempts to find me in space. Mom watched the musical game intently. The last time, I landed in the space that signaled the beginning of the gathering song - calling all the children and adults to join in the music circle. Michael and Mom were now positioned facing into the group, and Michael and I had a direct line of sight and hearing. Despite all the other children and grownups in the group, Michael's posture and facial gaze remained firmly focused on me as the source of the music.

Gathering songs (Schwartz, 2009) are a technique used in early childhood music therapy to bring everyone together in the music space. They have strong, steady rhythm along with musical gestures and are clearly structured. Michael began bouncing in response to this new song, and his delight in the sound and movement was shared by his mother, whose body relaxed as she released her tight hold on him. It was almost as if she could begin to let go, since the music would hold her child safe.

By session three and four, our greeting song had become routine, and Michael would begin looking for me even before I had time to sing. I would purposefully move toward the other children in the group and shake their hands as I sang Michael's "Good Morning" song. As Michael searched for his music, I would in essence transfer my greeting to his peers through my singing to them. In the music circle, I asked Michael's mom to sit in a different spot each time so that Michael would have the opportunity to experience the sounds from all different locations – something he could not do for himself due to his movement limitations. As the gathering song began, Michael had the experience of the music all around him, and was afforded the opportunity to gain awareness of the people and objects in his immediate environment. The lyrics and melodic rhythm of the gathering song supported this awareness of self and others. Adapted from the tune of an American folk song "Go In and Out My Window," the exciting rhythmic movement of 'clap hands in the circle' was followed by an accented, sung exclamation – "Here" – with two beats of silence afterwards. Then, suddenly, "There!" pointing outward across the circle, "Friends are everywhere." Michael's mother joined in singing and helped Michael to point out toward the others in the music circle. The duo engaged happily in the musical awareness of themselves and all the others within the music group. Both Michael and Mom shared in the joy of becoming aware. Instead of the inward focus that limited Michael's awareness of anything other than his family and could have been the cause of his frustration (seen in the biting and banging), Michael and his mother joined together in opening up to the world through the joy of a shared musical experience.

Peter: Learning to Trust

Peter's initial sessions in My Grownup and Me were marked by moments of calm and attention followed by screams and running away. When he was finally able to enter the room, he would walk straight through the others and sometimes over children and toys to get what he wanted. Once he found the object, he would intimately examine it to the exclusion of all else and tantrum if it were taken away. When the toys were cleaned up and the music began, Peter would throw himself on the floor, kicking or hitting his mother. Peter's mother would become visibly upset and appeared to be embarrassed by her son's behavior. She would chase after him or try to restrain him, but with little success.

The fleeting nature of the music experience in early childhood is matched by a technique called embedded music (Schwartz, 2009). In embedded music, very short musical phrases or simple intervals are sung or played that match the activity in which the child is engaged. The duration and the timing of musical fragments are sporadic and in the moment themselves. As Peter lay on the floor manipulating his chosen toy, I would lay down next to him with my face close to his. I chanted very insistently "A toy on my knee, a toy on my toe, a toy on my belly, now time to go." The meter of the chant was very deliberate, falling on every other beat. On the word 'go,' my voice would glissando down two octaves as I rolled away from Peter. Each time, his eyes would flicker and meet mine directly for a brief second. I came back again and again and again, each time repeating the same silly musical game. The flicker of attention grew longer and there was a hint of a smile. Peter's mom watched the game with a relaxed look on her face, perhaps glad to see such moments of happiness. I invited her to join me in the chant. She learned it quickly and took over this musical play with Peter.

All this ended as the session moved into the gathering song. It was apparent that the intimacy of the music circle and the joint music making was more than Peter could handle at that time. I encouraged Mom to stay in the group and allow Peter to watch from afar. I suspect she felt foolish participating in the songs and instrument play without a child on her lap, but she had given me her trust and was willing to try this new kind of interaction. Peter wandered but kept turning back to watch us both.

My Grownup and Me provides for a great number of music therapy interventions within the session, a strategy that matches the attending abilities of young children. After the closeness of the gathering and mutual play songs, the group changes to a less cohesive activity and everyone stands to move around the room using marching, running and jumping. The musical material keeps the group together through strong rhythm, consistent tempo, defined meter and clear structure. As the group swept past Peter (Mom included), all marching to the beat, he began to move his body in synchrony with the drum. His whole body started to respond and then he picked up his feet and joined us. The strong finish of the song was followed by several long moments of silence. Peter and the other children stood absolutely still. When the silence hung heavy in the room, I sang "Uh, Oh" on a descending fourth followed by a very deliberate perfect fifth from sol to do. "Listen!" Peter did not move. "Run," I shouted, and Peter ran. "Uh, oh. Listen!" "Jump," I shouted, and Peter jumped. Now it was Mom's turn to stand still as she admired the wonder of her son listening and doing.

At session five, Mom entered the room complaining. "All he wants to do at home is march," she explained with a twinkle in her eye. "What do you do?" I asked. "We march," she said with determination. Peter was now able to walk by himself into the room. He most often made his way to me and molded his whole body into mine for a few seconds as a way of saying hello. Sometimes he would actually say "hi." On week six, Peter entered independently, looked me in the eye and sang "Good morning!" using a pitched interval that approximated the downward fifth heard later as "listen."

He would now sit on my lap for the "Toy Song" and at the final glissando would send his toy car careening across the room to his mother. Mom would then send it back to him, imitating "Goooooooo!" Sometimes I would make the car go, and it would veer off course toward another child. While Peter was able to trust his mother with the car, the game and with himself, he was not yet ready to let go with his peers. Mom saw the new aspect to the game, and I could see she understood how the music could engage other children with Peter.

Peter's greatest musical participation was still during the active music and movement part of the session. He sang along now with pitched intervals on "Uh, Oh. Listen." He also took command of his actions and that of the group by shouting "march." He could now pick up his feet and place them firmly on the ground in rhythm, and his marching had become deliberate and sure.

For an active boy who thrived on rhythm, meter and structure, the music gave him an auditory and physical space in which to be organized and whole, instead of scattered and disconnected. His mother also had a predictable place in which to meet Peter at his best, and her delight was evident.

Many children like Peter find it difficult to be held, to be confined, or to be immersed in environments that provide too much unanticipated sensory information. Being a parent to a child like Peter means that the traditionally accepted physical closeness marking the mother/child relationship, such as holding or rocking, is rebuffed by the child. The parent most often misunderstands the child's aversion and interprets it as a form of rejection. This sense of rejection causes the parent to mistrust his/her instincts and pull away from the child, making the situation even more difficult. Feelings of failure as a parent often follow.

The closure of My Grownup and Me begins the only planned harmonic intervention of the session. Resonator bells tuned to the pentatonic are set out in the middle of the circle, and the children are motioned to leave the movement play and come once again into the center. Each child takes a bell and a mallet. Some give a bell to their caregiver, and some give a bell to a peer. None of them play the two handed instruments very effectively at this age, so the grownups must each become an active part of the group, providing the musical accompaniment to our "Good bye." Peter, as with many children with similar musical sensibilities, is drawn into the delicate, warm timbre of the instrument. The melody makes use of the minor third that is prevalent in the pentatonic, and the rhythmic flow is reminiscent of a mother rocking her baby. Peter plops down on the floor, wedged between his mother and me. The melody and rhythm do not stop. Peter lays his head on Mom's lap and she scoops him up in her arms. He stares intently into her face and calmly lets her rock him to the music.

Emma: Feeling Free

Emma had no difficulty entering the music room, and in making herself comfortable amid the toys and the other children. She carefully selected the toy that she wanted and sat very contentedly playing with it. Although she allowed her mother to take off her jacket and hat, she wasted no time in getting down to solitary play. If another child approached her, she simply stood up, took her things and went to play in another area of the room. She was able to use single words to comment on things, but she did not use this skill to communicate with either her peers, her mom or me. Since she accomplished most actions on her own, it was as if she had no need for spoken language. To someone viewing from the outside, she might look like a very independent child.

It was a whole different Emma, though, once the music of the gathering song began. Emma sat primly in her mother's lap and did not take her eyes off me for a second. Within the first few measures, she began to clap or pat or stamp as the words of the song directed. She began, very quietly, to sing along with precise use of pitch and simple intervals in imitation of the melody. Although the consonants and vowels of the words were unclear, the music was accurate. Mom looked very proud, but did not sing along. As soon as the song ended, Emma bolted out of the circle and toward the other side of the room. Mom quickly chased after her and brought her back without a word. Emma never looked at her.

But then, the maracas! Emma came hurrying back to the circle and took hold of two Chiquita or mini-size maracas. She shook them fiercely with a clenched intensity. It was in direct contrast to the Latin flavored swing of the maracas song that I chose. "I like this song," I sang calmly, swaying from side to side with a syncopated pattern. Emma shook the maracas furiously.

Early childhood music at this level relies on contrast and change, offering the child the opportunity to experience and make musical choices. The B section of this maracas song abruptly moves into a strong 2/4 meter, with very straight, even rhythmic patterns. The lyrics include the words "Yes, I can!" This section of the music fit Emma's intensity and tempo perfectly, and she joined in singing "Yes, I Can."

The song ends just as abruptly, with a vocal crescendo leading to the word "Stop." Emma stopped and then bolted again! Mom got up and chased Emma. I sat, planted firmly in the middle of the circle, picked up the maracas and began to calmly sing the lilting A section. Emma moved with Mom back to the circle and took up her maracas. Again, her shaking was matched by the B section of the song. The crescendo toward "stop" was long and drawn out. Emma shook and waited and waited and then joined in the word "Stop." As before, she left the circle, but I indicated to Mom to stay seated and calm in the circle. Emma ran a short distance and then looked back toward us. I once again began the maracas song.

Emma stood and watched. Mom sat and played. Emma independently moved closer, picked up maracas from the middle of the circle, and happily joined in.

By week four of the sessions, Emma was able to remain in the 'music circle' as long as the music was familiar to her. Instead of moving through rigid response patterns of fleeing and then being chased, Emma was making a choice to be a music maker, finally independent of the rigidity that had controlled her, preventing her from being truly independent.

During week five and six Emma showed, through her actions and behavior, that she was anticipating the maracas song. She would position herself close to me, allow me to take her hands, shake together while moving rhythmically to the gentle sway of the song. The furious shaking seen in the first sessions had been replaced by a true musical reaction to the choices provided by the tempo, meter and dynamic changes of the song.

The next week, Emma came to me with a toy and proceeded to 'tell' me a very long and involved story using vocal inflection, intonation and scattered consonants that let me know these were words. The details of the story were lost in her poor articulation, but the impact of relating her thoughts to another person vocally was very clear. I looked over at Mom and then back at Emma, "and what happened next?" I asked. Mom moved closer and Emma continued to 'tell her story' to both of us in a lovely spoken song.

SUMMARY

Michael, Peter and Emma all have a long developmental journey ahead. Some will go farther than others. The caregivers of these little ones might not fully understand all that happened during these sessions. However, over the many years that this program has been provided, the impact of the music lingers, as evidenced by the number of parents who have come back to me years later remembering in vivid detail the songs, chants and musical fun that they shared with their child.

For Michael, his alertness to the timbre and pitch of my voice provided the encouragement to attend outside of himself and become aware first of the music, his mother and me, and then to the other children. Rhythm and musical structure gave Peter the repeated, predictable comfort he seemed to require to allow him to trust in his mother, in me and in his environment. Emma's musical responsiveness allowed her to experience choices in melody, rhythm and movement and gave her the opportunity to be supported by her mother and me as she moved away from rigid patterns toward greater freedom and independence.

Becoming aware, learning to trust, being independent and free from the confines of a disability happened through the music shared among the child, caregiver, therapist and group. My Grownup and Me relies on music experiences to promote healthy development and assist the family in helping the child to 'grow up.' While the children described above had the benefits of other supportive services, music was where their strength and potential was given a place to shine. Music was the common ground where the grownup and child could meet in mutually understood play. It was in music that the necessary movement toward growth was experienced.

REFERENCES

Briggs, C. A. (1991). A model for understanding musical development. *Music Therapy*, 10 (1), 1–21.

Bredekamp, S & Copple, C. (Eds.) (2009). *Developmentally Appropriate Practices in Early Childhood Programs Serving Children from Birth through Age 8,* Washington D.C.: National Association for the Education of Young Children.

De L'Etoile, S. K. (2006). Infant-directed singing: A theory for clinical intervention. *Music Therapy Perspectives, 24*(2), 22–29.

Erickson, E. H. (1963). *Childhood and Society.* New York: Norton.

Ginsberg, H. & Opper, S. (1969). *Piaget's Theory of Intellectual Development: An Introduction.* New Jersey: Prentice-Hall.

Gordon, E. E. (2003). *A Music Learning Theory for Newborn and Young Children.* Chicago: GIA Publications, Inc. (Originally published 1990).

Humpal, M. E. & Colwell, C. C. (2006). *Effective Clinical Practices in Music Therapy: Early Childhood and School Age Educational Settings.* Silver Spring, MD: American Music Therapy Association, Inc.

Kegan, R. (1982). *The Evolving Self.* Cambridge, MA: Harvard University Press.
Mahler, M., Pine, F. & Bergman, A. (1975). *The Psychological Birth of the Human Infant.* London: H. Karnac Ltd.
McDonald, D. T. & Simons, G. M. (1989). *Musical Growth and Development: Birth Through Six.* New York: Schirmer Books.
Schwartz, E. K. (2008). *Music, Therapy, and Early Childhood: A Developmental Approach.* Gilsum, NH: Barcelona Publishers.
Schwartz, E. K. (2009). In the Beginning: Music therapy in early intervention Groups. *Imagine Early Childhood Newsletter*, Volume 15, 13-14.
Stern, D. (1985). *The Interpersonal World of the Infant.* New York: Basic Books.
Wilson, F. R. & Roehmann, F. L. (1990). *Music and Child Development.* St. Louis, MO: MMB Music, Inc.

Chapter Four

UNRAVELING HIDDEN RESOURCES OF A GIRL WITH RETT SYNDROME

Cochavit Elefant

Three-year-old Lisa was continuously crying in her nursery school. She came eagerly to music therapy, yet after a few songs she fell asleep on my lap and would remain so until the end of the session. This continued for three months and I could not understand the meaning of these sessions. After returning from my vacation, I was told that during my absence, Lisa had stood in front of my picture and touched it while tears rolled down her cheeks. Only then did I realize the meaning of our music therapy sessions. To me, this was a lesson never forgotten and a beginning of a journey into the world of Rett Syndrome.

(Elefant, 1989)

INTRODUCTION

This chapter describes music therapy with Ella, a girl with Rett Syndrome (RS). We will follow Ella from the moment I began working with her at age six at a center for children with special needs in Israel, and will revisit her during different points of her life until age 18. RS is a genetic disorder that primarily affects females (Amir, et. al., 1999; 2000). The disorder causes a developmental arrest that manifests itself in a variety of disabilities such as loss of functional hand use, loss of acquired speech, apraxia, ataxia, dysfunction in the autonomic system, epilepsy, breathing abnormalities, failure to thrive, orthopedic problems and muscle tone irregularities (Hagberg et.al., 1983; Lotan, 2006; Witt Engerström & Kerr, 1998).

It isn't difficult to notice the above definition uses the word 'loss of...' as a central description of this debilitating syndrome. However, in this chapter I would like to propose a more positive perspective. This stance stems from many years of work with persons with RS in music therapy: a frame that could offer therapeutic work through some of the 'losses,' by finding and nourishing traces of hidden resources.

In so doing, this chapter will focus on Ella's emotional and communicative circumstances and how these were influenced and changed in relation to her immediate surroundings. Unfortunately, Ella's own voice is left unheard, but I hope it will still resonate as a result of our many years of musical and personal encounters.

FOUNDATIONAL CONCEPTS

Rett Syndrome (RS) is a constellation of complex difficulties. Despite their severe developmental disabilities, most children have normal emotional, communicative, cognitive and motor development at first (Burford, 2005; Einspieler et al., 2005; Nomura, Kerr & Witt Engerström, 2005), with the appearance of abnormality between six months and two years of age (Hagberg et al., 1993). The external observer can easily focus on the extremely severe 'lost skills.' These may be perceived as not retrievable and, even worse, in constant regression. Surely, the losses are brutal; however, this type of assumption can be deceptive and easily mislead caregivers in handling and relating to the girls in a pessimistic way. This in turn can be communicated to the girls, who may fall into hopelessness and apathy. Conversely, today we are witnessing girls who are regaining walking (Lotan, 2008), hand use (Budden, 2008), and improving communicative and cognitive abilities (Elefant, 2002, 2005, 2006, 2009; Elefant & Wigram, 2005; Wigram & Elefant, 2009). These girls seem to thrive emotionally and are motivated and eager to further explore as these positive changes take place. How could the girls be so misleading? How is it possible that these 'silent angels,' with deep and penetrating expressive eyes, seemingly don't perceive what is happening to them and around them? To answer these questions, I would like to explore the theoretical perspective of Stern (2000) and Malloch and Trevarthen (2009), which I find relevant when thinking about the emotional and communicative development of girls with RS.

With the point of reference that a girl with RS usually experiences normal development at the beginning of her life, we can presume that her interactions with primary caregivers will have been similar to an infant with normal development (Elefant, 2008). This means that both the child and the adult have had meaningful emotional experiences through pre-verbal communicative dialogues. The infant and the parent identify with each other's facial expressions, gestures, explore different vocal interactions through 'affect attunement' (Stern et al., 1985; Stern, 2000) and find pleasure in the experience of interacting within the frame of 'communicative musicality' (Malloch, 1999; Malloch & Trevarthen, 2009; Trevarthen & Malloch, 2002). Holck (2002) explains that "in mutual interplay, both partners participate in turn-organisation, and therefore an analysis of cues indicating turn-taking and turn-yielding can give information on the participants' social skills, whether or not the dialogue is verbal" (p. 402). Parents of children with RS have reported that they have had these enriching experiences with their daughters until the onset of the disorder (Burford, 2005).

If we look at the developmental condition of RS and compare it to Stern's (1985; 2000) account of the development of 'the five senses of self' in infancy, it seems that most girls with RS developed through an 'emergent self,' the 'core self with others,' the 'inter-subjective self,' and many have even begun to develop the 'verbal self' at the age of 12 months, acquiring spoken language. As a result of the drastic stage II declines (the 'destructive stage' of this disorder, occurring between 6–24 months), there will be a change in the girl's interactions with others and a change in their responses and expressions toward her. This stormy period, troubling for both the girl and her family (Kerr & Witt Engerström, 2001), interrupts the flow in emotional communication that mediates inter-subjectivity (Wigram & Elefant, 2009). It isn't difficult then for the child and her family to be situated in a feeling of 'total loss,' and the inevitable belief that what had been lost may never be retrieved or reclaimed again.

This perspective has a direct implication on music therapy work with girls with RS. Each girl enters music therapy carrying the emotional grief of her loss, feels dysfunctional, helpless and in a state of disarray and confusion. The music therapist may choose to 'work through' these emotional hurdles with her but should also remember and remind the girl of the many meaningful experiences of her past. In other words, the therapist can express that "this is an extremely difficult condition to be in, but I know you have an array of possibilities waiting to emerge whenever you are ready." When the therapist manages to sincerely convey this message, the beginnings of trust and a therapeutic dialogue can take place. The girl needs an outlet for different types of feelings and a space where she can feel understood. When she does feel understood, her motivation and willingness to communicate are enhanced.

The music therapist can use 'musical communication' as interactive play where both partners are engaged in mutual interaction (Malloch, 1999; Trevarthen & Malloch, 2002; Wigram & Elefant, 2009). The therapist can develop awareness of the girl's physical and facial gestures and vocalizations as an indication of her relatedness, and express them in a musical form. These types of 'communicative musicality' (Malloch, 1999; Malloch & Trevarthen, 2009; Trevarthen & Malloch, 2002) are shared as a therapeutic dialogue. These communicative forms are unique to each girl and need to be created in each therapeutic encounter.

When interacting musically while attuning to the girl's emotional state, improvisation and pre-composed songs can be used (Elefant, 2005; Wigram & Elefant, 2009). These musical exchanges can address each girl's need to become self-aware, and in so doing rebuild lost self image. These interactions also provide an opportunity to discover hidden resources that may not be readily accessed because of the disability. With each such positive shift in these musical interactions, the girls can become empowered and driven toward new challenges that enhance growth.

THE CLIENT

I first met Ella when she was six years old. She attended a classroom with eight other children with developmental disabilities in a special education center in Israel. Ella was a beautiful, slim girl with deep brown eyes and long, dark hair. She was the eldest child in her family, with two younger brothers.

Ella was developing normally until the onset of RS at the age of nearly two years. Her parents described her as a very alert, intelligent, curious and a social girl who acquired normal motor and speech milestones before the onset of RS. She loved singing songs, reading books and taking walks with her parents and grandparents, eagerly waiting to look and smell beautiful flowers. Her development came to a halt (stage II of RS) quite suddenly, and she began losing hand function and speech. Stereotypic hand movement began to take over. She retreated to her 'own world,' isolated, with no interest in having contact with others – a crying, helpless state. She received the diagnosis of RS shortly after this period and, within a few months, became stable (stage III of RS). Her autistic-like features disappeared and she began showing better emotional stability, seeking contact with her immediate surroundings. Her parents reported:

> *From time to time she would cry as if she was grieving over the loss. We know she understands and has a desire to communicate. Her eyes tell it all.*

Ella had just arrived to her new classroom when I first met her. She tried to make contact with the staff around her; they looked at her, smiled and stroked her head. She tried to make contact again by touching them, looking into their eyes while vocalizing. After a few attempts, she went to the mattress, lay down and fell asleep. This ritual repeated itself day after day.

I worked with Ella's class twice a week. During these music therapy group sessions she expressed emotions of happiness; she laughed, attended, swayed to the music, leaned forward and vocalized. Her facial expression changed when the 'goodbye' song was sung. She became serious, began to scratch her eyes and turned her head away. After realizing how expressive and communicative Ella was during group music therapy, she was offered individual music therapy sessions with me. I assumed she understood my offer because she began laughing while walking next to me to the music therapy room.

Assessment

The focus of my assessment was not only to gather information about Ella's functional and physical disabilities, but to understand her resources, motivations, attention, interests and desires. This would help in making future therapeutic decisions. Ella's initial assessment was through group music therapy, in which she had shown emotional and communicative expressiveness and investment. During the group, I asked Ella to choose between two pictographs of songs. She scanned both pictures using eye tracking and ended up focusing on one. This took over one minute. She was beside herself when the song was sung following her choice. After a few such choice trials, her response time diminished and she began choosing with her nose and later with her hand.

During individual music therapy assessment, Ella sat and listened attentively to the greeting song. I suggested that she could indicate if she wished to hear the song again by either looking at me or by pressing the 'Big Mack' switch (alternative augmentative communication device) with a picture of the guitar and a message saying "I want more music." She touched the 'Big Mack' with her nose, and I began singing and playing the greeting song once more. I explained to Ella that we will explore different instruments and activities during this session and introduced her to 'yes' and 'no' communication cards that she could also use during the session.

Ella chose the piano and I began playing and singing a song while she played along using alternating hands on the piano. I then started to improvise around the song and from time to time added glissandos at the end of the phrase. She began laughing each time I added a surprise to the song. She then used her hand to beat the ocean drum while I played the guitar and sang, matching her beat. When I offered her a mallet in order to try out the xylophone, she dropped it. We then moved and danced to fast tempo pre-recorded music. She moved her body wildly from side to side while holding my hands. She seemed extremely happy and laughed out loud.

During the assessment Ella was very attentive, active, motivated and emotionally expressive, but she did not vocalize. She seemed flexible in trying out different instruments, used her hands to play the piano and strum the guitar, but did not manage to hold the mallet. It was a good start for both of us, yet I felt a challenge and desire to find ways to 'hear' Ella and to be able to address her requests.

THE THERAPEUTIC PROCESS

The therapeutic process that follows lasted six years, until Ella was twelve years old. After that, we met intermittently as she was transferred to a new school at age twelve. Ella and I had established a good rapport in group music therapy, and this was strengthened in her individual sessions. The purpose for the individual sessions was to provide Ella with a space in which she could find ways of expressing herself emotionally and communicatively. These sessions took place twice a week for 30–45 minutes.

Song Choice to Build Personal Autonomy and Communication

Ella came eagerly to the music therapy room and sat on a chair waiting for the greeting song. The song was usually the same opening song, but the text could change according to Ella's response and age. She was then offered a choice from a repertoire of familiar and unfamiliar songs, followed by my singing the song to her. She ended up choosing songs from a repertoire of over 20 pictographs (representing songs) which kept changing as she got older. She tried out new songs, but enjoyed returning to the old ones.

Generally, Ella preferred songs with faster tempi and greater variability in rhythm, dynamics and melody. She also enjoyed songs with vocal humour or playfulness. These choices changed with her mood at the time of the session. Her emotional expression changed with each song, and it seemed as if the songs had a different emotional meaning to her. The songs were age appropriate, which led me to believe that a child like Ella (who developed normally until around age two) had experienced normal interaction with her primary caregiver throughout the development of the 'verbal self' (Stern, 1985; 2000). She had experienced a communicative foundation, including affect attunement, which is important for her emotional development (ibid).

Ella vocalized during these songs, moved her body from side to side, moved her legs and wrung her hands (stereotypic hand movement typical to RS) in tempo with the music. My approach to singing the songs was a combination of holding the distinctive tempo, rhythm and melody of the musical form while attuning to the emotional and communicative impulses that Ella conveyed in response to my singing. The regulating motives of communicative musicality were activated as Ella and I conversed emotionally with one another by sharing the songs (Trevarthen & Malloch, 2002). Each time I sang the same song, it was as if a new narrative was told (Wigram & Elefant, 2009).

Ella loved taking control. She was empowered by her choice-making and by my immediate responses to her. There were times that I wasn't sure of her choices and let Ella know that we were attempting to find a common communicative understanding. This was a challenge that was important to both of us as it deepened our understanding of one another and helped to further develop her communicative abilities (Elefant, 2009).

'Musical Conversations' as Personal and Emotional Growth

Choice-making of songs was a music therapy approach we used throughout the six years we worked together. Following the singing, Ella and I would engage in another type of practice I called 'musical conversations:' a form of 'communicative musicality' (Malloch & Trevarthen, 2009). 'Musical conversations' were musical improvisations with text, conversing on a certain topic that related to and addressed some of Ella's concerns and desires. She could choose from a few topics I had gathered from either reading her 'communication journal' or from a conversation with her teacher. Ella listened intently to the list of topics as I asked her to indicate whether any of these topics could suit a 'musical conversation.' Examples for such topics were: the birth of her baby brother; spending the night at her grandparents; feeling sad/frustrated/angry/happy; going/returning from vacation, and more.

Ella chose each topic with 'yes' and 'no' cards or by looking at me when the right topic came along. To work out this type of communication and choice-making we had to develop a common emotional and communicative understanding (Trevarthen & Burford, 2001). We had to create a space for Ella to be able to express herself in a way that she felt understood. This was delicate because the conversations were limited to the fact that I had spoken language, while she didn't. It was similar to a mother-infant conversation, but the content was on a different level, with the assumption that Ella understood most of what was said. It was the intent of these 'narratives of the experiencing self' to reflect and attune to her internal world in order to confirm her inner emotions and intentions (Stern, 1985; 2000). The music always supported the narrative so the intent was conveyed either by the music, the narrative or both.

These 'musical conversations' were not always easy for Ella. She 'worked' hard and had to deal with intense emotions during some of the more difficult topics. The starting point for these 'musical conversations' was an agreed upon topic in order to convey to her that much of the therapeutic responsibility was hers. During the first couple of years, when she was still young, these 'musical conversations' were short and ended up with a simple song around the topic. As she grew older, these 'conversations' took a larger space in the session and touched on more emotionally challenging topics. Of course, there were times when she also chose fun and gossipy topics.

After the topic had been chosen, I began improvising on either the piano or guitar, singing and constructing the content as we went along. The style for the improvisation corresponded to the topic. The idea was to express a message in music and words about something Ella was concerned with. The following is an example for such a 'musical conversation.'

Ella had cried most of the day in school because of a stomach ache due to constipation (common and painful phenomena in children with RS). She came to our music therapy session quite exhausted and chose to 'talk' about it immediately following the greeting song. I began playing a chord progression on the guitar in an andante tempo, repeating it for the purpose of grounding. On top of the chord progression I began a vocal improvisation with the following text, and Ella 'replied' with her body and facial gestures. The parentheses are subjective interpretations:

Cochavit: I heard from your teacher that your day was hard.
Your stomach was hurting and it was quite tough. *(Informative)*
Ella: Wanders around the room
Cochavit: You lay on the mattress and wept softly till you fell asleep *(Informative)*
Ella: Stands for a moment quietly while looking at me.
Comes close to me *(Attentive)*
Cochavit: Was this really what happened, Ella?
Was the pain taking over everything you did? *(Verification)*
Ella: Brings her face towards mine *(Confirming)*
Cochavit: Oh Ella, it is never easy when it happens to you.
When you least expect it and you don't know what to do *(Empathy and support)*
Ella: Sits on a chair in front of me *(Relaxing)*
Cochavit: It's a situation your parents are trying to solve.
They're attempting to understand how to deal with this all *(Revealing)*

Ella: Smiles and looks straight into my eyes.
Begins to vocalize *(Agreement)*
Cochavit: Going from one doctor to another to get some answers while you are trying out different medications that might work *(informative)*
Ella: Continues to smile and to vocalize
Cochavit: In the meantime, Ella, what can you do to relieve this pain? Can you try to think of something that could put you at ease? *(Placing the responsibility)*
Ella: Turns her back to me. Goes to the door and stays there.
Vocalizes with a loud intensity, even shouts *(Resisting)*
Cochavit: I know you would rather it didn't exist *(Acknowledge the difficulty)*
Ella: Looks at the 'yes' card *(Approving)*
Cochavit: But there may be some things you can do to ease this awful pain.
How about if you listen to your favourite songs?
Maybe this could be a way to relax and calm you down *(Suggesting a solution)*
Ella: Looks at the 'yes' card
Comes closer to me. Brings her face close to mine.
Smiles and vocalizes *(Approving and accepting)*
Cochavit: I am glad we found something that you can do to relieve this pain.
When we go back to your classroom we will tell your teacher about what we have come up with. *(Reiterating)*
The music can soothe and can help the painful situation when it comes
Ella: Laughs out loud.
Goes to the door and grabs the doorknob *(Empowered)*

The emotional intent of this musical conversation coincided and changed in accordance with Ella's response to it. Small nuances occurred in tempo, rhythm, dynamics and melodic contour during these conversations. The narrative of the conversation is told via the music as well as the text. This adjustment of timing and expression was a natural interaction and is similar to the interaction that takes place between a caregiver and an infant (Burford & Trevarthen, 1997; Stern, 1985; 2000). It confirmed that Ella's affectionate communications and attuned expressive behaviour had been retained, without the presence of language (Merker & Wallin, 2001). In this type of communicative musicality, the child grows emotionally and socially, and the relationship between the caregiver and the child changes with each such encounter (Malloch, 1999; Malloch & Trevarthen, 2009; Trevarthen, 2002).

I believe that it was the discrepancy in our affective attunement that helped the therapy to move forward. In other words, it was when I suggested to Ella that 'she try to find a solution to relieve her pain' that her initial response was not to cooperate. It was only after I had suggested that she could 'maybe listen to [her] favorite songs' that she had felt that she had taken some responsibility: hopefully toward the acceptance that this pain is part of her life. The discrepancy can only happen after the client feels secure and safe in the relationship with the therapist.

Playing Instruments: Retrieving Use of Hand Loss

Ella enjoyed playing instruments such as the piano, ocean drum and chimes. However, she didn't like to play instruments that demanded hand grasp. Her beat became more and more synchronous with the tempo of the music and she enjoyed activities such as 'fill in the blank.' At the end of a phrase, she played a few beats and then burst into laughter. It was interesting to see the progression she made in this type of play from the time we began at age six until she was twelve. Initially, Ella would look at me, then at the instrument, look away, and then look at the instrument when finally playing it. This process could take almost two minutes. However, with many musical opportunities, her response time diminished, until she managed to play at the right time. This type of process helped Ella to realize that she was competent enough to explore and play instruments. It was the music that gave her the motivation to persist and try. With each attempt her success was greater. Her delayed response became smaller and smaller, and she became more secure.

Social Inclusion: Affirmation of Capabilities and Resources

Ella and other children from the centre were integrated into a regular school during music group for about two years (see Stige, Ansdell, Elefant & Pavlicevic, 2010). Ella was loved by the other children and was extremely excited to have contact with them. This gave us many topics to discuss during our individual music therapy sessions. Here is a vignette from one of the integrative music groups:

> *During music integration group we celebrated one of the girl's birthday. While we sang and danced and gave attention to the birthday girl, one of the pupils said: "Ella is crying." No one understood what was wrong until the caregivers shouted 'Oh my G-d, it is Ella's birthday today too....' Ella burst into laughter and one of the school children said: "She can't speak, but she sure knows how to express herself."*

This inclusion program helped Ella to experience interactions with children similar to those she had before the onset of RS. She listened intently to the girls' conversations, laughed, moved and vocalized with the same intensity and expression as the other children. She recognized her social strength and initiated intimate contact with them. They in turn found new ways of relating to Ella and the other children with special needs.

Second Personal Loss

When Ella turned twelve she left the special education centre and went to a new school. She had developed in a number of important ways, showing emotional stability and the ability to comprehend around 100 written words that she could also communicate with others.

After one year at her new school, the Israeli National RS Evaluation Team (in which I serve as music therapist) made an evaluation of Ella in her new school. The staff at the school had been concerned about her emotional stability. She was becoming more withdrawn and cried a lot. Ella had been their first pupil with RS, and they felt they were unable to reach her.

I met Ella at her new school in order to gain some understanding of what was happening to her. Although our exchange was extensive, I will only describe a small portion of the meeting here:

> *When I approached Ella, she seemed puzzled at first. I began improvising a 'hello' song, expressing my excitement at seeing her. I began asking her, in 'musical conversation,' what was*

> *happening to her. She showed me a picture symbol of being sad. We began singing familiar songs and she became very happy. After a while, I suggested that she should try to communicate with her teachers in order to be understood and reminded her that it was a mutual responsibility.*

We were informed that after my visit Ella began accepting her new school and seemed to thrive for awhile. The staff managed to find a communication channel with Ella, and she continued to progress.

A few years later, however, at age 17, our RS team went to visit Ella again. She had moved to a new class and the new staff felt that she was in distress. In addition, they reported that she didn't seem to "understand pictures or any other kind of communication symbols." This assumption is quite common. It isn't always easy for people to reach these girls and as a result, it isn't difficult for the girls to become passive and apathetic whenever they feel misunderstood. This behavior was described by Lindberg (2006) as "being under a cloud," and one can only wonder why they choose to stay there with some people, while flourishing with others.

The following 'musical conversation' took place during our meeting:

Cochavit: Started singing a 'Hello' song: Hi Ella. It has been a very long time since we saw each other
Ella: Looks down
Cochavit: I am glad to see you, so grown up, etc…
Ella: Looks at me. Brings her head towards mine
Cochavit: I want to continue singing/talking to you, Ella, but I want you to tell me if you want me to
Ella: Looks at 'yes' symbol
Cochavit: I am so excited to be here and see you again, Ella
Ella: Gets close to my face
Ella and Cochavit: We both start weeping
Cochavit: I am so sad to see that you haven't been communicating; it is as if you have lost your 'voice'
Ella and Cochavit: Continue weeping
Cochavit: Please, show me again if you want me to continue singing/talking

Ella: Looks at the 'Yes' card, puts her face on it, gives the symbol a big slap with her hand
Cochavit: Begins to laugh and sing to Ella that she sure showed me and the people around her what she wants. I tell her that she needs to trust herself and show what she knows. This could result in others responding to her.

Ella had obviously given up! Her new teachers were not able to recognise her resources, and she didn't make much effort to convince the staff otherwise. The staff was convinced after this meeting that there was much more to Ella than they had understood.

Postlude

A year has passed after my last visit, and Ella had turned eighteen. A remarkable change had occurred and Ella was back on track. She was alive, motivated and seemed to thrive as long as she had a supportive environment that could see beyond her losses.

SUMMARY

In this chapter I have told the story of Ella, a girl with RS. My desire to make her voice heard came from recognizing that she could still interact and understand, despite her losses. Ella's story is similar to many other girls with RS who experience a complex and debilitating disorder. On one hand, they experience a loss of abilities, while on the other, they seem to retrieve, regain and learn when given the opportunity. This incomplete and confusing image is distressing for the child and one can see that it isn't easy to rebuild self image over and over again (Lindberg, 2006).

Based on my practice, I propose a musical relating experience including affect attunement. These experiences could take the form of songs, musical improvisation and musical conversations; a combination of music and verbal processing, which can strengthen self-image and help these children move forward. Through musical and verbal interactions, children with RS can realize that, despite their losses, it is possible to identify hidden resources and find new possibilities. For this to happen, they need a supportive environment that believes in their abilities.

Additionally, I propose that the child with RS and her caregivers understand the mutual responsibility of shared intention that builds common communication channels. The process of reaching a shared understanding and communication is individually based and requires patience, creativity and resilience. In Ella's case we saw how easily her emotional and communicative state changed with each person she had contact with. At times, she thrived and showed a deep desire to communicate. At other times, she fell into passivity, acting as if not knowing. Through music therapy experiences, Ella expressed her feelings and came to realize that she could easily become helpless if she did not take some responsibility for reaching out in order to be understood. My experiences have taught me about the powerful affect music therapy can have on individuals with RS. Time after time I have met individuals with RS of all ages that managed to unravel hidden emotional and communicative resources. When this happens, it becomes quite profound for both the therapist and the client.

REFERENCES

Amir, R., Van Den Veyver, I., Wan, M., Tran, C., Francke, U. & Zoghbi, H. (1999). Rett syndrome is caused by mutations in X-linked MECP2, encoding methyl-CpG-binding protein 2. *Nature Genetics, 23*(2), 185-188.

Amir, R., Van den Veyver, I., Schultz, R., Malicki, D., Tran, C., Dahle, E., Philippi, A., Timer, L., Percy, A., Motil, K., Lichtarge, O., Smith, E., Glaze, D. & Zoghbi, H. (2000). Influence of mutation type and X chromosome inactivation on Rett Syndrome phenotypes. *Annals of Neurology, 47*, 670–679.

Budden, S. (2008). Management of Rett Syndrome both from the medical and therapeutic approach. Israeli Rett Association Seminar, Shiba Hospital, Israel.

Burford, B. (2005). Perturbations in the development of infants with Rett disorder and the implications for early diagnosis. *Brain & Development, 27*(1), 3-7.

Burford, B. & Trevarthen, C. (1997). Evoking communication in Rett Syndrome: Comparisons with conversations and games in mother-infant interaction. *European Child and Adolescent Psychiatry, 6*(1), 26-30.

Einspieler, C., Kerr, A. & Prechtl, H. (2005). Abnormal general movements in girls with Rett disorder: The first four months of life. *Brain and Development,* 27(1), S8-S13.

Elefant, C. (1989). Personal Logbook.

Elefant, C. (2002). Enhancing communication in girls with Rett Syndrome through songs in music therapy. Unpublished dissertation.

Elefant, C. (2009). Rett Syndrome and music therapy. *International Journal of Disability and Human Development,* 8(4), 359-368.

Elefant, C. (2005). The use of single case designs in testing a specific hypothesis. In D. Aldridge (Ed.) *Case Study Designs in Music Therapy.* London: Jessica Kingsley Publishers.

Elefant, C. (2006). Communicative and emotional expression through music in individuals with Rett Syndrome (Hebrew). *Israeli National Newsletter,* Tel Aviv, Israel.

Elefant, C. (2008).Unveiling hidden resources: Communication and learning in individuals with Rett Syndrome through music therapy. Paper presented at the 6th World Rett Syndrome Congress. Paris, France.

Elefant, C. & Wigram, T. (2005). Learning ability in children with Rett Syndrome. *Journal of Brain and Development,* 27, 97-101.

Hagberg, B., Aicardi, J., Dias, K. & Ramos, O. (1983). A progressive syndrome of autism, dementia, ataxia, and loss of purposeful hand use in girls. Rett's syndrome: Report of 35 cases. *Annals of Neurology, 14,* 471-479.

Hagberg, B., Anuret, M. & Wahlstrom, J. (1993). *Rett Syndrome: Clinical and Biological Aspects.* London & Cambridge: Cambridge University Press (Clinics in Developmental Medicine, No. 127).

Holck, U. (2002). 'Kommunikalsk' Samspil i Musikterapi ['Comusical' Interplay in Music Therapy. Qualitative Video Analyses of Musical and Gestural Interactions with Children with Severe Functional Limitations, including Children with Autism]. Unpublished PhD thesis, Aalborg University.

Kerr, A. & Witt Engerström, I. (2001). *Rett Disorder and the Developing Brain.* Oxford: Oxford University Press.

Lindberg, B. (2006). *Understanding Rett Syndrome* (2nd ed.). New York: Hogrefe & Huber.

Lotan, M. (2006). *Angels of Silence: Caring for Rett Syndrome.* (Hebrew). Israeli Rett Syndrome Center, Israel: Rotem Publication.

Lotan, M. (2008). The time is now – Appropriate therapeutic intervention for individuals with Rett Syndrome. Keynote presentation: National Conference of the Irish Rett Syndrome Association. Limerick, Ireland.

Malloch, S. (1999). Mother and infants and communicative musicality. In "Rhythms, musical narrative, and the origins of human communication". *Musicae Scientiae,* Special Issue, 1999-2000, pp. 29-57. Liège: European Society for the Cognitive Sciences of Music.

Malloch, S. & Trevarthen, C. (2009). *Communicative Musicality: Exploring the Basis of Human Companionship.* Oxford: Oxford University Press.

Merker, B. & Wallin, N. (2001). Musical responsiveness in Rett Disorder. In A. Kerr and I. Witt Engerström (Eds.), *Rett Disorder and the Developing Brain* (pp. 327-338). Oxford: Oxford University Press.

Nomura, Y., Kerr, A. & Witt Engerström, I. (2005). Rett Syndrome: Early behavior and possibilities for intervention. *Brain and Development, 27*(Supplement 1), S101.

Stern, D.N. (2000). *The Interpersonal World of the Infant* (2nd ed.) New York: Basic Books.

Stige, B., Ansdell, G., Elefant, C. & Pavlicevic, M. (2010). *Where Music Helps. Community Music Therapy in Action and Reflection.* Aldershot, UK: Ashgate

Trevarthen, C. (2002). Origins of musical identity: Evidence from infancy for musical social awareness. In R. MacDonald, D. Hargreaves and D. Miell (Eds.) *Musical Identities* (pp. 21-38). Oxford: Oxford University Press.

Trevarthen, C. & Burford, B. (2001). Early communication and the Rett disorder. In A. Kerr and I. Witt Engerström (Eds.), *Rett Disorder and the Developing Brain* (pp. 303-326). Oxford: Oxford University Press.

Trevarthen, C. & Malloch, S. (2002). Musicality and music before three: Human vitality and invention shared with pride. *Zero to Three, 25*(1), 10-18.

Wigram, T. & Elefant, C. (2009). Therapeutic dialogues in music: Nurturing musicality of communication in children with autistic spectrum disorder and Rett syndrome. In S. Malloch and C. Trevarthen (Eds.), *Communicative Musicality: Exploring the Basis of Human Companionship* (pp. 423-445). Oxford: Oxford University Press.

Witt Engerström, I. & Kerr, A. (1998). Workshop on autonomic functions in Rett Syndrome. Swedish Rett Center, Froson, Sweden, May 1998. *Brain and Development, 5,* 323-326.

Chapter Five

EXPLORING ISSUES OF CONTROL THROUGH INTERACTIVE, IMPROVISED MUSIC MAKING: MUSIC THERAPY DIAGNOSTIC ASSESSMENT AND SHORT TERM TREATMENT WITH A MOTHER AND DAUGHTER IN A PSYCHIATRIC UNIT

Amelia Oldfield

INTRODUCTION

Olivia was admitted to a child and family psychiatric unit in Cambridge, England when she was ten years old. As with many of the admissions to this unit, Olivia and her family had complex needs rather than one clear diagnosis. Olivia was displaying difficult behaviors at home, hearing voices and suspected of having mild Autistic Spectrum Disorder (Richer, 2001). During their eight week admission it became clear that the problems Olivia was experiencing had more to do with relationships within the family than specifically because of an underlying psychiatric condition. In this case study, I will describe Olivia's initial Music Therapy Diagnostic Assessment (MTDA), her work in the weekly music therapy group with her peers, and the six family music therapy sessions Olivia attended with her mother. Although the MTDA and the group work were separate from the work with her mother, all three interventions informed and influenced one another.

This clinical work takes place in a small community-based psychiatric unit funded through the United Kingdom Health Service. It admits children up to twelve years old who have a wide range of psychiatric difficulties. It is unique to the UK in that it admits not only the children, but also their families, on a residential basis. The thinking behind this practice is that children with complex psychiatric profiles need to be assessed and treated within the context of their family in order to best address their needs. Children usually have a combination of difficulties including Autistic Spectrum Disorder, attention deficit disorder, eating disorders, Tourette's syndrome, attachment disorders and Post Traumatic Stress Disorders.

This clinical work will be contextualised around Interactive Music Therapy (Oldfield 2006a; 2006b), an approach that I developed in working with children with a wide variety of diagnoses. In Interactive Music Therapy (IMT), non-verbal improvised musical interactions are central to the therapy. I focus largely on the enjoyable, playful and motivating force of music-making, helping children and parents to gain confidence through these positive experiences. Winnicott's theories (1960; 1971) of 'holding and caring' and being a 'good enough mother' are often relevant to the work I am doing both with children and their parents: both of whom frequently require care and mothering. Stern's writing (1985; 1995) on pre-verbal babbling between mothers and infants also comes to mind as a parallel to the non-verbal musical interactions I have with the children and the families (Oldfield, 2006a).

FOUNDATIONAL CONCEPTS:

An Interactive Approach to Music Therapy

Music therapy has been an established part of the treatment milieu at this psychiatric unit for over 20 years. I take an interactive approach, using mainly improvised music (Oldfield, 2006a). Children and families are invited to play and make music that I support and take part in. Patterns and types of interactions that occur are reflected upon and analysed, sometimes in the moment, but more frequently after the playing, often using video analysis. (Oldfield & Franke, 2005; Oldfield, 2006b). Interactive music therapy enables families who are struggling to interact verbally to spend time playing instruments together without needing to make specific attempts at communication. Through the improvised playing, supported by the music therapist, tension can be released and parents and children may relax and re-discover how to be playful. The music therapist can then guide the improvisations to enable more specific exchanges to occur between the parents and the child. Issues such as 'leadership,' 'control' and 'listening to one another' often emerge as themes in this stage of work.

Every week the children and their families are discussed in a large multi-disciplinary management team meeting. It is here that the role of music therapy becomes clear, and how this role differs from, or overlaps with, the work taking place in other settings. I often find that I have a different impression or view of a family than the rest of the team in these management meetings. Improvised music making brings out skills and difficulties that have not been noted in other settings, making music therapy a valuable addition to other specialist interventions in child and family psychiatry.

In addition to providing short term music therapy treatment for children and parents, I contribute to the diagnostic assessment of each child's difficulties through Music Therapy Diagnostic Assessments (MTDAs) (Oldfield, 2004). Assessments consist of two half-hour individual sessions that occur at the same time on two consecutive weeks. I invite the child to sit down opposite me, having explained that all the children at the psychiatric unit usually have two music sessions with me at the beginning of their admission. The sessions begin with a 'Hello' song that I sing to the child, accompanying myself by playing chords on the guitar. The sessions end with a shared percussion duet on the bongo drums where I say or sing 'Goodbye' and sometimes discuss what we have done together. In between the 'Hello' and the 'Goodbye,' I explain that we will take turns to choose what to do together. I can find out a great deal from the ways in which the child chooses instruments and activities. When it is my turn to choose, I can set up situations and make suggestions that I feel will help me to understand and gain insight into the child's strengths and difficulties. For most children, between six to nine of the following activities are included in the MTDA:

1. 'Hello' song
2. Child plays drum kit and I play the piano or another set of drums
3. Child and I play wind instruments such as a reed horn, melodicas, harmonicas, or Penny whistles (sometimes I will play my clarinet)
4. Improvised stories accompanied by percussion and the piano

5. Child plays the open strings of a violin and I accompany on the piano or the guitar
6. Child and I play small percussion instruments on the floor together or on chairs opposite one another
7. Child and I share an instrument such as the bass xylophone or the autoharp
8. Kazoo dialogue
9. Piano dialogue
10. Child plays an instrument such as the electric organ and I listen
11. I teach the child a simple tune
12. Rhythmic call-and-response on percussion
13. 'Goodbye' on the bongo drums (Oldfield, 2006b)

Each of these activities will provide me with different information. For example, in our shared improvised music making, I will be able to assess how spontaneous a child can be, whether they tend to follow or initiate, and whether they get stuck in particular patterns of playing. The song stories may provide insight into a child's inner world and their particular fears or concerns, while the kazoo exchanges can show me whether a child is able to pick up on different moods and emotions.

Based upon further research into the MTDA (Oldfield, 2004; 2006b), I developed a scoring system that allowed me to compare the MTDA to the Autism Diagnostic Observation Schedule (ADOS) (Lord et al, 1989). In each category (autism, attention deficit disorder, emotional difficulties and learning disabilities) a series of questions are asked relating to symptomatic behaviors that might be observed in sessions. Scores for each question are added up and cut-off points for diagnostic categories are indicated.

An ongoing weekly music therapy group takes place at the Croft for all the children on the unit (Carter & Oldfield, 2002; Oldfield, 2006b). This group enables the team to evaluate the children's strengths and difficulties in a non-verbal setting, as well as addressing some of the children's difficulties in a group setting. In these sessions, children will take part in a number of different musical activities that vary depending on the age of the children, how many children are in the group and the children's strengths and difficulties. The group usually starts with a warm-up activity where I invite the children to copy the rhythm I am playing on a tambour. This rhythmic exchange then turns into a greeting song which ends with the words "…..hello to the person….with pink stripes on their socks." This particular child will then take over the leadership with the tambour, eventually passing it on to another child until all the children and staff in the group have had a turn. Other activities involve group playing, where each of the children joins in on small percussion instruments while I improvise on the piano. My improvisations have several different purposes: to provide a clear rhythmic pulse; to make space for quiet instruments to be heard, and; to give playing an overall structure through instigating clear beginnings and endings. We might also take turns to play a particular instrument, or children may be invited to conduct the group in various ways. The group usually ends with a clapping game or improvised 'rap' where we might reflect on what we will all remember about a child who is about to leave the unit. We might also think about what we have done in the group on that particular day.

The music therapy work at the Croft often makes it possible for families who struggle to interact to spend a positive time together, or to rediscover how to be playful. Many parents find it easier to be part of a non-verbal group improvisation with their children than to engage in an activity where they have to communicate verbally (Oldfield, 2006b).

THE CLIENT
Olivia

Ten-year-old Olivia was admitted to the Croft as an in-patient with her mother, Kath. The family was struggling with Olivia's difficult behaviors at home and there was a concern that she might have an Autistic Spectrum Disorder. Kath felt she was sometimes unable to control her daughter's behaviors. Kath had a history of depression for which she had taken medication on several occasions.

Music Therapy Diagnostic Assessment

Olivia seemed happy to come to the music room with me, telling me confidently on the way that she knew where the room was as she had been there already the previous evening. She appeared as a confident, grownup ten year old. I explained to her that she would have two music therapy diagnostic sessions with me, at the same time on two consecutive weeks.

When I sang the 'Hello' song to her, having explained that this was how I started the session, she smiled and then put her thumb in her mouth, emotionally responding as a younger child would when hearing a warm and predictable melody. She reacted in exactly the same way to the 'Hello' song in her second MTDA session.

After the greeting, I explained that we would take turns choosing instruments and asked her whether she would like to choose first. Olivia seemed to be stuck in her 'young' mode. With her thumb still in her mouth she looked at me coyly and mumbled "Amelia choose."

I chose a large standing drum and a cymbal for Olivia, and went to the piano. Olivia immediately started to play loudly in fast regular semiquavers. I picked up her rhythm on the piano and within seconds we were 'jamming' together. She had an excellent sense of rhythm and liked initiating ideas, noticing and delighting in the fact that I would play these back to her. She was also able to pick up rhythmical phrases that I initiated, showing that she could listen and adapt to my playing. Nevertheless, in our improvised exchange, I took care to keep putting her in control as I quickly realised that I lost the sense of connection with her if I expected her to follow me for too long.

During this improvisation, Olivia seemed to have regained her initial confidence and was then able to choose the drum-kit for herself and a large conga drum for me to play. Her playing was very energetic and almost manic at times. However, she would occasionally stop her continuous loud playing to experiment with a rhythmic sequence on different drums and cymbals. When I imitated her rhythmic phrase, thereby inviting her to continue this experimentation, she kept going briefly, but then quickly went back to her energetic flurries, drowning out my responses. After about five minutes, I suggested that she might like to find a way to end our shared improvisation, which she was able to do effectively.

Next I chose a large bass xylophone for the two of us to play together, sitting opposite one another with the instrument between us. She immediately started playing in her fast energetic style, but when I suggested that we could have a musical conversation and take it in turns to play, she was able to do this with ease. After a few exchanges, she started to hit the xylophone so the notes bounced off it, giggling at what she perceived to be mischievous behavior, or 'startling' me with sudden loud beats on the wood at either end of the instrument. At one point I played the tune 'I hear Thunder' (Frères Jacques). Olivia was keen to learn to play and memorize this melody, focusing on the learning process and persevering when she made mistakes. However, it was noticeable that she always wanted to go back to the beginning when she made a mistake and appeared to want to play it perfectly from the beginning to the end. She seemed to gain a real sense of achievement from the learning of this tune and asked me whether she could play it to the other children on the unit.

In the second MTDA the following week, I gave Olivia a large metallophone and a cymbal on a stand and went to the piano myself. After some free playing together, I suggested that we make up a story while continuing to improvise on the instruments. Olivia wanted the story to be about a white horse called Bella. Bella had a friend called 'Ralph,' who was dark brown. Together they went to a lake and took a boat. When a crocodile appeared (my suggestion) they kicked it away "as far as it could go." They then came to a desert island and had a baby called Bambi who was chestnut coloured. Bambi was beautiful and very clever and they lived happily ever after. Throughout the story, Olivia's playing was lively and loud, and she quickly filled in the dramatic silence I left after the crocodile made his appearance. She did not respond to my dramatic tremolos, but added some glissandos when the horses kicked the crocodile away.

Later in this same session, Olivia and I both played kazoos. Olivia quickly entered into humorous vocal exchanges, laughing with delight at the funny noises we were making. She picked up on my sad and angry sounds briefly but quickly redirected me to silly or funny exchanges.

Reflections

Olivia's responses during the MTDA did not put her into any of the following categories: autistic spectrum disorder, attention deficit disorder, emotional difficulties or learning disabilities (Oldfield, 2006a). I felt it was easy to have musical dialogues with her and that she was able to listen and respond to my suggestions in addition to initiating her own. She was also able to respond to and pick up on changes of mood and emotion during our improvising.

On only one occasion during her entire admission at the unit did Olivia mention hearing voices. This seemed to be in relation to a stressful situation rather than a significant psychiatric symptom.

In the multi-disciplinary management meeting that occurred after my second MTDA with Olivia, I reflected on the fact that I seemed to have encountered two very different Olivias. One was a "toddler-like" little girl who wanted to be looked after and directed by me; and one was an outgoing, energetic and slightly manic ten year old who liked to be in control and direct me. I wondered whether this need to control me, and her manic energetic playing, was a way of avoiding sad or reflective music, which might have brought up difficult emotions. Although the second Olivia appeared confident in some ways, I felt that in other ways, she lacked self-confidence, was desperate to get things right, and was only satisfied when things were perfect. In the story she created, I felt that she did not want to confront adversity (the crocodile) and that perhaps she wanted to be a 'perfect' baby who was beautiful and clever. In our kazoo exchange she showed she was capable of recognising different emotions, but was much happier remaining with the 'safe' ones. While the team had seen glimpses of Olivia's toddler-like behaviors when observing her with her mother, it was only in the music therapy sessions that Olivia had clearly switched from one extreme to the other, and shown us her need to be in control. This was probably because Olivia was very motivated to play the instruments and engage in music making, and because I was able to assess her need for control through non-verbal musical interactions.

We decided to offer Olivia and her mother six joint music therapy sessions, with a view to helping the two of them to have fun together, enabling Olivia to find a middle ground between being a dependent toddler and needing to control her mother. In addition, we felt that these sessions would potentially provide opportunities for Olivia's mom, Kath, to experience and develop more self-confidence in her abilities to parent. Olivia also continued to attend the weekly music therapy group with the other children attending the Croft.

THE THERAPEUTIC PROCESS

Group Music Therapy

In the music therapy group, Olivia was excited and engaged, enjoying playing and interacting through free improvisation. She was constructive and helpful with her younger peers and a very positive influence on the group, clearly wanting to be part of the group music making. She did not display any of the shy and baby-like behaviours she showed in the individual sessions, and if anything appeared a little "high" and overly confident. She enjoyed conducting and playing solos but was also able to wait and listen to others.

In the fourth and fifth group sessions, Olivia would occasionally get a little stuck at the beginning of session, quietly making a point of opting out or not quite conforming. This might have been because she was frustrated with younger peers' slightly disruptive behaviors, and felt that she could not influence or control the group in the way that she wanted. However, as the sessions progressed, her enthusiasm for music making took over and she once again became very engaged in the playing.

Although she did not appear to have the same need to be in control of her peers as she did in the sessions with her mother and myself, I did feel that her opting out in sessions four and five was a way of controlling the adults and making sure we gave her special attention.

Family Music Therapy with Olivia and Kath

Olivia was delighted at the prospect of having music sessions with her mother, Kath. Kath was also happy with the idea and I explained to her that we would make music together and then she and I would have a chance to talk about the sessions after they had taken place. Olivia did not appear to mind that Kath and I would review our sessions without her.

Olivia

Although Olivia was willing to come, she became the "toddler-like" Olivia when I went to collect them both, talking in a young voice and putting her thumb in her mouth. Once in the music room, she was initially very shy, sat very close to her mother, and put her arm through her mother's arm. Olivia did not answer when I asked her whether she would like to choose instruments for us to play, so I went to get some large drums and a cymbal, which I placed in front of her. I offered Kath two beaters and put two on the drum in front of Olivia. I then went to the piano and started playing a rhythmic 12-bar blues. Kath immediately joined in following my beat, clearly enjoying playing. Olivia picked up both beaters in one hand (the thumb of her other hand was still in her mouth) and played briefly without enthusiasm. Suddenly, after her mother and I had been enjoying improvising together for several minutes, Olivia played very loudly, startling her mother, who laughed and looked at me to see what I would do. I immediately incorporated some loud and sudden chords into my playing and the three of us became louder and faster together. Olivia's second hand came out of her mouth and she once again became the more confident and engaged ten year old whom I had seen in previous sessions. This pattern remained similar throughout the six sessions. However, as the sessions progressed, Olivia's young behaviors became less obvious and pronounced. As Olivia and Kath both became involved in improvised music making, Olivia would always become more and more spontaneous and engaged in her playing, shedding her coyness the more involved she became.

Once Olivia joined in with our playing, she had clear ideas about how she wanted to play, often repeating short phrases and requesting that we stop playing together so she could perform her creations for her mother and I to listen to. She seemed to gain a sense of achievement from these performances and I felt they were a way of boosting her self esteem. I also felt that she was showing us that she liked being in control and organizing us. The big sudden beat she had played in our first session was perhaps a sign that she was bored, wanted our attention, and wanted the playing to be on her terms rather than the two adults playing together without her.

In the third session, I pointed out to Olivia that she seemed to enjoy leading and being in control. Olivia immediately looked cross and sulky and put her thumb in her mouth. She did not seem to want to be seen to be in control and I wondered whether in the past she had had to be in control at home when her mother had been depressed. It occurred to me that reverting to toddler behavior was a way of being dependent on adults, a safer position than being responsible for her mother.

In the fourth session Olivia chose to make up a song story in the same way she and I had done in the earlier Music Therapy Diagnostic Assessment. In this story, Olivia chose Chris (the name of her older brother) as the main character, as well as his mate Trevor. In the story, they defied authority and attacked the police. Olivia was clearly excited by this idea, as well as indicating that she felt this was what one might expect from 13-year-old boys. During the story, Kath tried to make the two boys come home and protested that they didn't attack the police. However, Olivia was adamant that her version was the one we should use. When we improvised around Olivia's suggestions, Kath was evidently ill at ease, making placating comments to me such as "he's not really like that...." It was clear that during the story, Olivia was aware of and possibly mischievously enjoying the fact that her mother was embarrassed by this account. In this story, Olivia was bringing up a sensitive family topic relating to events in which her mother had lost control. Interestingly, she did not allow her mother to modify her version of the story. Perhaps it was safer for Olivia to take control as the adults clearly weren't always in control of her brother.

In spite of this moment when Olivia enjoyed embarrassing her mother in a slightly adolescent way, Olivia was at ease playing with her mother and was thoughtful and caring toward her. In contrast, Olivia was quite sensitive to even mild criticism or constructive suggestions. However, she could easily be diverted from these upsets through humorous, playful interactions or engaging in rhythmic patterns.

In the last two sessions, I introduced several conducting activities where we alternated between following Olivia and Kath. Although Olivia clearly much preferred leading herself, she was also able to enjoy following her mother and was more able than previously to acknowledge that this was something she sometimes found difficult. Although the focus was on the musical interchange, both Olivia and Kath were aware that we were experimenting with issues of control, and we reflected on parallel situations at home where either Olivia and Kath were in charge.

Kath

Overall, Kath enjoyed playing the instruments and had no difficulty being playful with Olivia through our musical improvisations. She was a little diffident at first, saying that she had failed grade 1 cornet as a child and that the rest of her family was more musical than she was. However, this did not stop her enjoying playing freely in the sessions. In the second session she was able to say that she really wanted to play the piano, on which she then enjoyed experimenting.

In the first two sessions, Kath was sometimes a little stuck in trying to tell Olivia how to play instruments 'properly.' When we discussed the session together, she agreed that it would be more useful to explore creative non-verbal exchanges rather than give Olivia instructions. When reviewing the first two sessions with me, Kath was generally very positive, saying that she felt the sessions provided Olivia with an opportunity to 'let off steam' and express her frustrations. When Olivia chose to play very loudly and forcefully, Kath was able to support her and allow her to do this, even when she clearly would have preferred quieter playing. She was happy to accept my guidance to ignore Olivia's attention seeking through taking on baby-like behaviors or becoming excessively shy and coy.

After our first two sessions, I suggested to Olivia and Kath that it might be helpful to video the sessions so that we could look back at them and reflect upon what we had been doing. They both agreed to this. Olivia enjoyed watching the beginnings of a couple of sessions but quickly became bored and rejoined her peers, leaving Kath and I to spend more time looking at the sessions together.

Video Review

When I commented that it appeared that Kath really enjoyed music making, she again mentioned how she was not as musical as the rest of her family. I suggested that the important thing was that she was able to be spontaneous and enjoy playing, something that Olivia had clearly picked up from her. Kath was really pleased that something she was doing was having a beneficial effect on her daughter, and this seemed to give her the confidence to allow Olivia to play freely rather than feel she had to instruct her or tell her what to do.

We also talked about how Kath felt she needed to tell Olivia how to play because she was different from other children. This led to a conversation about Olivia's psychiatric symptoms and what might be wrong with her. I suggested that I could not see any obvious symptoms in the videos, and I asked Kath whether she had noticed anything she would like to point out to me. Kath agreed that Olivia was engaged and spontaneous in these sessions. As she felt stronger in herself, she seemed more able to see and recognise the healthy aspects of her daughter's behaviors.

We looked at Olivia's toddler-like behaviors, and Kath said she felt that Olivia was attention seeking. On reflection, she also said that it had been easier looking after Olivia when she was little, as she had felt more confident then than now. She was able to consider whether sometimes she enjoyed treating Olivia as a younger child for this reason. I suggested that we used the spontaneous musical interactions to be equal, each taking 'leading and following' roles, removing Olivia from situations where she was either a dependent 'toddler,' or omnipotent and in control.

When reviewing the fourth session, wherein Olivia had told the story about her 'deviant brother,' Kath again hastened to reassure me that her son was not 'like that.' I suggested to Kath that I saw it as a healthy sign that Olivia now felt safe enough with her mother that she was able to tease her in this way, obviously saying things she knew her mother would react to and be embarrassed by. I pointed out that this was normal pre-adolescent behavior, and that perhaps Olivia shared her mother's sense of humor.

In watching the videos, Kath enjoyed seeing Olivia's creative way of conducting us in the fifth and sixth sessions. She was able to see Olivia's leadership skills as a strength rather than being overwhelming, while at other times also realizing that Olivia needed to be able to accept direction from her.

SUMMARY

In this case study, I have shown that the Music Therapy Diagnostic Assessment helped the psychiatric team to highlight Olivia's strengths and difficulties and exclude a diagnosis of Autistic Spectrum Disorder. The six music therapy sessions with Olivia and her mother, as well as the group music therapy sessions with her peers, helped us to understand Olivia's need for control.

Kath became more confident in her ability to mother Olivia, acknowledging that her mood could affect Olivia. She also noted that her own ability to be playful had had a positive effect on her daughter. She recognized that different styles of parenting were appropriate for children of different ages and that some aspects of Olivia's need to be in control could be seen as normal pre-adolescent behavior. With the team's support, she was able to accept that we were not giving Olivia a psychiatric diagnosis, without feeling that this meant that she was to blame for Olivia's difficulties.

REFERENCES

Carter, C. & Oldfield, A. (2002). A music therapy group to assist clinical diagnoses in child and family psychiatry. In A. Davies and E. Richards (Eds.) *Group Work in Music Therapy* (pp. 149-163). Jessica Kingsley Publications.

Lord, C., Rutter, M., Goode, S., Heemsberger, J., Jordan, H., Manwood, L. & Schopler, E. (1989). Autistic diagnostic observation schedule: A standardised observation of communicative and social behaviour. *Journal of Autism and Developmental Disorders,* 19(2), 185-212.

Oldfield, A. (2004). Music therapy with children on the autistic spectrum: Approaches derived from clinical practice and research. Unpublished Ph.D. Thesis, Anglia Ruskin University.

Oldfield, A. (2006a). *Interactive Music Therapy: A Positive Approach. Music therapy at a Child Development Centre.* London: Jessica Kingsley Publishers

Oldfield, A. (2006b). *Interactive Music Therapy in Child and Family Psychiatry: Clinical Practice, Research and Teaching.* London: Jessica Kingsley Publishers.

Oldfield, A. & Franke C. (2005). Improvised songs and stories in Music Therapy Diagnostic Assessments at a Unit for Child and Family Psychiatry: A music therapist's and a psychotherapist's perspective/ In T. Wigram and F. Baker (Eds.) *Songwriting: Methods, Techniques and Clinical Applications for Music Therapy Clini-*

cians, Educators and Students (pp. 24-44). London: Jessica Kingsley Publishers.

Richer, J. (2001). The insufficient integration of self and other in autism: Evolutionary and developmental perspectives. In J. Richer and S. Coates (Eds.), *Autism: The Search for Coherence*. London: Jessica Kingsley Publishers.

Stern, D. (1985) *The Interpersonal World of the Infant*. New York: Basic Books.

Stern, D. (1995) *The Motherhood Constellation: A Unified View of Parent–Infant Psychotherapy*. New York: Basic Books.

Winnicott, D. (1960) *Playing and Reality*. UK: Pelican Publications.

Winnicott, D. (1971) *Holding and Interpretation*. New York: Grove Press.

Chapter Six

ESTABLISHING COMMUNICATION WITH A BOY WITH AUTISM UTILIZING RECORDED MUSIC

Barbara J. Crowe

INTRODUCTION

This chapter documents a year and a half of music therapy treatment with a four-year-old boy diagnosed with autism. The client presented with typical essential features of autism, including echolalia, immature speech, active withdrawal from others, stereotypical mannerisms and short attention span. The music therapy sessions were held at a university Music Therapy Clinic, and follow the first three semesters of treatment. Initially, techniques based on the Heimlich paraverbal approach were used to gather assessment information and establish a relationship with the client. As therapy progressed, interventions used were primarily a modified behavioral approach with selected interventions based on a sensory integration model. In the middle of the second semester of treatment, the Heimlich paraverbal therapy approach was again employed, with an emphasis on recorded music.

FOUNDATIONAL CONCEPTS

This music therapist's general approach to music therapy practice is eclectic, utilizing whatever methodology, approach, model, or music therapy intervention meets the client's needs at any given time. In the author's clinical work, several approaches are routinely used during a session, with approaches changing as therapy progresses, as occurred in this case. This approach is based on the strong belief that a disorder like autism is so complex and has so many facets that no one theoretical approach alone can adequately address the client's wide-ranging problems and needs (Crowe, 2004). This case had two distinct phases utilizing differing theoretical models and approaches. In the first phase of treatment, a paraverbal approach (Heimlich, 1983) was initially used, followed by behavioral music therapy techniques with some sensory integration incorporated. The second phase of treatment was fully based on the Heimlich paraverbal technique.

The behavioral model of therapy emphasizes external behavior and the relationship of behavior(s) to environment. In this model, behavior change is the focus of therapeutic effort (Wheeler, 1981). An environmental change produces the behavioral change based on the principles of stimulus-response. In behavioral music therapy, the music is both an element of the environment stimulating change, and a reinforcement so that the change is lasting. As such, behavioral music therapy is "...primarily concerned with the function of music as an independent variable acting upon a dependent variable such as the behavior of the patient" (Ruud, 1978 p. 29). Behavioral music therapy was utilized in this way for the case under discussion. Early interventions involved "compliance training," where the client was presented with a stimulus such as a song and was then expected to respond in the desired way (clapping along). The music became both the stimulus to the behavior and the reward for compliance. Specific interventions included action songs, songs with animal sounds or other forms of limited participation, stopping and starting instrument playing to a recording, and using music to reinforce a desired behavior. In this instance, the client's favorite popular songs were played after he had responded with a targeted behavior, such as making eye contact. The therapist's goal was to create and present music therapy interventions that would best stimulate the desired behavior change, and to verbally and musically reinforce that behavior when it occurred.

In addition to the behavioral approach used in phase one of therapy, some sensory integration interventions were used. In general, sensory integration involves the organization of sensation (locating, sorting, and ordering) arriving in the brain from all sensory channels. This leads to the formation of perception, the ability to assign meaning to and functionally use the sensory input. According to Ayres (1979), sensory integration is developed when a child is engaged in a purposeful, goal-directed response to multisensory activities (Crowe, 2004). In this approach, music, especially physical engagement in music making, is such an activity. Examples of sensory integration activities in music therapy used for this case include deep pressure on joints in rhythm to the beat of the music, rocking to music, vibro-tactile stimulation from the physical experience of music vibrations and multi-sensory activities combining balancing on a T-stool while catching and throwing a ball rhythmically to a song. The music both engages the client in these activities and provides direct therapeutic benefit through rhythmic input, vibration, and sensory input to the brain.

In the assessment period and the second phase of the therapy in this case, approaches and techniques based on Heimlich Paraverbal Therapy (PVT) were employed. This approach was developed by Evelyn Heimlich (1983) for children who are non-communicative and react negatively to verbal interaction, are treatment resistive, and/or who are unresponsive to conventional psychotherapy methods (Bruscia, 1987). It is used as an alternative to verbal expression and release of feelings. The method uses multi-sensory stimulation emphasizing pleasurable play, reciprocal interactions as the basis of relationship development, and free expressions of emotions through improvisations. The method literally involves "...playing in sound and movement" (Bruscia, 1987 p. 269) and utilizes a wide range of channels, media and materials for expression and communication. The intent is to replace speech with sensorimotor communication. The basic premise of PVT is to ensure that the client and therapist are engaged in the media, experiences and materials that are pleasurable, and in so doing, decrease the client's anxiety. The interventions used should never seem like work, teaching or compliance training, nor should they place demands on the client. It is the client's needs, interests, and preferences that determine what media and active interventions are used in the session (Bruscia, 1987). "The rationale for paraverbal therapy is that if the child can be pleasurably engaged through multisensory media and improvised play, which meet his/her ongoing needs, and if the child can be made to feel accepted and cared for, a therapeutic relationship can be established" (Bruscia, 1987 p. 270). According to Heimlich (1983), opening lines of communication is the primary, overall goal of PVT. Specific goals addressed by PVT include:

1. Fulfillment of basic needs
2. Development of a sense of self

3. Freedom of self-expression
4. Communication with others
5. Relief from painful emotions
6. Elimination of symptoms such as mutism, aggression, withdrawal, hyperactivity, anxiety stress, and ritualistic behaviors
(Bruscia, 1987 pp. 276-277)

PVT is used for clients with emotional and/or communications problems (Joseph & Heimlich, 1959; Heimlich, 1983, for clients diagnosed with mental illness (Heimlich, 1983, for problems in neurological functioning (Heimlich, 1975), specific learning disabilities (Heimlich, 1980), hospitalized children (McDonald, 1979; 1984) and for clients with multiple disabilities (Grob, 1979; 1981).

A PVT session attempts to address the expressive and communicative needs of the client moment to moment throughout the session. The therapist observes the client intensely and must be sensitive to the smallest reactions and behaviors indicating the client's emotional state (Heimlich, 1983). PVT theory is based on the premise that regardless of existing communication difficulties, overt behavior, facial expression, body posture, vocalizations and lack of response can all be apprehended as modes of communication (Bruscia, 1987). When the therapist perceives the cues being presented by the client, he/she responds to the client flexibly and spontaneously to meet the client's needs. The therapist does not force the client to do anything and presents as options media, materials, and activity interventions that the client enjoys (Bruscia, 1987). PVT incorporated a wide variety of nonverbal modes of communication, including sensorimotor experiences from the components of music, all forms of musical expression, musical instruments to explore, spontaneous dance and movement to music, art expressions, mime and psychodrama. Various props are employed, such as art materials, scarves, streamers, toys, balls and balloons and devices to encourage movement such as a trampoline.

Bruscia (1987) notes that Heimlich drew a distinction between music therapy and PVT. Typically, music therapists using paraverbal techniques identify their work as music therapy, employing techniques such as those used in the case being presented (Grob, 1979; McDonnell, 1970, 1983). Because PVT emphasizes play, pleasure, freedom of choice, spontaneity, flexibility and reciprocal interactions, the music therapist wishing to use paraverbal techniques frequently employs musical improvisation (Bruscia, 1987). This also distinguishes music therapy from PVT in that the spontaneous music making becomes a vital component to the paraverbal therapy. Improvisation is used by the therapist to accompany spontaneous songs, to mirror feelings and behavior, to engage in instrument dialogue, to stimulate movement and instrument playing and to prompt art expression. These become a direct expressive tool for the client. The music becomes a vital component of the therapeutic effort since it is the stimulus for client interaction and the way the client expresses emotions and presents issues. The music therapist's role is to observe all aspects of the client's reactions and respond with matching improvisations. As such, this approach shares aspects of Nordoff-Robbins's Creative Music Therapy (Nordoff & Robbins, 1971).

THE CLIENT

Mark was referred to a university Music Therapy Clinic by his mother. Though four years of age at the time of the referral, he was receiving no other therapy services and did not attend a pre-school program. His mother sought out music therapy because of his demonstrated interest in, and response to, music. Mark's parents were young, 20 and 21 years old, and kept the television in their home tuned to the MTV video music channel most of the time. Mark spent 4-5 hours per day watching music videos on MTV. His mother reported that he sang along to popular songs and played a toy guitar regularly. Mark's mother also reported that her son had initially been diagnosed with a speech delay and attention deficit disorder, but had then been diagnosed with autism just prior to his referral to music therapy.

Mark's assessment was based primarily on the therapist's observation of his behavior and response during involvement in music therapy activities. Mark was a physically beautiful blond, blue-eyed boy with a strong physique and age appropriate motor skills. He demonstrated a short attention span (15-20 seconds) and was easily distracted by visual stimuli. Typically, he would run around the Clinic in a frenzied motion, grabbing instruments and throwing them down. He was unable to maintain attention to task and was unable to complete an activity once started. Mark did not respond to any structure imposed on him by the therapist.

In fact, when the therapist would try to join him in an activity he had initiated (such as using the microphone), he would immediately stop the activity and run to the other side of the room. Mark displayed extreme tactile defensiveness and would actively withdraw from physical contact with the therapist. If touched or approached, he would scream, kick, spit, and try to flee from the room, which once included attempting to jump out the window. Mark initiated limited speech, utilizing one and two word phrases to make needs known ("play guitar" or "no Michael Jackson"). He also displayed classic echolalia, mimicking not only words used by the therapist, but the pitch and inflection of her voice as well. However, Mark's response to verbal interaction and commands clearly indicated he had strong respective language skills. For example, he would move to the piano when the therapist would say, "Piano, Mark?" He was unable to make eye contact or eye/face contact for the most part, though in some instances would hold eye contact for an inappropriate amount of time. Mark displayed a number of stereotypical, self-stimulating mannerisms, including rocking, stimulating his belly button and rhythmic, repetitive sucking on his fingers and shirt.

At the same time, Mark demonstrated a high level of response to music and musical stimuli. He was most responsive to current popular music, singing along with songs and mimicking guitar playing and a rock-n-roll "stance." Mark typically reacted best to recorded music, though live piano playing and drumming did engage him to some extent. He was interested in playing and exploring a wide range of musical instruments, especially drums, piano and an amplified microphone for singing.

Based on this assessment, the follow needs were determined:

1. Decrease tactile defensiveness
2. Increase attention span and attention to task
3. Develop communication skills in general and speech and language skills specifically
4. Increase tolerance to external structure
5. Improve social awareness and interaction, especially eye contact

THE THERAPEUTIC PROCESS

Assessment Phase

After the initial assessment session determined that Mark would probably benefit from music therapy, the next three sessions were designed to gather more detailed assessment information. To accomplish this, a paraverbal approach was used wherein a range of musical experiences and activities were introduced to Mark during each 50-minute session. A wide variety of musical instruments and equipment, toys and art material were placed around the clinic. These materials included an electronic keyboard, hand percussion instruments, drums including a children's trap drum set, piano, guitar, autoharp, omnichord, tone chimes, reed horns, a Native American flute, a violin, a cello and a dulcimer. Mark was verbally encouraged to freely interact with and use this equipment. When verbal prompting failed, the music therapist would play the various instruments and observe Mark carefully to see if he showed any interest or reaction to a particular instrument. If Mark touched or tried to use an instrument, the therapist would improvise a song or accompaniment on guitar in response to his behavior. Mark was somewhat responsive to these activities and would engage in the interaction for various amounts of time. In the third session, a microphone with amplification and reverberation sound was introduced to encourage vocalization. Mark became very invested in this activity and would spontaneously make a variety of vocalizations into the microphone. He would also become fixated by his own reflection in the mirror and would mimic the postures of rock and roll artists. During this phase, the therapist also improvised on the piano in response to Mark's movement patterns and vocalizations. Additionally, Mark was placed at the piano and encouraged to improvise with the therapist providing supportive accompaniment. Mark's response to these activities varied from session to session.

    Several activities based on a sensory integration model were also introduced during the assessment phase. This included rocking to music while being held by the therapist, and the application of deep pressure to his arms and legs in rhythm with the beat of recorded music or a song. The rocking to music was completely unsuccessful as Mark would violently pull away from the therapist and kick and scream. He did, however, tolerate the deep pressure activity and would visibly relax when this was going on. A bean bag chair was also provided for Mark to lie in for periods of rest and to decrease anxiety. Quiet classical music was played during the times he was in this chair. This was one of Mark's favorite activities. He would return 2-3 times per session to the chair.

Structured songs were also introduced both to encourage singing and to assess receptive language through his ability to comply with directions given within the lyrics of the song ("Put your finger in the air"). Mark did not sing in response to songs presented, but would irregularly respond to cues and commands in the lyrics. Structured movement to music was also attempted, though Mark did not respond to these activities in any way. Once the assessment period concluded, Phase 1 of Mark's music therapy began.

Phase 1

Based on the assessment information obtained, it was determined that a modified behavioral approach to the music therapy sessions (emphasizing compliance) would be used with the inclusion of some interventions based on a sensory integration approach to address neurological and cognitive deficits. A typical session would begin with moving Mark to the "music chair" and singing a hello song. During this song, Mark was asked to remain seated until the end and, utilizing verbal prompting, make eye contact with the therapist at least once. After the hello song, the session moved into free choice activities based on the paraverbal approach, where Mark was presented with a variety of music instruments and the amplified microphone, and allowed to use them in any way he wished. During this time the therapist observed Mark closely and, when an interest was shown in a particular instrument, provided a musical accompaniment through singing or playing guitar. The therapist's playing reflected the type, intensity and duration of Mark's involvement. In this way, the music was used to reinforce Mark's participation and reflect his expression. When Mark was using the microphone, the therapist would vocally imitate the sounds he produced and model other sounds in an effort to increase his repertoire of vocalizations.

After a period of 5-10 minutes of free-choice time, the session shifted to a more structured set of interventions emphasizing compliance.

Activity interventions included shake and stop, where the client is asked to play a rhythm instrument while the therapist plays piano or guitar, and action songs, where a movement or sound is required by the lyrics of the song. The music itself was used primarily to motivate participation and response, though verbal prompting was also used.

Interspersed with these activities were music therapy interventions based on a sensory integration approach. These activities included:

- Tactile modeling by applying deep pressure to joints in the arms and legs in rhythm to a recording or sung song
- Vibrotactile stimulation provided in two main forms: 1) by having the client lie on an Orff bass bar while a steady beat pulse was played, or 2) sitting against a stereo speaker
- Engaging in multi-sensory tasks such as balancing on a t-stool while catching a ball to a song sung by the music therapist
- Rolling on a large drum while a beat is played

For these interventions, the music and/or sound vibration provided direct therapeutic input through sensory stimulation in order to re-shape or re-mediate neurological problems. The therapist's role was to provide these sensory inputs and observe Mark's reactions closely. The therapist reacted to his behavior by introducing new activities or modifying the ones in use to meet his needs and interests of the client on a moment to moment basis.

Other activity interventions were used, including 1) the therapist improvising on piano or guitar to the client's behavior and vocalizations, and 2) the client improvising on piano while the therapist mirrored intervals, rhythms, and dynamics. These activities were used to give Mark opportunities to initiate and lead the musical interaction. Sessions ended with a structure goodbye song.

Throughout this phase of the music therapy, Mark's responses and behavior varied, and in this way, progress was not linear. Generally, he was minimally responsive to the structured, compliance-based interventions. He would often tolerate an action song for a short period of time, but would quickly run over to instruments or other equipment. The free choice activities were much more successful in holding Mark's attention, especially vocalizing into the amplified microphone. During the time Mark engaged in using a particular instrument, the music therapist would interact with him musically. His attention to task improved for these free choice activities, and he allowed more interaction with the therapist. He remained, however, tactilely sensitive and would quickly move away if the therapist got too close. The exception to this was during the tactile modeling activity using deep pressure touch to a strong auditory beat. Mark tolerated this activity for increasing amounts of time, and at times would indicate his desire for the activity by pulling the therapist's hand toward his legs. Improvised vocalizations into the microphone supported spontaneous vocalization, and he would say one to two words per session. Other sensory integration activities were also well tolerated. Visible muscle relaxation would occur when he experienced vibrotactile stimulation, or was listening to quietening music while sitting in the bean bag chair. During these times, his hyperactivity decreased, and he was better able to tolerate the therapist's physical proximity.

The therapy continued in this fashion through the first ten weeks of sessions and into the first four weeks of the next semester. In the fifth session, however, there was a dramatic and drastic change in Mark's behavior and response. This session began with Mark coming down the hallway toward the music therapy clinic screaming "no music, no music" at the top of his lungs. When his mother dragged him into the room, he immediately kicked the therapist and hid behind the piano. Efforts to engage him in any activity, including his favorites (like vocalizing into the microphone), were met with hysterical screaming, frantic kicking, and an escalation of rage and anxiety. At one point, he climbed on top of the piano and tried to jump out of the window. In discussion with his mother, the therapist learned that Mark was behaving this way at home and that the behavior had started when a group of out-of-town family members had arrived for a visit. This complete lack of response, active avoidance of the therapist and aggression continued for the next two sessions. It became clear that the current approach to Mark's music therapy had to change, and so Phase 2 of treatment was instigated.

Phase 2

Mark's sudden change in response and behavior coincided with disruptions in his home life and indicated that he was experiencing a strong emotional reaction and high level of stress to this change. As he was nonverbal, he had no way of expressing or dealing with these emotions. Because Mark had previously been responsive to the free choice activities used in Phase 1, it was decided to expand use of techniques from a paraverbal approach to re-establish a relationship with him. In addition to musical expression expanding, other art forms were introduced. In this case, the paraverbal technique was not used as a psychotherapy approach per se, but to help Mark discharge tension and pent-up feelings. Since he was completely resistant to therapist-initiated activities, it was felt that he would benefit from the sense of control offered by the paraverbal approach. He could make his needs known through art expressions and the music therapist could meet those needs non-verbally and in a non-threatening way.

Phase 2 of Mark's therapy began with the music therapist preparing the room with several bean bag chairs and placing musical instruments and the microphone around the room. Recordings of Mark's favorite popular music were played on the stereo system. As Mark entered the room, the therapist withdrew to a far corner and did not interact with him. Mark was free to use anything in the room with no interference from the therapist. During this time, the therapist observed Mark intensely and noted in writing the behaviors he displayed, the instruments he touched and used, for how long, and what kind of affect he displayed, including physical tension. In the second session of Phase 2, the session progressed as before, except that the therapist improvised quietly on guitar in response to Mark's actions and behaviors. During this session, Mark glanced at the therapist several times, but did not interact in any way. This pattern continued for two more sessions during which time the therapist moved physically closer to where Mark was sitting. Mark was now able to tolerate the presence of the therapist and some short verbal interactions, mainly verbal reinforcement.

At this point, the therapist also introduced paper and crayons to encourage Mark to draw. In the second of these sessions, Mark picked up a crayon and drew several jagged slashes in black and brown. The therapist responded with, "good picture, Mark." At this point, Mark looked directly at the therapist, picked up the crayon and wrote the word 'picture.' This was particularly noteworthy since Mark had not attended school up to this point and was now known to be able to read or write.

In the next session, Mark entered without resistance, though he immediately climbed on top of the instrument cabinet and would not come down. A song by Michael Jackson was playing on the stereo and Mark said, "No Michael Jackson. Billy Ocean." The therapist immediately played a Billy Ocean song and involved herself in playing the dulcimer, drawing on the paper, and modeling clay. Mark remained distant and non-interactive, though he did come down from the cupboard to get some clay. He then pounded the clay for a short time. When the therapist changed the recording, Mark yelled "No, no, no. Billy Ocean." This request was always met so that the Billy Ocean song "Sad Songs to Make You Cry" was played 10 times during the session. Though Mark continued to ignore the therapist, his mother reported that he constantly asked at home to go to "music class." Sessions continued in this manner with Mark distancing himself from the therapist and the therapist meeting his expressed and implied needs, including playing specific popular songs.

In a subsequent session, Mark entered the room and said, "Music class today, no thank you," ran to the far side of the room and lay on the floor. He displayed no interest in any of the activities or equipment offered him until he was finally coaxed to use the paper and crayons. At this point, he picked up the crayon and wrote the entire identification material for a particular song as displayed during the MTV videos:

>Gloria Esteban
>1-2-3
>EMI Records

This recording was quickly played on the stereo. When it finished, Mark wrote another identification for a song. This was also played for him. He began to verbally request songs using the full MTV identification, which the therapist would write down. At one point, the therapist wrote it incorrectly, and Mark picked up the crayon and corrected it. It was clear at this point that Mark was using written communication to make his needs known. In subsequent sessions, the therapist would prompt him with, "Write what you want to hear," and Mark would write his requests for songs. The therapist would then meet his request. Mark was also able to respond to more complex written questions such as "What side do you want" or "Who sings this song?"

Mark and the therapist began true two-way interactions at this point. The approach shifted from a paraverbal treatment to written, verbal interactions. However, the paraverbal techniques allowed this level of communication to occur. From this new means of communication, Mark's resistive behavior toward the therapist decreased. He allowed the therapist to sit closer to him and even sat in her lap on a number of occasions. Therapy progressed in this manner until the end of the semester. Toward the end of their time together, the therapist could write requests for Mark (play the bass drum 1 time and the cymbal 2 times), to which he would comply, and Mark could make his needs known to the therapist through writing.

Many of Mark's behaviors and reactions, such as hyperactivity, lack of attention to the task, active withdrawal for the therapist and stereotypical mannerisms decreased or disappeared as Mark was able to express himself, to have his needs known and met and to exercise control over the session. In this way, the use of the paraverbal techniques supported his move toward more normalized functioning. The music, in this case recorded popular music, was the motivating factor and catalyst for his improved interactions with the therapist. The music became a transitional object to buffer the client as he learned to relate to and communicate with the therapist. In this way, the recorded music allowed a therapeutic relationship to develop that could subsequently be used to work on other goals, and lead Mark to independent living.

Postlude

Music therapy continued in this manner for a year and a half until his family moved to another area. Some years later, the therapist had contact with Mark and learned that he had graduated from high school, held a job, lived semi-independently, and taught Sunday school. He was a happy, well-adjusted young man who was obsessed with music and computers. He remembered every piece of music ever used in his music therapy sessions and could list them all to prove it.

SUMMARY

This case involved a young boy diagnosed with autism who presented with behaviors, reactions, and problems typical of that diagnosis. After an assessment process involving case history information and observation of behavior and reaction, a two-phase treatment plan utilizing several treatment models was developed. In Phase 1, a general paraverbal and modified behavioral approach were used. In addition, activity interventions based on the sensory integration model were employed to address the underlying neurological difficulties associated with autism. After a major setback in the client's behavior and response, paraverbal approaches were used exclusively to allow Mark expression of emotions in order to re-establish a therapeutic relationship. From this, a two-way written interaction developed based on recorded popular music. For Mark, music was the motivation for participation in music therapy experiences, was a direct sensory stimulation for the central nervous system, and became the transitional object allowing the development of the therapeutic relationship.

REFERENCES

Ayers, A. J. (1979). *Sensory Integration and the Child.* Los Angeles: Western Psychological Services.

Bruscia, K. E. (1987). *Improvisational Models of Music Therapy.* Springfield, IL: Charles C. Thomas.

Crowe, B. J. (2004). *Music and Soulmaking: Toward a New Theory of Music Therapy.* Latham, MD: Scarecrow Press.

Grob, H. M. (1979). Music therapy. In P.J. Vallelutti and F. Christophos (Eds.), *Preventing Physical and Mental Disability: A Multidisciplinary Approach* (pp. 197-210). Baltimore, MD: University Park Press.

Grob, H. M. (1981). Music therapy utilizing paraverbal techniques. In R.F.D. Cuice and R.B. Kugel (Eds.), *Into the light: Helping People with Handicaps at Flower Hospital* (pp. 95-96). New York: New York Medical Publishing Corp.

Heimlich, E. P. (1972). Paraverbal techniques in the therapy of childhood communication disorders. *International Journal of Child Psychotherapy,* 1(1), 65-83.

Heimlich, E. P. (1983). Using a patient as "assistant therapist" in paraverbal therapy. *International Journal of Child Psychotherapy*, I(1), 84-101.

Heimlich, E. P. (1980). Paraverbal techniques: A new approach for communication with children having learning difficulties. *Journal of Learning Disabilities*, 13(9), 16-18.

Heimlich, E. P. (1983). The metaphoric use of song lyrics as a paraverbal communication. *Child Psychiatry and Human Development,* 14(2), 67-75.

Joseph, H. & Heimlich, E. P. (1959). The therapeutic use of music with "treatment resistant" children. *American Journal of Mental Deficiency,* 63(7), 41-49.

McDonnell, L. (1970). Paraverbal therapy in pediatric cases with emotional complications. *American Journal of Orthopsychiatry,* 49(1), 44-52.

McDonnell, L. (1983). Music therapy: Meeting the psychosocial needs of hospitalized children. *Journal of the Association for the Care of Children's Health,* 12(1), 29-33.

Nordoff, P. & Robbins, C. (1971). *Music Therapy for Handicapped Children.* New York: St. Martin's Press.

Ruud, E. (1978). *Music Therapy and its Relationship to Current Treatment Theories.* St. Louis, MO: Magnamusic-Baton, Inc.

Wheeler, B. L. (1981). The relationship between music therapy and theories of psychotherapy. *Music Therapy,* 1(1), 9-16.

Chapter Seven

ADDRESSING CORE FEATURES OF AUTISM: INTEGRATING NORDOFF-ROBBINS MUSIC THERAPY WITHIN THE DEVELOPMENTAL, INDIVIDUAL-DIFFERENCE, RELATIONSHIP-BASED DIR®/FLOORTIME™ MODEL

John A. Carpente

INTRODUCTION

This chapter is based on the author's clinical experiences developing a music therapy program at a Developmental, Individual-Difference, Relationship-based (DIR®) school in a large metropolitan area in the United States. Although terms, concepts, and philosophy are grounded in Nordoff-Robbins Music Therapy (NRMT), definitions, clinical interpretations and rationale have been modified based on the DIR® Model in an attempt to integrate NRMT and DIR®/Floortime™ (Greenspan & Weider, 2006a). The rationale for this is an attempt to develop a population-based music therapy assessment and treatment intervention that focuses on establishing and achieving musical goals in relation to social-emotional development in children with neurodevelopmental disorders that affect relating and communicating, specifically autism spectrum disorders. To that end, assessment and conceptualizing the child to determine intervention planning, includes both DIR® and NRMT.

Clinical Setting

This clinical work takes place at a Developmental, Individual-Difference, Relationship-based (DIR®) school located in New York City. The school serves 107 children, ages four to eighteen, with neurodevelopmental disorders of relating and communicating, including Pervasive Developmental Disorders (PDD). The school offers a variety of services, including music and art therapy, speech therapy, occupational and physical therapy, psychology and social work.

This case study details individual music therapy with Matthew, a seven-year-old boy diagnosed with Pervasive Developmental Disorder-Not Otherwise Specified (PDD-NOS) who displayed difficulties in his ability to self-regulate, engage, relate and communicate. In this clinical work, NRMT and the DIR®/Floortime™ model were used in tandem. The chapter describes a five-month process in which interactive musical experiences helped to facilitate Matthew's ability to self-regulate, engage, relate, and purposefully communicate. NRMT was used as the primary treatment approach, and focused primarily on musical goals and the establishment of musical relationships between therapists (intern and therapist) and child. DIR® was used as the primary means of conceptualizing and assessing the child's strengths and needs and evaluating the child's progress in these areas (Carpente, 2009).

FOUNDATION CONCEPTS

NRMT and the DIR®/Floortime™ Model

The DIR® model, developed by Drs. Greenspan and Weider (Greenspan & Weider, 2006b), provides a comprehensive framework for assessing and treating the child. It centers on facilitating foundational components of child development in the areas of relating, communicating and thinking through the development of relationships via interactive play - Floortime™ (Greenspan & Weider, 2006a; 2006b). Rather than simply focusing on isolated behaviors, the model takes a global perspective of the child regarding functional developmental capacities, biological processing differences and emotional interactions between the child and caregiver (Greenspan & Weider, 2006a; 2006b).

The term "Development" refers to where the child is developmentally, based on social-emotional development. According to Greenspan and Weider (2006a) developmental milestones include six levels of emotional development (Functional Emotional Developmental Levels or FEDL) important to children with autism spectrum disorders (ASD) of any age:

1. Regulation and shared attention
2. Engagement and relatedness
3. Two-way purposeful communication
4. Shared problem solving
5. Creative use of ideas
6. Building bridges between ideas

The Term "Individual-Difference" refers to how the child processes information such as motor and sensory capacities, touch, sound, and other sensations. It also includes auditory and visual-spatial processing, motor-planning and sequencing abilities. For each of the six developmental stages described above, the therapist looks at the particular "individual-differences" of the child, and determines how they interfere with the child's development (Greenspan & Weider, 2006b).

Finally, the term "Relationships" in the DIR® model refers to how the child interacts with others and what patterns of interaction, and affects, should be included in the treatment plan to support and enhance the child's development.

As can be seen, each component of the DIR® model complements the other. First, it is important to understand at what level the child is functioning developmentally. Secondly, one must ascertain what stands in the way of a child's development, in regard to how the child is processing information about him or herself. Lastly, it is critical to know how the child relates to others in the world. Once there is a developmental picture and a sensory profile of the child, the therapist can guide the child into ways of interacting and relating that will provide the proper sensory input necessary to move him/her up the developmental ladder (Greenspan & Weider, 2006a).

Nordoff-Robbins Music Therapy and the DIR® Model

The driving force of the DIR ® model, which parallels NRMT, is Floortime™. Floortime™ (Greenspan & Weider, 2006a) is a systematic way of using play to help the child to develop. Similarities between Floortime™ and NRMT are that they both involve improvisation, creativity, spontaneity, emotionality and a playful spirit. The main difference between Floortime™ and NRMT is in the medium. NRMT primarily involves the use of live interactive musical experiences, while Floortime™ primarily involves the use of objects and symbolic and sensory toys.

In NRMT, the therapist (music maker) observes the child and follows his/her lead using music as the primary medium. The music being improvised attempts to create affective and emotionally charged experiences intended to help the child regulate, musically engage and interact in a joint musical relationship (Carpente, 2009). Both are action-based approaches in which the child is an active and leading participant in the process. Both approaches view relationships as a core component of child development. Both focus on the creative process (dynamics) between the child and therapist. Finally, both models respect the individual differences of each child and view whatever the child is doing as important (e.g., respecting idiosyncratic and self-stimulatory behaviors without attempting to extinguish them, but to embrace them and help make them interactive and communicative). The primary focus of both approaches is to bring the child into a shared world from isolation. The idea is not to pull the child "kicking and screaming," but have the child want to be in the shared world.

Role of Therapist/Music

The therapist's task is to improvise music built around the child's musical responses, reactions, and/or movements, while considering the child's individual differences (Carpente, 2009). The primary focus of the improvised music is to create and offer experiences that will facilitate musical relatedness and communication in order to help the child move up the developmental ladder. Because the primary focus is on the quality of musical interactions between the child and therapist, "the musical process is the clinical process" (Aigen, 2005, p. 94). This means that the therapist's primary concern is to develop and incorporate musical interventions that deepen the child's musical engagement and interaction in order to increase relatedness and communication. In short, musical goals are clinical goals (Aigen, 2005). What a child accomplishes musically is regarded as a clinical or therapeutic accomplishment. However, although the focus is on musical goals and the widening of the child's musical experiences, it is clear that these goal areas can also address cognitive, expressive, sensory, communication and social areas. In considering all that is involved in achieving the above musical goals (motor planning, auditory cuing, fine and gross motor skills, visual-spatial processing and sensory modulation), it becomes clear that developmental goals are realized through musical goals and experiences (Carpente, 2009).

BACKGROUND AND CURRENT INFORMATION

History

Reportedly, Matthew was the product of an uncomplicated, full-term pregnancy and C-section delivery. He weighed 6 lbs. 8 oz. at birth and no complications were indicated. Developmental milestones were met within normal limits by age two; however speech was delayed.

Matthew was three years old when he was diagnosed with Pervasive Developmental Disorder-Not Otherwise Specified (PDD-NOS) and speech apraxia. In addition, testing revealed a Mental Development Index of <50 on the *Bayley Scales of Infant Development,* suggesting a rating of Significantly Delayed Performance. On the *Vineland Adaptive Behavior Scales*, Matthew obtained an Adaptive Composite score of 57, at the Low Level. All other domains were also in the low range, except motor skills, which were within the Moderately Low range.

Matthew resided with his mother, his maternal grandparents, aunt, and cousin. He saw his father occasionally.

Matthew had been attending his current school for two months prior to beginning individual music therapy. During this time Matthew was also receiving occupational, speech, and physical therapies five times per week, individually for 30 minutes.

DIR® Profile

Matthew presented as an active, sensory seeking child. He has difficulty maintaining self-regulation (the ability to be calm and available to interact), shared attention with the therapist (level I) and displayed intermittent capacities of engagement and relating (level II). He sought movement, and was in constant motion, which appeared to be a strategy to self-regulate when exposed to an over-stimulating environment, demonstrating his need for vestibular input.

Matthew displayed islands of capacities in his ability to engage in two-way purposeful communication (level III); however, he had difficulty sustaining this due to an inability to maintain self-regulation and engagement for extended periods. His intent to communicate was often demonstrated through nonverbal gestures as well as attempts at word approximations. In addition, Matthew appeared to have difficulty processing and filtering auditory stimulation, and would "melt down" in an aggressive manner (i.e., biting, pinching, hitting, etc.) when the environment was over-stimulating.

Music Therapy Assessment

The music therapy assessment was guided by Greenspan and Weider's Functional Emotional Developmental Levels (FEDL) (2006a), focusing on seven areas of musical responsiveness (Carpente, 2008; 2009):

1. *Musical Awareness*: the child's ability to respond or react in a reflexive or intentional manner related to any of the musical elements being offered.
2. *Musical Relatedness*: the child's ability to engage musically in an intentionally and related manner to the therapist's music.
3. *Relationship within Musical Play*: the child's ability to display an emotional interest in connecting with the music and therapist, based on his/her (child's) own initiative.
4. *Music Interresponsiveness*: the child's ability to imitate or copy a musical idea, and then incorporate it into musical play with the therapist.
5. *Musical Communicativeness*: the child's ability to open (initiate a musical idea) and close circles of musical communication (end or complete a musical phrase) during musical play, including the ability to engage in call-and-response interplay and cause-and-effect based play.
6. *Musical Interrelatedness*: the child's ability to connect his/her musical idea with the therapist's idea, and then elaborate on it during musical play.
7. *Musical Expressiveness*: the child's ability to play musically using range of musical elements (e.g. dynamics, tempo, etc.).

The music therapy room was set up with a variety of percussive and melodic instruments, an assortment of different sized mallets with various handle textures, pitched horns, and a variety of sensory based items (i.e. scarves, play-doh, mini-trampoline, etc.). The assessment focused on Matthew's ability to interact during musical play with the therapist. Matthew's assessment took place during the course of two 30-minute sessions. Clinical improvisation was used during the assessment in that the therapist improvised music built around Matthew's emotionality, and his behavioral responses and reactions to the music.

During the assessment, Matthew's primary mode of interacting was through vocalizations. Due to his tactile sensitivities, he displayed difficulty holding mallets for extended periods but would occasionally play the tambourine and other hand-played drums for brief periods when prompted (1–2 measures).

When Matthew was unable to be emotionally calm and available for engagement (dysregulated), he exhibited a low level of musical awareness. At these times he would only occasionally present reflexive tonal responses interspersed with bouts of intense crying and screaming while covering his ears with his hands, a sign of auditory overload to his sensory system.

His inability to maintain self-regulation inhibited Matthew from engaging in a musically related or communicative manner for extended periods. In addition, he exhibited no desire to initiate musical or interpersonal contact with the therapist, and would attempt to climb on window ledges, the piano and large drums, before attempting to leave the room in an aggressive and agitated state.

When Matthew was able to self-regulate, his level of musical awareness and relatedness increased. During these moments he demonstrated his ability to imitate and fill–in the ends of musical phrases (closing circles of communication) through both nonverbal and verbal (word approximations) singing, prompted by musical cues (displaying receptive language skills, and sequencing ability). In addition, when vocalizing, Matthew displayed islands of capacities in the areas of musical interrelatedness and communicativeness; however, he showed a limited ability to expand on the therapist's musical ideas, or to initiate musical ideas (open circles of musical communication).

The assessment indicated that Matthew's main areas of difficulty were in his inability to maintain self-regulation (ability to be calm and available for engagement) and musical engagement due to 1) his difficulties with language processing (specifically expressive), 2) a mixed reactive sensory system (hyper and hypo sensitive to sensory stimuli), and 3) auditory processing difficulties.

To that end, Matthew's sensory integration and language processing difficulties appeared to limit his ability to display musical awareness and the ability to use music in a related and/or interresponsive manner. Although he displayed islands of capacities in his ability to engage and relate in musical play, his self-regulatory challenges kept him from experiencing a continuous flow of musical communication for extended periods.

THE THERAPEUTIC PROCESS

Matthew's treatment consisted of twenty-five sessions over a five-month period. During this time, Matthew passed through four separate stages. In the first stage he exhibited self-regulatory challenges which impeded his ability to enter and remain in the music room, engage and relate during musical play. In the second stage, in providing Matthew with sensory input to facilitate self-regulation, he began to increase his ability to engage and relate during musical play. During stage three, a relationship (interpersonal and musical) began to develop as Matthew began to open (initiate) and close circles of musical communication during musical play. Finally, in stage four, Matthew's ability to engage in intentional and reciprocal musical interactions, while displaying causal thinking during musical play, began to develop.

Stage One: What's Getting in the Way? Developing the Playing Field While Considering Individual-Differences

Stage one included sessions one through six. This stage was considered a period of "getting to know" each other. Generally, sessions were very similar to the assessment sessions. Matthew would enter each session distressed and dysregulated and would usually lean on the wall (near the door), attempt to climb on something, or try to hide behind something.

His crying and screaming became extremely intense. Each session ended with Matthew desperately wanting to leave the room, which he would eventually do in a dysregulated manner.

Musically, I initially attempted to improvise music on the piano, around his "melt-downs," trying to meet the intensity of his crying in order to facilitate musical contact and relatedness. There were moments when Matthew's crying and screaming became increasingly related to my improvised music, both tonally and sequentially. Although he was clearly displaying musical awareness, his responses were reflexive, and did not demonstrate any intentionality in regard to relating to my music. Although the musical relationship, thus far, had been based on Matthew being resistive (Nordoff & Robbins, 2007) to the music making process, our musics (sounds) were related.

Looking at the interaction through the lens of the DIR® Model, Matthew had difficulty maintaining self-regulation, which prevented him from engagement. Although musically we were tonally connected, the music was fueling his "melt-downs" by overloading his auditory system. In addition, by solely focusing on music, I may have lost sight of his sensory needs.

The plan for subsequent sessions was to begin developing clinical parameters and boundaries in regard to time (length of session), pacing (i.e. when and how to transition into other music; the use of silence, and gauging the "rhythm" of the interaction) and sensory input from the environment. In addition, it was important for Matthew to leave each session in a regulated manner and to avoid a power struggle over when to leave music. To that end, sessions were shortened (5–10 minutes). Pacing, in terms of when to start and end improvisations, was controlled by Matthew's affect, emotionality, and the quality and "rhythm" of the musical interaction. Finally, the sensory environment was altered to cater to Matthew's individual-differences, including his auditory processing, tactile sensitivity and vestibular system (sensory system located in the inner ear that allows us to maintain balance and process movements).

Stage Two: Integrating Matthew's Sensory and Musical Profiles

Stage Two, sessions seven through twelve, consisted of balancing Matthew's sensory profile with the added musical stimuli to facilitate self-regulation and engagement. To do that, I incorporated a rolling chair, which spins around, in order to provide him with vestibular input. In addition, I shut off the rear room lights, to cater to his hypersensitivity to light, and brought Play-Doh into the room, in case he required tactile input. Musically, due to his auditory processing difficulties, I paid close attention to the register, dynamics, and chord voicings of my music.

Narrative 1: Pirouetting into Musical Awareness and Relatedness

Narrative 1 is taken from Matthew's seventh session. It illustrates the beginning of our musical relationship as Matthew enters the music room on his own initiative for the first time, displaying musical awareness, relatedness and engagement through movement.

Before the session had begun, Matthew was being escorted to the music room by two teacher's assistants (TAs). He was very resistant to entering the music room as he pinched and attempted to bite one of the TAs while sitting on a rolling chair outside of the room.

After 15 minutes of trying to coax Matthew into the room, Jean (intern) began to gently spin him in the chair. As Matthew was slowly spinning outside the music room, I accompanied him on the piano. In so doing, I created a repeated three-note melodic sequence (triplets) that matched his circular movements. As the music continued to play, Matthew stood up from the chair and began to pirouette into the room. This would be the first time that he entered the room on his own initiative, exhibiting self-regulation, musical awareness and engagement.

Stage Three: Developing the Musical Relationship: Initiating Circles of Musical Communication

Stage Three consisted of sessions thirteen through sixteen, and continued to follow the strategy of providing Matthew with the necessary sensory input to maintain self-regulation and engagement in intentional communication within the context of a musical relationship.

During this stage Matthew continued to develop his ability to be musically responsive (vocally) in a related and communicative fashion. The duration of each musical interaction also began to expand and our relationship, both musically and interpersonally, was developing. In addition, sessions began to increase in length (between 20–30 minutes).

The focal point of this musical communication was his ability to initiate circles of musical exchange (initiating and completing musical ideas in tandem with the therapist). In addition, intentional and reciprocal musical interactions, and the ability to understand cause-and-effect relationships within musical play, began to emerge.

Narrative 2: Rockin' for Musical Communicativeness

Narrative 2, from session fifteen, illustrates how the music "transformed" Matthew's isolated activity of rocking into a joint interactive musical experience, facilitating musical engagement and two-way purposeful communication.

Sessions fifteen and sixteen took place in Matthew's classroom while the rest of the class had gone to gym. Prior to each session, his teacher told me that he was having a difficult day and that it would be hard to get him out of the classroom. The session began with Matthew seated on a padded rocking chair that he used to rock forward and backward. He began to rock, providing himself with sensory input, while at the same time engaging in an isolating activity.

I began to improvise on the guitar, using the tempo of Matthew's rocking motion and developed a non-verbal melody. Occasionally, he acknowledged the connection between my music and his rocking through eye-contact. While I played I raised my right hand in front of him for him to hit, "transforming" it into a melodic/percussive instrument by accenting specific melodic notes each time he hit my hand.

After several minutes of this back-and-forth musical interaction, Matthew appeared to be getting distressed and dysregulated. He then looked at me directly, while rocking in his chair, and said, "no, no, no," in an agitated manner (communicating his desire to stop the interaction). I physically backed away from him, while simultaneously playing the guitar using a familiar harmonic structure (basing the rhythm and tempo on his rocking while singing with words), and in a calm and soft voice said, "ok, ok."

During this interaction, the rocking chair provided Matthew with a form of proprioceptive and vestibular input, while the hand-slapping provided tactile support. This, moving in tandem with musical stimuli facilitated an increase in his level of musical interaction, specifically in the area of musical communicativeness. In addition, Matthew was also experiencing a wide range of affects within the back-and-forth of two-way musical communication, engaging and imitation during the musical interaction. Furthermore, he was integrating and synchronizing multiple sensory stimuli (vestibular, tactile, proprioceptive, visual and auditory), while utilizing his expressive and receptive language within the context of musical play.

Narrative 3: Blowin' to the Blues with Intentionality: Musical Relatedness and Communicativeness

Narrative 3, excerpted from session sixteen, illustrates Matthew playing a pitched reed horn in a communicative manner with the therapist's music, relying solely on his auditory processing skills while being out of visual range of the therapist.

Session sixteen was also held in Matthew's classroom. The lights had been turned off prior to the session in order to help him self-regulate and calm down, as he had just came out of a serious "melt-down" before I entered the room. While he was lying down, on a padded chair, I offered him a pitched horn. He took it from my hand and began exploring the texture and look of the instrument. He began to blow into the horn as I improvised in a blues style. Initially, his blowing appeared to be disconnected from my music, and the horn seemed to be an object to fulfill his need for oral stimulation; however, Matthew's music began to find its way into my musical form, as I intentionally incorporated pauses and variations in the rhythm and tempo to connect our musics. His horn playing began to take on a rhythmic form that matched mine, followed by a self-initiated vocalization.

Stage Four: Moving up the Developmental Ladder: Assimilation and Integration

Sessions seventeen through twenty-five focused on strengthening Matthew's capacities in levels I, II, III, (self-regulation, engagement, and intentional communication) in order to help move him into higher levels of thinking (level IV) and music making (musical interresponsiveness).

Narrative 4: "Play-Doh" to facilitate Musical Interresponsivess

Narrative 4, taken from session twenty-five, illustrates Matthew's ability to engage in musical play while copying and initiating musical ideas in a related and communication fashion.

Ten minutes into the 25th session, with Play-Doh in hand, Matthew's attention and focus was completely on the Play-Doh, and he displayed no interest in interacting. Jean (intern) began to sing (improvise) a non-verbal melody in a gentle and legato manner, as she proceeded to apply light pressure to his legs by squeezing. I began to play the piano, accompanying both her melody and squeezing patterns. After several measures, Matthew began vocalizing in a related and communicative manner in relationship to the music being offered. The interaction moved into a call-and-response between Matthew and the co-therapist.

The interaction patterns moved beyond call-and-response interactions. In addition, Matthew explored his voice, utilizing new sounds and manipulating musical elements that enhanced his musical expressiveness. In short, it appeared that Matthew's ability to initiate was leading to musical independence. His independence, which in the past was self-directed and unrelated, could now be viewed as being related and communicative.

The above interaction began by providing Matthew with specific sensory input followed by musical accompaniment. The music was used as a way of taking an isolated behavior, such as squeezing Play-Doh, and making it into a joint interaction. This made it possible for Matthew to engage in musical communication and interresponsiveness.

SUMMARY

Client Process

Stage one, "What's Getting in the Way?: Developing the Playing Field While Considering Individual–Differences," included the first six sessions, where Matthew exhibited difficulty adapting to the new environment and medium of music due to his complex sensory system. To that end, it was difficult to engage him, musically or interpersonally, as he consistently "melted-down" before, during and at the end of music sessions. This stage ended when the therapist changed strategies, implementing clinical parameters that included shortening sessions, being sensitive to when and how to transition into other music, gauging the "rhythm" of the interaction, and the altering of the sensory environment to cater to Matthew's individual-differences.

Stage two, "Integrating Matthew's Sensory and Musical Profiles," consisted of sessions seven through twelve. During this time, in providing Matthew with the proper sensory input, his ability to maintain self-regulation for extended periods increased, which led, for brief moments, to an increase in his ability to engage in musical play in a related manner. In addition, during this stage, relationships (interpersonal and musical) were developing. This stage ended when the therapist began to increase the length of sessions, based on the emerging development of the relationship, and Matthew's increased ability to engage in musical play in a related fashion.

Stage three, "Developing the Musical Relationship: Initiating Circles of Musical Communication," featured sessions thirteen through sixteen. During this stage Matthew continued to increase his ability to engage in musical play in a related manner for longer periods; however, the key element during this phase was that he began to initiate ideas, opening and closing circles of musical communication. This stage ended when the therapist changed strategies in providing more opportunities for Matthew to "lead" and guide the musical improvisations; trusting the process between the music and the players (child, intern, and therapist) to facilitate independence and higher levels of thinking (e.g., initiating, reciprocating, and intentional and purposeful communication).

Finally, stage four, which consisted of sessions seventeen through twenty-five, "Moving up the Developmental Ladder: Assimilation and Integration," featured Matthew integrating and assimilating his abilities to musically engage, relate and communicate. To that end, he began to develop an increased sense of self, whereby exhibiting independence during musical play in a related and communicative manner. In addition, during this stage, he displayed his desire to be in a relationship for the sake of relating to another person, as opposed to relating for the purpose of fulfilling a sensory need. This new awareness also brought to light, for Matthew, that people were not objects to solely fulfill wants and needs (as seen by typical developing infants), but rather, social beings who want to be in relationship.

Therapist's Method

Focusing on what gets in the way (individual–differences) of a child's social-emotional development is at the crux of this treatment plan (Greenspan & Weider, 2006b). For Matthew, creating the proper sensory environment helped to facilitate his ability to self-regulate and be available for interactive musical experiences that provided an avenue for relationship, communication, and the exchange of ideas.

The non-verbal medium of music provided a non-threatening field of play for Matthew. Because of his difficulty with expressive language, music provided him with an outlet in which he could communicate and experience relatedness non-verbally.

Finally, during Matthew's treatment process, music not only became the vehicle for communication, but also the medium that converted his isolated sensory-motor play into joint musical interactions. The music helped Matthew make meaning out of something that had no meaning, in regard to relating to others, promoting a continuous flow of musical interaction that built a musical relationship, and the desire to be in a shared world.

REFERENCES

Aigen, K. (2005). *Music-centered Music Therapy*. Gilsum, NH: Barcelona Publishers.

Carpente, J. (2009). Contributions of Nordoff-Robbins Music Therapy within the Developmental, Individual-Difference, Relationship-based (DIR®)/Floortime™ framework to the treatment of children with autism: Four case studies. Doctoral Dissertation, Temple University, PA.

Carpente, J. (2008). Working in and Looking out of Music Experiences: Nordoff-Robbins Music Therapy within the DIR®/Floortime™ Model with Children on the Autism Spectrum. Paper presented at the annual conference of The American Music Therapy Association. Saint Louis, MO.

Nordoff, P. & Robbins, C. (2007). *Creative Music Therapy: A Guide to Fostering Clinical Musicianship*. Gilsum, NH: Barcelona Publishers.

Greenspan, S.I. & Weider, S. (1998). *The Child with Special Needs: Encouraging Intellectual and Emotional Growth*. Da Capo Lifelong Books.

Greenspan, S.I., & Weider, S. (2006a). *Engaging Autism: Using the Floortime Approach to Help Children Relate, Communicate, and Think*. Cambrigde, MA: Da Capo Press.

Greenspan, S.I. & Weider, S. (2006b). *Infant and Early Childhood Mental Nealth: A Comprehensive Developmental Approach to Assessment and Intervention*. Alington, VA: American Psychiatric Publishing.

Greenspan, S.I. & Weider, S. (1998). *The Child with Special Needs: Encouraging Intellectual and Emotional Growth*. Da Capo Lifelong Books.

Greenspan, S.I., DeGangi, G. & Weider, S. (2001). *The Functional Emotional Assessment Scale (FEAS) for Infancy and Early Childhood: Clinical and Research Applications*. Bethesda, MD: Interdisciplinary Council on Developmental and Learning. Disorders.

Chapter Eight

MUSIC THERAPY FOR CHILDREN IN HOSPITAL CARE: A STRESS AND COPING FRAMEWORK FOR PRACTICE

Jane Edwards and Jeanette Kennelly

INTRODUCTION

The experience of illness and/or injury and subsequent hospitalization is inevitably stressful. A range of theoretical perspectives inform and support therapeutic interventions with children and their families to manage stress following hospitalization. Crisis theory (Schaeffer & Moos, 1998) explains unexpected stress-inducing events as propelling individuals into turbulent and overwhelming cognitive and emotional experiences that challenge the resources available for maintaining equilibrium, or what is known as "coping." For children and their families, coping with their experiences of illness and/or injury leading to hospitalization can be additionally challenged by the developmental needs of the child. Offering support requires attention to children's perception of events, including attending to their comprehension of, and participation in, ongoing medical treatment.

This chapter describes a stress and coping framework that provides support to techniques used in music therapy services in a children's hospital. The authors present an outline of their approach, using case material to illustrate the application and integration of a framework incorporating theoretical constructs about stress, coping and adjustment within clinical practice.

FOUNDATIONAL CONCEPTS

Stress Management and Enhanced Coping for Hospitalised Children

Approaches from the psychological literature concerning stress and coping (for example, Lazarus & Folkman, 1999; Aldwin, 2007) have been adapted to provide a theoretical foundation in music therapy work with children facing the challenge of treatment for injury or illness (Edwards, 1999b). Other music therapists have also noted the usefulness of theories of stress and coping in work with hospitalized children and their families (Daveson, 1999; Robb, 2003). The stress and coping literature has provided us with a theoretical perspective with which to conceptualize children's responses within an overarching framework. Consequently, we were able to design and implement effective ways to offer help through music therapy.

As the child responds to the stress of his/her hospitalization, his/her capacity to adjust to the psychological and other demands can begin to manifest. Sometimes difficulties are demonstrated through such behaviors as not speaking, only speaking to particular people, refusing play opportunities, avoiding eating and drinking, mobilizing at a lower level than their ability, and being withdrawn or looking sad. It has been proposed that "successful adjustment is achieved when the child demonstrates skills in communication, play and perception consistent with skill levels prior to the injury, and when the child demonstrates verbalizations, interactions and other social skills as appropriate to chronological age and temperament" (Edwards, 1998, p. 22).

Four primary foundational concepts have informed this framework for practice:

1. Theories of stress, coping and adjustment
2. Transactional models of stress
3. Developmental theories
4. Family-centered care

In everyday clinical work it would be unusual for a practitioner to distinguish between these constructs in describing his/her thinking about interactions with patients, or in justifying the use of particular techniques. These constructs are learned, integrated and become useful as needed to elaborate experiences of the patients and their families, and are especially applicable when work is difficult or interactions are highly charged in some way. These concepts overlap and intertwine significantly and are produced discretely here to show the authors' applications within music therapy practice.

Stress, Coping and Adjustment

One of the foundational concepts within this framework is the management of stress to attain equilibrium through effective coping. Managing stress can be described as a process of undertaking the tasks of coping. In a hospital environment, these tasks have been described as:

1. Dealing with pain and symptoms
2. Dealing with the hospital environment and treatment procedures
3. Developing and maintaining positive relationships with medical, nursing, and allied health staff
4. Maintaining emotional equilibrium
5. Preserving a positive self-image, including maintaining competence and mastery
6. Sustaining relationships with friends, family and using these relationships as a means of support and information
7. Preparing for an uncertain future (adapted from Moos & Schaeffer, 1984)

Supporting the processes required to accomplish these tasks requires the therapist to attend sensitively to complex interactions between family members, the staff and the patient. The music therapist navigates a vast and challenging psychological terrain that is often encountered in the ward environment through observing and interpreting verbal and non-verbal behaviors of the various family members and staff.

Transactional Model of Stress

In the cognitive stress, appraisal and coping model proposed by Lazarus and Folkman (1991), psychological stress is defined as "a relationship between the person and the environment that is appraised by the person as taxing or exceeding his or her resources and endangering his or her well-being" (Lazarus & Folkman, 1991 p. 21). The individual's interpretation of the meaning or perceived threat of the experience, termed "appraisal," is a main contributing factor in a stress response. Using this model in practice can include, for example, attention to the ways in which the individual perceives the events that have occurred, and whether there are any aspects of this interpretation that may require external mediation, such as blaming or guilt responses (Lazarus & Folkman, 1991.

The transactional approach to stress modelling (Aldwin, 2007) represents a shift from what has been described as reductionism, or the scientific linear causal model, to an approach that emphasizes relationships and interactions between variables that are understood as multi-faceted and non-linear. In a transactional approach, the investigation of human experience is pursued with a range of potential and perceived complexities kept in mind (Aldwin, 2007). That is, the idea that the same event is experienced the same way by every person is relinquished, and a new theory of the relationship between the individual's prior experiences, current perspectives and context is proposed.

Within a transactional approach, three dimensions of the stress experience have been identified:

1. The strain experienced, which has emotional and physiological dimensions
2. The stressor, including the type of stress and its temporal dimensions, and
3. The transaction between these dimensions, including the person's cognitive appraisal of the stress and the perceived intensity of the stress that contribute to his/her responses (Aldwin, 2007)

That is, "the person, the situation and coping mutually affect each other in a process that evolves over time" (Aldwin, 2007 p. 99).

For the child in hospital, a range of issues in relation to the "situation" (point 2, above) impact on the child's coping, along with the coping of those who are caring for him/her. For example, a parent who seems highly stressed by their child's admission for a simple procedure may have previously been to the hospital with another child in more challenging health circumstances. Their presenting anxiety may stem from this history of their hospital experiences. The distance the rest of the family lives from the hospital, the supports available to that parent (for example, paid leave availability from their work), may all impact the experience of hospitalization, and the perception of threat and stress, apart from the immediate and/or ongoing medical needs of the child.

It brings to mind the story we were told at our hospital of a boy of six years of age admitted for appendicitis. The surgeon attended him at bedside and told him the details of the operation he would undertake to remove his appendix. The boy listened attentively. However, when the surgeon took a pen out of his pocket to write some notes, the boy showed signs of distress. It seemed he understood the operation was to take place then and there.

This story shows that even caring practitioners, who follow good practices for giving information to their young patients, sometimes miss the perception of the facts by the listener. The clinical team, including the music therapist, listen respectfully to the meaning of the events experienced by the children with whom they work, and try not to predict what a child will understand, or how they will deal with information or events. The starting point is providing children with a place to tell the story of their fears, their experiences, what they like about hospital, and what they miss from outside the hospital. It is proposed that this helps the child integrate the experience of hospitalization and to make sense of his/her injury or illness in his/her own way. At the same time, the therapist and the patient engage in mutual learning about the patient's circumstances and wishes.

Developmental Theory

Children's development is multi-faceted, involving cognitive, psychosocial, physical and moral dimensions of process and change from birth through early adulthood. While the development and capacities of any child are individual and unique, many theorists and practitioners in music therapy use developmental stage theories as well as theories and philosophy about identity, rights and family to provide a broad base for practice and writing in a range of fields related to understanding and working with children's needs (see Loewy, 1997; 2000). Stage models can also assist in understanding children's ability to manage and understand pain experiences (Edwards, 2005a; Gaffney, McGrath & Dick, 2003) and have been used to develop successful and effective assessment tools (Loewy, 2000).

Family Centered Care

At the hospital where the music therapy work described here was conducted, a family centered approach was embraced. Families were considered the main support available to children in managing their psychological adjustment to treatments and medical care. In addition, children were understood to benefit from strong attachment bonds with the family, and these bonds were considered vulnerable to damage through the possible physical and emotional separation that could occur when children were not able to cope with their experiences (see Jolley & Shields, 2009).

The music therapists worked with family members, where 'family' was considered to be the people with whom the child shared strong affectionate bonds of love and care, and the people on whom the child was dependent for their daily care needs. The therapists worked with the family as a whole as well as with individuals within the family, as needed.

Stress and Coping Responses Supported through Music Therapy

In the following case description, the reader is directed to the integration of aspects of this conceptual framework within the material presented. Some commentary following the case elaborates on how using a stress and coping framework helped in providing an effective therapeutic presence for this patient. However, we have also found this framework useful for other pediatric treatment arenas, including rehabilitation (Edwards & Kennelly, 2004; Kennelly & Brien-Elliott, 2001), intensive care (Kennelly & Edwards, 1997), and in general considerations of children's experience of hospitalization (Edwards, 2005c; Kennelly & Brien-Elliott, 2002).

THE CLIENT

Beni was eight years old at the time of his admission to the burns unit of a children's hospital. He was brought to the hospital following an accident that had caused 30% full thickness burns[1] to his back, posterior, arms, lower abdomen and thighs. His parents accompanied him to hospital and resided in a motel near the hospital during Beni's recovery. Although Beni was able to converse a little in English, he mainly spoke in his own community language. Hospital staff described him as being quiet, withdrawn and unresponsive, and only communicating with his parents. He demonstrated little interest or engagement when medical and nursing staff approached and would not join in any play activities initiated by therapy staff.

Beni was referred to music therapy by the clinical nurse consultant of the unit, Kerrie, one week after his admission. Kerrie expressed concerns about his adjustment to hospital and his injuries, observing that he did not engage verbally with staff and that this lack of ability or desire to do so may impact his treatment and the healing of his injuries. She also felt that giving Beni and his family opportunities to interact with staff during treatment procedures would assist Beni in his ability to self-express and potentially feel less isolated in this hospital environment.

Assessment

In the first assessment session, Jeanette went to Beni's room to find him alone, lying in bed. In this initial period of interaction Jeanette sought to determine what kinds of music Beni was interested in, whether music therapy was indicated, and if so, the ways in which it would be possible to communicate together. At the start of this first session, Beni was very quiet and still. While Jeanette improvised a song about the teddy bear above his bed, Beni smiled and nodded when asked if the bear was his.

---

[1] Full thickness burns involve damage and destruction to all layers of the skin and require surgical treatment, including skin grafts, to restore the skin.

Soon after, his parents arrived and Beni no longer acknowledged Jeanette's presence. He seemed to visibly withdraw and now looked toward the window on his right-hand side. Jeanette turned her attention to Beni's parents and discovered that his father played guitar in a band and had written his own songs. These songs discussed the customs, religious beliefs and practices, and the way of life in their community. Beni's parents both enjoyed singing, and they described Beni as sharing their love of music, especially instrumental playing. Toward the end of the session, Jeanette offered Beni's father the guitar, and, together with his partner, they sang two of their own community songs. They told Jeanette the titles were "Black Magic Man" and "Home Sweet Home." Previously, when Beni had been offered instruments, he had refused to play them. Now, together with his parents, he took the tambor and played with them using a syncopated ostinato pattern, smiling all the time.

After this session, Beni's music therapy goals were refined to focus on extending his available resources in coping with his burn injuries, hospitalization and treatment. The objectives included providing opportunities for self expression, support during treatment procedures and increased interaction between family members. Based upon this family interaction, it became clear that Beni's music therapy sessions would now begin by including his family in the recollection of familiar song material so as to provide a safe, known and supportive environment for music therapy to take place. Sessions centered around singing familiar Aboriginal songs from Beni's community, along with prominent Aboriginal bands. Improvisational experiences on tuned and untuned percussion instruments were also incorporated into sessions. These sessions took place before, during and after medical procedures, including his debridement baths[2], and also prior to and after surgery.

THE THERAPEUTIC PROCESS

Beni's music therapy program consisted of a total of 14 sessions that can be divided into three stages: "Turning Away" (session 1), "Songs of Place" (Sessions 2-12) and "I Want to go Outside/Goodbye" (Sessions 13-14).

---

[2] In the debridement bath, skin is cleaned gently with sponges to remove dead skin so as to promote healing, minimize infection and to reduce scarring. See Edwards (1998).

The therapeutic relationship between Beni and Jeanette changed as trust and greater interaction developed, supporting his adjustment to hospital and decreasing his stress and anxiety.

Turning Away

During the initial stage of Beni's program, the burns team dealt with a range of concerns that included promoting opportunities for Beni to communicate his experience of treatment, but which also related to a fear for his survival. Beni was about to undertake an intensive period of medical treatment that included numerous skin graft operations. Grafting requires ongoing debridements and many dressing changes, events that were potentially painful and distressing for Beni. Staff were concerned that because Beni and his family were isolated from their home environment, this perceived lack of family support could impact Beni's ability to cope with these procedures and his overall recovery. It was therefore important that opportunities were made available to provide Beni and his family to get the emotional and physical support they required.

In this first session, Beni's parents looked upset and concerned for their son. After some discussion between Jeanette and his parents about their family and home environment, Jeanette was introduced to one of Beni's favorite songs - a song sung in his native language. Jeanette invited Beni's father to take her guitar and play and sing the song for them. The father seemed reluctant but, with encouragement, eventually sang and played the song using a quiet tone. As the song was played, Beni began to smile, and he soon joined in singing with his father. Beni also sang quietly and continued to watch his parents engage with Jeanette. Beni's mother soon joined in with this singing and also played along using a tambor. By the end of the session, Jeanette and his parents were singing and smiling. Beni was even beginning to play the tambor with his mother's assistance.

This song helped Beni form a connection between hospital and home. The therapeutic rapport initiated in this first session was possible because of this familiar song. The alliance of trust and support that began through the connection between the music therapist and Beni's parents also facilitated the potential that was later realized. Through the choice of familiar song material recreated by a family member, music therapy was able to alleviate tension and anxiety for Beni. This session also provided opportunities for a means of communication, not only between Beni and Jeanette but also between Beni and other hospital staff as the program continued. Nursing, medical and allied health staff soon became familiar with Beni's songs and often encouraged Beni and his family to sing and talk of their home environment when Jeanette was not present. Music therapy assisted in increasing socialization between the family members and hospital staff and also assisted in normalizing the hospital environment for Beni and his family; and perhaps even for hospital staff themselves. These staff would often comment on the lovely sounds coming from Beni's room and the positive impact this music made on the hospital environment.

Songs of Place

During this stage (sessions 2–12,) Beni expressed a range of feelings and emotions relating to his hospitalization, his injuries and his isolation from home. Sessions now took place in a variety of settings, including the bathroom during debridements. Support was provided to assist pain management, using music as relaxation and distraction during debridement procedures. During these sessions, Beni would often request the songs "Black Magic Man" and "Home Sweet Home" and two songs that Jeanette wrote that were purposely based on similar chordal progressions from his two well-known songs.

Whenever injections were administered or dressings applied or removed, these were the songs that Beni requested. They were always played softly and calmly with an arpeggiated guitar pattern. Vocals were also sung softly, with 'oohs' and 'ahs' added instead of the lyrics, to promote a comforting, supportive environment.

These sessions were often quite long, commencing in Beni's individual hospital room, moving to the bathroom for his debridement bath, to the table in the bathroom for his dressings to be changed and finally back to his room where he often fell asleep. Music therapy remained a constant for Beni through these treatment stages. Music engaged him in different ways depending on his needs at the time. Jeanette would always invite Beni to take the lead in deciding which songs and instruments to use next. The time spent in the bathroom felt intense for Jeanette - not only due to the warm temperature of the bathroom (which is standard in burn care debridement), but also the intrusive nature of the procedure (Beni was semi-nude and in a bath) and the stress of anticipating Beni's distress when he experienced pain or distress.

During the debridements, Beni would watch Jeanette and listen to the music she played. This was usually guitar accompaniment and unaccompanied vocal improvisations. He would communicate with Jeanette using smiles and head nods/shakes to communicate his musical wishes. During one session, following the debridement when dressings were being reapplied, Beni appeared tired and looked as though he would fall asleep. Jeanette asked the nurse present if she should stay. The nurse replied, "it doesn't matter." As Jeanette softly said goodbye to Beni, he opened his eyes and called out, asking her to stay. The session continued until all dressings were completed and when Beni, assisted by his father, walked back to his hospital bed. He continued with the music therapy session in his room, engaging actively in instrumental improvisation with Jeanette using tambors, maracas and castanets.

Many of the sessions in this second stage of Beni's programme continued in this way. Jeanette would present him with a variety of instruments and together or with his parents present, would actively engage in creative musical play. It was not until Session 5 that Beni verbally spoke to Jeanette, asking to use a drum for an improvisation. During this session, Beni continued to dialogue with Jeanette, speaking of his home environment and reminiscing on past events that involved music making with his family. He requested the electronic keyboard and began experimenting with different rhythmic accompaniments and timbres. He seemed much more engaged and interactive now and eager to experiment with music and demonstrate his skills to Jeanette, his family and hospital staff.

During debridements, nursing staff started to comment on a more 'relaxed' Beni, who interacted more easily whenever the music therapist was present. Together with medical staff, they reported an increase in interactions with Beni during these procedures and were pleased that Beni attempted to communicate with them in English. Staff made positive and encouraging comments about Beni's drumming and told his parents how much they enjoyed listening to their community songs.

As therapy continued, recorded music and videos of a popular Australian Aboriginal band was provided for Beni. One of these songs,

"Freedom," became his favorite, and he often requested this song to be played and sung over and over. The song spoke of feeling alone and wanting things to happen in the world by being free. At the end of the song Beni would smile, laugh and play a loud sound on the tambor. He was able to express himself and his needs through this song - a desire to be free and away from the hospital environment.

Music therapy also provided other opportunities for Beni to express his feelings. In a session where he received an injection, Beni placed the sticker he had received as a reward for the procedure on the tambor and loudly struck the instrument several times. He would then ask the music therapist to play 'his song' - Beni's song, which the music therapist had improvised on guitar. Beni would then relax back into his bed and accompany the music therapist with his tambor, using a syncopated rhythm. Whenever he felt tired, he requested quiet and peaceful music – this often occurred after debridement when he was often exhausted after the traumatic experience.

Throughout this stage, the therapeutic process grew and matured into a trusting, safe and secure relationship where Beni felt he could be supported and understood. The music acted as the connection between home and hospital and assisted in alleviating the stress and anxiety that Beni had initially experienced upon his admission to hospital.

I Want to Go Outside/Goodbye

The final sessions (sessions 13–14) centered around preparation for Beni's discharge and return home. Beni began song-writing with Jeanette, creating lyrics about seeing his friends again and riding his bike. He also wrote about leaving hospital and how he would feel about arriving back home. During these sessions, Beni would take Jeanette's hand and show her the guitar chords that he wanted her to play. This interaction also demonstrated the close and trusting relationship that had developed between them. One of the final sessions involved Beni, his parents and Jeanette singing and playing instruments outside the playroom in the burns unit. Other patients, their families and hospital staff gathered around to watch and listen. Beni sang loudly and confidently and smiled from ear to ear as he shared his music with others around him. As the songs ended, everyone applauded. Jeanette left the final session as hospital staff continued to sing and play instruments with Beni and his parents, talking with him about his music and home life.

Music Therapy: Making a Difference in a Child's Experience of Hospital

Prior to music therapy intervention, Beni was described as a withdrawn and frightened child who only communicated with his parents and preferred to speak his native language. The music therapy program, conducted over 14 sessions, provided Beni with opportunities to improve his self expression, to feel safe and supported and to cope effectively with treatment procedures. In the final stages of the work, Beni was interacting with others outside of his immediate family and was demonstrating enjoyment through mastery, playing music for others.

In considering the experiences of a child who is far from home, both geographically and culturally, the music therapist must be sensitive to the circumstances he/she encounters with the child and his/her family members. It is important to find ways to cope with one's countertransference in the situation where a child is minimally responsive or seems afraid. The urge to embrace or engage the child must be resisted in order to be available as the child needs, rather than smother one's own anxieties about being a good enough therapist by overwhelming the child with either affection or enthusiasm (see also Edwards, 1999a). It is important to wait until the child is ready to use the potential opportunities provided in music therapy.

A family-centered approach considers that the family are a primary resource for the patient's coping and adjustment. In this case, Jeanette's ability to encourage and communicate with Beni's parents resulted in them sharing important musical material that became an aural lynch pin for Beni's feelings of connection between the challenges of hospital and the safety and security of home.

CONCLUSION

The music therapy literature attests that music can be a successful way to start a supportive dialogue with a young person experiencing a crisis (Daveson & Kennelly, 2000; Edwards, 1995; Ledger, 2001; Robb, 2003).

In order to provide a therapeutic service through music therapy to patients receiving care in hospital, we used concepts from the following four theoretical areas:

1. Theories of stress, coping and adjustment
2. Transactional models of stress
3. Developmental theories
4. Family centered care

With constructs from these theoretical approaches in mind, we were able to promote the necessary psychological support, mastery of effective coping skills, and family integration to improve Beni's hospital experience, making an otherwise difficult time more manageable. In order to do this effectively, his developmental level had to be acknowledged, including the psychological, emotional and physical dimensions of his life stage. This, in conjunction with consideration of his needs for independence/dependence and support, and his capacity to cope with difficult circumstances, allowed the therapeutic process to unfold.

We developed this way of thinking about patients through collaboration and dialogue around our clinical experiences. This in turn has led us to expand our theoretical understanding of stress and coping for children in hospital and their families. We hope that this work, and the resultant evolving framework, will continue to be a support to patients and their families in the most trying of circumstances, and in so doing, they may gain positive experiences from being offered, and engaging in, music therapy.

REFERENCES

Aldwin, C. (2007). *Stress, Coping and Development: A Integrative Perspective* (2nd ed.). London: Guilford Press.

Daveson, B. & Kennelly, J. (2000). Music therapy in palliative care for hospitalised children and adolescents. *Journal of Palliative Care*, 16, 35-38.

Daveson, B. (1999). A model of response: Coping mechanisms and music therapy techniques during debridement. *Music Therapy Perspectives*, 17(2), 92-98.

Edwards, J. (1995). "You are singing beautifully": Music therapy and the debridement bath. *The Arts in Psychotherapy*, 22(1), 53-55.

Edwards, J. (1998). Music therapy for children with severe burn injury. *Music Therapy Perspectives*, 16, 20-25.

Edwards, J. (1999a). Music therapy with children hospitalised for severe injury or illness. *British Journal of Music Therapy*, 13, 21-27

Edwards, J. (1999b). Anxiety management in pediatric music therapy. In Cheryl Dileo (Ed.), *Music Therapy and Medicine: Theoretical and Clinical Applications*. Silver Spring, MD: American Music Therapy Association.

Edwards, J. (2005a). Developing music therapy approaches to pain management in hospitalized children. In C. Dileo and J. Loewy (Eds.). *Music Therapy at End of Life* (pp. 57-64). Cherry Hill, NJ: Jeffrey Books.

Edwards, J. (2005b). The role of the music therapist in working with hospitalized children: A reflection on the development of a music therapy program in a children's hospital. *Music Therapy Perspectives*, 23(1), 36-44.

Edwards, J. (2005c). The contribution of music therapy to the process of therapeutic change for people receiving hospital care. Chapter 9 in Carole-Lynne Le Navenec & Laurel Bridges (Eds.). *Creating Connections between Nursing Care and Creative Arts Therapies*. Springfield: Charles C Thomas.

Edwards, J. & Kennelly, J. (2004). Music therapy in paediatric rehabilitation: The application of modified Grounded Theory to identify techniques used by a music therapist. *Nordic Journal of Music Therapy*, 13, 112-126.

Gaffney, A., McGrath, P.J. & Dick, B. (2003). Measuring pain in children: Developmental and instrument issues. In N. Schechter, B. Berde and M. Yaster (Eds.) *Pain in Infants, Children and Adolescents* (2nd ed.) (pp. 128-141). Philadelphia: Lippincott, Williams & Wilkins.

Jolley, J. & Shields, L. (2009). The evolution of family–centered care. *Journal of Pediatric Nursing*, 24, 164-170.

Kennelly, J. & Brien-Elliott, K. (2002). Music therapy for children in hospital. *Educating Young Children: Learning & Teaching in the Early Childhood Years*, 8, (3), 37-40.

Kennelly, J. & Brien-Elliott, K. (2001). The role of music therapy in paediatric rehabilitation. *Paediatric Rehabilitation*, 4(3), 137-143.

Kennelly, J. & Edwards, J. (1997). Providing music therapy to the unconscious child in the paediatric intensive care unit. *The Australian Journal of Music Therapy*, 8, 18-29.

Lazarus, R. & Folkman, S. (1991). The concept of coping. In A. Monat & R. Lazarus (Eds.) *Stress and Coping: An Anthology* (3rd Ed.(Ed.)

Loewy, J. V. (Ed.) (1997). *Music Therapy and Pediatric Pain*. New York: Sachnote Press.

Loewy, J. V. (2000). Music psychotherapy assessment. *Music Therapy Perspectives*, 18(1), 47-58.

Moos, R. H. & Schaefer, J.A. (1984) The crisis of physical illness: An overview and conceptual approach. In R. Moos (Ed.) *Coping with Physical Illness: New Perspectives*. New York: Plenum Press.

Robb, S. L. (2003). Designing music therapy interventions for hospitalized children and adolescents using a contextual support model of music therapy. *Music Therapy Perspectives*, 21, 27-40.

Schaefer, J. A. & Moos, R. M. (1998). The context for posttraumatic growth: Life crises, individual and social resources, and coping. In G. Tedeschi, C. Park & L. Calhoun (Eds.), *Posttraumatic Growth: Positive Changes in the Aftermath of Crisis* (pp. 99-125). New Jersey: Lawrence Erlbaum Associates.

Chapter Nine

DEVELOPING SPEECH WITH MUSIC: A NEURODEVELOPMENTAL APPROACH

A. Blythe LaGasse

INTRODUCTION

This chapter illustrates the use of Neurologic Music Therapy (NMT) with a child who has a neurodevelopment disorder. Daniel was a six-year-old boy with Down Syndrome whose parents sought music therapy in order to improve his speech communication abilities. He received services from a music therapy private practice that was housed within a Speech-Language Pathology center. Individualized treatment goals were speech specific and focused on speech intelligibility and a multimodal approach to functional communication. Based upon Neurological Music Therapy (Thaut, 2005), the treatment approach was determined by examining evidence utilizing the Rational-Scientific Mediating Model (R-SMM) and developing client-specific interventions using the steps set forth by the Transformational Design Model (Thaut, 2005).

FOUNDATIONAL CONCEPTS

Neurologic Music Therapy

Neurologic Music Therapy (NMT) is defined as "the therapeutic application of music to cognitive, sensory, and motor dysfunctions due to neurologic disease of the human nervous system" (Thaut, 2005 p. 126). NMT is an evidence-based approach that is based on scientific evidence supporting the use of specific music therapy interventions (Thaut, 2005). Neurologic Music Therapists utilize standardized techniques for functional rehabilitation training in sensorimotor, cognitive, and speech and language domains.

NMT is guided by the Rational-Scientific Mediating Model (R-SMM), a neuroscience model of music perception and production. This model is utilized to systematically examine the influence of music on changes in nonmusical function (Thaut, 2000). The R-SMM guides the development of evidence-based therapeutic interventions that are adaptable to each individual's needs and functional therapeutic goals. These treatment techniques have standardized terminology and application, based on functional therapeutic goals and the mechanism within the music that is facilitating change (Thaut, 2005). The design of the therapeutic interventions is not limited, but is rationally guided by technique standardization. The NMT practitioner is encouraged to use creativity in the construction of logical therapeutic music interventions.

The carefully crafted musical stimulus promotes physiologic change. NMT is heavily based on the role of rhythm in therapeutic intervention; however, the NMT practitioner must also consider all elements of music that promote change. Melody, harmony, musical structure, lyrics, range, dynamics and tempo are all elements that should be carefully considered (Thaut, 2005). Guided by research, the NMT practitioner is the creator of the therapeutic music experience and facilitates the use of music in therapy.

Treatment in NMT is subdivided into three areas of functioning: 1) cognitive rehabilitation, 2) sensorimotor rehabilitation, and 3) speech and language rehabilitation. Treatment interventions are based on evidence of musical responses within each of these domains, and how such evidence can be meaningfully translated into cognitive, affective and sensorimotor therapeutic responses. To help guide treatment in these areas, Thaut (2000) developed a five-step model called the Transformational Design Model (TDM), which aids the music therapist in translating the R-SMM into functional therapeutic music interventions. The TDM aids the NMT practitioner in developing creative therapeutic interventions while logically maintaining treatment focus.

Although NMT has been developed from research and evidence in neurological rehabilitation, NMT techniques can be utilized to address functional goals in children with neurodevelopment disabilities. There is a growing body of research demonstrating the effectiveness of NMT techniques with children (e.g., Claussen & Thaut, 1997; Krauss & Galloway, 1982; Kwak, 2000; Lim, 2010; Pasiali, 2008). According to Thaut, Mertel and Leins (2008), the major areas of focus with children who have disabilities include education, rehabilitation, and development. Educational goals focus on academic, social, emotional, and physical skills. Rehabilitative goals focus on remedial or compensatory therapy for physical and speech deficits. Developmental goals enhance the course of normal development by providing social, emotional, and sensorimotor experiences.

In order to properly utilize NMT techniques with children, it is essential to understand neurological development, as children with neurodevelopmental disorders will be learning skills for the first time and will not, in most cases, be re-learning skills. For instance, the development of motor synchronization abilities must be carefully considered when implementing techniques heavily based on rhythmic cueing. Research from the biomedical sciences provides support for the use of rhythmic cueing with children; however, the motor synchronization abilities of children differ from abilities of adults (e.g., Hurt-Thaut & Johnson, 2003; Mastrokalou & Hatziharistos, 2007; Smoll, 1974a, 1974b, 1975; Thomas & Moon, 1976; Volman & Geuze, 2000). This is just one example of why the NMT practitioner must carefully consider many aspects of child development (neurological, social, motor, linguistic, etc.) when implementing NMT techniques.

THE CLIENT

Daniel, a boy with Down Syndrome, was six years old at the time of his initial music therapy assessment. He had been reported as non-compliant and demonstrated negative behaviors during speech interventions at school. At the time of his evaluation, he was not receiving any private services for physical, cognitive, or speech needs. Daniel attended a private preschool and received 30 minutes of speech therapy once a week at school. According to his mother, he was becoming increasingly frustrated with his inability to communicate with others. His frustration resulted in tantrums and inappropriate behaviors such as yelling "no" or biting.

At the time of his assessment, Daniel's primary needs were in the area of functional communication. He exhibited severely delayed speech articulation, vocabulary use, sentence use and ability to use speech in communication. Daniel's speech was rapid, cluttered and accompanied by a series of fast gestures. His primary method of communication was a Picture Exchange Communication System (PECS) that was being implemented in school and at home. He was also learning sign language to express his wants and needs at school and home.

Daniel was warm and open to others, and was reported to quickly make friends with children in his class and in his community. His desire to interact was demonstrated through his ability to initiate conversation and attempt age-appropriate reciprocal communication. Daniel demonstrated excellent receptive language skills, as evidenced by his ability to follow directions and to respond to questions with signs or PECS. The primary factor that was limiting his social abilities was his verbal communication. When he attempted to communicate with others (including same-age peers), and his ideas were not understood, he would either shut down and cease communication attempts, or become visibly frustrated.

Daniel's mother had heard about music therapy for children with Down syndrome and decided to seek services since Daniel loved listening to music.

Assessment

The assessment process within NMT practice involves an in-depth look at a person's non-musical functioning, including any available non-musical testing measures, functional assessments, or gold standards (accepted measurements in the field). When available, non-musical measures are obtained from other professionals including speech-language pathologists, physical therapists, and occupational therapists. In addition to functional measures of ability, the Neurological Music Therapist will engage in non-musical observation of the client's behavior within the typical or targeted setting (i.e., school, speech-language pathology session, etc.). During the non-musical assessment, baseline data are collected in the identified areas of need.

After compilation of information about the client's non-musical functioning is completed, the Neurological Music Therapist will consult the R-SMM to determine what evidence-based techniques are appropriate for the client's needs. The final phase of the assessment is the application of NMT techniques to determine if there is a change in behaviors when musical stimuli are present. Changes in behavior are often immediately recognizable within this method and are documented in terms of possible treatment outcomes. The treatment plan is constructed from the baseline data, observed change in behavior with application of NMT techniques and the recommended course of NMT treatment.

Daniel's Assessment

Documentation about Daniel's current and past treatment was supplied by his mother and was reviewed during the assessment phase. His speech-language goals were of specific concern to his parents and therefore were the focus of the assessment. Daniel's other skills were also assessed (i.e., cognitive, motor, emotional, etc.); for the purposes of this chapter, however, I will focus on the speech assessment.

Daniel demonstrated the ability to produce four initial phonemes in words including /b, m, w, d/ (age-matched norms are able to produce most phonemes within words), and he had mastered signs including name signs for his family and different foods. He did not have the ability to produce want or need phrases, middle or ending consonants, or to verbally communicate thoughts. He attempted to pair verbalizations with mastered signs, although verbal intelligibility was very low. Daniel's receptive language was delayed in comparison with age-matched peers; however, he demonstrated stronger receptive than expressive language. When undergoing the non-musical assessment, he exhibited inattentiveness and frustration when not understood.

The music assessment was constructed to determine if Daniel's observed non-musical behaviors changed when musical stimulus was present. Observed changes included the ability to sequence speech and sign with rhythmic cueing. He was also able to produce two-word phrases with rhythmic prompting, although intelligibility was still low. Daniel's attention improved and his frustration when misunderstood decreased while engaged in music. Based on this information, Daniel's treatment plan included the recommendation to begin music therapy services once a week for 40 minutes per session, inclusive of a home treatment program to be carried out by the parents.

THE THERAPEUTIC PROCESS

Although NMT is a scientific approach, there is no lack of age-appropriate elements within sessions. The intention is to reach the targeted goals and objectives while implementing exercises that are motivating, exploratory, aesthetically pleasing and success-oriented. From the "welcome" song to the therapeutic music experiences, every exercise implemented within the session is a direct translation of the equivalent non-musical task, as facilitated by the steps of the TDM. The therapist is the researcher, the creator and the facilitator in this model — the *researcher* of the non-musical exercises that would be utilized within other disciplines to reach the target goal/objective; the *creator* of the isomorphic music experience that embodies the non-musical exercise while adding age-appropriate musical aesthetics; and, the *facilitator* who can modify and adapt to accommodate the client's needs and to promote success.

The therapeutic process in NMT also incorporates constant examination of research in the fields of neuroscience, neurodevelopment, learning and music in therapy. This constant inquiry into evidence-based practice aids the therapist in continually expanding his/her therapeutic repertoire, which ensures excellence in services provided to clients. The following description not only illustrates NMT techniques for verbal communication in a child with a developmental disorder, but also how research provided insight into techniques that were current and success-oriented.

Typical Session

Sessions began with an assessment of Daniel's arousal level (with observation of his activity, energy and attentiveness). After observation, a tempo that matched his arousal level was set on the metronome and played at that tempo for the entire duration of the session (at a comfortable volume). The metronome was utilized as a pacing device for priming motor movements. If the metronome tempo was too fast/slow for production of speech utterances, then the tempo was adjusted to promote success. Often during speech exercises, the tempo was twice that of the speech of the utterance/target syllable. Since Daniel's speech (when engaged in speech exercises) was often very slow, the extra metronome click provided an anticipatory cue for the words/syllables.

After assessment of his arousal level, Daniel was immediately engaged in a welcome song that emphasized utilizing common greeting phrases (e.g., "Hello, how are you?"). We would then explore different aspects of functional communication with age-appropriate musical experiences. This would typically begin with articulation practice using instruments to reinforce production (i.e., *Therapist:* I can say ba, ba, ba, ball, I can say *Client response:* ba, ba, ba, ball). Articulation practice was also paired with a large body movement such as playing a drum, bouncing on a therapy ball or moving his hands with the rhythm of the song. Articulation exercises were then embedded in other functional communication exercises.

The focus of the remainder of the session was on functional communication. A multifaceted communication approach was utilized in order to provide the client with as many tools as possible for success. This approach involved the use of pictorial communication, signed communication or gestural communication, along with verbal communication in order to promote success. The idea is that if the child's verbal utterances are not enough to express his thoughts, then the second mode of communication helps to complete the communicative gesture. These concepts were presented using the technique Developmental Speech and Language Training through Music (Thaut, 2005), which emphasizes age-appropriate speech and language experiences that are motivating.

For Daniel, different musical experiences were presented on a picture board and would include activities such as "frog song," "instrument playing," "singing," "dancing" and "drumming." Each picture card represented a functional communication exercise that could be completed. For example, the "instrument playing" application may utilize instruments to work on want/need phrases (i.e., *I want the ____*), whereas the "frog song" may work on describing the placement of an object (i.e., *Fred the frog is on/in/behind/under the table*). Other exercises worked on vocabulary. For instance, with "singing" we might pair word cards with actual items ("Apple" was paired with an apple/apple shaker, "ball" with an actual ball, etc.) and a song would be created to reinforce the vocabulary, including a description of the item (i.e., *I bounce the ball, the red ball, the <u>red ball</u>*) while Daniel was manipulating or attending to the object.

When engaged in these exercises, Daniel would be exposed to rhythmic cues from the metronome and the rhythmic structure of the songs created for the experience. He would often hear an example provided by myself and then would be cued by the rhythm and structure of the music to provide his own response (i.e., *Blythe likes the purple ball, purple ball, purple ball. I like the <u>client response</u>*). I would follow Daniel's lead in order to promote further exploration of language and vocabulary. If Daniel rolled the ball, our song would adapt to include language reflecting the new action. Therefore, the experiences were part therapist-directed and part client-driven.

Providing an experience in which the client would need to use his communication to change the experience was used to encourage spontaneous communication. For example, with instrument playing the client would choose an instrument to play and after time for exploration of the instrument, I would bring out two new instruments and play them. Daniel would see the new instruments and would need to communicate that he was "finished" with his instrument and initiate a phrase for acquiring a new instrument (i.e., "I want _____ please"). This allowed Daniel to practice learned phrases without adult prompting, in an effort to encourage spontaneous communication that he could use outside music therapy sessions.

After each experience, the targeted speech or language goal was reinforced non-musically, or if possible, in another location. For example if we were engaging in an experience about "stop" and "go," we would look outside at the traffic light and carry-on our experience non-musically waiting for the red light to turn to green by verbalizing "Let's stop" and "Let's go!" Transfer to outside objects/situations wasn't immediate, so a gradual transfer was often necessary. We would pair outside or new objects with the items we were just using, and then fade over time. Rhythm was still present when practicing speech without the melodic and structural cues, and Daniel was encouraged to self-cue by tapping on his leg with the rhythm when he had difficulty verbalizing.

Daniel responded more favorably to experiences that were more "play" oriented than the experiences that were more focused on "work," such as articulation applications. Although every effort was made to make all experiences engaging for Daniel, there was a difference in the more clinician-directed vs. child-directed experiences. However, a balance between the two allowed Daniel to practice all of the skills that were targeted, with maximal interest and participation. This also decreased the occurrence of tantrums and frustration.

First Three Months

Daniel's initial treatment period was three months, enough time to ascertain if NMT treatment was beneficial in reaching his non-musical goals and objectives. This period in NMT, as in other approaches, is a time in which a relationship is established. Daniel was immediately friendly, and for the first few weeks displayed developmentally appropriate behaviors of environmental exploration. This exploration of the environment was incorporated into the first few weeks of treatment, encouraging as much communication as possible while allowing for exploration. The relationship in NMT is built on success-oriented and aesthetically pleasing experiences. The therapeutic music experiences target goals and objectives *while* building a client-therapist relationship.

According to Kumin (2006), the typical child is 100% intelligible by four years of age. However, it is unusual for a person with Down Syndrome to be 100% intelligible at any age. Furthermore, delays in speech production in children with Down Syndrome have been documented to continue into adulthood, with significant delays in consonant acquisition (Kumin, Council, & Goodman, 1994). At six years of age, Daniel had extremely low intelligibility, with few acquired phonemes. During the first three months of services, the focus of treatment was on producing isolated phonemes, producing those phonemes in the initial position of words and producing simple two-word phrases. Interventions were also designed to increase prosodic elements of vocalizations. Each of the exercises implemented were developed utilizing the TDM. The non-musical exercise, as would be implemented in speech therapy, was first outlined. In order to achieve appropriate non-musical applications, speech-language pathologists, research and current texts on speech interventions were consulted. Music was then created to transform this non-musical exercise into a therapeutic music application.

Developmental Speech and Language Training through Music (DSLM) experiences utilized aspects of play and natural interaction, in combination with specific (directive) cues for responses within the play experience. Once the child produced the word when prompted, the prompts were faded in order to allow for spontaneous production within DSLM experiences. The typical structure of the music was a simple composition with instructions or prompts imbedded within the lyrics or musical structure that were utilized to elicit a response. This was in place of the verbal prompts given in speech therapy and provided a temporal cue for responses. An ongoing rhythmic stimulus (metronome) continued during the client's response time in order to promote the motor speech response. The songs composed were age-appropriate for a six-year-old child and combined elements of active engagement in speech production and "speech breaks," where participation in musical play was encouraged.

It was soon evident that Daniel was able to synchronize his speech to the stimulus provided by the metronome and harmonic instrument. An example of motor synchronization was his ability to repeat a learned phoneme, such as /ba/. When asked to repeat the phoneme without musical stimuli, he would exhibit a three-second pause between productions (if he were to produce the syllable a second time at all). With musical stimulus present at a functional tempo, he would produce three to six successive repetitions of the phoneme. This ability soon allowed for more oral motor practice of unlearned syllables within each exercise. Synchronization was also evident in the sequencing of phrases. Without rhythmic stimulus, he would require several verbal prompts and an extended pause for execution of the phrase. With rhythmic stimulus, the phrase was produced in time, or slightly after, the stimulus. This production was even more successful when the response followed a structured musical cue.

Daniel's treatment was supplemented at home, with weekly assignments that were given to his parents to complete throughout the week. These assignments focused on utilizing rhythmic cues for when his speech was unintelligible and redirections to use his augmentative communication methods (sign language and PECS). Any musical exercises that were to be carried out at home were demonstrated to Daniel's mother at the end of each session. The family was provided with a written explanation of each exercise to be implemented, when possible. These exercises were designed to take very little time or to be completed while engaged in play. The family was successful in implementing most of the prescribed exercises over the weeks and often asked for additional tools that would be useful. The implementation of such exercises not only provided added opportunities for Daniel to practice skills that he was learning, but also encouraged him to use those skills in his typical environment. This incorporated the family into the treatment process, rather than relying solely on the therapist-client interaction to facilitate change.

A non-musical re-evaluation was completed at the end of three months to determine if music therapy was an effective treatment method.

By the end of three months, Daniel was consistently producing four new phonemes within the initial position of words. He had increased spoken vocabulary to include eight additional (intelligible) words, increased sign vocabulary by nine signs, and was able to speak and sign the two-word phrase "I want" with minimal assistance. By this time in the treatment process, it was apparent that he had the ability and showed the desire to learn effective communication. Language learning in persons with Down Syndrome has been suggested to continue into adolescence (Rondal, 2003), and therefore, this was seen as an important period for growth. In order to provide the best treatment outcomes possible, Daniel's parents were referred to a local speech therapist.

Next Six Months

The next six months were filled with changes for Daniel. He was integrated into a new class, began receiving music therapy twice a week, and underwent a full speech-language pathology assessment. Following the speech assessment, he also began speech therapy sessions once a week. The speech therapy assessment was in agreement with the three-month music therapy re-evaluation.

During the next six months of Daniel's treatment, objectives for phoneme production continued, with emphasis on placing phonemes in the initial position and middle position of words. Increasing vocabulary was targeted, as well as production of two- to three-word phrases. By this time, he was back in school and his communication methods (speech, sign and PECS) were being utilized at home, in school, in speech therapy and in music therapy.

The implementation of therapeutic music experiences for functional phrases began with phrases targeted by his parents and school. He continued to work on "I want" phrases, adding verbalizations for the desired object or action word (i.e., "I want more" or "I want ball"). Additionally, he began working on a phrase for introducing himself to his peers at his new school. As in other experiences, a song was created in order to allow him to practice the targeted phrase in response to the question "What's your name?" Utilizing the rhythm and sign cues to sequence the speech of the phrase, Daniel graduated from imitative responses to an initiated response. In order to prepare him for school, the musical cues were faded and spoken cues were utilized. As in the first three months, rhythm was integral to all therapeutic music experiences for speech production and the DSLM was the primary technique utilized.

During this treatment period, attempts were made to decrease Daniel's dependence on someone else cueing him for speech. Therefore, he was encouraged to provide his own motor tapping cues on his leg, matching one tap to one syllable in order to learn a functional way to self-cue when he wished to speak. Although research regarding rhythm for speech production in children is in its infancy, there have been promising results for using rhythmic cues for speech communication in children (e.g., Carroll, 1996). He was also encouraged to sign (another type of motor movement pairing) while speaking a word in order to better facilitate functional communication. Rhythmic tapping/signing was encouraged whenever he was producing two-syllable words or phrases. Daniel was very successful with pairing sign language with speech. Rhythmic tapping was less natural, but he gradually became adept at cuing himself without prompts from an adult.

The progression to self-cue speech was completed by first practicing the pairing of syllabic speech with instrument playing (i.e., three instruments are placed on a white board under a written phrase with three syllables), then pairing syllabic speech with touching the actual syllables of the written word, and then cueing by tapping on his knee. The environment in which he cued himself was also changed periodically, as we would take "field trips" and meet other therapists or office workers that were unfamiliar to Daniel so that he could practice his speech and speech cueing with an unfamiliar listener. This was completed to reinforce step five of the TDM, which focuses on fading the musical cues and transitioning into the typical environment.

During this treatment period, Daniel was integrated into public school and was increasingly showing signs of frustration when he was not understood. When this occurred during the music therapy session, he would "shut down" verbally and physically. This shutdown involved a closed (often hunched over) position and refusal to talk. This often occurred when he was attempting to spontaneously tell a story about his new friends at school. Methods for preventing meltdowns were implemented, including adding his classmates to his PECS book, reminding him to slow down his speech and aiding him in cuing his speech. When meltdowns occurred, a short musical improvisation was often implemented, since exploratory behavior on an instrument usually redirected the client back to the music experience.

Final Three Months

Over the last three months of services, Daniel continued to learn sign language very quickly, as evidenced by his ability to spontaneously use new signs just a few weeks after learning the sign(s). A consultation with then current research supported the use of written words for language learning in children with Down Syndrome (Buckley, 2000) and this became an integral element in his music therapy sessions. It was soon apparent that he had the ability to sound out a written word. The combination of visual language (sign & written), spoken language and rhythmic cuing was observed to be the most beneficial for him. He had the ability to learn new words by sounding-out the written word (requiring some help) and practicing the sounds within the word. Words were always paired with the visual representation of the word (i.e., if the word was "ball" then he would find the ball or the picture of a ball). He also practiced writing the words that he would verbalize.

After 12 months of music therapy, sessions were terminated due to the occupational relocation of Daniel's family. It was recommended that he continue receiving speech-language and music therapy services with an emphasis on communication. The final report and progress note showed that Daniel made a number of improvements. Developmental Speech and Language Training through Music aided him in learning functional phrases that were generalized into his typical environments including "*I want _____,*" "*more please,*" "*my name is Daniel,*" "*shoes on/off*" and "*no thank you.*" In total, he improved from overall low intelligibility to more than ten consistently intelligible target phrases (up to four words). His success with new phrases (or self-generated phrases) was often dependent on the consonant-vowel combinations of the attempted phrase and his acquired phoneme repertoire. Focused attention on phoneme production increased his success with intelligible speech due to improvements on targeted phonemes in initial, middle and ending positions. He was able to consistently utilize targeted phonemes in the initial and middle position of words (91% success) and started placing phonemes in the final position of words. He was also more successful at initiating intelligible phrases utilizing self-cueing techniques, with 84% intelligibility for two-word phrases (identified by an unfamiliar listener).

When not understood verbally, Daniel was more consistent in initiating the use of signs or PECS to communicate. Furthermore, DSLM aided him in vocabulary learning through the use of motivating musical experiences, literature and music and age-appropriate language incorporated into musical play. Vocabulary gains were demonstrated in increased expressive vocabulary use (signs and spoken) and the increased ability to demonstrate receptive understanding (i.e., following more complex directives). In the final months of treatment, he had independently demonstrated the use of 19 unprompted signs. Furthermore, instances of frustration decreased, with only two instances of visible frustration in the last two months of treatment.

SUMMARY

Daniel made several important improvements in his expressive language through the use of DSLM and rhythmic cueing. Although there were some immediate improvements (such as sequencing oral motor movements with rhythm), the production of intelligible speech was a gradual process that involved practice in different environments.

The use of Neurologic Music Therapy for practice with children with developmental disabilities involves consideration of current literature in development, neuroscience, and music. The R-SMM and TDM helped to guide the Neurologic Music Therapist in developing treatment-specific applications that facilitate the functional goals of the client. Although NMT has been primarily researched with adults in neurological rehabilitation, using current research to guide practice in music therapy for children with developmental disabilities will aid music therapists in developing protocols that promote success in music therapy treatment.

REFERENCES

Buckley, S.J. (2000). Speech, language and communication for individuals with Down Syndrome — An overview. *Down Syndrome Issues and Information*. Retrieved from http://www.down-syndrome.org/information/language/overview/.

Carroll, D. (1996). A study of the effectiveness of an adaptation of melodic intonation therapy in increasing the communicative speech of children with Down syndrome. Unpublished doctoral dissertation, McGill University, Canada.

Claussen, D.W. & Thaut, M.H. (1997). Music as a mnemonic device for children with learning disabilities. *Canadian Journal of Music Therapy, 5,* 55–66.

Hurt-Thaut, C. & Johnson, S. (2003). Neurologic music therapy with children: Scientific foundations and clinical application. In S. Robb (Ed.), *Music Therapy in Pediatric Heathcare: Research and Evidence-based Practice* (p. 81-100). Silver Spring, MD: American Music Therapy Association.

Krauss, T. & Galloway, H. (1982). Melodic Intonation Therapy with language delayed apraxic children. *Journal of Music Therapy, 19*(2), 102-113.

Kumin L. (2006). Speech intelligibility and childhood verbal apraxia in children with Down syndrome. *Down Syndrome Research and Practice, 10*(1), 10-22.

Kumin, L., Council, C. & Goodman, M. (1994). A longitudinal study of the emergence of phonemes in children with Down Syndrome. *Journal of Communication Disorders, 27,* 293-303.

Kwak, E.E. (2000). Effect of rhythmic auditory stimulation on gait performance in children with spastic cerebral palsy. Unpublished Master's thesis. University of Kansas, Lawrence.

Lim, H.A. (2010). Effects of "Developmental Speech and Language Training through Music" on speech production in children with autism spectrum disorders. *Journal of Music Therapy, 47*(1), 2-26.

Mastrokalou, N. & Hatziharistos, D. (2007). Rhythmic ability in children and the effects of age, sex, and tempo. *Perceptual and Motor Skills, 104*(3, Pt 1), 901-912.

Pasiali, V. (2008). Music therapy and resiliency: A pilot project. Unpublished manuscript. Michigan State University.

Rondal, J.A. (2003). Maintenance training in older ages. In J.A. Rondal & S. Buckley (Eds.), *Speech and language intervention in Down syndrome* (pp. 166-183). London: Whurr Publishers Ltd.

Smoll, F.L. (1974a). Development of rhythmic ability in response to selected tempos. *Perceptual and Motor Skills, 39,* 767-772.

Smoll, F.L. (1974b). Development of spatial and temporal elements of rhythmic ability. *Journal of Motor Behavior, 6*, 53-58.

Smoll, F.L. (1975). Preferred tempo in performance of repetitive movements. *Perceptual and Motor Skills, 40*, 439-442.

Thaut, M.H. (2000). *A Scientific Model of Music in Therapy and Medicine*. San Antonio, TX: IMR Press.

Thaut, M.H. (2005). *Rhythm, Music, and the Brain.* London, England: Taylor & Francis.

Thaut, M.H., Mertel, K. & Leins, A.K. (2008). Music for children with physical disabilities. In W.B. Davis, K.E. Gfeller, & M.H. Thaut (Eds.), *An Introduction to Music Therapy: Theory and Practice* (3rd ed.) (pp. 143-180). Silver Spring, MD: American Music Therapy Association.

Thomas, J. R. & Moon, D. (1976). Measuring motor rhythmic ability in children. *Research Quarterly, 47,* 20-32.

Volman, M. J. M. & Geuze, R. H. (2000). Temporal stability of rhythmic tapping "on" and "off the beat": A developmental study. *Psychological Research, 63,* 62-69.

Chapter Ten

FROM VIOLENT RAP TO LOVELY BLUES: THE TRANSFORMATION OF AGGRESSIVE BEHAVIOR THROUGH VOCAL MUSIC THERAPY

Sylka Uhlig

INTRODUCTION

The voice as a primary therapeutic instrument will be addressed in this chapter. Through vocal expression, chaos can be transformed into order – crying into singing, aggressive shouting into the structure of a rap song. This transformation of emotions demonstrates the ability to change behavior and to stimulate neurological development (Uhlig, 2006; Cramer, 1998). This remarkable learning capacity will be evidenced by children with special needs in a public school setting in New York City. Children 'at-risk' demonstrate honesty in expressing their most personal desires and fears through vocal music therapy. Through this process, they discover their pure musicality. Cursing, shouting, singing, rapping, chanting and songwriting help them to survive their personal and familiar environments and increase their learning potential.

FOUNDATIONAL CONCEPTS

The idea of transforming emotions through music is rooted in the origins of spontaneous vocalizations in a speech-like (recitative) style (Uhlig, 2006; Clayton & Sager, 2005; Karolyi, 1998). Since the voice is our first instrument, we always use it as a primary form of expression: sighing, babbling, laughing, crying, shouting, screaming and groaning. More sophisticated forms of vocalization include humming, calling, talking and singing (Uhlig, 2006). I interpret these primary forms as ancient forms of rap because they include a recitative structure and melodic phrasing (see appendix A for an introduction to rap).

This primary form of vocal expression has been used for centuries to help transform emotions (Clayton, et al., 2005; Austin, 2009; Uhlig, 2006; Bossinger, 2005; Karolyi, 1998; Cramer, 1998). We cope with myriad issues through vocalization: working through sadness and pain, grief and loss, hard labor, along with happiness and pleasure. In the recitative songs of the slaves, for example, working men were able to express their frustrations with extremely hard labor, and directly transform these emotions into a spontaneous vocalization by putting shouts or strident words into a regular rhythm (Uhlig, 2006). In so doing, the Negro song was created. These simple, rhythmical songs helped to structure emotions in order to ease their hours, days and years of hard labor and oppression (Allen, Ware & Garrison, 1867).

The same transformational process is common for other emotions. By putting words of grief in a rhythm, weeping rituals were created by women all over the world to mourn death (Holst-Warhaft, 1992). By putting words of happiness and pleasure in a rhythm, like those used in sporting competitions, songs of encouragement and strength are spontaneously created (Uhlig, 2006). The lullaby is another example of placing vocal sounds in a simple rhythm: softly singing soothing sounds and words that are calming to a child (Austin, 2009; Aldridge, 2008; Bossinger, 2005; Cramer, 1998). These are all natural, culturally derived forms of human vocalization used as authentic tools for coping, healing and well-being (Austin, 2009; Uhlig, 2006). Clayton et. al. (2005) described these various vocal utterances as attempts for rhythmic coordination and entrainment, a natural search for homeostasis.

Throughout the world people have created these forms without musical training or instruction (Clayton, et. al., 2005; Uhlig, 2006). But the effect can be even stronger and more directed through musical instruction and repetition within the context of a helping relationship. In the section that follows, I link behavioral adaptation and academic learning with deeper neurological processes. My premise is that singing activates deeper brain structures, and in so doing, stimulates neurological development, healing emotional trauma and activating the child's learning potential.

Behavioral Adaptation

Research has shown that music therapy has the potential to transform aggressive behavior, resulting in a form of aggression regulation (Hakvoort, 2008; Turry & Marcus, 2004). For example. Choi, Lee and Lee (2008) demonstrated the effects of a group music intervention on aggression regulation and improved self-esteem in children with highly aggressive behavior. Similarly, Fouche and Torrance (2005) described how rap and hip-hop music brought local gangs and group members together, enabling them to address agressiveness and social differences within the gangs.

Academic Achievement

A growing body of literature suggests that music leaning promotes skill development in other areas. For example, Rauscher (2003) found that 'at-risk' children who received two years of individual keyboard instruction scored higher on a standardized arithmetic test than children in control groups. Similarly, Douglas and Willatts (1994) found that 8-11 year-old children with reading problems who received music instruction showed a significant improvement in overall reading performance when compared to children who did not receive instruction.

Speech and Language Development

Music experiences that focus on singing, including aural skills development, appear to remediate deficits in both reading and language development. Overy (2003) examined the connection between dyslexia and music perception, demonstrating how dyslectic children experience difficulties with musical timing, but not with musical pitch. Through careful intervention, she showed how focusing music instruction on pitch and tonal skills improved both phonological and spelling skills. Overy (2003) hypothesized that "singing might lead directly to phonologic development, while learning to read music might help with learning to read text" (p. 503).

Further, Kennedy & Scott (2005) examined the effect of music therapy interventions on the development of English as a second language for children of Hispanic ethnicity (ages 10-12). They developed an intervention that included storytelling, singing, chanting, playing instruments and engaging in musical games (like fill-in songs – providing answers in rhythm to therapist-chanted questions). Through listening to and singing songs while viewing the lyrics on a white board, children improved their speaking and writing skills after each month of intervention. Importantly, even after the intervention finished, children were able to continue using the vocal techniques in order to maintain and improve their language skills, particularly fluency, diction and rate of speech.

Finally, the emotional potential natural to the singing experience also seems important for the development of language. Singing can transform aggression into a personal experience of being heard, understood and accepted (Uhlig, 2006; Bossinger, 2005; Turry & Marcus, 2004). Singing can extend communication from inside into the world outside. Being heard and understood in the world outside improves self-identity and self esteem (Uhlig, 2006). Thus, for children who live in stressful environments, transforming difficult feelings into music underlies the learning process. Feelings need to be released, and in so doing they are transformed into healthy expression.

Neurological Development

Underlying the child's ability to learn music, and the implications this has for learning in other areas, is the specific effect this learning has on neurological processes. Schellenberg (2004) found that children with music instruction in keyboard and voice groups showed significant improvement in general intelligence compared to children in control groups who received drama or no lessons. In particular, singing activates sophisticated neurological processing within the brain (Cramer, 1998), bringing about the potential to heal trauma, change behavior and stimulate brain development at a neurological level (Schneck & Berger, 2006). This potential is particularly significant for children who are "at risk" because it suggests that musical experiences, and singing in particular, facilitate both primary emotional expression and behavioral adaptation necessary for learning and development.

Rohmert (1994, cited in Cramer, 1998) suggested that through singing, specific neurological areas are stimulated by vocal vibrations, spreading impulses to the cerebral cortex and transporting vital energy in the form of stimuli. These stimuli arouse the capacity for concentration, balance in the body and sensorial movement. Vocal activity stimulates concentration and cognition through articulating and memorizing words, and coordinates speech and movement through simultaneously singing, playing and dancing (Cramer, 1998; Schneck & Berger, 2006; Uhlig, 2006) . When vocalizing, the relaxing elements of this vibration, and the rhythmical pattern of breath control, carry the potential to decrease anxiety and develop entrainment (Clayton, et. al., 2005; Schneck & Berger, 2006; Uhlig, 2006; Loewy, 2004). Rhythmic engagement used in vocalizations – like rap – structures emotional expression and appears to decrease tension, worry and nervousness through a repeated and relaxed pattern. If the relaxation effect is felt by the rapper, this person is carried to a different level of perception, wherein the violent mood (as I will describe later in this chapter) is changed into a pleasurable state of fulfillment and developed entrainment.

This transformation of affect, observed in the music-making process, can be understood as a "fight-or-flight" response (Schneck & Berger, 2006). When children live in destructive situations, like those at the school I worked in, they learn to protect themselves at an early age. This protection strategy often manifests itself in aggressive behavior, or "acting out." If the frightening home situation continues, then this fight or flight response is reinforced. These children act as if they need to fight (violence) or flee (escape) the unsafe environment. Neglected and deprived of comfort, attention and understanding, they overcompensate against this enormous anxiety, and unhealthy behavior ensues.

Schneck and Berger (2006) explain that during these moments of high anxiety or fear, the homeostatic control mechanisms of the body are activated, and stress hormones are produced when homeostasis cannot be maintained. The central nervous system receives these alarm signals and perceives the stressor as a threat to its survival, shifting to an emergency mode. These stressors can influence the child's physiology enormously: heart rate, blood flow, respiration, pupil dilation, blood sugar level etc. can all be effected in response to the stressor (Schneck & Berger, 2006). Such stress responses are quite normal, and when activated, the child (or adult) responds to the environment in order to reduce their stress. However, if the stressor continues, or the child is unable to cope with or diminish the stress, his/her body can become flooded with excess hormones, leading to unhealthy or even pathological behavior. Importantly, cognitive function can also become seriously affected, further impeding the child's ability to adapt and respond to the stressor. Over time, exposure to such stressors may lead to a generalized impairment in cognitive functioning, which has significant implications for learning (Schneck & Berger, 2006).

Any therapeutic response to children who live in these kinds of stressful environments must address the underlying stress response at a physiological, emotional and cognitive level. When stress is ongoing, the child's ability to learn is blocked because of his/her anxiety: the brain is simply too busy protecting the body from danger (i.e. the amygdala shuts down during emergency) to analyze and respond. It is only after relief from anxiety, when relaxation and comfort are experienced during homeostasis, that cognition can begin again (Schneck & Berger, 2006).

Singing and composing songs about feelings and ideas directly addresses the child's emotional world, while simultaneously opening the child to learning and adaptation. Working on personal vocal expression, a song addresses speech development through the combination of rhythm, melodic line and lyrics. A song has the ability to structure time by establishing a rhythm. Through rhythm, the impulses of the child can be organized into an expressive form. Melody organizes the patterns of high or low tones and flows with the child's mood changes. Space for emotional expression can thereby be created and developed, activating the brain beyond "fight or flight." The child can therein experience emotional satisfaction when expressing pleasure, sadness or even aggression. Lyrics give meaning to the song and stimulate cognitive processes of concentration, memorization, pronunciation, phonology and spelling skills, as well as symbolic play. These musical elements can create a container in which the child can feel a sense of safety and decreased anxiety that are fundamental to exploration and development (Uhlig, 2006).

In the case of Richard that follows, singing, and rap in particular, was used to express his isolation and profound anger. Here, the music stirred and exposed qualities and capacities that had not been developed, resulting in behavioral change. Richard shows us the potential of these abilities in every child: an emotional and neurological potential waiting for somebody to awaken.

THE CLIENT

The public school I worked in served children with special needs (ages 5-12) in an underprivileged part of New York City. In addition to developmental delays, these children were also 'at risk' because of the environments they live in. They were often physically neglected, receiving a minimum of support at home. As a result, many of these children were extremely emotionally disturbed. Because of a lack of positive attention, they unconsciously altered their behavior to receive negative attention – apparently better than no attention at all. Consequently, their need for attention and personal expression was so profound they had difficulty developing the ability to constructively listen, cooperate and work together in the classroom.

To overcome these serious difficulties required a sensitive and attuned collaboration between teachers and therapists. During my years of work I have been fortunate enough to build strong collaborations with staff members, essential to any integrated learning experience. Together with classroom teachers and the speech pathologist, we found ways of combining our methods, wherein we experienced the power of music to hold the positive and negative emotions of the children in a structured, acceptable and enjoyable therapeutic experience – all centered around the form of the improvised song.

Richard

Richard was an underweight 11-year-old African American boy with developmental delays, average speech skills, erratic concentration and poor academic skills. He was often extremely violent, acted out and, paradoxically, also showed 'grown-up' behavior. Apparently, he had been masking his fears with misbehavior from a young age. Richard's constant severe mood changes, street-smart behavior and bad language, episodic irritability and wild tantrums, created regular conflicts at school. Once or twice a week, a simple conflict would suddenly escalate into a tantrum of extreme aggression. Richard would yell, scream and curse, hitting everything and everybody around him. During these tantrums, three or four staff members were called to help the teacher in the classroom. These helpers were trained to safely hold Richard's body close to the floor, preventing his classmates from being attacked, and then calming him down afterward. These incidents took between twenty and thirty minutes, and afterwards, everyone involved – classmates, teachers and Richard himself – needed a "time-out" to reorient and reorganize for the tasks at school. Richard's outbursts exhausted and annoyed everybody around him. Not only was his behavior disagreeable, it also limited his academic performance. These interruptions, combined with his lack of interest in school, blocked his cognitive progress: neurologically, his amygdale had shut down. A big change was needed.

The people in Richard's home environment were neither interested nor involved in his education. He lived with his mother in a shared home situation with additional adults and children. There was no structure or guidance in his life. In the morning, Richard would wear the clothes he found around the house. This could be a sweater of an adult or an unwashed t-shirt from the day before. He took care of himself – as much as this was possible for an 11-year-old. Although Richard's teacher had reached out to his mother, she had never visited the school, and everyone assumed she had no interest in his educational development.

Richard's teacher referred him to music therapy because of his extreme aggressive behavior. She hoped that the music could offer him a tool for relaxation to calm his temper. She also welcomed support and cooperation of another sort: all the children relaxed when Richard was out of the classroom during music therapy.

THE THERAPEUTIC PROCESS

I started working with Richard in a dyad during his first year in music therapy, but soon separated him from the other boy so that I could focus more specifically on his needs. In so doing, I discovered his tremendous musicality. For example, Richard intuitively acknowledged 'unusual' musical scales and their moods. After hearing a pentatonic scale at the piano, he described it as 'Chinese' sounding, sensing perfectly subtle differences in tonal center. When we played instruments together with untamed rhythmic patterns on drums and rich melodic variations on harmonica, his mood and facial expression changed visibly and his body moved to the rhythm of the music. He became intensely involved in music making, playing instruments with remarkable coordination and exhibiting significant auditory-motor and sensory-motor skills. However, he was most engaged when he vocally transformed parts of his aggression into rap, spontaneously experimenting with shouting sounds and screaming words. He vocalized more and more, and his speech-like articulations seemed gradually to release his tension. I supported his vocalizations with a simple repetitive chord progression on the piano or just the rhythm button of the keyboard, matching his rhythm. I also used a vocal rhythm pattern myself to offer a structured model to contain his sounds. I had to be sensitive in the ways I used my voice, not connecting too closely to him yet.

Richard finally became the music himself – he was in the flow – rapping about his deep frustration and anger, putting screaming sounds and words into a rhythm. Typically, his hard and violent vocalizations were like the aggressive outbursts I saw in the classroom. He expressed himself for weeks and months as follows:

> *(shouting sounds)*
> *Yeah, wow …*
> *Asshole, bitch, I am a nigger,*
> *I hate you,*
> *Be careful,*
> *Nobody can touch me,*
> *Yeah, yeah,*
> *Stay away, f…ing asshole,*
> *Don't f… with me,*
> *I am strong,*
> *Yeah, yeah, yeah*
> *Don't mess with me,*
> *Be careful,*
> *You don't know me,*
> *Wow, yeah, yeah…*
> *(shouting sounds)*

During our second year together, Richard went to a higher level, not only shouting, screaming and playing hard, but also creating beautiful and significant improvised songs. He started vocally to compose music that was touching in its purity. He expressed himself most verbally in a rhythmical pattern – still similar to rap – while I supported him with a simple chord progression on the piano, matching his characteristic rhythm. His need for personal expression would let him utter whole sentences such as 'I am a nigger from Jamaica,' 'don't mess with me,' 'nobody knows who I am' and 'I punch you right in your face.' He would also rap and sing freely about his teachers and people in his life, expressing shocking or very emotional truths. Musically and vocally supportive, I always contained his aggressive expression and sang and rapped to him, mirroring, provoking or inviting more articulations about his inner world.

In the beginning, he primarily expressed himself without answering my sounds. Later, he developed a sense of vocal dialogue with me. He surprised me with his responsiveness to special subjects during a rap like 'Twin-towers were knocked down September 11,' or suddenly 'Mr. B., I miss you,' about a teacher who left the school. Continuing the musical pattern on piano, I first wove vocal sounds like 'yeah' and 'wow' in a rhythmic pattern, and later added words into his meaningful messages. I also provoked his moods, for example when I sang "sometimes we don't know what we feel or what we do," addressing his aggressive behavior. Unexpectedly, he picked up on my words and often integrated them in the ongoing song. He sang back "...yeah, we don't know what we feel, yeah, yeah..." creating his own version of it. We never talked about the meaning of the words, but we improvised intensely together using non-verbal and verbal sounds, creating solos and refrains, and singing call and response patterns. At every moment our improvised songs carried different but very meaningful content. Rhythmically shouting and expressing what he needed to say seemed to be a release for his aggression. After these vocal outbursts, he appeared more relaxed. I did not judge or stop this primary expression when he musically - in rap form - cursed or expressed his feelings vocally.

Richard behaved like an adult who had learned to protect himself in a world of danger (fight-or-flight response). He was actually in a 'flow' while rapping, and he had learned to relax himself by searching for sounds and rhymes in his words. In between his aggressive shouts, he started to weave in soft words that sometimes included me. I was never sure if he really meant me, saw me or heard me – except when he answered my words. I never felt personally attacked and I never made an interpretation of his cursing words. I accepted them as his primary expression of hate and anxiety. Through playing piano rhythmically and repeating the vocalizations through rapping and countering his words, I offered a structure of safety where he could feel held. My positive musical and personal presence demonstrated that I accepted him, even when I was far from understanding him. Through these experiences, he could develop a sense of comfort and safety.

We worked this way for a further six months into his second year of music therapy. Gradually, little by little, Richard began to relax. In experiencing safety, and feeling understood, he could begin to develop a sense of others. He started to sing about people, especially about the children in his class. He demonstrated an unexpected softness, often surprising me with tender lyrics. We often sang together now, exchanging vocal sounds, improvising lyrics, and answering each other's words. We musically played together and created fill-in song constructions, improvising in a vocal dialogue. In these experiences I realized that Richard had noticed me as a person, present with him in the same room.

This kind of awareness extended into dialogues with others. He started with recitative forms of word construction, calling the names of teachers, and singing about his class as a whole group, he communicated with them in song. In this way, he was tremendously involved in putting these words into a fitting rhythm. One very touching song he created during this time was about love, especially for his own classmates. Instead of hate and anger, he sang about love. We took his original poem, written alone before he entered the music room, and thoughtfully worked to fit the text into a Blues form. Searching for a suitable accompaniment, Richard chose a slow 'bluesy' rhythm for his words, while I offered him a fitting pattern at the piano:

> *We are happy*
> *Love is happiness from the bottom of my heart*
> *God loves us from his heart*
> *We know we are a happy family*
> *The kids run around with me.*
> *Love is happy[ness] with my heart*
> *From class [...] love is happy[ness] with my heart*
> *To the kids from my heart*
> *I love when the kids play with each other*
> *When I am home the kids play with me*

The kids like to be happy

Richard was now engaged and relaxed in a way that showed me his homeostatic state had been modulated. A transformation had happened so that his soft rapping and singing lyrically, smiling and dancing, had exposed a totally different side of his personality. I had never before seen this kind of transformation in him and noticed how his behavior was also changing. In Richard grew a perception of the change he had made, but there was not yet full awareness. Fulfilled and proud of his personal song and musical experiences, combined with a feeling of being supported and understood, Richard planned to go on with 'making songs' and creating more lyrics. By working on various lyrics about his personal experiences, he became enthusiastically involved in learning to find the "correct" words. But more important was his wish to perform this song at his graduation party. He needed to satisfy his desire to perform, even "show off," so that he could be seen and noticed in a positive way. He was very well known at school – but sadly only through his negative behavior. Determined, he practiced the song in front of the video camera, controlling his movements and experimenting with his vocal and acting skills. His need for positive attention and recognition as a rapper, particularly within the culture of his African American school, showed how much his priorities and behavior had changed. Not only was he seeking recognition for his artistic abilities, he was seeking recognition from his community, one he now felt he belonged to.

Richard had performed once before during a holiday show, watched by his mother, who had visited her son's school for the first time. Preparing for the next performance, and her second visit, his excitement and awareness made him adopt the attitude of a 'star.' He imitated movements he had seen on video clips and infused his music and dance with great talent, transforming his art into his own personal context. The appreciation of his race and culture was acknowledged by his teachers, classmates and school in general. And I, a white European woman, supported, engaged and accepted his cultural progression. In so doing, his negative role vanished. His personal transformation from violent rap into lovely blues shifted not only on a musical level, but also on a cultural level into a positive identification.

During this time, whenever he saw me at school, he enthusiastically told me that he had made a new song – which we later practiced in the music therapy session. He was curious to learn how to read and write with more accuracy. Asking me for help with spelling and expression, he carried over his curiosity for learning into the classroom. His teacher, who personally supported his development and carefully noticed any changes, told me that his cognitive potential had been engaged. His reading and writing skills improved significantly and his motivation for learning increased. But most importantly, there was a big decrease in his tantrums – there had now been months without any aggressive outbursts.

On the day of the concert, Richard performed his rap-blues with enormous success. He was proud of his performance and received lots of acknowledgement from his schoolmates. He had illustrated perfectly his love and attention for his peers – and he was rewarded with their powerful appreciation after the show. His intensive musical interactions and positive experiences appeared to greatly strengthen his self-esteem. Above all, the teachers were pleased to have the opportunity to meet his mother again when she came for his second performance. Using time for a cooperative conversation with her about Richard's development, everybody shared their appreciation for his touching performance.

SUMMARY

Richard had made an emotional and cognitive transformation. He had become more conscious of himself, and in so doing, was able to acknowledge others and their feelings. His voice offered him a primary form of expression: shouting, screaming and rapping, supported by musical accompaniment. The significant effect of vocalization integrated his personal need to release emotional and physical tension. He experienced relaxation and comfort, developed a sense of safety, and opened his cognitive potential. His emotional expression strengthened subtle transformations of behavior, freeing up energy and relaxing tension, creating safety and comfort, and finding homeostatic balance. Above all, this process helped his brain to develop significantly, as he started to sing more words and to make up various lyrics himself, concentrating on fitting or rhyming words.

In Richard's case, the vocal activity of shouts, supported by music, was met with positive encouragement. This stimulation developed into relaxation, activating concentration and then cognition. His emotional involvement set larger neurological processes in motion and finally influenced his cognitive development, as well as his emotional and social well-being.

REFERENCES

Allen, W. F., Ware, C. P. & Garrison, L. M. (1867). *Slave Songs of the United States*. Bedford, Massachusetts: Applewood Books.

Aldridge, G. (2008). *Melody in Music Therapy, A Therapeutic Narrative Analysis*. Philadelphia PA: Jessica Kingsley Publishers.

Austin, D. (2009) *The Theory and Practice of Vocal Psychotherapy: Songs of the Self.* Philadelphia, PA: Jessica Kingsley Publishers.

Bossinger, W. (2005). *Die Heilende Kraft des Singens*. Germany: Norderstedt, Books on Demand GmbH.

Choi, A., Lee, M. & Lee, J. (2010). Group music intervention reduces aggression and improves self-esteem in children with highly aggressive behavior: A pilot controlled trial. *Evidence-based Complementary and Alternate Medicine*, 7(2), 213-217.

Clayton, M. & Sager, R. (2005). In time with the music: The concept of entrainment and its significance for ethnomusicology. In S. Hallam, I. Cross and M. Thaut (Eds.), *The Oxford Handbook of Music Psychology*. New York: Oxford University Press Inc.

Cramer, A. (1998). *Das Buch von der Stimme, Ihre Formende und Heilende Kraft Verstehen und Erfahren*. Zurich/Dusseldorf, Germany: Walter Verlag.

Douglas, S. & Willatts, P. (2003). *Can music instruction affect children's cognitive development? ERIC Digest*. ED480540. www.eric.ed.gov.

Elligan, D. E. (2004). *A Practical Guide for Communicating with Youth and Young Adults Through Rap Music*. New York: Kensington Publishing Corp.

Fouche, S. & Torrance, K. (2005). Lose yourself in the music, the moment, yo! Music therapy with an adolescent group involved in gangsterism. *VOICES: A World Forum of Music Therapy*, 5(3).

Hackvoort, L. (2008). Rapmuziektherapie, een muzikale methodiek. *Tijdschrift Voor Vaktherapie*, 4, 15-21.

Holst-Warhaft, G. (1992). *Dangerous Voices, Women's Laments and Greek literature*. London and New York: Routledge.

Karolyi, O. (1998*). Traditional African and Oriental music*. Middlesex, England: Penguin books.

Kennedy, R. & Scott, A. (2005). A pilot study: The effects of music therapy interventions on middle school students' ESL skills. *Journal of Music Therapy*, 42(4), 244-261.

Loewy, J. V. (2004). Integrating music, language and voice in music therapy. *VOICES: A World Forum of Music Therapy,* 4(1).

Overy, K. (2003) Dyslexia and Music, From Timing Deficits to Musical Intervention. *New York Academy of Sciences, 999*, 497-505.

Rainey Perry, M. & Ri, C. J. (2005). Developing intentional communication: A combined music and speech therapy approach. Paper presented at 11th *World Congress of Music Therapy*, July, Brisbane Australia.

Rauscher, F. H. (2003). Can music instruction affect children's cognitive development? *ERIC Digest* ED480540. www.eric.ed.gov.

Schneck, D. J. & Berger, D. (2006) *The Music Effect: Music Physiology and Clinical Applications.* Philadelphia, PA: Jessica Kingsley Publishers.

Schellenberg, E. G. (2004) Music lessons enhance IQ. *Psychological Science,*15(8), 511-514.

Tyson, E. H. (2002). Hip hop therapy: An exploratory study of a rap music intervention with at-risk and delinquent youth. *Journal of Poetry Therapy*, 15(3), 131-144.

Turry, A. & Marcus, D. (2004) *Musical Community: Music Therapy at Northeast Center for Special Care.* www.nordeastcnter.com Retrieved June 12th, 2010.

Uhlig, S. (2006) *Authentic Voices – Authentic Singing: A Multicultural Approach To Vocal Music Therapy.* Gilsum, NH: Barcelona Publishers.

APPENDIX A

Rap music has various forms, and as Elligan (2004) describes when discussing rap as therapy, is different from hip-hop. Rap is the music, the beats and the rhyme of a culture known as hip-hop. Elligan (2004) differentiates several forms of rap: Gangsta rap, Materialistic rap, Political/Protest rap, Positive rap, Spiritual rap and rap forms not otherwise specified. Rap songs critically analyze society. Rap songs create culture shock, exposing different cultural norms unfamiliar to others. The culture of rap provides the foundation for the development of a community, and like all communities, focuses on sharing the same interests and identities. Rap has primarily grown out of the interaction of poverty, music, dance, graffiti and fun (Elligan, 2004). For example, the aspects of anger, abuse, misery and inhuman circumstances of many people living in urban poor ghetto communities are expressed through Gangsta rap. Poor academic choices and a minimum of social and emotional care created a collective need to report about them through Political rap. Herein rap demonstrates its value as an educational tool, to bring into awareness issues important to the listener. Finally, rap has developed from an idiosyncratic form of expression in the ghettos of large cities into an important form of communication for communities of interest. Elligan (2004) calls for the use of rap therapy as a means of promoting positive behavioral change and improved insight into the lives of the clients through five steps:

1. Assessing the person's interest in rap music and hip-hop (clothing, videos, concerts) and developing a plan for using rap music with a person.

2. Building a relationship and alliance with the person through discussing the different types of rap songs to which he or she enjoys listening.

3. Challenging the person with the lyrics of his or her rap icons in order to reevaluate his or her thoughts and behaviors.

4. Asking the person to write raps about the desired changes they have set for themselves.

5. Monitoring and maintaining the progress made through continued discussion and feedback (p. 65).

Chapter Eleven

PUNKER, BASSGIRL AND DINGO-MAN: PERSPECTIVES ON ADOLESCENTS' MUSIC THERAPY

Jaakko Erkkilä

INTRODUCTION

During my years as a music therapist I have often thought about core guiding principles when working with adolescents. Although I use different clinical methods to meet the needs of this very diverse group, was there something that guided my thinking, attitude or stance to working with adolescents? After all, the concept of adolescence only refers to a certain phase of life, with its developmental characteristics, and not a specific illness or problem. In this chapter I will focus on the results of the above-mentioned thinking, illustrating core phenomena of my work with clinical examples.

In music therapy with adolescents, various models and clinical techniques are utilized (Gold, Voracek & Wigram, 2004). For example, I often found myself looking at the clinical situation from a different perspective depending on the goal of therapy in a given moment. Sometimes learning is the focus, sometimes change in behavior, sometimes a need to be accepted and to gain compensatory experiences. In other words, I find myself moving across behavioral, cognitive and psychodynamic theories (Erkkilä, 1997). Similarly, depending on the phase of the therapy, and the needs of the client, it is sometimes important to be flexible with clinical techniques as well. With many young clients I prefer a kind of soft start by employing receptive techniques at the beginning of therapy, and active techniques in later stages, for engaging them gradually in the therapeutic process. Interestingly, a meta-analysis of the effectiveness of music therapy with children and adolescents (Gold, Voracek, & Wigram,

2004) confirmed, amongst other things, that treatments with eclectic approaches proved the most effective.

However, none of these theoretical constructs or methods alone results in successful therapy if there is no real contact, motivation, trust, and mutual acceptance within the working alliance. It is this living relationship with the therapist that is primary to the effectiveness of psychotherapy and which, in turn, significantly influences method and technique (Wampold, 2001).

FOUNDATIONAL CONCEPTS

In my work with adolescents I soon learned that talking about the client's problems is seldom possible or beneficial, particularly in the earlier stages of therapy. In fact, you first have to make contact with the client (see Figure 1). At this point, it is good to avoid "difficult" topics. By difficult topics I mean a problem-orientated approach where the therapist immediately focuses directly on the client's problems as well as on therapeutic goals. For example, it is important to consider if the client seems to be noncommittal, or if there are any signs of resistance from his/her side. It is helpful to bear in mind that the adolescent has already met various health professionals (e.g., psychologists, doctors and psychiatrists) and may be tired of talking about his/her problems.

It is often a good idea to start by discussing hobbies and preferred music, and to ask the client to bring some of his/her favourite CD's to listen to and discuss in the session. That is, not to start with the client's problems (such as their emotional or behavioural issues), but to start with something that is part of his/her everyday life. This is both safe and accessible for the adolescent, as I've not yet met a client without a preference for a particular type of music! At this stage of the process, the therapist's role is typically more active (see figure 1). The aim is to create contact and trust as well as to get to know as much as possible about what is important for the client. The therapist's hidden agenda at this stage is to investigate what might be the most appropriate way to engage the client in creative work.

But why is it so important to find, or arouse one's creativity? It is because creativity is connected to symbolic process[1] and, when it is active, there is always a direct connection to one's emotional world. Practically all mental health problems are more or less emotionally related and thus, in order to deal with the emotions, it is important to enter the "world" of emotions, metaphors, symbols and associations – the *pre-conscious*[2]. Bruscia (1998) has defined the pre-conscious as kind of a mediating level between the unconscious and the conscious. Thus, whatever the content and form of the pre-conscious process, we can think of it as somehow linked to one's mental landscape – as well as to one's psychopathology – and therefore it is worthy of investigation.

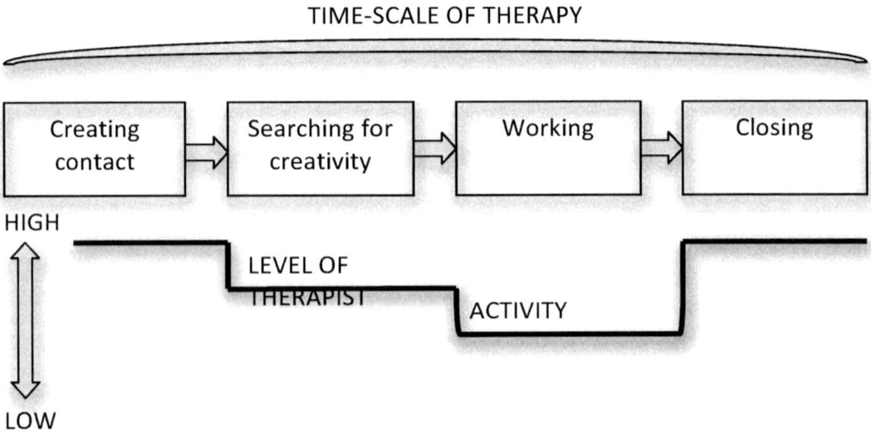

TIME-SCALE OF THERAPY

Creating contact → Searching for creativity → Working → Closing

HIGH
LEVEL OF THERAPIST ACTIVITY
LOW

Figure 1. Phases in the Music Therapy Process with Adolescents, and the Therapist's Role Within These Phases.

Music can be a powerful tool for entering the pre-conscious level and conveying various emotional and symbolic meanings (see Bruscia, 1998; Erkkilä, 1997, 2004). However, when working with children and adole-

---

[1] Symbolic process may be understood as an emergent property of the interplay of a variety of psychobiological functions and psychological capacities in the context of body, object, and interpersonal relations (Levin, 1989, p. iii).
[2] Several authors (Bruscia, 1998; Erkkilä, 1997;, 2004; Eschen, 2002; Lehtonen, 2007; Priestley, 1994) have dealt with the concept of pre-conscious in music therapy.

scents, the principle of *symbolic distance* is often important (Ahonen-Eerikainen, 1998). The therapist has to understand that the young client may not be ready to make connections between his/her own reality and the symbolic (music related), emotionally loaded expression linked to it. The connections may be very clear to the therapist, but the client may need some distance as if acting as a symbolic shelter against too painful or unbearable experiences. The therapist often feels a pressure to deal with the client's problems more concretely by discussing them. In my experience, adolescents can manage an amazing amount of psychic work on the symbolic level without ever really verbalizing their problems.

What then is the role of conscious processing in adolescents' therapy? In Figure 2, the term conscious processing refers to rational thinking including skills, knowledge and techniques. I have found that, with adults, this often means gaining insights about the meaning(s) of their emotionally loaded symbolic experiences. Adults may reflect on how these experiences are linked to their problems, for instance, but unlike adults, adolescents are not so eager, or competent, at making these kinds of direct connections. For adolescents, the zig-zag movement between conscious and unconscious processes may be based more on the interaction between practical elements (skills, knowledge, and techniques) of the session, and the creative musical act, with its emotionally loaded symbolic experiences. In particular, when creating contact and exploring the young client's creativity (first two phases in Figure 2), the therapist may find him/herself in the role of a teacher. It may be necessary to offer some basic advice on instrumental technique, or to help the client to find an appropriate form for their creative product (e.g., to structure a song writing experience). If the therapist understands the meaning of this process, s/he should not be worried about moving away from the role of a therapist and into the role of teacher. When the relationship and therapeutic process deepens, this relationship will naturally shift and the therapeutic nature of the sessions will solidify.

202   Jaakko Erkkilä

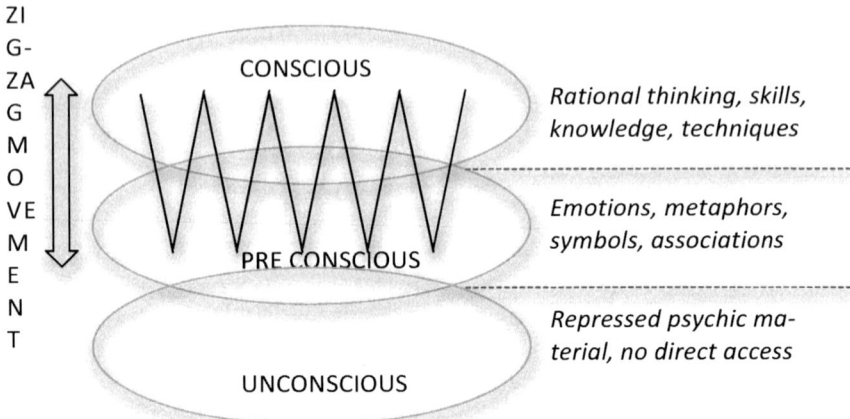

Figure 2. A Topographic Model of Mind Illustrating the Typical "Zigzag" Movement Between the Conscious and Pre-conscious in the Therapeutic Process.

The *working phase* (see Figure 1) starts when the client has found his/her personal way of expressing him/herself through musical activities. Attaining the working phase may take months, and sometimes even a year or more. The Finnish music therapist Kimmo Lehtonen demonstrated this in his work with "Jaska," whose music therapy began when he was 12 years old, and ended some five years later (Lehtonen, 1999). In Jaska's case, it took almost two years until the working phase really began. This was because Jaska had experienced a very traumatic childhood. His mistrust of adults, in particular men, was very deep, and he also suffered from severe psychotic disorders. The therapist had to work for a considerable amount of time to help strengthen Jaska's ego, to develop a trusting working alliance, and to explore the signs of normal functioning, free of paranoid or neurotic thinking and behavior.

In the working phase it is typical that the client is responsible for most of the content of the therapy. The therapist takes a few steps back, taking a more empathic role, and sometimes even acting as "a technical assistant" who enables the client's creative work. When the working phase has ended and the closing phase approaches, the role of the therapist becomes more active again. In this final phase, the client is often more interested in verbal discussion – partly because of the long, shared time together and increased sense of trust, but also because he/she is more mature and capable of verbal expression and interaction.

In my experience, adolescents are action oriented. Although it may be a good idea to begin therapy by utilizing receptive techniques, and to sit and discuss things with the client, it often happens that after this initial stage of the process, the client really wants to create something instead of just talking and listening to music. Most of my young clients have been able to find an interesting and motivating way to execute their creativity through music-related activity, and when doing so, I have observed that there is always part of the client's inner world attached to the creative product.

Song writing (Baker & Wigram, 2005) has been far the most often employed method with my young clients. This has been the case even though the relevant musical skills may not initially be present. If the client has or can attain the motivation to actively engage in music making, the drums (for example) are relatively easy to begin with. If the client has even minor musical skills when entering therapy, these can be used as a starting point. I have also had clients who are not so eager to play a musical instrument, but may want to write songs and then later sing them. In these cases, the client may have an inner vision of a song and then asks the therapist to create a musical framework based on that vision. Many young clients have written songs this way, which serve as a glimpse of their inner world.

THE CLIENTS

I have worked with adolescents in many contexts: in a psychiatric hospital, in a special school and in a psychiatric clinic. To illustrate my work in these contexts I have chosen three cases to refer to here. I will call them "Punker," "Bassgirl" and "Dingo-man." These clients provide contrasting examples of my clinical work because they had notably different reasons for entering therapy.

Punker was 16 years old when he started therapy. He did not show severe behavioral or emotional problems. However, because his family background was very challenging, and he had experienced many losses and traumatic events (such as the divorce and alcoholism of the parents, and an early move to a children's home), he was given as much additional support as possible to prevent minor symptoms, such as isolation and withdrawal, from getting worse. The Punker was rather withdrawn when I met him for the first time, which was not a good sign. But he loved punk music, which rather contradicted this inward presentation. The aim of therapy was to enrich his self-expression and communication skills as well as to support him in dealing with, and regulating, emotions.

Bassgirl was 15 years old when she started therapy. She was very anxious, with suicidal behavior, and used to slit her wrists when her anxiety became overwhelming. She had been living with her grandmother because her parents could not take care of her, but was now at an adolescent ward of a psychiatric hospital. Bassgirl used hard black makeup and had colored her hair black as well. My first impression was that she was distant and rather detached and cold in her demeanour and speech. The aim of her therapy was to reduce anxiety, support self-expression and deal with difficult emotions.

Dingo-man was 16 years old when he started therapy. He had rather difficult emotional problems and was very shy and fragile. One could describe him as a rare bird, a loner with few friends. I had no information about his domestic background when he began therapy. One day he just entered an open music therapy group and asked to listen to his favorite band, called Dingo. He loved to live in a fantasy world created around Dingo, and identified himself with the singer of the band. Soon afterward he started individual music therapy, the aim of which was to consolidate his self-esteem and support his growth in general.

Assessing Clients for Music Therapy

It is still not common practice to use specific, standardized music therapy assessment methods in Finland. Many music therapists advocate the use of non-structured methods, utilizing a range of data in the process of assessing the client (Ala-Ruona, 2005).

Ala-Ruona (2007) developed a model of music therapy assessment that is very helpful in providing a framework for assessment with adolescents. This model consists of four inter-related phases, each of which will be briefly described: 1) first contact/referral, 2) assessment meetings, 3) conclusions, and 4) reporting.

> 1) The *first contact* always begins through a referral. In some situations this may be made by the adolescent themselves, but it may also be made by a relative or other health care professional. While it is often the case that documents about the client's illness, history, previous treatment and goals are included with the referral, in some cases this information is gathered anecdotally. The less information readily available to the therapist, the more he/she has to rely on intuition and experience.

> 2) During the *assessment meetings* – the number of meetings may vary from two up to six meetings (usually 45 minutes each) depending on the setting – the therapeutic possibilities of music tend to utilize as much as possible. I am interested in the musical interaction between the client and myself, and in the client's overall relationship to music. Therefore, in addition to interviewing the client, I also focus on music making whenever possible. I have termed the phrase *creating contact* to describe an important element of this part of the assessment process. Creating contact serves two important functions: it helps in establishing a relationship with the client and in planning the appropriate musical activities and detailed goals of the therapy.

> 3) Drawing *conclusions* about the client and his/her therapy involves analyzing the data collected from the previous two phases. It is utilized to make a final decision about the suitability of music therapy for the client, and to frame the content and goals of therapy. Supervision and multidisciplinary meetings are often part of this decision-making process.

> 4) *Reporting* involves making a written or oral report about the conclusions. Here the client's opinion is also taken into consideration and reported. These kinds of statements are more general in today's music therapy practice – in particular because the initial assessment is often made by an independent music therapy

expert who is not supposed to be the clinician, and will not do the clinical work if therapy contract begins.

THE THERAPEUTIC PROCESS

Creating Contact

The music therapy room creates a musical environment that often helps the young client orient him/herself at the beginning of therapy. There are instruments, equipment, cds, etc. available – in other words, something to focus on and somewhere to start from when making *contact*. This kind of environment makes music therapy different from other therapeutic contexts, and it is often a good way to motivate the client. For instance, with all three clients discussed in this chapter, there was already a specific relationship to a musical style or band. The first important task of the therapist is to take advantage of this and do his/her best to find out as much as possible about the client's musical preferences, values and attitudes.

Hard-core punk fascinated Punker, and he carried the external signs of that sub-culture, seen in his black leather clothes, studs and piercings. Bassgirl loved heavy-rock music and wore the clothes that could be immediately connected to specific bands. She always wore black with striking, dramatic make-up. Dingo-man was not as easy to define because his presence and appearance did not reveal much about his values or orientation. However, he wanted to listen endlessly to the Finnish rock band "Dingo." In this way the first meetings were relatively easy, where the music (and even clothing) worked as a kind of a bridge between the client and the therapist. None of the clients spontaneously took the initiative to mention their problems during the first sessions. Nor was it sought out by the therapist. The music itself facilitated contact and fostered the possibilities of a therapeutic relationship.

Creating contact takes a varied amount of time. Punker did not need many sessions (only 3 or 4), because he soon knew what he really wanted to do. With Bassgirl and Dingo-man it took longer because unlike the Punker, they had no previous experience playing an instrument or making music. Thus, engaging them in creative musical activities, and supporting them in finding their creativity, took some more time. Furthermore, their own therapeutic issues were reflected in a longer period of creating contact, in particular with Dingo-man, who showed fragility and insecurity.

Searching for Creativity

Punker had played drums in a hard core punk band, and when he noticed that it was possible to record music with a multi-track system in therapy, he soon expressed his desire to make his own hard core punk songs. After a few sessions, he had created a method wherein I had a recording engineer's role, while he acted as a song-writer and musician.

With Bassgirl, we spent many sessions 'opening' the creative channel. She wanted to play bass guitar but first had to learn it. We devoted these sessions to playing songs with an easy bass line while I gave the necessary technical instruction. After approximately 10-15 of these sessions, Bassgirl brought in a lyric sheet, in English, of a song she had written. She was ready to take the next step – to write the music to these song lyrics. My help was still needed at the beginning of this process, in order to give structure and form to the songs. Importantly, though, the creative process had begun.

Dingo-man was fixated on his favorite Fin-rock band. He was, of course, not the only one in the country to have an obsessive interest in Dingo. But his dedication, and associated fantasies that emerged through listening to the band's music, were somewhat alarming. He was not interested in playing any instruments, or learning to play them. His favorite activity was to stand in front of the loudspeakers, sing along with the music (he had memorized all the lyrics), and ask the therapist every now and then whether his voice and movements were good.

I tried to encourage him to focus on other musical activities, for example, introducing different instruments and ways of playing them creatively. However, he remained non-committal about actively playing any instrument. It was not until later on that he started to compose and sing his own music. That is to say, Dingo-man found a rather unique way of using session time. Of his own initiative, he developed a numbered notation system, wherein he simply gave a number for each key of the keyboard and created a series of numbers (his own kind of notation) that represented a melody. He would then ask me to play the notes in numbered order. If he was not happy with the melody, he made some changes, until he was satisfied. Once completed, he allowed me to help him find structure and harmony for the songs. As this work developed, he began writing songs on the ward using his notation system, boosting our work in music therapy.

In my clinical thinking, I associate creativity with the ability and willingness to operate on the pre-concious level, which is the arena of emotions, metaphors, symbols and associations (see Figure 2). When the client feels secure enough, the activated pre-conscious processes can be transformed into a concrete object such as a song, lyrics etc. This kind of zig-zag movement between the conscious and the preconscious often exceeds the boundaries of the actual therapy sessions. Often the real creative work happens in the clients' private time, when they are writing lyrics or producing ideas for their songs. Thus, it might happen, as was often the case with Punker, that the real therapy session was rather functional; mostly staying at the conscious level because it was centered on ideas that were actually created elsewhere. It does not matter where the ideas come from, as long as the creative process occurs within the overall therapeutic experience.

Working Phase

The early stage of the working phase may be rather "cognitive." In other words, it may stay on a more or less conscious level (see Figure 2). I have never seen this as a problem because attaining trust, developing a working alliance and focusing the content of therapy all need time to develop. I have found that creative, emotional work (i.e., the pre-conscious level in Figure 2) often starts when the roles between the therapist and the client become clear, and when work becomes "automatic." By automatic, I mean the situation where both parties know their roles and tasks and there is no need for verbal planning of the sessions.

With Punker, the first clear sign of this change was when he brought his first lyrics to the session. The lyrics were surprisingly personal, emotional and sensitive, and dealt with issues such as loneliness, anxiety, love, dreams and family relationships. It was also interesting to see how all this sensitivity was hidden in the very noisy and fast music, and how his singing style (more like shouting) actually covered all the content. It was an absolute paradox, yet also a powerful example of how symbolic distance can be utilized. From that moment on, and for a long time thereafter, Punker did the work and I stayed in the background – still present and available, but not intrusively so.

With Bassgirl, it was a somewhat different process. The songs she wrote were perhaps not the most important part of her process - more like a bridge to something else. Her appearance and her songs reminded me of an imitation of how a heavy-rocker should look and sound, rather than a true musical passion. She did not express too much of her inner world in the music, but what really happened was that, outside the musical activities, she became more and more talkative and open. Her fixation on hiding behind a hard heavy ego decreased as well. The latter part of her working phase was based more on open discussion than on making music. There was a motivational shift from making music that was to some extent disconnected with her real inner world, to open, emotional discussion. In her case, music partly served as a mask that helped her to keep something inside her (symbolic distance) because she was not ready to open her inner world to anybody. Although I have emphasized the idea of symbolic distance and avoiding direct talking about problems when working with adolescents, the therapist must also be ready for that if the client is willing to talk.

In the working phase, Dingo-man wrote songs that were musically and lyrically very original. He had had long bouts of illness with lengthy periods at the hospital. His ego was still forming, and he had rather unrealistic thoughts about himself. Song-writing was, for him, a window to a normal world. When we made music, he was more structured – more like a normal adolescent – and able to deal with issues typical of his age group. As a pubescent boy, he was interested in girls and becoming aware of his sexuality, all topics that he dealt with in his songs.

Closing

It is sometimes difficult to work as a therapist with in-patients, because it is often impossible to know the exact length of their hospital stay - something that may endanger a long-term therapy process. Both Bassgirl and Dingo-man were in-patients and their closing phases were not overly prepared or "planned," as the therapist was informed that they would be leaving the hospital only a few weeks before their discharge date. This meant that the closing phase began whether it was appropriate or not. Fortunately, in both cases, the music therapy process had formed a relatively solid structure, which made the premature ending possible and not too damaging.

However, for Punker this was different because he was an outpatient, enabling a systematic therapy process with four phases. When Punker's music therapy was approaching the closing phase – which we both knew – he started to speed up the song-writing process because he wanted to get all the important songs finished. Here he was very systematic. When listening to the songs made during the working phase, it was easy to hear a change in his musical style. The last songs were in slower tempo, more melodic, and with some words distinguishable. A real surprise for the therapist was when he asked him to play a keyboard track on the last song. I felt really honoured to be invited – for the first time – to undertake such a demanding and important task. I also felt that this may have been a way for Punker to thank me for all that we had shared during the process. However, after the first take, my playing was clearly not what the Punker desired and he said "Man, this is not f---king jazz music!" So we recorded the track again, this time successfully.

After the last session, the Punker invited me to his home for coffee. The feeling of this meeting was relaxed, friendly and mutually respectful. I was able to leave feeling as though this young man would now cope with life.

With Bassgirl, we did not really have time to make a clear closing or resolution to her therapy. When she left, she appeared to be more resilient, and we made an agreement that she could return at a later stage - which she did, several months later. Interestingly, I did not recognize her immediately when she returned. Her dress code was totally different, with no dramatic make-up and more of the appearance of "a girl next door." She gave the impression of being much more mature and talked very openly about her current life. Amongst other things, she also told me that she was planning to go to nursing school. I had the feeling that her crisis was more or less resolved, and that music therapy had made some contribution to that process.

As Dingo-man's music therapy ended when the therapist stopped working in the hospital, we had our time to prepare closure. The therapist could not see dramatic change in Dingo-man's condition in either direction. Perhaps this was related to the fact that he was used to being a "patient" and had already lost touch with a normal adolescent's life some time ago. I have not see him since I left this work setting, and I can only hope that music therapy was positive for him. I think that the most important aspect of his music therapy was dealing with his developmental issues (pubescent) and the factors linked to these issues. Music therapy offered the possibility for purposeful, creative functioning instead of getting stuck in his inward-looking thoughts and behavior.

SUMMARY

Both the Punker and Bassgirl had essentially healthy psychic structures beneath their problems. However, the extent of their trauma, and the problems this created for them in their lives, meant that they needed therapeutic understanding and support. They had both created a kind of defensive wall between themselves and others (due to the effect of their traumatic experiences), and this had caused various emotional and/or behavioral disorders. It seems that such symbolic walls are something that prevents one from opening oneself to anybody, and which keeps one's inner feelings and emotions safely inside. The primary task of music therapy was to dismantle this wall, using the therapeutic possibilities inherent in music, combined with the therapist's own personality, experience and skills.

Dingo-man had more severe psychiatric problems. His ego structures were unformed, and his self-concept was unrealistic and undeveloped. In addition, he had been isolated from society for a long time due to his illness. His therapy probably did not include such rewarding moments of improvement and recovery, but it was possible to work with him in a similiar way to the two other cases, despite the fact that his condition was more challenging.

With all these cases, music served as the context for functioning, as well as a general framework for the content and shape of sessions. Most of the psychic work and development could also be seen in the music and musical processes themselves. Music enabled self-expression and helped these clients to describe their own personal reality, attitudes and values. Music was a meeting point between the client and the therapist, and also an irreplaceable motivational factor for the clients. However, this is true only when we speak of the clients' music, because the therapist must respect the client's musical world, accepting it unreservedly. Päivi Saukko, the Finnish music therapist and researcher, wrote that the most important thing for a music therapist working with children is unconditional acceptance, meeting the child in the here and now (Saukko, 2008). I would suggest that this holds true for adolescents' music therapy as well.

My role as music therapist with these clients was as a kind of empathic companion, who enabled their creativity and supported the therapeutic process whenever needed. As such, I had to be ready to step aside or enter in a more active role whenever appropriate and necessary.

Seldom does the therapist engage in therapeutic conversation with an adolescent. More often than not, s/he has to keep their interpretations inside and trust the functionality of the process, placing meaning and importance on the client's creative expression.

Sometimes young clients test the therapist. For example, by telling dubious and shocking facts about their experiences and life. Sometimes these facts are true and sometimes they are a "flight of fancy." Either way, their real meaning is probably to find out the therapist's attitude and responses. It may be also sort of a test where the client's real purpose is to find out the therapist's trustworthiness. In my experience, it is important for the therapist not to cling to these revelations, or overestimate their meaning; they may be of relevance for understanding the client, but the role of a moralist does not fit well to the therapist working with adolescents (Lehtonen, 1999).

In my experience, when working with adolescents, the music therapist has to take different positions in relation to activity and proximity issues. This may be sometimes challenging for a therapist, in particular, when the client is overtly productive and is carrying most of the responsibility of the session content and activities within it. The therapist may feel unprofessional or helpless if s/he does not understand the meaning and power of inactive presence. In my experience, working with adolescents requires that the therapist understands the significance of his/her presence for the client when s/he is not actively contributing to their way of being.

To summarize, the biggest moments of insight for an adolescent's music therapy are perhaps not found in spoken words, but in shared musical moments in which non-verbal interactions and shared experiences form the core of therapeutic change.

REFERENCES

Ahonen-Eerikainen, H. (1998). *"Musiikillinen dialogi" ja mutita musiikkiterapeuttien tyèoskentelytapoja ja lasten musiikiterapian muotoja.* Joensuu: University of Joensuu.

Ala-Ruona, E. (2005). Non-structured initial assessment of psychiatric client in music therapy, *Music Therapy Today,* 6(1), 23-47.

Ala-Ruona, E. (2007). Alkuarviointi kliinisenä käytäntönä psyykkisesti oireilevien asiakkaiden musiikkiterapiassa – Strategioita, menetelmiä ja apukeinoja. Unpublished Dissertation, University of Jyväskylä, Jyväskylä.

Baker, F. & Wigram, T. (2005). *Songwriting. Methods, Techniques and Clinical Applications for Music Therapy Clinicians, Educators and Students*. Philadelphia, PA: Jessica Kingsley Publishers.

Bruscia, K. E. (1998). *The Dynamics of Music Psychotherapy.* Gilsum, NH: Barcelona Publishers.

Erkkilä, J. (1997). Musical improvisation and drawings as tools in the music therapy of children. *Nordic Journal of Music Therapy,* 6(2), 112-120.

Erkkilä, J. (2004). From signs to symbols, from symbols to words - About the relationship between music and language, music therapy and psychotherapy. *Voices,* 4(2).

Eschen, J. T. (Ed.) (2002). *Analytical Music Therapy*. Philadelphia, PA: Jessica Kingsley Publishers.

Gold, C., Voracek, M. & Wigram, T. (2004). Effects of music therapy for children and adolescents with psychopathology: A meta-analysis. *Journal of Child Psychology and Psychiatry,* 6(45), 1054-1063.

Lehtonen, K. (1999). Rap-artisti JJ Kelan tapaus. *Musiikkiterapia,* 2, 71-92.

Lehtonen, K. (2007). *Musiikin symboliset ulottuvuudet*. Jyväskylä: Suomen musiikkiterapiayhdistys r.y.
Levin, C. D. (1989). An Essay on the Symbolic Process. Unpublished Dissertation, Concordia University, Montreal, Canada.
Priestley, M. (1994). *Essays on Analytical Music Therapy*. Phoenixville, PA: Barcelona Publishers.
Saukko, P. (2008). *Musiikkiterapian tavoitteet lapsen kuntoutuksessa*. Jyväskylä: University of Jyväskylä.
Wampold, B. E. (2001). *The Great Psychotherapy Debate*. London: Lawrence Erlbaum Associates.

Chapter Twelve

CROSSING THE DIVIDE: EXPLORING IDENTITIES WITHIN COMMUNITIES FRAGMENTED BY GANG VIOLENCE

Sunelle Fouche and Kerryn Torrance

INTRODUCTION

This case describes six group music therapy sessions that took place with adolescent boys who attended school in the Heideveld area, outside Cape Town's city centre, South Africa. This so-called 'colored'[1] community was established in the 1960's as part of the Apartheid Government's Group Areas Act and many of the older residents of Heideveld can still remember being forcefully moved here from inner city suburbs. Heideveld is plagued by a range of social problems including violence, poverty, unemployment and substance abuse. In the foreground of these depressing social features lies ongoing gang violence that has been part of this community for many generations and impacts every aspect of life in Heideveld.

The boys who attended these music therapy sessions are part of the Music Therapy Community Clinic's[2] (MTCC's) *Music for Life* program. This program takes place after school in one of the local school buildings and is facilitated by both community musicians and music the-

---

[1] In South Africa, the color of our skin is directly related to our cultural identities. In this chapter we therefore do refer to people as being 'Colored,' 'Black' and 'White'. Although the term 'Colored' might be seen as an offensive term to an international audience, in South Africa it is a term comfortably used by many 'people of color' to describe their specific cultural group. The writers agree with Zimitri Erasmus when he says: *"There is no such thing as the Black 'race'. Blackness, whiteness and colouredness exist, but they are cultural, historical and political identities"* (Erasmus, 2001 p .12).

[2] The Music Therapy Community Clinic (MTCC) is a non-profit organization that provides music therapy services and other music activities to previously disadvantaged and underprivileged communities in Cape Town, South Africa.

rapists. Approximately 120 children come from the surrounding schools at least once a week to take part in a group of their choice. Currently, we have a choir, two marimba groups and two drumming groups. The boys featured in this chapter are members of two of these groups. During school time, the very same classrooms are used by our music therapists to conduct music therapy sessions with children and youth referred by teachers.

While the focus of this chapter is the six music therapy sessions that took place with this group of boys, it is only a small part of their ongoing therapeutic work in the *Music for Life* program. It is therefore not possible to consider the work without understanding the broader context of the *Music for Life* program, the surrounding schools, the community of Heideveld, and even the townships that surround and impact the Heideveld community.

FOUNDATIONAL CONCEPTS

Understanding the context in which our work takes place and the ways we have adapted our music therapy approach have been central to the development of the MTCC. When we founded the MTCC in 2003, our music therapy program was limited to individual and closed group sessions for children traumatized by incidents such as the death of a close family member, exposure to violence, abuse, neglect or abandonment. We adopted the 'traditional' role of a music therapist and turned the room that the school provided us into a sacred music therapy space, where short-term clinical interventions happened once a week. However, children would bang on the music therapy room door and could not understand why only some children were allowed to partake in this new "music therapy thing." We realized that we were only reaching a small group of children in our music therapy program and that there were countless others who were confronted with the negative effects of living in a community ravaged by poverty, gang violence and substance abuse. We decided to offer an after-school music program that provided children with a space to learn musical skills, as well as a space where they could explore different experiences of themselves within this community. Children began to 'self-refer' and soon we realized that our music therapy practice seemed to be crossing the boundaries of what we perceived music therapy to be.

At a similar time, dialogue was beginning to take place within the music therapy community about the emergence of something called 'Community Music Therapy' (Stige 2002, Ansdell 2002). While those talking about it were reluctant to give it a definition (Ansdell & Pavlicevic, 2004), one thing emerged that resonated with many of the discussions we had been having – Community Music Therapy's basic premise was that it was a context- and culture-sensitive practice (Pavlicevic, 2004; Stige, 2004); meaning that it needed to be able to adapt to the ever-changing needs of the community it served. It also implied that the whole community can become the music therapy client (Stige, 2004), rather than addressing the individual alone and out of context.

One of these adaptations, discussed by Stige (2002, 2004), is the importance of collaboration and the need to expand music therapy practice "beyond the triad of client, therapists and music." As such, we began to include community musicians in our team. Our music therapists also began to take on roles not traditionally associated with music therapy clinical practice: supporter, organizer, co-facilitator, relationship builder, group process director and mentor, as well as using conventional music therapy skills in new and innovative ways (Oosthuizen, Fouche and Torrance, 2007).

Our community musicians have not been an 'added extra' to our project teams. Rather, they have been essential in being able to offer a culturally sensitive service. The children in Heideveld lack role models from their community; the boys in particular lack male role models as many of them have lost their fathers to violence, AIDS, long work shifts away from home or even the local jail. As 'white' females from completely different communities, there was little we could do to fill this gap. Furthermore, these musicians bring with them musical skill and knowledge that is very specific to their culture and which we view as vitally important to the development of the children's cultural identity (Stige, 2004; Oosthuizen, Fouche and Torrance, 2007).

Stige (2002, 2004) also spoke of Community Music Therapy's different venues for practice that included semi-public and public arenas of performance. This resonated strongly with the MTCC's practice, where clients often moved between the private arena of the music therapy room and the public arena of our *Music for Life* program, which affords opportunities for concerts and 'showing off' developing talent. We believe that both the private and public arenas provide different but equally important opportunities for the development of individual and group identities.

As the Heideveld Project has developed over the past eight years, we have found that most of the music therapists find working with groups (rather than individuals) more valuable. We suspect that this could be because the majority of our referrals are for socially-based issues that are best addressed in groups - reflecting the community at large. We use a variety of activities in our sessions, including improvisation, song-writing, movement, story telling and listening. We found the guiding principles expressed in McFerran and Wigram's (2002) review of current practices in group music therapy improvisation very valuable when reflecting on the therapeutic potential of music with this group of boys:

- Music offers the opportunity to express ideas and feelings that are abstract and vague, whereas words are exact and specific .
- All group members are able to speak together at once because music works both in time and on time .
- Music can be safer than words.
- Music can be used as a defense, or as a place to hide, by avoiding the kind of specific expression that words demand.
- Music is able to provide a way of expressing feelings that people are not willing to express verbally because it involves some risk.
- Group music-making is experienced as an interactive entity that overcomes individual issues , a joint creation that can be stepped into and shared by all participants.
- Each group becomes a miniature society.

THE CLIENTS

The twelve boys around whom this case study revolves are all between 12 and 15 years of age. The marimba group consists of six boys from the community of Heideveld. The drumming group, also consisting of six boys, contains two from Heideveld and four from the neighboring Xhosa[3] community of Gugulethu. A few of the boys referred themselves, as the opportunity to take part in a music group was appealing. However,

---
[3] The Xhosa people are one of South Africa's multiple cultural groups.

the majority of the boys were referred by their teachers for constantly fighting on the playground and general aggression toward teachers and peers. While their aggression may be more overt than that of other boys in their class, they are not unlike many of their peers. At this critical age, when they are beginning to form their adult identities, they are at risk of being inducted into local gangs.

Gangs have been part of the social structures of both these communities for many generations. They impact every aspect of the lives of their residents. Heideveld is divided into different sections that gangs proclaim as their territory. Children often 'inherit' their gang membership from their parents or older siblings and, armed with knifes and guns, these young boys are prepared to lay down their lives to protect their gang's pride and territory (Dissel, 1997).

Forced racial segregation – a legacy left by the Apartheid Government – is still playing itself out in the country, even though South Africa is 16 years into its democracy. Gugulethu is a 'Black,' Xhosa-speaking Township. Heideveld is a 'colored,' Afrikaans-speaking community. For the past few years, some Xhosa children have been attending local Heideveld schools. We have noticed that territorial thinking, the notion of 'us vs. them,' is playing itself out in the schools in what looks like racially motivated fighting. As our *Music for Life* groups naturally reflect the larger communities from which the children come, we were not surprised when one afternoon a fight occurred after the two groups had finished rehearsing. Their perceived differences - different music groups, different cultures, different communities, different languages - had caused a divide, and they were responding to this in the only way they knew.

After some discussion amongst the MTCC's music therapists and community musicians, it was decided that these two groups would benefit from coming together in the music therapy room, while simultaneously continuing with their *Music for Life* groups. For this reason, it was difficult to define where the therapeutic process began or ended with this group of boys. While they had only six 'official' music therapy sessions together, we took a more holistic view of what was therapeutic, viewing both the *Music for Life* program and the music therapy sessions as crucial to their process. Later in the chapter, we will therefore reflect on the six music therapy sessions within the broader context of the

MTCC's approach to therapeutic intervention within the community of Heideveld.

Assessment

A key learning for us in the MTCC's Heideveld Project has revolved around flexibility in order to respond to the ever-changing needs of this dynamic community. The process of assessment and reflection is therefore a crucial and continuous part of our practice. However, how, where and when our assessment takes place is not bound by conventional norms and means. Due to the fact that we work within the midst of communities, our assessment tools and procedures involve more than just the therapist and client. We rely on the community at large.

The fact that the MTCC team witnessed the fight that broke out between the boys meant that we could respond immediately. Furthermore, working in this community week after week, and having worked with the boys in weekly music rehearsals, meant that we had some sense of how these boys presented themselves within their communities. We also had a sense of how the community – teachers, parents, peers – perceived them, and we had first-hand experience of the 'troublesome' behavior that the community was informing us about.

In an assessment meeting that included the community musicians and music therapists, we discussed the incident and the possible reasons and 'meaning' behind it. The fight was racially motivated, rooted in the boys' preconceived ideas about each other. We suspected that these perceptions had been passed on to them by the older generation that lived within a very different political and cultural world than that of present day South Africa. One of the goals of our *Music for Life* program was to offer these children the opportunity to celebrate diversity through music. It was decided that bringing the two groups together in a music therapy space could offer opportunities for experiencing themselves and each other in a different way. At the following rehearsals, the idea of bringing the groups together was discussed with the two separate groups. While they were aware that the reason behind the temporary amalgamation was due to the fight, the discussions revolved around the musical potential of joining the groups. In typical adolescent style, they nonchalantly agreed to our proposal.

THE THERAPEUTIC PROCESS

The following two vignettes (1a and 1b) are a depiction of the two separate groups at their weekly *Music for Life* rehearsals before the amalgamation for music therapy sessions.

Vignette 1a – Thursday Afternoon, Djembe Drumming Group.

The boys walk into the room. They don't have much to say. They're from different schools, different communities and it all feels a little uncomfortable. They respond with mono-syllabic grunts and a cautious nod to the community musician's questions. The music starts – it provides a relief to the awkwardness. The drums are all the same size, with the potential to make the same sounds – it's almost as if the drums make everyone equal. But there are still moments when each person has a chance to play a solo – to be heard as the individual that he is. The drumming begins to grow into something quite raucous. It feels as if there is very little silence for the rest of the session. The drumming is loud and powerful and noisy – its potential is limitless. The music therapist leaves with a headache.

Vignette 1b – Thursday Afternoon, Marimba Group.

The boys are walking towards the Music for Life *room and the energy is palpable – they're excited, eager to get going, mocking and swearing at other children along the way. They enter the room and pass a cheeky comment to the music therapist. There's no time for talking as this keeps them from playing. The community musician hasn't even arrived yet but there is no way to restrain them – someone starts playing and very quickly everyone is playing on their own marimba. It is immediately clear that playing these instruments is physically demanding and the music absorbs the high energy that the boys exude. It is also obvious that each group member has a role to play, and each role is respected. Someone needs to play the bass, someone else the melody and each part is equally valued.*

The above vignettes paint a picture of how the *Music for Life* rehearsals are able to elicit and contain the high energy levels of these boys. The community musicians who run the sessions are skilled at teaching marimba and djembe drums, understanding the cultural significance of these powerful instruments. We believe that the instruments themselves have played an "important role in these boys' development of self and identity in relation to their community" (Stige 2004). In both communities that the boys come from (Gugulethu and Heideveld), musicians are highly respected and valued role models. This is one of the many reasons that the MTCC's practice includes these community musicians. The role of the music therapist in these sessions, however, is still of great importance. She needed to assist the community musician in managing group dynamics and therapeutic process to ensure that the rehearsals were not about transference of musical skill only. This collaboration has been a vital part of providing a service that is both culturally and contextually sensitive.

Vignette 2: 'Step into the Circle,' From Session 2 of the Music Therapy Sessions

The week after the two groups had the fight, a discussion was held between the involved music therapists, community musicians and the boys from both groups. After they all agreed to the amalgamation, the groups came together for music therapy sessions the very next week. The first session consisted of introductions, greeting rituals and semi-structured group improvisations. The following vignette describes a pivotal moment and an activity from session two, which was then used and developed each week.

The group members, consisting of the twelve boys, two community musicians and three music therapists, are seated on chairs organized in a circle with four big drums placed in the centre. The atmosphere in the room is tense... but I expected this: bringing these two groups together usually causes tension, which has on previous occasions led to fighting. Today I have decided to do an activity that will confirm the group members' differences, but hopefully also highlight similarities. I ask them to step into the circle and play on the drum if they live in Gugulethu: two boys and one community musician stand up and they beat on the drums. I then ask them to step into the circle and beat the drum if they live in Heideveld: four boys respond. I ask the members to step into the circle and beat the drum if they have lost a parent: Several boys and adults stand up and I notice that as they beat the drums, they also take a moment to make eye contact with the others in the inner circle. I ask the group to step into the circle and beat the drum if they have seen (in their communities) people who are older than them fighting, stabbing or shooting each other: the majority of the group stands up. I ask the group to step into the circle if that scares them sometimes: I am surprised that the ones who often boast about not being scared of anything stand up and beat the drum. I ask that they beat the drum if they are sometimes bullied, and I am very proud of Luvuyo, who is usually the 'underdog,' when he stands up and beats the drum with conviction. I ask that they beat the drum when they are sometimes the ones doing the bullying: at first, no one moves, and then two of his closest friends indicate to Damian that he will have to stand up...which he does. I ask the group to step into the circle and beat the drums if they like playing music: they move like one, and the sounds coming from the drums are boisterous.

This activity was very structured in order to provide safe and containing guidelines for the group members to participate. On reflection, the directing music therapist commented that she had felt the need to address the division as early on in the therapeutic process as possible and in a direct manner. Her sense was that in order for the boys to shift their preconceived ideas about each other, they would need to enter into a potentially vulnerable space where they would be quite exposed in front of their peers. Her role now was to finely attune to the non-verbal cues and decide on the right moments to ask the 'heavy' or 'light' questions. This, combined with music as the buffer, and the fact that everyone, including the other music therapists and community musicians were responding, resulted in a rich and rewarding experience for all.

The activity described above was used in each subsequent session as it was a powerful way to 'sound out' similarities and differences between the boys. It gave musical expression to things that were difficult to talk about. Being able to play their answers seemed much safer than speaking them. On the other hand, moving into the circle was a brave and bold act, giving physical expression to their answers and allowing the others to witness them. Group members could 'speak' at the same time in the music, which for a group of awkward adolescents can be a less risky option than having to talk. Furthermore, due to the fact that music has the ability to express abstract ideas, the manner in which they played on the drum was able to express something of the complex emotions surrounding the particular question to which they were responding.

Also evident from the above vignette is that there were three music therapists and two community musicians present in the six music therapy sessions. What may not be so clear is the reason why. One music therapist was responsible for running the sessions. She was not linked to the two groups of boys and was thus able to take on a neutral role. The other two music therapists and the community musicians were now seen as part of the groups as they facilitated the marimba and drumming groups each week. In the music therapy sessions, the community musician's roles shifted and instead of being 'teachers' and 'leaders,' they simply became role models – fellow community members – with little expectation of the boys to 'perform' or behave in a particular way. The presence of the music therapists (from another cultural group) meant that there were five adults present in the sessions who could model healthy relationships across different cultures.

Sessions also included free improvisations, but the music therapist felt that these either felt quite superficial or became 'messy,' and the boys did not feel secure enough (as you can imagine) to reflect on them. The 'Step into the Circle' activity, on the other hand, provided sufficient guidance to contain the group members, while allowing more and more flexibility each week as the boys began to trust the structure. By the last session, they had made it their own song.

Vignette 3: Last Session Song

We are about 20 minutes into the session. This will be our last session, as a three-week school vacation is starting tomorrow. There is a lot of excitement in the room. We are all sitting on chairs in a big circle. For the past 20 minutes we have been working on putting a rap song together. The chorus repeats the line 'Step into the circle and play on the drum if....,' and then each group member has a turn to respond with a line that has become meaningful to them over the past few weeks, which the rest of the group then repeats. Kyle, from the marimba group, is keeping the beat on a djembe drum and Vuyo, community musician from the drumming group, is accompanying with a shaker. The style of the song is Hip-Hop and some of the boys fall right into the groove – tapping their feet, moving their bodies and making hand gestures – imitating their idols like Eminem and Tupac. Their contributions to this communal song include the following:

> *Step into the circle and play in the drum if....*
> *You love the people*
> *You're happy*
> *You love peace*
> *You've lost a friend*
> *You live in Heideveld*
> *You've been in love*
> *You love your mother*
> *You've lost your dad*
> *You love music.*

The song ends and Damien gets up to get a drink of water from the tap in the corner of the room. He comes back with a glass of water for Abongile who is sitting next to him. Two months ago, Damien and Abongile were the instigators of the fight outside the music room that set this whole process in motion.

The above song was written by the whole group, and it was obvious that it developed from the second session's 'Step into the Circle' activity. As the weeks progressed, the activity began to change and develop organically. Each person brought something to the creative process, be it a contribution of words, how it was orchestrated, who should say or sing what and when – the boys, the music therapists and the community musicians all contributed to this closing session product. The sentiments expressed in the song include the desire for peace, the issue of loss, as well as typical adolescent topics of being in love and their relationship with their mothers. In all likelihood, this song was a message to their broader communities, who were struggling with violence, untimely death of children, siblings and parents, and gender issues.

Moments like these are common in our music therapy program, and songs such as these often find their way into *Music for Life* performances, where the applause reveals that there are others who agree wholeheartedly with the message. We view this group of boys (and other groups like them) as a micro-representation of the societies from which they come, and it is clear to see why the MTCC resonates with the Community Music Therapy idea that the whole community is, in actual fact, the client (Stige, 2004.

Vignette 4: End of Year Concert

The hall is packed, and it's been a raucous evening of performances and audience participation. Parents, from both Heideveld and Gugulethu, peers, some teachers and curious residents from the surrounding area have been cheering, dancing (some a little inebriated) and supporting the children on stage. It is the annual end-of-year Music for Life *concert that is held in a local church hall, 500 meters from the school that the MTCC works from. It is the final item on the evening's program, and all of the Music for Life groups have combined for the 'Grand Finale.' To those who don't know the background, the fact that the drumming group is perched on the stage, directly above the marimba group, is nothing to be noted. But there they are, uncomfortably close, both groups playing their instruments with conviction and great skill. The occasional taunt flies from one group to the other, but it is more lighthearted and sibling-like. Apart from playing together for some of the verses, each group gets to accompany the choir on their own. No doubt, there is an air of competition about whose accompaniment sounds better – but they function as two units of the same whole, and their pride is obvious.*

While we are very aware that this process did not magically heal the divide that exists between these boys, we believe that in the moments of creating music together (and especially as they experienced their joint product), the metaphor of musical interaction made a lasting impression on how they experience both their individual and group identity.

The end-of-year concert took place five months after the final music therapy session with these twelve boys. The groups continued with their weekly *Music for Life* rehearsals, and as the concert drew closer, there was more emphasis on perfecting the music for their performance. Moving into the arena of performance had its own therapeutic value for these boys. More willingly, they began to focus their energy on creating something that sounded 'good.' Being received and validated by their communities as talented and skilled musicians stood in stark contrast to the identities that they may have portrayed as 'trouble makers.' Once again, this is where viewing the community as client holds immense value. This concert was a celebration of some of the successes of the therapeutic journey that these boys continue to make. We also hope that it was of therapeutic value to disillusioned parents, teachers, principals and community members and an opportunity for them to hear (in musical form) the intrinsic possibility of community unity.

SUMMARY

This case study has described the therapeutic journey of twelve boys from our *Music for Life* project. These boys were involved in a fight on the school premises that was rooted in racial tension and perceived differences between the members of two separate after-school music groups. While the after-school music groups and therapy sessions described in the chapter took place on the premises of a local primary school, we are more inclined to describe the context of our work as the broader community of Heideveld and the surrounding townships. This is because we view the children and the issues with which they present as a micro-representation of the communities from which they come.

The twelve boys discussed in this chapter moved between two of the MTCC's programs as the need arose. In fact, some of the boys are still involved with some of our community musicians and music therapists as part of the *Music for Life* program. The six music therapy sessions discussed made use of semi-structured improvisations and song-writing. The structure contained the boys and their adolescent vulnerability, while the music provided opportunities for them to sound out and express their similarities and differences in a way that was more abstract and less threatening than verbal discussion.

Lastly, we could not discuss this case study without referring to the journey of the music therapists and community musicians. We believe that we could not have provided a culturally appropriate service without collaborating with community musicians from the local communities.

Our roles as music therapists have also been challenged and extended as we adopt a less traditional role in order to ensure that we maintain a practice that is sensitive to the ever-changing needs of the community within which we work.

We believe that the above observations of collaboration, adaptation and flexible spontaneity are in line with the principles of Community Music Therapy practice. By employing this practice, we believe that we have provided different opportunities for these boys to develop both their personal and social identities. The dream is that healthier identities will lead to healthier communities.

REFERENCES

Ansdell, G. (2002). Community Music Therapy and the winds of change. *Voices: A World Forum for Music Therapy, 2(2).* http://www.voices.no/mainissues/Voices2(2)ansdell.html.

Dissel, A. (1997). Youth, street gangs and violence in South Africa. In *Proceedings of International Symposium: Youth, Street Culture and Urban Violence in Africa.* Abidjan, Ivory Coast.

Erasmus, Z (Ed.) (2001). *Coloured by History, Shaped by Place.* Cape Town: Kwela Books.

McFerran, K. & Wigram, T. (2002). A review of current practice in group music therapy improvisations. *British Journal of Music Therapy*, 16(1), 46-55.

Oosthuizen, H., Fouché, S. & Torrance, K. (2007). Collaborative work: Negotiations between music therapists and community musicians in the development of a South African Community Music Therapy Project. *Voices: A World Forum for Music Therapy*, 7(3). http://www.voices.no/mainissues/mi40007000243.php.

Pavlicevic, M. & Ansdell, G. (Eds.) (2004). *Community Music Therapy.* London: Jessica Kingsley Publishers.

Pavlicevic, M. (2004). Learning from *Thembalethu:* Towards responsive and responsible practice in Community Music Therapy. In M. Pavlicevic and G. Ansdell (Eds.), *Community Music Therapy.* London: Jessica Kingsley Publishers.

Stige, B. (2002). *Culture-Centered Music Therapy.* Gilsum, NH: Barcelona Publishers.

Stige, B. (2004). Community Music Therapy: Culture, care and welfare. In M. Pavlicevic and G. Ansdell (Eds.), *Community Music Therapy*. London: Jessica Kingsley Publishers.

Chapter Thirteen

OUR PATH TO PEACE: SONGWRITING-BASED BRIEF MUSIC THERAPY WITH BEREAVED ADOLESCENTS

Robert E. Krout

INTRODUCTION

Experiencing the death of a child is one of the most difficult losses for family members to accept, cope with, and adjust to (Children's Hospice International, 2005; Fletcher, 2002; Pavlicevic, 2005; Robb, 2003; Rosof, 1994). Even when a child has a life-limiting illness, such as a terminal cancer, and is expected to die, few families know what to do when that child does die (Armstrong-Dailey & Zarbock, 2001; De Cinque, Monterosso, Dadd, Sidhu, & Lucas, 2004). Parents and caregivers are challenged as to how to help themselves, as well as surviving siblings (Bright, 2002). The death of a sibling can be an especially difficult and significant life-impacting event for adolescents (Birenbaum, 2000; Doka, 2000). The grieving process interacts with core adolescent concerns of gaining mastery and control over their environment, having a sense of belonging, and seeking fairness and justice in their lives (Fleming & Adolph, 1986). This chapter describes the use of strategic songwriting-based brief music therapy with a group of young adolescents during a single session that took place at a three-day family bereavement retreat. This approach incorporated concepts from brief therapy, cognitive therapy and insight therapy (Krout, 2005a; 2006).

FOUNDATIONAL CONCEPTS

Moos (1995) describes how bereaved adolescents adapt to the death of a loved one through establishing the personal meaning of the loss, maintaining an emotional balance, sustaining interpersonal relationships, and preserving a satisfactory self-image. Balk (1996) articulates a cognitive approach to bereavement therapy with grieving adolescents, emphasizing the need for them to develop a variety of coping skills, including dealing with the reality of the loss and learning how to respond to life changes as a result of the death. Many adolescents have a strong need to belong and not seem different from peers that may cause them to hide outward signs or expressions of grieving (Corr & Corr, 1996). Forward and Garlie (2003) describe the adolescent bereavement process as variable, encompassing five stages of finding out, avoiding reality, facing reality, turning the corner and finding new meaning versus ending the search. In each of these stages, the adolescent focuses on the basic psychological process of the search for new meaning.

Group activities may help adolescents organize the confusing experience of grief and facilitate their gaining insight into what they are going through, as they may feel a frightening loss of control (Duncan, Joselow & Hilden, 2006; Holliday, 2002; Perschy, 2004; Snyder, 2008). Among group grief services for siblings of children who have died are complementary modalities such as creative arts interventions (Bright, 2002; Brooks & O'Rourke, 2002; Desai, Ng, & Bryant, 2002; Hasenfus & Franceschi, 2003; Hilliard, 2001; Jimerson, 2005; Krout, 2002, 2005b; Lehmann, Jimerson, & Gaasch, 2001a, 2001b, 2001c, 2001d; Mondanaro, 2005; Rufin, Creed & Jarvis, 1997). These address a wide range of concerns, with a particular focus on self expression.

The use of music therapy experiences in grief interventions for bereaved children and adolescents are designed to help them with issues relating to the validation, identification, clarification, normalization and expression of feelings (Bright, 2002; Dalton & Krout, 2005, 2006; Gilmer, 2002; Hilliard, 2001, 2007, 2008; Hogan & Roberts, 2005; Krout, 1999, 2002, 2005b, 2006; Krout & Jones, 2005; McFerran-Skewes, 2000; McFerran-Skewes & Grocke, 2000; McFerran-Skewes & Erdonmez-Grocke, 2000; Roberts, 2006; Skewes, 2000; Skewes & Grocke, 2000; Teahan, 2000). For example, McFerran-Skewes (2001) investigated a psychodynamic approach to music therapy group work with younger, bereaved adolescents. The author conducted and analyzed in-depth interviews with the participants following a course of ten music therapy sessions. She reported that their desires for freedom, control, fun and achievement of cohesion within the group were essential in successfully addressing their grief needs (McFerran-Skewes, 2001).

Music therapy bereavement interventions for adolescents have included the specific use of song-writing-based experiences. In one two-part study, Dalton and Krout (2005, 2006) described the development and implementation of the Grief Song-Writing Process (GSWP) with bereaved adolescents. First, a thematic analysis was completed of 123 songs previously written by bereaved adolescents in individual music therapy sessions that expressed core concerns regarding the death of their loved one and how they were coping since the death. Second, existing grief models were compared with these song theme areas, and an integrated grief model was developed that included five identified grief process areas. Next, a systematized seven-session group GSWP protocol was developed and implemented, during which adolescents created music and wrote original lyrics to songs that focused on each of the five grief process areas: understanding, feeling, remembering, integrating and growing. These last two process areas, integrating and growing, may be related to the model described as continuing bonds (Webb, 2004). Webb (2004) and others have suggested that siblings should not be encouraged to disengage from the deceased but to continue their bonds, thus aiding in their developmental task of mastery. Packman, Horsley, Davies and Kramer (2006) discussed the unique and continued relationships formed by bereaved children and adolescents following the death of a sibling.

In the present example, a group of young adolescents served as a single case for this chapter, which combined design elements of a naturalistic treatment case study with an outcome–based evaluative case study (Bruscia, 1991; Smeijsters, 2005). I incorporated several theoretical approaches represented through a songwriting-based approach to music therapy, including brief therapy, cognitive therapy, insight therapy, process-oriented songwriting and strategic songwriting (Brunk, 1998; Darrow, 2004; Hanser, 1999; Krout, 2005a, 2006). Treatment occurred during one session. Although unusual for case studies, a single session approach may be appropriate in grief and bereavement work when the clinician knows in advance that there will only be one session and a single opportunity to work with a specific group of clients due to the nature of the treatment setting, client goals, and advance scheduling (Krout, 2005a, 2006).

In this session, the young adolescents re-wrote lyrics to a song I composed for the sole purpose of working with this group on this occasion. The song represented the overall theme for the retreat, that of each family (and family member) finding their own "path to peace" as part of their unique grief journeys. This theme was developed during retreat staff planning sessions in which I took part. It is important to note that the weekend retreat was designed to be supportive in nature, and was not intended to substitute for intensive or on-going counseling for the parents and sibling participants. Instead, it was designed to incorporate and reflect what Teahan (2000) termed the "V.I.N.E." concept, which refers to the use of creative arts therapies in facilitating the validation, identification, normalization and expression of feelings, thoughts and emotions of bereaved family members as part of a natural and organic grieving process.

THE CLIENTS

This songwriting-based music therapy session took place with a group of young bereaved adolescents at a three-day family bereavement retreat run by a not-for-profit bereavement organization. The adolescents were all part of attending families who had experienced the death of a sibling/child. The services of the bereavement organization were offered to the families in a number of ways. Brochures about the organization were available at pediatric hospitals, cancer care centers and hospice facilities in the area. Social workers and child life specialists at these facilities were also made aware of the available services by the organization, and as such, families often knew about the grief services before or shortly after the death of their child. As a result, families who were interested in the services of the organization visited the web site for specific programs offered or contacted the organization by phone or e-mail. The family weekend retreat, offered twice per year, was one of the programs offered and described.

Assessment

Prior to the retreat weekend, I was provided with information regarding how many young adolescents were scheduled to be in my group (nine), their grief and loss backgrounds (included both sudden and anticipated sibling deaths), their ages (11-13) and their genders (four males and five females). Intake and assessment information on all sibling participants was provided by parents as part of the application process. This included information about the deceased child, such as dates of child's birth, death and cause of death. Causes of death included neuroblastoma, leukemia, kidney and renal failures, metabolic disorder, immune deficiency, trisomy, congenital heart defect and staph infection. Information on each sibling participant was also provided, including their age at the time of the death, current home and school placement information, age of and relationships with other surviving siblings, nature of any grief services provided before or after the death (including participation in retreats offered by our organization) and how the sibling had been coping since the death. Other relevant information such as sibling medical conditions and medications currently being taken was also provided.

Another portion of the application asked parents to describe what they wanted to "get out of" the retreat for both themselves and their children. The information was reviewed by retreat staff, who were all mental health professionals volunteering for the retreat. All staff had previous experience working with bereaved families, and many worked as clinicians at local pediatric hospitals or hospice organizations. If a family appeared to be appropriate for the retreat after review of their application, they were invited to take part. If the family did not appear to be appropriate for the retreat (for example, the death being less than one month prior), or that parents described what appeared to be symptoms of complicated mourning (Rando, 1993), the family was contacted by staff and offered other alternatives to the retreat. These alternatives included grief counseling for the family.

The overall goal of the retreat, as described to the parents, was to provide the children, adolescents and adults with a safe and supportive environment in which to share their losses and the changes in their lives since these losses. The retreat was also intended to provide interventions and experiences to help them identify and express feelings and emotions, as well as to explore adaptive strategies suited to their unique situations.

THE THERAPEUTIC PROCESS

During the retreat, siblings were seen in separate process and recreation groups, and were organized into groups by age (3-4 year olds, 5 year olds, 6-7 year olds, 8-10 year olds, 11-13 year olds, and 14 years and older). There were also process-oriented family sessions and experiences in which they took part. Additional separate process groups were held for parents as couples, and for moms and dads separately. A music therapy facilitator served as co-leader of each sibling group. At this weekend retreat, I co-facilitated a process group with a child life specialist who worked full-time at a pediatric cancer center and who had experience in working with bereaved children and adolescents. The group included nine 11-13 year olds; four males and five females. Although music therapy experiences were included in three of the group sessions with these nine participants, the songwriting itself took place during one 90-minute session.

The method of therapy involved engaging the group in a songwriting experience, creating new lyrics to the song "Our Path to Peace" (see Table 1). At the time I wrote the song, the retreat staff had an idea of how many young adolescents were likely to register, their grief and loss backgrounds, and their genders. With this information in mind, I wanted to create a song that could be used with the group and individualized via active songwriting for each participant in the group. Again, the "path to peace" title and focus was chosen for the song due to the fact that this was the theme selected by the retreat staff for the entire weekend. When families registered for the retreat, this "path to peace" title and theme was featured in the registration information and application.

For the music therapist using songwriting as an intervention, the issue of who actually writes the song is crucial (Krout, 2005b). One important consideration is how much session time and how many sessions can be devoted to this, as a song may take several sessions to complete if working from scratch. I knew that our songwriting session would take place during one 90-minute session. As such, I wrote the song prior to the retreat, but planned to involve the participants in re-writing the lyrics during the session. This approach represents a combination of strategic songwriting (song written ahead of time for clinical use), process songwriting (song written as a process experience by/with the participants) and lyric re-writing (Baker & Wigram, 2005; Brunk, 1998; Krout, 2006). I did this because of how I wanted to use the song in the group, and how much time (one session) was available for this music therapy intervention.

I wanted to engage the participants in exploring the theme for the retreat and to use the song to foster discussion regarding each participant's relationship to the theme via the concepts and metaphors embedded in the song. This song was designed to serve as a departure point for sharing, and the beginning of a group process for the weekend. I wanted to share some thoughts and concepts for the participants to react to, and to use the song in fostering discussion regarding these concepts.

The session began with introductions and a review of confidentiality guidelines (i.e., "What we say here stays here"). Each group member was invited to "tell their story" and share about his/her sibling who had died. Most of the group members shared briefly, and only three participants elaborated on their losses for more than several sentences. This was expected, as for adolescents, sharing about their personal sibling loss histories can be both difficult and intimidating (Birenbaum, 2000). Both myself and my co-leader assured the participants that they did not have to share more than they felt comfortable with at that time.

I next told the participants "Here is a song I wrote that relates to the theme of this retreat and to some of the issues we will explore this weekend. For now, just listen to the song, and we can talk about it afterwards if you wish. You can also re-write the lyrics if you want to make the song your own. I am passing out copies of the lyrics so you can follow along." I felt that starting with a receptive experience in which I played and sang the song while the participants just listened would be a safe and non-threatening experience for them. The original lyrics, as well as the lyrics re-written by the group, can be seen in Table 1. A lead sheet for the song as re-written (verse 1 and chorus) can be seen in Appendix 1.

I then played and sang the song with guitar accompaniment. Following the song, I asked if anyone in the group wanted to comment on or talk about the lyrics. After a moment of (anticipated) silence, one

12-year-old boy whose younger sister had died the year before of renal failure, began the discussion by saying that the path to peace might be found inside of us rather than externally like a path one walks on. Several participants agreed with him, and a 13-year-old girl followed up, suggesting that the path might be in heaven, where she thinks her baby sister is. Conversation continued, and we explored a number of concepts imbedded in the original lyrics.

I next asked if the group would like to re-write some of the lyrics, to which the participants responded positively. I wrote the original lyrics in the first person plural so that the singer would be in the voice of, and represent, the point of view of the group. I also wanted the song to help contribute to these individualized processes within the environment of this particular session and the grief retreat as a whole. This appeared to work, as participants discussed the lyrics, related them to their own losses and situations and offered new lyrics. The songwriting process also offered participants opportunities to reflect on and process their unique grief situations both as individuals and as a group, which was the clinical intention. This can be seen in the new lyrics, which include personal pronouns that are both first person singular and plural (e.g., you, we), as well as first person and plural possessive pronouns (e.g., your, our).

Although several participants made multiple suggestions for lyric changes, all group members offered at least one suggested lyric change. In addition, all suggested lyrics were explored and discussed by the group, which made the decision on whether or not to include the newly suggested lyrics in the song, or stick with the original lyrics. I served as scribe for the group, writing down the suggested lyrics and reading them back to the group for reflection, discussion, clarification or alteration. After new lyrics were suggested and discussed, I sang the new song line containing the lyrics so the group could hear how it sounded when sung. Some of the participants began to sing along with me after I invited them to do so.

Table 1. Lyrics to "Our Path to Peace".

Original Lyrics	Re-Written Group Lyrics
<u>Verse 1</u> From this journey we are on Come the moments which have grown To bring the rising of the dawn And you before us	<u>Verse 1</u> We wait for you and love you We wait for you and miss you To bring the rising of the dawn And you to join us
So as this new day comes to pass Changing shape and moving fast Forming memories that will last Of you within us	So as your life comes to pass Shaping lives and leaving fast Storing memories that will last Of you within us
<u>Chorus</u> We are standing here Remembering you and holding dear The light of love Reflections of The hearts that will not cease	<u>Chorus</u> We will stop here To remember you and hold you dear The light of love Reflections of Our hearts that go on forever
To move forward still As days grow bright our journey will Begin each day To show the way Along our path to peace	To move forward still As days grow bright journey will Begin each day And show the way Along our path to our peace
<u>Verse 2</u> Today we turn our thoughts to you All the dreams that we've been through	<u>Verse 2</u> Today we turn our love to you All the thoughts that we've gone through
Living every day anew Your light among us	Living every day anew You're flying among us
So here we share our hopes and touch	So here we share our hopes and touch
A future bright you are with us	Our future bright, now you're with us
Each step we take it means so much You're walking with us	Each step we take you mean so much And you're holding onto us

The lyric changes for the second half of verse two also seemed significant. The sentence "Each step we take it means so much, you're walking with us" was changed to "Each step we take you mean so much, and you're holding onto us." The boy who offered this change shared that they (the surviving siblings) were the ones walking on their grief journeys. He said that their deceased brothers and sisters couldn't walk anymore (being dead), but that their spirits could hold onto them as they walked. In this way, they would be together throughout their lives. This prompted another group member to suggest a change for the second verse. She changed "Living every day anew, your light among us" to "Living every day anew, you're flying among us," observing that the spirits can fly even if they can't walk.

The discussion and lyric re-writing took about 45 minutes. At the conclusion of the process, we discussed the new song in total and how it was now uniquely theirs. I asked the group if they would like to change the title of the song, but they chose to keep the original title. Finally, I asked the group if they would like to sing the song with me at the closing remembrance service and ceremony or record it so a CD of the song could be played at the service. The group chose to record the song rather than sing it live, and we recorded the song to a CD with me playing guitar and the group singing with me (see Appendix A for the music and lyrics).

A remembrance service at noon on Sunday concluded the retreat. It was held in an outdoor chapel, which consisted of a beautiful open limestone structure with a small creek flowing through it. There were seats around the perimeter, as well as stone benches facing a raised stone platform, with a stone wall behind it. The goal of the non-denominational service was to honor and remember the deceased children. After an induction by a chaplain and remarks from the retreat leader, each deceased child was honored with a flower placed on a wreath by his/her family. The name of each child was read by the chaplain, along with the dates of the child's birth and death, the child's age at death and how the child died. During this time, the family brought the flower forward. After all the names had been read, I introduced the song, its relationship to the retreat theme, and shared how the group had re-written the lyrics. At this point, several of the group members came up to the front of the space and stood next to me. This was self-initiated and suggested that they felt ownership for the song and how it was being shared with their families.

Copies of the song lyrics were distributed by several members of our songwriting group. Our song was then played via a CD player hooked into the PA system. The service concluded with remarks and a blessing from the chaplain. After the service, I gave each group member a copy of the CD we had made.

The families then dispersed and the retreat was over. During this time, most of the group members came over to say good-bye, and several shared how meaningful the songwriting process was for them. Several parents also said that their children had discussed and shared the song with them during informal times during the weekend. In written evaluations of the retreat, all group participants rated the songwriting experience as positive, indicating they would like to take part in a similar group in the future.

SUMMARY

For family members, grieving has been described as a shared, universal and natural expression in response to loss such as the death of a sibling (Bruce, 2002). For adolescents grieving the death of a sibling, music therapy can facilitate this natural grieving (Teahan, 2000), and music therapy songwriting-based interventions can be a significant part of this process (Krout, 2005b). As Bruscia (1998) wrote, "They (*songs*) express who we are and how we feel, they bring us closer to others, they keep us company when we are alone. They articulate our beliefs and values. As the years pass, songs bear witness to our lives. They allow us to relive the past, examine the present, and to voice our dreams of the future. Songs weave tales of our joys and sorrows, they reveal our innermost secrets, and they express our hopes and disappointments, our fears and our triumphs. They are our musical diaries, our life-stories. They are the sounds of our personal development" (p. 9).

In music therapy group work, the use of therapist-composed songs can facilitate participant connections and goals between and for participants during a single session, even when those participants have not interacted prior to that session (Krout, 2005a). For adolescents, songs can function as powerful catalysts for individual and group identity formation and the construction of feelings of self (Laiho, 2004). The music and lyrics of group-composed songs can provide creative and safe containers in, and through which, bereaved adolescents can experience, explore and process their grief (Dalton & Krout, 2006). The songwriting experience in which I involved the group of bereaved young adolescents at this grief retreat appeared to facilitate the validation, identification, normalization and expression of their feelings relating to both their deceased siblings and their own on-going grief journeys and processes. Although this group process lasted for only 90-minutes, it allowed the group members to take part in a meaningful group experience, while also examining and reflecting on their own unique grief situations in a creative and non-threatening way.

242 Robert Krout

APPENDIX A Lyrics and Music to "Our Path to Peace."

REFERENCES

Armstrong-Dailey, A. & Zarbock, S. (Eds.) (2001). *Hospice Care for Children* (2nd ed.). London: Oxford University Press.

Baker, F. & Wigram, T. (2005). *Songwriting: Methods, Techniques and Clinical Applications for Music Clinicians, Educators and Students*. Philadelphia, PA: Jessica Kingsley Publishers.

Balk, D. (1996). Models for understanding adolescent coping with bereavement. *Death Studies, 20* (4), 367-387.

Birenbaum, L. (2000). Assessing children's and teenagers' bereavement when a sibling dies from cancer: A secondary analysis. *Child: Care, Health and Development*, 26(5), 381-400.

Bright, R. (2002). *Supportive Eclectic Music Therapy for Grief and Loss*. St. Louis: MMB Music.

Brooks, M. & O'Rourke, A. (2002). *Opening Doors: Music Therapy in Hospitals and Hospices.* Wellington, NZ: Wellington Society for Music Therapy.

Bruce, C. A. (2002). The grief process for patient, family, and physician. *Journal of the American Osteopath Association, 102* (9 Supplement 3), 28-32.

Brunk, B. K. (1998). *Songwriting for Music Therapists*. Grapevine, TX : Prelude Music Therapy.

Bruscia, K. (Ed.) (1991). *Case Studies in Music Therapy.* Phoenixville, PA: Barcelona Publishers.

Bruscia, K. (1998). *The Dynamics of Music Psychotherapy*. Phoenixville, PA: Barcelona Publishers.

Children's Hospice International (2005). *Approaching Grief.* http://www.chionline.org/resources/approaching_grief.pdf. Retrieved June 22, 2005.

Corr, C. & Corr, D. (Eds.) (1996). *Handbook of Adolescent Death and Bereavement.* New York: Springer Publishing.

Dalton, T. & Krout, R. (2006). The Grief Song-Writing Process with bereaved adolescents: An integrated grief model and music therapy protocol. *Music Therapy Perspectives, 24*(2), 94-107.

Dalton, T. & Krout, R. (2005). Development of the Grief Process Scale through music therapy songwriting with bereaved adolescents. *Arts in Psychotherapy, 32*(2), 131-143.

Darrow, A. A. (2004). *Introduction to Approaches in Music Therapy.* Silver Spring, MD: American Music Therapy Associaiton.

De Cinque, N., Monterosso, L., Dadd, G., Sidhu, R. & Lucas R. (2004). Bereavement support for families following the death of a child from cancer: practice characteristics of Australian and New Zealand paediatric oncology units. *Journal of Paediatrics and Child Health, 40*(3), 131-135.

Desai, P., Ng, J. & Bryant, S. (2002). Care of children and families in the CICU: A focus on their developmental, psychosocial, and spiritual needs. *Critical Care Nursing Quarterly, 25*(3), 88-97.

Doka, K. (Ed.) (2000). *Living with Grief: Children, Adolescents, and Loss.* Washington, D.C.: Hospice Foundation of America.

Duncan, J., Joselow, M. & Hilden, J. (2006). Program interventions for children at the end of life and their siblings. *Child and Adolescent Psychiatric Clinics of North America,* 15(3), 739-758.

Fleming, S. & Adolph, R. (1986). Helping bereaved adolescents: Needs and responses. In C. A. Corr and J. N. McNeil (Eds.), *Adolescence and Death* (pp. 97-118). New York: Springer.

Fletcher, P. N. (2002). Experiences in family bereavement. *Family Community Health, 2* (1), 57-70.

Forward, D. & Garlie, N. (2003). Search for new meaning: Adolescent bereavement after the sudden death of a sibling. *Canadian Journal of School Psychology,* 18(1-2), 23-53.

Gilmer, M. J. (2002). Pediatric palliative care: a family-centered model for critical care. *Critical Care Nursing Clinics in North America, 14*(2), 207-214.

Hanser, S. (1999). *The New Music Therapist's Handbook.* Boston, MA: Berklee Press.

Hasenfus, E. & Franceschi, A. (2003). Collaboration of nursing and child life: A palette of professional practice. *Journal of Pediatric Nursing, 18*(5), 359-365.

Hilliard, R. (2001). The effects of music therapy-based bereavement groups on mood and behavior of grieving children: A Pilot study. *Journal of Music Therapy 38(4),* 291-306.

Hilliard, R. (2007). The effects of Orff-based music therapy and social work groups on childhood grief symptoms and behaviors. *Journal of Music Therapy,* 44(2), 123-138.

Hilliard, R. (2008). Music and grief work with children and adolescents. In C. A. Malchiodi (Ed.), *Creative Interventions with Traumatized Children* (pp. 62-80). New York: Guilford Press.

Hogan, B. & Roberts, M. (2005). "Why did you leave me alone...?": Investigating music therapy's value for bereaved children/adolescents. Paper presented at the 11th World Congress of Music Therapy, Brisbane, Australia. July.

Holliday, J. (2002). *A Review of Sibling Bereavement – Impact and Interventions.* Basildon, Essex, UK: Barnardos Publications.

Jimerson, S. R. (2005). *Project LOSS: A Focus on Youth for a Better Tomorrow.* http://www.education.ucsb.edu/jimerson/loss.html. Retrieved June 22, 2005.

Krout, R. (1999). *Songs from Sorrow, Songs from Joy. Original Music to Facilitate Creative Grief Processing with Bereaved Children and Youth* (book and accompanying compact disc recording). St. Louis, MO: MMB Music.

Krout, R. (2002). The use of therapist-composed songs to facilitate multi-modal grief processing and expression with bereaved children in group music therapy. *Annual Journal of the New Zealand Society for Music Therapy*, 1, 21-35.

Krout, R. (2005a). Applications of music therapist-composed songs in creating participant connections and facilitating goals and rituals during one-time bereavement support groups and programs. *Music Therapy Perspectives, 23*(2), 118-128.

Krout, R. (2005b). The music therapist as singer-songwriter: Applications with bereaved teens. In F. Baker & T. Wigram (Eds.), *Song Writing Methods, Techniques and Clinical Applications for Music Therapy Clinicians, Educators and Students* (pp. 206-223). London: Jessica Kingsley Publishers.

Krout, R. E. (2006). Following the death of a child: Music therapy helping to heal the family heart. *New Zealand Journal of Music Therapy. 4, 6-22.*

Krout, R. & Jones, L. (2005). When a child dies – music therapy in facilitating family grief processing. Paper presented at the Annual Conference of the American Music Therapy Association, Orlando, Florida. November.

Laiho, S. (2004). The psychological functions of music in adolescence. *Nordic Journal of Music Therapy, 13*(1), 47-63.

Lehmann, L., Jimerson, S. & Gaasch, A. (2001a). *Grief Support Curriculum: Facilitator's Handbook.* New York: Brunner-Routledge.

Lehmann, L., Jimerson, S. & Gaasch, A. (2001b). *Mourning Child Grief Support Group Curriculum: Early childhood Edition: Kindergarten-grade 2.* New York: Brunner-Routledge.

Lehmann, L., Jimerson, S. & Gaasch, A. (2001c). *Mourning Child Grief Support Group Curriculum: Middle Childhood Edition: Grades 3-6.* New York: Brunner-Routledge.

Lehmann, L., Jimerson, S. & Gaasch, A. (2001d). *Teens Together Grief Support Curriculum.* New York: Brunner-Routledge.

McFerran-Skewes, K. (2000). From the mouth of babes: The response of six younger, bereaved teenagers to the experience of psychodynamic group music therapy. *Australian Journal of Music Therapy, 11,* 3-22.

McFerran-Skewes, K. & Erdonmez-Grocke, D. (2000). Group music therapy for young bereaved teenagers. *European Journal of Palliative Care, 7*(6), 227-229.

McFerran-Skewes, K. & Grocke, D (2000). What do grieving young people and music therapy have in common: Exploring the match between creativity and younger adolescents. *European Journal of Palliative Care, 7*(6), 227-230.

Mondanaro, J. (2005). Interfacing music therapy with other arts modalities to address anticipatory grief in pediatrics. In C. Dileo & J. Loewy (Eds.), *Music Therapy at the End of Life* (pp. 25-32). Cherry Hill, NJ: Jeffrey Publishers.

Moos, N. L. (1995). An integrated model of grief. *Death Studies, 19*(4), 337-364.

Packman, W., Horsley, H., Davies, B. & Kramer, R. (2006). Sibling bereavement and continuing bonds. *Death Studies*, 30(9), 817-841.

Pavlicevic, M. (Ed.) (2005). *Music Therapy In Children's Hospices: Jessie's Fund in Action.* London: Jessica Kinsgley Publishers.

Perschy, M. (2004). *Helping Teens Work Through Grief* (2nd ed.). Bristol, PA: Accelerated Development.

Rando, T. (1993). *Treatment of Complicated Mourning.* Champaign, IL: Research Press.

Robb, S. (Ed.) (2003). *Music Therapy in Pediatric Healthcare: Research and Evidence-based Practice.* Silver Spring, MD: American Music Therapy Association.

Roberts, M. (2006). "I want to play and sing my story": Home-based songwriting for bereaved children and adolescents. *Australian Journal of Music Therapy, 17,* 18-34.

Rosof, B. (1994). *The Worst Loss: How Families Heal from the Death of a Child.* New York: Henry Holt and Company.

Rufin, J., Creed, J. & Jarvis, C. (1997). A retreat for families of children recently diagnosed with cancer. *Cancer Practice, 5*(2), 99-104.

Skewes, K. (2000). From the mouths of babes: The response of six younger, bereaved teenagers to the experience of psychodynamic group music therapy. *The Australian Journal of Music Therapy, 11,* 3-22.

Skewes, K. & Grocke, D. (2000). What does group music therapy offer to bereaved young people: A rounded approach to the grieving adolescent. *Grief Matters: The Australian Journal of Loss and Grief, 3*(3), 54-61.

Smeijsters, H. (2005). Quantitative single case designs. In B. L. Wheeler, (Ed.), *Music Rherapy Research* (2nd Ed.) (pp. 293-305). Gilsum, NH: Barcelona.

Snyder, L. (2008). Qualitative research on the culture and theology of the teen grief experience for a teen grief ministry: An ethnographic approach. *Dissertation Abstracts International Section A: Humanities and Social Sciences,* Vol 68(7-A), pp. 2992.

Teahan, M. (2000). Grief interventions. In M. Teahan and T. Dalton, (Eds.) *Helping Children and Adolescents Cope with Grief and Bereavement.* Symposium conducted at the Alumni Conference of the Barry University School of Social Work, Miami, FL.

Webb, N. (2004). *Helping Bereaved Children: A Handbook for Practitioners* (2nd Ed.). New York: Guilford Publications.

Chapter Fourteen

MOVING OUT OF YOUR COMFORT ZONE: GROUP MUSIC THERAPY WITH ADOLESCENTS WHO HAVE MISUSED DRUGS

Katrina McFerran

INTRODUCTION

As I sit casually clutching my guitar, I watch seven older adolescents enter the house where the music therapy program is going to run for the next ten weeks. They are an intimidating crew, dressed predominantly in black with a range of styles from Emo[1] to ultra-conservative. They are from diverse cultural backgrounds, including Maltese, Vietnamese, Chinese, Singaporean, Italian and two Skips[2]. The three males and four females glance at me, and I smile warmly and try to look cool. I wonder how this will go since it is a new environment for me and a new group. They certainly won't think that I am cool!

The young people involved in this program are all 16-20-year-olds wishing to remain abstinent from their drug of choice – usually Ice or Heroin. They have previously been involved in a residential rehabilitation program and have now progressed to supported accommodation that includes weekly therapeutic sessions and house meetings. Music therapy is one of a range of programs they will experience over the twelve months they spend in this stable but independent environment. The workers who engaged me to run the sessions have briefed me on the backgrounds of each participant, but without meeting the individuals, it is difficult to understand the ramifications of their histories. The experiences they have had don't explain how it has affected them, and this is of greater interest to me. But before I can begin to understand that, I will

---

[1] Short for Emotional – a type of heavy rock music that is also associated with traditional black makeup and clothing.
[2] Slang for "of Australian origin" – based on the 1970s television series 'Skippy the Bush Kangaroo.'

want to know what kind of music they like, and that will be the first thing they want to know about me. From there, we will get to know one another and learn in relationship about what possibilities for action are relevant.

FOUNDATIONAL CONCEPTS

Theoretical Orientation

> "It is the client who knows what hurts, what directions to go, what problems are crucial, what experiences have been deeply buried" (Rogers, 1961 p. 12)

The writings of humanist scholars have informed my orientation to music therapy since training in the early 1990s with Denise Grocke in Australia. I fundamentally believe that each person is full of potential and that the meaning of therapy lies in the creation of a relationship wherein that potential can be actualised (Maslow, 1968). The fact that this relationship is actively musical is critical for me because it further extends the potential for growth by drawing on an inherent capacity for musical communicativeness (Trevarthen & Malloch, 2000). In my experience, the sense of emotional synchronicity that can be achieved in music therapy interactions is the mechanism for change, occurring at an implicit level that frequently does not require verbal consolidation (Bruschweiler-Stern, et al., 2002). This is essential in my work with adolescents who, for various reasons, are not inclined to engage at an analytic discursive level. Adolescence is marked by the beginnings of abstract thinking and expression (Piaget & Inhelder, 1958), often accompanied by rebellious attitudes and risk-taking behavior that are understood as identity formation (Erikson, 1965). Epstein (2007) argues that this is a cultural, rather than biological construction, noting that this stage of development is not differentiated in many non-western countries. Stige (2002) thoroughly articulates the relationships between these individual, biological and social influences, drawing on the concept of musicking. His perspective is that, together, these frameworks support the premise that music in therapy is the performance of the relationship (p.84). This develops Ruud's (1997) contention that music is the performance of identity. My work with adolescents draws on all of these perspectives as a framework for growth. They support my experiences of music therapy, where music, identity and relationships interplay in a journey toward better health (McFerran, 2010).

Practical Approach

> "As much as they love to dish it out, teens appreciate an adult who, if momentarily rattled, can take it in stride and in good humour (with ego intact – outside the door, of course)." (Malekoff, 1997 p. 22)

A humanist orientation tinged by a belief in the power of musicking is one thing. Facing up to music therapy with a group of adolescents is quite another. A number of practical perspectives shape this endeavor, influencing my understandings of both the nature of adolescent group work and the use of music within that. The emphasis on group work comes from my belief that, whether they are physically present in the therapy room or not, the peer group is essential to any adolescents' growth, and it makes sense to deal with some aspects of peer relationships within the therapeutic encounter. By implication, the interpersonal dynamics that exist within the group are important, and an awareness of the stages of group development often provide an anchor amongst the chaos that ensues after the initial stages of group formation (McFerran, 2005; Morgenstern, 1982). Yalom's (1995) playful identification of the different personalities that often present in groups is another useful source of information, particularly his emphasis that understanding the motivations behind behavior are the basis for understanding and compassion, rather than judgement.

Apart from the security blanket of group dynamics, my other area for consideration in adolescent group work is leadership. Malekoff (1997) reminds leaders to leave their egos at the door and prepare to be tested as they work with teenagers. Instead of trying to be youth-savvy, he emphasizes the need for an authentic stance, since teenagers are the masters of disguise as they slip on one mask after another in their constant experimentation with identity. An authentic and grounded group leadership style is also congruent with Lewin's (Lewin, Lippit & White, 1939) ideas of democratic, as opposed to autocratic or laissez-faire styles of leadership. In my experience, teenagers respond to a constant, unflappable and understanding leader who does not control and direct, but rather allows and recognizes their experiments for what they are – self-discovery.

Many teenagers naturally use music as a vehicle for self exploration and spend impressive amounts of time engaging with songs on a daily basis (North & Hargreaves, 2000). For this reason, songs play an important role in music therapy practice with adolescents in Australia (Hunt, 2008; McFerran, 2004) and are reported as being used in the majority of articles describing music therapy and substance misuse (Freed, 1987; James, 1988; Jones, 1998; Murphy, 1983; Walker, 1995). Group improvisation is less prominent in the literature, but elements of improvisation have been described as improving connectedness for people struggling with substance misuse (Soshensky, 2001; Wheeler, 1985). This method also has obvious relevance for adolescents who struggle with articulating and expressing the issues which challenge them, but this has not been described previously, except in the context of my own research with bereaved adolescents (McFerran-Skewes, 2000). Both of these active methods are usually central to my work with teenagers and were so in the group being described in this chapter.

THE PARTICIPANTS

The young people involved in this program came from diverse backgrounds, both culturally and in terms of family support. Many of them had spent time living on the street and putting themselves at great risk to score drugs – whether that involved stealing, selling themselves, or simply allowing themselves to be treated badly in order to maintain their habit. Across the course of the group, some of the young people did share details about their history, but they more often described their current struggle to establish a new identity without drugs. Seven teenagers attended the group with support from their workers, and the various individuals made for an interesting group. The 'Rock Chicks,' as they were known by group members, were two sixteen-year-old women who had just joined the program and were living together in supported accommodation. They played music together regularly, and Elizabeth was a talented guitarist, while Sarah was a drummer with a wavering sense of tempo. Seventeen-year-old Flash had no previous experience in active music making but had a strong connection with pop music and an unfulfilled desire to sing. She was further through the rehabilitative process than the

Rock Chicks and due to graduate from the program in the coming months. Phantom was similarly placed in the time-continuum of the program, and had learned piano as a young boy as well as having a brother who worked as a DJ, so he considered himself to have a musical background. Nineteen-year-old Shen's interest in music was mostly related to backing tracks for computer games, and he showed little interest in music generally. Seventeen-year old Van was an electronic music aficionado and had a broad knowledge of the genre. Both were mid-way through the program, and although they were not strongly connected to the group, they appeared to be travelling successfully. The final young woman, eighteen-year-old Kai-Ying, expressed an interest in R'n'B and other pop genres, but did not elaborate.

THE THERAPEUTIC PROCESS

This group took place over ten consecutive weeks, running for two or three hours on a weekly basis. During this time, the influence of previous and/or current misuse of heroin was evident in the significant interpersonal difficulties experienced by group members. These social challenges may have precipitated the participants' use of substances in the first place, as a resilient strategy to seek out less challenging situations such as the 'wasted' group hang out. Or the lack of interpersonal skills may be the result of the cognitive deficits that haunt chronic heroin users (Ornstein et al., 2000). The real-life experience of trying to relate to other people without the assistance of substances is comparatively challenging, both because it feels less successful and also more boring. At the conclusion of the group, interviews were conducted with five of the young people who had participated regularly. The following descriptions of the group process draw on the perspectives shared in these interviews, as well as interviews with other involved staff, my own session notes and reflections, and also the insights gleaned from the music created by the group.

Week 1: Let's Make Some Music

One of the differences between community based groups and institutionalized populations is that you never know if anyone will show up. Having arranged the instruments in the middle of the lounge room floor of the sheltered group home, I plugged in the keyboard and CD player and casually placed my song book on a soft chair. It was now time to wait and see. I played through some songs on the guitar, preparing myself mentally to communicate a stance of welcoming acceptance.

Less than 30 minutes later, the group of seven young people was laughing at me for suggesting that we would play the instruments together – and play different 'feelings' of all things. Ten weeks after this moment, Phantom would make a public speech in the final session of the group where he expressed amazement at this phenomenon of 'going beyond your comfort zone' in the music therapy group. When I followed this up in an interview, he said:

> *You grow, you learn how you can do things that you wouldn't want to do alright, you know... Yeah, and realising that, you know, you don't have to be able to play the guitar to make music, sort of thing.*

But a positive reflection about my radical suggestion of instrument playing was still a long way ahead, and in this first session I felt that the ability of the group leader to 'survive' the banter of the group was critical (Malekoff, 1997). After all, I was asking them to do something very strange, even though I did briefly justify it by saying that some people felt relieved once they had played their feelings out. I wanted them to experience musical communicativeness through active and shared playing, and I knew that the only way it would happen was if I introduced it with complete confidence.

I also introduced the concept of song-writing. This idea is usually successful in attracting the attention of teenagers since they customarily listen to songs that relate to their own experiences. Drawing on my past experiences, I felt confident that this method would provide the basis for task interdependence – where the members of the group are dependent upon one another to achieve group goals (Lewin, 1948). I took a more directive role in this first song creation, actively facilitating the brain-storming process and modelling the process through some contribution of ideas (McFerran, 2004).

We had the whole afternoon, so there was time to cover a number of musical bases, even allowing for multiple cigarette breaks. By the time the young people left at the end of the afternoon, we had created some lyrics that they rapped over a beat based on German Electronica and progressed through three simple minor chords. Introductions were complete.

Week 1 Song
I'm not cashed up
Got low self esteem
But at least I've got my cigarettes
And my caffeine

Shit might seem f__ked up
But it's really OK
Playing normal peoples games
Is not my forte

Chorus
I'm brave and I'm proud
And I'll shout it out loud

Week 2: Oh No!

A short excerpt from the scribbled notes in my journal reveals how challenged I was by the events (or non-events) of session two:

> *Ahhh – what just happened. Maybe they thought it was boring, or they couldn't see the relevance, or they didn't respond to the music, or the music was too strong. Must remember LET CLIENTS GUIDE THE PROCESS – it should not be therapist directed.*

After such a powerful first session, I had expected to build to greater levels of intimacy in week two. Instead, I had to consider that my perception of the group had been different to what the young people had experienced, since only three young people came to the group and only one (Rock Chick Elizabeth) came with any intention of action. To further complicate matters, Elizabeth had expected me to bring a guitar amplifier, as promised in the previous week, but I had not been able to borrow one. During the session, Shen and Kai-Ying responded to questions but did not engage with either of us any more deeply. The session was short and polite, but all in attendance were conscious of those people and equipment not present. We played a little, they smoked a lot of cigarettes, and I tried to achieve a stance of interest rather than feeling stressed. After significant debriefing from the support workers and a full turn-out the following week, I accepted that the responsibility for this poor attendance was not necessarily due to poor facilitation of the first session. I was still unaccustomed to the chaotic lives of this group of young people and was more used to working with teenagers whose parents shuttled them back and forth to services. When I asked the group members in the final interviews about their reasons for non-attendance in the second week, none of them could remember what I was referring to (whereas I will never forget it!).

Week 3: They're Back!

All group members attended the following session, some with nonchalant apologies for their absence the week before. Things to do, people to see. I tried to contain my excitement and offered a choice between free improvisation, improvised songs without words and song-writing. The unfamiliar option of creating a song without words was chosen, driven by Elizabeth, who showed a brief interest in the guitar amplifier but was more interested in jamming on the other instruments. She seemed to defer to her fellow Rock Chick, and I got the impression that she was trying to make sure that she did not outshine her friend.

This negotiation of power seemed to be reflected in the group improvisation[3]. It began with an introductory period where there was no shared tempi, but from the one-minute mark, a leadership role was established by the 'Rock Chicks' through the provision of a rhythmic ground and figures on the doumbek (Sarah) that were mostly integrated with a repeating melodic shape on the metallaphone (Elizabeth). At times this partnership seemed fused, but the level of tension in the rhythmic role contrasted with the calm and cyclic nature of the melody. The music therapist acted as partner on an acoustic guitar, integrating with the two in a follower role. Other group members also contributed to the improvisation with smaller percussion instruments, including a tambourine (Phantom), shaker (Kai-Ying) and sliding whistle (Flash), but these

---

[3] This description has been developed using Bruscia's IAPs (1987).

contributions were incongruent in their lesser volume, emphasizing their roles as followers. The group described the improvisation afterwards as 'musical' and 'relaxing,' although I felt that the group dynamics were more a representation of power than peace. This difference may have been because I was listening to the group playing together, whereas they were likely listening only to their own individual contribution. I asked Elizabeth about her desire to empower her friend at the expense of her own musical expressivity in the interviews conducted at the end of the group. Instead of agreeing with my interpretation, she reflected on how much she enjoyed her chosen level of participation in the music making, which I accepted.

> *Yeah, a lot of it was improvisation and that's good, that's what I usually do, just improvise, but every now and then, put a structure to it. Well that first one, and then there was one I wanted to work on a bit more ... you know, I love that music, like that kind of music and I've written a fair few songs from that.*

Individual dynamics aside, by the end of this third session the group was an entity, complete with the usual dynamics of sub-groups, monopolizers and non-contributors (Yalom, 1995). The centrality of my role as leader had passed, and there was no more need for torturous self-questioning about a possible inclination to push the group too quickly. This change of role felt more comfortable for me, and I anticipated the developmental stage that lay ahead as the group moved from norming to storming (McFerran, 2001). I did not have very long to wait.

Week 4: Whose Story is this Anyway?

By week four, the battle for leadership had begun in earnest and the 'teams' that emerged could be classified as those who were 'getting off the gear' versus those who could not quite break the habit. The second group was made up of the two 'Rock Chick' musicians who had dominated the group dynamics thus far. Flash was the most vocal of the opposing team and was brave enough to contribute a significant portion of lyrics in this session, with her main counterpart, Phantom, offering to sing them with her. The song they composed used metaphoric language to describe the act of receiving daily methadone doses from the local chemist. The song could equally be interpreted as the story of scoring heroin and the dual meanings caused some overt conflict in the group. On reflection, Flash felt that the confusion added credibility to her writing ability and said:

> *That was alright, but I think she (Sarah) turned around and said 'that's like scoring' or whatever, but then that was a kind of illusional song anyway. She thought I was talking about scoring, but I was talking about the 'done'[4]. So that was pretty cool, it was good.*

Sarah and Elizabeth refused to accept the methadone option, both in the song and in their lives, and cast doubt on the lyricist's intention. This frustration was still present in the final interviews, where they made specific references to the song in a way that suggested they had ruminated on this topic in the weeks that had passed.

> *It makes me feel sick in the stomach, that song. I couldn't stand that.*

The group dynamics were mounting, and there were a number of verbal confrontations within the group as they argued about lyrical meanings and musical decisions related to the song creation. The tension between the two groups was also clear in their body language, with small groups leaving to smoke together and then returning in time for the next subgroup to take a break. The content of sessions was becoming more authentic. What could happen next?

Week 5: Agreeing to Disagree

Almost as soon as the tension mounted, it resolved. In Week 5, the group chose to write a song about the complexities of home life and participants were no longer poised in opposing camps. The lyrics described

---

[4] A street term for methodone – a depressant prescribed by the Australian Government for assistance in ceasing the use of illegal depressants such as heroin.

experiences that were shared and the group's capacity to survive the storming of the week before resulted in a level of cohesion where members could contribute honestly to the song creation. In the absence of the other two males who often fought over playing the beats on the keyboard, Shen took responsibility for selecting a House beat from the samples available. His musical contribution was then used to frame the song. Group members played a range of percussion instruments along with the beat and asked me to sing the melody line that week. The lyrics were as follows.

<u>Week 5 Song</u>
My home is full of memories
Some I'd like to forget
My silk sheets have been laid on my rest
Everything happening at the right time
Any choices determine my time of play
And the rest of my day is time away

Home is where I feel secure
Home is my own place
Home is my time
Home can be hell

It was a quiet session of consolidation and the time passed quickly. Shen later described the session when I asked him about how it felt to take on such a significant role.

It was alright. You know, there were a few cool weeks and then it just got boring.

This was one of the cool weeks apparently.

Week 6: Getting Personal

It was a small group again in Week 6, and the absence of both Elizabeth and Sarah opened up a significant opportunity for musical participation without critique. Those in attendance chose to substitute the lyrics to a song by the Red Hot Chilli Peppers about heroin use, 'Under the Bridge'

(1991). The retitled song addressed the loneliness many of the group experienced in achieving abstinence and seemed to inspire further connections between group members.

<u>Week 6 Song: My Companion</u>
Sometimes I feel like I don't have a partner
Sometimes I feel like my only companion
Is the pussy I live with, who knows how I'm feeling
We snuggle and cuddle, it purrs while I cry

The keys are the doorway, to the other side
My peaceful home where I always smile
There is no pressure, no forced expectations
I feel so happy, being who I am

CHORUS:
I don't ever want to feel
Knowing I was lonely
I don't ever want to feel
That I can't have my way
I don't ever want to die
Knowing that life has passed me by

This was a significant moment for the attending group members who were taking greater risks in their personal expression. This was most clearly visible for Phantom, who sang the lyrics 'solo' for the recording. Later he reflected on this experience:

> *SINGING! I can't believe it, I'd never sing, especially that sort of stuff, but I did... Yeah, coz it's embarrassing, it's vulnerable to cop it basically, I dunno what it is. Yeah, if you don't have high self-esteem, it's hard to do something like that, especially if that's not your type of thing ... Ummm, and yeah, just to remember that I can do things that I didn't think I could do, or wouldn't do.*

Other group members commented later about how much they admired the risks taken by individuals at this time. It was a peak experience for the group of participants who were successfully managing their withdrawal, but it also represented the moment where the other two group members seemed to slip away.

> *Yeah, and you could kind of see when the Rock Chicks came to music that they were going off the rails anyway ... I really don't have much respect for them, you know. And if I was doing the same thing I'm sure they wouldn't have no respect for me either. They're on their last legs.*

The success was therefore tinged with a conscious sorrow.

Week 7: Daring to Feel

In week seven, only two group members made their way to the session. Phantom and Flash chose to sing songs from the song book during this time, and Flash commented that it was easier to use her voice when she was sharing the experience with her friend.

> *Coz I thought his voice would drown me out (laughs). Basically, I didn't want to sing by myself and he didn't want to sing by himself, so we had to compromise there and sing together... well that was hard because I know what my voice sounds like and it's like, it just doesn't ... I know I sound bad singing along to a song, so you know, having to sing and make the voice myself was pretty hard, but I thought maybe with a bit of practice it could get a bit better. So it was good doing that.*

Flash did sing with a monotone voice, possibly a response to her chronic drug use or a representation of her depressed state as she struggled to resurrect her life. During the session, we talked about how her interest in vocal development was closely linked with her commitment to achieving a full range of emotional expression and this intimate session provided a possibility for action. In the final interview she noted that her relationship with Phantom developed further after this session and was still progressing well. She was also pleased to be experiencing emotions without needing to escape. Phantom expressed similar struggles with emotional connection, trying to distance himself from personal interactions through humor and sarcasm, but requiring only minimal encouragement to contribute more personal material. Immediately following a discussion about not feeling emotions anymore, Phantom elected to sing 'The Rose' (Middler, 1979). This classic song describes the challenges of daring to love and allowed an ongoing engagement with the topic at hand. It was an emotional moment.

Week 8: Individual Voices

The sporadic attendance continued during the eighth week, and in this session, the work was largely individual. Van, who had been an active but mostly non-verbal group member, took the opportunity to monopolize the keyboard and created a Trance track that incorporated a range of melodic loops available through the keyboard. In listening back to his improvisation, Van was thrilled. One of the support workers commented on this.

> *I won't forget these images of the end of the sessions with two people sharing your walkman thingy, listening to their music, bopping away and smiling!*

It was a small enough group to allow for this kind of individual achievements and the level of cohesion was sufficient for active listening as well as participating. Elizabeth practiced and recorded a guitar riff she had been working on. Kai-Ying commented on the achievements of both individuals and chose two songs for us to sing, but did not actively participate. I had a number of one-to-one discussions with group members as we worked on their contributions and took the opportunity to acknowledge the contribution each had made to the group. Closure felt imminent.

Week 9: Preparing to say Goodbye

Loss and grief underpin many young people's misuse of substances, and for this reason, closure had been on my mind from the beginning. Week nine was the last opportunity to make any recordings, and at my initiation, the group agreed to address closure by writing a song on that theme.

The piece that emerged did not fulfill my expectations regarding the gravity of the moment, however. Instead, the group took my very serious idea and turned it into a satiric yarn, complete with humorous vocalizations, a pop-sounding harmonic frame, and Elizabeth even played a guitar strum that echoed my own natural style[5]. The group members worked hard to perfect their teasing, and I enjoyed the game equally, sitting back and offering playful analyses of their need to joke at such a profound moment. We recorded the song a number of times, since the group kept dissolving into laughter as they interjected with spontaneous raps and lyrics. I experienced this light-hearted moment as a gift from the group as they humorously acknowledged the therapeutic process. I was sad that we would only meet one more time.

<u>Week 9 Song</u>
Saying Goodbye to our friendship tie
Would do the opposite of saying 'Hi'
It's the end to something good we had
Saying goodbye to you will make me sad

But when I'm alone and everything's looking bad
I picture you in my mind and I feel glad

Now you have gone, you've left me feeling empty
When I want but can't see you, my head gets tempy

I miss your hugs and smiles, they lasted for miles
Your happiness and spirit, that you bought to us here

I miss you now as I will always
From the morning time to the end of my days
But, I know I'll be OK

Week 10: Saying Goodbye

The support workers had arranged a feast for the final session and the party atmosphere that ensued left no room for further therapeutic process. I played the group the compilation CD that contained their musical

---

[5] Robert Krout MT-BC has been known to call this particular style 'the music therapist's strum'!

material from each week. This totalled more than 40 minutes of music, which was too much for most to sit through at once. People wandered in and out of the lounge room, getting food from the kitchen and having cigarettes on the front porch. Each person was suddenly present for the songs that they had contributed to, if not on the first, then on the second play through. The members helped me pack my instruments into the car and promised to be in touch for interviews. I felt a little empty as I drove away.

LEARNINGS AND REFLECTIONS

From this group of young people I learned two things. The first was to do with the quality of the musical recordings, which on reflection did not seem good enough. The adolescents in this group were grappling with forming a new identity in the wake of their reliance on substances and they considered themselves to be reflected in the music they had made. Although many teenagers I have worked with do not have the auditory discrimination skills to distinguish between a high quality and a casually recorded song, the musicians in this group were conscious of the difference. he fast pace of the group process had been designed to maintain their attention and need for stimulation, however the Rock Chicks described craving an opportunity to perfect and perform their work:

> *Yeah, like maybe, take a couple of weeks out at the end of it, maybe each individual has organised a piece and they can all put bits into it, like maybe stick to one beat and the guitar for someone else. And maybe have this concert where each person can do their original piece that they did themselves and then everybody's bit of work together.*

At one level, this suggests that when group members identify as musicians, there will likely be an aesthetic judgement applied to the quality of the musical outcome and this should be anticipated and incorporated from the beginning. I also learned that it is important to recognize that adolescents are in a constant process of identity formation and that more time should be allocated for the technical requirements of high-quality recording. My tendency to emphasize the expressive and connective properties of music did not leave sufficient room for this requirement during the group described.

My second learning experience was related to the poor social confidence of this group. The chaotic nature of each group was one indication of this, and the support workers commented on the challenges faced by individuals at different times in the final interviews.

> *My observations of the young peoples' behaviours and attendance during the group varied from session to session and was often largely contingent upon what else was happening in their lives. Having said that, I would also add that at some critical point, the group would, as a whole, settle and focus on the session.*

From a young person's perspective, Phantom took the opportunity in Week seven to let me know that he thought my positive and confident style was a little over the top. When I offered to contain my enthusiasm, he quickly reneged and explained that it simply felt unfamiliar since life as a junkie does not usually result in people treating you well. It was only in that discussion that my theoretical knowledge merged with my real life understandings. Phantom's statement clearly illustrated the complex web of the social challenges facing the young people, where they were viewed as failures by nearly all those they came across outside the program. This realization clarified the importance of the emerging discourse on community music therapy (Pavlicevic & Ansdell, 2004) and the role that performance might play in music therapy for people who are further along the health continuum (O'Grady, 2007). For this group of young people, bridging to the community as part of the music therapy process may have added further value to their experience of boding within the group (Stige, 2002).

SUMMARY

The music therapy group challenged many group participants to move beyond their comfort zone and to increase their sense of personal competence. Whether it was by singing, playing or simply attending, the achievement of group cohesion created a community where participants were able to contribute in their own way. Nonetheless, all participants experienced difficulties in relating to one another at various times, and sometimes struggled with the differences that became evident. Some participants also noted a desire to achieve something concrete from the experience - evidence of the quality of their combined and individual abilities. In order to further the outcomes of the group experience, a longer time frame with a more developed outcome could be considered. This would potentially consist of the creation of a CD that includes individual and group songs that reflect a greater level of achievement than the recordings completed in this project. It may also involve performance opportunities as part of a CD 'launch' where family, friends and others involved in the organization may attend. This awareness of a musical life that exists beyond the group may facilitate the transition being made by participants and support further identity development as they strive to live a life that is not dependent on substances.

REFERENCES

Bruschweiler-Stern, N., Harrison, A. M., Lyons-Ruth, K., Morgan, A. C., Nahum, J. P., Sandler, L. W., et al. (2002). Explicating the implicit: The local level and the microprocess of change in the analytic situation. *International Journal of Psychoanalysis, 83*, 1051-1062.

Bruscia, K. E. (1987). *Improvisational Models of Music Therapy*. Springfield, Il: Charles C. Thomas.

Epstein, R. (2007). *The Case Against Adolescence: Rediscovering the Adult in Every Teen*. Sanger, CA: Quill Driver Books.

Erikson, E. (1965). *Childhood and Society*. London: Penguin Books.

Freed, B. S. (1987). Songwriting with the chemically dependent. *Music Therapy Perspectives, 4*, 13-18.

Hunt, M. (2008). When in doubt return to the music: Group music therapy with adolescents who are inpatients with an eating disorder. Paper presented at the 35th National Australian Music Therapy Association Conference.

James, M. R. (1988). Music therapy values clarification: A positive influence on perceived locus of control. *Journal of Music Therapy, 25*(4), 206-215.

Jones, J. D. (1998). A comparison of songwriting and lyric analysis techniques to evoke emotional changes in a single session with chemically dependent clients. Unpublished Master's Thesis, Florida State University, Tallahassee.

Lewin, K. (Ed.). (1948). *Field Theory in Social Science: Selected Theoretical Papers.* New York: Harper and Row.

Lewin, K., Lippit, R. & White, R. K. (1939). Patterns of aggressive behavior in experimentally created social climates. *Journal of Social Psychology, 10,* 271-301.

Malekoff, A. (1997). *Group Work with Adolescents.* New York: Guildford Press.

Maslow, A. (1968). *Toward a Psychology of Being* (3rd ed.). New York: John Wiley and Sons.

McFerran-Skewes, K. (2000). From the mouths of babes: The response of six younger bereaved teenagers to the experience of psychodynamic group music therapy. *Australian Journal of Music Therapy, 11,* 3-22.

McFerran, K. (2001). The experience of group music therapy for six younger bereaved adolescents. Unpublished Doctoral Dissertation, University of Melbourne.

McFerran, K. (2004). Using songs with groups of teenagers: How does it work? *Social Work with Groups, 27*(2), 143-157.

McFerran, K. (2005). Articulating the dynamics of music therapy group improvisations. *Nordic Journal of Music Therapy, 14*(1), 33-46.

McFerran, K. (2010). *Adolescents, Music and Music Therapy: Methods and Techniques for Clinicians, Educators and Students.* London: Jessica Kingsley Publishers.

Middler, B. (1979). The Rose - Original Soundtrack Recording. Berlin, Germany: Rhino Atlantic.

Morgenstern, A. (1982). Group therapy: A timely strategy for music therapists. *Music Therapy Perspectives, 1,* 16-20.

Murphy, M. (1983). Music therapy: A self-help group experience for substance abuse patients. *Music Therapy, 1,* 52-62.

North, A. C. & Hargreaves, D. J. (2000). The importance of music to adolescents. *British Journal of Educational Psychology, 70,* 255-272.

O'Grady, L. (2007). Community music therapy and its relationship to community music: Where does it end? *Nordic Journal of Music Therapy, 16*(1), 14-26.

Ornstein, T., Iddon, J., Baldacchino, A., Sahakian, B., London, M., Everitt, B., et al. (2000). Profiles of cognitive dysfunction in chronic amphetamine and heroin abusers. *Neuropsychopharmacology, 23*(2), 113-126.

Pavlicevic, M. & Ansdell, G. (Eds.). (2004). *Community Music Therapy*. London: Jessica Kingsley Publishers.

Piaget, J. & Inhelder, B. (1958). *The Growth of Logical Thinking from Childhood to Adolescence* (A. Parsons & S. Seagrin, Trans.). New York: Basic Books.

Red Hot Chilli Peppers (1991). Blood Sugar Sex Magik. Los Angeles: Warner Brothers.

Rogers, C. (1961). *On Becoming a Person: A Therapist's View of Psychotherapy*. London: Constable.

Ruud, E. (1997). Music and identity. *Nordic Journal of Music Therapy, 6*(1), 3-13.

Soshensky, R. (2001). Music therapy and addiction. *Music Therapy Perspectives, 19*(1), 22-39.

Stige, B. (2002). *Culture-Centered Music Therapy*. Gilsum, NH: Barcelona Publishers.

Trevarthen, C. & Malloch, S. (2000). The dance of wellbeing: Defining the musical therapeutic effect. *Nordic Journal of Music Therapy, 9*(2), 4-17.

Walker, J. (1995). Music therapy, spirituality, and chemically dependent clients. *Journal of Chemical Dependency Treatment, 5*(2), 145-166.

Wheeler, B. (1985). The relationship between musical and activity elements of music therapy sessions and client responses: An exploratory study. *Music Therapy, 1*, 52-60.

Yalom, I. (1995). *The Theory and Practice of Group Psychotherapy* (4th ed.). New York, NY: Basic Books.

Chapter Fifteen

JUST DON'T DO IT: A GROUP'S MICRO JOURNEY INTO MUSIC AND LIFE[1]

Mercédès Pavlicevic

INTRODUCTION

This chapter focuses on some three minutes of a musical journey that happened in group music therapy, contextualized within the session as a whole. This three-minute focus is due to the richness and complexity of this particular aspect of this group's music therapy work. This focus is further informed by two threads, the first being that Nordoff-Robbins clinicians are trained to index their work, necessitating a focused and detailed listening to the musical recording of sessions. This level of detail, in turn, often informs their therapeutic thinking (Nordoff & Robbins, 1977). The second thread links to recent discussions on music research that consider the importance of finding the 'right level' of generality to maximize meaning while being prepared to engage in detailed observation and analysis (DeNora, 2003). Like reflexive researchers, reflective music therapy practitioners need to decide how much (or how little) detail suffices for their endeavours. This is a different stance from 'doing detail' for its own sake. Thus, in this chapter, the decision to limit the case study to three minutes is a decision based upon the therapeutic significance of the segment.

The three minutes described here happened in South Africa, in a place called Eersterust, east of the capital city of Pretoria. Eersterust is a (so-called) 'coloured' urban area, so designated in the apartheid government's 'separate development' policies. It remains today an area of lower socioeconomic status than the better resourced metropolis that is Preto-

---

[1] I am grateful to Carol Lotter for permission to draw from her work, for the purposes of this chapter.

ria, some twenty minutes car journey away. Eersterust is characterized by high unemployment and associated problems recognizable in any part of the world: high substance abuse, crime, and a dearth of socially engaged and responsible male role models (Springveldt, 2008). The music therapy work happened in a community based organization called YDO (Youth Development Outreach), founded in order to keep Eersterust's young people off streets, and committed to providing skills training and social programs to young offenders. Its clientele are young people in conflict with the law, and they are referred to YDO by the juvenile courts.

Carol Lotter, who developed the YDO Program, serves as music therapist in this session. The three minutes frame the journey of a song, entitled "Just Don't Do It," from its embryonic stage to its completion. At the end of three minutes, the song is 'performed' by the group, as an entity. This narrative concentrates on the musical-social micro-events that enabled this rapid and skillful transition, and describes the micro-phases of this event, focusing on the swift creating, exchanging and sharing of skills, meaning, and music (for further analysis, see Davidson & Good, 2002; Wosch & Wigram, 2007).

FOUNDATIONAL CONCEPTS

The music therapy programme at YDO is informed by a Community Music Therapy stance (Pavlicevic & Ansdell, 2004), which endeavours to be responsive and appropriate to 'time, place and persons,' as well as engaging with (and indeed becoming a part of) socio-cultural and political contexts of the site of work. In practice, the music therapist engages with YDO's ethos and core values, as well as with its other music practices, familiarizing herself with current adolescent music genres, and music being played on the streets. This 'streetwork' can be understood as the music therapist's acknowledgement of popular music's powerful social imperatives on the life of young people (Martin, 2006; Miell, MacDonald & Hargreaves, 2005). In keeping with Community Music Therapy's extended spectrum of work (Pavlicevic & Ansdell, 2004), Carol's practice includes 'private and confidential' work with individual clients and small groups, open-ended group work, where clients come and go from week to week, and public music performances for larger groups. Carol runs guitar classes and teaches skills such as song-writing and performance. In addition, Carol provides other music sessions from week to week, depending on what is happening within and around YDO. Much of the time, these music practices run in tandem with one another, with clients moving between various formats on offer. YDO mentors (i.e., staff members) at times participate in music sessions alongside their charges, and Carol also works with visiting musicians and community musicians. The music therapist engages with the entire organization and its needs, running open workshops for all members of the organization when the need arises. This can be understood as developing an organizational socio-musical identity; where relationships can be based on shared *musicing* rather than only on the basis of YDO or Eersterust hierarchy and status.

The Community Music Therapy work is informed by Nordoff-Robbins' music-centered stance (Aigen, 2006; Ansdell, 2004; Nordoff & Robbins, 1977). Here, musical action *per se* is understood to be the therapeutic locus, based on an understanding that co-improvisation in music therapy engages and repairs our neuro-psycho-biological capacities for human communication, as well as our cultural musicing experience (Pavlicevic, 2000; Pavlicevic & Ansdell, 2008; Stige, 2002; Trevarthen & Malloch, 2000). Not only does co-musicing in music therapy enable participants to regulate themselves in relation to others, but this very act enables a reframing of social identity: from youth at risk to youth in music. In the words of music psychologist Ian Cross (2003), it is music's "floating ambiguity" (p. 27) that is advantageous in enabling what we might call a "floating identity" to be explored, improvised and stabilized. Group musicing's demands for precise shared coordination – both as individuals and as a collective – enables participants to enact and experience an investment in 'present time.' This experience, according to Daniel Stern, has powerful implications for social bonding (Stern, 2004).

This shared experience leads naturally to another ethos underpinning this work: that of 'social and interactive' health. In contrast to a western medicine and psychology's understanding of illness or health as situated within the delineated, individual self (with corresponding treatment and 'cure') (Billington, Hockey & Strawbridge, 1998), health and empowerment are enacted between persons, and situated in social contexts (Rolvsjord, 2004). The UN's Millenium Report makes a compelling case for linking diseases to poverty, malnutrition and geographical characteristics (Annan, 2000). This suggests that health, or the lack of it, are at the very least, contextual. The experiences of health include being able to participate in society; having a sense of belonging in, and with, one's social world; experiencing neighborliness, usefulness, social reciprocity and support (Blaxter, 2004). In this sense, collective personal marginalization and a sense of 'uselessness' (Sennett, 2006) are often refractions of socially disabling environments. At Eersterust, where the environment might be considered disabling, one of music therapy's tasks is to enact health-giving social experiences through musicing, embedded in YDO's ethos and values. Music therapy at YDO can be characterized as 'social health musicing' (Stige, 2003) geared towards creating social bonds, enabling persons to participate in their social worlds. As such, they experience a sense of belonging, and 'rehearse' skills that are socially useful. This stands in contrast to the kind of social recognition and status that come from being 'good' at crime and brinkmanship.

THE CLIENTS

The clients portrayed in this chapter are four young men from Eersterust who participated in YDO's Adolescent Development Program. Little else is known about them, in keeping with the social rehabilitation and empowerment ethos for YDO programs. This ethos also fits with the music therapist's stance of engaging YDO's clientele as well-resourced *musicians*, with a potential to participate in communal musicing, rather than engaging with them as 'youth at risk' who need therapy.

The case study happened as part of open group work. Two of the clients (Jabu and William) attended music therapy the previous week, while the other two (Benji and Michael) were new to the group. Consistent with Community Music Therapy philosophy, no formal music therapy assessment took place before the group. Instead, the music therapist contributed to, and participated in, discussions of group members and significant events within the community that might emerge as themes in sessions.

THERAPEUTIC PROCESS

The Session Unfolds

This element of the session centers on the 'rehearsal' and 'performance' of a song, written by Jabu. In the previous week, Jabu and Carol spoke of ways to convey a message to young people in Eersterust about crime and how it ruins your life. Jabu has first-hand experience of this, and was keen that others (especially those younger than him) be alerted to the dangers of crime. Carol suggested he write a song and bring it in the following week for the group to work on together. This was when this excerpt was recorded. Jabu used newspaper headlines to put together a text, and with Carol's help, subverted Nike's 'Just do it' into 'Just don't do it' as the song's refrain.

The words are:

> *Please guys, drugs and crime are no solution to any problem in life*
> *Instead they lead one to end up in jail or dead*
> ……………..Just don't do it………………
> *Today's youth have no future / Due to dangerous substances / It leads them to steal and commit a lot of crime*
> ……………Just don't do it ………………..
> *Parents, teachers, the police and the community / Must stand together to fight evil deeds*
> ……………Just don't do it ………………..

The words are in the form of a plea, addressing various social groups within Eersterust. Verse 1 warns young folk that crime doesn't pay, while in the third verse, directly addressing elders in the community (parents, teachers, police) implies their failure to prevent evil deeds and protect their young people. The second verse is a more general narrative – possibly addressing the song's audience, recounting the poorly resourced environment in which the future for young people is bleak. During the delineated session time, the five participants (four young men and Carol) transform the words on the page into a heartfelt, quasi rapped performance. This happens swiftly – so swiftly that had the excerpts not been subjected to micro-analysis, it would have been difficult to account for how a written text became 'performed' from scratch in under three minutes.

The three-minute segment was further segmented by Carol and myself using straightforward criteria: 'when something changed' or 'when something happened.' These subjective, perceptual-temporal delineations remained stable throughout repeated viewings. The segments were indexed using Nordoff-Robbins' (1977) descriptive listening techniques over a real time base, where each segment was subjected to thick description and temporal micro-analysis. The latter focused on body movement, communicative and expressive gesture, and the musical utterances. In addition, Carol and I studied the segments together, discussing their content and possible meanings. The following section presents a summary of each segment, with a heading to characterise it.

Unfolding Segments

Four young men, William, Benji, Jabu and Michael, aged 17-19 years, are on chairs drawn into a semi-circle, together with Carol. All look at writing on a large flipchart sheet on the floor: the text of 'Just Don't Do It.' Another scribbled version of the text is on a flipchart stand next to the group, behind William. Behind Carol is a piano, with the lid closed. She sits with her back to the piano.

Segment 1 – Gathering, Preparing, Attuning. (9 seconds)

Jabu talks to the group (which includes Carol), and conducts three beats (he says 1, 2, 3!). On his fourth beat, all begin reciting the song's words while Jabu continues conducting. The group's movements and voices are out of alignment at first, but soon begin co-ordinating and aligning with one another. There is a gradual build-up of momentum as the recitation progresses. Shortly after, however, the recitation begins to lose momentum and energy.

Segment 2 – Suggesting, Directing, Modifying (11 seconds)

Carol suggests that the group takes the song from the beginning, and asks whether William (who's holding a drum) would like to play it. Someone says, "No, you play the piano." Jabu nods in agreement, looking at Carol. She asks in a surprised voice, "me?" The group responds with "yes!" She turns to the piano behind her with a swift decisive movement and opens the piano lid. She now has her back to the semi-circle. She plays repeated accented chords in E minor, following the earlier tempo of the group recitation, entering seamlessly into the beat and tempo as well as dynamic level of the recitation. (While watching the segments together, Carol told me she had no idea what to play at that moment.) We noted that her role had shifted from suggesting (let's take it from the beginning) to being guided by the group to play the piano. The group restarts reciting the words together, re-pitching their voices in relation to the piano's E minor chords. At the second repeat of the refrain (Just Don't Do It), the singing loses tightness and alignment.

Segment 3 – Checking Direction (21 seconds)

Carol continues to play through the group's loss of momentum, and attempts to re-energize the group by slightly tightening the tempo and emphasizing the accents. During this 'bridge' passage, Jabu looks down at the sheet on the floor while still sustaining clapping/upper body movement. He seems to have withdrawn his gaze from the rest of the group. Benji follows Jabu's gaze and also looks at the words on the floor, while William points at the flipchart stand while looking at Jabu (as though asking which words they should follow). Benji and Michael also look up and around to the flipchart. Jabu looks up from the floor to the flipchart in response to William, shakes his head as a 'no,' then returns to looking intently at the words on the floor.

Musically there are various possibilities as to where the next verse can begin. Carol continues to play repeated chords. There is some indecision as to where to start, while all continue clapping and tapping their feet with the piano.

Segment 4 – Checking and Acknowledging Roles (9 seconds)

Carol looks round at Jabu, and he returns her gaze. They watch one another intently, while her playing slightly eases in intensity to a slower rock. Carol seems to be waiting for Jabu's cues as to how to proceed.

Jabu listens to Carol's playing and seems to tacitly encourage her to continue. The rest of the group listen and watch both Jabu and Carol. In this brief segment, there is a sense of high attentiveness between all group members.

Segment 5 – Checking Roles (8 seconds)

With split-second accuracy and seamless alignment of intensity, Jabu cues in the group to begin at the very moment that Carol forcefully says 'let's go!' accompanied by stronger piano playing. The young men begin nodding, clapping, tapping their feet and moving their bodies, with Carol providing a harmonic pulsed ground. The energy of the music has picked up, and this is reflected in the young men's body movements and clapping. Michael points to the sheet as though asking Jabu, "Is it my turn?"

Segment 6 – Directing, Supporting and Rehearsing (85 seconds)

Jabu nods emphatically to Michael and the group falls into collectively practicing the words, seamlessly entering the piano's pulsed harmonic stream. The recitation begins to sound like singing. The song gathers momentum and intensity, supported by the piano, and Jabu signals to William to move closer into the group. In response, he draws his chair in. The circle is closed, the space between the participants is tighter and closed, refracting the tightening of the music's pulse and phrasing.

Segment 7 - Towards Spontaneous Performance and Elaboration (28 seconds)

The group now shifts into a different musical gear. The song is 'performed' with no more interruptions or hesitation. As one unified organism, they clap, tap their feet and move their bodies, while Jabu seamlessly signals as to who recites each verse. During the refrain, the group shifts from recitation to singing, and as the song progresses towards the end, Jabu ceases to direct or conduct. At the last reciting of the verse, Jabu spontaneously exclaims, *"Please GUYS! Just don't do it!"* On the last chord Carol spins round and exclaims excitedly, *"NICE!"*

The momentum from this session led the group members to explore the possibility of performing the song in public, using it as a way of educating their peers about the dangers of drugs. With Carol they discuss the possibility of recording the song onto a CD and sending it to a local radio station.

Soon after this discussion, a spontaneous semi-public performance of 'Just Don't Do It' happened at YDO. A visiting jazz musician provided keyboard backing, and one of the YDO mentors took the role of compère/MC. Jabu, microphone in hand, performed the song powerfully while the small attentive audience sang the refrain. At the end of the song, the mentor saluted Jabu to the 'audience.' The event had all the ingredients of a popular music happening.

Reflections on the Session Experience

This musical journey conveys the transformative power of 'collaborative musicing' (Pavlicevic & Ansdell, 2008). In this brief group musicing event, people's experiences of making music together can be seen to be as much social as musical. All participants closely monitor one another's participation as social-musical beings, attending to fluid roles of leading, suggesting, prompting, following, reciprocating, supporting and simply finding the best and most enjoyable way of being part of this event. During this musical journey, the song's cultural-musical imperatives invite all participants to engage in a particular way of being together. Although 'Just Don't Do It' was created 'in vivo,' it draws from local musical genres familiar (more or less) to the five participants. These genre-specific characteristics place a powerful (and, one could suggest) non-negotiable attitude and commitment on the five. For the song to do its social-musical transformative work, everyone needs to collaborate. Here are five persons who find themselves in the same physical space-time, but share little in terms of language (with the exception of Carol, English is a second language), background (from Eersterust, Mamelodi and Pretoria) and social status. Despite all these differences, what they do share is a willingness to make this song work.

How does this happen? And what does the music therapist have to do with this? Is her presence necessary? Indeed, watching the session video, it would appear that Jabu could have managed this event as the musical director. The music therapist appears to play second fiddle. Close study of this and other excerpts reveal that it is not so much what the music therapist 'does' that matters, but her stance. Her stance is anchored in an unshakeable belief in musicing's transformative powers; a belief anchored in her direct experiencing of music therapy over the years. The music therapist's skill, I propose, does not come from 'book knowledge:' it is grown through her stance, grown from the ongoing experiencing and honing of the subtle skills needed for the crafting and evoking of transformative musicing. Her stance, then, is one of acute alertness and still listening, constantly attentive to what needs to happen: when, and how. She navigates with a light touch, appearing to do very little. However, when she 'acts,' it is with musical decisiveness and impeccable timing. Her skill is in creating an optimally alive, liminal musicing experience. This is about creating the best possible musical product (a song that grooves, swings and rocks), the best social product (that conveys clearly and powerfully that crime doesn't pay) and the best possible collaborative musicing. The 'magic' of this liminal experience transforms the experiencing of 'life;' crystallising in each participant an optimal quality of bonding, collaborating and enjoyment. In this time-space, rather than folk with identities of 'young folk in conflict with the law,' 'middle aged woman,' 'music therapist' or 'gang members,' a shared identity as musicians is enacted. Such musicians choreograph a social space with elegance, nuance and skill; knowing when to lead, who needs to lead, how to listen, to respond, to contradict, to ensure that music does its work. Their skills resemble those of skilled amateur and professional musical groups rehearsing, improvising and performing (Davidson & Good, 2002; Sawyer, 2005).

SUMMARY

This three-minute music therapy journey reveals rich and complex aspects of music therapy work. These include the music therapist's expertise in being acutely still and engaged so as to invite expertise from all; all participants' social elegance enables this collaborative experience; and the music therapist's stance, which is to do as little as necessary to ensure that all do as much as possible. Close analysis of the brief musical journey of 'Just Don't Do It' reveals the micro patterns and networks of optimal collaborative musicing: ways of being together that are charged with musicing's transformative power; transformative power that may propel the song onto a journey culminating in a radio station broadcast.

REFERENCES

Aigen, K. (2006). *Music Centered Music Therapy*. Gilsum, NH: Barcelona Publishers.

Annan, K. A. (2000) We the Peoples. *United Nations Millennium Report* http://www.un.org/millennium/sg/report/summ.htm Accessed April 29, 2010.

Ansdell, G. (2004). Rethinking music and community: Theoretical perspectives in support of community music therapy. In M.Pavlicevic & G. Ansdell (Eds.), *Community Music Therapy* (pp. 65-90). London: Jessica Kingsley Publishers.

Billington, R., Hockey, J. & Strawbridge, S. (1998). *Exploring Self and Society*. Houndmills: Palgrave.

Blaxter, M. (2004). *Health*. Cambridge: Polity Press.

Cross, I. (2003). Music and Biocultural Evolution. In M. Clayton, T. Herbert and R. Middleton (Eds.), *The Cultural Study of Music - A Critical Introduction* (pp. 19-30). New York and London: Routledge.

Davidson, J. & Good, J. (2002). Social and musical co-ordination between members of a sting quartet: An exploratory study. *Psychology of Music, 30,* 186-201.

DeNora, T. (2003). *After Adorno. Rethinking Music Sociology*. Cambridge: Cambridge University Press.

Martin, P. J. (2006). *Music and the Sociological Gaze. Art Worlds and Cultural Production*. Manchester: Manchester University Press.

Miell, D., MacDonald, R. & Hargreaves, D. (2005). *Musical Communication*. Oxford: Oxford University Press.

Nordoff, P. & Robbins, C. (1977). *Creative Music Therapy*. New York: John Day.

Pavlicevic, M. (2000). Improvisation in music therapy: Human communication in sound. *Journal of Music Therapy* 37(4), 269-285.

Pavlicevic, M. & Ansdell, G. (2008). Collaborative musicing. In S. Malloch & C. Trevarthen (Eds.), *Communicative Musicality*. Oxford: Oxford University Press.

Pavlicevic, M. & Ansdell, G. (2004). *Community Music Therapy*. London: Jessica Kingsley Publishers.

Rolvsjord, R. (2004). Therapy as empowerment: Clinical and political implications of empowerment philosophy in mental health practices of music therapy. *Nordic Journal of Music Therapy,* 13(2), 99-111.

Sawyer, R. K. (2005). Music and conversation. In D. Miell, R. MacDonald, & D. Hargreaves (Eds.), *Musical Communication* (pp. 45-60). Oxford: University Press.

Sennett, R. (2006). *The Culture of the New Capitalism*. New Haven & London: Yale University Press.

Springveldt, I. C. (2008). The relationship between local government and welfare organisations in Eersterust. Unpublished Masters Thesis Pretoria: University of South Africa.

Stern, D. (2004). *The Present Moment in Psychotherapy and Everyday Life.* New York: Norton.

Stige, B. (2002). *Culture-Centered Music Therapy.* Gilsum, NH: Barcelona Publishers.

Stige, B. (2003). Elaborations Towards a Notion of Community Music Therapy. Doctoral Dissertation, University of Oslo, Norway. Published by Unipub.

Trevarthen, C. & Malloch, S. N. (2000). The dance of wellbeing: Defining the musical therapeutic effect. *Nordic Journal of Music Therapy, 9,* 3-17.

Wosch, T. & Wigram, T. (2007). *Microanalysis in Music Therapy*. London: Jessica Kingsley Publishers.

Chapter Sixteen

FACILITATING NEUROLOGICAL REORGANIZATION THROUGH MUSIC THERAPY: A CASE EXAMPLE OF MODIFIED MELODIC INTONATION THERAPY IN THE TREATMENT OF A PERSON WITH APHASIA

Felicity Baker

INTRODUCTION

In the rehabilitation setting in Australia, the interdisciplinary team works together to provide effective rehabilitation programs for people who have neurological damage, with the ultimate goal being re-integration to the client's premorbid lifestyle and community. The primary focus of rehabilitation programs during the initial period post-trauma is addressing functional outcomes, specifically physical (motor), cognitive, communicative, and activities of daily living, due to current understandings that early intervention maximizes functional outcomes (e.g., Mateer & Kerns, 2000). This can, and frequently does, present a significant challenge for music therapy practitioners who may have to make choices with respect to the overall purpose of the music therapy program and the approaches used within those programs. I consider addressing the client's psychological and emotional adjustment to his/her acquired disability a necessary component of the rehabilitation process. However, this need is not always acknowledged by the interdisciplinary team who seem more interested in what music therapy can offer with respect to addressing functional outcomes. The clinical case presented here illustrates how music therapy interventions, specifically melodic intonation therapy (MIT) (Sparks, Helm, & Albert, 1973), target functional outcomes while simultaneously responding sensitively to the psychological adjustment of the client.

FOUNDATIONAL CONCEPTS

The Clinical Context

Working in a neurorehabilitation setting involves working together with the clients, interdisciplinary team members and family members to reduce the severity of the acquired impairment. The clients I worked with were adults (usually young adults aged 18-35 years) and were almost exclusively traumatically brain-injured as a result of a road traffic accident. Dependent upon the severity of the injury, and their phase of recovery, these clients may be in a coma, requiring a high level of care (completely dependent for all functional activities of daily living), semi-independent (living within the hospital but in units containing their own kitchenette and laundry), or integrated into the community and returning to the hospital as outpatients. Client progress can be rapid (some clients may only be in hospital for weeks), steady (hospitalized from 3-6 months), or slow (more than 6 months and sometimes years after the acquired brain injury). Therefore, the work of the music therapist is wide ranging and requires the experience to work with minimally responsive clients as well as highly independent clients, all of whom vary in their recovery pace. The clients' needs and therapy approaches selected are influenced by these factors.

Regardless of the severity of injury and their phase of recovery, clients often present with a combination of physical, communication, cognitive and emotional impairments (Baker & Tamplin, 2006). Physical impairments may range from limited range of movement, decreased coordination of movement, dyspraxia (impaired sequencing of movement), reduced muscle strength and endurance, poor trunk control, hemispheric neglect or perseveration. Cognitive and behavioral impairments typically range from poor concentration, poor abstract thinking, poor on-going memory or poor frustration tolerance, to disinhibited behaviors. Importantly, and often neglected, clients have extensive emotional adjustment needs – loss of independence, loss of role, loss of self-concept, loss of physical appearance, feelings of guilt and self-blame, feelings of anger toward others, and feelings of anger with hospitalization and the therapeutic process.

When addressing the client's therapy needs, it is important for the clinician to be aware that each physical, cognitive, communicative, behavioral and emotional adjustment impacts all other areas of the client's therapeutic outcomes. So, a holistic approach within a functional framework is required.

Of particular relevance to this chapter, clients with neurological damage may display a range of communication impairments, including aphasia (of various forms), dyspraxia, dysphasia and dysphonia. Broca's aphasia is a communication disorder caused by damage to the Broca's area of the brain in the posterior–inferior frontal gyrus of the left hemisphere. It is classified as one of the expressive aphasias and is characterized by non-fluent, effortful, slow, halting and uneven speech (Helms-Estabrooks, 1992). Clients will commonly have limited word output, with short phrases and sentences. They will misarticulate or distort sounds, their speech may be agrammatical, they may have impaired naming of objects, and they may not be able to repeat back words or sentences if modeled first by another person. However, their comprehension of language may be relatively intact with only slight impairments.

Neuroplasticity and Rehabilitative Potentials

Music therapy's effectiveness in neurorehabilitation is not itself a new concept. In fact, clinicians have published work in neurorehabilitation since the 1950's (e.g., Claeys, Miller, Dallow-Rampersad & Kollar, 1989; Cohen, 1988; Fields, 1954; Lucia, 1987). However, recent knowledge acquired in neuroscience and clinical neuromusicology have allowed music therapy clinicians to reflect upon their approaches and refine them accordingly (e.g., Baker et al., 2005; Kim & Koh, 2005; Magee, 2007; Särkämö et al., 2008; Schaulag et al., 2008; Tamplin & Grocke, 2008; Wheeler et al., 2003).

Perhaps the most important concept informing my work is that of neuroplasticity. Neuroplasticity is the term used to describe the process that the brain undergoes during recovering from injury. What is known now is that the brain is not structurally static, but capable of self modification and reorganization (Kolb 2004; Kolb & Gibb, 1999; Mateer &

Kerns, 2000). This means that if one part of the brain that was responsible for performing a certain behavior has been damaged, there is the potential for the brain to reorganize itself and another part of the brain will "take on" the responsibility for that function.

An important finding in neuroscience is that neuroplasticity doesn't just happen on its own. It is dependent upon the client being engaged in experiences that encourage the use of the behavior that is lost or impaired. And we know this because studies that have scanned the brains of people from certain professions show that their neuronal morphology differs slightly to those not engaged in such activities (Patel, 2008). For example, when compared with the general population, secretaries and appliance repairman develop advanced finger dexterity over sustained periods of use (Kolb & Gibb, 1999). Brain scans showed differences in trunk and finger neurones in their brains when compared with other people.

Relevant for music therapy practice, the same types of observations have been noted when people engage in making music. For example, the digit fingers in the left hands of string players show increased cortical representation when compared with the left thumb, yet no such differences were found in the cortical representation of the right hand (Elbert et. al., 1995). These findings show that the more frequently a skill is performed or practiced, the more the neural connections are strengthened and thus, the more likely the client will be able to perform that skill again, with more accuracy, for longer duration, and/or with greater efficiency.

There is mounting evidence that early intensive therapeutic intervention (2-3 times per week minimum), as opposed to less often (e.g., once per week) increases the chances for maximum cortical reorganization (neuroplasticity) (e.g., Mateer & Kerns, 2000). Mateer and Kerns (2000) and Nudo (2007) also provide evidence that varied approaches to developing a skill are more effective than pure repetition because they encourage multiple neural connections that increase the chances of developing and strengthening neuroactivity. In relation to my own practice as a music therapist, I therefore tend to work with clients intensively and engage varied activities to promote neural connectivity and facilitate the neuroplastic process.

The potential for music-based interventions to facilitate recovery of speech and language is supported by music and imaging studies that show how neuronal networks responsible for music processing are widely distributed throughout the brain (e.g., Patel et al., 1998 Sergent et al., 1992; Zatorre et al., 1992; 1996). Further, many of these music processing sites are in areas of the brain that are adjacent to, or overlap with, the areas of the brain involved in language and speech functioning, and are therefore relevant and influential in my understanding of my work with clients with communication disorders, including that of aphasia. To illustrate just a few:

- engagement in speech and music activates some of the same areas of the primary auditory regions of the brain (Zatorre et. al., 1992)
- listening to music (scales and auditory imagery for sounds) and words activate the same areas of the secondary auditory regions (Falk, 2000; Sergent et. al., 1992; Zatorre et. al., 1996), and
- Broca's area (known to be involved in the motor activity related to language) is also activated when playing music (Sergent et. al., 1992) and when musicians are engaged in a rhythmic task (Patel et al., 1998).

Given this knowledge, music-based interventions have a strong potential to stimulate neuronal changes by encouraging the areas of the brain responsible for music to take over responsibility for the speech skills that were previously controlled by the now neurologically adjacent and overlapping damaged areas of the brain. What we hope will happen during music therapy is that existing neural pathways will be strengthened, and that new neural pathways connecting undamaged areas of the brain will be created.

Melodic Intonation Therapy

As described in the previous section, because music is processed through varied areas of the brain, particularly those that overlap with areas of speech, and because repetition/active participation in music making can alter the brain's neuronal morphology, music-based techniques that engage unimpaired areas of the brain responsible for music making are well suited to assist with the rehabilitation of speech. Originally developed by Sparks, Helm & Albert (1973), Melodic Intonation Therapy (MIT) is a technique developed to facilitate the production of language in people with mild to moderate non-fluent aphasia. The approach described in this chapter is a modified version of MIT (referred to here as MMIT) which was adapted to assist those with severe non-fluent aphasia regain some verbal communication. Readers wanting more information about traditional MIT and the differences between MIT and the approach presented here are encouraged to read Baker (2000).

MMIT is a structured intervention whereby phrases or short sentences are set to music. These phrases are repeatedly sung to the client with the intention being that he/she will learn to sing them, internalize them, and eventually say them in a functional setting. My approach incorporates four components – preparing material for use in the sessions, implementing the intervention with the client, providing homework and practice tasks for the client, and then assessing and regularly reassessing client progress. These components are described in more detail in the case study below.

THE THERAPEUTIC PROCESS

The Client

At the time I met Tara, she was a 32-year-old woman who had been struck by a car four months earlier. Born and raised in the Philippines, she was on vacation in Australia, visiting her sister, while recuperating from the loss of her first child (who, at age eight, had recently died of a brain tumor). She also had a younger child, aged six, who was in the Philippines and living with her estranged husband. At the time of her accident, Tara was employed with an international company and spoke English fluently.

The accident left Tara with severe head injuries. On admission to emergency care, she was unconscious, intubated, and remained so for two months. Brain scans indicated Tara had sustained severe damage to the left hemisphere of her brain. Right hemispheric damage was also sustained. Several interventions were performed during the first few months post-accident, including two craniotomies. Once medically stable, Tara was transferred to a specialist traumatic brain injury rehabilitation hospital.

Assessment of Client

Three months post-injury, Tara regained consciousness, and prior to her referral to music therapy, completed a range of functional skills assessments including an assessment of her speech and language skills. Tests indicated speech difficulties including severe right hemiparesis affecting her right facial muscles, severe non-fluent aphasia (Broca's), and dyspraxia (a motor planning problem). Tara demonstrated that she had retained English verbal comprehension.

Tara began participating in active rehabilitation programs which were comprised of physiotherapy, occupational therapy, speech pathology and counseling. During speech pathology, various interventions were implemented to promote verbal output, and despite Tara's high level of motivation, she was unresponsive. A book of compics (pictorial communication system) was created for Tara so she could communicate her basic needs and wants while speech therapy continued.

A month later (four months post-injury), a staff member at the hospital witnessed Tara singing the words to a Beatles' song playing on the radio and had reported to the speech pathologist that Tara was singing the words to the song with clarity. It was at this point that Tara was referred to music therapy. On assessment, it was ascertained that Tara regularly participated in karaoke singing while in the Philippines. She had a beautiful sounding and controlled singing voice, and had a large repertoire of Western "pop" songs. She was a particular fan of Mariah Carey. Most importantly, she sang the words of familiar songs with remarkably accurate articulation. Her music skills appeared to be unaffected by her injury and this suggested that the areas of the brain responsible for music production were not damaged.

Initial Music Therapy Program

After consultation with the speech pathologist, and in keeping with the view that regular therapy is necessary in the early phase of rehabilitation, it was recommended that Tara receive five half-hour sessions of music therapy each week in addition to the four one-hour sessions of speech pathology she was already receiving. The music therapy sessions focused on singing popular love songs that Tara knew well, which aimed at 1) providing Tara with an opportunity to use her voice in an enjoyable activity that was guaranteed to be successful, and 2) practicing articulating words clearly (to support the work being done in speech pathology). The speech pathology program focused on conducting intensive drills aimed at improving Tara's verbal output. In spite of the intensive efforts of both speech pathologist and myself, after two months, Tara was unable to produce simple consonant and vowel combinations even when paired with gestural cues, pictures of mouth shapes, or modeling. While only brain imaging could prove this, it might suggest that there was extensive damage to certain areas responsible for speech, reducing her responsiveness to traditional speech approaches in areas that were not adjacent to the areas activated by the music-based approaches.

Introducing Melodic Intonation Therapy

Because Tara continued to sing beautifully, with motivation and clear articulation, discussion between the speech pathologist and myself led us to try Melodic Intonation Therapy. Here, it was actually the speech pathologist who implemented the program over the following three months, while I continued to provide Tara with opportunities to sing in order to maintain her clarity of articulation.

Integral to the therapeutic process with Tara was the need to simultaneously address her psycho-emotional needs and processes. Here, the singing and ensuing therapeutic relationship that we developed allowed Tara to express issues that could potentially lead to low therapy motivation. By singing songs that were either enjoyable or meaningful, Tara was able to express her frustration, anger or grief around her acquired disability and the loss of her daughter. For example, she would frequently arrive for music therapy distressed, and due to her language impairments, was unable to verbally articulate what was going on for her. Instead, we perused songbooks together and I would play the keyboard to accompany her singing. Singing released different emotions at different times – sadness (tears), tension (relaxed body) and happiness (smiling, laughing) – in ways that allowed her to work through her grief and loss.

Modifying MIT: A Ten Week Trial

Despite intensive efforts by the speech pathologist and myself, Tara remained unable to generate words independently outside of a singing context. Not deterred by her lack of progress, the speech pathologist and I were convinced that because Tara could sing, music would be key to any success she would have in speech therapy. We needed to rethink what we were doing and vary our approach. I suggested we make best use of the intact music skills Tara was displaying and introduce a modified version of MIT, which we would trial over ten weeks.

Step 1: Preparing the Musical Phrases

The speech pathologist first selected ten common words (herein called "keywords:" e.g., door, chair, bed, book), each of which were placed at the end of a phrase. For example, for the keywords coffee, bed, chair and door, the phrases could be constructed as "I want a cup of *coffee*, go to *bed*, sit on a *chair*, knock at the *door*." My clinical experience has shown that clients are more likely to recall the final word of the phrase than other words in the phrase (Baker & Tamplin, 2006).

Once I had constructed these phrases, I then set them to music. I created a melody for each phrase using a limited pitch range (usually no greater than a Major 6th) and composed at a register that aligned with Tara's vocal range. It was important that she was presented with "singable" melodies, otherwise she may have felt uncomfortable singing, and this may have limited her participation and therefore negatively affect outcomes. I constructed the melodies so they could be joined together to form a song. However, I was careful to ensure that each phrase had an individual melody distinct from the others in the set and did not resemble the sound of any other song phrase that Tara was likely to know. For example, creating a song phrase that used the melodic line from the opening phrase of "happy birthday" may confuse Tara, resulting in her singing the words of "happy birthday" instead of the target phrase.

Another feature of the phrases I composed for Tara was that they were composed around a central harmonic structure. I found creating a set of phrases in this way provided maximum potential for the client to internalize the phrases. Figure 1 provides an example of some of the phrases that I used in Tara's program.

Figure 1. Sample Phrases Composed Specifically for Tara

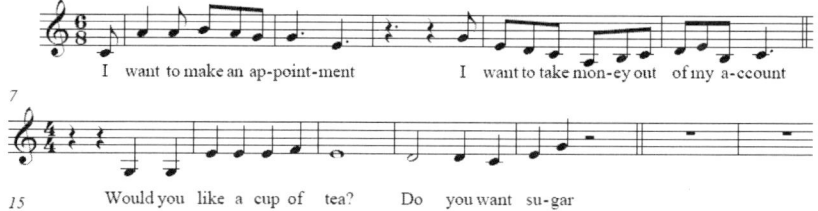

Step 2: Introducing the Phrases in the Session

When commencing MMIT in a typical session with Tara, I first started by singing the musical phrases to her a number of times while accompanying my singing on the keyboard. I sang the words of the phrases with very clear articulation. After several repetitions, I invited Tara to join in and "sing along" with me. Tara enjoyed this and joined in enthusiastically. Her articulation improved quite dramatically from the frequent incorrect sounds (caused by her co-morbid dyspraxia), and over the course of a couple of minutes, I noticed she was becoming more confident in her singing – singing louder and less tentatively, giving the impression she was aware of her improving performance. Following intensive daily practice of these phrases over four weeks, I gradually withdrew my participation and encouraged Tara to sing the phrases unaided. My role at this point was to assist her in becoming more independent in her singing. When her singing began to break down or she lost the melody, I would prompt her by choosing one of the following options:

1. Return to singing in unison with her.
2. Sing the phrase that immediately preceded the "target phrase" to cue Tara.
3. Sing the first word/s of the target phrase, leaving Tara to complete the phrase.

It was important for me to recognize that Tara's performance varied substantially from session to session as she began to internalize the phrases. More consistency in the generation of specific phrases occurred over time.

To promote Tara's independence in melodic recall, I encouraged Tara to sing her favorite songs at intermittent points throughout the session. This provided Tara with the often needed "break" from the hard work of therapy. Importantly, it also provided a distraction from the melodies to ensure that Tara would not perseverate on the "practiced" phrases. Perseveration is common in brain injured people. Tara enjoyed the singing but was always anxious to return to the practicing of the phrases. I explained to her that the singing of songs has therapeutic benefit: i.e. that it is like a test to see if she can recall the MMIT melodies once another tune was going around in her head. Once she understood this, she was able to enjoy the singing more.

Step 3: Moving Towards Independence

The final step in the MMIT process was to encourage Tara to use the target words in normal conversation. To achieve this, I asked Tara questions to test her independent word generation. For example, it is hoped that she would generate the word "soap" in response to the question "What do you wash yourself with in the shower?" Or "cappuccino" in response to the question "What are you going to order at the café?" At times this was quite a frustrating step for Tara, as her performance was initially inconsistent. However, with support from me, and continual practice, Tara managed to improve her output. Within two months, Tara had internalized the melodic phrases as a strategy, and was able to generate the ten words when cued. This relatively slow progress can be understood in terms of the neurological reorganization taking place in the brain. Initially, we are trying to encourage the use of certain neural pathways that have not been used in this way before. It takes time for the brain to adjust to this new way of doing things. Neurological research referred to earlier indicated that the more frequently a pathway is activated as a consequence of engaging in a task (like singing), the stronger the connection will become. This suggests that over time, we would expect that Tara would improve in this domain should she continue to engage in the program.

Tara's Rapid Progress

Tara's slow but steady progress was so encouraging that the therapy team recommended increasing her music therapy program to four hours per week. At this time, the speech pathologist and I introduced new target words. Tara indicated that she wanted to be able to call her family members by their names, so this was the focus of the next phase in her program. She was very motivated by this task – the words had more personal meaning for her – and so she often arrived at the music therapy office asking whether she could have more sessions. To address her request for more therapy, I introduced a homework program for her to implement between sessions. This program involved her playing an audio recording of all the melodic phrases so she could sing along with the recording. This approach aligns with the modern views of rehabilitation which indicate that during the initial phase of recovery, frequent sessions (even if they are short in length) are needed to maximize recovery. This self-initiated practice resulted in Tara learning new words at a faster pace.

I monitored Tara's progress regularly to determine how many phrases she was able to independently generate and how many still required musical prompts. I did this by beginning each session with a recap of what had been addressed in previous sessions without providing any music (cues). Another important feature of Tara's program was that while I may have introduced new material, I would often revisit and reassess previous material to ensure she was maintaining her ability to self-generate the phrases rehearsed earlier.

The next stage in Tara's MMIT program was to introduce functional words suggested by the occupational therapist. These targeted words included personal hygiene items such as soap, lipstick, makeup, brush and the names of clothing items such as shoes, shirt and jumper. This enhanced her activities of daily living by enabling Tara to name the various items she was manipulating or wearing. Within six months of commencing MMIT, Tara was learning one or two new words each week and was able to independently generate 25 of the 32 words that she had been introduced to. Of the remaining seven, she was able to recall six of these when musical cues were provided by the therapist.

Tara is Reintegrated into the Community

The four-times weekly MMIT program continued until Tara's discharge to a shared community house 12 months after initially commencing MMIT (18 months post-injury). At that time, Tara's music therapy program was reduced to one outpatient session per week. She was also discharged from speech therapy. Tara continued to utilize the audio recorded program to practice between each session.

On commencement of her community living program, the occupational therapist requested that I teach Tara to verbalize words and/or phrases that would assist her in communicating with others in the community. Phrases that were added to the program included "I want a 2-hour ticket, zone 1 and 2" (referring to a transit ticket), "I want to take money out of my account," "I want a taxi to Saint Albans," "I want to make an appointment" and "Where are the toilets?" As part of her rehabilitation program, Tara and I would have music therapy sessions in the community. We visited a bank, a doctor's surgery, a coffee shop and a toyshop, and Tara practiced independently using these phrases so she could perform her banking needs, make doctor's appointments and have a cappuccino. My role was to facilitate this process, be a back-up person, prompt her to use her musical cues should she have problems generating words, and assess her independence in the community. Tara was initially motivated to use her language within the community but found it difficult when members of the public were impatient with her. My support was crucial in maintaining her motivation to keep trying. Perhaps the most significant moment for Tara was when she managed to communicate with the bank teller her request to withdraw money from her account. I witnessed the first time that she was able to achieve this task independently. She gained so much confidence from this one event – it was moving to witness

Figure 2 illustrates the changes over the course of the MMIT program in terms of the number of phrases in the program, the number Tara could recall independently, and the number she could recall when given musical prompts. The figure shows that Tara's progress was initially slow, but over time, her progress accelerated, particularly in relation to how many words/phrases she could independently generate.

Figure 2. Tara's Progress in her Production of Target Phrases

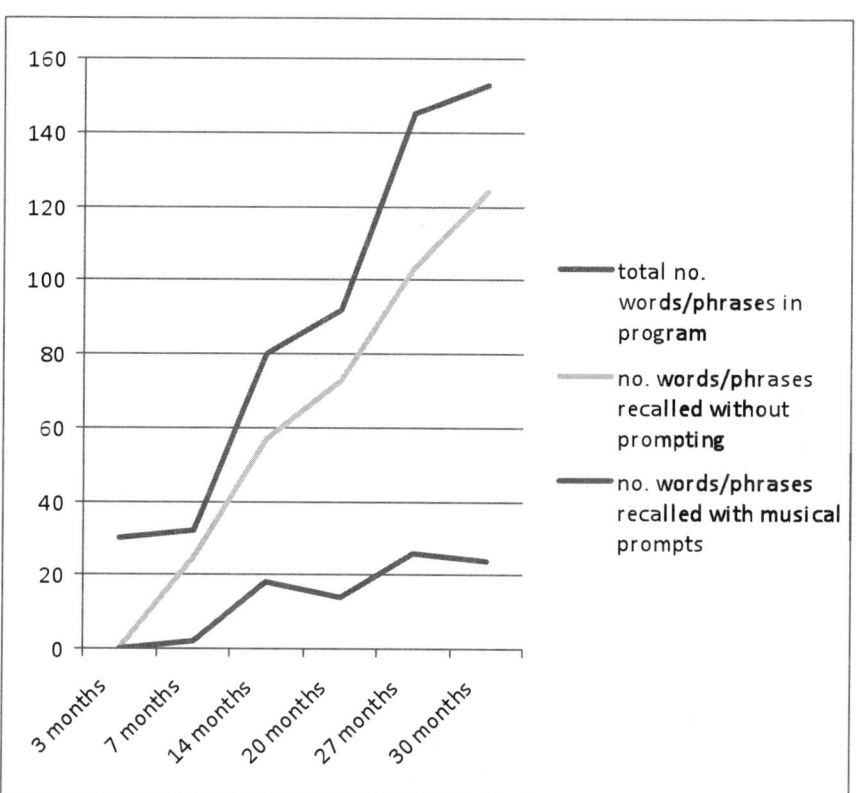

This might suggest that neural pathways were connecting and strengthening at a more rapid rate, with each connection increasing the probability that Tara's brain would reactivate the pathway on a subsequent occasion. On final assessment, after 30 months using MMIT both as an inpatient and then as an outpatient, Tara had acquired a functional language of 148 words/phrases, of which she was able to initiate 124 of these independently and the remaining 24 were recalled following musical cues. She was able to express her immediate needs, feelings and interests. Without the modifications made to the traditional MIT program, Tara may not have been able to use verbal language at all.

CONCLUSION

The case study of Tara indicates the value that MMIT can have in assisting a person with neurological damage to regain some speech function. Although a speech pathologist would normally implement an MIT program, the necessity to create phrases with predictable but individual melodic and rhythmic structures indicates the need for a music therapist's input into the MMIT program. It suggests that the musical centers of the brain, when activated, facilitated a neuronal reorganization that allowed Tara's brain to access language again. Further, consideration for Tara's emotional well-being and the support that can be offered through music therapy was instrumental in maintaining Tara's motivation for therapy, a reward for her hard work, and an outlet to explore her feelings associated with receiving the traumatic brain injury.

REFERENCES

Baker, F. & Tamplin, J. (2006). *Music Therapy in Neurorehabilitation: A Clinician's Manual*. London: Jessica Kingsley Publishers.

Baker, F. (2000). Modifying melodic intonation therapy programs for adults with severe non-fluent aphasia. *Music Therapy Perspectives,* 18(2), 107-111.

Baker, F., Wigram, T. & Gold, C. (2005). The effects of a song-singing programme on the affective speaking intonation of people with traumatic brain injury. *Brain Injury,* 19(7), 519–528.

Claeys, M. S., Miller, A. C., Dallow-Rampersad, R. & Kollar, M. (1989). The role of music therapy in the rehabilitation of traumatically brain injury clients. *Music Therapy Perspectives*, 6, 71-76.

Cohen, N. (1988). The use of superimposed rhythms to decrease the rate of speech in a brain damaged adolescent. *Journal of Music Therapy, 25(2)*, 85-93.

Elbert, T., Pantev, C., Wienbruch, C., Rockstroh, B. & Taub, E. (1995). Increased cortical representation of the fingers of the left hand in string players, *Science, 270*, 305–307.

Falk, D. (2000). Hominid brain evolution in music. In N.L. Wallin, B. Merker, and S. Brown (Eds.), *The Origins of Music* (pp. 197–216). Cambridge, MA: Massachusetts Institute of Technology.

Fields, B. (1954). Music as an adjunct in the treatment of brain-damaged patients. *American Journal of Physical Medicine, 33*, 273-283.

Helms-Estabrooks, N. (1992). *Aphasia Diagnostic Profiles.* Austin Tx: Pro-Ed.

Kim, S. J. & Koh, l. (2005). The effects of music on pain perception of stroke patients during upper extremity joint exercises. *Journal of Music Therapy, 42*, 1, 81-92.

Kolb, B. (2004). Mechamisms for cortical plasticity after neuronal injury. In J. Ponsford (Ed.), *Cognitive and Behavioral Rehabilitation: From Neurobiology to Clinical Practice.* New york: Guilford Press.

Lucia, C. M. (1987). Towards developing a model of music therapy intervention in the rehabilitation of head injured clients. *Music Therapy Perspectives, 4*, 34-37.

Magee, W. (2007). Development of a music therapy assessment tool for patients in low awareness states. *NeuroRehabilitation, 22*(4), 319-324.

Mateer, C. A. & Kerns, K. A. (2000). Capitalizing on neuroplasticity. *Brain and Cognition, 41*(1), 106-109.

Nudo, R. (2003). Adaptive plasticity in motor cortex: Implications for rehabilitation after brain injury. *Journal of Rehabilitation Medicine*, 35(suppl. 41), 7-11.

Patel, A. D. (2008). *Music, Language, and the Brain.* New York: Oxford University Press.

Patel, A., Peretz, I., Tramo, M. & Labreque, R. (1998). Processing prosodic and musical patterns: A neuropsychological investigation. *Brain and Language, 61*, 123-144.

Särkämö, T., Tervaniemi, M., Laitinen, S., Forsblom, A., Soinila, S., Mikkonen, M., Autti, T., Silvennoinen, H. M., Erkkilä, J., Laine, M., Peretz, I. & Hietanen, M. (2008). Music listening enhances cognitive recovery and mood after middle cerebral artery stroke. *Brain: A Journal of Neurology, 13*(3), 866-876.

Schlaug, G., Marchina, S. & Norton, A. (2008). From singing to speaking: Why singing may lead to recovery of expressive language function in patients with Broca's aphasia. *Music Perception, 25*(4), 315-323.

Sergent, J., Zuck, E., Terriah, S. & Macdonald, B. (1992). Distributed neural network underlying musical sight-reading and keyboard performance. *Science, 25,* 106-109.

Sparks, R.W. & Deck, J.W. (1986). Melodic intonation therapy. In R. Chipley (Ed.), *Language Intervention Strategies in Adult Aphasia* (pp. 320-332). Baltimore: Williams & Wilkins.

Sparks, R.W., Helm, N.A. & Albert, M.L. (1973). Melodic intonation therapy for aphasia. *Archives of Neurology, 29,* 130-131.

Tamplin, J. & Grocke, D. (2008). A music therapy treatment protocol for acquired dysarthria rehabilitation. *Music Therapy Perspectives, 26*(1), 23-29.

Wheeler, B., Shiflett, S. & Nayak, S. (2003). Effects of number of sessions and group or individual music therapy on the mood and behavior of people who have had strokes or traumatic brain injuries. *Nordic Journal of Music Therapy*, 12(2), 139-151.

Zatorre, R.J., Evans, A.C., Meyer, E. & Gjedde, A. (1992). Lateralisation of phonetic pitch discrimination in speech processing. *Science, 256,* 846-849.

Zatorre, R.J., Halpern, A. R, Perry, D.W., Meyer, E. & Evans, A.C. (1996). Hearing in the mind's ear: a PET investigation of musical imagery and perception. *Journal of Cognitive Neuroscience, 8*(1), 29-46.

I wish to thank the editor of Music Therapy Perspectives who kindly gave permission for me to include some previously published material (Baker, 2000).

Chapter Seventeen

THE CASE OF PAULA: MUSIC PSYCHOTHERAPY WITH A MUSICIAN

Joanne Loewy and Stephan Quentzel

INTRODUCTION

This chapter is based on music psychotherapy sessions that took place at an outpatient center for musicians. This center is part of a large medical institution in New York. Paula was a musical prodigy who was referred to our center by a fellow musician and friend. She was involved in 44 individual sessions over a period of approximately 14 months. Central to this treatment were aspects of self care, musical intimacy, awareness and trust. This included using music for self-care, which often was in contrast to the music Paula might have played in performance. One important philosophy of our work with musicians, illustrated in this chapter, is the desire to recover creativity and aspects of health and spontaneity, which eventually lead to integration of the 'true self' with the 'performer self.' Specifically, musical play was addressed as a forum for repartee - an expansion of the ability to seek an authenticity of self through discovery of music used in the context of its application to the self.

FOUNDATIONAL CONCEPTS

The Center for Music and Medicine, from which this chapter is drawn, treats musicians and performing artists who have specific medical and health needs related to the unique physical, mental and emotional demands of their profession. This includes treating musicians whose performance may be stifled by overuse injuries, psychiatric challenges, anxiety, chronic fatigue, focusing difficulties and/or the various side effects of medications (e.g., tendon inflammation). Performers often report a high incidence of depression and chemical dependency (Cuyjet & Tolson, 2007), and this has been reported in the literature for jazz musicians as early as the 1960's (Winick, 1960). The mission of the Center is to provide musicians and performing artists with health services tailored to their unique needs. Each musician and performing artist can receive low-cost medical treatment in conjunction with select, specialized music therapy services. Our clinic's medical director specializes in integrative medicine and psychiatry, while the music therapists specialize in music psychotherapy. The Center's integrative-bio-psycho musical approach (Quentzel & Loewy, 2010) addresses the unique ailments specific to performing artists and musicians. The Center's interdisciplinary team of medical professionals and music therapists provide traditional medicine with complementary mind-body approaches.

Each musician, upon intake, receives both medical and music therapy consultations, which include a comprehensive history and physical exam, review and evaluation of his/her chief complaint, and proposals for treatment modalities. The music therapy assessment (Quentzel & Loewy, 2010) includes a full music history, music psychotherapy evaluation, and a performance history along with an assessment of future music therapy interventions that might address the patient's symptoms and potential. In follow-up medical treatment, referrals to our team of consulting physicians cover a wide range of specialties that include neurology, acupuncture, pulmonology, pain medicine and palliative care, neuromuscular and electromyography neurology, rehabilitation and internal medicine. Follow-up music therapy services may include treatments by our team of consulting music therapists in the following areas: 1) *Music ergonomic-posturing*, which focuses upon adjusting and/or altering the way music is played and the musical environment in which one plays, to assist in the avoidance of overuse that contributes to repetitive strain injury, 2) *Music visualization,* which focuses on relaxing mind and body to alter one's perception of tension and/or to evoke the potential of healthy inner resources, 3) *Sound vibration*, in which vibratory instruments are used to address and alter the client's perception of pain and/or anxiety, 4) *Music and breath entrainment*, which uses the inherent structure and shape of music to create flow and enhance the patient's feeling of space, in order to ease the fear and constraints of breathing, 5) *Tonal intervallic synthesis*, (Loewy, 2011) in which tones and sounds are used to create consonance within the body, and 6) *Rhythmic release*, where repetitive rhythms, drumming and triplet metered holding (in both structured and non-structured musical motifs) can provide a physical/emotional/spiritual release.

Music Psychotherapy

Since music is often a musician's means of livelihood, and is strongly associated with feelings of self worth and/or self hate, it can often be a source of problems for a musician. Being inside the music experience with the musician client can address these issues in a unique yet delicate way.

Using the 'Tour of the Room' assessment approach (Loewy, 2000) presents opportunities to explore the musician's musical and performance history. The 'Tour of the Room' also includes demonstrations of all the sounds/instruments in the room and provides a means for the client to make associations with each of these sounds. Playing music of choice for and with the therapist may further elicit memories or expand current experiences. This might include stories related to the experience of performance. The outcomes may include identifying problems related to pain from overuse, chronic fatigue, anxiety and/or a host of other situations that are accompanied by fears, anxiety, loss of confidence, or renewed feelings of success that shape the musician's identity.

Central to the *Center for Music and Medicine's* approach to clinical care is music psychotherapy, which utilizes music and the context of a musical relationship, to provide opportunity for self-growth and insight. Clinical music improvisation is vital to this approach and involves creating spontaneous live music by oneself or with a music therapist on an instrument (or instruments) that is either familiar or unknown. The created music can provide a spontaneous forum that uncovers intrapsychic tendencies. Clinical improvisation may give insight into unconscious issues, and into the interpersonal tendencies that are often encapsulated by the role one tends to assign to the music. Analyzing and making conscious one's relationship with music, musical others and the subtle referential role that music and musicians tend to play in everyday living can be life-changing. The musical relationship that develops in the treatment of musicians is complicated in the sense that the music therapist is constantly seeking to understand the transference, and counter transference, not only in the relationship between client and therapist, but also between the client and the music, and in doing so, providing insight into the problems and resources of the client.

THE CLIENT

Reflections On Treating A Music Prodigy

Paula was a renowned jazz musician who was referred by a friend who was concerned that the client had not been able to leave her apartment for several years. He was worried that her medical condition was worsening, though he could not say exactly what it was she was suffering from. Nevertheless, he believed that our Center was using what he referred to as "music-based healing" and upon arranging an appointment, promised that her nurse would be able to accompany her to come see us, if we could arrange car service.

Two weeks later, Paula was rolled into our clinic on a stretcher. The transport medics lifted her from the stretcher to a special large padded electronic wheelchair that we borrowed from the day surgery department. This is only important to know because the transport team and the process of lifting Paula from the stretcher to the modified gurney each week became a ritual, and as such, there were notable transitional elements.

Paula was a large woman. This, combined with her rapid-fire nervous joking, her disarming though somewhat gruff and unfailing ability to say the right thing to the transport medics, and her uncanny ability to use flirtation coupled with her dramatic cries if not touched exactly the right way, made for a prolonged transition from stretcher to chair. It was a memorable weekly experience. This is not to imply that physical motion was not a true hardship for her, or that we were not empathic to her continuous apparent discomfort in moving. There was, however, an undeniable ease yet simultaneous sense of entitlement in the way she treated the five people assisting her in the weekly transition that seemed to be indicative of her many years of concert touring. She was the quintessential diva! Memorable were Paula's familiarity with the entourage and her grace in entertaining everyone involved as she demanded as much as possible from every person around her during transitions in and out of her music therapy sessions. Her grace, however, taken one step further, resembled manipulation more than it did charm. This giant of the jazz world was insecure and rejection-sensitive enough to feel drawn to test how far she could push our loyalty and responsiveness.

Today, approximately seven months after her death, we find ourselves still feeling compelled to review and rediscover the extremely sensitive aspects of treatment that emerged, especially in the cross transferences between music prodigy and music psychotherapist. We are grateful to have recorded a pivotal mid-point music therapy session on DVD, which we analyzed as part of this chapter. This case highlights a few of the significant and delicate issues, nuances and treatment perspectives that can arise when treating performers.

Paula's History

Paula was an African American woman, one of two sisters from a large family. She studied classical piano as a young girl in the 1930s. In her music therapy sessions, she often remembered playing the piano for governor's events in his mansion at the age of two. Paula was a frequent music contest winner as a child and her early interest in jazz as a teen afforded her an invitation to play in neighborhood bars. Eventually, as a very young woman, she earned opportunities to play music abroad with several well-known big band leaders. Paula studied at a mid-Western university and worked with local west coast bands in the late 1940s, well before graduating. She relocated to New York City in the mid 1950s, playing cocktail lounges and developing her own style as a singer and performer. At the same time, she accompanied a variety of well known jazz vocalists. Her compositions include several recognized jazz tunes. Her big band recordings number in the hundreds. Paula was chosen to perform at the Kennedy Center in the late 1990s and at the Apollo Theater at a national jazz event several months before her death.

THE THERAPEUTIC PROCESS

The First Meeting

We distinctly recall approaching Paula in the hallway outside our clinic in preparation for our first session. She was screaming, complaining of pain and refusing to move off the stretcher onto the wheelchair in order to enter our clinic. The transport team was in need of the stretcher Paula was lying on in order to go to their next job. They seemed frustrated and were concerned about being late for their next pick-up, but our wheelchair was standard and not perceived as comfortable by Paula. As she caused this great commotion, Dr. Quentzel, knowing of an oversized padded electric wheelchair in the surgery recovery room, went to retrieve it for Paula.

Early in the transportation process, upon hearing her moaning and the commotion outside our clinic, and not quite knowing what to expect, I grabbed my guitar and met Paula with music outside in the hall. My hands fell into a bass line vamp that was grounded in the key of her screams. Amidst her delight and quieted moans, I worked myself into an "I Can't Give You Anything But Love" improvisation with lyrics of "…soon we'll go on in the music room…P-a-u-l-a (spelling out her name).

This delighted Paula and she sang back to me and the medics as we waited for Dr. Quentzel to retrieve the recovery room chair. She also improvised to strangers passing by the hallway - patients and families going to other clinics. She was receptive to me and called me "darling." In two bars, she had the medics smiling and dancing, seemingly forgetting about their other routes. She had mustered a small crowd around her and appeared to be slowly rising to a 'sit-up' position on the stretcher. My bass line kept flowing effortlessly, and we were scatting in harmony. Before Paula had ever appeared inside our clinic, she had our medical director serving as a transport aide and her new music therapist holding a walking bass on guitar. At the final cadence of "I Can't Give you Anything But Love" we glided into "Oh What a Beautiful Morning," Ray Charles-style, in 3… "I played for him (Charles)…" she announced. We were all listening, as my bass line shifted into chords. I thought to myself: how did she know I liked to play in three quarter time? We were all in the 'music sphere' - a manager from another clinic whom we rarely saw outside of her office, the director of phlebotomy, and the chief pediatrician from another clinic. Everyone was watching and some were even singing. This was a like a gig, I thought to myself, and we were all musically infatuated.

Treating Paula

Infatuation soon led to heavy reflection and several consultations with our team prior to her second session. We prepared in advance for the padded electric wheel chair to be ready so as to generate an easier transition for the medical transport team that was bringing Paula to session two.

We learned from session one much of Paula's medical and psychosocial history. She was 75 years old and the youngest of eight children. She had been bedridden for years due to her legs being crushed by an auto hit-and-run accident some years earlier. Her medical problems were multiple: diabetes mellitus, cataracts, hypertension, multiple motor vehicle accidents, gross atrophy of lower limbs, peripheral neuropathy, peripheral vascular disease, degenerative disease of the lumbar spine, vision problems and moderate anxiety.

Her husband had died 25 years ago. Her only son died in a shooting in his late 20s. Paula was alone, with several friends and home health aide, but "mostly alone," as she explained.

The First Six Months

The first stage of treatment usually involves listening. In a music psychotherapy context, this entails building trust. Though tempting to come quickly and directly into musical play, the building of a dynamic emerges most naturally when the therapist hears from the musician and listens openly: "What does the musician come in with, and what is s/he choosing to play in the first moments of our musical meeting?" These are essential questions to ask early in the music psychotherapy relationship.

The first month of Paula's sessions was spent listening: listening to her music, listening to her stories about musicians, and to the litany of ups and downs she had experienced in playing with many prominent jazz musicians. Notably, as I eased my way into playing with Paula, there were recognizable resistances. She would typically speed up her tempo and transpose us into a key a half step higher than the one we had begun in. At first this seemed to be a natural elevation, but at other times, this would not occur at a cadence or bridge, but seemingly would occur 'out of nowhere.' It felt as if it was a challenge, or more specifically a test: Could I follow? It was a challenge I rather enjoyed!

Paula's greatest acceptance of me musically was when I would harmonize with her. She remained on the melody and would smile with delight when I decorated her melodies. This happened in the latter parts of our work together. She also enjoyed medleys of her own design, which occurred as part of the musical soliloquies she would share. Paula had countless stories of traveling on the road through her relationships with jazz greats and movie stars. I worked hard to discern what was important and applicable to Paula's issues and what was merely 'sensational' and seductive to our musical and personal relationship.

A Turning Point

Paula's favorite tunes to sing and play included "Tomorrow" (jazzy arrangement), "Feliz Navidad" (jazz style) and "Lush Life" (slow and heart-felt). She was a personal friend of Billy Strayhorn, and the story I heard her repeat more often than any other was the day he happened to step into a bar in which she was practicing piano. She had not seen nor heard anyone enter and was unaware that her practice was being evaluated. Evidently, Strayhorn (the composer of "Lush Life") was taken by Paula's interpretation of "Lush Life" and relayed that her rendition was the way he had "meant it to be played," and the finest he had heard. For Paula, the rest was history. One of Paula's favorites to play was "Lush Life."

This story reminds me of how the musician often builds a significant repertoire based on the feedback of others, rather than the inclusion of repertoire based on the performer him/herself. How one gauges one's own creative process often takes a back seat in repertoire building. This inner nurturance can be replaced by an outer image, which is built upon the feedback and approval of others. In a way, this takes away our own feeling about our music and how we play it, and in so doing, we may be diminishing an authentic level of self growth and discovery. This aspect of 'art,' as representative of the 'self,' involves a critical self-evaluative process that many musicians and performers find is worth investigating because it not only influences how they play, but can permeate into themes of self-fulfillment outside of music.

For Paula, there were often instances where she would recall stories of jazz greats, people with whom she had enjoyed playing, which included those who had appreciated her genius. At the same time, there was a marked separation in what she had identified as her own process versus what others had demanded of her. There were feelings related to stories of being "burned" or mistreated, and these often involved the ideas and egos of other musicians, whom she did not feel appreciated her enough. There was a part of Paula and her music that she saw as being taken advantage of.

Session 24 was particularly important in Paula's therapy, providing insight into several dimensions of the therapeutic process: the sequence of the session, the main issue(s), the treatment strategy, the music and our musical relationship (see Table 1). At this juncture, we were reflecting on the session prior, where Paula had ended with a poignant rendition of "Little Girl Blue:"

> *Sit there and count the raindrops, falling down on you. Old girl, you're through. All you can do is count the raindrops. Unlucky, little girl blue.*

This session was unusual in that she had trusted my song selection, and then worked with my tempo and arrangement. At this point she had been going through a particularly difficult time. She shared that her home health aide had hit her and taken her wallet. Evidently the police had taken their time in responding to her call. She reflected that most of her home health aides had been inattentive and that several had robbed her. Playing "Little Girl Blue" toward the end of our session seemed to reflect a point of tenderness and hopelessness for Paula.

Once she had been transferred to her chair and the keyboard placed on top of it, I brought up the last session and how her rendition of "Little Girl Blue" had stayed with me.

Table 1. Unfolding Session Sequence of "Little Girl Blue"

Sequence	Issue	Strategy	Music
Joanne: "I've been hearing your 'Little Girl Blue' all week"	Hopelessness	Joanne supports Paula, letting her know she has penetrated Joanne's song-consious mind and that this is a critical issue for Paula	
Joanne and Paula begin playing "Little Girl Blue" together		Moving into the shadow: Can we go into what it means for you to be depressed?	Key of D flat - Paula starts on the phrase before the bridge but she does not sing the words, suggesting she is thinking
A bridge is sung by Paula, but the words are not sung – they are avoided. "No use old girl... you may as well surrender... your hope is getting slender"	Despair	Reflection through words: "Music has taken you through many things"	Paula is smearing the song- She is improvising the feeling - perhaps it is too much – the music is getting darker and yet the words acknowledge what is gone... she has never done this in music. Joanne joins her in the music, harmonizing.
Silence		Silence	Grand Pause

Sequence	Issue	Strategy	Music
Joanne and Paula: How can we address being depressed?	Depression	Paula: "My music chills others out." Joanne: "I wonder how can it help you through this so you can take advantage of it - for *you*?" Joanne tries to connect Paula to her own resources	
Reflecting on issues with others, Paula reviews her musical history "I played since I was two, musicians always call on me." Joanne: How can music address your needs?	Finding strength within herself	Prompts self reflection -seeking strength – she has reached a vulnerable position	As she sings, Paula changes key into E, then F, F#, and then G - and goes into a potentially new theme
Paula: "I was singing in the ambulance on the way here…I am realizing, with everything I am going through, I have to find ways to keep myself happy…around the abusive nurses, the psychotic aids…I wanna be in a better place…a clearer head….how can I when everyone mistreats me?"	Finding happiness when things feel chaotic	Prior to working with the sadness and depression, Joanne senses there is anger to be addressed and released	Joanne takes a cymbal and acknowledges: "I am hearing *Get Happy* but I am also hearing *You Took Advantage of Me*"
After singing with Joanne, Paula says: "I know how to	Finding strength in music	Help Paula feel strength without using performance as a de-	Paula complains about the keyboard: "It's out of tune."

make myself happy" and begins playing a song of her own choosing		fense	She begins scatting on "Make Someone Happy" dropping down to the key to F, she sings about "Making people happy…"

After a brief pause, the session continues:

Sequence	Issue	Strategy	Music
Joanne investigates the lyrics of "Make Someone Happy" with Paula	Keeping Paula connected to her own needs and not those of her audience	To bring it back into self reflection - defining the needs of the performer beyond performance	Joanne sings to the tune : "What would make Paula happy – I wonder what would make you really really happy?"
Paula responds verbally, still playing	Joanne is the audience: Paula is still trying to please her, and thereby distancing herself	Hold/contain Paula in the music	Paula says: " I am happy - I just need to be where I can play and give of myself". She sings: "Now I'm making up the lyrics so you can be happy too"

Joanne moves into the music, searching for a way to collaborate as equals	Transition	Making music together and reflecting on Paula's issue can bring us into a better place for investigating the things that are giving her pain and avoidance.	With a cymbal brush accompaniment, Joanne sings in up-tempo: "I want to be happy - but I can't be happy - 'till I make you happy too...'
Paula takes the lead and scats out to Dr. Quentzel as he passes. She reflects: "Doc, the way you're looking at me is dangerous!"	Reaching out and feeling good about her music	We are connected in the music	Paula continues the music, even when the song ought to end - repeating cadence indicating that she does not want it to end
Joanne moves into "Happy Talk," seeking to further the medley	Accepting intimacy	Extending an intimate musical connection-at the bridge Joanne suggests that she wants to keep going, but Paula starts to talk	Paula stops the music to tell of her musical relationship with the singer who made "Happy Talk" famous.

Paula continues, "That's the problem with them [famous musicians]...the magic is tragic. We had a great day when we first played together. It's sad because the stars see themselves doing what they were doing, before when all the lights were on, and when the lights were dimming, they can't face it." Realizing that she has not only disclosed about the "Happy Talk" star, but perhaps also about herself, she reflects on her own struggles with her sister growing up. "My older sister was sent to a conservatory while I always traveled with people who saw themselves in 'lights.' I'm not really needing to know how to take care of myself, I can do that...."

I respond, "I know you can do that, I see you can do that...this film will show you directing with lots of song themes of how to make yourself happy...and...you know how you say you always trust ME, well I trust YOU...especially the things that come for YOU when you play, very important themes...." Paula then reflects "I need to get away from people that are trying to hurt me..." (referring to aides and nurses).

Joanne directs Paula back to music improvisation based on a good-bye theme. Paula speaks about her upcoming gig, the first in ten years. We discuss resourcing options for a wheelchair and transportation.

Session Reflection

For the first time, Paula allowed me to play with her for an extended period, and furthermore, she allowed me to lead. Much of my work in previous sessions had been listening to her play and talk. This was critical to our relationship, but also seemed to reflect her general sense of isolation. Listening to her in earlier sessions led us to this point of improvisatory play. In so doing, it helped her to admit her depression and lead her to find resources to cope. The more she sang and played, the more she was able to recognize her deep need to perform again.

Paula became more collaborative in future sessions, especially once we had watched the film of the session. She reflected that "we had good musical ideas" and she also claimed to understand music therapy and was impressed by how it visibly influenced her mood and sense of self, especially in our improvisatory moments.

After this session, Paula complained less and seemed to be excited about getting back on the stage. Her desire to perform and to become more physically independent reflected greater risk-taking and increased coping skills.

Throughout her turbulent final years of life, several themes emerged and crystallized in the course of her music therapy treatment at our center. The strongest, ironically, was her deep desire to walk. This grossly unrealistic desire came alongside her weekly resistance to discuss the use of a wheelchair. She adamantly claimed that using a wheelchair would limit her and would keep her from her ultimate goal of walking. This belief did not seem to foster resilience, but rather built unreasonable expectations, which ultimately would seem to defeat her ability to recover her own ability to be mobile. Her unstated goal, of freezing herself in the 'sick' role, worked like a charm."I will walk again — wait and see" she would say, accepting little discussion that "any wheelchair" would be a first step to sitting up and gaining independence. It was believed by the team that the only reason she used the oversized wheelchair to come into the music therapy center was because the stretcher would not fit through the door.

Incidentally, she also used this type of wheelchair in her last public performance at a jazz event that occurred at the Apollo Theatre a few months before her death. She told us that at that performance, she had reconnected with a podiatrist who promised her he would treat her personally and would have her walking again in several months. The first step to this process was to admit her to a nursing care facility near to his office, which he did several months before her death.

We received several calls from Paula from that facility. The first two were shortly after her admission. She was seemingly positive, yet there were no details about how her ambulation challenges were being treated. She avoided the topic altogether. It seemed she mostly wanted a personal connection with me. "I miss you girl...and how is Quentzel?" she said a few times. A month later, she called and spoke of being in "hell" and that she was "trying to get out." We had no access or phone number for the nursing home, and the podiatrist's number was disconnected. Paula promised to be back at our Center soon.

Three months later, Paula passed away, but we did not hear for several months until her referring friend called to invite us to her memorial service, which would be attended by an international mix of jazz greats.

CONCLUSION

We have appreciated the opportunity to study, research, present and share this work. In an important way, Paula's brilliance and our learning of how to treat issues delicate to music and musicians remain significant for us. Music resistances as well as the vulnerabilities of what genius musicians can tweak in the music psychotherapist provide a deep learning and perhaps a path for Paula's legacy to live on through the understanding of focal themes within this treatment context.

REFERENCES

Cuyjet, M. & Tolson, G. (2007). Jazz and substance abuse: Road to creative genius or pathway to premature death. *International Journal of Law and Psychiatry*, 30(6), 530-538.

Loewy, J. (2011). Tonal intervallic synthesis as integration in medical music therapy. In F. Baker & S. Uhlig (Eds.), *Voicework in Music Therapy* (pp. 253-266). London: Jessica Kingsley Press.

Loewy, J. (2000). Music psychotherapy assessment. *Music Therapy Perspectives*, 18(1), 47-58.

Quentzel, S. & Loewy, J. (2010). An integrative bio-psycho-musical assessment model for the treatment of musicians: Part I-A continuum of support, *Music and Medicine*, 2 (2), 117-120.

Quentzel, S. & Loewy, J. (2010). An integrative bio-psycho-musical assessment model for the treatment of musicians: Part II—Intake and assessment, *Music and Medicine*, 2(2), 121-125.

Winick, C. (1959/1960) The use of drugs by jazz musicians. *Social Problems*, 7, 420-253.

APPENDIX OF SONGS

"I Can't Give You Anything But Love, Baby" (1921) by McHugh and Fields, Columbia Records.

"Oh What A Beautiful Morning" (1943) by Rodgers and Hammerstein, Williamson Music.

"Tomorrow" (1982) by Strouse and Charni, CBS.

"Lush Life" (1949) by Billy Strayhorn, Verve

"Little Girl Blue" (1957) by Rodgers and Hart, AMC

"Make Someone Happy" (1935) by Styne, Comden and Green, DRG.

"Happy Talk" (1947) by Rodgers and Hammerstein, Columbia.

Chapter Eighteen

FROM THE HIGHEST HEIGHT TO THE LOWEST DEPTH: MUSIC THERAPY WITH A PARAPLEGIC SOLDIER

"me'igra rama le'bira amikta"[1]

Chava Sekeles

INTRODUCTION

I met Dor[2] at the suggestion of his nursing team at the institute where he was undergoing rehabilitation therapy. Dor had suffered serious injuries to his lower spine after having a military accident that left him a paraplegic.[3] Another soldier was slightly wounded, and a third was killed instantly. Since Dor refused to comply with his proposed treatments, the nursing team suggested bringing in a music therapist from outside the institute. At that time, Dor was about twenty. He was a soldier in routine service in the army and his parent's only child. Before the accident he had been an excellent sportsman, had played electric guitar in an amateur band, had enjoyed nature and hiking and had been considered intelligent, joyful and sociable.

---

[1] This locution is in the Aramaic language, and the meaning is a sudden fall from a good situation to a bad one. Igra = roof; rama = high; bira = pit; amikta= deep: A Rabbi was reading from the Book of Lamentations. As he reached the verse "Its heavenly splendor he has turned into ruins" (Lamentations, 2, 1) the book fell from his hands. He said: "me'igra rama le'bira amikta." From the highest height to the lowest depth (Hagiga 5, page 2).

[2] Dor: A pseudonym used, in order to abide by professional ethics, with permission. All the names, and some details have been changed to protect the privacy of the patient.

[3] Paraplegia: full paralysis of lower part of the body, including legs, below the location of spinal injury (see Appendix A)

Dor's music therapy process was based on the Developmental-Integrative Model in Music Therapy[4] (DIMT) (Sekeles, 2006) which integrates neurological as well as psychological facets. The overall goal was to enable Dor to return, as much as possible, to his music and hobbies, and to facilitate his psychological rehabilitation. In our first meeting, these goals seemed to be overly ambitious and impossible to reach. The changes were slow and gradual and required significant patience. In this chapter, I will de scribe and analyze the obstacle course the patient and therapist passed through together, the necessity for flexibility on one hand, and of a clear and supportive framework on the other, the meaning of mutual trust, and the struggles gaining and maintaining that trust.

FOUNDATIONAL CONCEPTS

A Basic Foundation of Beliefs and Principles

As music therapists, and trainers of music therapists, we frequently examine our own psycho-musical sources, the profound influence music has on our spiritual and physical life and the place music holds in our personal life. As far as I have observed and investigated, models of music therapy were established and assembled by professionals based on and influenced by their personal history and culture, as well as by practical and theoretical thinking that connected music to relevant subjects and developed into one body. Moreover, over the course of years I learned that therapists who strongly believe in the healing power of music began their relationship with music at an early stage in their lives, and music became metaphorically intertwined with their physical and spiritual organism, like fine threads of silk. Throughout the many years in which I gradually defined my own model (DIMT), I underwent the same process by carefully examining my musical history, and by performing a kind of musical psychoanalysis. This analysis brought me to the clear conclusion that the basic principles of the DIMT model were rooted in my personal developmental path and in the integration of my multi-faceted studies: music,

---

[4] I chose this model, not only because I myself defined it and assessed its effectiveness over the course of many years of activity, but mainly because of the necessities I faced dealing with a young man whose injuries required care of physical as well as of emotional aspects. Indeed, the DIMT touches on basic aspects of life: movement, senses, vocality, emotion, cognition and socialization, and as such facilitates integrative treatment and strives to achieve balance and compensation.

occupational therapy, psychology, ethno-psychology and musicology. Another factor is my belief that music is like food, faith and love: natural ingredients necessary for a healthy, meaningful life.

Music may be the language of therapy, but can we conduct therapy without words? Furthermore, can we utilize words and movement without knowledge of psychological and medical processes? In music therapy, there are approaches and models which claim that psychological thinking and medical knowledge are almost irrelevant vis-à-vis the knowledge and therapeutic potential of the music. Others claim that medical knowledge is secondary and stress the importance of psychological considerations for any kind of patient problems. I happen to believe in a therapy of integration and balance, and cannot accept either view stated. It is true that we are supposed to make therapeutic use of music and its components, but we cannot separate the process from medical knowledge and psychological thinking, just as we cannot ignore the patient's stage of development and cultural background, and apply the same material/approach/technique to everyone.

As such, I developed a model of music therapy that seeks to integrate my personal and professional experiences in a way that acknowledges psychological and medical processes. The central components are outlined below, wherein I articulate their *developmental* and *integrative* elements.

The Developmental-Integrative Model in Music Therapy: DIMT

Developmental implies a basic concept of Man as a being who passes through various stages of development during his lifetime, including certain vital functions of his senses and sensations, vocality, motion, emotion and cognition. Developmental psychology and physiology maintain that growth is characterized by supra-cultural or universal processes. Science seeks to describe, investigate and measure these, as well as to study deviations from their norms. Such research into deviationary patterns has indeed advanced our potential of understanding and treating future pathologies. Despite the apparent differences between various current psychological approaches, it would seem that rather than contradicting each other, their different accentuations tend to support the overall accepted view of infant development. As a result of long-term observation of infants, children, adolescents, adults and the elderly (employing music), DIMT arrived at the following conclusions regarding its definitions:

Developmental:

> 1. Part of human health is determined by the degree of maturity and integration that exists within and between the vital systems that contribute to development. Observation by means of music can pinpoint deficits, gaps, regression and fixation. This is because music itself influences these very same life systems.
> 2. Should there be any health malfunction, this must be examined according to its developmental significance. Identifying the developmental stage is an essential part of the intake and observation phase of music therapy. Without such data, the therapist is unable to evaluate and consider any form of treatment.
> 3. There exists a certain parallel between the development of the persona in general and its development in music therapy. By observing musical activity, we can identify stages of physical, psychological, cognitive and social development.
> 4. DIMT sees each hour of therapy as a developmental microcosm and follows the patient's development as though it were parallel to the life continuum.
> 5. DIMT stresses the need to stimulate and develop the surviving and healthy functions of the patient, without ignoring deficits and gaps, in order to bring about positive changes and to improve the quality of life. (for additional discussion of these dimensions see Sekeles, 1996 pp. 147–155).

Integrative:

> 1. The integrative treatment of deficits and gaps.
> 2. A holistic treatment of the complete individual (sensory-motor integration, motion-emotion integration, etc.).
> 3. The integration of the physiological and the psychological persona, and the treatment of the whole person as far as music

permits, whether or not the handicaps are defined as either physical or emotional.

4. Integration of the problems as diagnosed and the therapeutic approach, techniques, and the musical and verbal means at the disposal of the therapist.

5. Integration of methods and techniques in music therapy with knowledge acquired from relevant fields (music, musicology and ethno-musicology; psychology, psychiatry, neurology and other basic subjects in psychology and medicine), in order to render as effective a treatment as possible.

This model can be either active or receptive, depending on the needs of the individual patient. However, the most desirable aim is to achieve a balance between a receptive (being) and active (doing) approach. Since development is perceived in terms of human relationships, even a receptive approach finds its fullest expression in the contact established between therapist and patient.

In order to use the model efficiently, the following standards are mandatory for the music therapist:

1. To be a professional and flexible musician.
2. To be educated on all the relevant subjects mentioned before (music, medicine, psychology, etc.).
2. To be educated on different psychological approaches.
3. To undergo his/her own psychotherapy.
4. To continue with complementary studies in music, music therapy and required therapeutic education and to be equipped to meet the needs and requirements of each patient (for additional reading, see Sekeles, 1996 pp. 25–63).

THE CLIENT

At our first meeting I found Dor lying in bed, his face turned toward the wall, eyes open. I introduced myself. Dor did not respond. After twenty minutes of mutual silence, he turned his head toward me and asked:

> *What do you want from me?* I answered: *I came to find out with you if you are interested, and if you could be helped by music therapy in order to improve your situation.* Dor reacted: *I never heard of such nonsense. I don't believe in any help.* I replied: *What do you think it is?* Dor, showing lack of interest and apathy: *What? Listen to music? I can't play anymore, and what do you know about my music anyway? You must be my mother's age, and you sure don't know a thing about rock and all...*[5]

This was the first spontaneous welcome by Dor, but despite his depressed-angry mood, I detected in his resistance some aspects of strength. I said:

> *Every therapy means embarking together on a journey of quest and discovery. I know that you play electric guitar, and that you took part in a rock band in high school. If you'd like, we could start on this subject of "your music." You could share with me and teach me the music you know and love. We could begin with records and then continue with playing the guitar together and other instruments that I could bring you.* Dor replied: *Leave me alone, I don't believe you, or any therapy, nobody can give me back my legs. I am not ready to live as half a man. I prefer to die.*

I decided to refrain from an answer, and asked if I could return a few days later. Dor's reaction was not positive, but neither negative. In my heart I pondered his feelings of frustration and guilt over the death of a comrade, the injury suffered by another, the sense of the terrible burden of the "punishment" inflicted on him, the loss of freedom, his bruised manhood, the sudden dependence on others — mostly strangers — and, probably, his anxiety concerning the future.

It should also be mentioned that in Israel, with its multitude of war-injured people, sports for the handicapped are high on the list and considered important beyond their physical aspects, because they restore some of the self-confidence and self-respect that are usually lost. Indeed, the emotional aspect of loss of motility, of bowel control, and of auton-

---

[5] Throughout the chapter, I quote from the reports I wrote immediately following the therapy session, or from the recordings routinely made with the consent of the patient.

omy, may trigger a severely depressed reaction. In the case of young people like soldiers, the difficult task of accepting a new image, the loss of masculinity, the uncertainty of their further development as men, and the loss of control over their lives, are extremely detrimental. Dor expressed this at a later stage of therapy:

> *Hands are not sufficient, pain accumulates in the heart, and the mind enhances it. I know that it could be worse if my hands and my upper body were paralyzed, too, but right now this is of no comfort to me. I feel like a marionette that must be moved by others, because it has no living drive of its own.*

In the meantime, I found out that during the first month after the accident, he had harshly driven away the girl who had been his companion for two years, and had thrown her out of the hospital. After a series of rejections, the girl, a joyous person full of life, gave up and severed her relations with him. His parents took turns at his bedside, but he rejected them too, and they had a hard time coping with the tragedy and with their son's state of mind. Dor seemed to cooperate with the physiotherapist, grudgingly tolerated passive exercises, but was not yet ready to activate his healthy limbs and to practice movements that were meant to allow him to develop some form of autonomy. Dor refused to talk with a social worker, and he did not believe in psychotherapy. His resistance, which was strong and unbending, actually served as an ineffective defense mechanism against seriously coping with his situation. It was a period in which things were not yet clear, and perhaps Dor still had some hope that a miracle would occur, and that the paralysis would go away.

THE THERAPEUTIC PROCESS

Stage One: Resistance as a Defense Mechanism

In principle, the term resistance refers to any action of the body, or the spirit, that opposes a force or stands against it, undermines that force, or is immune to it. Sometimes resistance is a personal trait and indicates unwillingness to carry out orders, to respond to social pressure, and so on (Reber, 1982). In psychoanalysis, resistance is seen as the refusal to allow unconscious contents (thoughts, feelings, repressed desires) to become conscious. Even in cases of conscious resistance, the assumption is that the unwillingness to disclose information originates from unconscious motives (Rosenheim, 1990). In the technique of psychoanalytic treatment, the interpretation of resistance is considered extremely valuable. The term appeared at an early stage in Freud's writings, and was an important aspect of psychoanalytic theory. At first, resistance was defined as an obstacle to the elucidation of the symptoms and to the progress of the treatment. Freud tried a persuasive approach, but he came to the conclusion that resistance itself could bring about an unveiling of repressed material and of the secrets of the neurosis. And indeed, the interpretation of resistance and transference are the central bases of psychoanalytic treatment:

> *"Resistance during treatment arises from the same higher strata and systems of the mind which originally carried repression"* (Laplanche & Pontalis, 1985 p. 395).

According to Hadley (2002), resistance arises when the patient rejects treatment in various ways, and prevents the possibility of beneficial change. In Priestley's Analytical Music Therapy (1994), resistance can be expressed in words, and also in music. In music, we may find that the patient refrains from making use of voice, or instrument, or remains compulsively stuck on the same musical theme. Resistance can also be expressed through musical activity without sequence of verbal elaboration, or, on the other hand, verbal activity that occupies most of the therapeutic hour, and leaves very little space for music (Hadley, 2002). In severely disabled individuals suffering from neuro-psychological problems, and in particular during the first "mourning" phase, resistance could originate from various factors:

> a. It is difficult to immediately muster the energy necessary to cope with hardship while you are in a state of mourning that depletes all your strength (Parks, 1972). We should not forget that in addition to Dor's injury, he was feeling responsible for the death of a comrade, and the wounding of another soldier.

Such facts can lower the drive to live, and direct the focus to feelings of mourning, guilt and frustration.

b. Sometimes it is easier to relinquish difficult rehabilitation steps and to indulge in idleness and disability rather than to cope with the necessity of taking the long and painful path of rehabilitation.

c. From an objective point of view, Dor lost his legs, losing the ability to change his position (sitting, walking, lying and exercising) easily. He was compelled to adapt himself to a new flawed body image, his voiding system (urine, feces) became defective, he lost normal sexual function, his status and his self-esteem. All this severely impaired his ability to function in body and in mind. In his resistance I detected, as indicated before, an expression of energy, which could be perceived as a positive force. I wish to point out that we must also consider another aspect: Dor did not yet know what kind of future was in store for him. Would some functions be restored? What studies and occupation could he acquire? What might he do? Would he have to face a court trial? What would happen if he would start exercising his upper body in order to compensate for the paralyzed parts? In fact, strengthening the upper body, which usually does not function to carry weight, might cause pain and problems in the shoulders, wrist joints and more (Trieschmann, 1987; Greenstein, 1999).

Stage Two: Cautious Progress

The next meeting took place a week later. Dor was lying on the bed, and the physiotherapist exercised him passively. Dor, sour-faced, was silent, and he suddenly uttered to the therapist:

You are only wasting time on me. This will not help. My legs are not coming back, I am just a nothing.

In Dor's case, I carried in my bag a few recordings from different musical categories, some composed by myself. In anticipation of the session, I had prepared and recorded with a friend a composition of my own for viola and piano. This was a short piece, with moderate tempo and limited octave range. It was meant for listening (receptive activity) and relaxing movement. I said to Dor and to the physiotherapist:

> *I see you have a tape-recorder here. Would you mind continuing with your work while being accompanied by some background music?*

The physiotherapist accepted immediately. Dor kept silent, but did not object. I played the recording and the therapy session went on as before. Dor continued to be quiet, and finally commented:

> *It was bearable, but this is not my music. This is the music of Methuselah's generation.*

During the next two weeks I continued to attend the physiotherapist's sessions. At first I brought recordings of instrumental music.[6] Later, I also brought a guitar, and I accompanied the exercises with instrumental as well as vocal improvisations. About six weeks elapsed before I instigated a conversation about Dor's feelings during the physiotherapy exercises accompanied by recorded or live music. I was very careful not to hurry with any kind of verbal investigation and processing of his thoughts, feelings and experiences. My observation had been that Dor was in a very sensitive, somewhat adolescent mood, and that verbalization might be experienced by him as intrusive and inappropriate. I waited for clear cues from him, and refrained from accelerating the process for the sole reason that we, the therapists, are short on time or have run out of patience (Sekeles, 2008).

In general, the Israeli dynamic favors the kind of heroic, macho soldiers, who are not inclined to share feelings. Throughout the course of years of activity, and in particular after the Yom Kippur war (October 1973), though one could notice changes in this regard, my assumption was that I should wait patiently.

---

[6] I chose instrumental music in order to avoid inflicting on Dor the increased intimacy related to vocal music, and the immediate connotations to feelings. In this regard, the guitar is also quite intimate, specifically as it is often played while the therapist sits facing the patient.

During the following two weeks, I saw Dor every day for only half an hour. The physiotherapist began to sense that Dor was a little more serene, peaceful and accepting. Sometimes he even peeled away a thin layer of bitterness and rigidity, and revealed a bit of a smile, almost hidden. After two weeks I asked him if he could take over the role of the guitarist, thereby allowing me to play another instrument and extend musical activity beyond physiotherapy exercise. Dor responded:

> *How come? I haven't played classical guitar for years. I can't play in a wheelchair, and I am not in a mood for that.* I replied: *When you feel that you can do it, we'll try to improvise together, perhaps in the style of blues?*

This proposition surprised Dor:

> *What do you know about blues?*[7] I replied: *I like the blues, and sometimes improvise for my own enjoyment or when needed in therapy.* Dor: *Okay, bring something and we'll try.*

I tried to refrain from appearing over-excited, and the next day I brought a well-known piece of blues with its lyrics. Dor appeared very anxious. He asked for the guitar, I helped him to stabilize his sitting position with a temporary support around his back and chest, and he played the piece by himself. At a certain point he asked:

> *Will you sing or won't you?*

I sang, and from that moment a window of musical communication opened, which did not yet touch directly on his problems, nor bring about verbal expression of feelings.

---

[7] I recall my first experience in a psychiatric institution abroad, where I was working with a psychotic 17-year-old, who had a job on a freight ship. His music was indeed very far from me — heavy rock - and he rejected me immediately. I asked him offhand if he knew the latest hit that was raging and exciting at that time in the Netherlands. While asking, I played the tune on the piano, and he started, without even realizing, to join in, drumming and singing. This was a decisive, swift turning point, which resulted in four solid years of therapy, until his last day of hospitalization. I stress this subject because one of the principles in music therapy is to learn and know as many different musical cultures and styles as possible, in order to establish a positive inter-relationship with the patient.

We often speak of subjects like empathy, establishing trust with the patient, containing, supporting, setting boundaries and so on, and I keep asking myself how these terms can be expressed in our therapeutic language and communication through music. What can we do if we are not familiar with the culture of the patient in general, and in particular with his or her musical preferences and rejections? With age-related culture? With the cultural background from which he, or she, came to Israel (if they were not born here), and occasionally also the culture of the disease (as with drug-addicts)? We ought to remember that music is not an international language, but rather a multi-faceted medium, and that we, as therapists, must make an effort in order to learn, understand, and be able to perform and collaborate with the patient, even if his or her music is painful and bothersome to our ears. This is one of the reasons why we, as therapists, must constantly listen to music of various categories, to different radio stations, and also continue to perform and improvise freely.

Empathy is different from the identification of the therapist with the patient, where the distinction between the two becomes blurred and the therapist cannot help any more (Sekeles, 2008). In music therapy, empathy is not only expressed in the form described in psychology:

> *Empathy is based on controlled and cautious use of transference. The therapist imagines that under certain conditions, the patient experiences something similar to what the therapist would have experienced in the same conditions* (Rosenheim, 1990 p. 9).

In addition to this, in music therapy we can express empathy through our specific therapeutic medium, that is to say music, which stresses its importance as a common language connecting the patient and therapist. Other themes abovementioned are also expressed in musical activity itself: we establish relations of trust, refraining from intrusion into the musical universe of the patient, lending support, and containing the music produced and performed by the patient. Support and containing can be created by "being and/or doing together." For example, by listening to music with the patient, providing harmonic accompaniment to the patient's music, joining the musical style of the patient, and showing respect for his creations, etc.

Indeed, according to my model (DIMT), music serves as our main therapeutic language, thus the different techniques and approaches used in psychology can be applied and worked through sound. This brings us to the next stage of therapy:

Stage Three: "Music can Speak"

During this stage, I began working with Dor with the consent of the physician in charge of rehabilitation, on mobility, beyond the aspects covered by the physiotherapist, without interfering in the therapy provided by her. Dor started practicing movements to a piece of jazz music I gave him upon his request, and in accordance with his taste. At the same time, we began to work with free improvisation: Dor began to respond to improvisations representing key themes in his life. For example, he played an improvisation on the synthesizer that he called "feet versus hands." In this piece, the feet are represented by a long note (organ point), like the long line that shows up on the electrocardiogram screen in hospitals and indicates that life has come to an end. At the same time, he represented the hands by a series of hard rhythmical strokes. In the subsequent conversation, Dor said that by the long note he wanted to express the fact that his legs were not functioning anymore, and that his hands were strong and capable of expressing anger and rage.

Another example came when he began to speak of the sorrow he felt for the soldier who was killed, and for this he chose not to play, but to listen to an Israeli song "Every Man" that spoke to his somber mood, and enabled him to later talk about the pain, and of his wish to forget and to escape.

Every Man[8]

Don't say: see, a man is marching straight, secure
He wanders happily on his path
The burden of his sorrow blown away
And nothing left from yesterday.

---

[8] Lyrics by Abraham Ben Ze'ev. Music by David Zahavi. (Translated into English by permission of the poet Avraham Ben Zeev). Sheet music: Appendix B.

Don't say that, for I know too well
Can't get away from the past...
Every man wants to find a quiet beach
In the endless night of cold
Every man runs away from something
Tries to reach the dawn, the light.
Appears marching happily on his path,
A day of spring fading away
A bunch of hopes withered
A grave – a lonely pit, forgotten
And a friend lying there.
In every man's heart there is
A gloomy secret, pitiful
An echo from battle, not the last
Will rise again, again to burn.
But do not wonder, do not ask the flying man
And do not plow his field.
He goes on, in silence like the moon
Leaving his garden forever.
Thirsty as a desert he walks away, tries to forget,
To flee from the fangs of secret.
But his secret like thistles will rise and flourish,
And the man will go on wandering.

The music David Zahavi chose to compose for this poem sounds like a tale, generating a very peaceful atmosphere. This peacefulness is also a desire of the heart, a kind of shield against the tragic secret one carries within, the secret the poet describes as thistles that rise and flourish, which prevents the man from escaping its fangs. I was much surprised when Dor requested to listen to this song, which he had just heard on the radio, and was very distant from his musical taste. His choice gave me a glance at a layer I hadn't realized existed before, and showed me once again the power music possesses when it is linked with words to symbolically summarize our innermost longings.

At this stage, music became more and more meaningful to Dor, and he began collaborating in full, except for when he was depressed. At such moments, I would usually sit quietly at his side, without attempting to suggest anything to play or listen to. By maintaining the silence, my intention was to show respect for Dor's grief – his grief for others and for himself. But there was also an additional aspect, which entered my mind only later: through this I could provide his parents with the model they needed. A model saying "one must not constantly try to cure Dor." Dor had a wide universe of suffering and sorrow, and one should not intrude without his permission and consent. Dor's parents were what we call "the salt of the earth" of our country, and they had a strong desire to be helpful. This desire was sometimes counteracting because it irritated Dor and triggered aggression and rejection toward them (Rubin, 1990). His parents did not attend our sessions, which took place in a small adjacent room, but they saw me sitting quietly at Dor's side during situations in which he did not cooperate. Perhaps this silence surreptitiously reached their hearts, and created some space of calmness. In this matter, I wish to mention a book by the Israeli Dan Ben-Amoz "I Don't Give a Damn" in which he writes of a paraplegic soldier in the process of rehabilitation, and of the conflicts between him and his parents. Among other things, his father says of his wife: "He is the one paralyzed, but she is the wounded one" (Ben-Amoz, 1973 p.97).

I found this to be a typical picture. Families often cannot accept the situation they find themselves in, and react with denial and false hopes. Instead of showing empathy, they project their own problems on the disabled, and in their agony they neglect the fact that the patient needs their strength. The fact that the injured person is dependent on his family intensifies his anger and leads to situations in which he simultaneously rejects his parents while still retaining his dependence on them. He assumes that their smiles are fake and that they are concentrating on their own pain. In such situations, the team in charge of the therapy must contact the family and teach them the very words to use in conversations with their son and the right moments to employ nonverbal communication. This kind of procedure is followed only rarely. In most cases, the workload on the medical-nursing team is so intense that they are unable to find much time to deal with the accompanying family.

Stage Four: New Therapeutic Space

Four months passed by. At a certain point in time, I considered the possibility of holding our two weekly sessions alternatively in my clinic and at the rehabilitation facility. At the latter we would focus on physical aspects of movements accompanied by music. The transfer to the music therapy clinic involved transportation and complicated arrangements, but Dor's excitement and the good will of his parents and nursing team made it possible.

The music therapy clinic is set up as follows: in a corner, there is a table and armchairs for conversations. The floor is carpeted, and musical instruments hang on the walls all around in such a way that most of the room is still an open space. In this space, one is at liberty to play various instruments (regular-classic, ethnic, self-made), to sing with the accompaniment of various instruments, to move around inspired by the music, to make a recording of the therapeutic session, to videotape, and so on

Dor liked to be in this room. He said that in his view, therapy already began with the journey along the wooded mountain road leading to the clinic. Indeed, we should remember that we offer the patient not only meaning of internal content, but also — since we deal with arts — aesthetics and beauty. In this space, unlike the one at the rehabilitation facility where he lived at that time, Dor could get away from the atmosphere of malady and from everything related to it, like the equipment, sounds, smells, and interferences of treatments; or for other reasons. At that time, he had the electric guitar brought to the hospital, and began to play it whenever he had a chance. I wish to point out that he never requested to bring his guitar to my clinic, and that the atmosphere created there was quite different from the one he was familiar with. We practiced relaxation, exercised specific movements I invented for his sore hands, and created improvisations and composition from the material he discovered when he played on different instruments, including music and poetry. The lyrics of his songs were impressive (man and nature, falling leaves, me the child in the moon…) revealing the level of tenderness I detected when he chose to listen to "Every Man."

At this stage, playing music with Dor allowed me to discover that besides his favored rock music, he also liked jazz music, and had even experimented with it with his band. The band itself had existed a few years before. It dissolved when the members were enlisted for army service, and Dor did not tell any of them of his accident. Since I had a collection of a variety of jazz music, we were able to play it, to listen and to sometimes discuss certain issues while listening to it as a soothing background. In addition, I practiced with him the Chinese movement exercises known as "Chi Gong," in which I have many years of training and which can be done with music and just the upper body. The Chi Gong presented to his body and soul a combination of soft movement and stable grounding.

Stage Five: An End That is Not an End

Dor made progress in all facets of his rehabilitation. He collaborated in physiotherapy, participated in occupational therapy, and joined group conversations. He played music, and twice a week had music therapy sessions. His emotional state was much more stable, but he still became depressed from time to time, which worried the nursing team very much. Eventually, the time would come for Dor to leave the rehabilitation facility, move to his parents' home, and eventually find a suitable apartment while continuing with his rehabilitation, his studies and with life. At this time he knew for certain of the seriousness of his injury, the paralysis of his legs, the problems related with sex and exertion, and so on. Despite the progress he made, I felt he was quite worried about his fate, and I was not certain that his future would be bright, as in the song:

> *Leaving his garden forever. Thirsty as a desert he walks away, tries to forget, to flee from the fangs of secret. But his secret like thistles will rise and flourish, and the man will go on wandering.*

After seven months of hospitalization, Dor was released from the facility. He had to move, reluctantly, to his parent's home, which they tried very much to adapt to his needs, in order to enable him to perform everyday activities as easily as possible. Dor temporarily discontinued music therapy until he could reorganize transportation, and for a few weeks we were out of touch. After these arrangements were made, he called me asking to re-start sessions again. We set a date and agreed that he would take care of the technicalities of transportation and arrival. Two days prior to our meeting, while Dor was sitting in his wheelchair in front of his house waiting for transportation to a medical checkup, a truck passing on the street lost control, hit the sidewalk, ran over Dor and killed him. Dor stopped "wandering." I still remember the thought that crossed my mind after his death:

> *In fact, he had wanted to die...he worked and overcame resistance, but something inside him could not accept disability, and the misery around him...that truck realized his fantasy that something would come and help him get away from his problems and from the whole world...as he said: Hands are not sufficient...I feel like a marionette that must be moved by others, because it has no living drive of its own.*

THERAPEUTIC CLOSURE

It took me a few months to reach the possibility for emotional and cognitive closure — to cope with the process that Dor passed, the personal feeling of failure and loss that accompanied me as a therapist, and the summary of the therapeutic stages until the time of death.

From a musical therapy point of view, Dor had first passed through resistance with no use of music and rather short conversations. The second stage involved pre-composed recorded or live music that accompanied the work of the physiotherapist and could be defined as a receptive process. In the third stage, Dor actually began to use the guitar in an interaction with a second instrument played by me. The next step involved mobility. Dor moved in his wheelchair to the sound of jazz music, and by doing that, freed his souring body. From there developed clinical improvisation with which Dor represented key issues in a symbolic way and turned hurt feelings into art. The last stage was moving the therapy in part to my clinic and opening his eyes to the multi-possibilities of music therapy in a calm environment.

The general feeling of working in developmental stages and achieving integration became clear to both patient and therapist, as well as Dor's ability and will to continue music therapy. From this short summary, it is obvious that the Developmental-Integrative-Model directed us physically and emotionally toward a better acceptance of the situation, and contributed more energy to coping with the future. Dor's father said at his son's funeral that at the end of his life, music therapy gave Dor "drops of faith and for that we have to be thankful." With this thought I dedicate the paper to Dor, who after his death compelled his family and his therapists to dive into the world of mourning and find these drops of faith.

REFERENCES

Ben Amotz, D. (1973). *I Don't Give a Damn*. Tel Aviv: Bitan Publishers (Hebrew).
Colman, A. M. (2001). *Oxford Dictionary of Psychology*. Oxford: Oxford University Press.
Greenstein, I. (1999). Late Complications of Over-use of Upper Extremities in Paraplegia. Be'er Sheva: Medical Center, The Faculty of Health Science, Ben Gurion University of the Negev (Hebrew).
Hadley, S. (2002). Theoretical bases of Analytical Music Therapy. In J. Eschen (Ed.), *Analytical Music Therapy*. London: Jessica Kingsley Publishers.
Laplanche, J. & Pontalis, J. B. (1985). *The Language of Psycho-Analysis*. London: Hogarth Press.
Parks, C. M. (1972). *Bereavement – Studies of Grief in Adult Life*. New York: International University Press, Inc.
Priestley, M. (1994). *Essays on Analytical Music Therapy*. Phoenixville, PA: Barcelona Publishers.
Reber, A. S. (1992). *Dictionary of Psychology (Hebrew Edition)*. Jerusalem: Keter.
Rosenheim, E. (1990). *A Man Meets Himself. Psychotherapy: Experience and Process*. Tel Aviv: Schocken Publishing House (Hebrew).
Rubin, S. (1990). Death of the future. An outcome study of bereaved parents in Israel. *Omega*, 20: 323–339.
Sekeles, C. (1996). *Music Therapy: Motion and Emotion*. St. Louis: MMB Music, Inc.
Sekeles, C. (2006). The Developmental-Integrative Model in Music Therapy. *Nordic Journal of Music Therapy*, 15 (1), 58–82.
Sekeles, C. (2007). *Music Therapy: Death and Grief*. Gilsum, N.H: Barcelona Publishers.
Sekeles, C. (2008). *Revised Version of Diagnostic Charts in Music Therapy*. Jerusalem: David Yellin Academic College (1st Hebrew version 1990).

Trieschmann, R. (1987). *Spinal Cord Injuries: Psychological, Social, and Vocational Rehabilitation.* New York: Demos.
Trombly, C. A. (Ed.) (1983). *Occupational Therapy for Physical Dysfunction.* London: Williams & Wilkins.

APPENDIX A

Paraplegia

As indicated in the abstract, paraplegia is characterized by motor and/or sensory loss in the lower limbs and trunk. Some of the people affected also exhibit paralysis of internal organs below the waist. Paralysis is the consequence of a sudden or gradual lesion of the spine and affects the body below the point of impact. The condition could be caused by a variety of agents: a disease of the spine, cancer, fractures, partial or transversal slashes due to injuries from war or by accident, and so on. In some cases, the damage is limited, but it is usually extensive and irreversible. Treatment and rehabilitation include physiotherapy, adaptation of mechanical devices for the improvement of everyday functions (activities of daily living), occupational therapy, psychotherapy and arts therapies. Some of these therapies are administered on an individual basis and some in support groups. Full invalidity (as in Dor's case) means the inability to walk and the need for a wheelchair, urinating and defecating problems, lack of sexual function, and additional problems caused by reduced motility (decubitus ulcers, thrombosis, pneumonia and so on). Therapy encourages movement, standing up (with supporting frame), compensative strengthening of the upper body and extremities and as much meaningful activity as possible, despite the severe handicap (Further information in Trombley, 1983 chapter 21).

From the Highest Height 333

APPENDIX B

Every Man

Abraham Ben Ze'ev David Zahavi

Chapter Nineteen

MUSIC THERAPY AND ADDICTION: ADDRESSING ESSENTIAL COMPONENTS IN THE RECOVERY PROCESS

Jim Borling

Addiction is the ultimate condition of separation
(Sparks, 1993 p. 199)

INTRODUCTION

Addiction: a word that is difficult to define, assign or characterize in one simple phrase. *Recovery*: an even more complex concept that involves a process of treatment and lifestyle change (i.e., therapy, intervention, commitment, etc.) that may be more qualitative and on-going in nature than one would initially expect. May (1988) suggests that recovery is not a guarantee of serenity and fulfillment, rather that we find truth in recovery. We come to understand that "we were never meant to be completely satisfied" (p. 179). Recovery, as we know it, may be more of a process than a destination.

Implied in the above statements is that recovery from addiction is a process that encourages the client to begin taking responsibility for his or her life, conditions and choices. Through the development of tools and strategies, as well as experiential processes, an individual is given the opportunity to reclaim a productive and meaningful lifestyle that is consistent with the moral, ethical, and spiritual standards by which he or she wishes to live.

This chapter, involving several vignettes and clients, takes place at an Intensive Outpatient Program (IOP), Avenues to Recovery. The IOP meets three nights a week (total of 9 hours per week) for up to 19 weeks.

Group Music Therapy meets one time per week over this treatment period.

FOUNDATIONAL CONCEPTS

The approach to music therapy at Avenues to Recovery involves several interrelated levels or stages. The first level is bio-physical: addressing the initial needs of the client as he/she enters a new life without his/her drug of choice. The second level is psycho-emotional: providing the client with an opportunity to explore his or her own emotional recovery process. As such, psychodynamic issues begin to surface as the client begins to re-discover or re-connect with his or her authentic self that is often lost through the addictive process. During this stage, the client is also encouraged to engage in new, yet safe behaviors, in a secure and protected environment. The third and final stage addresses the psycho-spiritual dimensions of recovery. As Carl Jung so clearly stated in a personal letter to Bill W., one of the co-founders of the twelve step program of Alcoholics Anonymous (AA), "Spiritus contra Spiritum," which means: *The alcoholics' craving for alcohol was the equivalent, on a low level, of the spiritual thirst of our being for wholeness...the union with God* (Alcoholics Anonymous, 1984 p. 348). The 12 steps make regular reference to a Higher Power, which should be a part of any healthy and on-going recovery process.

Fundamental to this model of music therapy with addictions is the suggestion that answers to recovery must come from within the client. Voiced another way, we all hold an elemental wisdom within. The goal of treatment, then, is to engage this inner resource. By finding meaning in life and focusing on a process of 'becoming,' we can honor the core ideas stated in the humanistic psychology movement (Schneider et al., 2001). The simple ideas of symptom alleviation are far removed from core concepts that include personal growth, self understanding and the pursuit of meaning. It would be important here to acknowledge the influence of "psychodynamic" thought as well. For the purposes of this case, psychodynamic thinking shall be defined as thoughts, feelings and behaviors as manifestations of inner drives and the interactions they have among each other (Waldrond-Skinner, 1986).

Essential when working with this population is a firm understanding of the 12-step process that is often employed and/or strongly supported by most treatment centers and programs. Alcoholics Anonymous (AA) considers itself a fellowship of men and women who, through common experiences, are able to share their knowledge in the hopes of solving problems common to them all as they enter into a life of recovery. Any good treatment program (and therapist within that program for that matter) will have a solid understanding of the 12-step process and how it can relate to the inner workings of the treatment setting. It is important to understand that AA is an autonomous organization with no direct ties to treatment facilities. Off-shoots of AA include Narcotics Anonymous (NA), Gamblers Anonymous (GA), Cocaine Anonymous (CA) and so on.[1]

The concepts presented in these cases are often tied to the 12-step process. For the sake of simplicity, the ideas of surrender (steps 1–3), honesty (steps 4–7), accountability and responsibility (steps 8–9), and stability (steps 10–12) will often be referred to as a way to show connections between the 12 steps and the music therapy process.

Additionally, aspects of the Transpersonal Model of Addiction (Firman and Gila, 1997) will be considered. Transpersonal experiences, as discussed by Grof (1988), suggests that under certain circumstances we have access to unlimited resources well beyond our traditionally defined 'self.' These resources may, in fact, contribute to the recovery process. The role of the transpersonal experience, and recovery from a spiritual perspective, will be discussed later in this chapter.

THE CLIENTS

The clients discussed here participated in a 19-week Intensive Outpatient Program (IOP) for addiction to, and dependence on, a chemical substance. Whether referring to drug addiction, substance dependence, chemical dependency or substance abuse, these clients are fundamentally dealing with a compulsive use of their drug of choice to the point where the user has no effective option but to continue this addictive behavior.

---

[1] I strongly recommend that any therapist working with this population find 12-step meetings in their local area and attend these meetings for the purpose of learning and professional growth. One need not be in active recovery to attend many of the meetings offered by these 12-step programs. Meetings considered 'open' are for anyone interested in learning more about the 12-step process; 'closed' meetings are for those directly dealing with an addiction.

For the purposes of this chapter, I will use the term 'addiction' to refer to a chronic disorder involving compulsive use of a drug or drugs. Most of our clients are dealing with addiction to one of the following chemicals: opiates (heroin or strong pain medications), alcohol, cocaine (including crack cocaine), benzodiazepines (anti-anxiety medications) and/or methamphetamine.

These individuals come from all walks of life, with the majority from the middle to upper-middle classes. Regardless of socioeconomic status, the needs for each individual are typically consistent from client to client. The IOP largely focuses on the following aspects of recovery:

- *Psycho-educational:* learning about the addictive process and how it impacts various aspects of one's life
- *Psycho-social:* providing for insight and the development of social systems
- *Experiential:* focusing on physical, psycho-emotional, and psycho-spiritual issues of recovery
- *Medical:* understanding the physiological effects of addiction and beginning the process of healing both mind and body

Assessment

This particular IOP undertakes a single comprehensive assessment. This assessment involves the following elements: determination of appropriateness for program participation, and consideration of bio-psychosocial issues that relate to recovery. Assessment also includes a general history, extensive alcohol and drug use history, urine drug screening, patient and family interview, and administration of a substance abuse screening inventory. The goals for each client are consistent across disciplines. They include:

- increased insight into the disease model of addiction
- improved psycho-emotional expression and understanding
- abstinence from substance use/abuse
- identification of faulty beliefs and underlying feelings that fuel substance use

- increased social interface, particularly through the 12-step recovery community
- adoption of new coping mechanisms to deal with the stressors of everyday living
- exploration of the core concepts of physical, emotional, and spiritual recovery

THE THERAPEUTIC PROCESS

Addiction is often considered to be a three-pronged illness: physical, emotional and spiritual. Recovery can and should occur in all three areas to be considered effective and long lasting. Music therapy at the IOP is designed to address all three of these areas as needed by the client.

Bio-physical

While all aspects of recovery are based on the idea of abstinence, physical recovery is typically the first area of challenge for an individual dealing with an addiction. An opiate addict, for example, will experience severe withdrawal symptoms often known as 'dope sickness.' These symptoms may include diarrhea, cold chills, insomnia, muscle pain, irritability and anxiety. Withdrawal from other substances may cause very similar symptoms. It is here that the music therapist can address the bio-physical process of recovery.

Jerry entered treatment at the age of 61. He was heavily addicted to both opiates and methamphetamine. While the medical director was assisting with some of the more dramatic withdrawal symptoms, Jerry was experiencing regular bouts of panic, insomnia and general irritability. Jerry found it very difficult to simply quiet his mind and separate from what his body was experiencing (as a bio-physical 'healing').

It is important to note that symptoms of withdrawal from any substance can be a strong trigger or stimulus to go back to using the initial drug of choice, and Jerry was struggling with this on a daily basis. In this case, Jerry was not convinced that the irritation of withdrawal was worth the promised physical benefits of being chemically free.

The music therapy strategies that Jerry responded to most effectively with regard to bio-physical recovery involved the following elements:

- *Stress management:* engaging him in a body-centered, tense/release relaxation process using non-evocative and supportive music. Breathing techniques were always at the center of this process.
- *Physical movement:* through dance and exercise to music (this would often address the psycho-emotional aspect of recovery as well through risk-taking in a supportive environment).
- *Drumming:* while the music therapist provided a rhythmic and musical foundation, the client physically explored and released through simple instrument playing. Often, an authentic African rhythm would be taught to provide a container within which to have this physical experience.

The intention of using these stress management techniques for Jerry was not to create a one-time, feel-good experience. It would always be packaged as part of a strategy that was to be used away from the facility as well. Customarily, an educational discussion on the role of stress and relapse would precede the actual exercise in group. Over time, with regular practice (3–4 times per week) of this stress management technique, Jerry was able to deal in much healthier ways with stress, anxiety, and most importantly, the strong cravings to use his drug of choice. Jerry was able to take responsibility for his reactions to, and responses toward, the physical sensations he was experiencing as well as the daily stressors he would encounter.

Psycho-emotional

Once the general physical symptoms of withdrawal have diminished and the process of bio-physical recovery is underway, emotional issues may begin to surface that the client is unprepared to deal with in a clean and sober manner. Additionally, cognitive strategies may be exposed that are now a detriment to the recovery process. These strategies, often designed to keep one distanced from the true progression of addiction, may include such terms as denial, rationalizing and minimizing, terms that could easily be categorized as irrational beliefs (Ellis, 1992) or distorted thinking (Beck et al., 1993).

Additionally, it is important for the music therapist to be attentive to the potential of co-morbidity as an issue with psycho-emotional recovery. What may often surface is an underlying depression or anxiety disorder that has gone undiagnosed due to the process of self-medication (drug use). Debate exists among clinicians regarding the relationship between addiction and other clinical diagnoses. In other words, "which came first, the chicken or the egg?" Bill W., co-founder of Alcoholics Anonymous, stated that "very deep, sometimes quite forgotten, damaging emotional conflicts exist below the level of consciousness" (Alcoholics Anonymous, 1952 pp. 79–80).

Cognitive goals traditionally addressed in the treatment setting may include the enhancement of sense of control, personal empowerment, increased self-esteem and well-being, choice making and initiation of behavior change.

Emotional goals addressed in the music therapy setting will likely include enhancement of relationships, reliance on a support system, increased emotional maturity and honesty, increased emotional expression in a group setting and decreased isolation.

Shirley entered treatment at the age of 35. She was a single mother of two. After several violent episodes with family and friends, she made the hard decision to receive help for her alcoholism. Shirley presented as a rather soft-spoken, humble woman who was able to immediately assume responsibility for her actions and the consequences that brought her to the treatment setting.

Shirley did not experience many of the physical withdrawal symptoms often associated with alcoholism. She did, however, enter the IOP with considerable emotional heaviness and distress. In her own words, she stated "I feel ashamed for what I have done. I hold guilt deep within... I know that I must take a hard look at who I truly am." Upon hearing these words, it was apparent to me that she was ready for some psycho-emotional work.

Music therapy strategies often employed at this stage of work include the following:

- *Lyric Discussion:* choosing a song to sing or listen to and providing the client an opportunity to reflect and connect with the message contained within.
- *Song Writing*: contributing, in a group setting, to the lyrics of a verse that may center around a specific topic or subject matter that is particularly relevant at that point in time.
- *Structured Imagery Work:* within a structured relaxation exercise, somewhat evocative music will be employed, providing the client an opportunity to explore an area of recovery that lies just below his or her threshold of awareness. Topics of exploration may include meeting an inner wisdom figure, connecting with a phrase like 'one day at a time,' 'let go, let God' or 'easy does it.' It is the author's experience that exercises like this can provide a more personal relationship with the many phrases and concepts that are encountered in the 12-step environment.

Shirley had asked to discuss the lyrics of the song "Crossroads" by Don McLean. She particularly resonated with the lyrics from verse one:

> But I'm all tied up on the inside,
> No one knows quite what I've got;
> And I know that on the outside
> What I used to be, I'm not anymore.

Shirley spoke of her deep religious convictions and of her separation from these ideals. She very honestly and emotionally shared the experience of numbness she had developed about being a mother and the responsibilities that came with that role. She openly wept as group members listened and provided supportive feedback. Shirley was ready for growth and healing on the psycho-emotional level.

Through this experience, Shirley took the chance to speak from her authentic self, while at the same time clearly acknowledging that her family and friends were correct: she was not what she 'used to be.'

It was in this same group that Jerry identified a part of the song that was particularly meaningful to him. Verse two contained the following:

> You know I've heard about people like me,
> But I never made the connection.
> They walk one road to set them free
> And find they've gone the wrong direction.

Jerry, at age 61, described having no idea who he truly was. He knew that he could play any role or part needed, given the situation, but when it came down to being authentic, he was lost. He shared about his decades of drug use, showing how it had taken him further and further from himself. When asked how it felt to share his story from this perspective, he said that it felt raw inside, as if a wound was opening for the first time in years.

I reminded Jerry that when we get honest in the recovery process, we often find that an inner healing begins to surface and can be experienced as quite uncomfortable. He very clearly asked me "Do you mean like PTSD?" I said yes...perhaps. As the group intently supported Jerry's words, I gently asked him, "Are you a Vet?" He quietly emoted, shared some of his story of being in Vietnam, and finished by saying that this was the first time he had spoken of his military experiences in nearly 40 years.

Shirley and Jerry are representative of people in recovery who are ready for the psycho-emotional dimension of healing. Through the process of group lyric discussion, possibilities for growth and healing emerge. Patients are given opportunities to tell their stories, and in so doing to risk having their stories witnessed and acknowledged.

While this is not 12-step work in the truest sense of the word, themes of surrender, honesty, accountability and responsibility were all at play here. Both clients were able to personalize the lyrics of the song and tap into their search for meaning. In humanistic terms, they were in the process of becoming (Schneider et al., 2001).

The experience of song writing presents some unique dynamics in the context of recovery work. Lyric writing can take on many forms. Sometimes it is humorous, other times very serious. It almost always involves risk-taking behavior that is new, raw and revealing of a vulnerability necessary for the recovery process. Clients are encouraged to write their verse in a manner that is connected to the recovery process.

Through the experience of song writing, clients are generally asked to sing a verse that has already been composed by the music therapist. This is followed by the creation of the patient's own verses. The music therapist provides a success-oriented structure that virtually ensures that their lyrics will fit musically. The final challenge of this exercise is to sing one's original verse for the group, accompanied by guitar (or piano).

As stated earlier, music therapy exercises often parallel the 12-step process. In the case of song writing, Step 4 (honesty) is often addressed. Step 4 suggests the client undertake a searching and fearless moral inventory of one's self. It is strongly suggested that this personal inventory is shared (Step 5) with another human being (and God). Steps 6 and 7 speak directly to the identification of certain shortcomings or character defects that might hold one in a pattern of substance abuse. After the song writing exercise is completed, a discussion of Steps 4–7 follows. It is suggested to clients that while singing for peers was a fairly vulnerable act, no one failed. In fact, it is quite common for clients to identify a sense of liberation after the exercise. This is what Steps 4–7 are all about. It appears that involvement in music therapy may allow the client to deal with the deeper emotions and conflicts without being overwhelmed by them. True integration of the positive and negative sides of the self must happen at a deep level for it to elicit the type of change necessary for long-term sobriety and true recovery.

Structured Imagery Work

Structured imagery work might be considered a more advanced approach to working with clients in early recovery. While this work is not considered the Bonny Method of Guided Imagery and Music (GIM) (Bruscia & Grocke, 2002), it does hold some core concepts of GIM.[2] Fundamentally, the structured imagery approach makes use of both scripted and non-scripted experiences. It is common in structured imagery work to provide

---

[2] It is beyond the scope of this chapter to fully discuss the Bonny Method but I refer you to: Bruscia, K. & Grocke, D. (2002) *Guided Imagery and Music: The Bonny Method and Beyond*. Gilsum, NH: Barcelona Publishers.

clients with a seed image — an image from which an experience may begin. Further, clients are encouraged to enter this experience with a direction or intention already in mind. If these variables are in place, the client is able to work with issues that may lie just below the threshold of awareness. Structured imagery work, used in a group format, allows a client to work from a broader span of consciousness, beyond the traditional constraints of cognitive or linear thinking often found in other forms of therapy. It also honors the natural desire of the psyche to move toward healing and wholeness, thereby allowing the client to have his or her unique experience in the context of this structured work.

Tonight, the group was offered several song titles along with the words to each song. Each client was encouraged to identify one song that seemed to carry a message that was particularly relevant to them at that point in their recovery. Once identified, the client was asked to simply read for the group a part of the song that resonated with him or her.

Jerry chose the song "Hiding in Myself" by Kenny Rankin. He read the following words directly from the song:

> I've been so alone all my life
> Couldn't give my heart to anyone...
>
> So I hid inside 'til I almost died
> Yes I hid inside and I cried
> A loving heart in a sensitive man
> Hiding inside myself

For Jerry, this became the focus for his structured imagery work that night. As the group entered into the relaxed state, using the floor, pillows, blankets and focusing on the breath, each was invited to cross an emotional threshold, beyond which they would further examine the essence of the song and lyric they had chosen. The music used for this imagery exercise was 'Air on the G String' by J. S. Bach.

Through the process of spontaneous imagery, originating from within, Jerry was able to encounter the 'sensitive man...hiding inside.' He was able to observe, feel, even dialogue with this inner part of his being. In the truest sense, Jerry was reclaiming this part of his authentic self and engaged in the process of psycho-emotional healing.

May (1988) suggested that an addiction may be a reflection of a blessed pain. This blessed pain, often felt but rarely embraced, may paradoxically represent an underlying willingness to enter the recovery process. It would appear that Jerry, in this state of readiness, was connecting with the emotional pain of the "ultimate condition of separation" (Sparks, 1993 p. 199). Psycho-emotional recovery is an on-going and long-term commitment. When a client expresses a sincere desire to stay clean and sober, prognosis is good. Both the 12-step community and supportive counseling are integral components of this commitment to this recovery.

Psycho-spiritual

Let us now examine the level of recovery that most consider absolutely essential if recovery is to be long-lasting. Spiritual recovery is a phrase that can be widely interpreted by people in recovery, as well as professionals in the addictions community. Sometimes this level of recovery is simply referred to as an adoption of spiritual principles in one's daily activities that may be quite separate from any religious traditions, while at other times there may, in fact, be a strong re-acquaintance with lost traditions and religious activities.

Alcoholics Anonymous speaks very freely of a Higher Power (HP) and suggests that an awareness of an HP is the final chapter in effecting a change in one's outlook and working toward quality recovery and long-term sobriety. I wish to re-emphasize that recovery, as we are discussing it in this case, is neither a linear process nor a step-by-step formula that, when adhered to, gives promise to a quality life of sobriety. It is not uncommon at all that a client in the treatment setting may have spiritual insights anywhere along the path of treatment.

It is also important to note that this HP, as AA speaks of it, can be whatever the client in recovery needs it to be. Often it is the God of the churches (e.g., Catholicism), but it need not be. More times than not, the Higher Power is something that is intimately personal and private to the individual, and something that may be felt/experienced/acknowledged throughout one's whole being. It is here that the authority of psycho-spiritual recovery resides.

However it is viewed, it is generally agreed that spiritual recovery is essential if long-term abstinence and a general sense of well-being is to be sustained. In both AA and in the professional community, it is well accepted that recovery must include growth along spiritual lines in addition to the adoption of spiritual principles in the areas of daily living (Alcoholics Anonymous, 1984).

The music therapist is in a unique position to assist with this developing relationship with one's own Higher Power. Music, by its very nature, has the ability to touch us very deeply and to call forward those aspects of our being that are ready for growth and healing. For some, the reclamation of feelings of human-ness is spiritual in nature. I encourage all clinicians, when working with psycho-spiritual issues, to remain very open-minded and unbiased when this topic arises.

Shirley had been struggling with her deep religious convictions while in treatment for alcoholism. Her behavior, internal feelings toward others, and general guilt of the overall experience were profoundly inconsistent with what she knew as a spiritual life. As a young child, the fundamental tenets of her church were acutely adhered to and were a strong part of her family life.

In group, we were to do an imagery exercise designed to help the client develop a stronger relationship with some of the phrases often heard around 12-step meetings. I asked "what do you hear?" How do you integrate these slogans into your daily life? Some of the typical phrases heard at meetings include 'Easy does It,' 'One Day at a Time,' 'Let Go, Let God' and 'First Things First,' to name a few.

Each client was to choose the slogan that they wished to explore more deeply through relaxation, evocative music and imagery. Shirley chose "Let Go, Let God." The music chosen for this exercise included two selections: "Pastorale" and "Sigma" from the Secret Garden (1996, tracks 2, 4). The instructions from the music therapist were very simple.

> *As we relax, imagine yourself connecting with the core message of the chosen slogan. For some of you, this may feel immediate, for others, there may be a time of searching. Be open...allowing...trust that your inner wisdom has something for you to hear.*

Shirley almost immediately connected with her chosen phrase "Let Go, Let God." The inner message was clear: Forgiveness was the key. She felt forgiven by her Higher Power; she understood forgiveness of self; she felt, not just thought about, but actually felt the process of forgiveness that was emerging within her extended family and friends.

During the post imagery processing, Shirley was able to give voice to her experience. She stated that she felt a new relationship with her Higher Power. She affirmed that He knew she was not alone in this process of recovery. She understood that this chapter of her life was there for reasons beyond her understanding, but that with this deep connection she now knew that there was hope, trust and a shift in perspective. The opening was akin to what AA would refer to as a Spiritual Awakening.

As Shirley shared her experience, tears streamed down her cheeks. The group members witnessed her words and affirmed for her that this was real; it was to be given its due reverence. I reassured her that this image, this message, came from within. It would take time for her to fully integrate what she had just experienced, but I encouraged her to build this experience into her daily recovery process.

Small (1991) speaks of the process of hitting bottom from a spiritual perspective. She suggests that when hitting bottom is viewed through a spiritual lens we may, paradoxically, view this as an opportunity, a sacred function that allows us to give birth (or re-birth) to the creative spirit. Peck (1985) spoke of addiction as a 'Sacred Disease.' May (1988) felt that being brought to our knees may strangely enough also be the channel for the powerful flow of grace.

Could it be that this simple exercise of exploring the slogan "Let Go, Let God" enabled Shirley to move beyond the prison of her ego and enter into the realm of psycho-spiritual healing? It seems reasonable to consider that this experience was the beginning of her psycho-spiritual process of recovery. Maslow (1968) believed that we possess a biologically-based drive toward spiritual self-actualization. Perhaps it is this drive within Shirley that has been awakened.

SUMMARY

Addiction is any compulsive, habitual behavior that limits the freedom of human desire... (May, 1988 p. 24)

The case vignettes described above speak to a three-pronged approach to music therapy with addicts. They speak to the multifaceted nature of music therapy clinical practice with this population and the need for the music therapist to be open and prepared to work on a variety of levels. Each level of recovery presents unique challenges to patients and clinicians, and while practice can be understood from these three dimensions, they are by no means linear. Patients' journeys into recovery are complex, difficult and represent an entirely new way of being in the world.

Recovery on the physical, emotional, and spiritual levels suggests a process of reconnection and reintegration. And while addiction may be viewed as the ultimate condition of separation (Sparks, 1993), recovery is the reclamation of freedom and the reawakening of what it means to be fully human.

REFERENCES

Alcoholics Anonymous World Services, Inc. (1952). *Twelve Steps and Twelve Traditions*. New York: Alcoholics Anonymous World Services, Inc.

Alcoholics Anonymous World Services, Inc. (1984). *Alcoholics Anonymous* (3rd ed.). New York: Alcoholics Anonymous World Services, Inc.

Alcoholics Anonymous World Services, Inc. (1984). *Pass It On: Bill Wilson and the A.A. Message*. New York: Alcoholics Anonymous World Services, Inc.

Bach, J. S. (1993). Aria (Air on a G String). *Stokowski's Symphonic Bach* [CD] England: Chandos Records Ltd.

Beck, A., Wright, F., Newman, C. & Liese, C. (1993). *Cognitive Therapy of Substance Abuse*. New York: Guilford Press.

Bruscia, K. & Grocke, D. (Eds.) (2002). *Guided Imagery and Music: The Bonny Method and Beyond*. Gilsum, NH: Barcelona Publishers.

Ellis, A. (1992). *Addictive Personalities [sound recording]: Rational-Emotive Approaches to Treatment.* New York, NY: Institute for Rational Emotive Therapy.

Firman, J. & Gila, A. (1997). *The Primal Wound: A Transpersonal View of Trauma, Addiction, and Growth.* Albany, NY: State University of New York.

Grof, S. (1988). *The Adventure of Self-Discovery: Dimensions of Consciousness and New Perspectives in Psychotherapy and Inner Exploration.* Albany, NY: State University of New York.

Maslow, A. (1968). *Toward a Psychology of Being.* Princeton, NJ: Van Nostrand.

May, G. (1988). *Addiction and Grace: Love and Spirituality in the Healing of Addictions.* New York: Harper SanFrancisco.

Peck, M. S. (1985). *The Road Less Traveled: A New Psychology of Love, Traditional Values and Spiritual Growth.* New York: Simon and Schuster.

Schneider, K. J., Bugental, J. F. & Pierson, J. F. (Eds.) (2001) *The Handbook of Humanistic Psychology: Leading Edges in Theory, Research, and Practice.* Thousand Oaks, California: Sage Publications.

Secret Garden (1996). Pastorale and sigma. *Songs form a Secret Garden* [CD]. Norway: Polygram Studios.

Small, J. (1991). *Awakening in Time.* New York: Bantam.

Sparks, T. (1993). *The Wide Open Door: The Twelve Steps, Spiritual Tradition, and the New Psychology.* Santa Cruz, CA: Hanford Mead Publications.

Waldrond-Skinner, S. (1986). *Dictionary of Psychotherapy.* London: Routledge and Kegan-Paul.

Chapter Twenty

MAKING MY BODY A SAFE PLACE TO STAY: A PSYCHOTHERAPEUTICALLY ORIENTED APPROACH TO VIBROACOUSTIC THERAPY IN DRUG REHABILITATION

Marko Punkanen and Esa Ala-Ruona

INTRODUCTION

This chapter describes a psychotherapeutically oriented approach to vibroacoustic therapy, called physioacoustic therapy, for a woman in drug rehabilitation. Sara was 23 when she began therapy and had been using drugs for ten years. Sara's therapy started as a follow-up treatment after a six-month period in a drug rehabilitation centre. She was directed to music therapy by a local social and health services organization and the therapy process occurred in a private practice. Sara had great difficulty in regulating and tolerating strong and negative emotions, and this became the main focus of our work. The whole therapy process lasted six months and was divided into three phases, in which the intensity of the therapy sessions varied from two sessions per day to one session per week. In a secure therapeutic relationship, it gradually became possible for Sara to notice and experience bodily sensations related to different emotions and thoughts, and also tolerate and regulate emotions, which she had earlier thought to be intolerable without drugs.

The clinical method described here, physioacoustic therapy (Lehikoinen, 1997), is a form of music therapy that uses low frequency sound waves and music listening to address emotional, cognitive and social problems, along with bodily sensations. The method is psychotherapeutically oriented (Ala-Ruona & Punkanen, 2007).

FOUNDATIONAL CONCEPTS

Physioacoustic Therapy in a Context of Music Therapy and Drug Rehabilitation

According to Reed (1994), drug addiction is often defined according to how often drugs are used, which drugs are used, how large the doses are, and how long they have been used. Although these are important factors to consider, they do not fully define the concept of drug addiction. According to Reed (1994), addiction is not so much a question of continuous drug use, but is defined above all by compulsive use, combined with loss of control, denial of the problem, and the continuation of use regardless of the negative consequences (Reed, 1994).

Drug rehabilitation can be divided into two main phases: the acute phase, also called detoxification, and the follow-up phase. The possibilities that music therapy offers in the treatment of different kinds of addiction have been studied throughout Europe and the United States (e.g., Baker et al., 2007; Erkkilä & Eerola, 2001; Ghetti, 2004; Hairo-Lax, 2005; Horesh, 2006; Punkanen, 2002; Punkanen, 2006a; Robin, 2005; Ross et al., 2008; Ryynänen, 2004; Soshensky, 2001). According to Punkanen (2006a), music therapy in drug rehabilitation should be very intensive in the acute phase. In practice, this means up to two sessions per day. This helps the client to engage in the therapeutic process. In the follow-up phase of treatment, the frequency of therapy should be two to three times per week, and in order to maximize the potential for ongoing recovery, should last two to three years.

Vibroacoustic therapy is traditionally considered to be a physical and receptive form of music therapy, which uses pulsed, sinusoidal, low frequency sound on a specially designed bed or chair (Skille & Wigram, 1995; Wigram et al., 2002). Vibroacoustic therapy is used with various client groups, and different kinds of technical devices have been developed in Norway, Finland and the USA (Hooper, 2002). The vibroacoustic device described in this case study is a Finnish application called the physioacoustic chair. This computer-controlled device produces low frequency sinusoidal sound vibration between 27 and 113 Hz, and the main adjustable sound parameters are pulsation, scanning and direction (Lehikoinen, 1997). Six loudspeakers divided in four channels are located in the treatment chair. The chair is adjustable for comfort, and treatment programs can be created and edited with special software. These individual treatment programs can be saved for later use.

Physioacoustic therapy uses this combination of low frequency sound vibration and music listening to work with different levels of experience (sensations, emotions, images, memories and thoughts). Verbal reflection is also part of the process. This kind of multimodal approach enables one to work with the client's physiological and psychological experiences at the same time, in a flexible way. Use of these key elements varies between client groups and also depends on the framework, training and competence of the therapist (Ala-Ruona, 1999; 2003). Figure 1 provides an overview of the relationship between physioacoustic therapy and vibroacoustic therapy, of which a more detailed discussion of the central elements of physioacoustic therapy are presented in the following section.

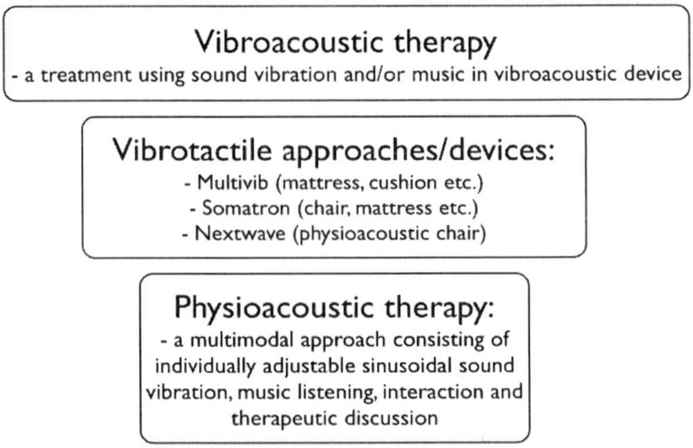

Vibroacoustic therapy
- a treatment using sound vibration and/or music in vibroacoustic device

Vibrotactile approaches/devices:
- Multivib (mattress, cushion etc.)
- Somatron (chair, mattress etc.)
- Nextwave (physioacoustic chair)

Physioacoustic therapy:
- a multimodal approach consisting of individually adjustable sinusoidal sound vibration, music listening, interaction and therapeutic discussion

Figure 1. Physioacoustic Therapy in a Context of Vibroacoustic Therapy

The Role of Sound Vibration

Low frequency sound vibration is central to the therapeutic process. As such, it can be used for either relaxation or activation. In most cases, the main aim is to help the client calm down and reach a state of deep relaxation. This can be achieved by using the three main sound parameters of the physioacoustic device: pulsation, scanning and direction. Slow pulsation is used for relaxation and faster pulsation for activation. Scanning changes the frequency of sound in a chosen range. This allows the therapist to find the ideal sound frequency to resonate with the affected area of the body. Each time a muscle resonates with a sound stimulus, it will deepen the relaxation of the muscle. Sound can be directed to move from the legs toward the head, or in reverse direction. Based upon clinical anecdotes, changing the direction of the sound appears to be beneficial in the treatment of stress-related symptoms and muscle tension. When combined, these adjustable sound parameters provide diverse possibilities in designing and editing treatment programs to meet individual therapeutic needs (Lehikoinen, 1997).

The Music Listening Experience

The role of the music listening experience in physioacoustic therapy can be entertaining, relaxing or activating in nature (Ala-Ruona & Punkanen, 2007). According to Punkanen (2007), in the context of drug rehabilitation, it is closely related to the stage of treatment. In the acute phase, the entertaining and relaxing aspects of music are most important. As such, the main objectives are to increase the client's feelings of relaxation and safety (e.g., Pelletier, 2004; Bartlett, 1996). In the follow-up phase, the role of music is both relaxing and activating. Here it is important that the therapist sensitively assesses when the client is able to use music that activates strong emotions, images and memories and when there is need to use music that calms the client and helps him/her to relax (Punkanen, 2006b).

The Role of Therapist

The role of the therapist in this approach is multifaceted. In the beginning of the process, the therapist is active in creating therapeutic conditions where safety and trust can develop. The therapist begins by describing the basics of the treatment procedure and methods used during the therapy process. The aim here is to reduce the client's anxiety toward a new and unfamiliar situation, and to help a client to adhere to the treatment. The therapist encourages the client to engage in reflection and share emerging experiences by working with bodily sensations, emotions, images, memories, thoughts and beliefs. Finally, the therapist helps the client to integrate these experiences and insights into his/her current life situation and personal history (Ala-Ruona & Punkanen, 2007).

The therapist is sensitive in observing the client's psychobiological states and he/she works as an interactive regulator for the client's dysregulated states (Ogden et al., 2006; Siegel, 1999). When there is enough safety in the therapeutic relationship, the therapist also confronts and challenges the client to find alternative views to problematic issues. The therapist's interventions can be verbal or centered on choosing music or treatment programs.

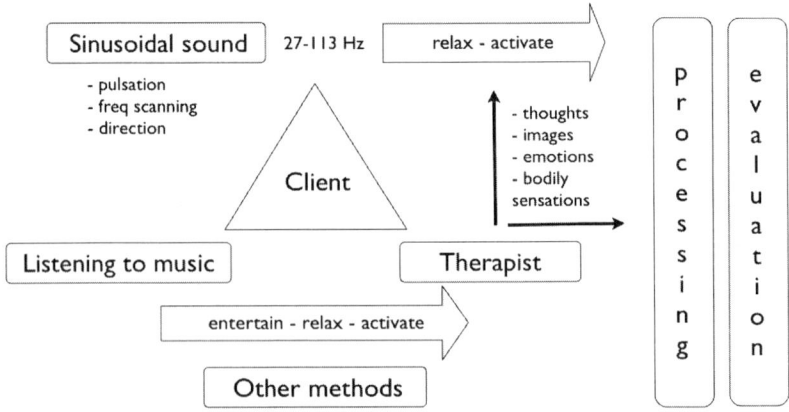

Figure 2. Key Elements of Physioacoustic Therapy

To summarize, the key elements of physioacoustic therapy are described in Figure 2. In the center is the client, because the basis of this approach is to actively engage the client in the process. The main elements in treatment are the effect of sinusoidal sound, the effect of music, and the effect of the therapist — how s/he contributes to the formation of the therapeutic alliance, mutual interaction, and how s/he helps the client to process emerging experiences. The areas of experiences to be discussed include thoughts (cognitive level), images (symbolic level), emotions (emotional level) and bodily sensations (sensorimotor level). Conducting the therapeutic discussion on these levels enables the development of an individually tailored and meaningful therapeutic process, along with the evaluation of the physical, emotional and cognitive areas of a client. This approach can also be utilized as a part of other therapeutic methods (e.g., clinical improvisation) or with related treatments (e.g., physical therapy).

THE CLIENT

Sara was a 23-year-old woman who lived together with her spouse Matti. They didn't have children together, but Matti's two children from his earlier marriage visited them regularly. During physioacoustic therapy, Sara was participating in an outpatient program. Before attending this program, she had spent six months in a drug rehabilitation centre, and physioacoustic therapy was planned for her as a follow-up after returning home from the centre. When the therapy process started, Sara had been off drugs for six months.

Sara had a ten-year history of drug use. She started to smoke when she was thirteen, and one year later started to use cannabis and then amphetamines. Her drug of choice was amphetamines, although she had also tried ecstasy, cocaine and heroin. Drug addiction had caused many problems in Sara's life, and now she was in a situation where she was very motivated to work with the issues related to her addictive behavior.

Sara felt that returning from the rehabilitation centre to her hometown was challenging and wanted to have as much support as possible to maintain the changes she had made. She felt very lonely because she had to sever all the relationships that were related to her drug use. Sara felt scared to start living without drugs in an environment where drug use had been the main part of her life. Sara was particularly scared about how to handle all the strong and difficult emotions and memories that she had previously regulated through drug use.

Assessment

The initial assessment was conducted by using a semi-structured interview that consisted of five main themes: history of substance abuse, relationship to music, relationships, emotions and emotional processing, and aims and expectations of the therapy process.

When talking about music and its meaning, Sara spoke of how she listened to lots of music and that song lyrics were the most meaningful part of music for her. She said that she often found themes from song lyrics, and that she selected music for listening based on her emotional state at the time.

Sara said that for her, a good relationship meant that there was trust, where each person could be honest with the other. She felt that she had that kind of relationship with her spouse, Matti. Sara also felt that she currently had quite a good relationship with her parents and brothers. Earlier, there had been many problems in her relationship with her parents and spouse because of her drug use. All her friends who weren't involved in drugs had disappeared from her life. Now that she had stopped using drugs, she had to break up with those friends who were also drug users.

When talking about emotions, Sara spoke of how she was very sensitive on an emotional level. At first she said that emotional processing of all kinds was easy for her when she was sober. However, as the interview continued, it became clear that getting angry was impossible for her, even though she wanted to be angry. Sara said that it was easier for her to handle all kinds of emotions when she used drugs, because once on drugs, she was no longer so sensitive. She said that when she was sober she was always stressed and thought too much about things in her life. So, it was a relief for her to reduce that sensitivity by using drugs:

> *When you take drugs you don't have to think anything. There is nothing that makes you feel bad. It is easier to be in that way, or that's how I thought earlier. But of course it is better to stay with your real emotions and try to find ways to handle them without drugs.*

When Sara reflected on her style of emotional expression, she recognized that it was easier for her to express positive emotions than negative ones. Positive emotions for her were joy and happiness, while negative ones were anger and sorrow. Sara described how she had been bullied at school, and felt that she had to be stronger and harder to be able to survive in relationships. She spoke of having taken on a kind of protective shell, which included being rude and unfriendly. She felt that this role was very contradictory to what she felt inside her. It had become a way to survive in life and cope with threatening emotions. Sara noticed that her experiences of being bullied had a direct link to starting to use drugs. It gave her relief from her emotions and provided a social group where she felt safe and accepted.

Sara identified working with negative emotions as the main theme for her therapy. She said that expressing anger was so difficult for her that, when she had a quarrel with her spouse, she totally froze. She described these situations as follows:

> *I become like a little helpless child. I can't do anything. And then I am totally hysterical. I feel that everything will fall apart until someone solves the situation.*

THE THERAPEUTIC PROCESS

Sara's therapy lasted six months and was divided into three phases. The first phase was very intensive in nature, as therapy sessions were held twice a day. This phase lasted only one week, but helped Sara to engage in the therapy process. The second phase was over two months, where sessions were held twice a week. In the third phase, sessions were held once a week, and this period lasted four months.

The basic structure of every session included an initial discussion, which lasted about ten minutes. During this discussion, general issues in Sara's current situation were addressed and preparations were made for her physioacoustic treatment, including the choice of music she would listen to. The physioacoustic program and music listening method that followed lasted from 25 to 30 minutes. After this came a therapeutic discussion wherein Sara's sensations, emotions, images, memories and thoughts raised during the physioacoustic and music listening program were reflected upon and integrated. Each session lasted 60 to 70 minutes.

Phase One (sessions 1–10)

In Sara's first session, the therapist chose a modified relaxation program, which used frequencies from 27 to 80 Hz with slow pulsation and mild strength. Music used in the first session was from Kitaro's Silk Road IV, which is Oriental instrumental music with a slow tempo and a stable rhythm. Melody lines in Kitaro's music are slow and sustained, and the dynamics of his music are also very soft, which works well with the physioacoustic program used.

After the physioacoustic and music listening experiences, Sara felt very relaxed and safe. Music awoke images of water, a small river and a beautiful summer's day. During the therapeutic discussion Sara started to talk about her feelings of insecurity that she often felt when she was home alone. She said that she didn't know how to be alone and that made her feel vulnerable and insecure. When exploring these feelings of insecurity, Sara said that she didn't feel insecure when she was a child and these feelings began when she was being bullied at school. In the first session, the therapist also started to ask questions that helped her to be aware of what was happening in her body. According to Ogden et al. (2006), the therapist can teach the client to be mindful of his/her body experience by asking questions that require awareness of bodily sensations in the present moment. Sara noticed positive sensations all over her body. She was somewhat surprised because normally she was only aware of negative sensations linked to negative emotions; emotions that she wanted to get rid of. Now she was connected with positive body sensations related to feelings of security and relaxation, along with the positive images evoked by the music.

In the second session the same physioacoustic program was used. This program was used, with small adjustments, as the main program in Sara's therapy. This time classical music was used (Albinoni's *Adagio for Strings*), and it evoked strong emotions of sorrow in Sara. She didn't feel insecure, but she said that it wouldn't be possible for her to listen to that kind of music by herself at home. Sorrow was something that she couldn't imagine herself feeling while alone. She said that it was good and important for her to feel it now in therapy. The therapist helped her to relate her bodily sensations to her feelings of sorrow, and she noticed that it was hard to breathe. She also noticed that there was a lot of tension in her stomach and chest area. Noticing this and integrating it with feelings of sorrow connected her to images about church, funerals and her grandfather's death. Her grandfather had died two years before, and this experience helped her to integrate his death at all levels of information processing. According to Ogden et al. (2006), it is important to link sensorimotor, emotional and cognitive levels of information processing together when processing traumatic memories with the client. Caldwell (1996) talks about the addictive spiral that begins with an intolerable experience. It is typical that this kind of experience is felt as a threat to one's physical, mental or emotional survival. An intolerable experience stimulates a fight or flight reaction that makes us search for a relief from the situation. The deep sorrow that Sara brought up in this session revealed this kind of intolerable experience, which she wasn't able to handle by herself. She needed someone to help her tolerate and regulate these strong emotions.

In the seventh session Sara felt very relaxed and happy after the physioacoustic program and music listening. However, she had difficulty trusting these feelings and was afraid they would be taken away from her:

I am so happy now, but it has always been so that when I am happy, I don't dare to feel that way because I am afraid of what will happen next. So now I am waiting for what horrible things would happen next. I can't be happy. But on the other hand, I think that finally it is time for me to be happy.

Trying to control situations and experiences through denial is part of the addictive spiral (Caldwell, 1996). Sara's comments reflect a basic mistrust of life. She seemed to be prepared for the worst, even though things were quite good at that moment. Her belief about the outside world was negatively colored. However, now that she was in therapy, she was able to reflect and discuss all these things with the therapist, as she was experiencing them, and without the use of drugs.

During the first week of intensive therapy, Sara had many good compensatory experiences from the therapy sessions. She noticed that it was possible to experience positive body sensations and emotions without drugs. She was also able to experience negative feelings without getting overwhelmed by them. That made her motivated to continue therapy, and built trust with the therapist.

Phase Two (sessions 11–26)

In the second phase of the therapy, we started to go deeper into themes and emotions that had emerged during the first phase.

In session 17, when music identical to the first session was used (Kitaro), images relating to water rose again, and Sara surprisingly spoke of how she was afraid of water. However, in music-based images, water had also appeared to her as a place of safety. This strengthened the link between images of water, positive sensations and feelings of safety. In discussions about fears, Sara said that being alone at home made her hysterical sometimes. In those situations, she felt strong negative sensations in her body. It was intolerable to stay with these painful sensations and feelings and she felt that she wanted to leave her body because of them.

Sara described drug use as an effective way for her to escape those intolerable experiences. Drugs certainly can be a relief for this kind of situation. According to Caldwell (1996), when using drugs, control loosens and we feel freer for a while. Through this, an illusion is created in which we feel that we are taken care of. At the end of this session, the therapist guided Sara to visualize this positive water image again, and at the same time asked her to notice what was happening in her body. Sara reported sensations of warmth in her chest and hands and the therapist encouraged her to just feel those sensations and stay with them for a while. According to Siegel (2007), it is important to notice that "sensing" is different from "noticing" because they involve two different streams of our awareness. In integrative therapy work, we want to bring both these streams into balance, increasing our client's integration of both. In Sara's case, she was now willing and able to stay with these sensations, "just sensing" what happened in her body and mind.

In session 24, a more activating program from the physioacoustic device was used with progressive and stimulating music from Finnish composer Pekka Pohjola. Memories started to emerge for Sara. She remembered her first day at school, and it was quite a traumatic memory. She remembered that her parents drove her to school, and then she had an image of herself standing in front of school, crying and looking at her parents going away. She was afraid and didn't want to stay there. She felt like running away, but couldn't move. As the image of this forgotten memory was rekindled in Sara's body, she felt herself tense up as she re-experienced the same emotions that were experienced on that day. The therapist helped Sara to link these body sensations to the image of her standing at the school. He asked her how she felt and, if it were possible, to stay with those sensations and emotions. Sara answered that she was sad and felt sorry for that little girl standing there alone, but it was tolerable for her. The therapist asked if it was possible for her to reassure that little girl that everything was fine now; and that she was not alone anymore. An image was used where Sara was an adult, standing with that little girl, holding her hand, and telling her that everything was okay.

After a while the therapist directed Sara to be aware of her body sensations and emotions again. She noticed that her breathing had become deeper and her body didn't feel as tense anymore. She also noticed tears in her eyes but said that it actually felt good to cry. At the end of the session, Sara was very surprised that this memory had come to mind because she hadn't remembered it for many years. She also made a connection between her body sensations during this memory and those body sensations she had to face in her life now. Sara spoke of how she reacted before coming home from the rehabilitation centre:

I was so scared about coming home that for two weeks I threw up several times a day. I reacted so strongly. That has happened to me before when there has been a lot of stress or anxiety in my life. I start to react in a psychosomatic way.

According to McDougall (1989), psychosomatic symptoms are sometimes connected to drug addiction problems. It is probable that psychosomatic vulnerability increases with people who use drugs, as protection against psychic pain when recalling an emotion would be a more suitable way to deal with the pain.

At the end of the second phase of therapy, Sara said that she was going back to the job that she had before drug rehabilitation. She had allowed her boss to tell everyone why she had been away for so long. Sara felt that being honest about this made it easier for her to go back. She was unsure about how she could adapt to a 'normal' daily routine in her life again, as this meant getting up early in the morning and working the whole day. But, she was ready to try.

Phase Three (sessions 27–42)

The aim of the therapy during phase three was to strengthen Sara's resources and insights discovered during phases one and two. Two traumatic memories that surfaced during the physioacoustic program and music listening were processed. These memories were not fully explored or integrated, so Sara began work in these areas. The first of these was in session 32, when Sara started to talk about her parent's divorce:

> *When my parents divorced I stayed with my mother. I always waited for those days when I was able to spend time with my father, just the two of us together. I remembered when my father's new girlfriend moved to my father's house with her son and her son started to call my father 'his father.' It felt so bad to me.*

Sara was thirteen at the time, and it was very difficult for her to accept that her parents didn't live together anymore. Sara recognized feelings of jealousy toward her father's girlfriend. She was also very angry about the situation and blamed herself. The therapist helped Sara to understand how it often happens that children will blame themselves for what happens around the separation of their parents, even though they are not responsible for this happening. The therapist also encouraged Sara to feel the anger inside her and express it both verbally and with movement. The therapist directed her to just be aware of what her body would like to do with all that anger, and she started to clench her fists. Encouraging her to verbalize that movement, Sara said *"I am so angry because they divorced and broke our family."* The therapist continued to encourage and support her expressions of anger, affirming that it was safe for her to do it now. After staying with that emotion for a while, its intensity started to fade, and she said that she was not so angry anymore.

In session 36, Sara listened to music by the Finnish composer and musician Jukka Leppilampi. His music is very powerful and shamanic in nature, using singing without any words. This music evoked strong emotions of being held by sound and voice. In the therapeutic discussion, Sara talked about how important Matti was to her. She started to cry:

> It was so close that I would have lost him. He had taken my epilepsy medicines, and when the ambulance came, they were quite sure that he wouldn't survive from that. They didn't even allow me to go with the ambulance. When I called the hospital they told me that if I didn't come soon I wouldn't see him alive anymore. But he survived...and after that I was ready to go to the rehabilitation centre. And I made him come with me. There were no other choices anymore.

That memory, along with the emotions and bodily reactions related to it, were processed for the next three sessions and helped Sara to integrate this very traumatic episode into her newly emerging identity. It was no longer something that made her hysterical, where she would experience tremendous panic whenever she talked about it or remembered how it felt. It became part of her life story — something that she could say had happened to her, but was now over.

CONCLUSION

At the end of therapy, Sara felt much more confident and stronger in herself. She felt that physioacoustic therapy had created a safe place for her, like being held by someone you can trust, where there was no need to be afraid. This place had given her a space and time to reflect on her experiences and be aware as a whole. It also gave her the support to return successfully to work, fulfilling her duties appropriately.

According to Kurtz (1990), "the goal of therapy is not any particular experience" but "a change which organizes all experiences differently" (p. 139). This means that the client's way of experiencing themselves and the world around them will change. In Sara's case, this change was clear. She started to give more value to her bodily experiences and emotions so that they were more balanced with her cognition. Physioacoustic therapy created the conditions for Sara to process a whole range of experiences, including emotions that had previously been intolerable. In so doing, Sara discovered that there were many surprising and unexpected things within, and that by staying with these sensations, emotions and memories, she rediscovered the fullness of herself:

> *It was sometimes so surprising how all those old memories came to my mind. And even though they were difficult memories to talk about, it felt right to do so. It really gave me a relief to feel those emotions and express them in here, in safety. I am also very happy that I have been able to enjoy my bodily sensations. It is not just a source of anxiety and distress anymore. My body is now a much safer place to stay in.*

REFERENCES

Ala-Ruona, E. (1999). *Fysioakustisen Hoidon Kehittämisprojekti Seinäjoen Sairaalassa* [Project for Developing the Physioacoustic Treatment in Central Hospital of Seinäjoki]. Seinäjoki: Etelä-Pohjanmaan sairaanhoitopiirin kuntayhtymä, Fysiatria/Musiikkiterapia.

Ala-Ruona, E. (2003). *Fysioakustinen Hoito Osana Erikoissairaanhoitoa ja Kuntoutustutkimusta* [The Physioacoustic Treatment as a Part of Rehabilitation Assessment. in Spesialized Health Care]. In E. Ala-Ruona, J. Erkkilä, R. Jukkola and K. Lehtonen (Eds.), *Muistoissa Petri Lehikoinen. Jyväskylä: Suomen musiikkiterapiayhdistys* r.y.

Ala-Ruona, E. & Punkanen, M. (2007). *The Physioacoustic Treatment: The Training Manual*. Jyväskylä: Eino Roiha Institute.

Baker, F. A., Gleadhill, L. M. & Dingle, G. A. (2007). Music therapy and emotional exploration: Exposing substance abuse clients to the experiences of non-drug-induced emotions. *The Arts in Psychotherapy*, 34(4), 321–330.

Bartlett, D. L. (1996). Physiological responses to music and sound stimuli. In D. A. Hodges (Ed.), *Handbook of Music Psychology*. San Antonio: IMR Press.

Caldwell, C. (1996). *Getting Our Bodies Back. Recovery, Healing, and Transformation Through Body-centered Psychotherapy*. Boston & London: Shambhala Publications.

Erkkilä, J. & Eerola, T. (2001). *Hallitsetko sinä pelejä vai pelit sinua* [Research on Multimethod Rehabilitation Project with Gambling Addiction]. Jyväskylä: Suomen Musiikkiterapiayhdistys r.y.

Ghetti, C. M. (2004). Incorporating music therapy into the harm reduction approach to managing substance use problems. *Music Therapy Perspectives*, 22(2), 84–90.

Hairo-Lax, U. (2005). *Musiikkiterapiaprosessin merkittävät tekijät ja merkittävät hetket päihteettömän elämäntavan tukijoina* [Significant Moments and Significant Factors of Music Therapy in the Process of Supporting an Intoxicant-Free Way of Life]. Sibelius-Akatemia. Musiikkikasvatuksen osasto. Studia Musica 27. Väitöskirja (Doctoral dissertation).

Hooper, J. (2002). Is VA therapy, music therapy? *Music Therapy Today* (online), available at http://musictherapyworld.net.

Horesh, T. (2006). Dangerous music: Working with the destructive and healing powers of popular music in the treatment of substance abusers. In D. Aldridge and J. Fachner (Eds.), *Music and Altered States: Consciousness Transcendence, Therapy and Addictions*. London & Philadelphia: Jessica Kingsley Publishers.

Kurtz, R. (1990). *Body-centered Psychotherapy: The Hakomi Method*. Mendicino, CA: LifeRhythm.

Lehikoinen, P. (1997). The physioacoustic method. In T. Wigram, & C. Dileo (Eds.), *Music, Vibration and Health*. Cherry Hill, NJ: Jeffrey Books.

McDougall, J. (1989). *Theaters Of The Body: A Psychoanalytic Approach to Psychosomatic Illness*. New York & London: W. W. Norton & Company.

Ogden, P., Minton, K., & Pain, C. (2006). *Trauma and the Body: A Sensorimotor Approach to Psychotherapy*. New York & London: W. W. Norton & Company.

Pelletier, C. L. (2004). The effect of music on decreasing arousal due to stress: A meta-analysis, *Journal of Music Therapy*, 41(3), 192–214.

Punkanen, M. 2002. "Matkalla mieleen ja tunteisiin". Fysioakustinen menetelmä ja musiikkiterapia huumekuntoutuksessa [The Physioacoustic Method and Music Therapy in Drug Rehabilitation]. Jyväskylän yliopisto, Musiikkitieteen laitos. Pro gradu-tutkielma (Master's Thesis).

Punkanen, M. 2006a. Musiikkiterapia osana huumekuntoutusta: hoitoon kiinnittämisestä kokemusmaailman integroimiseen [Music Therapy as a Part of Drug Rehabilitation]. Jyväskylän yliopisto, Musiikin laitos. Lisensiaatintyö (Licenciate's Thesis).

Punkanen, M. (2006b). On a journey to somatic memory. Theoretical and clinical approaches for the treatment of traumatic memories in music therapy-based drug rehabilitation. In D. Aldridge and J. Fachner (Eds.), *Music and Altered States: Consciousness, Transcendence, Therapy and Addictions.* London: Jessica Kingsley Publishers.

Punkanen, M. (2007). Music therapy as a part of drug rehabilitation. *Music Therapy Today*, 8(3). Available at http://www.musictherapyworld.net.

Reed, E. C. (1994). Basic principles of drug use. In M. J. Landry (Ed.), *Understanding Drugs of Abuse: The Processes of Addiction, Treatment, and Recovery* (pp. 7–28). Washington D.C.: American Psychiatric Press, Inc.

Robin, R. (2005). Adults in Recovery: A year with members of the choirhouse. *Nordic Journal of Music Therapy*, 14(2), 107–119.

Ross, S., Cidambi, I., Dermatis, H., Weinstein, J., Ziedonis, D., Roth, S. & Galanter, M. (2008). Music therapy: A novel motivational approach for dually diagnosed patients. *Journal of Addictive Diseases*, 27(1), 41–53.

Ryynänen, E. (2004). "Mie haluun hoitaa itteni kuntoon" Hoitomallin kehittämisprojekti huumevieroituspotilaan kuntoutumisen käynnistäjänä [Developing the Treatment Model of a Patient in Drug Rehabilitation – An Action Research Study]. Jyväskylän yliopisto, Musiikkitieteen laitos. Pro gradu-tutkielma (Master's Thesis).

Siegel, D. J. (1999). *The Developing Mind. How Relationships and the Brain Interact to Shape Who We Are.* New York & London: The Guilford Press.

Siegel, D. J. (2007). *The Mindful Brain. Reflection and Attunement in the Cultivation of Well-Being.* New York & London: W. W. Norton & Company.

Skille, O. & Wigram, T. (1995). Vibroacoustic therapy. In T. Wigram, B. Saperston and R. West (Eds.), *The Art & Science of Music Therapy: A Handbook*. Amsterdam: Harwood Academic Publishers.

Soshensky, R. (2001). Music therapy and addiction. *Music Therapy Perspectives*, 19(1), 45–52.

Wigram, T., Nygaard-Pedersen, I. & Bonde, L. O. (2002). *A Comprehensive Guide to Music Therapy: Theory, Clinical Practice, Research and Training*. London: Jessica Kingley Publishers.

Chapter Twenty One

A FLASH OF THE OBVIOUS: MUSIC THERAPY AND TRAUMA

Julie Sutton

INTRODUCTION

This chapter is an exploration of work with a female psychiatric patient[1] attending a National Health Service primary care outpatient unit in the United Kingdom. The unit is staffed with psychotherapists, psychiatrists, a cognitive behavioral therapist, an art psychotherapist and a music psychotherapist. The team stance is psychoanalytic.

I will describe what emerges from the work with the patient at different points in the therapy. This includes what appears out of her music (sounded and silent), her words and her silences. I place this alongside my experiences of listening and sitting with her, and from further reflection within the supervision context. I aim to show how staying with thoughts about music can offer a particular way of being attentive to the patient. I believe that this can open up spaces for unexpected ways of coming to an understanding of the therapeutic work that both goes beyond, but is also simultaneously and fundamentally grounded in, the music itself.

Our attitude to the music made in music therapy sessions defines us as therapists. While almost all the literature is focused on sounds produced in the clinic room, I believe that silences are an essential part of our work (Sutton, 2001; 2002; 2006; 2007; Sutton & De Backer, 2009). In this chapter, I concentrate on what was not sounded in the sessions. Some may ask, 'is this *music* therapy?' I will argue that it is indeed music therapy, and as this chapter unfolds, I will demonstrate how focusing on the silent music in the sessions allows us the space to think about what lies before, during and after each musical sound.

---

[1] As the work takes place within a health service setting, I use the term 'patient' rather than client.

FOUNDATIONAL CONCEPTS

Clinical Stance: An Unseen Hand

My clinical focus is on the music in music therapy. This way of thinking owes much to a concept of musical listening, which is a way of putting one's attention fundamentally in music, in what is produced musically, and in how it is produced in relation to the self and the other. The ways in which the therapist experiences and thinks about listening is core to this. I think of listening as potentially a way of sensing the present moment in the clinical room as openly as possible. In this context, music is not a noun, but a verb — music is something created in time, within and between people. Music is not something that happens in isolation. It exists in an ongoing process that takes place and requires people to be part of it, whether actively producing sounds or not. The great pianist Alfred Brendel (2001) described this process as "an unseen hand that keeps its hold over player and listeners alike for the duration of these timeless moments" (p. 360).

Part of music's unique potential as an art form is that it is always in a state of becoming. This concept incorporates awareness of time being something that not only goes on, but is also fluid and in flux. More than any other art form, music works through a flexible relationship between actual and perceived time, where present and past might meet and move towarda an as yet unknown future (Sabbadini, 1996; Sutton, 2006; 2007). This is both a reality of the individual's experience of the world and others in the world (Winnicott, 1971; Bion, 1984), as well as something that directly links with the infant's experiences of his/her first relationship (Stern, 1977; Trevarthen & Aitken, 2001).

Related to this, musical listening describes not only what the therapist does when she allows her attention to be caught by the patient and by the quality of this process, but also how a kind of musical preoccupation in the therapist enables us to think in detailed ways about the patient. This thinking is undertaken in the context of a kind of curiosity about the inner and outer worlds of the patient, of what takes place within the therapist while he/she is with the patient, and of how this is thought about both inside and outside sessions.

Over many years of clinical work, I have become increasingly convinced of the value of a particular kind of waiting that I link to a type of listening that is inherently musical. It is musical because of the qualities of music that are both going-on-in-time and stretching time. This is something that can be experienced and simultaneously heard via musical production in improvisations in the clinic room, but is often held silently in the analytic situation, either behind words spoken, or in what is not spoken. In music therapy sessions, this occurs in verbal or musical silences, as well as what is heard in the content of the music played. We can note, in addition, the work of sitting with the desire to seek out neat explanations for what occurs in the therapy room, particularly when one part of a therapist's role is to help the patient to come to forms of understanding about his/her life. This idea is present in Bion's (1974) observation that one "is usually so busy looking for something out of the ordinary that one ignores the obvious as if it were of no importance" (p. 103).

Bion's (1974) recommendation to approach each session without memory or desire goes further than proposing that the therapist remain in an open receptive state, because within his statement is an implication that when one is expecting to discover more about the patient, or for therapy to move forward in any particular way, one is no longer available to the patient. Therefore, the therapist's memory, desire, and sense of anticipation of the content of a session works directly against his/her ability to stay in the present moment and to feel the present unfolding in the patient while he/she sits with the therapist, and the therapist sits with the patient. Ogden (1997) developed this idea using the term the *intersubjective analytic third*, which he describes as "not…a static entity; rather, I understand it as an evolving experience that is continually in a state of flux as the intersubjectivity of the analytic process is transformed by the understandings generated by the analytic pair" (p. 30). This experience is not identical for both, but meanings are negotiated between both. In musical terms, we might think of a form of free-improvised duet, where one, or both, or neither might play, but where there can be a listening to the duet that *is not being sounded,* is nonetheless silently present (or potentially so). This jointly negotiated potential way of 'being' musically places the emphasis on the therapeutic relationship. The therapist pays attention to nuances and changes from moment to moment, to how patterns emerge over time, and how a shift or hiatus can bring new ways of thinking about what happens between patient and therapist while in the clinic room. Therefore, meanings may be musical experiences that are shared or not shared, and may be transformed further into words that can be thought about and linked with feelings and sensations.

While many of these ideas are connected to psychoanalytic theory, and while my work includes a psychoanalytic stance, I also place an emphasis on music and music therapy research. In particular, I am interested in the ways that a patient's music enables us to hear his/her inner state as it unfolds in ongoing time (movement toward a future), and also backward and forward across time (the past emerging in the present). Compared with the main body of music therapy research, there is relatively little published material dealing in any depth with traumatic material presented musically, a notable exception being De Backer's concept of *sensorial play* (a description of the musical and psychic phenomena of the patient's inner traumatized state) and the identification of a musical-personal process moving toward the appearance of *musical form*. Both concepts represent significant contributions to our understanding of the unique place that music therapy has in the treatment of the traumatized patient (De Backer, 2008, Sutton & De Backer, 2009).

I believe that ideas about the development of a personality can be thought about musically, making it possible to identify a process that traces a parallel developmental pathway from the infant's first experience of being at one with mother, to experiencing relationship (oneself in the context of two people), but which process is found in altered form in the pathological presentation of the traumatized patient (from sensorial play to musical form). More specifically, I am concerned with the unexpected emergence of what De Backer (2008) terms *moments of synchronicity*, which he defines as spaces that open up in the repetitive, endless, meaningless sensorial play through which emerge brief moments of potential for intersubjectivity. De Backer described these moments as when:

> *the music already anticipates something, which is not yet there, a type of structure, within which the patient possibly can enter [into]* (De Backer & Wigram, 2007 p. 132).

De Backer (2007) links this with the ways in which "structures originate [in music] to which we escape" (p. 132) and with an experience described by Lacan (1966) as mirroring, where, to simplify a complex process, one perceives oneself one step removed, and where one senses oneself as no longer quite alone. In sensorial play, one could say that the therapist takes on the task of *echo* in order to be nearby the traumatic, and it is the space in which the music itself comes into existence, as it lives in the therapist, that makes this possible. In order for this to happen, the therapist is making use of the way of being that Bion and Odgen have described as reverie and the emergence of an analytic third, as cited previously. While there is a personal experience of what takes place in the space between and within patient and therapist, it is the music itself, and its presence inside the therapist (and then potentially inside the patient, and between patient and therapist) that makes this possible.

A Few Words About Trauma

In the case study that follows, much of the musical listening was to the traumatic material presented musically by the patient. This material had no meaning other than being a sounded statement of the patient's inner world, where time had ceased to exist and where there was repetition but no development. When a patient plays in this way, trauma is presented as a form of enactment, heard in the endless musical material, trapped and destined to repeat over and over, but not to move forward or onward, nor to have reference to the past.

The theoretical thinking about trauma and music therapy outlined in this chapter is relevant to all types of traumatic experiences, and speaks particularly to the complex interplay between earliest and later traumatic events, and between developmental and single event trauma. The case presented here is of someone whose life spanned the 30 years of the Northern Ireland conflict, and like everyone else living in N. Ireland, someone who would have experienced life in a part of the world where paramilitary and military activity was taking place. While this patient was not referred to psychological services specifically because of conflict trauma, her experience of what was taking place in the community was part of a complexity of influences on her mental state, and would have had an impact on her sense of feeling safe in the world.

The case material explored here is not the full story of the therapy with this patient. It was a deliberate decision to focus only on the earlier part of the therapeutic process. The theme running through this chapter is that of the therapist's sitting with the unknown in the therapy room, and of suspending expectation of any particular outcome for the work. As emphasized earlier, this stance encourages the therapist to aim to be as open and receptive as possible in his/her listening attitude to the patient. In this chapter, I make use of the theme in a way that will leave the reader similarly 'suspended' regarding full details of the entire therapy process. There is no neat ending provided, to enable the reader to fully focus on the theme of sitting with 'not knowing.' It is acknowledged that experienced clinicians will be familiar with this idea and will recognize the kind of inner space this requires in the therapist, while trainee therapists will come to connect with this through their experiences during and after reading this text, and from further reading and clinical experience.

THE CLIENT

Vicky

Vicky was a woman in her thirties with a history of self-harm and acting out dramatically as a teenager. Vicky's notes show that she had cut herself and had made a number of suicide attempts, none as serious as the recent attempt, from which she had to be resuscitated. Her early history indicated that she had been with one foster family before arriving with a second foster family who eventually adopted her at the age of six months. The circumstances of the first six months of her life are sketchy, but suggest a rather confusing and unboundaried immediate environment.

Vicky was referred initially to the Centre during the aftermath of a suicide attempt. At this point, it had not been possible to obtain a clear picture of her psycho-emotional state, due to brain damage from the suicide attempt, and it was decided to offer a music therapy assessment, where Vicky would have available both words and music. Vicky attended her first meeting with me eight months after her suicide attempt, at a point at which her physical condition had stabilized, she was out of hospital and resident in a nursing home. At this point, the primary concern and medical input had related to her brain injury. The assessment was Vicky's first post-hospital contact with psychological services. At this point, she was using a wheelchair, was unable to bear weight and showed high muscle tone in her legs and lower arms. She spoke with some difficulty, but managed to form words that could be understood. Vicky was brought to her session by her adoptive mother.

Assessment

Vicky was referred by her neuropsychiatrist to the consultant psychiatrist for the team within which I worked. The consultant psychiatrist saw Vicky six months after her suicide attempt, when she was out of hospital and residing in a nursing home. Her chart showed that Vicky had a complex psychiatric history from adolescence onward.

Vicky's neuropsychiatrist requested a psychological assessment. This was because up to this point it had been difficult to ascertain if Vicky's responses were influenced by physical, cognitive and/or memory issues related to her brain injury, or underlying psycho-emotional factors related to her past. There was a sense that she was not always able to be engaged sufficiently to give coherent answers to questions, but the cause of this was unclear. However there was a feeling that a multi-disciplinary approach to Vicky's treatment was important, and that this should include both physical and psychological therapies.

This referral was more unusual for our out-patient psychiatric facility because of the extent of the brain injury. In view of this, the assessment process was carefully undertaken. For example, it had not been possible for Vicky to complete the detailed questionnaire that was an important part of team discussion between the initial referral and any assessment appointment. This was due to Vicky's presenting cognitive impairment and the not-fully-known impact on her mind of the situation before and after such a traumatic incident. Neither was it possible for Vicky to attend the new patient clinic, meet with a psychotherapist in order for a detailed history to be taken, and then wait for the discussion between the therapist and consultant to be completed before discussing and deciding the way forward with them.

The consultant psychiatrist visited Vicky and undertook an interview, reporting afterward that Vicky showed a significant degree of hypoxic brain injury. It was clear that she made unreliable responses to questions, but it was not possible to identify how far the disturbance in her thinking was as a result of brain injury or psychological defense mechanisms. It was felt by the team that verbal engagement would be too difficult for Vicky at this stage, and a further referral was made for music therapy.

Vicky attended an initial music therapy session, with a view to a 4–6 session assessment. However, I believe that a therapeutic process began in our initial meeting, and have therefore detailed the first session within the main body of this chapter. It is important to note that while also observing that Vicky's responses to me seemed to be influenced by a mixture of functional and emotional factors (that in themselves were as yet unclear), I found myself caught up in wondering what had happened to her that might have caused the current situation she found herself in. I think that this was linked to a sense that while Vicky had an acquired brain injury, there was an intact psychological factor underlying this.

In many ways, the main purpose and value of this process of assessment was that it was largely completed before the referral to music therapy, by the two consultants involved. The main purpose of our first meeting was to see how Vicky would respond to the setting and to me. Once she had agreed to continue meeting with me, my role was to suspend a belief that there was a single cause for what Vicky was presenting, or that therapy would progress in any pre-ordained fashion; I kept an open mind and acknowledged the unknown complexity of this patient's presentation. I do not think that the music therapy assessment can be separated from the therapeutic process as a whole. This is an important point because of the meanings that may be present during any first meeting with a patient: one can think of the first session with a patient as containing everything about the therapy to come, with the therapeutic process the space in which this unfolds and is processed. This was true of Vicky's first meeting with me.

THE THERAPEUTIC PROCESS

Three aspects of the sessions demonstrate how I came to understand the ways that Vicky could have experienced her sessions, and how these have linked what happened in the room to Vicky's past and present, and her inner and outer worlds. I have chosen to take these examples from the first six months of her therapy. While her therapy continued after this, I feel that these earlier meetings have value because they reveal much of what emerges from working with a disturbed patient such as Vicky, and the detailed musical listening and thinking that takes place in the therapist. As noted earlier, this also allows the reader the opportunity to connect with the processes relating to this. I begin with the first meeting, within which there was a sense that a therapeutic process might have begun.

Meeting for the First Time and an Intense Musical Contact

Vicky arrived in a wheelchair and, as observed already, her physical state showed clear signs of hypoxic brain injury. Her speech was labored but largely clear and understandable. She looked around the room and told me that she had played a few instruments, but that she could not play anymore. Her face was mask-like. After the session, I found myself thinking about what might be behind the mask, and while the mask invited me to have these thoughts, I did not have an idea of Vicky wanting me to be curious about this.

In the third session, we sat together at the piano, at Vicky's suggestion. For a few minutes we played single black notes in turn. The mood was very quiet and serious, and I found myself concentrating intensely on how one note sounded, then another, and another. I realize that I must have been joining the sounds together in my mind, and hearing the music as a whole, rather than as several disconnected sounds. It was a way of keeping a sense of the nature of the space in the room, into which the notes emerged. But Vicky's notes did not seem to exist for very long, they seemed to be like echoes of sounds, and barely there at all. On the other hand, she sometimes attached a note to the previous one I had played. Somewhere hidden in the intense concentration inside me was also a sense of something not quite working, and a painful after-effect.

Vicky had no reflections after this music. She returned for her next session in a distressed state. She told me about a previous music teacher who had had a terrible accident, and although she had no way of contacting her, she wanted her to know that she thought about her a great deal. There was a very sad and anxious feeling in the air, but at the same time I was confused about when this had happened, and about what was past and present. In supervision I thought about ways in which this communication from Vicky might have meaning, and particularly the ways her experiences of the previous session may have been held in the figure of the teacher who seemed to be both her and me. Perhaps a lack of clarity about what belonged to which of us was picked up in my confusion.

Sleeping Away the Session and Silenced Music

After the experience of this intense musical contact, Vicky told me that she was very worried about playing again. I took her seriously about this because patients with Vicky's kind of early history can have a fundamental terror of emotional connection with another. This *'other'* is felt to be a terrible, threatening invader who must at all costs be kept at bay. Without protection, there would be an experience of unbearable emotional pain, for to be *connected with* is to be destroyed in the most awful way (Rosenfeld, 1987). In addition, once connected, one would ultimately have to lose the connectedness and experience being alone in a state of loss. One must remain in an impregnable place, protected against all attempts others might make to intrude. In order to achieve this, one remains vigilant to the extent that a state of nothingness is preferable to the terrible anxiety experienced when someone comes near. Contact is not only shunned, it is actively repelled. In Vicky's case, she broke any attempt at linking by her therapist. Vicky initially closed her eyes, then apparently fell asleep. She seemed to put herself into an altered state where she was completely protected from the therapist and from anything in the therapy room that might get in.

In this instance, at the time, I felt intuitively that this psychotic withdrawal should not be broken. To try to make a link would be experienced as a terrible intrusion so early in the therapy. Therefore, I waited quietly with Vicky, until the session came to an end, at which point I spoke her name and informed her that we had completed the session. Vicky showed a hint of interest in this but otherwise remained quite blank. In subsequent sessions, it was also possible to make quite neutrally the observation that I had seen Vicky close her eyes and go to sleep. My statements had a musical quality, placed in the mid-low vocal range, paced slowly and carefully, and were quiet, calm and serious. Vicky's reaction to these words was ambivalence — she both welcomed the fact that I had sat quietly with her, but hated me for being there at all, whether silent, or making sounds. Later, I was able to wonder aloud whether or not Vicky had been dreaming when she slept, again saying this with a similar musical vocal quality. Vicky simply said, "no, I don't dream. I am nowhere." This had the effect of shutting a door on any further contact, giving me the message that there could be no hope of anything living, or anything coming to life in the space within which Vicky sat.

Additionally, when Vicky sat with her eyes shut, I found my attention was drawn to thoughts about her suicide attempt. On one occasion, I found it difficult to catch my breath, and I had to concentrate on my breathing in order to remain in the room. This body sensation helped me to understand something of the quality of Vicky's terrible anxiety about a connection with a woman that could link her directly with her earliest experiences of her mother. Later in the same session, I found myself imagining a lullaby, accompanied by feelings of tenderness toward Vicky. Such a maternal transference, and the nature of the music imagined, also linked me with a completely vulnerable infant who needed delicate and gentle holding. We can wonder what an infant does to survive when he/she had experienced such a devastating threat to his/her sense of safety and where, as Rosenfeld (1987/2005) puts it, "something which should have been pleasurable and satisfying, and could have been the basis of security and love, created terror and misery" (p. 152). How could such an infant ever trust anyone, when the source of comfort is also the source of overwhelming, terrible anxiety? How fundamentally these early experiences would color attitudes and responses to future relationships.

I wondered about Vicky's experience of being with me, while I was in the sessions, during the time that I wrote my notes, during post-session musical reverie[2] and in supervision. There was a sense of a terrible dilemma between us: at times we seemed to move a little closer to each other, but this mood immediately frayed at the edges and fell away into a kind of colorless nothingness. I had no sense of any music that could exist there, and the quality of silence in the room was thin, shapeless and timeless. There was not enough of anything present that could be called a silence. In these moments, I found that something in me disappeared. My mind wandered to a place outside the room, and it took considerable effort to bring myself back into the space and exist as a living being. However, once or twice a gentle lullaby began to appear in my mind, and I was overcome with feelings of tenderness along with a deep sadness. I think this is where there was something in Vicky's music therapy that came alive and I will expand on this point in the next section of the text.

A Flash of the Obvious and Music that Cannot yet Become

After weeks of quietly sitting with Vicky, I found myself increasingly being able to observe nuances in her state. It is important to note that this indicated something happening between us, found in my growing awareness, attunement to and discovery of different kinds of qualities in Vicky. These were indistinct but nonetheless present, and here one might find it helpful to think of the image of shapes appearing briefly in the formless mist of a session, existing for the briefest of moments before returning to an overall shapeless fog. In musical terms, this comprises a process in the therapist that involves listening to the echo of a refrain, of a song yet to be sung, as suggested by Williams (2010). While an active process in the therapist, it requires an overall internal stillness and a different kind of refrain — a refrain*ing* from acting on one's responses and a 'staying with' the overall mood of a session until something begins to emerge more clearly from the patient's material. This is part of a staying-with the unknown, as recommended by

---

[2] Musical reverie is a way of further processing material from sessions, via improvising, with the patient in mind. I also find it useful to improvise when a patient is unable to attend a session, with my mind preoccupied with them as I play.

Bion, and paraphrased as being without memory, desire or the need to understand (Bion, 1967; 1984; Symington & Symington, 1966).

Working in this way, I also noticed a clearer sense of tension in Vicky, and it became quite possible to sense when she was about to cut off any connection with me. At the beginning of one session, when this seemed to be happening, I said, "Vicky, I am sitting here with you, and I am thinking how hard all this is. How something goes on that cannot work and is always doomed to fail." Vicky stared hard at me, looked very serious and said, "yes, you understand." At this point, and for a short while, something lived between us. I experienced this as moving towards a moment of synchronicity, and something that I think is meant by Paul Williams' (2010) description of a particular kind of potential space. In another form, this was almost the beginning of a silence before music could be sounded.

This also reminds me of Williams' (2010) comments when sitting with very disturbed patients, of his definition of love as being able to make time for another. I think this includes making time for an 'other' when the other does reciprocate, as with Vicky, who was not able to allow a space for me to exist in the room, and therefore could not make time for me. However, when I discovered time and space became alive in me, as described earlier, there existed a potential that was otherwise deadened. This would not have been possible without attention paid to the process described previously, of listening to 'the refrain that was from a song yet to be sung.' This, while undertaken silently, is part of music therapy, and of the therapist's own internal work, via personal psychotherapy and regular clinical supervision.

I noted that Vicky's apparently impermeable state nullified any attempt to be present with her, or to sit with her. There was no music that could be sounded, although as her therapist, I could begin to imagine a gentle lullaby that linked me to tender and deeply sad feelings about her early experiences, without knowing what these were. This imagined lullaby provided something alive in the deadened silence created by Vicky, who would sometimes become aware of my efforts to be present with her without despising me for it. Much later in her therapy, she described how she could feel the therapy was pointless (because nothing could be allowed to enter her dreamless sanctuary), but sometimes felt something different via my presence in the room. I wondered if this indicated a potential for Vicky to also become aware of the song yet to be sung, in a way that was fleetingly manageable. This was the most delicate thread between us and one that was always broken or smashed. Remaining open to remember the moments where this 'thread' was managed and could also be imagined, was one of the most important aspects of the work with Vicky, who actively forgot in order to protect herself. Along with Rosenfeld (1987/2005), we can only continue to wonder about what was at stake for Vicky and what unbearable terrors could emerge if such a song was allowed to be sung, be listened to, or be heard.

CONCLUSION

Final Thoughts: A Flash of the Obvious

Vicky came into therapy as a result of unanswered questions about her rehabilitation following a suicide attempt that had resulted in significant hypoxic brain injury. Answers that had been unavailable through the usual psychological assessment procedures emerged in the music therapy room through using musical perspectives (via musical listening and thinking), to experience and think about Vicky. Attention to the detail of the sessions during lengthy periods of silence was fundamental to this, with the therapist allowing moments to pass without acting upon them, remaining open to how this resonated in her, and how impressions, sensations and thoughts appeared as if musical motifs in the silence. Without searching for answers, this left the therapist open to experience the patient as fully as she could. As Bion (1973) noted, this stance enabled freedom for the unexpected to emerge:

> *I found that I could experience a flash of the obvious. One is usually so busy looking for something out of the ordinary that one ignores the obvious as if it were of no importance. Indeed, one of the reasons for thinking it is time to give an interpretation is that nobody has seen something that is obvious* (p. 67).

As Bion also seemed to imply, when we do experience the present in its intensity, then the past and the future are powerfully brought together to produce a 'timeless' state. In Bion's (1973) words "A present experience is past, is present, and is future; it is timeless" (p. 88). This kind of timelessness is alive to what might pop up, and should be placed alongside Vicky's deadened timelessness that destroys any possibility for this. Awareness of the distinction between these two forms of timelessness provides a clue about how to understand the meaninglessness of traumatic material. This awareness can only be developed via the therapist's willingness to open up thinking and feeling spaces both inside and outside the therapy room, and why personal psychotherapy and supervision are essential when working with those traumatized.

In work with severely disturbed patients, our task is about discovering ways of remaining musically present in the clinic room, and therefore, also open to what is not sounded. Vicky taught me more about this essential task, and I hope her story also opens up a thinking space for the reader that will lead to potential new discoveries. As we leave Vicky's story poised here, I hope that within this musical pause, the unknown future comes alive in the reader, waiting to be found in a flash of the obvious.

REFERENCES

De Backer, J. (2006). *Music and psychosis.* Unpublished doctoral dissertation, University of Aalborg.
De Backer, J., Wigram, T. (2007). Analysis of notated music examples selected from improvisations of psychotic patients (pp. 120–133). In: T. Wosch and T. Wigram (Eds), *Microanalysis in Music Therapy.* London: Jessica Kingsley Books.
De Backer, J. (2008). Music and psychosis: A research report detailing the transition from sensorial play to musical form by psychotic patients. *Nordic Journal of Music Therapy*, 17(2), 89–104.
Bion, W. R. (1984). *Attention and Interpretation.* London: Karnac Books Ltd.
Bion, W. R. (1973/1990). *Brazilian Lectures.* London: Karnac Books Ltd.
Bion, W. R. (1967). Notes on memory and desire. *Psychoanalytic Forum, 2, 271–280.*
Brendel, A. (2001) *On Music.* London: Robson Books.

Freud, S. (2003) *An Outline of Psychoanalysis.* London: Penguin Books (The New Penguin Freud Series).

Lacan, J. (1966). Le stade du miroir comme formateur de la function de Je. *Ecrits.* Paris: Seuil.

Ogden, T. (1997/ 1999). *Reverie and Interpretation: Sensing Something Human.* London: Karnac Books.

Ogden, T. (2002). *Conversations at the Frontier of Dreaming.* London: Karnac Books.

Rosenfeld, H. (1987/2005). *Impasse and Interpretation: Therapeutic and Anti-therapeutic Factors in the Psychoanalytic Treatment of Psychotic, Borderline, and Neurotic Patients.* London: Tavistock.

Sabbadini, A. (1996). On sounds, children, identity and a 'quite unmusical man'. Paper presented at a Study Day on Psychoanalysis and Music at the Centre for Psychoanalytic Studies, University of Kent, Canterbury. Retrieved April 24, 2008, from http://www.ukc.ac.uk/sdfva/sound-journal/sabbadini981.html.

Stern, D. (1977). *The First Relationship. Infant and Mother.* Cambridge Massachusetts, Harvard University Press.

Sutton, J. P. (2001). The pause that follows… Silence, improvised music and music therapy. *Nordic Journal of Music Therapy, 11*(1), 27–38.

Sutton, J. (2002). *Music, Music Therapy and Trauma: International Perspectives.* London, Jessica Kingsley.

Sutton, J. P. (2006). Hidden music: An exploration of silence in music and music therapy. In I. Deliège and G. Wiggins (Eds.), *Musical Creativity: Multidisciplinary Research in Theory and Practice* (pp. 252–271). East Sussex: Psychology Press.

Sutton, J. P. (2007). The air between two hands: Silence, music and communication. In N. Losseff and J. Doctor (Eds.), *Silence, Music, Silent Music* (pp. 169–186). Hampshire: Ashgate Publishing Ltd.

Sutton, J. & De Backer, J. (2009). Music, trauma and silence: The state of the art. *The Arts in Psychotherapy* 36 pp. 75–83.

Symington, J. & Symington, N. (1966). Without memory or desire. In J. Symington and N. Symington (Eds.), *The Clinical Thinking of Wilfred Bion.* London: Routledge.

Trevarthen, C. & Aitken K. (2001). Infant intersubjectivity: Research, theory, and clinical applications. *Journal of Child Psychology and Psychiatry, and Allied Disciplines*, 42(1), 3–48.

Williams, P. (2010). *Invasive Objects: Minds Under Siege.* London: Karnac Books.

Williams, P. (2007.) The worm that flies in the night. *British Journal of Psychotherapy, 23*(3), 343–364.

Winnicott, D. W. (1971). *Playing and Reality.* London: Routledge.

Chapter Twenty Two

FROM EGO DISINTEGRATION TO RECOVERY OF SELF: THE CONTRIBUTION OF LACAN'S THEORIES IN UNDERSTANDING THE ROLE OF MUSIC THERAPY IN THE TREATMENT OF A WOMAN WITH PSYCHOSIS

Lillian Eyre

What is the psychotic phenomenon? It is the emergence in reality of an enormous meaning that has the appearance of being nothing at all — in so far as it cannot be tied to anything, since it has never entered into the system of symbolization — but under certain conditions it can threaten the entire edifice (Lacan, 1993 p.85).

INTRODUCTION

This chapter describes the music therapy process with Julie, a 24-year-old woman who was treated for three years in the psychiatric outpatient and inpatient departments of an urban teaching hospital. When Julie was first seen as an outpatient, she had experienced three major traumas beginning at the age of 16. Consequently, Julie suffered from anxiety, reclusiveness and bizarre behaviors. Over time, Julie fell into psychosis, unable to eat, care for herself or speak. Various diagnoses were proposed, each one resulting in a trial of different medications, yet none seemed to help. Eventually, Julie's anorexia created a life-threatening electrolyte imbalance, and the last recourse was to prescribe Electroconvulsive Therapy (ECT).

I worked with Julie throughout her admissions, often seeing her individually three times a week during her deepest phase of psychosis. In a parallel process, Julie's months of internal darkness were mirrored by an intellectual darkness that I experienced when I grappled to understand how music might help Julie to engage with the world. Jacques Lacan, a French psychoanalyst who worked with psychotic patients, wrote a seminal work on psychosis (1993), and it was in this work that I began to glimpse what Julie's constellation of psychotic symptoms might mean. This, along with Lacan's semiotic theories of identity formation (Muller, 1996), provided me with a therapeutic direction. Eventually, music proved to be the means by which Julie was able to break through her isolation and begin to relate to herself and others.

FOUNDATIONAL CONCEPTS

Lacan's Three Orders

Confronted with a client who seemed to initiate and maintain a strong barrier against the world, I sought a theory that would provide me with an understanding of self and other in psychosis. Jacques Lacan's (Benvenuto & Kennedy, 1986) constructivist theory of psychoanalysis was based on Freud's (1905/1977) concept of psychosexual development. Lacan (1988) explored psychosexual developmental stages from the perspective of semiotics and the development of language. Central to Lacan's theory was the concept of the contribution of interpersonal interactions and dialogue in the construction of identity. He suggested that knowledge, self and reality were constructed by way of linguistic structures that organized not only our conscious but also our unconscious lives (Felluga, 2003, Module I). Lacan's concept of the structure of the psyche was expressed in three registers, also called orders or dimensions: the Symbolic, the Imaginary and the Real. Lacan's concepts bring insight into the communicative process and shed new light on infant-caregiver communication, particularly as it applies to music therapy.

In the Symbolic order, one acquires and uses language in a co-constructed and cultural context. This order corresponds to Freud's psychosexual developmental stage where the child passes through the Oedipal complex (Eagleton, 1983). In the Imaginary order, the self is constructed through images that are evoked in relationships, corresponding to Freud's anal stage when the infant moves from primal need to the stage of demand and mastery as s/he begins to form ego identity. Lacan's concept of the 'Gaze' is important in the achievement of a sense of mastery, which occurs when one sees the image of oneself as the ideal ego mirrored in the Gaze of the 'Other' (Muller, 1996). The Real order is linked to both unconscious and psychotic states. The Real, as experienced in early infancy, can be described as an oceanic state in which there are no boundaries and no separation between oneself and the external world. In adulthood, intrusions of the Real may be experienced as feelings of loss or failure, and are described as dumbfounding, painful, incomprehensible, confusing or horrific (Neubert, 2003). Conversely, the Real is also the feeling that leaves us speechless when we come upon ecstasy or inexpressible beauty (Muller, 1996). Real events cannot be fully expressed in the Symbolic order of language, nor do they completely fit into known or lived experience that has been assimilated into the Imaginary.

Psychosis and the Real Order

This brief introduction to Lacan's theory of the structure of the psyche provides a basis for a discussion of psychosis in Lacanian terms. In psychosis, the unconscious is brought to the surface and becomes conscious (Lacan, 1993). Thus, psychosis can be described as a falling into the Real, a phenomenon that occurs when words in the Symbolic order no longer function adequately, and "the patient is left with only the fantastic quality of images with which to grab hold of their import. These images alternately terrify or seduce, promising destruction or paradise…the isolation is extreme" (Muller, 1996). Another essential characteristic of psychosis is the non-existence of the Other: "…in psychosis, the Other, where being is realized through the avowal of speech, is excluded." Instead, the subject has a "relationship of internal echo to his own discourse" (Lacan, 1993).

The dimension of the Real is the essential element in trauma. When trauma cannot be adequately expressed in language, it is excluded from the Symbolic order and cannot be assimilated into the psyche. Thus, it must be repeated. The trauma confronts the subject with an "ever-missed encounter with this 'real' object of anxiety that cannot be named" (Lacan, cited in Patsalides & Patsalides, 2001). The traumatic residue reappears in the Real as psychotic symptoms (Benvenuto & Kennedy, 1986). Lacan (1993) stated, "it can happen that a subject refuses access to his symbolic world to something that he nevertheless experienced; …what comes under the effect of repression returns …expressed in a perfectly articulate manner in symptoms and a host of other phenomena." In the same process, the place of the Other is deleted or seriously disordered because of this gap in the Symbolic order (Benvenuto & Kennedy, 1986).

The task then, in the treatment of psychosis, is to integrate and bring into the Imaginary and Symbolic orders, that which has emerged in the Real, "for the subject represents something of himself that he has never symbolized" (Lacan, 1993). With regard to treatment of psychosis, Lacan (1993) stated that "[i]n order for the human being to establish...relations, a third party has to intervene, one that is the image of something successful, the model of some harmony." Lacan further stated, "the ambiguity and the gap in the imaginary relation requires something that maintains a relation, a function, and a distance."

Music Process in Lacan's Conceptual Frame

Lacan's conceptual framework describes how a rupture in intrapersonal communication can be seen as the fundamental problem in psychosis, while withdrawal from the world and lack of interpersonal communication can be understood as a breakdown in the psyche. This provided me with therapeutic direction in my work with Julie: music might be used to re-establish communication and integration within the Real, Imaginary and Symbolic orders. In the course of my work with Julie, there emerged eight roles that music played in the treatment of her psychosis: 1) as a mediator between the Real and the Imaginary order; 2) as a mirror to facilitate ego awareness in the Imaginary order; 3) as a mediator to symbolize the trauma of the Real in the Imaginary and Symbolic orders; 4) as a semiotic code creating awareness of the Other in the Imaginary order; 5) to elicit desire, motivation, intention and will; 6) as a transitional object leading to a relationship with the Other in the Symbolic order; 7) as a facilitator of ego reconstruction and identity formation in the Imaginary order; and 8) as a facilitator of ego integration in the Symbolic order. These functions will appear in italics as they relate to specific events in the therapeutic process.

My role throughout the therapeutic process was to: 1) maintain the necessary balance between distance and intimacy to create safety so that Julie might accept the music; 2) facilitate Julie's intrapersonal communication in the three orders by singing songs and playing instrumental selections or improvisations that matched Julie's energy, mood and vitality states; 3) establish interpersonal communication through trust established in the musical relationship; 4) help Julie gain access to calm, soothing, internal states when she was traumatized by the chaos of the Real; 5) provide Julie's mother with appropriate recorded music that she might use with Julie in my absence; 6) facilitate, through music, the integration of the three orders; 7) facilitate, through music, Julie's ability to articulate whatever she was capable of regarding her experiences in the Symbolic order; and 8) support Julie's emerging identity through music.

BACKGROUND AND ASSESSMENT PROCESS

I first met Julie in the outpatient department where her mother provided a history of the events leading to Julie's difficulties. Julie's early life was one of apparent promise; she was gifted and had tested with an I.Q. of 170. When she was 14, she experienced adjustment difficulties when she moved from a small town to a large city. A few months after her sixteenth birthday, Julie was date-raped by her older boyfriend. Confused and guilt-ridden, she did not tell anyone about it. Six months after the rape, Julie gradually began to avoid contact with most of her friends and eventually refused to go to school.

The second trauma occurred two years later when Julie's father was diagnosed with cancer and died within six months. It was likely that because of Julie's dissociated state of mind from her first trauma, she was not able to fully mourn her father's death, and this provoked a complicated grief reaction that exacerbated her trauma.

Two years after the death of her father, at the age of 20, Julie's third trauma occurred when she had a motor vehicle accident (MVA). Julie was in a coma for three days, registering 4 out of 15 on the Glasgow Coma Scale. Following the MVA, Julie remained reclusive and had minor cognitive difficulties. Two years later, alarmed by Julie's request for a gun for her birthday so that she could kill herself, Julie's mother brought her to an emergency room, where she was diagnosed with non-specified psychosis and referred to the outpatient program.

Julie isolated herself in the outpatient group program and spoke very little. After two weeks, her mother found it impossible to motivate her to come to the program, and I did not see her again until five months later when she was admitted to hospital as an inpatient. At this time, music sessions occurred most often at Julie's bedside, sometimes with the

the aid of, or in the presence of, her mother. Julie was withdrawn; she did not play an instrument or sing. I used a guitar, voice and keyboard to sing pre-composed songs with occasional lyric substitution; I improvised with gentle humming. Because Julie's verbal communication was minimal, her mother was crucial during the assessment, providing me with information regarding Julie's symptoms and her music preferences. Julie's psychotic ideation was formulated around a refusal to urinate because she believed that she would pollute the water supply; she refused to eat or drink, and she believed she could not walk. The goal of music therapy during this phase of her illness was to ease her distress and to establish contact with her through music.

Julie made some progress, and when she was able to walk again, she left the hospital without discharge. This was a pattern that occurred for the next six months. At times, her mother returned to the hospital with her; at times, she took over Julie's care at home. During these admissions, I attempted to work with Julie in the Symbolic and Imaginary orders. In individual sessions, I focused on ego structuring experiences, for example, teaching Julie how to play a song her mother said she liked. I used song choice and suggested instrumental improvisation to develop a relationship with her. She often refused to choose a song, and when she did, she became distressed and rejected the song soon after I began to sing. She became more distracted and distressed when she was out of her room, and my goal was to use recreative and receptive music experiences to keep her in the music session for up to 30 minutes.

It was clear from her numerous admissions that the course of Julie's illness was mysterious and complicated. Likely, this was a neurophysiological response to the emotional traumas she had experienced, as well as unidentified brain damage from the MVA. Over the following months, Julie regressed considerably. In addition to being almost mute, she was anorexic. After a few courses of neuroleptic medications were unsuccessful, Julie was given a series of 32 ECTs. On the basis of the trust we had established, and my knowledge of her ability to relate to music, I continued to provide music at Julie's bedside one to three times a week. The goals were to provide comfort, to maintain trust, and to encourage interaction with an external stimulus.

THERAPEUTIC PROCESS

Phase one: Terror and Soothing in the Real and Imaginary Orders

As Julie used less speech, it became evident that she was losing her ability to function in the Symbolic order. In this period, I often improvised vocally over guitar accompaniment to match her mood and to calm her, thus using *music as a mediator between the Real and Imaginary orders (1)*. When one dwells in the Real it is all-encompassing. Thus, in order to mediate between the Real and Imaginary orders, a boundary must be delineated in the Real. For Julie, this was achieved by using music to help her access and identify soothing feeling states that she might recall from her past experience in the Imaginary order. For example, after ECTs, Julie became less fearful and allowed herself to be comforted when I sang songs such as "The Rose."[1]

One evening, however, instead of being calmed, Julie began to tremble; her state of terror was induced and exacerbated by my presence. Uncertain how to proceed, and unwilling to leave her alone, I sat in silence with her. I noticed that Julie was joining her thumb and second finger of both hands to form a circle. Thinking this might be significant, I imitated Julie's sign with my left hand. She stared at my hand, began to breathe more calmly, and relaxed physically. I began to improvise vocally again, picking open strings while making this sign in my left hand for the rest of the session while Julie watched my hand. When she was able to speak in her recovery phase, I asked Julie what the sign meant; she told me that it symbolized a circle of protection. In this situation, music was not enough to create the boundary; only when a boundary in the Real order had been created through a symbolic act of interpersonal resonance, could Julie utilize the music in the Imaginary order where she had a sense of self.

Over the next month, Julie completely lost her ability to function in the Symbolic order. Falling into a deep state of psychosis in the Real order, she lay in her bed, eyes averted, speechless, showing no signs of recognition of her mother or anyone else. I continued to sing songs to her. Six weeks after the beginning of ECTs, Julie began to react to songs I

---

[1] Written by Amanda McBroom, 1977.

sang with subtle physical movements, which I interpreted as a communication of her song preferences.

Phase Two: Awareness of Self and Other in the Imaginary and Symbolic Orders

Though Julie continued to look at the wall and give no indication that she knew I was present, she began to respond to songs with particular behaviors, such as silently mouthing undecipherable words to the music I sang. As she became animated with her internal representation of the song in her Imaginary order, she expressed her feelings through gestures. For example, when I sang "What if God was one of us, just a slob like one of us,"[2] Julie at first shook her fist at the ceiling, then weeks later, she humorously stuck her tongue out in mock anger against God. In calm songs such as "Scarborough Fair"[3] and "Like a Bird on the Wire,"[4] Julie became physically quiet and listened to every word intently. If I substituted different words for a line or verse of the lyrics, her body language expressed her awareness of the change. Julie recognized the music was something outside herself that nevertheless corresponded to her experience of being "like me," or "not like me." In discovering how the musical affect matched her internal world, she became more aware of her identity. She often used nonverbal signs to communicate how she felt about the music that was chosen for her. She became, in Lacanian terms, "iconically captured by the image which lured her narcissistic investment" (Lacan, cited in Muller, 1996 p.139). In this situation, the musical affect was the "image" to which Lacan referred, and in this process, *music was used as a mirror to facilitate ego awareness in the Imaginary order (2).*

In creating silent words to the music, in her gestures, and by living through the emotions evoked by the music, Julie used the Imaginary order to create personal rituals that expressed the traumas that she was experiencing in the Real: rape, death, loss and being physically put in restraints. Muller (1996) stated that when dealing with trauma, the psychotic person's symptoms "have as their context a specific field in a rela-

---

[2] Written by Eric Bazilian, released by Joan Osborne, 1995.
[3] Anonymous. Traditional English Ballad.
[4] Written by Leonard Cohen, 1968.

tionship where the representation of an unnamed catastrophe has to be killed ... and the symbolic killing occurs through naming. This naming can be done in words or ritual, even by gesture or by the use of transitional objects." Music was the transitional object that facilitated the identification of unbearable affect, created boundaries around it, and made it bearable. Though Julie was not speaking words out loud, it was evident that she was using language internally. Thus, she confronted the traumas she experienced in the Real and used *music as a mediator to symbolize the catastrophe in the Imaginary and Symbolic orders (3).*

Gradually, Julie became less invested in avoiding contact. She was not only aware of herself, but she was also aware of the music, and by extension, aware of me as the Other who was the agent of the music. She began to develop more energy and often became so animated after ECTs that she was put into restraints for her own protection. One day after ECT, Julie was in a combative mood; she had thrown her lunch against the wall and was repeating something like *uh-uh* softly under her breath. Interpreting this as a negation reflecting her rejection of life, I used these sounds to improvise on the keyboard. At first, I imitated and supported the *uh-uh's* (No) with a diminished seventh chord resolving on C minor triad, then I challenged the *uh-uhs* with light, operatic *um-hms* (Yes) with an arpeggiated C major triad. We "conversed" for over thirty minutes; Julie seemed to derive pleasure from it, insisting playfully on the *uh-uh's* with a loud whisper when I challenged her with *um-hm's*. Twice during this session, she forgot to be mute and laughed; she said, "Oh God," then clapped her hand to her mouth to stop the sound. This was the first time she had used audible language in months. In the musical dialogue, Julie was not only asserting her identity with *uh-uh*, but she was recognizing the difference between *uh-uh* and *um-hm,* the "me" and the "not me." Caught up in the playfulness of the musical expression of sameness and difference, she entered into dyadic contact. Thus, creative musical play substituted for the speech that Julie was not capable of expressing in the Imaginary order. *Music functioned as a semiotic code creating awareness of the Other in the Imaginary order (4).*

When Julie was feeling intense energy after ECTs, I played and sang rock and roll music as vigorously as possible. On one occasion, shadowed by her mother for protection, she danced wildly and threw herself around the room with no awareness of her physical safety. When she had spent all her energy, she collapsed, and I sang "Like a Bird on the

Wire" as she fell asleep on the floor in her mother's lap. By expressing her internal states of tension and energy in physical movement through her resonance with the music, Julie expressed her needs, her desire and her will. In doing so, Julie was feeling the impact of the presence of the Other (therapist, music and mother), which also awakened her *desire for the Other (5)*.

Another way that *music elicited desire for the Other and evoked motivation, intention and will (5)*, was in the vocabulary of gestures that Julie developed to indicate her feelings about the songs I chose to sing for her. She used signs such as scratching the sheet, tapping her arm or blinking yes or no to indicate whether or not she wanted to hear a particular song. I could not always understand the personal meaning that Julie associated with a gesture. When Julie had regained speech, she explained that the gesture of tapping her arm was related to a childhood memory of a nurse who tapped her dying grandmother's arm to administer an intravenous drip to keep her alive. Julie had used this gesture to communicate to me that the song was bringing life into her veins. By expressing her desire or lack of interest for a particular song, she was engaged in co-creating her identity with music and with the Other.

Phase Three: Meeting the Other in the Imaginary and Symbolic Orders

By using gesture to communicate desire, Julie was beginning to use *music as a transitional object to relate to the Other in the Symbolic order (6)*. In her reliance on the Other to meet her desires, Julie was also creating the possibility that misattunement might occur. An example of misattunement that drew Julie more directly into relationship with the Other occurred when I put on a 20-minute tape of Bach for her to listen to while I went to a meeting. When I returned, Julie was sitting on the floor in what appeared to be urine. I immediately recognized my poor judgment; the music had brought up difficult emotions, and I had left her alone with no way of defending herself, since she couldn't manipulate the boom box. I wondered if Julie's incontinence might have been intentional, and without expecting a response, I said, "I left you all alone with the music." She nodded yes, and I added, "I'm thinking maybe that wasn't very good for you," to which she again nodded in agreement. This was the first time that Julie responded directly to a verbal communication since she had fallen into muteness eight months previously. I discovered that she had not been sitting in urine, but in apple juice, which she had purposely spilled on the floor. I interpreted this act as an attempt to communicate her anger toward me and her frustration in her situation of being unable to stop the music.

Since music was a powerful means of connecting with Julie, her mother often played music I had selected for her when they were together. One morning, she played and replayed Schubert chamber music while Julie stood and stared at the wall. After a few hours, she turned to her mother and had a conversation, asking what had happened to her. This was the first time Julie had conversed in nine months. After this event, Julie established a pattern of attempts to communicate with speech followed by regression into mutism. Two days after speaking, Julie knocked over the boom box and said that she was angry that she had been brought out of her isolation by "that music." Gradually, Julie was able to consistently give one-word answers to questions and showed other signs of being aware of being in relationship with others in the world. For example, she demonstrated empathy toward me; when I told her I was sad that I was unable to understand something she was trying to communicate, she reached out to console me. She also displayed emotions of joy and happiness in the music and when she saw her mother or myself. Thus, music served as a *transitional object in awakening relationships with the Other in the Symbolic order (6)*.

As Julie regained more speech, she was able to choose songs and express her desire to hear Heavy Metal or fast-paced rock music with lyrics that carried a tone of anger or cynicism. Julie now had no recollection of the last year she had spent in the hospital when she had lost her speech. She began to reject hearing all the songs that had sustained her this past year. Since these songs would have evoked the now unconscious and repressed chaotic feelings she had experienced in the Real order, her rejection of them suggested that Julie was establishing her own protective defenses against the Real.

Phase Four: Integration of the Orders and Identity Reconstruction

Very rapidly after regaining her ability to speak and re-establish her connection with the Symbolic order, Julie began in earnest to reconstruct her identity. She refused to be addressed by her given name, reconstructing her ego based on a fantasy that she was a male, African-American rapper. In a symbolic act, she took a musical instrument, an African shaker that consisted of two balls tied together on a string, and wore it on the belt loop of her jeans for weeks; this object transformed her into the male gender, thereby decreasing her female vulnerability, the source of much of her trauma. She also occasionally joined the music group where she interacted with others, particularly males. Her musical interest was exclusively rap music, as she used *music to facilitate her ego reconstruction and identity formation in the Imaginary order (7)*.

Julie had regained more speech, but she was still very disorganized and had difficulty functioning in the world. Her affective world was problematic, and she was sad and confused. During this time, Julie was still focused on her identity as a male rapper, but she presented another persona: the vulnerable Julie. The rapper was the vulnerable Julie's protector. We improvised on various instruments, but Julie had difficulty sustaining any interaction musically for more than a few seconds. During one session, Julie said that she had to "bring in the big boys to take over" when she was tied down in restraints in the hospital because "Julie" was too weak to tolerate being restrained. She said, "I left her [Julie] curled up there in a ball in the same position they had left her when they raped her." The vulnerable Julie was not able to take care of herself, so she split off from her and abandoned her, becoming instead, a strong rapper who was capable of defying the external world. It is significant that in addition to the two personas, the "I" also emerged at this time.

Julie was discharged and I saw her three times as an outpatient. During these sessions, Julie fluidly slipped in and out of psychosis, cried in sadness and fear, and presented dream-like material as reality. For example, she said she felt like she had been raped many times, and couldn't tell which of them was real anymore. When she talked about the rape, she also talked about the restraints that had been used in the hospital, associating them to the rape because in both situations she had been held down. She was beginning to articulate the violations against herself and describe her traumas in the Symbolic order.

It was important to work on integrating the two parts of Julie that she had identified — the protective male rapper and the vulnerable female Julie. This split, which had been initially helpful in protecting her and helping her to gain a sense of self while she was in a vulnerable state in the Imaginary order, was now inhibiting her experience of herself as an integrated person. For example, she was preoccupied with the polarities of God and the Devil, stating that the Devil was her friend. We found sounds for the Devil and God, then put the sound of them together, which she said brought her comfort. We also worked on the images of the rose (which she chose for the vulnerable Julie) and the dragon (which represented the rapper — strength). I asked Julie to consider what each image (dragon and rose) could bring to the other so that the two of them might communicate. Two weeks later, Julie spontaneously created the story of the rose and the dragon while she strummed on the guitar:

> Lillian: Can you tell me about the rose?
> Julie: The rose? ... The rapper is kind of like the dragon; it used to be that the rose was surrounded by the dragon and the dragon stomped on the rose. Now the dragon has a corona, a garland of roses around his neck — like a wish bone — a revelation; he's a pretty dragon; he and the rose are married. ...The dragon switched his colors.
> Lillian: How did it happen?
> Julie: The Queen and King of the Roses went up to the dragon and said, "Why are you stepping on our people, dragon?" But the dragon didn't have much to say because the dragon's a Taurus. ... He said that he had been stomping on roses for centuries, but now that the Queen and King had come to him and there were petals falling from the sky, he said, "I don't have to be breathing fire and stomping on these roses, they're beautiful roses, I don't want to damage them." So the dragon changed his colors. He found out he could change; he was still the same person, still had the same skin, but his color could change.

In these sessions, Julie worked on the integration of her Real order experiences of trauma and aggression, vulnerability and self-protection, in both the Imaginary and Symbolic orders. Thus, she was using *music as a facilitator of ego integration in the Symbolic order (8)*.

Phase Five: Endings

Julie's sessions occurred in the music room that was in the inpatient unit of the hospital. Because she was an outpatient, I could not see Julie privately. For Julie, coming to the hospital brought up memories of being restrained and made her very fearful that she would not be allowed to return home again. After three sessions, she refused to continue, and I supported her decision because there were signs of regression in her behavior. I visited her in her home a few weeks later for closure. At that time, she was under the care of a psychiatrist who specialized in dissociative identity disorders. She refused to continue to see him after two sessions, stating that he made her talk about things that made her feel confused. She was withdrawn and had some bizarre behaviors, but she still possessed the ability to use speech and to communicate in the Symbolic order.

SUMMARY

Emotional health requires an integration of the three orders that are based on an assimilation of psychic phenomena. This requires the ability to use defenses, such as repression, to avoid falling into the Real, while at the same time remaining sufficiently aware of one's Real events to be able to adequately symbolize them in the Imaginary and Symbolic orders. Once the Real has been inhabited, it exerts a strong magnetic pull on the individual to fall back into it. To continue on her path to integration, Julie had to be able to recognize what was healthy for her, to use whatever could bring her out of Real, and to avoid what could bring her back into it. Julie remained under her mother's care for three more years. Eventually, she had integrated her psyche well enough to be able to attend a long-term residential psychiatric rehabilitation facility from where she successfully began her university education.

Music reached Julie when she was lost in the Real order and it was essential to her return to the Imaginary and Symbolic orders. But this could not have been accomplished without the courage and will demonstrated by both Julie and her mother through a long sojourn that baffled her psychiatric practitioners. Music was able to reach inside to find Julie, and following the music, Julie found her way back out to those who loved her.

REFERENCES

Benvenuto, B. & Kennedy, R. (1986). *The Works of Jacques Lacan; An Introduction*. London: Free Association Books.

Eagleton, T. (1983). *Literary Theory: An Introduction*. Oxford, England: Basil Blackwell.

Felluga, D. (2003). *Modules on Psychoanalysis*: *Introductory Guide to Critical Theory*. November 2003. Purdue University. http://www.purdue.edu/guidetotheory/psychoanalysis/psychmodules.html. Retrieved March 13, 2005.

Freud, S. (1977). *Three Essays on the Theory of Sexuality and Other Works*. (James Strachey, Trans.) Hammondsworth: Penguin Books. (Original work published 1905).

Lacan, J. (1988). *The Seminar of Jacques Lacan: Book I. Frued's Papers on Technique* 1953–1954. (J. Forrester, Trans.). Cambridge: Cambridge University Press.

Lacan, J. (1993). *The Seminar of Jacques Lacan: Book III. The Psychoses* 1981.

Muller, J. (1996). *Beyond the Psychoanalytic Dyad: Developmental Semiotics in Freud, Peirce, and Lacan*. New York: Routledge.

Neubert, S. (2003). *Some Perspectives of Interactive Constructivism on the Theory of Education*. University of Cologne. http://www.uni-koeln.de/ew-fak/konstrukt/texte/download/introduction.pdf. Retrieved October 13, 2005.

Patsalides, B. & Patsalides, A. (2001). Butterflies caught in the network of signifiers: The goals of psychoanalysis according to Jacques Lacan. *Psychoanalytic Quarterly, 70*: 201–229.

Chapter Twenty Three

SINGING IN THE RECOVERY MODEL WITH A CHRONIC MENTALLY ILL OFFENDER

Vaughn Kaser

INTRODUCTION

The adult male forensic mental health setting is typically thought of as a challenging work environment. In addition to being diagnosed with a major mental illness, most of the residents at this large forensic state hospital have also committed some type of felony. Serious assaultive criminal behavior often occurs as a symptom of the individual's mental illness. This type of behavior is often related to the individual's Axis II diagnosis[1] (i.e., personality disorder). As in many psychiatric treatment settings, substance abuse issues are often an additional part of the problem and can also lead to serious criminal behavior problems. Some drugs can lead to violence with extended usage, whether the individual is mentally ill or not.

Many of the individuals being treated in adult forensic mental health facilities have similar diagnostic combinations and can be a significant challenge to work with therapeutically. Response to medication, intellectual functioning, family and community support systems, and acquired life skills are all important factors related to how an individual might respond to therapy. This, in turn, affects their chances for being released back into the community.

Despite the challenges many of the individuals face in this setting, the first step or steps are often the most important and difficult to make. Despite the numerous problems confronting them, some may continue to be resistive to treatment and in denial of their problems. For others, their symptoms are more severe and do not respond successfully to medica-

---

[1] DSM IV-R

tions. Individuals in this category are often assigned the label of "chronically" mentally ill and are by nature the most difficult to treat.

This chapter describes music therapy with Alex, a man suffering from a severe mental illness who was able to engage in a range of music therapy experiences to express and release feelings related to earlier life experiences and his current life circumstances. His struggles to maintain participation in groups and verbally process experiences reflected deep struggles with his mental illness and recovery.

FOUNDATIONAL CONCEPTS

A Prison Recovery Model

The forensic state hospital system discussed in this chapter has adopted the Mental Health Recovery Model as a treatment philosophy (Anthony, 1993; Deegan, 1988; Magler et al., 2001). Early components of this model began in the late 1980's and borrowed elements of the 12-step substance abuse treatment program (Alcoholics Anonymous, 1976). Recovery has been referred to as "both a conceptual framework for understanding mental illness and a system of care to provide supports and opportunities for personal development. Recovery emphasizes that while individuals may not be able to have full control over their symptoms, they can have full control of their lives. Recovery asserts that persons with psychiatric disabilities can achieve not only affective stability and social rehabilitation, but transcend limits imposed by both mental illness and social barriers to achieve their highest goals and aspirations" (Anthony, 1993; Deegan, 1988; Magler et al., 2001).

In the Recovery Model, individuals (the terms patients or residents are also acceptable in this model) are encouraged to more fully participate in their own treatment. As such, they are empowered and encouraged by the treatment team to take an active role in both determining and deciding the course of their own treatment program. In the Mentally Disordered Offender (MDO)[2] program these men are encouraged to select

---

[2] The Mentally Disordered Offender (MDO) law applies only to prisoners whose crimes were committed on or after January 1, 1986. The statutes governing the MDO program are contained in Penal Code (PC) Sections 2960-2981. The law requires that a prisoner who meets six specific MDO criteria shall be ordered by the Board of Prison Terms (BPT) to be treated by the Department of Mental

from a wide variety of treatment groups and activities. They are also given the choice to attend therapy groups without fear of some sort of disciplinary action by the treatment team. During team meetings, the individual Wellness and Recovery Treatment Plan is projected onto a wall for them to view and discuss with members of the team. Progress reports and changes in the plan are also discussed.

This Recovery Model also includes what is referred to as a Treatment Group Mall Program. In this type of program, groups are offered to individuals throughout the entire facility. Individuals are given the opportunity to choose groups they would like to be involved in. All therapy groups are based on 12-week lesson plans designed to address specific areas of treatment outlined by the Wellness and Recovery Plan. In this model an individual might select an activity group involving playing music designed to address specific therapy goals that address barriers for them to be released back to the community.

Individual Barriers to Discharge are identified within the first seven days as Recovery begins from the first day of admission. The focus of treatment and the interventions (treatment groups) are assigned to address what the individual will need to do in order to be discharged to the next least restrictive anticipated placement setting.[3]

The Role of Music Therapy

When attempting to motivate unstable problematic resistant individuals to attend a music therapy group in a long-term adult forensic mental health setting, it is recommended considering the following guidelines. Try to create and offer a group experience that is well structured and supportive as much as it is musically and socially enjoyable for the entire group. Nothing can be accomplished therapeutically if the men don't come to group! The therapist should be active in the musical improvisa-

---

Health (DMH) as a condition of parole. An MDO patient is a parolee who meets the criteria and is paroled on the condition that he or she receives DMH treatment.

[3] There are 11 separate areas of treatment, including Psychiatric Symptoms, Social Skill development, Anger Management and Impulsive Behavior, and Substance Abuse. All groups, including the music therapy treatment groups, are designed to address a specific focus of treatment. The treatment team can then select from a variety of groups provided by the various disciplines to address each focus. Groups provided for this focus are also designed to address the level of motivation or treatment readiness of the individuals and are referred to as "The Stage of Change."

tion with the rest of the group. When the music therapist engages in the group experience this way he/she becomes more like another member of the group. In this interactive role, staff may appear less authoritarian, less threatening, and this supports a therapeutic alliance in which everyone shares their personal expressions. Any discussions the therapist might facilitate after an improvisation should be designed primarily to elicit verbal comments directly related to the improvisation. Positive comments related to the focus of treatment are targeted in addition to feedback in support of how the group can achieve a healthy sounding musical creation.

This approach is primarily in support of the notion that it is the actual musical expression that provides the most therapeutic benefits to these men. Spontaneous musical group expression contributes to helping integrate the individual, both internally and externally (with the rest of the group). This integration occurs through the simultaneous use of cognitive, emotional (visceral and psychological), and kinesthetic movement experiences (Schneck & Berger, 2006). In discussing this multi-level integration, Schneck and Berger (2006) examine music from a biomedical/physiological engineering perspective and draw parallels between the complexity of the music created by patients and their multidimensional health. A music therapy improvisation group, when offered to a more challenged individual who has an emotional investment in musical expression, can begin to address multiple symptoms of their mental illness while at the same time helping to develop their ability to focus, tolerate others and interact more successfully in a group setting:

- Self integration supports grounding and reality testing problems related to symptoms of a patient's Axis I disorder
- Problems encountered with social interactions related to Axis II personality disorders are confronted directly in support of listening and responding spontaneously to others in a musical improvisation
- Agitation, stress and anxiety are often reduced through playing musical instruments by supporting the expression of feelings and the physical process of moving, playing instruments or singing

THE CLIENT

Alex was a 47-year-old single white male who had been transferred from a regional county jail pursuant to PC 2972 (MDO). His controlling offense, Assault with a Deadly Weapon (ADW), with prior incarcerations, occurred some years earlier. His County CONREP[4] caretakers readmitted Alex to the hospital. His first arrest was at age 16 for petty theft. He was placed in jail at age 18 for receiving stolen property. Adult arrests and convictions include: reckless driving, burglary, trespassing, resisting arrest, vehicle theft, exhibiting a deadly weapon, lewd and indecent exposure, disorderly conduct, loitering, defrauding an innkeeper and multiple counts of battery. Alex has had prior admissions to a state hospital in 1984, 1988, and from 1995–1998. He had also been admitted to regular psychiatric inpatient facilities for the treatment of his mental illness.

Alex was adopted at a young age and has no siblings. It was reported that Alex became depressed and started using drugs after his mother died of cancer when he was 17 years old. His father died from cancer when he was 24. Drug use has included marijuana, cocaine, methamphetamines and alcohol. He has previously been diagnosed with ADHD and was treated with Ritalin. Alex attended special education classes and dropped out of high school in the 11th grade. He has had no employment history except for working as a gardener for his father's mobile home park.

Upon evaluation at the prison, Alex was given the following diagnosis according to DSM IV-R criteria: Axis: I 295.70 Schizo-affective Disorder. Axis: I Polysubstance Dependence. Axis: II Anti-social Personality Disorder.

At the time the music therapy treatment began, Alex was struggling with various problematic interpersonal behaviors on the unit. He was often observed by staff to be making nonsensical comments, stating that he was agitated, and requesting a PRN for agitation and making bizarre hand gestures in the patient dining room serving line. He was having difficulty following the unit daily routine and was thought to a have cognitive impairment. Twice in the last few months he had been in physical altercations with peers, resulting in slight injuries. There were almost

---

[4] Conditional Release Program. A County mental health system in California where patients, who are accepted, receive follow-up care in the county where they committed their crime.

daily reports from both staff and peers that Alex initiated annoying behavior toward his peers. He was receptive to taking his psychiatric medications and was thought to be responding well to them. However, Alex was refusing all of his assigned treatment groups.[5] It was often difficult enough for Alex to tolerate a brief informal conversation with one staff person if he was not interested in the topic of the conversation. An interactive group setting was very difficult for him in terms of staying focused, listening and absorbing the material being presented, and being able to tolerate the presence of others.

Assessment

Alex had been in hospital for over one year before beginning the therapeutic work described in this chapter. He had not begun to address any of his seven barriers to discharge in the treatment groups assigned to him. Three of these barriers included: 1) maintaining a period of psychiatric and behavioral stability, 2) remaining free of physical and verbal assaults or threats, and 3) acknowledging the presence of a mental illness and the need for treatment. Alex's behavior was such that he has not been able to tolerate the treatment group setting.

During the initial Rehabilitation Therapy (which included music therapy) an assessment referred to as the *Initial Assessment of Rehabilitation Therapy* revealed that Alex had a particularly keen interest in rock music. He had been observed engaging in informal interactions with the nursing staff during which Alex would accurately imitate various guitar riffs with his voice and hands. Alex would also sing the lyrics to parts of each song. He would occasionally ask to play the unit acoustic guitar, though his "playing" ability was exclusively limited to reproducing the opening guitar lines of Deep Purple's "Smoke on the Water."

At that time, Alex was assigned to begin two music therapy groups being offered to the residents on the unit: An improvisation group called *Interacting Through Music*, and the on-unit informal music listening group *Fun With Music*. Alex would also be encouraged to attend the evening leisure karaoke singing group.

---

[5] Anger Management; Mental Illness Awareness and Wellness; Recovery Action Planning (relapse prevention and community reentry group); substance abuse treatment.

One of the main goals of the music therapy program would be to attempt to use Alex's interest in music to help reduce his resistance to attending therapy groups, develop his social interaction skills and help reduce anxiety and agitation by developing frustration tolerance for others.

THE THERAPEUTIC PROCESS

Stage 1: Inconsistence

For the first two months Alex was assigned to a small free improvisation group, with about four or five men attending fairly regularly. However, Alex was not one of them. His attendance was very sporadic, and when he did attend, he would repeatedly ask to leave soon after arriving (usually so he could go to the courtyard to smoke). The two times he stayed to play, Alex was interested in trying out most of the percussion instruments in the room including the bass and tenor xylophones, a percussion table and the drum set. His playing on all these instruments was disorganized rhythmically, with little connection to what others were playing. He played with both hands simultaneously, striking random notes softly on the xylophone. He would often stop in the middle of an improvisation and require verbal guidance before starting again.

The role of the therapist in this group was very focused and supportive. The therapist was responsible for selecting the various percussion instruments, drums and xylophones, the manner in which the instruments were set up in the room, and determining the method for how the group was going to begin each improvisation. After a moment of silence, the group was free to begin playing however they wanted. There was no set structure for how the improvisations were to end and no direction from the therapist to initiate the ending. The group members were allowed to move freely between the instruments if they wished. The therapist facilitated a brief discussion after each improvisation. The intent was to allow the group to voice how they felt about the improv-isation and to indirectly suggest ways of improving the experience by asking questions such as "Who were you listening to during the improvisation?" or "Could everyone hear all the instruments?"

After eight weeks, Alex attended his fourth improvisation group. During the third improvisation of the group, he was able to organize his rhythm on the xylophone with the rest of the group. This was the first time Alex made an attempt to engage with the group while playing any instrument. He was also becoming more familiar with the process of improvising, how to play the instruments, as well as the playing of the rest of the group. He appeared relaxed and focused enough to actually play and listen simultaneously, at least for a moment. On this particular day, Alex had been in a fairly positive mood before starting. He had sung a guitar part from a song by Dio (a heavy metal band led by Ronnie James Dio) on his way to the music area. This was the sort of thing Alex enjoyed doing on the unit when he was in a good mood.

Around this time, Alex began participating in the evening leisure karaoke group. He sang two songs, including "Don't Fear the Reaper" by Blue Oyster Cult. Alex sang in a low monotone voice, but in rhythm and on pitch with the recording well enough to tell he was familiar with the song. Singing a song he was familiar with appeared to offer Alex the additional structure he needed to stay organized in relationship to the music.

Stage 2: An Isolated Voice

It would then be three weeks before Alex was willing to attend the music improvisation group again. The week before he did attend the karaoke group on the unit and sang two songs: "Caribbean Queen" by Billy Ocean and "Thriller" by Michael Jackson. It should be noted at this point that in both the informal karaoke group and the music therapy improvisation group, Alex would rarely interact with others in the group outside of a few polite words of acknowledgement.

It was becoming apparent that Alex had a preference for attending groups only when and if he felt like it, no matter how much he might enjoy the activity when he did attend. His attendance at the improvisation group was inconsistent, and though we felt he would benefit more if he came regularly, some positive signs were beginning to appear. Among the three different groups, he was being seen almost every week in some type of music group.

During the third month, Alex attended the improvisation group for two weeks in a row. Though he had again insisted on leaving the group right after he first arrived, the staff on the unit were able to convince him to return. While playing the drum set, Alex began playing in rhythm with the rest of the group, using the mounted toms and a cymbal. While he was playing, the therapist began to imitate his rhythm on another drum. Alex responded by making eye contact. This was the first time Alex had responded to the music of someone else in the group. On the way back to the unit Alex stated: "That was fun." The following week Alex again requested to leave early. He appeared agitated and distracted, but agreed to stay and play the bass xylophone for part of the first improvisation before leaving.

At the same time, Alex was attending the karaoke group. He sang several songs including "Sexual Healing" (M. Gaye), "Yesterday" (Beatles), "The One That You Love" (Air Supply) and "Paradise City" (Guns & Roses). Alex continued to display his knowledge of a wide variety of songs, singing them all fairly accurately without assistance from the therapist or the rest of those in attendance. At this point it was felt that Alex might enjoy the structured improvisation music group where familiar songs are utilized to help structure the improvisational experience.

Alex attended his new music therapy group the first two weeks in a row and stayed the entire 50 minutes both times. At the beginning of the first group he did make a request to leave but he was able to stay without requesting again. He played the wind chimes while the group improvised to "Heaven's Door" (B. Dylan). For the next song, Alex made a request for the group to play "Drive" by the Cars. He sang and played the bass xylophone. He sang the song well, with little prompting, in his usual low, soft voice. For the third and final song, Alex was able to play an organized steady beat on the drum set to the song "Can't Help Falling in Love." The next week Alex had a similar experience when he sang two more songs, including "Hotel California" (Eagles).

It now appeared Alex was poised to become more consistently and actively involved in the music improvisation group. However, this did not eventuate. Alex's music therapist had three weeks vacation scheduled and this, combined with Alex's refusal to attend any groups, meant that he did not rejoin the music therapy group for another two months. This is a typical pattern for many chronically mentally ill patients. Just when they seem to be moving in a positive direction in a certain group, they suddenly stop attending. They are inconsistent, ambivalent and unpredictable. It certainly did not help that the therapist went on vacation and disrupted a pattern of Alex beginning to attend more consistently. However, Alex had not been forming any particular interest in playing instruments. He always seemed more interested in singing. His anxiety level, when off the unit, was always fairly high and he often had complaints concerning various individuals in the music improvisation group, whether staff or peers. Though he did not attend regularly or even stay for long when in the group, the music therapy groups were still the only groups Alex attended at all.

Stage 3: A Fuller Voice

During the next three months, Alex ended up attending the new music therapy structured improvisation group only three times out of the nine sessions held. However, he attended the karaoke group eight of the nine sessions. Alex would stay for most of each group, requested and sang several songs when he had the opportunity, and requested different songs almost every week. By now it was becoming quite clear that Alex was primarily interested in singing and more successful musically when doing so.

The music therapy improvisation group known as "interacting through music," was specifically designed to address Alex's socials skills deficits as part of his Wellness and Recovery Plan (WRP) and was considered to be a treatment group. The karaoke group, on the other hand, is held in the evening, and was not considered to be a treatment group. It was known as an "Enrichment group." It was this fun, informal singing group, that had emerged to become Alex's primary treatment.

The karaoke group experience had several specific advantages. Alex was able to sing without the rest of the group improvising on instruments, hearing himself with fewer distractions. This more informal group was held on the unit and allowed Alex the option of leaving anytime he felt uncomfortable. Alex attended regularly and enjoyed singing the various songs he chose. There were a wide variety of songs for Alex to select from that allowed him to express a range of feelings. Being able to express these feelings through the songs appeared to be a significant emotional release for him — a release we felt was probably related to the trauma of losing his parents (Kaser, 1993).

In the following months, Alex requested and sang 26 different songs in the 14 karaoke groups he attended. Of these 26 songs, 15 share some lyric content related to the expression of feelings of a lost love, experiencing the memory of a better time with a loved one, a desire to reunite or be together again, physical touching or holding a loved one and missing something that is now gone (see Appendix A).

There was no discussion or processing of Alex's thoughts or feelings related to these songs. However, during his monthly treatment team review in September, Alex described how he had been thinking a lot about his mother. It was around the time of his mother's death that Alex began using drugs and living on the street. His first criminal activities also began at that time. Perhaps Alex was now beginning to connect to and express some of these feelings. Our hope was that such expression would lead him more deeply into his emotional world, and help him build tolerance for being with others

For the next month, Alex attended the Karaoke group twice. During one of the groups he sang "Sara" (Starship) for the first time. This song contains the lyrics:

Go now, don't look back, we've drawn the line,
Move on, it's no good to go back in time.
I'll never find another girl like you,
For happy endings it takes two.

During this group it was noted that Alex made a rare direct verbal comment, using my first name and thanking me, something he rarely did. For the most part Alex avoided any type of verbal exchange with staff beyond initiating a request for something, complaining about another patient bothering him or saying hello.

During the karaoke group Alex rarely spoke to anyone beyond initiating his request for the song he wanted to sing. He would occasionally offer praise to someone after they finished singing their song. He would often come and go from the room during the group without commenting. Outside of group, Alex would almost always be the one to initiate any contact. If he was not in the mood he would usually wave staff away with a backhanded flick of his wrist and walk briskly away. His affect would often be stern and he might mutter something like "Don't talk to me."

Alex would not attend the Karaoke group for the next three months. It was also around the Christmas holiday, often a time when individuals enjoy getting together with others to sing. The time of the group was changed to 3:30 pm, and it was still up to Alex to decide if he wanted to go or not. It was not uncommon for Alex to be sleeping during the new group time, whereas he was almost always awake during 7.00 pm group time. It was at this time that Alex initiated a discussion in which he stated he would no longer be coming to the karaoke group. He added that he did not want to go because it was making him think about his mom and dad and this was bothering him. He recalled the last time he went into the room and, after he sat down and I tried to hand him one of the song lists, he waved me off and left the room. During this brief discussion Alex appeared more relaxed and he spoke directly, clearly and with good eye contact.

A few weeks after this discussion Alex attended two more karaoke groups, both of which he attended briefly. He requested the song "Sara" again but did not stay to finish singing it. He appeared to struggle to find the melody and read the lyrics in time to the music. The final week Alex requested "Paradise City" by Guns & Roses. This song contains these lyrics:

>*Take me home (oh, won't you please take me home)*
>*Just an urchin livin' under the street,*
>*I'm a hard case that's tough to beat.*
>*I'm your charity case.*
>*Strapped in the chair of the city's gas chamber,*
>*Why I'm here, I can't quite remember.*
>*He said turn me around and take me back to the start,*
>*I must be losing my mind.*
>*Are you blind?!*
>*I've seen it all a million times.*
>*I want to go, I want to know,*
>*Oh, won't you please take me home.*

A week later Alex learned that his CONREP has decided to accept him, and the process for his release and return to community care was put into place. Alex appeared both very happy and apprehensive about the news. After, I asked him if this meant that he wouldn't be coming to the Karaoke group any longer. He looked at me sternly, flicked his hand back with a "don't talk to me!" gesture, turned his back, and walked away.

SUMMARY

Given the severity of Alex's mental illness and the difficulty he had forming meaningful relationships in order to process his feelings, expressing himself musically through songs appeared to help him reduce the emotional tension and anxiety related to traumatic events of his past. The relief of tension and the possible processing of long held feelings were the beginning of Alex's journey into recovery.

Alex presented important challenges for the music therapist. He had a chronic mental illness that was not in total remission, and as a result he was not able to tolerate treatment for his Axis I Poly Substance Abuse problem. He was also resistant to getting involved in most of the therapy programs being offered that would address these barriers to discharge. However, Alex enjoyed music and had the opportunity to get involved in three separate groups, all of which had the potential to help him.

Our therapeutic focus was initially placed on the music therapy improvisation group (interacting through music) where he had both the opportunity to play instruments and to sing with a small group of his peers. However, we soon learned that he could tolerate this level of interaction and expression.

In the end, the music therapy group Alex preferred was technically not considered a treatment group in the Recovery Model. Despite this, Alex attended the karaoke group regularly and appeared to gain something very positive from this experience. As Alex had difficulty socializing with others and expressing himself verbally, the many songs he chose to sing gave him a way of expressing significant emotional events in his life.

Mentally ill individuals like Alex, with anger management issues, have difficulty expressing feelings of anger, frustration and anxiety effectively in order to prevent themselves from acting out aggressively. When given the opportunity to express feelings through the creative act of singing, Alex was able to manage his overall stress levels sufficiently to avoid being overwhelmed by anger when difficult circumstances arose on the unit.

Alex's work over the course of this 12-month time period attests to the difficulties of working with severely mentally ill persons. Alex was very resistant to change, and the instability of his mental state contributed to, or was expressed as, difficulties engaging in therapy. The karaoke group represented the first stage in this treatment process — one that would likely be very long term. While it was easy to see that Alex needed to work musically in a group in order to address his core problems, he was not ready to do so. Singing in the evenings allowed him time to build strength internally without the tension of having to work with others while doing so.

REFERENCES

Alcoholics Anonymous World Services, Inc. (1976). *Alcoholics Anonymous* (3rd ed.). New York: Alcoholics Anonymous World Services, Inc.

Anthony, W. (1993). Recovery from mental illness: The guiding vision of the mental health service system in the 1990s. *Psychological Rehabilitation Journal*, 16(4), 11–24.

Deegan, P. E. (1988). Recovery: The lived experience of rehabilitation. *Psychological Rehabilitation Journal*, 11(4), 11–19.

Kaser, V. (1993) Musical expressions of subconscious feelings: A clinical perspective. *Music Therapy Perspectives*, 11(1), 16.

Magler, D., Tavano, P., Gerard T. & Baber, D. (2001). The recovery model: A conceptual implementation plan. Contra Costa County Mental Health Recovery Task Force, October, 1–8.

Schneck, D. & Berger, D. (2006). *The Music Effect: Music Physiology and Clinical Applications*. Philadelphia, PA: Jessica Kingsley Publishers.

APPENDIX A

1. "Caribbean Queen" B. Ocean,
   > Now we're sharing the same dream,
   > and our hearts they beat as one
   > no more love on the run
2. "One That You love" Air Supply
   > Tell me we can stay
   > Hold me in your arms for just another day
3. "Yesterday" Beatles
   > Why she had to go I don't know, she wouldn't say,
   > Now I long for yesterday,
   > Now I need a place to hide away,
   > Oh, I believe in yesterday
4. "We've Only Just Begun" Carpenters
   > We start our walking,
   > Talking it over just the two of us,
   > Working together day to day,
   > Together
5. "Sweet Child O Mine" Guns N Roses
   > She's got a smile that it seems to me, Reminds me of my childhood memories, Where everything, Was as fresh as the bright blue sky,
   > Now and then when I see her face, She takes me away to that special place, And if I'd stare too long, I'd probably break down and cry
6. "Groovy Kind of Love" Phil Collins
   > When I'm feeling blue, all I have to do, Is take a look at you, Then Im not so blue, When you're close to me, I can feel your heart beat, I can hear you breathing near my ear. When I'm in your arms, nothing seems to matter, My whole world could shatter, I don't care
7. "Make it With You" Bread
   > And if I chose the one I'd like to help me through, I'd like to make it with you. I really think that we can make it girl
8. "Dust in the Wind" Kansas
   > I close my eyes, only for a moment, and the moments gone,
   > All my dreams, pass before my eyes,
   > Nothing lasts forever, It slips away
9. "Born to be My Baby" Bon Jovi

I don't need nothing when I'm by your side, We got something that'll never die, So Hold me close better hold on tight, If we stand side by side, There's a chance we'll get by, And I'll know that you'll be live, In my heart till the day that I die, My heart beat like a drum, one to one, And I'll never let go cause, There's something I know deep inside

10. "Thriller" M. Jackson

    They're out to get you, there's demons closing in on every side, Now is the time for you and I to cuddle close together, All thru the night I'll save you from the terror on the screen

11. "Yesterday Once More" Carpenters

    Lookin' back on how it was, In years gone by, And The good Times that I had, Makes today seem rather sad, So much has changed. I'd memorize each word Those old Melodies still sound good to me. All my best memories come back clearly to me

12. "Crazy for You" Madonna

    Two by Two their bodies become one. You're so close but still a world away, What I'm dying to say is that. Im crazy for you, Touch me once more, Soon we two are standing still in time

13. "I Don't Want to Live Without You" Foreigner

    I want you now and forever, close to me, I'm longing for the day, hoping that you will promise to be mine and never go away, I don't want to live without you, I could never live without you, You see I'm lost without your love

14. "Don't Fear the Reaper" BOC

    Love of two is one, Here but now they're gone, Came the last night of sadness and it was clear she couldn't go on, And she ran to him, They looked backward and said goodbye, She had taken his hand, Come on Baby

15. "All Out of Love" Air Supply

    I want you to come back and carry me home, Away from this long lonely night, I'm reaching for you, There's no easy way, it gets harder each day. Please love me or I'll be gone

Chapter Twenty Four

THE DOORS AND WINDOWS OF THE DRESSING ROOM: CULTURE-CENTERED MUSIC THERAPY IN A MENTAL HEALTH SETTING

Brynjulf Stige

INTRODUCTION

Living a troubled life in a rural area of Norway, Ramona encountered the possibilities of music therapy when she was hospitalized due to deep depression and suicidal tendencies. When she first came to the mental health center, she wanted to leave this world and she wanted to live. Vacillating between these inclinations, she one day heard sounds from the music therapy room and asked one of the other inpatients about this. She was informed that there is something called music therapy, which — the other client suggested — could be good. Later Ramona told me how she immediately had a strong feeling that she needed to find out if this could be something helpful for her.

Ramona referred herself to music therapy and was invited to an initial mutual assessment period of four sessions. After this we decided to work together and we collaborated for another 62 sessions over a period of two and a half years. She then decided to leave music therapy because she felt that the worst crisis was over and that she was ready for "going back to the world," as she would put it.

The music therapy room became a space where Ramona could sing and play, listen and be listened to, move and be moved, act and reflect. Her journey from depression and suppression to vitality and healthier interdependence was long and windy. Music therapy was not her only support, but an essential one with a unique contribution. The story that I will present in this chapter is based upon my own field notes from the therapy process and interviews with Ramona where she talked about her experience of music therapy.

FOUNDATIONAL CONCEPTS

I have written about parts of Ramona's story previously.[1] When I now approach her story again, it is with a different purpose and mode of presentation, with less orientation toward the theoretical ideas of the author and more focus upon the process and what the client tells about her experiences of music therapy. By taking one step back in order to let the client step up, I hope to be able to illuminate how culture-centered perspectives imply an integration of client-centered and contextual practice.

In my previous presentations of Ramona's story, I described how my work was informed by narrative therapy (White & Epston, 1990; McLeod, 1997), Nordoff and Robbins's (1977) approach to clinical improvisation, Mary Priestley's (1994) combination of free improvisation and verbal processing, Diane Austin's (1999) approach to vocal improvisation and modified versions of Helen Bonny's method of Guided Imagery and Music (Summer, 1988; Moe, 1998). This is a broad range of influences indeed, and in some ways many of them are incompatible, given the fact that they are informed by very different assumptions about the nature of music, humans, health and therapy. Reviewing my previous attempts of communicating the therapy approach taken, I think that the following sentence may be one of the more important: "These techniques were integrated in an approach designed to suit Ramona's needs and resources and my strengths and weaknesses as a therapist" (Stige, 2003 p. 288). This simple statement — which suggests that the approach was to not have a predefined approach — requires some elaboration.

The idea that therapy is recreated in each new encounter is not new. It could, to a large degree, be contained in the humanistic tradition of psychotherapy, as developed by Carl Rogers (1951/1999) and Rollo May (1969/1977) and extended by many music therapists. Anderson and Goolishian's (1992) ideas on the client as expert and the therapist as "not-knowing" is another source of inspiration. These terms make sense if you focus upon humans as meaning-generating beings. As "not-knowing therapist," you enter the therapy dialogue with a focus upon the client's

---

[1] I have discussed aspects of Ramona's story in order to illuminate the relevance of culture-centered perspectives for music psychotherapy (Stige, 2002 pp. 155–177). I have also discussed her story in a chapter of my dissertation on community music therapy (Stige, 2003 pp. 285–343.)

client's narrative truth rather than your own pre-defined knowledge. This questions the traditional idea that the professional is the one who knows (Ulvestad et al., 2007), but as I have suggested previously, it takes a lot of knowledge to take a not-knowing position, since it requires that you flexibly adjust to the client's theory of change without losing hold of your own judgment and experience (Stige, 2001).

In relation to therapy practice, two ideas that seem to be based upon incompatible premises have been much debated lately, namely the idea of evidence-based practice and the idea of empowerment and user-involvement. The first is based upon a deductive premise; pre-existing knowledge on what (usually) works should inform your practice decisions. The second is based upon an inductive premise; the work should evolve from the goals and values of the participants of each context (Stige, 2008). It is beyond the scope of this chapter to discuss this schism, but the attempt of Duncan, Miller and Sparks (2004) to suggest a new path should be mentioned, since it reflects the above-mentioned focus upon the client as expert, adding a concern for what works. These authors suggest that the effectiveness of therapy could be improved through client-directed, outcome-informed therapy. This implies a focus upon *practice-based evidence* and a radical breach from the medical thinking that informs the evidence-based practice movement. The logic of the medical model has influenced most models of psychotherapy, these authors suggest, so that therapists tend to focus upon the effect of specific interventions based upon a diagnosis of the client. The alternative they offer is to focus upon client resources and resilience, client theories of change and client feedback about the fit and benefit of service. In her elaboration of resource-oriented music therapy, Randi Rolvsjord (2007; 2010) has explored similar perspectives for music therapy in mental health care.

To link client-centered and contextual perspectives requires a rethinking of conventional therapeutic practice. To take interest in everyday life experiences, and to reflect upon them during the therapy process, is standard procedure in most models of psychotherapy, but to think of the client's use of everyday activities as an integrated and essential part of the therapy process is not. These contemporary debates contextualize some of the ideas that I tried to develop in *Culture-Centered Music Therapy* (Stige, 2002). I did not attempt to develop another model of music therapy but a meta-perspective that implies a reorientation of music therapy practice in relational and contextual directions. I therefore defined music therapy practice not as an intervention but as a process of collaboration. In discussing therapy processes I suggested that we should take interest in the availability of a range of resources, such as the *arena* and *agenda* and the involved *agents, activities* and *artifacts* (see also Stige, in press).

When we take interest in the possibilities of resources such as these, the client is often the one who is competent to take the lead. Therapists could not rely on a predefined model and might need tools to redefine their roles and navigate within the clients' view and world. In an attempt to illuminate such a relational and contextual perspective, I developed a figure that I here will present in a slightly modified version:

Figure 1. Illustration of the Music Therapy Process in a relational and Contextual Perspective (after Stige, 2002 p. 209).

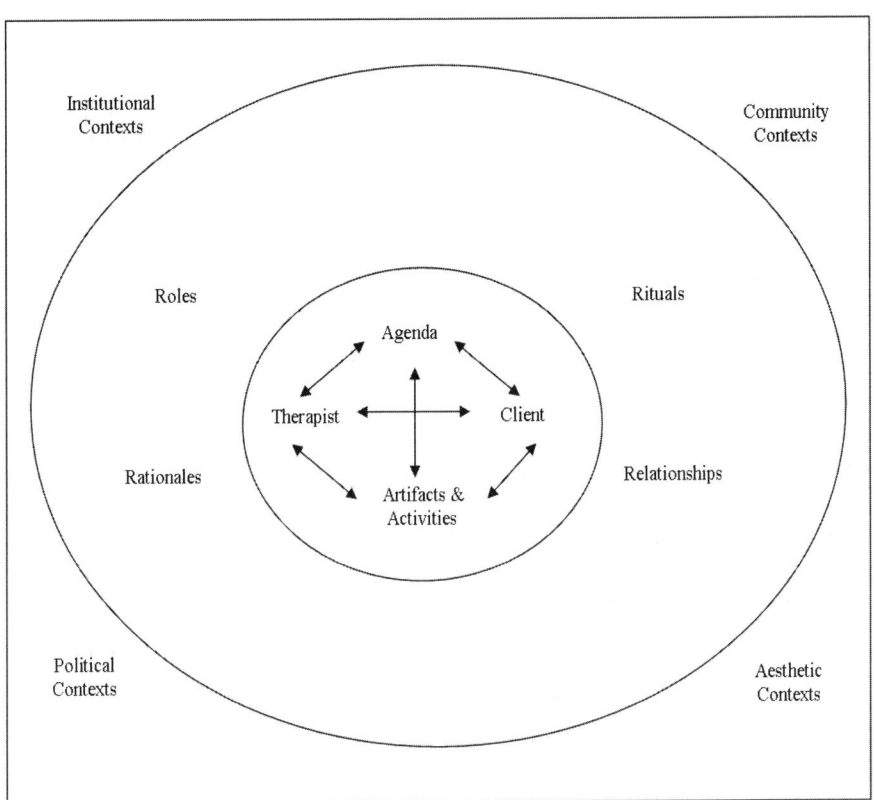

In the figure, music is included in the modes of artifact and activity, as these are two of the central ways in which we encounter music: we search or stumble upon songs and instruments and other artifacts that enable us to take part in various activities, such as singing, playing, listening, dancing and reflecting. How we use the artifacts and take part in the activities is embedded in interpersonal relationships and the agenda of the collaboration. These microsystem processes may involve appropriation of mesosystem resources such as roles, rituals, rationales and relationships from other contexts (often in the local community). It is also colored by various macrosystem influences, such as institutional, aesthetic and political contexts.

This description of music therapy processes is abstract, and intentionally so. Concrete models would more easily be interpreted as prescriptive or regulatory at the level of technique, while what is proposed here is not technique but a radical willingness to listen to the clients in the context of the lives they live. The rationale for this is grounded in a relational conception of health:

> Health is a quality of mutual care in human co-existence and a set of developing personal qualifications for participation. As such, health is the process of building resources for the individual, the community, and the relationship between individual and community (Stige, 2003 p. 207).

A relational conception of health exemplifies a relational understanding of human life, where freedom is understood not just as self-realization but also as self-care and care for others (Vetlesen, 2004).

THE CLIENT

Ramona was a married woman in her late forties and a mother of three children. Due to her family and life situation, she had limited experience with paid work. In the mental health center, she was diagnosed according to the conventions of the medical model. For an understanding of Ramona's music therapy process, this is of less relevance than how she presented herself and perceived herself in the therapy process.

When Ramona first came to music therapy, she spoke with a shy and low voice. I was struck by the emotional suffering that I could feel and the restless energy that still seemed to be there. Some of the apparent contradictions in how she presented herself were demonstrated in the second session by the way she approached a djembe that she spotted among the other music instruments. In the middle of a conversation where she shared aspects of her traumatic personal history, she discovered the djembe. With some curiosity, she asked what kind of an instrument that would be. I explained briefly and asked if she wanted to try to play it. She said she was not sure, but there was something in her posture that I interpreted as an eagerness to try. Just a few seconds later, she was playing quite loudly on the djembe and I was improvising on the piano. I was surprised by this quick start, but the improvisation ended as abruptly as it had started. After less than 30 seconds of music, she stopped and asked, with a voice I could barely hear, if her playing was OK and if she was doing the right thing.

This question seemed to relate to the story she had been telling, about a childhood of sexual abuse and an adult life with a relationship in which she was also abused and suppressed in various ways. Maybe it was not so surprising that she would almost automatically take a subordinate position in relation to me and ask if she was doing the right thing. There was one important discrepancy involved, however, and that was the way she played the djembe. Her playing was lively, with strong and vigorous movements, a stunning contrast to how she presented herself verbally.

Throughout the therapy process I gradually became more informed about Ramona's story, suffering, and resilience. Together we explored how the music activities would relate to her verbal narratives, sometimes in analogy, other times in thought-provoking contrast.

ASSESSMENT AND EVALUATION

Some authors promoting client-directed therapy have developed rating scales that can be used to monitor client change (Duncan et al., 2004). I did not use such scales with Ramona, one obvious reason being that I was not aware of these authors' work at that time. The approach to assessment and evaluation that I used was careful attention to client statements in sessions, combined with qualitative interviews for meta-reflection. I consider this to be a relevant alternative or supplement to the use of rating scales. It is a more time consuming approach and it may also be less helpful if the therapeutic relationship does not work too well. But it is an approach with many advantages, the main one probably being that it is congruent with the therapeutic process; it is dialogic and gives space for unexpected comments and directions.

One of the things Ramona told me in the first session was that she had "lost her music." She used to sing, but now she could not. The only songs she knew were hymns and other religious songs, and she explained to me that she did not feel that these songs were true anymore. Some years earlier she almost lost one of her children, due to an acute illness. The child survived, but was seriously handicapped. After this, Ramona's struggle to endure emotionally had become even tougher. She told me how she first approached the situation with all the fighting spirit she could muster. Then she collapsed and became confused and depressed, suicidal at times, and no longer able to function in the everyday roles that she was expected to fulfill. She had then been offered anti-psychotic medication and individual verbal psychotherapy. She told me that she felt she needed this but that something was missing. These services could not address the fact that she was not able to sing anymore, and that was one of the reasons why she came to music therapy. She wanted to learn new songs: "Ordinary songs, songs that ordinary people sing." This was seemingly a trivial request, but in the light of her story I believed it was an important one. I heard it as an expression of a will to redefine her life

I informed Ramona that to learn new songs certainly would be a possibility in music therapy and that there were also many other ways of using music that she could try if she wanted to. We could improvise instrumentally and vocally, we could listen to music, and we could move, write or draw to music. I suggested that we could arrange a sequence of four assessment sessions and then evaluate whether we thought it would be worthwhile to continue working together. She accepted this idea, and in the next few sessions we tried out a range of activities. She told me she was interested in trying these things, as long as I could promise not to force her to sing when she did not want to. She also stressed that any movement to music was absolutely out of the question.

Ramona found some pleasure in all the musical activities that we tried out, but things also developed in ways she had not expected. In response to her wish to learn new songs, we had taken a traditional song book from the shelf and started to practice a well-known song called *Lykkeliten*. Many people think of this as a rather sweet little song, but the lyrics about a little child in a tough world drew Ramona in other directions. All of a sudden, she was filled with strong feelings of grief for her handicapped daughter. Ramona told me that previously she had not allowed herself to be in contact with the grief, not even in verbal therapy. As she shed tears, she expressed that it surprised her that music could create such strong feelings.

When we evaluated the four assessment sessions together, this was one of the episodes Ramona talked about. She felt that, until this moment, she had repressed her grief and — since she had experienced how emotional the experience of music could be — she now speculated about the lack of contact with her emotions as one reason why she had lost her music in everyday life. She therefore expressed that she wanted to continue in music therapy and to expand her ideas about activities, to include improvisation and music listening. She was still interested in learning songs, but added that she now knew that there could be a range of emotional experiences linked to that activity and that we therefore would need to relate to her life situation and story. This resonated with my experience of the four assessment sessions, and we agreed to continue to work together.

We decided to have weekly sessions of one hour and to supplement the sessions with interviews where she could reflect upon her experiences of the process. These interviews were originally conceived as research interviews, but they turned out to be an important part of the therapy process also.[2] Ramona's voice, as documented in the interviews, will therefore be part of the presentation of the process.

THE THERAPEUTIC PROCESS

When describing therapy processes, there are many possible trajectories to explore, including changes in the activities, in the relationships and in the client's experience and participation, both in the therapy sessions and in everyday contexts. One pertinent place to start in relation to Ramona's

---

[2] For discussion of relationships between qualitative research and therapy process, see Stige (1998). For explication of the specific research methods used in this case, see Stige (2003 pp. 289–306).

process is to describe the negotiations around agenda. They reveal changes along several dimensions and were central to her process and to my understanding of how she was using music therapy. As described above, negotiations about agenda started already in the initial assessment sessions. She came to music therapy with a concrete plan; she wanted to learn some new songs. The experience of the first few sessions made her realize that this plan implied some other things that she had not considered consciously, such as relationships to her emotions, to me, and to her life story.

From the beginning, we established a simple ritual; every session would start with a conversation about how she would like to use this music therapy session. The ritual was open; she could choose whether she wanted to go directly to a music activity or whether it was helpful for her to share verbally some of her personal history, either from the last week or from earlier periods of her life. This ritual also served to clarify that alteration between action and reflection was a possibility that she could choose to use at any point in any session. Given the fact that Ramona had some experience with verbal psychotherapy, the idea of verbal reflection was not alien to her. What was new was the possibility of combining this with musical activity.

After just a few sessions, she would share that the ritual stressed her. Several days before each session she would start worrying about which song to sing and what else to do the next time she met me. She wondered whether I could help her and suggest things to do. I responded that to think about the sessions during the week could be a good thing, because that would help her discover relationships between music therapy and her everyday life. I also suggested that to come to a session without knowing what to do would be completely legitimate. We could always come up with something together and maybe in a session she would discover wishes that were not so clear the day before. These types of negotiations continued in session after session, and they opened up reflections about many themes, including the roles, rituals, rationales and relationships that characterized her everyday life.

She discovered that the role she would take in our negotiations was not so different from some other everyday rituals of her life, where she tended to take on a subordinate role and want the other to decide. One of the processes that seemed to challenge this in music therapy was a negotiation about rationale. She came to music therapy because she wanted to learn some music, but what exactly do the words "learning" and "music" mean? This became much more than abstract questions for Ramona. In the first few sessions, she often played percussion instruments while I played the piano. She would then be surprised when I used the term "music" about what we had done. "To me it's only noise," she would say, and then add that she was talking about her own contribution. The "name of the game" was something we talked about over a long period of time. To open up the possibility that what she did could be accepted as music was a slow process, even though she had some breakthroughs quite early on, such as in session seven when we agreed to try to free ourselves from the "tyranny of pretty chords" by playing together on the piano, as "ugly" as possible. We both enjoyed the experience, and it was one of the steps she would take in order to open up her conception of what music could be. This seemed to open up other things too. After a year in music therapy, she looked back at the process in an interview, and this was one of the things she commented upon:

> When I asked to start in music therapy I thought: "Now I will at any rate have a chance to *learn some music*." But I have discovered that the main thing would not be to *learn* music, but to have the possibility to be *in charge* of the sounds myself. How should I explain? The alphabet has letters that can be made into words. It is me who decides *what* words. I had a picture of music as being a ready-made world, something I had to learn and memorize; to learn chords, to learn where I could find the different sounds. But you have contributed to making it into *another world* than what I had thought of. The sounds have become mine, I can put together the sounds I want, I can say that this is to "play music," even though it's nothing that I've been taught. It's impulsive, it's the *use of sounds*.

This statement clearly reveals that to work with her conception of music was a relational experience for Ramona. Gradually, during this first year in music therapy, our relationship had become part of the agenda, together with the relationships of her everyday life. This happened in conjunction with an increased interest in metaphorical use of music, especially linked to the activities of listening and improvisation. Music as an analogy and a contrast to her everyday life would increasingly become a topic of conversation.

My field notes from session 28 illuminate this: The session started with dialogue on the dilemma she experienced concerning balancing care for others and care for herself. She then said that she was afraid that I would throw her out of music therapy and close the door. As in many sessions previously, the theme of not trusting that she deserved what was good for her was prominent. After a while, she wanted to play, and she picked out some new instruments in the music therapy room. First, she played softly on pipe chimes and then she wanted to try the ocean drum. She had never played that instrument before, and it fascinated her. I improvised on the piano and the music lasted almost 30 minutes. While playing I was enthralled by the musical interaction, which was sensitive, creative and collaborative. The contrast to how she communicated musically earlier in the therapy process was striking. There was much more mutual trust now. After the improvisation she did not comment upon this, however, but shared a metaphoric experience she had had while playing: "I'm just like one of those small hailstones in the ocean drum, I move automatically." The paradox of this statement, expressed after an improvisation where she had taken considerable responsibility and many initiatives, did not escape her.

The theme of being in charge was existentially significant for Ramona, given the history she had of being abused and suppressed by men. Gradually, she started to trust that she could share that she was terrified by the idea of relating to me emotionally, since she was then afraid that I would exploit her, as men usually did. She added that maybe I was different, but she was not sure. The way she worked with this theme reveals how she gradually took responsibility in using the possibilities that being in charge of the music therapy agenda offered her. She started to use music therapy in tandem with the support that she increasingly was able to muster in other contexts. For instance, after two years of music therapy, she decided to join a summer camp arranged by an indemnity group by and for abused women. When she came back, something had changed. She told me that she felt empowered by the sisterhood and that the courage of the other women who insisted upon the right to "take their bodies back" had really been important for her. She declared that she now wanted to use music therapy in a new way. "I almost want to dance a waltz with you. Well, that would be too much, but I'd like to move to music." We agreed about various ways of doing this, starting with me improvising on the piano with my eyes closed, so that she did not need to worry about being watched. Gradually she trusted me to open my eyes, and after a few weeks, we ended up doing movement improvisation together, mirroring, leading and following each other. I was moved and astonished. The memory of how misplaced the idea of movement had been two years ago was still vivid.

This would not be the only thing that surprised me this autumn. Ramona was now able to make many changes in her life, and she was both determined and energetic. Some months previously she had divorced her husband. Now she had met a man who she felt was good for her. And this was not the only change. She started to sing in a choir in the community, which is something the feeling of "not being worthy" had stopped her from doing previously. Also, and this was especially important, she started to attend high school classes. As a young woman, she had been forced to drop out of high school when she had her first child. Now, as a middle-aged woman, she felt that she had a new beginning. This was also the beginning of the end of her music therapy process.

Ramona started to air that she was now so occupied with school, the choir and her new personal relationship that maybe she would soon be ready to conclude our music therapy collaboration. We agreed upon a period of closure, where we looked back at what she had achieved and worked through many of the activities that she had enjoyed. In one of the last sessions, we did a long piano improvisation together. Before we started playing I asked if she wanted any givens or rules for the improvisation. She said "No, I can play here or I can play there. I can play in my own space or move toward your space, and you can do the same. That's fine." We started to improvise, first in a sequence with no established tonality. Then we moved into a succession of fifths and ended up in the B flat Dorian mode. After a transition in C minor, we moved to C major and the rhythm of the music gradually changed. After a while Ramona stopped playing, smiled, and asked: "That was triple time, wasn't it?" I responded positively, and she said: "Hmm, so finally there was a waltz for me in music therapy… That was a good rhythm for me; it gave me this feeling of space."

It was time for closure. Ramona summed up her experience of music therapy and shared that she had been thinking about her depression lately. Some doctors would call it a disease, but she felt it was a struggle, a struggle for survival. If she only could manage to maintain the space she had created for herself, in her inner dialogues as well as in her everyday life, then she felt she could have a chance in this struggle. Music was a part of this now, she said. She had started to enjoy daring combinations in music and she related this to her life situation, which she described as a struggle requiring courage. "Music therapy has been a workshop for me..., no, more than that, it has been a holy space where I could do things I never thought I would be able to do."

When ending the therapeutic relationship we agreed upon meeting a few more times, for interviews where she could look back at the therapy process. I met her some months later, and we talked for an hour, but not in the format of a research interview. At this point, she was so overwhelmed by the complexity of her life situation that I suggested that we just talked about whatever was important for her to talk about. She told me that one of her kids was in serious trouble with the law and that this was very upsetting for her. Also, going to school was stimulating but also quite stressful. She had top grades in mathematics and history, but was toiling with the Norwegian literature. Previously she had not felt that she had the permission to read novels, so this was new territory again. The total life situation was quite overwhelming, she told me. As an addition to and possibly also a symptom of all this she had just crashed her car in an accident that could have been very dangerous. "And now I'm going to marry again in a few months," she then added, in a tone that reflected both despair and hope.

I interviewed her again 17 months later, almost two years after the closure of the therapy process. Things were now much calmer in her life. She had moved to a different part of the country and felt that her new environment was much better for her. She enjoyed being married to a more respectful man, her children were doing reasonably well, and she herself was doing fine in high school and was even considering going to college. Within this context, she felt she was ready to look back and think about how she had experienced and used music therapy.

> I think I can say that I experienced the music-therapy-corner that we had together as kind of the "interspace" that I needed in order to find courage to open up, from the heart of my inner life.[3] The expressions, the moods...to create a space for myself, to hear my voice, to hear all the sounds whether from the instruments or from my voice, or...to feel the movements of my body, and then — to find the courage to join a choir...and to hear my own voice together with the others. To have that experience; "This is fun." So that was *something*; from just being afraid and wanting to hide [and then] to be able to experience that there are good things with being with others. And to sing — to *express* myself in the presence of others.

She continued by talking about how she gradually had understood that she had the freedom to participate in various public situations: "...today my platform is much more solid. That is, I have a much better understanding of my rights," she said and continued by elaborating some of the metaphors she had used in describing music therapy.

> Do you know where I would have placed music therapy today?...Eh, you know...that place where the women put on their make-up, a place of preparation before one goes out. Or to be with the hairdresser. That is; it's like a private corner where you...make yourself ready and aware of who you are...and that you shall express yourself in a way or another.

We elaborated upon this image of music therapy as a dressing room, which she explained as a place in between a private and public space:

> Not the therapy process in itself...but the *products* become public. It's a place where things are created, and what comes out of it is yourself as a new product, and this becomes public...But my music therapy in itself was to meet you as a

---

[3] In translating her statement I use the neologism "interspace" even though Ramona used an established Norwegian compound. The word she uses – "mellomrom" – literally means "interspace" but usually refers to a crevice or interval and not to a "space in between" which could be used, but this seems to be how Ramona uses the word here.

therapist...and I think that you affected my music therapy...Well, maybe I should not say that you have been dominating in my inner world, but I think you have been an invisible factor there. I don't think that my music therapy would have been the same irrespective of what person was there...For me you represented safety, which helped me to cross my borders...I could come to the music therapy room with anxiety and fear, but – I could tell it to you, I could be open...

In real life I have in fact no experience with using make-up, so it's kind of funny that this is...what I find it natural to compare music therapy with, but, you know...maybe that's the next step, that I start to use make-up? [chuckles] I can see myself in front of the mirror becoming conscious about *who* I am, and that I have several alternatives to choose among. And I can try them out. I guess that's what I feel...And, there is another human being there, who helps me try things out...That's why I also came up with the image of a hairdresser...There is another person there, with me, and I can say: "I'd like to try it a little bit shorter today." "Should we put some color in it today?" You see? We are two persons in front of the mirror all the time...That mirror is important.

I thanked her for the collaboration and expressed that I did appreciate that she could use music therapy and the relationship to me in this way.

SUMMARY

Ramona experienced music therapy as an "interspace," allowing for movements inward (contact with her emotions and her body) and outwards (participation in activities and relationships). The metaphor of music therapy as a "dressing room" captured much of this. The subsequent elaboration of the metaphor highlighted the interplay between private, interpersonal, and public aspects of the music therapy process. In spite of the conventional format of individual music therapy, Ramona strongly focused upon public aspects of the music therapy process. This did not make her downplay the private and interpersonal aspects. She worked with her own capacities for *emotion* and *expression* and at the same time she was concerned about how she *presented herself* to others. She did this not only through use of the activities and relationships offered in the music therapy sessions but through creative use of the possibilities and challenges of her everyday life. The dressing room that she was using had mirrors but also doors and windows. This relates to the idea of health as participation and mutual care, described in the beginning of the chapter.

The connotations that the phrase dressing room may give to the backstage of a theatre were not commented upon by Ramona but are of relevance for our understanding of the metaphor, if we take Goffman's (1959/1990) dramaturgical approach to the understanding of everyday life into consideration. Music therapy sessions seem to have the potential of representing an intermediary arena, bridging private explorations of self ("backstage performances") with more public presentations of self ("front stage performances"). In music-making, we may integrate the biologically given capacity for non-verbal communication that we all share with our own personal narratives as well as the available sociocultural resources for participation in a given context (Stige, 2002). Music, therefore, is a powerful medium for a client-directed yet relational and contextual approach to therapy. Music therapy, according to this way of thinking, is a collaborative and interactive search for health-promoting *connections*.

REFERENCES

Anderson, H. & Goolishian, H. (1992). The client is the expert: A not-knowing approach to therapy. In S. McNamee and K. Gergen (Eds.), *Therapy as Social Construction.* London, United Kingdom: Sage Publications.

Austin, D. (1999). Vocal improvisation in analytically oriented music therapy with adults. In T. Wigram & J. De Backer (Eds.), *Clinical Applications of Music Therapy in Psychiatry.* London: Jessica Kingsley Publishers.

Duncan, B. L., Miller, S. D. & Sparks, J. A. (2004). *The Heroic Client. A Revolutionary Way to Improve Effectiveness through Client-Directed Outcome-Informed Therapy.* San Francisco, CA: Jossey-Bass.

Goffman, E. (1959/1990). *The Presentation of Self in Everyday Life.* London: Penguin Books Ltd.
May, R. (1969/1977). *Kjærlighet og vilje* [Original title: Love and Will (Translated to Norwegian by Daisy Schjelderup and Hilde Andresen)]. Oslo: Dreyers Forlag.
McLeod, J. (1997). *Narrative and Psychotherapy.* London: Sage Publications.
Moe, T. (1998). Musikterapiforløb med en skizotypisk patient udfra en modifikation af metoden [A Schizotypical patient's music therapy process through use of a modified version of Guided Imagery and Music]. *Nordic Journal of Music Therapy,* 7(1), 14–23.
Nordoff, P. & Robbins, C. (1977). *Creative Music Therapy.* New York: John Day.
Priestley, M. (1994). *Essays on Analytical Music Therapy.* Phoenixville, PA: Barcelona Publishers.
Rogers, C. (1951/1999). *Client-Centered Therapy.* London: Constable.
Rolvsjord, R. (2007). "Blackbirds Singing": Explorations of Resource-Oriented Music Therapy in Mental Health Care. Unpublished doctoral thesis, Aalborg Universitet.
Rolvsjord, R. (2010). *Resource-Oriented Music Therapy in Mental Health Care.* Gilsum, NH: Barcelona Publishers.
Stige, B. (1998). Qualitative research interviews as a part of the music therapy process. *Musiikkiterapia* (Finnish Journal of Music Therapy), 2.
Stige, B. (2001). The fostering of not-knowing barefoot supervisors. In M. Forinash (Ed.), *Music Therapy Supervision.* Gilsum, NH: Barcelona Publishers.
Stige, B. (2002). *Culture-Centered Music Therapy.* Gilsum, NH: Barcelona Publishers.
Stige, B. (2003). Elaborations toward a notion of Community Music Therapy. Doctoral thesis, University of Oslo. Published by Unipub.
Stige, B. (2008). Implications of various perspectives on evidence for music therapy assessment, treatment, and outcomes. Invited paper for the Mid-Atlantic Region Chapter of the American Music Therapy Association, Cherry Hills, New Jersey, March.

Stige, B. (in press). Health musicing – A perspective on music and health as action and performance. In R. MacDonald, G. Kreutz and L. Mitchell (Eds.), *Music, Health and Wellbeing.* New York: Oxford University Press.
Summer, L. (1988). *Guided Imagery and Music in the Institutional Setting.* St. Louis, MO: Magna-Music Baton.
Ulvestad, A. K., Henriksen, A. K., Tuseth, A.-G. & Fjeldstad, T. (2007). *Klienten – den glemte terapeut. Brukerstyring i psykisk helsearbeid* [The Client – The Forgotten Therapist. User-directed Mental Health Work]. Oslo, Norway: Gyldendal akademisk.
Vetlesen, A. J. (2004). Det frie mennesket? Et sosialfilosofisk blikk på patologiene i opsjonssamfunnet. [Are humans free? A view from social philosophy on the pathologies of the option society]. In H. Nafstad (Ed.), Det omsorgsfulle mennesket. *Et psykologisk alternativ [The Caring Human. A Psychological Alternative].* Oslo, Norway: Gyldendal Akademisk.
White, M. & Epston, E. (1990). *Narrative Means to Therapeutic Ends.* New York: W.W. Norton.

Chapter Twenty Five

MUSIC IS ABOUT FEELINGS: MUSIC THERAPY WITH A YOUNG MAN SUFFERING FROM ANOREXIA NERVOSA

Gro Trondalen

I did never believe I would dare to try the piano ... but I did ... Music describes feelings. At least it does to me ... Music is about movement, rhythm, strength and intensity.

(Simon, 19)

INTRODUCTION

This chapter addresses expressive individual music therapy in an outpatient setting with a young man suffering from Anorexia Nervosa (AN/B). The therapeutic approach includes musical improvisations and verbal exchange. A central focus was to empower the client by fostering his creative health resources through musical improvisations, verbal communication and the use of instruments.

The theoretical framework is rooted in humanistic ideas (Ruud, 2010), while the clinical theory is informed by developments in relational psychology, highlighting an intersubjective perspective (Benjamin, 1990, 2004; Stern, 2000).

In this chapter, health is understood as a positive relationship between the dimensions of physical/mental health and existential wellbeing, which may be understood as a way of finding meaning and fulfilment by "being-in-the-world" (Sigurdson, 2008). The relationship between the client and the therapist is of vital importance, and may be termed "Fellow Travelers" (Yalom, 2002).

THEORETICAL FOUNDATIONS

A Talking Body

Traditionally, anorexia has been reported with reference to women in the Western world, understood as an internal and external expectation to fulfil images exposed in the media (e.g., Nasser & Di Nicola, 2001). However, men also suffer from eating disorders (Andersen, 2002; Kjelsås & Augestad, 2004). Hsu (1996) suggests a prevalence of 0.5 percent for anorexia in the general population. Similar figures have been described by Fairburn and Harrison (2003), who suggest an incidence of 19 females and two males per 100,000 people.

From a psychological point of view, suffering from an eating disorder generally reflects insufficiently reliable self-soothing, tension and mood regulation (Garner & Garfield, 1997; Lask & Bryant-Waugh, 1999). The body is used as an external, concrete tool for promoting internal life ("embodiment") (Duesund & Skårderud, 2003). Literature on eating disorders also draws attention to difficulties in connecting body and mind; that is, relating inner feelings to words (alexithymia) (Cochrane et al., 1993).

Literature on individual music therapy with people suffering from anorexia suggests that musical improvisation provides a basis for connecting non-verbal senses of self and allows for a recreation of self through active music making (Robarts, 2000; Smeijsters, 1996; Trondalen, 2003). Free movement and improvisation may support creative processes, which in turn challenges rigid patterns of behavior (Trondalen, 2005) and allows for confused and aggressive feelings to be expressed (Eckhoff, 1997; Frederiksen, 1999; Loos, 1994; Parente, 1989). Improvisational experiences may also be processed verbally and subsequently support connectedness between body and mind, which is an important objective for people suffering from anorexia (Lejonclou & Trondalen, 2009; Robarts & Sloboda, 1994).

Sounding Relationships: A Music Therapeutic Soundboard

The music therapy approach undertaken by the author included free improvisations and verbal exchange. The improvisations and handling of instruments did not require musical skills and were not evaluated according to performance criteria (Alvin, 1966; Bruscia, 1987). Improvisations were usually programmatic and referential in nature. On occasion, the client also listened to recordings of his improvisations after playing, a form of "self-listening" (Bruscia, 1998 p. 125).

This music therapy approach was inspired by Alvin's Free Improvisation model focusing on the use of instruments (Alvin, 1966) and Nordoff and Robbins' client-centered model concentrating on the development of a musical/therapeutic relationship (Nordoff & Robbins, 1977). The creation of themes followed by a verbal reworking after the improvisation was informed by Priestley's Analytical Music Therapy (Priestley, 1994). The theme for an improvisation always emerged from whatever the client brought to therapy. The client chose instruments for himself, and then the music therapist made her choice(s). From this sounding relationship emerged a playful exchange of musical ideas and themes.

To conclude sessions, the client was often asked to write (i.e., a word, phrase or sentence) or draw to "sum up" the session. This served several different purposes. It allowed for closure, created a concrete image of client's inner experiences, created a symbol or metaphor for the session and gave coherence and continuity to the music therapy process as a whole (Trondalen, 2006). Examples of such intuitive phrases include "a possibility of peace in mind" and "I am happy – but I hope I am not going to jump that much up and down from joy that I lose even more weight."

A Theoretical Stratum

The theoretical framework of this approach is rooted in humanistic ideas (Ruud, 2010) and is inspired by developments in relational psychology (Benjamin, 1990; 2004), while focusing on an intersubjective perspective (Stern, 2000; Bråten 1998; Trevarthen, 1999; Trevarthen & Mallock, 2000).

The basic assumption is that the relating experience itself is the driving force of human development and growth (Stern, 2000). Using music as a relating experience (to oneself and another) is understood as a way of "being-in-the-world" (Trondalen, 2008). Stated in another way, music serves as an expression of performing personal identity (Ruud, 1997). Such a humanistic-existential perspective may be interpreted as self-caring (self-actualization) (Ruud, 2010). From a philosophical point of view, the human being is understood as *homo communicans*, with an inherent humanity able to share experiences and actions. Such exchange allows for recognition and partaking in one another's life at an existential level (Trondalen, 2004).

In western society today, health is more often linked with quality of life connected to individual, collective and social ways of living, rather than focusing on sanitary conditions and the fight against contagious diseases carried out through history (Sigurdson, 2008). The theologian Sigurdson suggests that health is a relationship; a positive relationship between the dimensions of physical/mental health and existential wellbeing. Physical and mental health are not to be understood in a categorical way, but seen as a continuum wherein bodily functions influence our mental state of being — and vice versa. Together they form a unit. The existential aspect of health is connected to human existence in a broad sense, including cultural, political, reflective, religious and social dimensions. Approaching health in such a broad way provides a context in which our cultures are conditioned by history and given meaning through discourse (Ibid.). Health, a positive relation between the dimensions of physical/mental and existential wellbeing, may be understood as a way of finding meaning and fulfilment by "being-in-the-world."

A central emphasis in this approach to music therapy is to empower the client by fostering his/her creative health resources through musical and verbal dialogue (Trondalen, 2008). Empowering[1] is always linked to context. In this music therapy setting, it is connected to psychological empowerment at an individual level (Zimmermann, 2000), which includes changes in behavior, cognition and emotions. Focusing em-

---

[1] Empowerment may also be understood as a consequence (i.e., intrinsic) of music therapy in general (Daveson, 2001) or as a philosophy guiding the music therapy practice, inherent in both political and relational aspects (Proctor, 2002). For an introduction to and discussion of perspectives from empowerment philosophy related to music therapy, see Rolvsjord, 2004 (pp. 99–111) and 2007 (pp. 77–90).

powerment by supporting creative health resources in such an aesthetic practice in modern society seems to be linked to "an assemblage of activities designed to promote health and prevent sickness" (Aldridge, 2004 p. 37), rather than a focus on personal health management in response to sickness. Health becomes a creative performance linked to personal values and cultural norms. Accordingly, health is understood through experience rather than the objective measurement of bodily functions. This implies that the music therapist downplays pathological aspects of a person's life in favor of healthy dimensions, in order to allow for self-actualization and the search for meaning within a relational context. Such a humanistic and resource-oriented perspective[2] still takes the person's illness (bio-medical perspective) into consideration, however in a *dialogical* way by focusing positive creative resources to cope with a variety of constraints.

The relationship between the client and the therapist is of vital importance and may be termed "Fellow Travelers" (Yalom, 2002 p. 8). From a philosophical point of view, this indicates a subject-subject position, as opposed to the client being an "object" that is treated in therapy. Being a fellow traveler does not allow the therapist to disclaim responsibility for understanding and monitoring the therapeutic process (at a practical and theoretical level). It does, however, abolish the "distinctions between "them" (the afflicted) and "us" (the healers): "we are all in this together" (loc.cit.). From this follows an attention toward what emerges *between* equal human beings, as this relationship is seen as the basis of development and growth.

This clinical theory is drawn from developmental psychology, oriented toward clinical research on infants, highlighting an intersubjective perspective (Benjamin, 1990, 2004; Bråten, 1998; Stern, 2000; Trevarthen, 1999). Such theoretical thinking is fundamentally dyadic and understands communication as a *process*, making a shift from a stage-like to a layered model of development. Core elements are the child's experience of "senses of self" in relation to oneself and others. These inner experiences of "senses of self" organize the child's development (Stern, 2000, p. xxv). Being together with another person is seen as a process of "moving along," which implies implicit knowledge of "how to

---

[2] For an elaboration of Rolvsjord's concept *Resource-oriented music therapy in mental health care* see Rolvsjord, 2010.

be intimate with others" at a non-verbal level (Stern, 1998, Lyons-Ruth, 1998). The process of "moving along" includes two consecutive goals. One goal is to explore the theme of the communication; for example, talking about the family situation. The other goal is to participate in the moving along process itself. What is at stake is *how* the interaction moves along, rather than merely the themes or the concrete actions per se.

Transferred to music therapy, such a process of "moving along" simultaneously includes an exchange of musical ideas and gestures (e.g., beat, key and dynamic expression), and an awareness of how it *feels* to be with the other person at an existential level. Further, it is most important to recognize *how* the musical interaction moves along, rather than only the themes/phrases in the music or the musical actions as such. From a therapeutic point of view, this allows the client to feel recognized within the musical relationship at an existential level, even if the client does not have any musical skills.

From a therapeutic point of view, there may be a need for verbal processing to contextualize, develop, and interpret the musical interaction, not least in the client's case because he found it hard to connect inner feelings to words (cf. alexithymia). However, such a reworking is not necessary when it comes to the origin of the interaction's immediate power. The music in these relating experiences was both an agent (non-referral) and a tool for dialoguing (frame and medium). The aim in music therapy was to maintain immediate mutuality, since sharing musical experiences (intersubjective behavior) was seen as the basis for the development and continuity of the musical relationship.

THE CLIENT

A Traveler

Simon, a young man of 19, came to music therapy while attending college. During a stay abroad, it became obvious he was suffering from an eating disorder, namely Anorexia Nervosa, bulimic type (AN/B, American Psychiatric Association, 1994). Simon struggled with concentration, was hardly eating anything and used to vomit after meals. Suffering from anorexia limited his personal development and reduced his quality of life during the previous one and a half years.

Simon's daily activities used to be winter sports, reading and listening to music, but it was difficult for him to keep up with these interests due to his physical condition. He had a warm sense of humor and wonderful sense of irony. Simon was the youngest of two, with an older sister. He grew up in a small town, belonged to a supportive and well-resourced family and had friends he spoke of highly. Simon had always been connected to music, even though he had never played any instrument before. He loved to listen to music through headphones: "funky music with real lyrics," he would say.

Simon alternated biweekly between music therapy and verbal psychotherapy. The psychiatrist and music therapist talked frequently about their work with Simon, and he was happy with this collaboration. There was also one joint family meeting, in the initial phase of therapy.

Simon came to music therapy because he was curious. During the process, he often expressed great pleasure in participating. "After I've been to music therapy I don't have to throw up the half slice of bread I've had today," he said at one occasion.

His music therapy lasted for one year and included 19 sessions. Sessions usually lasted for one hour, but the duration had to be adjusted in accordance with Simon's physical and mental condition. The heating in the room also had to be high, otherwise Simon would start freezing, which reduced his concentration and capacity to engage.

THERAPEUTIC PROCESS[3]

Moving Along

Simon had never learned to play any instruments or improvised music before. He often seemed restless, and his arms and legs appeared to be "spread everywhere." It seemed as if he struggled to connect to himself and others. "I do not know — I do not know anything," he often said.

---

[3] The music therapy process was documented by audiotape of the sessions, which were transcribed. In addition, there was a semi-structured interview with Simon, which took place two months after the completion of music therapy.

Throughout the music therapy process, he explored a variety of instruments, from xylophones and maracas to piano and percussion. The music therapist played different instruments and sang, which Simon never did, except for some spontaneous humming. Musically, the improvisations covered pentatonic modes, blues, a Spanish mode, standard scales and atonal expression.

When examined as a whole, the music therapy process can be divided into three phases: 1) sessions 1–10, 2) sessions 11–17 and 3) sessions 18–19.

The First Phase: Sessions 1–10

In the first phase of therapy, Simon chose the xylophone as his favorite instrument. He said he had a "passion for knocking on objects." The therapist would sometimes play another xylophone together with Simon, while at other times, piano or djembe. Simon often said he was exhausted after playing, but "enjoyed being tired." It allowed him "to be absorbed in the music." In summing up session one, Simon said "improvisation gives energy." I found this encouraging, since Simon talked a lot about being "limp and tired."

This first long phase of therapy was characterized by a search for security in the relationship ("I am afraid of trying all these new things"), a period of trying out the instruments ("important to try all these things") and of "having fun." He was very fond of "the strange" pentatonic scale.

Musically, Simon explored the instruments predominantly through single tones and rhythmic patterns. In the tenth session, he discovered the big tubular bells, which were hung in a frame. From this point on, it seemed as if Simon explored *emotional* expressions in the music in a broader way than earlier, very different from his first rhythmic expressions.

The Second Phase: Sessions 11–17

In the second phase, Simon took a greater interest in bigger instruments like the piano, djembe and drum kit. He seemed to move from small instruments to bigger, while exploring rhythmic and melodic patterns musically. "Playing on a set of drums demands concentration and my concentration is getting better," he wrote after the eleventh session.

In session twelve, Simon told me *he* had realized his vomiting was related to times when he felt "angry, lost sight and felt overwhelmed." In the same session, he also recognized his musical progression by saying "I do manage the rhythm better than before."

In the fifteenth session, *regulation* was a term that emerged after the improvisation. We explored the notion together, relating both to the musical improvisation and how he regulated himself (e.g., in a party, in daily life). Simon said he knew he was going to reflect on "regulation" on his way home. In summing up, he wrote the word "regulation" within a rectangle.

Within this phase, the music became more accentuated and 'groovy,' and there was a new awareness between Simon and myself in the music. Simon commented on this development in the sessions: "We are adjusting to each other — I do regulate too" and "it does not necessarily *sound* better, but it *feels* better ... I am fully in the music ... I hear you are playing the same tone as I do. Are you teasing me?" (session sixteen). He also related feelings to playing on instruments in a referential way saying "I do not want to play a set of drums because I am not so angry today."

The seventeenth session included an improvisation that Simon said was important. This was due to 1) him daring to play the piano, and 2) what emerged in the music while playing. Before beginning this improvisation, Simon told me he was afraid of improvising on the piano. Nevertheless, he did choose the piano, and the music therapist played a drum kit. The improvisation lasted for nearly fourteen minutes. After this shared improvisation, there were some seconds of condensed awareness. It was as if "*I* know that *you* know that *I* know we've been very close to each other" (intersubjectivity). This was observable immediately after the improvisation through a momentary glance at each other, a microsecond of a pause, bursting into a smile, and a deep relaxed breath before a vocalization (i.e., "mmm" with a smile).[4] Afterwards, Simon said that "music is about movement and feelings."[5]

The Third Phase: Sessions 18–19

The third phase represented the termination of expressive music therapy and consisted of only two sessions. In this closing phase, Simon improvised more freely than earlier. He talked a lot between the improvisations in sessions eighteen and nineteen and expressed a new belief that he could actually manage to learn to play an instrument, if he really wanted to (session eighteen). He also came to understand that "music and feelings are connected ... It is something to relate to when I am alone. Music and feeling — the music reflects my feelings." On his frequent choice of xylophones, Simon said "it is not a *nice* instrument, but gives me a lot of fun." The last improvisation was performed on two equally large African drums, one for each of us.

DISCUSSION

The discussion of Simon's music therapy has three main foci: 1) a healthy body, 2) the ambiguity of instruments, and 3) musical relating experiences as potential for change.

A Healthy Body

Simon was very constrained by his anorexia. He struggled with concentration and his arms and legs often seemed to be "spread everywhere." However, it was obvious he leaned *intentionally* toward the instruments to perform music. Such a bodily directedness (intentionality) is a functional action in the situation and related to the subjective body. With reference to the French philosopher Merleau-Ponty (1945/1994 p.35ff.), "the living body" is able to grasp (physically) and perceive (mentally) at the same time from an inside perspective ("double-sensing"). In music

---

[4] This chain of events is audible on the minidisk recording and is commented in the music therapist's reflective notes from the session.
[5] For an elaboration on *"Significant moments"* in this improvisation, see the analyses of the improvisation inspired by a phenomenological procedure (Trondalen, 2004, 2005, 2007).

therapy, Simon used his living (subjective) body to direct awareness and express inner feelings through music. Such a beneficial body focus and mood regulation are the opposite of a rigid and stiffened (inner and outer) body (anorectic), which does not allow for personal feelings (objective body) ("embodiment"; Duesund & Skårderud, 2003). Connecting music to feelings in such a way promoted inner healing resources and contributed to a living bridge between inner and outer reality (Lejonclou & Trondalen, 2009), as Simon started to verbalize how his inner feelings and visible behavior were connected.

In music therapy, Simon moved rhythmically to the music. The performance of his subjective body seemed to promote vitality, create energy and the feeling of being alive. He said that "improvisation gives energy … it does not necessarily *sound* better but it *feels* better … I am fully in the music … music and feelings are connected." Such comments imply that Simon was able to *recognize* his own musical initiative and appreciate the interplay with the therapist (Trondalen & Skårderud, 2007). From a clinical point of view, this is a positive development, as letting go of control and allowing himself to be influenced by another was a constant challenge for Simon.

Simon's musical expression was a way of "being-in-the-world." Mutual appreciative recognition through musical and verbal dialogue seemed to support Simon's sense of belonging to time and space. An example is Simon's comment: "I know I can become well with a little help from you and the psychiatrist. I know. Music therapy is good for me." Such a statement can be interpreted as psychological empowerment at an individual level (Zimmermann, 2000), where Simon experienced control and understood the music therapy setting in his personal context, building on his own competencies. Such a psychologically sufficient self-soothing (Garner & Garfield, 1997; Lask & Bryant-Waugh, 1999) and appreciative "self-actualisation" (Ruud, 2010) support a positive self-image. Self-actualization and the ability to take care of oneself is of vital importance to people suffering from an eating disorder, where performing life in a negative way often is the case (Claude-Pierre, 1999). Hence, the music therapy process supported Simon's positive bonding between the dimensions of physical/mental and existential well-being (Sigurdson, 2008).

The Ambiguity of Instruments

Playing instruments had different functions for Simon. They were a concrete means of expression, a referent of an affect, an extension of his body and a symbol (Trondalen, 2006). Other elements influencing Simon's experience of music-making on instruments seemed to be the instrument's material, size, visual appearance, texture and sound. He favored the xylophones, but throughout the therapy process, he selected a variety of instruments, which he connected to his own feelings and bodily affects. An example was when he firmly decided *not* to play the drum kit because he was "not so angry today." Instead, he chose the big tubular bells to express softer emotions.

Simon seemed to be empowered through his personal choices to speak, remain silent, play/not play music, choose an instrument, along with the personal meta-reflection he developed within the context of music therapy. This was observable in his own deliberate awareness of changes in his emotions, which followed his actions. It was obvious he felt he had the right to personal choices, a position connected to individual empowerment (Zimmermann, 2000; Rolvsjord, 2004).

Simon also used instruments as a way of "projecting" physical, mental and existential dimensions of himself into the instruments in the musical relationship (Alvin, 1966), while experiencing neither loss of control nor destruction of the relationship. This was evident in the last improvisation performed on two equally large African drums, an improvisation that Simon enjoyed very much. The musical relationship seemed to function as a relating space, allowing for regulation of inner tension and social interaction (Frederiksen, 1999; Robarts, 2000; Stern, 1985/2000). Simon explored dynamic and rhythmic patterns, which created an illusion of moving toward controlled "spreading out" and controlled "holding back," from a psychological point of view. "I am not so afraid any more," he said in session ten. This statement was observable in his life outside therapy as well: little by little he returned to college, found a girlfriend and slowly decreased his sessions in psychotherapy and music therapy. He seemed to acquire renewed self-esteem, believing he could manage his life in a normal way again.

One important experience for Simon was connected to performing on the piano (session seventeen), an instrument that may be interpreted as a transformative social symbol. On the one hand, the piano is a powerful solo instrument. On the other hand, it belongs to a group of instruments (e.g., an orchestra). Perhaps unconsciously, Simon wanted to try out a social practice; an experience of participating in a socially normal relationship both at a personal and relational level. A sense of belonging, in addition to a personal pleasure of music making, are important elements for developing musical identity (Ruud, 1997).

Musical Relating Experiences as Potentials for Change

In his daily life, Simon struggled to connect to himself and others. "I do not know — I do not know anything," he often said. Nevertheless, in music therapy Simon *decided* to make personal choices of action by selecting instruments and participating in the musical improvisation. From a theoretical point of view, such an experience of being able to influence at a concrete and interpersonal level supports the development of a "core self" (Stern, 2000 p. 69ff.). At a practical level, Simon was empowered through personal choices, observable through a change in behavior and a new awareness of his personal emotions.

Playing music together allowed for joint experiences of processes of "moving along." Sometimes the musical actions were in the foreground, at other times the most important thing was how it felt to be together in the music (implicit knowledge) (Lyons-Ruth, 1998; Stern, 1998). "It does not necessarily *sound* better, but it *feels* better," Simon said after one improvisation. Another example of shared experience (i.e., intersubjectivity) is the event including the condensed awareness and a smile after the long improvisation in session seventeen. Such joint experiences, although not identical, seemed to support appreciative recognition at an existential level, and supported Simon's ability to share inner feeling states. Accordingly, he seemed to benefit from such an interpersonal tension and mood exploration in the musical relationship (Lask & Bryant-Waugh, 1999; Robarts & Sloboda, 1994).

In the therapy process, Simon and the therapist also explored these musical experiences through verbal exchange. Such dialogues, where both have been actively involved in the music, allowed for a verbal exchange rooted in a shared — but individually informed — form of vitality. Such a sharing of non-verbal experiences, of "dynamic forms of vitality"[6] at a non-verbal level, is connected to any temporally based human activity that evokes a felt experience of another. Following, dynamic forms of vitality concern "how" something is done and not the "what" or "why" (Stern, 2009). To Simon, the musical sharing really seemed to support dynamic forms of vitality from an 'inside perspective' and was related to his feeling of being alive: "Improvisation gives energy" and "the music reflects my feelings."

The verbal dialogues where lived experiences were explored in a relating context seemed to support Simon's connection between inner and outer life. From a therapeutic point of view, this may mean a closer connection between *lived* experiences and experiences that are verbally *narrated*. Such a combination of the client's personal inner and outer stories may challenge and change the client's perception of him/herself (Stern, 2000, Trondalen & Skårderud, 2007). When lived experiences and the narrative based on real experiences are connected in real life, as in Simon's case, a fusion of the two stories support meaning and symbolic emergence. This is particularly relevant in anorexia nervosa, where alexithymia, an inability to connect words and feelings, is often a central characteristic (Cochrane et al., 1993; Trondalen & Skårderud, 2007).

SUMMARY

This chapter addresses expressive individual music therapy in an outpatient setting with a young man suffering from anorexia (AN/B). The theoretical framework is rooted in humanistic ideas and the relational turn in psychology, highlighting an intersubjective perspective. Accordingly, the relating experience itself is seen as the driving force of human growth. A central focus in this music therapy process was to empower the client by fostering his creative health resources through musical improvisations, verbal communication and the use of instruments.

---

[6] Previously named "vitality affects" by Stern (2000).

REFERENCES

Aldridge, D. (2004). *Health, the Individual and Integrated Medicine: Revising an Aesthetic of Health Care*. London: Jessica Kingsley Publishers.

Alvin, J. (1966). *Music Therapy*. London: John Baker.

American Psychiatric Association. (1994). *Diagnostic and Statistical Manual of Mental Disorders* (4th ed.). Washington D.C.

Andersen, A. E. (2002). Eating disorders in males. In C. G. Fairburn and K. D. Brownell (Eds.), *Eating Disorders and Obesity — A Comprehensive Handbook* (2nd ed., pp. 188–193). New York: The Guilford Press.

Benjamin, J. (1990). An outline of intersubjectivity: The development of recognition. *Psychoanalytic Psychology, 7(suppl.)*, 33–43.

Benjamin, J. (2004). Beyond doer and done to: An intersubjective view of thirdness. *Psychoanalytic Quarterly, New York, LXXIII*, 5–46.

Bråten, S. (1998). *Intersubjective Communication and Emotion in Early Ontogeny*. Cambridge University Press.

Bruscia, K. E. (1987). *Improvisational Models of Music Therapy*. Springfield, Illinois: Charles C. Thomas publishers.

Bruscia, K. E. (1998). *Defining Music Therapy* (Second Edition.). Gilsum, NH: Barcelona Publishers.

Claude-Pierre, P. (1999). *The Secret Language of Eating Disorders* (2nd ed.). New York: Random House, Inc.

Cochrane, C. E., Brewerton, T. D., Wilson, D. B. & Hodges, E. L. (1993). Alexithymia in eating disorders. *International Journal of Eating Disorders, 14*, 219–222.

Daveson, B. (2001). Empowerment: An intrinsic process and consequence of music therapy practice. *The Australian Journal of Music Therapy, 12*, 29–37.

Duesund, L. & Skårderud, F. (2003). Use the body, and forget the body: Treating anorexia nervosa with adapted physical activity. *Clinical Child Psychology and Psychiatry, 8*(1), 53–72.

Eckhoff, R. (1997). Musikk og kropp. Filosofisk grunnlag og metodisk anvendelse i musikkterapi med psykiatriske pasienter. [Music and body: Philosophical basis and methodological application in

music therapy with psychiatric patients]. *Musikkterapi, 22*(4), 17–39.
Fairburn, C. & Harrison, P. J. (2003). Eating disorders. *The Lancet, 361*, 407–416.
Frederiksen, B. V. (1999). Analysis of musical improvisations to understand and work with elements of resistance in a client with anorexia nervosa. In T. Wigram & J. de Backer (Eds.), *Clinical Applications of Music Therapy in Psychiatry* (pp. 211–231). London, Philadelphia: Jessica Kingsley Publishers.
Garner, D. M. & Garfield, P. E. (1997). *Handbook of Treatment for Eating Disorders*. New York, London: The Guildford Press.
Hsu, L. K. G. (1996). Epidemiology of the eating disorders. *The Psychiatric Clinics of North America, 19*, 681–700.
Kjelsås, E. & Augestad, L. B. (2004). Gender, eating behavior, and personality characteristics in physically active students. *Scandinavian journal of medicine & science in sports, 14*(4), 258–268.
Lask, B. & Bryant-Waugh, R. (Eds.) (1999). *Anorexia Nervosa and Related Eating Disorders in Childhood and Adolescence* (2nd ed.). London: Psychology Press.
Lejonclou, A. & Trondalen, G. (2009). "I've started to move into my own body": Music therapy with women suffering from eating disorders. *Nordic Journal of Music Therapy, 18*(1), 79–92.
Loos, G. K. (1994). *Spiel-Raüme der Magersucht. Musiktherapie und Körperwahrnehmung mit frühgestörten Pasienten* (Vol. Band 7). Stuttgard, Jena, New York, Barenreiter Verlag, Kassel, Basel, London, Prag: Gustav Fischer Verlag.
Lyons-Ruth, K. (1998). Implicit relational knowing: Its role in development and psychoanalytic treatment. *Infant Mental Health Journal, 19*(3), 282–289.
Merleau-Ponty, M. (1945/1994). *Kroppens Fenomenologi [Phenomenology of Perceptions]*. (B. Nake, Trans.). Oslo: Pax Forlag A/S.
Nasser, M. & Di Nicola, V. (2001). Changing bodies, changing cultures: An intercultural dialogue on the body as the final frontier. In M. Nasser, M. A. Katzman and R. A. Gordon (Eds.), *Eating Disorders and Cultural Transitions*. New York: Brunner-Routledge.
Nordoff, P. & Robbins, C. (1977). *Creative Music Therapy: Individual Treatment for the Handicapped Child*. New York: John Day.

Parente, A. B. (1989). Music as a therapeutic tool in treating anorexia nervosa. In L. M. Hornyak and E. K. Baker (Eds.), *Experimental Therapies for Eating Disorders* (pp. 305–328). New York, London: The Guildford Press.

Procter, S. (2002). Empowering and enabling: Music therapy in non-medical mental health provision. In C. Kenny and B. Stige (Eds.), *Contemporary Voices in Music Therapy* (pp. 95–108). Oslo: UniPub Forlag.

Priestley, M. (1994). *Essays on Analytical Music Therapy*. Phoenixville, PA: Barcelona Publishers.

Robarts, J. (2000). Music therapy and adolescents with anorexia nervosa. *Nordic Journal of Music Therapy, 9*(1), 3–12.

Robarts, J. & Sloboda, A. (1994). Perspectives on music therapy with people suffering from anorexia nervosa. *British Journal of Music Therapy, 8*(1), 7–14.

Rolvsjord, R. (2004). Therapy as empowerment: Clinical and political implications of empowerment philosophy in mental health practices of music therapy. *Nordic Journal of Music Therapy, 13*(2), 99–111.

Rolvsjord, R. (2007). "Blackbird Singing": Explorations of Resource-Oriented Music Therapy in Mental Health Care. Unpublished Ph.D., Aalborg University, Aalborg.

Rolvsjord, R. (2010). *Resource Oriented Music Therapy in Mental Health Care*. Gilsum, NH: Barcelona publishers.

Ruud, E. (1997). Music and identity. *Nordic Journal of Music Therapy, 6*(1), 3–13.

Ruud, E. (2010). *Music Therapy: A Perspective from the Humanities*. Gilsum, NH: Barcelona Publishers.

Sigurdson, O. (2008). Vil du bli frisk? [Do you want to become well?]. In G. Bjursell and L. V. Westerhäll (Eds.), *Kulturen och Hälsen: Essäer om Sambandet Mellan Kulturens Yttringar och Hälsans Tilstånd [Essays on Culture and Health]* (pp. 189–218). Stockholm: Santérus Förlag.

Smeijsters, H. (1996). Music therapy with anorexia nervosa: An integrative theoretical and methodological perspective. *British Journal of Music Therapy, 10*(2), 3–13.

Stern, D. N. (2009). The issue of vitality. Keynote at the Sounding Relationships. 6th Nordic Music Therapy Conference. Aalborg University. May 2nd.

Stern, D. N. (2000). *The Interpersonal World of the Infant: A View from Psychoanalysis & Developmental Psychology*. New York: Basic Books.

Stern, D. N. (1998). The process of therapeutic change involving implicit knowledge: Some implications of developmental observations for adult psychotherapy. *Infant Mental Health Journal, 19*(3), 300–308.

Trevarthen, C. (1999). Musicality and the intrinsic motive pulse: Evidence from human psychobiology and infant communication. *Musicæ Scientiæ. Escom European Society for the Cognitive Sciences of Music* (Special issue 1999-2000), 155–215.

Trevarthen, C. & Mallock, S. (2000). The dance of well-being: Defining the musical therapeutic effect. *Nordic Journal of Music Therapy, 9*(2), 3–17.

Trondalen, G. (2003). "Self-listening" in music therapy with a young woman suffering from anorexia nervosa. *Nordic Journal of Music Therapy, 12*(1), 3–17.

Trondalen, G. (2004). Klingende Relasjoner: En Musikkterapistudie av "Signifikante øyeblikk" i Musikalsk Samspill med Unge Mennesker med Anoreksi. ['Sounding Relationships': A Music Therapy Study of 'Significant Moments' in Musical Interplay with Young People Suffering from Anorexia Nervosa]. Ph.D. NMH-Publications. Oslo: Norges Musikkhøgskole.

Trondalen, G. (2005). 'Significant moments' in music therapy with young persons suffering from anorexia nervosa. *Music Therapy Today (online), VI*(3), 396-429. Available online at http://www.MusicTherapyWorld.net.

Trondalen, G. (2006). "Musikk er sjela mi" — musikkterapi med unge mennesker med anoreksi. ["Music is my inner being" — music therapy with young people suffering from anorexia]. In T. Aasgaard (Ed.), *Musikk og Helse [Music and Health]* (pp. 122–138). Oslo: Cappelen.

Trondalen, G. (2007). A phenomenologically oriented approach to microanalyses in music therapy. In T. Wosch and T. Wigram (Eds.), *Microanalysis in Music Therapy: Methods, Techniques* and *Applications for Clinicians, Researchers, Educators and Students* (pp. 198–210). London: Jessica Kingsley Publishers.

Trondalen, G. (2008). Musikkterapi - et relasjonelt perspektiv [Music therapy — a relational perspective]. In G. Trondalen and E. Ruud (Eds.), *Perspek-tiver på Musikk og Helse. 30 år med norsk musikkterapi [Perspectives on Music and Health. 30 years of music therapy in Norway]*. Oslo: Cappelen.

Trondalen, G. & Skårderud, F. (2007). Playing with affects: And the importance of "affect attunement". *Nordic Journal of Music Therapy, 16*(2), 100-111.

Yalom, I. D. (2002). *The Gift of Therapy: Reflections on Being a Therapist*. London: Judy Piatkus Ltd.

Zimmermann, M. (2000). Empowerment theory: Psychological, organizational and community levels of analyses. In J. Rappaport and E. Seidman (Eds.), *Handbook of Community Psychology* (pp. 43–63). New York: Academic/Plenum Publishers.

Chapter Twenty Six

"TAKING A CLOSE LOOK": EMOTIONAL AWARENESS AS A CORE PRINCIPLE IN THE MUSIC THERAPY TREATMENT OF A PATIENT WITH AN ANXIOUS-AVOIDANT PERSONALITY DISORDER

Ulrike Haase and Axel Reinhardt

INTRODUCTION

In this chapter, we present an overview on the music therapy approach developed by Schwabe (1978, 1979, 1983, 2003, 2005, 2007, 2008) and its application in the treatment of Andreas, a patient with an anxious-avoidant personality disorder. Schwabe's music therapy approach has been applied successfully in group and individual settings in the treatment of patients with diverse disorders including affective, psychosomatic, and personality disorders. Integrating active and receptive methods, the approach lays particular emphasis on fostering awareness, especially emotional awareness. We begin by presenting basic concepts of Schwabe's approach. We then show how this approach was applied successfully in the case of Andreas. After a suicide attempt, Andreas was diagnosed with an anxious-avoidant personality disorder and treated at a psychiatric university hospital in Germany. We present major steps in the music therapy treatment of Andreas, which, as part of a multi-component treatment approach, eventually led to major and lasting improvements in functioning.

FOUNDATIONAL CONCEPTS

Awareness as a Core Principle

Fostering awareness is a central aim of the music therapy approach developed by Christoph Schwabe (e.g., Schwabe, 1978, 1979, 1983, 2003,

2005, 2007; Schwabe & Haase, 2008; Schwabe & Reinhardt, 2006; Schwabe & Röhrborn, 1996). Schwabe's approach is based on a biopsychosocial disorder and treatment model (Kohler, 1968; Schwabe & Haase, 2008) and has been applied successfully in diverse clinical and nonclinical contexts, in therapy, rehabilitation, and prevention. This broad applicability is possible because the approach is based on an integrative psychotherapeutic concept (Haase, 2009). Schwabe's approach did not grow out of a specific psychotherapeutic school. Rather, the approach is situated at the interface of medical sciences, psychology, social sciences and education. It utilizes therapeutic functions of music and integrates them within a psychotherapeutic action-oriented treatment approach. Central emphasis is placed on psychological concepts such as awareness or verbal and nonverbal expression, as well as on processes of social interaction. All these aspects play a central role in human experience and behavior across the life span, which explains the broad applicability of the approach.

A core principle is the *awareness-oriented action principle*. *Awareness* is a process by which an individual creates a subjective reality of all that he or she perceives inside and outside of him/her. This subjective reality serves as guidance for individual action. The less biased and more precise the awareness process functions, the more adaptive an individual action and functioning becomes. The awareness-oriented action principle seeks to broaden and to differentiate awareness by encouraging an open tuning of the patient toward his or her internal and external reality, toward physical, emotional and cognitive experiences, even if they are burdening or scary. In this process, which, of course, takes time, the patient develops an open tuning toward reality holding as little preconceptions as possible. Eventually, this open tuning can pave the way toward experiencing partly or completely unconscious material, particularly suppressed emotions. In order to render these experiences consciously accessible, it is important that the patient tries to verbalize them. Only this verbalization, which we call *awareness reflection*, makes it possible to bring these experiences to consciousness, and to understand and change them. Eventually, fostering awareness, particularly emotional awareness, will stabilize a patient's psychological structure (Schwabe & Reinhardt, 2006).

The Role of the Therapist

What is the function of the therapist? In Schwabe's approach, the therapist does not offer guiding interpretations. Rather, he or she stimulates action processes (see below) and supports the patient in "taking a close look" at all the things that he/she might prefer not to take a look at. The awareness-oriented action principle hence implies that the overarching aim of any therapeutic action is to stimulate an open tuning of the patient toward his or her internal and external reality. In this process, the therapist has to carefully regulate the balance between emotional exploration and stabilization (Schwabe & Haase, 2008), while guiding the patient on a path toward adaptive development. The ultimate aim of any therapeutic action is not only to reduce pathologies, but to strengthen a patient's resources. That is, to further positive aspects of functioning (Schwabe, 2005). Strengthening resources in turn does not only mean strengthening positive aspects of the self, but also empowering the patient to actively cope with his or her disorder. We call this *treatment through action* (in German "Behandlung durch Handlung").

Schwabe's approach targets those aspects of a disorder that are linked to experience and behavior. Across various disorders, including affective disorders, psychosomatic disorders and personality disorders, pathologies in these areas manifest themselves in distorted perceptions of both internal and the external reality, disturbances in self-expression, disturbances in self and social relations, and psychosomatic symptoms. The therapeutic process aims to evoke *actions* in exactly those domains where distorted perceptions, disturbances and symptoms appear. These domains include the *intrapersonal*, the *social* and the *creative* domain.

Treatment typically takes place in a group setting but can also take place in individual therapy, depending on whether a patient is physically and psychologically able to enter a group setting. Importantly, in a music therapy group setting, the therapist does not function as a co-player. Rather, the therapist has two main functions: 1) stimulating action processes using various music therapeutic methods (see below), and 2) stimulating awareness reflection. Action processes are stimulated not by formulating specific goals, but by providing suggestions. These suggestions can be highly open (e.g., "Make some music") or more structured (e.g., "Make some music. Take care that not everyone plays at the same time, but that nobody plays alone"), depending on the therapeutic situation. After action processes have taken place, the therapist stimulates a verbal discussion (i.e., awareness reflection) so that patients can enter an awareness process, in convergence with the therapeutic goals. During this process, possible cognitive limitations of the patient have to be taken into account as these may limit the potential for change.

The Role of the Group

What is the function of the group in Schwabe's approach? The group is seen as an important factor in the treatment process — a "social laboratory" if you like — that serves two main functions. On the one hand, the group provides a protected situation where processes may take place that mirror a patient's real-life experiences. These can be burdening, scary, or disturbing experiences that limit the patient, and are therefore important to address. With the help of the therapist and the group, the patient can become aware, understand and change these experiences. Thus, the group creates opportunities for individual growth. On the other hand, the group provides containment, security and a sense of community where the individual can enact creative resources and experience him/herself as competent (Schwabe, 2005). Ideally, the therapeutic process capitalizes on both functions of the group.

The Role of Music

When discussing the functions of music in Schwabe's approach, we first need to note that music always has effects when people experience it, either as listeners or as producers. Undoubtedly, music releases forces which, however, are not necessarily healing in and of themselves. Music can unfold its therapeutic potential only if the therapist stimulates action impulses in relation to music. Importantly, music does not act as a sort of medication with which patients are treated. Music functions as a carrier and transmitter of meaning, much like human language (Koelsch, 2004; Koelsch & Fritz, 2007a; 2007b). Music is a basic nonverbal instrument to express oneself, to form social relations and to create something together with others (see Jacoby, 1921). Moreover, music is also a part of the patient's external reality, which can be perceived and described as a placeholder for other external realities, thereby fostering awareness. This is particularly indicated in patients with personality disorders for whom an immediate confrontation with one's self and relationships to others could induce anxiety and, in the end, maintain or even increase defense mechanisms. Finally, listening to music can facilitate getting into contact with oneself if awareness is directed toward intrapersonal — physical, emotional and cognitive — processes, which can enter consciousness during awareness reflection.

Schwabe's music therapeutic approach uses active (e.g., musical improvisation) and receptive (e.g., listening) methods, as well as other creative modes of expression (e.g., painting to music). We present a variety of music therapeutic methods and their therapeutic functions:

1) Instrumental improvisation is particularly helpful in treatment processes that aim to enhance social interactions. This method helps patients to develop social skills, particularly skills necessary for regulating proximity and distance.

2) Movement improvisation (typically with classical music) is especially suited to fostering awareness. This method provides stimulation, encourages patients to express emotions with the body, and helps them to broaden and differentiate awareness.

3) Group singing is particularly appropriate for fostering feelings of community in the group. The group offers security and relief as well as physical, emotional and cognitive activation.

4) Group dancing is another method that fosters feelings of community in the group as well as physical, emotional and cognitive activation. Moreover, and in contrast to movement improvisation where individuals freely improvise, group dances provide clear rules and offer structure and orientation. This method is therefore particularly suited to individuals who would be overburdened by free improvisation.

5) Painting to music is especially suited for enhancing creativity and awareness. Moreover, this method can foster positive relations to one's self and to others.

6) Regulatory Music Therapy (RMT) is a receptive music therapy method that is especially suited for broadening and differentiating awareness. In RMT, patients are encouraged to become aware of their actual internal reality, bodily sensations, emotions and thoughts, including those that are only partly conscious before the awareness process begins. Moreover, awareness of the external reality is encouraged. Music as a structure of sound, rhythm and dynamics, is also a part of this external reality. Moreover, music has an effect on the internal reality of the patient as it stimulates experiences, emotions and thoughts, and brings them into awareness. In RMT, patients are encouraged to close their eyes while listening to music, typically classical instrumental music, and let their awareness swing between the internal and the external reality without voluntary effort. Gradually, these swings help to loosen an anxious fixation on only one element in the internal or external reality; for example, a fixation on a particular psychosomatic symptom. After the music has ended, patients are encouraged to verbalize their awareness experiences (i.e., awareness reflection) so that they may enter consciousness.

All these methods can be used alone or in combination, in individual as well as in group settings. We can only discuss some basic therapeutic functions of these methods in this chapter (for further reading see Schwabe, 1979, 1983, 2007; Schwabe & Haase, 2008). Their actual application always depends on the context and the therapeutic goals. Importantly, the method serves the patient and not the other way around.

After presenting basic concepts of Schwabe's music therapeutic approach, we now provide an in-depth discussion of how this approach was applied in the successful treatment of a patient with an anxious-avoidant personality disorder — Andreas.

THE CLIENT

Born two months early, Andreas spent the first six weeks of his life separated from his mother in an incubator. From early childhood until the age of 18, he suffered from asthma and, due to a weak immune system, from several other illnesses. At an age at which other children built attachment, formed social bonds and gained social skills, he mostly stayed at home, sick. Early on, he wrote in his reflections (Andreas, 2008) that he was aware of the resulting deficits. He often felt insecure, an outsider, and increasingly began to withdraw from others.

Relationships to his family members likewise did not provide much containment or security. His mother and stepbrother were often overburdened and unable to attend to Andreas' needs. He never really got to know his father.

At about 15, Andreas started to think about death and, in particular, his mortality. He finished school with an average GPA and obtained the certificate necessary to enter university in Germany. When his asthma disappeared at about the age of 18, Andreas was diagnosed with ulcerative colitis. Triggered by the information that his illness carried an increased risk for visceral cancer, Andreas began contemplating suicide. During this time, he also began experimenting with drugs and soon became a regular abuser. In his reflections, he describes his drug abuse as the reason for dropping out of university, where he was studying computer sciences. This drop out, in turn, led to an increase in his drug use.

One year later, he had successfully stopped drug abuse, "got clean" and underwent treatment. However, when he returned to university, he failed again due to the same problems. This repeated failure and resumption of drug use led to a serious crisis and eventually a suicide attempt. According to Andreas, the decision to commit suicide — his ultimate escape from misery — had not been difficult.

Diagnosis and Treatment Approach

After his suicide attempt, Andreas was treated at a psychiatric university hospital in Dresden, Germany. He was diagnosed using a multidimensional diagnostic approach drawing from a holistic biopsychosocial disorder and treatment model (Knothe & Reinhardt, 2006). The diagnostic process included a psychological personality diagnosis combining anamnesis, clinical observation, psychometric and projective tests, an assessment of the patient's resources and an ego-structure oriented diagnosis. This instrument, since standardized, draws upon an interpretation of unconscious conflicts and underlying personality structure when making a diagnosis (Kernberg, 1971a, 1971b; Rudolf, 2002, 2005; Rudolf, Grande, & Henningsen, 2002).

Kernberg (1971a, 1971b) distinguishes four levels of personality organization: the normal, the neurotic, the borderline and the psychotic (ordered by increasing pathological relevance) (Rudolf, 2002, 2005). These levels develop as a result of early experiences which, in turn, lead to the development of a coherent or incoherent ego structure. Individuals with different levels of personality organization differ in their use of mature or immature defense mechanisms, their competency for emotional regulation, as well as in the quality of their social relationships. In the case of Andreas, the diagnosis suggested an impaired ego function at the level of borderline personality organization, which, importantly, is not to be confused with a borderline personality disorder. Borderline personality disorder is only one of various disorders that can result from a borderline personality organization. In the case of Andreas, the borderline personality organization manifested itself in an anxious-avoidant, self-insecure personality disorder.

Building on this diagnosis, a complex psychotherapeutic treatment was developed, which combined group music therapy (using various music therapeutic methods) and individual psychotherapy. Long-term clinical experience and empirical studies (cf. Knothe & Reinhardt, 2006) show that awareness and awareness reflection promote the development, stabilization and differentiation of basic ego functions, which show multiple impairments in patients with a borderline personality organization. The core and unifying element, which guided the therapeutic process, was the awareness-oriented action principle. According to Rudolf (2002), emotional awareness or "access to one's emotions can be seen as the royal road in the treatment of a patient with an ego-structure disorder as it promotes the understanding of one's own personality and its conflicts" (p. 257).

THE THERAPEUTIC PROCESS

Music therapy, like any other psychotherapy, begins with a first encounter. In our treatment context, these encounters typically take place during the ward round or a joint coffee break at the end of the week. Thus, the first encounter happens before the patient has played the first tune, sung the first song, and encountered the music therapy setting. These first encounters are often crucial for the success or failure of music therapy. Sometimes a music therapist may fail because he or she overestimates the medium, music, and eagerly waits for the patient's first free improvisation, while not listening to the symphony, which has already started playing. From the first encounter onward, the patient sends musical signals in the form of basic signs of expression and communication: his voice, his laughter, crying, silence, movements, the rhythm of his steps and even his sighs. The art of therapy is to become aware of all these signals in their complexity, paying attention to them, and becoming aware of one's own responses to them — all against the backdrop of the diagnosis and the patient's biography. This also requires the therapist to *not interpret* these signals prematurely, but embrace them and respond with transparency, authenticity, openness, and empathy.

The music therapist met Andreas first during a ward round, several days after he had been transferred to the day unit. He met a young man who was still fragile and visibly affected by his suicide attempt. With a friendly smile, Andreas tried to show adjusted behavior in order to fulfil what he thought was expected of him. However, he also expressed his scepticism toward yet another psychotherapy, referring to his many negative experiences. According to him, he did not believe that the treatment would help much. Maybe it would help him to survive the next year or two. After that, everything would repeat itself anyway. He did not need anyone. This was the situation he was familiar with, much as he was familiar with contemplating death.

When he underwent group treatment for substance use, he had learned only to allow for loose, superficial contacts with others in order to get through. Opening up, making authentic contact with others, and maybe even showing his emotions, would only lead to hurt and disappointment. He would obey the rules and somehow get through.

This attitude was somehow impressive. It made Andreas appear brave, both provocative and nihilistic at the same time. It even suggested a kind of flirtation with his own mortality. The therapist still remembers his response to this cool, well-articulated statement, which evoked in him the image of an anxious, deeply insecure, sad, angry and lonely little boy. At the same time, he became aware that Andreas was completely out of touch with this part of his personality. He had split this part off and buried it under mountains of cognitive rationalizations. This first statement also reflected Andreas' previous relationship experiences and gave an idea of the relationship patterns to be expected in the therapy process.

Three modes of interaction appeared to be dominant in Andreas: 1) a friendly, adjusted, superficially active, emotionally disconnected mode, 2) a refusing, rationalizing, devaluing mode, and 3) a euphoric and idealizing mode. In the treatment process, the therapist would possibly encounter a different interaction mode or a particular combination of interaction modes every day. With these thoughts in mind, he entered the first group singing session with Andreas.

The Therapy Process Unfolds

A first quote from Andreas' writings (2008) sums up his initial experience:

Terrible! I wondered what I had gotten myself into. Thirty or forty people sitting in a room and singing folk and children's songs. My first reaction? Refusal. Why? This was just too stupid for me. I was not yet ready for an honest answer, also to myself. I sat still the whole time with a stoic expression on my face. When Mr. Reinhardt looked at me, I looked back at him in a defiant and provocative manner. 'Come on! Tell me that I should sing along,' this was what this look meant to say.

And this is exactly what the therapist did not do. He had instinctively become aware of the trap. His response therefore did not meet what Andreas had expected based on his previous relationship experiences. Had the therapist made a suggestion or, even worse, evaluated Andreas' open refusal, this would have carried the message: "I do not care about your feelings. I want you to follow the rules and adjust your behavior." Such a message would only have perpetuated Andreas' pathological relationship with himself and others. A pathological psychodynamic constellation, which ran like a red line through Andreas' life, would have only repeated itself in the music therapy process.

Situations in which the patient initially refuses to join the music therapy process are challenging and can potentially cause the whole treatment to fail. However, challenges can also arise in other situations and sometimes, ironically, may stem from the therapist's perception of the patient's affinity toward music. Patients are often deemed particularly suitable for music therapy when they have a strong connection with music. However, the decision as to whether a patient should receive music therapy treatment should not be based on whether a patient likes music or not. Such a decision would ignore the multitude of contextual factors,

factors, particularly the psychodynamics rooted in the patient's biography, which influence his or her current affinity to music. Moreover, such a decision may overestimate the importance of music in music therapy and, finally, ignore that a pronounced affinity toward music can also serve a patient's defense mechanisms. Thus, a therapist should remain particularly cautious when a patient willingly accepts musical suggestions at the beginning, or even joins the treatment with particular enthusiasm.

Andreas had opted for refusal. What to do? After the twelfth group singing session, the therapist approached Andreas and made clear to him that he accepted his behavior. But he further suggested that Andreas try to become interested, to take a closer look at what prevented him from becoming actively engaged. Andreas (2008) experienced this encounter in the following way:

> *Dismissingly I told him that I already knew the answer, which I did. I had just not been able to face it. But this situation was different. He had gotten to my ego, maybe my arrogance. In any case, I was angry. And suddenly I began throwing all the reasons at him, the real ones. I was scared of making a fool of myself, I was jealous of the others who had fun. I was afraid of letting go and having fun myself and I felt inferior. Well, now I had said it, and after I had said it I could finally begin to change it.*

When the therapist suggested Andreas become interested in his refusal, he also made a relationship statement: "I am interested in your experiences and your refusal and I am trying to understand the motives behind it." This approach was not random; it reflected the therapeutic goal of the music therapy process, the awareness-based action principle. Besides, it was based on a conscious decision for a structure-enhancing focus, geared toward the development and differentiation of awareness and reflection skills aimed at cognitive and emotional processes. Thus, a conflict focus was temporarily put aside (e.g., Rudolf, 2002).

Andreas reflected on his experiences in group singing further in his individual sessions. Several weeks after the encounter with the therapist, he described it as a key experience, which had enabled him to get in touch with another person and consequently, to truly enter treatment. Andreas began to raise his voice, express his fears and insecurities, experience community and cooperation in the group, learn how to enjoy these relationships, discover his own body and explore the multitude of instruments available to him as opportunities for expression and communication.

Classical music, which he had not liked before and deemed too difficult to understand, opened a new space for him and helped him to observe and listen to his own internal world. In a RMT session toward the end of the treatment, the second part of Beethoven's Piano Concerto No. 1 was played. After the music had played, Andreas first described heavy physical symptoms that he had become aware of while listening to the music. He had felt a rapidly rising pulse in different parts of his body, in sharp contrast to the tempo of the music. Moreover, he had felt a heavy burden on his chest, which took away his breath. His thoughts had first focused on the calm and beauty of the music. Then he had become aware of the contrast between the harmony in the music, the sensations in his body and his own inner turmoil. On the one hand, he had not felt that joyful and happy in a long time, full of pride about his accomplishments. On the other hand, he felt extreme anger that his last attempt to negate everything and commit suicide seemed to be closed now and forever. Initially, he wanted to leave the session and destroy something, much as he contemplated during his first RMT session. But this time he had been able to tolerate the tension and he had felt a new strength in himself that he had not known before.

All these experiences were transferred broadly and lastingly beyond the treatment context into his "real" life. Step by step, Andreas learned to approach his deep sadness, disappointment, anger and especially his complex fears and insecurities. He expressed them through music and through body movements, linked them to colors, gave them names and discovered their relations and origins in his biography. In the many group sessions, he was gradually able to let go of his mask, to put his coolness and rationalizing arrogance aside, and face his fear of conflict and acceptance. Andreas matured through these experiences. He became a constructive and esteemed group member who was immediately liked by others. This caused his prior nihilistic image of himself and the world to crumble. The therapist observed this development with joy and deep contentment.

However, it became clear that this development would also imply new distress for Andreas. The more his situation stabilized, the more his hopes for a fulfilled future rose, the more he experienced acceptance and love, the more the destructive parts of his personality tried to come into play again. Promising him familiarity and security, the old patterns seduced him and led him to develop fantasies of destruction. Contained by the therapeutic relationship and by the group, Andreas learned to confront these destructive impulses and to verbalize and understand them. Eventually, they lost their power over him. Looking back at his experiences in movement improvisation and RMT Andreas (2008) wrote:

I took part in many group sessions for more than half a year, but I hated nothing more than movement improvisation. It is true; in movement improvisation you can experience and train all kinds of encounters between different people. Conflicts — Do I want to be led by others or not? Where do I draw the line? Do I want this or that in a given moment? How can I make others take notice of me? Communication — How can I coordinate both parts of my body? Do I try different movements on the right and the left side? Joy, self-reflection. How do I react to others, how do they react to me? As I said, I never liked it, but nevertheless, I exposed myself to this situation each time intentionally and consciously. I began to experience and to name my insecurities, my fears, and all the other reasons for my dislike. Slowly things started to change. I drew boundaries to determine what I was willing to do and what not. Not only in the group but also in my private life. I learned how to deal with criticism and how to express it; I became more self-secure, stronger and more assertive. The most difficult thing for me was to become aware of the chaos in my emotional experiences, to face these experiences and to learn how to describe them. I still remember my first session of Regulatory Music Therapy very vividly like it had just happened. During the session I was overcome with regret to still be alive. This in turn produced an insane anger, which was looking for a way out. I hit a drawer in front of the therapy room; one could probably hear the noise in the whole house. In situations like these, it was always good to have an individual session right afterwards or the next day. Because when I could not or did not want to express my experiences in the group, I could express them in the individual session. Gradu-

ally I began to realize and understand the links and functions of these and other thoughts. For example: Suicidal thoughts are well-known thoughts to me, like 'old friends' if you like. These thoughts show me that I am afraid of something or that I feel overburdened. They are a sort of escape because they distract me from the real problem and, paradoxically, give me some security, the security of something familiar. Today, some thoughts reflect the urge to destroy what I have achieved because I have rarely experienced in my life the situation I am experiencing now — I am happy! I could name a dozen other examples and fill many more pages. The result would be the same. In all the group sessions I have encountered myself, tested my boundaries and enlarged them. The most important thing, however, was that I have learned to cope with my feelings and to accept them. The combination of music therapy and individual sessions and my own tenaciousness have helped me to follow this path and, of course, my music therapist who showed lots of patience, energy and heart. Even if we did not always agree.

Andreas' treatment in music therapy lasted six months. A core principle in the therapeutic process was the persistent and patient emphasis on broadening and differentiating awareness. Andreas increased his ability to experience and become aware of his emotions in a differentiated manner and to express them on a verbal-symbolic level. His emotional regulation skills improved significantly and he increasingly gained a differentiated understanding of their meaning. Of particular importance was his psychological maturation brought about by an increased acceptance of negative emotions such as fear, sadness, anger and shame. This also led to increases in security and empathy in interpersonal relations. His emotional outbursts decreased. Through his increased ability to become aware of and accept the present, Andreas gained control over the parts of his personality that caused him trouble, but which had lost their destructive power over him.

CONCLUSION

Finding Closure

The question of when to end therapy is as crucial as the question of when to begin; and it calls for a differentiated perspective, much like the first encounter. In a dialogue characterized by openness and transparency, the patient and the therapist should define a certain time frame in which the good-bye process can take place, with the patient's release as the end date. Saying good-bye needs space and time for all the emotions that may arise in the patient, the other group members and the therapist: nostalgia and sadness about what has been overcome and what is left behind; joy about what has been achieved, but also hope and fear with regard to the future. All of these emotions should be expressed, communicated and understood. Only when one is able to say good-bye properly can one start something new; and this applies to the patient as well as the therapist. Saying good-bye means letting go, leaving behind, but also taking something with you.

According to Andreas, he carried the voice of his music therapist with him; an inner voice, a close companion, which reminded him in times of trouble: "Take a close look." An internalized authority, which reminded him to get in touch with himself, to become aware of his strengths and to accept the responsibility for making something out of each day. This was the opposite of introjected dependency on a therapist.

Andreas is currently applying for vocational training. He has given himself the chance to live a full life.

REFERENCES

Andreas (2008). Selbstreflexion meiner Erfahrungen mit Musiktherapie [A reflection on my experiences in music therapy]. Dresden, Germany, Unpublished manuscript.

Haase, U. (2009). Die psychotherapeutische Identität von Musiktherapie – zwei Entwicklungslinien in Ost und West [The psychotherapeutic identity of music therapy – Two developmental pathways in East and West Germany]. *Musiktherapeutische Umschau, 30,* 203–216.

Jacoby, H. (1921/1984). *Jenseits von „Musikalisch" und „Unmusikalisch"* [Beyond Musically "Talented" and "Untalented"]. Berlin, Germany: Christians Verlag.

Kernberg, O. F. (1971a). Prognostic considerations regarding borderline personality organizations. *Journal of the American Psychoanalytic Association, 19,* 594–635.

Kernberg, O. F. (1971b). The structural diagnosis of borderline personality organisations. In P. Hartocollis (Ed.), *Borderline Personality Disorders* (pp. 87–121). New York: International University Press.

Knothe, K. & Reinhardt, A. (2006). *Stellung, Bedeutung und Effektivität der Musiktherapie in der Behandlung psychiatrischer Patienten* [Position, Relevance, and Effectiveness of Music Therapy in the Treatment of Psychiatric Patients]. Aachen, Germany: Shaker Verlag.

Koelsch, S. (2004). *Das Verstehen der Bedeutung von Musik* [Understanding the meaning of music]. Retrieved online November 17, 2008 from http://www.mpg.de/bilderBerichteDokumente/dokumentation/jahrbuch/2004/neuropsych_forschung/forschungsSchwerpunkt/pdf.pdf.

Koelsch, S. & Fritz, T. (2007a). Ein neurokognitives Modell der Musikperzeption [A neurocognitive model of music perception]. *Musiktherapeutische Umschau, 26,* 365–381.

Koelsch, S. & Fritz, T. (2007b). Neuronale Korrelate der Musikverarbeitung [The neural correlates of music processing]. *Verhaltenstherapie und Verhaltensmedizin, 28,* 23–38.

Kohler, C. (1968). *Kommunikative Psychotherapie* [Communication Psychotherapy]. Jena, Germany: Gustav Fischer.

Rudolf, G., Grande, T. & Henningsen, P. (Eds.). (2002). *Die Struktur der Persönlichkeit* [The Structure of Personality]. Stuttgart, Germany: Schattauer.

Rudolf, G. (2002). Konfliktaufdeckende und strukturfördernde Zielsetzungen in der tiefenpsychologisch fundierten Psychotherapie [Conflict-revealing and structure-enhancing approaches in psychodynamic psychotherapy]. *Zeitschrift für Psychosomatische Medizin und Psychotherapie, 48*, 163–174.

Rudolf, G. (2005). *Strukturbezogene Psychotherapie* [Structure-oriented Psychotherapy]. Stuttgart, Germany: Schattauer.

Schwabe, C. (1978). *Die Methodik der Musiktherapie und deren theoretische Grundlagen* [The Method of Music Therapy and its Theoretical Foundations] (1st ed.). Leipzig, Germany: Johann Ambrosius Barth.

Schwabe, C. (1979). *Regulative Musiktherapie* [Regulatory Music Therapy] (1st ed.). Jena, Germany: Gustav Fischer.

Schwabe, C. (1983). *Aktive Gruppenmusiktherapie für erwachsene Patienten* [Active Group Music Therapy for adult Patients] (1st ed.). Leipzig, Germany/New York: Georg Thieme.

Schwabe, C. (2003). *Regulative Musiktherapie (RMT). Die Entwicklung einer Methode zu einer Konzeption* [Regulatory Music Therapy (RMT). The Theory-Driven Development of a Method]. Bad Klosterlausnitz, Germany: Akademie für angewandte Musiktherapie Crossen.

Schwabe, C. (2005). Resource-oriented music therapy. *Nordic Journal of Music Therapy, 14*, 49–57.

Schwabe, C. (2007). Regulatory Music Therapy (RMT) — Milestones of a conceptual development. In I. Frohne-Hagemann (Ed.), *Receptive Music Therapy* (pp. 203–210). Wiesbaden, Germany: Reichert-Verlag.

Schwabe, C. & Haase, U. (2008). *Die Sozialmusiktherapie (SMT). Das musiktherapeutische Konzept nach Christoph Schwabe* [Social Music Therapy (SMT). Christoph Schwabe's Music Therapeutic Approach] (3rd ed.) Bad Klosterlausnitz, Germany: Akademie für angewandte Musiktherapie Crossen.

Schwabe, C. & Reinhardt, A. (2006). *Das Kausalitätsprinzip musictherapeutischen Handelns* [The Causality Principle in Music Therapeutic Action]. Bad Klosterlausnitz, Germany: Akademie für angewandte Musiktherapie Crossen.

Schwabe, C. & Röhrborn, H. (1996). *Regulative Musiktherapie (RMT)* [Regulatory Music Therapy (RMT)]. (3rd ed.). Jena: Gustav Fischer.

The authors would like to thank Tony Meadows for his insightful comments and Claudia M. Haase for translating this chapter.

Chapter Twenty Seven

THE USE OF ELEMENTAL MUSIC ALIGNMENT IN THE JOURNEY FROM SINGER TO HEALER/THERAPIST

Frank Bosco

INTRODUCTION

This chapter describes the clinical application of Elemental Music Alignment (EMA) with a middle-aged woman challenged by traumas and issues of insecurity. EMA combines music with touch (bodywork) in order to address issues that clients initially find too difficult or disconcerting to talk about. When focused on touch, the principles and practices of Polarity Therapy serve as a foundation in understanding this aspect of the EMA process. Once the client encounters and begins to process these experiences verbally, Gestalt Therapy theory serves to frame and contextualize verbal exchange. Aspects of the early stages of Clara's work will be described, along with updates from our nearly 12 years of work together.

FOUNDATIONAL CONCEPTS

Elemental Music Alignment (EMA) is a unique approach that I designed to combine the power of two therapeutic modalities that bring about change and growth for adults in individual therapy (Bosco, 1992). As I discuss this case, I will attempt to describe how these two therapeutic modalities, bodywork (massage) and music, are combined to enhance the power of music and broaden the experience of therapy. EMA involves making specific connections between music and touch that are determined by the client's particular needs, and then both sound and touch are altered or adjusted by the therapist in accordance with the client's moment-to-moment responses. Musical qualities and events are matched with the specific nature of the bodywork, which can include for example, the degree of pressure, the speed of movements, the pressing, holding, rocking, shaking, and/or lifting of body parts and contacting the specific areas of the body with respect to how they relate structurally and theoretically to Polarity Therapy theory (see Stone, 1986).

The verbal processing in this case, surrounding and supporting the EMA work, was primarily based in Gestalt Therapy theory (Perls et al., 1994). While Polarity Therapy recognizes the importance of establishing emotional balance as part of the overall healing process, it offers no specific techniques or unified approach to verbal processing. It does, however, address how emotions relate to the body, and in that regard, become a spawning ground for Gestalt experiments (Perls et al, 1994). Such experiments are suggested by a therapist and/or client to explore and experience novelty through an expanded awareness of the present, given the real or imagined circumstances of the experiment. Generally, we might opt for doing an EMA session as a form of Gestalt experiment to deal with issues that arise in a verbal process. Conversely, an EMA session would tend to bring to light topics to discuss and further process verbally. Since some of the issues in this case interrupted the client's ability to engage in verbal processing, EMA became instrumental in taking the process further, and then allowed movement back into verbal work.

Elemental Assessment

In order to associate music with a person's current condition and needs, I feel it is most helpful to make an assessment in a language that is consistent with both human nature and the nature of music. Music, from a purely scientific perspective, is a function of vibration or wave forms that we experience in nature as the movement (compression and decompression) of air molecules within a space; and yet, as an art form, we might agree that it somehow expresses or adequately represents our human nature (Kahn, 1983). Therefore, it seems a logical fit to utilize a theory of the human condition that is based on understanding nature by breaking it down into its most basic structural categories or *elements;* earth, water, fire, air and space.

Element theories come from ancient traditions of which the most widely considered is probably the Oriental five element system that serves as the basis for acupuncture (Kaptchuck, 1983). Many indigenous cultures have taken on this idea which, in essence, was an attempt to arrive at organizing principles by which to better understand human life. In other words, five element theories are a form of ancient science. The element theory that I mainly utilize is from Ayurveda (Lad, 1984), developed in India in alignment with yogic traditions. This theory became the basis for much of the work of Stone (1986) in the development of what he called Polarity Therapy (Sills, 1989; Stone, 1986). Stone was a doctor of osteopathy who challenged himself to find out why his patients would not maintain the adjustments he would give them. His search for answers led him to discover and incorporate element theories as they attempt to address the notion of life energy.

In 1981, I began to study Polarity Therapy as a system for understanding the connection between the innate structure of music and the innate structure of human beings. After studying the application of five element theory to the quality and expression of the human voice (Beaulieu, 1987), I extended this work to include polyphony so that any and all musical expression could be understood in terms of the Ayurvedic five elements: earth, water, fire, air and *ether* (i.e., "space"). I devised a system for analyzing music in detail for specific applications in this approach that I call EMA, to bring about balance as needed in the human condition. From this point on I will make references to these elements using parentheses — earth(E), water(W), fire(F), air(A) and ether(e) — as they relate to certain descriptive words or concepts in this case.

One way that I have come to understand the idea of balance in the human condition that is consistent with element theory is to compare our needs to the needs of a plant. Starting with the notion that growth only happens under certain conditions that will then yield varying results ranging from dismal to optimal depending on the nature of those conditions, we can visualize a working elemental metaphor for therapy. We are like the seed that needs enough water and warmth(F) to germinate (i.e., to begin a growth process; for example conception). Next, we open to the earth's nutrients, but can only get enough if we break through to the air (e.g., the birth process) in order to siphon up the water that will carry those nutrients through to where they are needed. Indeed, as this process continues, it is bound to ultimately repeat as the plant bears fruit and the life cycle continues. It is this kind of thinking that informs me in a way that I feel is both simple and profound. Applications of these elemental metaphors provides understandings of the therapy process at any level from the moment-to-moment minutiae of the client/therapist interaction to the over-all stages of the therapy process. I would encourage the reader to be open to such references as I have used them to outline the case that follows.

THE CLIENT

Not a "Diva"

Clara was 52 when she came to see me. In her 20's, she achieved some notoriety in a performance that caught the eye of some prominent people in and around the New York opera scene. To many, she showed promise. She was an attractive young talent with a huge "Wagnerian" soprano voice, but there was a crack in her foundation(E). Clara was not exactly "Diva" material. She had a great voice and the necessary intellectual fortitude to "fit the bill," but at the core, her self-confidence faltered, resulting in some unpredictable performance disasters. She encountered issues like losing her voice just before or after a performance, or freezing in fear(E) on stage. She had no sense of what was causing the interruption, which she described as "having the rug pulled out from under me." This was clearly an earth element issue since it relates to the polarities of structure, support and security. She needed a solid foundation of fertile ground to grow confidence in her vocal expression. Fertile ground supports growth through a balanced infusion of all the elements.

Many of Clara's problems seemed to be related to her father. He was a powerfully assertive man who realized the American dream as he developed a major manufacturing company. All through her childhood, Clara would engage in "battles of the will"(F) trying to resist her father's patriarchal rule, often in support of her mother or siblings. As she would win some of these fights, she would eventually learn to *expect the unexpected* in a surprise attack her father would launch to get back at her by embarrassing her in the presence of other people.

It wasn't until she was well into her teens that Clara learned to sometimes counter-attack by getting others to see what he was doing to her. Unfortunately, by that time the damage was already done. She learned to be very careful about leaving herself open(e) and vulnerable to attack. With any situation that required intimacy or personal exposure, she would tend to be on guard or go into a reactive mode of behavior. She became overly defensive and even reclusive later in her 20's as she managed bouts of anorexia and bulimia on her own in a constant struggle with embarrassment due to her poor body image. Out of fear(E) of being seen as "fat" she even resorted to constantly donning a raincoat to hide her body. Elementally, this represented a kind of earthen regression back to a sense of safety that might come with being inside a womb, like a pod, or a shell provided for a seed.

THE THERAPEUTIC PROCESS

One of Clara's original reasons for beginning therapy was that she wanted to gain more comfort(E) with her "big" voice. She was aware of how it felt cut off or stifled in her throat(e) and solar plexus(F). It was a bit like a static charge needing grounding(E) or discharge. It would build up in her body and then, when she could release her voice, the sound(e) would feel out of control like she was somehow not producing it. In fear(E), Clara would lift her chest up to get more air into her body as would be needed for a "fight or flight" situation. But, without a clear threat to respond to, she would not be able to release this energy. Consequently, she would not be able to take in much air on her next inhalation and would then start to panic, having closed off the physical gates for her expression. Excessive tension in the thoracic region — particularly the intercostals and scalene muscles — would effectively flatten the dome-like shape of the diaphragm, and leave her with a confounding feeling of discomfort and disconnection with her body. She was, as it became quite clear later on, describing a pattern of dissociation that began in childhood and would for now become the central focus of our work together.

In terms of elements, *balance* supports life. Clara's lack of emotional support(E) gave her a quality of frozen(E) ground with muscular tensions that made her body too rigid for the powerful voice within her to flow(W) freely out into the world around her. She could not claim the necessary space(e) she needed for her "big" voice, and so her expression(e) was stifled much like a plant that has out-grown its pot and become root-bound.

Stage 1: Thawing and Tilling the Soil, Sowing the Seed...

For roughly the first three years of our work, the challenge was to deconstruct the shaky ground that Clara had become accustomed to and reconstruct a more solid and consistently secure ground/Earth for her to stand on. This involved a kind of re-forging of the configuration of her elements so that her desires(A) could be willfully(F) expressed with a clear sense of her Self/identity(E). Her early struggles with her father left her in a predicament where he, in essence, rather than supporting her to express herself, took up the space she needed for her voice to come forward by constantly asserting his authority over her. While her ability to defend herself was compromised by this lack of a consistent support, she learned to fight with her father and became a valiant defender of others. In harnessing this ability, we did many sessions where she learned to defend herself against oppressors and perpetrators of the past. We enacted many *experiments* based on reviewing challenging events both from her past and from current relationships using Gestalt techniques (Perls et al., 1994) and Somatic Experiencing (Levine, 1997) to support aspects of her expression that she was not originally able to access because of earlier trauma. At this point, she was not yet ready to try an experiment where she would confront her (deceased) father directly for his offensive behaviors. In fact, she would tend to defend him at the suggestion that he was not a good father, even after discussing these offenses. She needed to feel a good, strong connection to him and to the part of herself that felt proud of him. She could feel a sense of having inherited some of his strengths during these experiments as she was experiencing a greater sense of personal power.

It was our third session when she brought up the "raincoat" and described how it gave her a sense of security — like a shell that protected her from the embarrassment of being fat. She showed me the fearful posture that she imagined she held under the coat. As this moved into a spontaneous experiment, I picked up a drum and started to pound in a sporadic manner to emphasize and represent the external world as I repeated back to her the negative thoughts about herself (introjects) that she had just expressed to me. She held herself in fear and hiding with her head tucked down into her arms held tightly across her chest. I supported this posture with drumming that was sharp and strong(F), irregular and syncopated(A), to represent the ceramic quality (E: dried = no water and, compressed = no e) of her shell-like containment(E).

Next, seeing her in what I believe Keleman (1985) might describe as a posture of "rigidity, aversion [and] fear" (p. 69), I asked her if she could move from this internal experience to begin feeling her arms as a self-loving embrace. To support this musically, I needed to introduce some *water* to be warmed by the available *fire* and moved by this combination with *air*. I did this by establishing a moderate, regular beat with predictable accents and a flowing wavelike quality. Her head began to rise up as she appeared to embody a proud, serene and noble looking posture. I asked her to hear and relax into the rhythm like it was water all around her. Soon I began slowing down(E) and simplifying the rhythm, relating it to a gentle heartbeat, and gradually fading the volume lower(E) down to silence(e), giving her time and space(e) to return to the present. When she came back from this experience, she had an awareness that her main issue in life was, just as with her voice, her difficulty in maintaining a consistent and self-replenishing output of energy. She acknowledged how great she was at supporting others, referring to a song she sang entitled "As long as he needs me" (Bart, 1960), to indicate that the only thing she would need in return for her efforts was external validation. She was beginning to realize that she needed to learn how to be there for herself in the spirit of the embrace she had just experienced.

We continued working on this theme with bodywork and EMA sessions on my sound table — a massage table with built-in speakers to enhance the physical experience of recorded sound or music. Breathwork became the most compelling focus for us at this point as the tensions she experienced while performing also disturbed her ability to speak freely. She would often not finish sentences in a way that seemed to correlate with her tendency to not finish her exhalations. Issues associated with these tensions constantly created hesitations in her speaking when she would attempt to communicate and make contact in a meaningful way. This was a clear example of a common understanding in Gestalt therapy theory of how holding back physically and emotionally can be linked (Perls et al., 1994).

Typically, I would use music to provide a sense of safety in these moments when Clara would tend to freeze up in reaction to some memory that caused involuntary shaking, as her body attempted to manage or discharge this bound energy. Depending on the circumstances of the moments, I might either attempt to quell this reaction, perhaps with more soothing elemental qualities, or encourage the symptom toward fuller expression and release. In one such session, I was playing a recording of a shakuhachi (bamboo flute) and koto composition (Somei Satoh) which presented *ether of Air*, as long stretched-out tones were surrounded by silences(e). With Clara lying face up, I began pressing gently but firmly into her neck region to release her tightly held scalene muscles (these emanate from the mid-to-lower cervical vertebra and insert or attach into the first two ribs). The music had a direct elemental correlation to the body area I was working in as this is precisely where the heart chakra(A) and the throat chakra(e) meet. Both the music and the bodywork helped her to release emotions that she held deep in the realm of her body. We were contacting a physical boundary that gave her a needed layer of protection similar to what the "raincoat" once provided. But softening this inner shell required a more tactful approach. The air and ether of this music presented a rather cold, barren and isolated atmosphere, much like a frozen(E of W) Arctic tundra. Grief(e) was apparent, but her deep sadness was not being released as fear(E) was overwhelming her ability to feel it and let it go. Her earth element needed some warmth to thaw so that insecure frozen ground could shift into a secure and fertile ground where emotions could flow and growth could be experienced through proper nurturing.

    So, keeping one hand on her shoulder so as not to let her feel abandoned, I reached over to my CD player controls and faded out the somewhat stark flute sounds and quickly switched to the *Adagio for Strings* by Samuel Barber. The slow and steady process of this piece provided the necessary elements to support Clara through an expression of profound grief. The nature of this piece is such that it builds gradually on a connected, flowing and stepwise(W,W,W) string(F) theme through the entire range of elements from a quiet(E) pool to a gentle, slow boil(F of W and A). Using principles and techniques from Polarity Therapy, I worked contact points in coordination with this music. I was constantly working to integrate at least two different elements as they were represented in the music and in accordance with Polarity bodywork. For instance, in the beginning of this piece I shifted my right hand from her shoulder(A) to her neck(E) and placed my left hand just under her navel, contacting the second(W) chakra. With gentle rocking and firm full hand contacts, I soon moved down to her left foot(W) and knee(E). From there I worked upward again by matching contacts with the changing elements in the music. Clara seemed to be almost crying when, near the climax of the piece, I found myself again gently pressing into her diaphragm up under the ribs with one hand and down under the clavicle (collar bone) into the anterior scalene muscle with the other. Suddenly, she let out a deep howl, releasing her chest and exhaling completely as she broke into a sobbing that she later described as being "not as much about feeling her pain, but rather finding release from it."

Clara cried through the pause in this piece, which comes after the building of a dynamic melodic pinnacle. During this silence, Clara seemed to make some connection(e) to what she needed to feel and by the end of the piece she was in fact feeling peace. She briefly made eye contact with me and with an acknowledgement of where we had just gone. In the verbal processing that followed, Clara told me this session was all about her learning to be less dependent on others to help her feel safe. She was feeling this infantile place like a child who grieves a loved toy that is somehow broken beyond repair. She was shedding a false sense of protection that she had wished was truly provided by her father but that she could never really count on. Facing this sad reality, she felt the loss of a dream and at the same time a new awareness that she could take care of herself.

Stage 2: Breaking through the Soil...

The raincoat was off. The shell had broken open naturally, and the process of germination had begun. Like a child taking its first breath, Clara could now get the air needed to fan her own fire; and there was much to do with that fire. We entered into a phase that focused on her ability to express her anger in an empowered way. About eight months into our work, she had a recovered memory while driving home from a voice lesson where her male teacher was touching her neck to assist in a new technique for vocal production. She recalled a date she had during a trip to Italy when she was 22 years old and suddenly moved into the memory that she was raped. She pulled the car over immediately and called me after releasing what reportedly, and to her credit, were some "very loud sounds." I supported her to recoup and get home safely, and we scheduled an extra session to revisit this event. Two days later, as she was sitting in my office recounting the scene with a man in Italy, she started to collapse, almost losing consciousness. I encouraged her to stand up and feel what was happening in the moment. She had a hard time accessing her anger, but eventually I got her to mobilize some emotional energy by pounding on a big cushion. However, she could not yet make any sounds with the pounding. I tried to keep her moving through this, but she fell into a kind of post-traumatic reaction, shaking and crying.

I helped her to the table and played a soft and slow, watery clarinet piece called *Begin Sweet World* by Richard Stoltzman, holding contacts on her body to match its nurturing mix of elements — *warm, moist and aerated earth*. As she settled into her body again she was able to tell me that she had never really dated before this event, which happened just after losing a lot of weight. Indeed, feeling more attractive made her feel more vulnerable to an overpowering sneak attack just like she had suffered many times before with her father. The same feelings of embarrassment and entrapment came up for her with the addition of some guilt over feeling some degree of sexual arousal before she realized this young man was taking advantage of her and acting against her will(F).

Two days later, as we were again working on her ability to stand up and defend herself from attack, it became clear how Clara was caught in a traumatic re-enactment pattern stemming from these issues with her father. She told me that she had successfully deterred sexual advances from some football player who also tried to force himself on her when she was just twenty years old. The problem was that she felt subsequently that she failed somehow because she let this guy down and upset him. It was the same old demoralizing feeling that she would get when she won an argument with her dad. For, even if she got her father to apologize for something he did, she knew it was only a matter of time before he would stab her in the back with some insult that would reestablish his dominance. This also reinforced her feeling that it was not safe to win battles against people with whom she had a degree of intimacy. It was this pattern that made her actually apologize to the football player for messing up his play and perhaps, by beating him back, she was set up to lose against the surprise attack that would come two years later in Italy.

Clara's comfort with me at this point, and her ability to see how ludicrous it was to apologize to her rejected rapist, led us into what started as a light-hearted role play inspired by the fact that I had forgotten to turn off the ringer on my phone. Just as we were getting into the subject of saying "no!" as a means of setting a protective boundary, my phone rang. Playing with her, I went for the phone saying, "Oh, you won't mind if I get that will you...?" Realizing that she was not about to use this opportunity to playfully respond to me by practicing "No!" I paused right before picking up and asked, "Clara, can you tell me what you are feeling right now?" We both realized her nervous system was activated, and she knew she should be protesting and angry but she could only feel frantic and shaky. We spent the next half hour working up her fire and earth until she could shout "no!" in various ways, coordinated with rhythmic beating again, on the *cushion* and then sparring with me as we both played on conga drums. Most significantly, she did this with some real strength and without losing her intensity, anger or determination.

Stage 3: Reaching for the Light

In the next stage of her work, Clara came face-to-face with her inner demons. Standing up for herself and feeling safe in the world was no longer her main issue. Instead, she was in touch with feelings of depression connected to the fact that, with the exception of her mother, she had never had a deeply committed love relationship. At about a year and a half into our work, she told me that if her mother (whom she lived with and took care of) was to die now, she would want to die as well. Clara was managing her life but still seemed to need to support someone else to give her life meaning. Some sort of fear was limiting the joy of the connection she was having to her mother and also to her new-found sense of self.

I was inspired by some toning (Keyes, 1973) work that we had recently done to do some EMA work to Steve Reich's *Tehillim*. I often combine toning with EMA to stimulate energy for creative expression, and this particular piece has a buoyant and stimulating quality that I thought might get her in touch with the joy of having this precious time with her mother.

We started working on the table, and as she seemed to become activated by fear in her body, I could see her back away from it and suppress it rather than release it. I intuitively thought this music would support her and provide some ground for opening up her heart chakra/area(A) for expression. I felt that the energy of the voices(A), warmed by the gentle syncopated(A) accents(F) combined with a steady rhythmic background(E), could persuade her frozen earth to melt and move. Following the music with some very active jostling of her shoulders(A) helped to release some formidable knots, but when I reached her abdominal(E) area I could feel her defenses and I kept a gentle pressure there so that she could remain aware of her fear and internal holding. At some point in the piece I did sense a deep relaxation throughout her body, but we did not speak until the piece ended. In the ensuing silence I briefly checked in verbally to see how she was doing. Clara was not ready to talk, but she gave a subtle nod indicating that she was in *a good place* and did not want to move or speak. I put on *Om nama shiva ya*, a quiet(E) and peaceful Hindu chant that offers a mix of voices(A) with a slow(E), flowing(W) texture like elongated(e) breathing patterns quite devoid of accents(F). I let Clara bask in this peace as I stood at her feet, gently holding her ankles(e contacts). She soon began to tell me about her experience. She said she had never heard music in this way before and that she felt pain, but all of the sudden it just lifted and she went into the music. She said that it filled her body and, as the different overlapping voices entered, she was aware of feeling them in her back and running through her limbs. It was the most amazing sensation of connectedness that she had ever had — an experience of healing, she said.

Stage 4: Choosing Life — Braving the Elements and Receiving the Sun's Light

With Clara's increasing strength and independence, she took on many new challenges as many traumas from her past continued to emerge over the next couple of years. She began to study several health and healing approaches, and incorporated other self-help tools and techniques she had learned previously. Opening herself to others, she soon had a budding private therapy practice. However, the more she learned in the interest of helping others, the more she had to grapple with her own issues. She was growing fast and making many important life adjustments, such as changing what she would tolerate in friendships and family relations, dealing with authority issues with new teachers, and learning to let go of her ailing mother. However, feeling isolated and unable to focus on creating new, loving relationships, she was still suffering bouts of depression.

We first addressed this theme just nine months into our work when she experienced it as something of a distant memory of an old despair. Using the first part of Bruch's Concerto no. 1, we did an EMA session that she reported had a transformational effect on her mood. Three years later, when I thought she was feeling strong enough to embrace the tumultuous musical conflicts inherent in the compositions of Gustav Mahler, we did an EMA session using Mahler's Second Symphony (*The Resurrection*) to revisit Clara's looming death theme. Indeed, this music lived up to its name. The elements at play in this piece took her through an extraordinary journey, and while she shared some words during the process, I encouraged her to speak minimally so as to stay in her body sensations relative to the imagery she was actively experiencing. Given that there was not much time left in the session to talk after the music, and the fact that talking immediately after an EMA session can interrupt the necessary digestion and assimilation of the experience, I asked her to consider writing about what had happened so we could discuss it later. The following is taken from what she wrote:

> ...I didn't want to die but the desire to live was only a thread and the opportunity to go out of my body was there for me...So many times I could feel the music giving me the choice to die and ascend and go into ether (*she understood this from my talk of Polarity*) as I felt a sweet sinking, but then the desire to live would present itself and I would fight. I was fighting for my survival. I wanted to live. I had a life with promise and I wanted to live it. All my energy, every bit of me was focusing on my next breath...The music penetrated my soul and carried me along when I felt too weak. In retrospect I can say this session was life changing. I have for so long questioned my passion and desire to live this life. This session tapped into my passion, my desire, my love of life, my need to survive, and my strength and power. I didn't want to leave this life without completing. Completing is a big issue for me. I have things to do and a life to live. I felt this whole session had to do with giving up or fighting to survive. I was supported through this whole process.

CONCLUSION

Indeed Clara's life did change after this. Naturally, she continued to struggle in her life, but she never again questioned the point or purpose of her life. She continued to take on more challenging studies with various teachers and trainings so that she could better herself as a health and healing practitioner. As her work developed, we naturally blended personal therapy with supervision by addressing issues related to counter-transference as they became apparent.

In these years of working with Clara, I have witnessed her overcoming huge obstacles. To summarize these elementally, the process involved fanning Clara's fire (A&F) to get it hot enough to melt the faulty and insecure aspects of her familial foundation(E) and then utilize the creative(W) movement provided by music (hearing = e) and touch(A) to mold a new form of support from a ground (E) substance that was now more purely hers — free of infiltration and unwanted introjects. Going forward, such a profound transformation has enabled Clara to have the sense of space and clarity(e) for herself to express the presence and solidity needed to take other people through the same kinds of troubled waters that she has now successfully navigated.

Recordings

"Om nama shiva ya" Sidda Foundation
"Symphony No. 2" Gustov Mahler
"Begin Sweet World" by Richard Stoltzman
"Tehillim" by Steve Reich
"Adagio for Strings" by Samuel Barber
"Kougetsu" by Somei Satoh

REFERENCES

Bart, L. (1960). *Oliver.* Musical
Beaulieu, J. (1987). *Music and Sound in the Healing Arts.* New York: Station Hill Press.
Bonny, H. (1978). *Facilitating Guided Imagery and Music sessions.* Salina, KS: Bonny Foundation.
Bosco, F. (1992). Elemental Music Alignment. Unpublished master's thesis. New York University. New York, NY.
Bosco, F. (1997). Sensing and resonating with pain: A process-oriented approach to focusing the body/mind using music therapy. In J. Loewy (Ed.), *Music Therapy and Pediatric Pain.* Cherry Hill, New Jersey: Jeffrey Books.
Bosco, F. (2002). Daring, dread, discharge, and delight. In J. Loewy and A. Frisch-Hara (Eds.), *Caring for the Caregiver: The Use of Music and Music Therapy in Grief and Trauma.* Silver Spring, MD: American Music Therapy Association, Inc.
Kahn, H. I. (1983). The music of life. New Lebanon, NY: Omega Press.
Kaptchuk, T.J. (1983). *The Web that has no Weaver.* New York, NY: Congdon & Weed, Inc.
Keleman, S. (1985). *Emotional Anatomy.* Berkeley, California: Center Press.
Keyes, E.L. (1973). *Toning: The Creative Power of the Voice.* California: DeVorss.
Lad, V. (1984). *Ayurveda: The Science of Self-Healing.* Santa Fe: Lotus Press.
Levine, P. (1997) *Waking the Tiger.* Berkeley, California: North Atlantic Books.
Loewy, J.V. & Frisch-Hara, A. (2002). *Caring for the Caregiver: The Use of Music and Music Therapy in Grief and Trauma.* Silver Spring, MD: American Music Therapy Association, Inc.
Lowen, A. (1976). *Bioenergetics.* New York, NY: Penguin Books.
Perls, F., Hefferline, R. & Goodman, P. (1994). *Gestalt Therapy: Excitement and Growth in the Human Personality.* Highland, NY: The Gestalt Journal Press, Inc.
Sills, F. (1989). *The Polarity Process: Life as a Healing Art.* Longmead, Shaftesbury, Dorset: Element Books Limited.

Stone, R. (1986). *Polarity Therapy: The Complete Collected Works (Vol. I & II)*. Sebastopol, CA.: CRCS Publications. (Reprint of works originally published 1954–1957).

Chapter Twenty Eight

MUSIC THERAPY AND DEPRESSION: UNCOVERING RESOURCES IN MUSIC AND IMAGERY

Lisa Summer

INTRODUCTION

This case study illustrates how I adapted the Bonny Method of Guided Imagery and Music (Bonny, 1978; 1980) to address my client Kyle's depressive symptoms. Initially, GIM with its emphasis upon inner exploration and reconstruction, exacerbated his symptoms. But through trial and error, I learned to rework the basic components of GIM. This reworking, over time, led to the discovery of the supportive and re-educative levels of practice in music and imagery. Each level of practice — supportive, re-educative and reconstructive — is concerned with transcending the emotional limitations that brought the client into therapy, yet each uses a different approach to this end. Supportive music and imagery uses positive inductions with simple, repetitive music with little harmonic tension. The re-educative approach uses symptom-oriented inductions with repetitive music that matches the symptom with harmonic tension, but contains little structural development. In both levels of practice, the client is given a directed task during the music to hold him in a singular image. After the music, verbal processing techniques encourage the client's in-depth relation to the image.

Kyle's sessions illustrate how the supportive approach circumvented his symptoms in order to connect him with positive resources lying dormant in his internal world. Subsequently, re-educative music and imagery brought Kyle new perspectives that enabled him to transcend his heavily ingrained and emotionally limiting symptoms.

FOUNDATIONAL CONCEPTS

In the early 1970's at the Maryland Psychiatric Research Center and the Institute for Consciousness and Music, Helen Bonny created specific procedures for an in-depth, humanistic music listening session and called it Guided Imagery and Music (GIM; also called the Bonny Method of GIM) (Bonny & Pahnke, 1972/2002; Bonny, 1995/2002). Bonny's goal was a broad-based, free exploration of the unconscious. To achieve this, GIM utilized an altered state of consciousness and an exploratory, open-ended induction, paired with a 30-minute program of evocative classical music (Bonny, 1980/2002). Bonny created a series of eighteen music programs, each with a different therapeutic contour (Bonny, 1978/2002). The musical selections used in the Bonny programs can be classified into three different categories (Summer, 2009). Supportive classical pieces, such as the Warlock *Pieds en l'air* from his *Capriol Suite*, have a simplistic use of all musical elements, a simple structure and little tension. Within a GIM session these serve a restful, or re-fueling, function for the client. Re-educative classical pieces contain significant tension yet have a simple, straightforward and repetitive structure (often an ABA structure). These are evocative, "working" pieces, such as the Barber *Adagio for Strings*, whose function in the session is to match and hold a client's tension. Reconstructive classical pieces are those "working" pieces that are characterized by significant development sections in which the musical material is extended significantly beyond its original exposition, and beyond a simply stated ABA format. These stimulative pieces function to "work through" and transform the client's symptom. Each GIM program links these three types of music together into a unique intensity contour that consists of supportive, re-educative and reconstructive pieces. The GIM client experiences the music program in a completely individual and subjective way, but usually follows the contour of the program, refueling with positive resources during the supportive selections, exploring conflictual areas during the re-educative selections, and ultimately traveling to unknown territory with the reconstructive selections.

Since GIM was primarily designed for use with well adults, the case study of Kyle illustrates how I made changes in my practice of GIM when I first encountered clients in a real-world practice. In essence, when working with a depressed client, I found the need to slow down and separate the GIM process into its three constituent parts: refueling, working and transforming. Many sessions, especially at the beginning of a therapeutic process, consisted of only one of these aspects. My approach and terminology came to be basically aligned with Wheeler's levels of music therapy practice (1983): supportive, re-educative and reconstructive (taken from Wolberg, 1977), which actually represent a flexible continuum of clinical practice in music and imagery.

All levels of this continuum have the same ultimate goal as derived from Bonny's (2002) foundational goals for GIM: transcendence — transcendence of the external reality in which we are all immersed, with its practical limitations, in favor of the internal world which has no limitations but that of the individual's imagination. The central assumption of the use of music and imagery is that the freedom we possess in our imagination transcends the limitations imposed upon us by external forces (parents, society, the expectations of peers and the like). The supportive level addresses the development of positive internal resources, the re-educative level directly addresses the client's specific symptoms and the reconstructive level goes to the root of the resources and symptoms within the unconscious (Summer, 2002).

The Setting

The setting for this case study was within a private practice in the U.S. Virgin Islands. The practice consisted of a family physician, two verbal psychotherapists and myself. Most of our clients were diagnosed with drug addiction, anxiety or mood disorders; about a third of the clients were on medication (they saw a psychiatrist to monitor their medication), and the majority were in recovery from alcohol or drug addiction. The verbal therapists took a psychodynamic approach and referred clients to me when they were "stuck" — having gained cognitive insights or symptom relief, yet without enough life change. When clients were referred to me for music and imagery, I consulted frequently with their verbal therapist, sometimes having co-therapy to integrate the music and verbal therapy. Kyle, one of my first clients, illustrates the development of the music and imagery continuum of practice as it unfolded in my music psychotherapy practice.

THE CLIENT

Kyle, a physician, came to our first session in an expensive and stylish suit and tie, a starched white and monogrammed shirt. Referred to me by his primary therapist as depressed and obsessive-compulsive, he seemed so articulate, healthy, aware of himself and in control, that even when he talked about being depressed and obsessive, I wondered whether he was simply confabulating. Despite that, he was working obsessively — at least ten hours a day, six days per week — and he could not rid himself of the feeling that his work was inadequate. Married, with two children, the fifty-year-old professional was on medication for obsessive-compulsive disorder and major depression. He had been in verbal therapy for about two years. Verbal therapy and medication had improved many of his depressive symptoms, but his primary therapist had reached an impasse in her work with him to lessen his hours at work, to slow down his pace while he was at work and to deal with his feelings of inadequacy.

Kyle spoke with celerity and perspicacity, changing topics faster than the island's chameleons changed color. In an early session, I played for Kyle a Bonny program containing chatoyant impressionistic music with a great deal of musical tension, my goal being to match his demeanor. In a GIM session, when you can match a client's in-the-moment state with music, they feel "understood" and "heard" on an emotional level. Having matched his state, the music stimulated an experience, as Kyle told me once the music concluded, exactly analogous to how he viewed his life. As Kyle listened, he reported fleeting and disturbing images:

I see swirls, they are coming at me very quickly...now there are sketches, like black and white drawings of birds...it is very dark...Everything is coming and going so fast, I can hardly recognize anything; I am trying to slow things down, but they won't listen to me...I am in a tomb – a grave, it is so dark and empty, I think I am in the tomb; I am trying to get out but I can't.

I tried several different pieces of music to see if the change in music would elicit a change in the nature or pace of his experience. No change in the music resulted in significant changes in his imagery. These unvarying images, Kyle told me, were akin to "symptoms" that afflicted him in his everyday life, a life he described as unconnected and distant. Nothing, he insisted, had real meaning to him, and he felt powerless to make any changes, as if he were simply an ineffectual observer of a life consisting of a series of mostly unpleasant events. Work, relationships, events, were all remote from him emotionally; and the prosperity, success and intellectual achievements that he had obtained were without meaning.

Kyle worked obsessively to feel accomplished, bringing him fleeting positive thoughts, but kept himself emotionally distant from the fruits of his labor. Intellectually, he justified his disengagement as a necessity, paradoxically denying himself the joy of the rewards he worked so hard to accomplish. The momentary positive feelings generated by his accomplishments were destroyed by what was underneath, in the unconscious: an internalized (introjected) version of his mother (a depressed, needy perfectionist who was emotionally abusive to Kyle and whose behavior was highly inconsistent in his childhood) and his father (who was highly critical, emotionally abusive and paid little attention to Kyle). The internalized figures of his parents continued the abuse and criticism of his childhood and thus denied him any lasting feelings of self-worth. Instead, as revealed in his imagery, his inner world consisted of shells of defensiveness, nested in further shells of defensiveness. Feelings of sadness, helplessness, powerlessness, anger, despair, vulnerability — all the responses he had had as a child to his parent's emotional abuse — were, by this time, chronically patterned in his unconscious. His imagery also uncovered the dark roots beneath his depressive defenses: a deep existential fear of death. When younger, he had periods of intense nightmares and night terrors that his parents had not addressed in any way.

Using GIM had yielded, for Kyle, imagery that was fragmentary, fleeting and out of control, but I believed that this session would be helpful to him; that it would help him face his difficulties and bring him a new understanding of himself. Experiencing how out of control his life was, I thought, should bring him motivation to change — to work less, slow down, to become more engaged and thereby live life more fully. But when Kyle returned for his next session, it was clear that his condition had seriously worsened due to the GIM session. He reported to me that in the previous session he had realized how out of control his life was, and that during the previous week, he had felt an increased sense of hopelessness about himself. Instead of relief and reinvigoration, he was despondent. He had become acutely aware of his wife and children's complaints about his emotional distance from them, and yet he could not respond. He was pale, could not look me in the eye, seemed totally miserable, and his manner of speaking was more fragmented than in his previous session.

Though most people have had some injurious parenting in their childhood, there are nearly always aspects of positive nurturance as well. When imagery is conflictual, one can expect some evidence of ego strength (positive resources, positive adaptations to tension and abuse), and even when such is not evident in a client's imagery, there is likely to be evidence in the client's positive response to the images. Kyle had no positive feelings whatsoever. If there was any ego strength, it was completely obscured by his unremitting depression. Though I did not expect to be able to remedy every client's symptoms, it seemed here that I had actually made the situation worse. I wanted to rescue Kyle from himself, to give him some relief from his horrible and fragmented world, but I was at a loss as to how to proceed.

THE THERAPEUTIC PROCESS

Supportive Music and Imagery

It was clear to me that GIM would not help Kyle address and improve his symptoms. I had not yet worked with a client whose positive internal resources were so unavailable to him — even with the help of psychiatric medication. There had to be a positive experience upon which to rebuild his ego: a positive, innocent Kyle that existed prior to his abuse. But I did not know how far back in the past this true positive self remained, nor how deeply buried it was within his unconscious. As a beginning therapist, I was determined to help him find this positive kernel, but I did not have the technique or skills to locate it. I needed an approach to music and imagery that was lighter, more structured and more directive than GIM. For several sessions I explored different approaches: relaxation techniques, music without imagery, imagery without music, though I was anxious myself about whether I was doing any good. At least, I thought, let me do no more harm.

A breakthrough came in the eighth session. I asked Kyle to tell me if he had had even one positive, quiet moment by himself within the last few years. He had not, but he had had a vacation with his wife, and they had risen at dawn to see a sunrise, a thought which Kyle found pleasant. Nervous as I was to introduce drawing to a man dressed in an Armani suit, I suggested (in an induction prior to the first movement of the Dvorak String Serenade, Opus 22) that Kyle recall the memory of watching the sunrise, and that he draw the experience on the page in front of him. As the music started, I could see he was self-conscious about the idea of drawing a picture. After about a minute of hectic illustrating, Kyle relaxed. With the pace of his drawing slowed down, his arms began moving every once in a while with the rhythm of the music. Listening deeply, he allowed the beauty of the music to shape what he was drawing. I played the piece over and over again. Rolling up his starched, monogrammed white shirt Kyle proceeded to get it filthy with all the colors of the chalk he used — without any concern to his previously immaculate garb. He used pastel colors, putting them on the page and then using his hands to blend them together. When he had covered the entire page, and it seemed that he was finished, I stopped the music. After all the layering of pastels, his drawing appeared to be softly green, blue and purple inside the circle: with soft yellows and reds, respectively on the left and right side of the page outside the circle.

"Contentment"

He was transformed, totally at ease and comfortable, the music and the drawing having created some kind of idyllic, positive experience. I did not really know how to verbally process what had just occurred, but, speaking slowly, I asked him to describe his experience.

Kyle expressed that he had felt "focused," "involved" and "creative" while he was drawing. He had tried, he confessed, to draw the sunrise in a literal way, but let go of that goal in favor of just expressing the feelings of the sunrise. He expressed gratitude that there were "no interruptions," unlike the interruptions that flooded his daily life (by which he meant his obsessive, depressive, fleeting thoughts). He was truly able to relax and enjoy the music. For the first time, Kyle had made contact with positive feelings in a session. He did so by initially recalling the memory of a sunrise as a visual image. Then, the music helped to focus him on the memory, and the simplicity and aesthetic beauty of the Dvorak *Serenade* held him in the image and called forth, into the present, the true and positive feelings contained within that image. The repetition of the movement (which I played four times) allowed the positive feelings that had emerged to gain strength. Kyle's state of consciousness had totally transformed from the beginning of the session, when he entered feeling "pressured, left over from work," to "content." This change held throughout our discussion and continued until the end of the session. He titled his drawing "Contentment."

Kyle was pleased with the results of this session and came back to the next session with a positive attitude about the therapy. I continued to use the same format in all of Kyle's supportive sessions: a positive induction tied to the task of drawing, with classical music. These sessions resulted in the following drawings: "Trying to blend chaos and pleasantness," "Father and son dolphins, frolicking," and "In touch." Within two months of our work together, Kyle found that he was capable of establishing contact with positive resources (positive feelings) within himself. He described himself changing in his everyday life, finding focus, presence, openness, acceptance, hope, availability, relaxation and contentment. In addition, he reported that he experienced — for the first time in his life that he ever remembered — really feeling what he knew were normal feelings of compassion for another person. This occurred at work when a client told him about her impending divorce, and for the first time, rather than offering the professional, artificial compassion that he employed only as a tool in his trade, he felt able to emotionally empathize with a patient. The supportive music and imagery sessions in which Kyle was in touch with positive feelings had crossed over into the real world and had already begun to take hold. He was developing a constant positive internal object, the beginnings of a healthy ego, previously absent due to his parents' abusive and inconsistent nurturance. The repetition of internal visits to his positive core with classical music had taught his psyche about positive feelings, and was beginning to take root outside the session, even with people outside his immediate family. For the first time, he reported, he had been able to make a truly human connection with a patient, an amazing confession — coming as it did — from a physician.

Over a period of approximately two months, the supportive music and imagery sessions allowed Kyle to discover a state of consciousness that was unattached to his usual psychological patterns. During the music, he was able to free himself from the omnipresent levels of defenses that otherwise plagued his every waking hour: the negative parental introjects, his depressive feelings and his existential fear of death. Kyle's weekly "immersion" in a positive, healthy state with music began to free his psyche from psychologically debilitating defenses. Though these symptoms would always return, little by little Kyle generalized parts of this healthy state of consciousness into his daily life.

The Process Deepens: Re-educative Music and Imagery

Although supportive music and imagery was changing the quality of Kyle's daily life, it had not adequately or directly addressed his general anxiety or work-related problems. That required a deepening of his inner experiences that I have called re-educative music and imagery. In order to directly address Kyle's symptoms, I kept the basic structure of using drawing with a piece of classical music. Yet I began to directly introduce his symptoms as an entrance point, an induction into the music, and I utilized evocative music that could match the tension of his identified symptom.

Kyle's therapy sessions were scheduled after work, and he arrived at sessions with a long list of complaints from the day. In one re-educative music and imagery session, Kyle initiated the session with his usual complaints about his day's work. Although it was evident that he wanted to unburden himself with each successive complaint he stated, I asked him to close his eyes and rather than *think* about the frustration or *talk* about it, to allow himself to *feel* it. He described: "It's a trapped feeling, a pressure, a tension in my chest. It wants to get out but I feel it's trapped there." As he described these internal sensations, I could better choose a piece of music to match his experience. I felt that the *Passacaglia and Fugue in C* by Bach, orchestrated by Stokowski, would match Kyle's tension. With the suggestion that he let the music help him express his internal experience in drawing, Kyle began to draw a road on his page. With the music, he depicted a winding road, colored in black and dark blue with patches of mustard yellow. It wound around the page with several large curves in it. After the road was complete, he added, at different points outside the path, seven round figures. Each figure had a strong center and several small, bright fluorescent pink arms extended, touching the outside of the path. After the music had ended, we began to discuss the drawing, which he titled "No Exit." Kyle described the feeling he had as one akin to being trapped on the road. "It meanders, it goes no place, it has nothing to offer." As he described the drawing, the feelings became stronger. We went back and forth, referring to his feeling, referring to the image. He identified the feeling as frustration. Furthermore, he explained that the seven figures were people in his office who were ready to help him. However, he felt these figures — not as potential helpers, but rather — as a burden. They only served to cement his frustration with feelings of inadequacy. I continued to work with the image and his feelings until I saw that he had more fully accepted the two feelings: frustration and inadequacy. After this, Kyle's perspective about the seven figures shifted. His expressions of inadequacy were replaced with a new feeling of desire to ask a secretary in his office for help. This is the hallmark of re-educative music and imagery. The therapist brings matching pieces of music to bear on a problem. But rather than becoming stuck in the problem as a client is wont to do, the client is "re-educated," by which I mean that he/she gains a new perspective. In re-educative music and imagery, the image does not change; the client changes his relation to the image. Kyle's perspective on the "no exit" drawing changed from frustration to inadequacy to acceptance and, finally, he arrived at a desire to ask for help.

"No Exit"

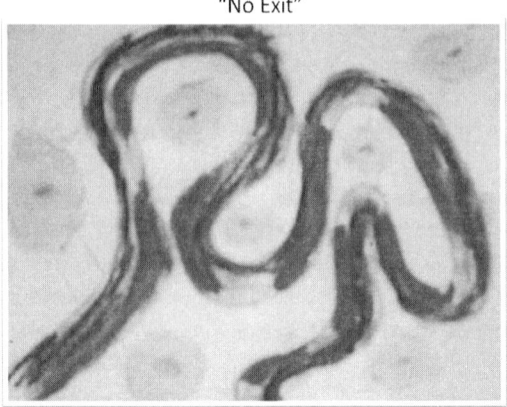

In Kyle's session, the strong, constant repetition in the music — Bach's *Passacaglia and Fugue* — paired with the focus (induction) had held him in the internal feeling of frustration. The drawing had allowed him a full, yet contained, expression of feeling trapped, frustrated and inadequate, in an aesthetic image. The verbal processing of the "no exit" image further held Kyle in a here-and-now experience of the symptoms he had been experiencing on a daily basis at work. Each of these components contributed to Kyle's "re-education."

The first step of Kyle's re-education occurred when he was able to separate and identify the specific symptoms, frustration and inadequacy, that were keeping him trapped in his depression and unable to ask for help. The second re-educative step occurred when he was willing to accept, on a new level, the reality of his feelings. On the surface, it may appear odd to suggest that it was a positive result for Kyle to deepen the feeling and acceptance of being trapped since the goal of our therapy was to alleviate his symptoms. But this is a prerequisite to the amelioration of symptoms and a prerequisite to new insights and perspectives.

Re-educative music and imagery sessions usually end with the verbal processing of the client's new perspective, and I could have ended Kyle's session after the first or second re-educative step had been achieved. But I sensed Kyle's readiness to solidify his new perspective with another music experience. Therefore, I asked Kyle not to think about what just happened, but to embrace this new perspective in a second drawing as he listened deeply to another piece of music. I chose the second movement from Beethoven's *Piano Concerto #5*, a supportive piece. He drew three concentric circles growing progressively larger from the center. Beginning in the center, the circles were bright yellow, light blue and fluorescent pink. Three green curving lines flowed through the center, and one green line circled around the center. Kyle reflected:

> *I just need to do it. I have an opportunity to do it. It's safe to do it here. I need to make the effort [at work] — it may not work out, but I think I have it within me now. I can take some time out and then ask someone to help me.* He called the drawing "Opportunity," and our discussion centered upon his feeling that there was a way out for him.

This additional supportive music and imagery experience helped him to more firmly access the feeling of opportunity, and with it, the possibility of asking for the additional help he needed at work. In effective re-educative music and imagery, the therapist's aim is to stimulate within the client a new perspective that can be made usable in daily life. In fact, after his music and imagery sessions, Kyle often utilized his imagery to help him confront issues in his life.

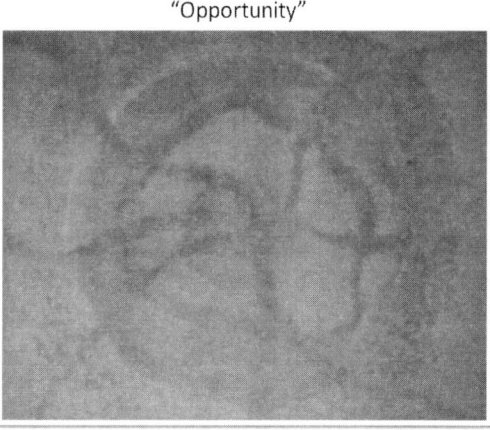

"Opportunity"

CONCLUSION

Kyle's internal and external world were filled with symptoms that were unmanageable and rigidly fixed. His distance from everyone had caused his relationships to be devoid of feeling, his character to be devoid of depth, and his life to be devoid of meaning. Since his inner life was so fragmented any time he had closed his eyes in therapy, he was inundated with negative images of death and hopelessness. Immersing Kyle in his symptoms while playing music had availed him nothing. In fact, it had exacerbated his distress. Neither had positive inductions with light repetitive music offered respite from the horror because he did not have the ego strength to utilize the positive imagery he generated, until I had added the external task of drawing to enable him to successfully hold the positive experience and assimilate it. Using positive inductions paired with simple, repetitive music, Kyle was able to develop compassionate responses within the therapy sessions that were then made useable in his real life — both with his patients and family. Re-educative music and imagery using simple inductions focused upon his symptoms, paired with music that contained harmonic tension and little development, helped Kyle accept and gain new perspectives in his daily life. The re-educative sessions significantly improved Kyle's life by reducing his symptoms and giving him an increased healthy repertoire of responses to life events.

Kyle's therapy progressed in a flexible way, moving between supportive and re-educative approaches for three years. Through supportive and re-educative music and imagery, instead of simply ameliorating his depressive symptoms through medication, Kyle transcended the ingrained negative patterns that had limited his everyday life and supplanted these with his previously buried positive internal responses to life.

REFERENCES

Bonny, H. L. (2002). *Music and Consciousness: The Evolution of Guided Imagery and Music* (L. Summer, Ed.). Gilsum, NH: Barcelona Publishers.

Bonny, H. L. (1978/2002). The role of taped music programs in the guided imagery and music process. In L. Summer (Ed.), *Music and Con-sciousness: The Evolution of Guided Imagery and Music* (pp. 299–324). Gilsum, NH: Barcelona Publishers.

Bonny, H. L. (1980/2002). The early development of guided imagery and music (GIM). In L. Summer (Ed.), *Music and Consciousness: The Evolution of Guided Imagery and Music* (pp. 54–68). Gilsum, NH: Barcelona Publishers.

Bonny, H. L. (1995/2002). Guided imagery and music: The discovery of the method. In L. Summer (Ed.), *Music and Consciousness: The Evolution of Guided Imagery and Music* (pp. 43–52). Gilsum, NH: Barcelona Publishers.

Bonny, H. L. & Pahnke, W. (1972/2002). The use of music in psychedelic (LSD) psychotherapy. In L. Summer (Ed.), *Music and Consciousness: The Evolution of Guided Imagery and Music* (pp. 20–41). Gilsum, NH: Barcelona Publishers.

Summer, L. (1988). *Guided Imagery and Music in the Institutional Setting.* St. Louis, MO: MMB Music, Inc.

Summer, L. (2002). Group music and imagery therapy: An emergent music therapy. In K. Bruscia & D. Grocke (Eds.), *Guided Imagery and Music: The Bonny Method and Beyond* (pp. 297–306). Gilsum, NH: Barcelona Publishers.

Summer, L. (2009). Client perspectives on the music in guided imagery and music (GIM). Doctoral dissertation, Aalborg University, Denmark.

Summer, L. & Chong, H. J. (2006). Music and imagery techniques with an emphasis on the Bonny method of guided imagery and music. In H.J. Chong (Ed.), *Music Therapy: Techniques, Methods, and Models.* (Kor-ean language). Seoul, Korea: Hakjisa Publishing Company.

Wheeler, B. (1983). A psychotherapeutic classification of music therapy practices: A continuum of procedures. *Music Therapy Perspectives, 1*(2), 8–12.

Wolberg, L. R. (1977). *The Technique of Psychotherapy* (3rd ed., Pt. 1). New York: Grune & Stratton.

Part of this case study was published in the Korean language in Summer, L. & Chong, H. (2006). Music and imagery techniques with an emphasis on the Bonny method of guided imagery and music. In H. Chong (Ed.), *Music Therapy: Techniques, Methods and Models*. Seoul, Korea: Hakjisa Publishing. With permission.

Chapter Twenty Nine

BRINGING LIGHT INTO DARKNESS: GUIDED IMAGERY AND MUSIC, BEREAVEMENT, LOSS AND WORKING THROUGH TRAUMA

Leslie Bunt

INTRODUCTION

This is the story of a courageous woman who used a series of seventeen Guided Imagery and Music (GIM) sessions to bring light and healing into very dark and troubled places. Fiona was originally referred for bereavement support following the loss of her partner, but as the case narrative unfolds it will become apparent that working through this specific loss triggered exploration of earlier losses and traumas resulting from periods of childhood abuse. GIM can provide a safe setting for containing the expression of some of the complex feelings associated with the grieving process, including sadness, isolation, guilt and anger, and can also assist a client to strengthen the inner resources required to allow other deeply buried losses to be recalled and moved into the light of consciousness. Given sufficient ego strength (as was the case with Fiona) it is then possible for further mourning of these earlier losses to be reconstructed and worked through in the present moment. Reflecting on Fiona's entire journey benefited from insights gained during discussions with my supervisor, a Jungian analyst. The chapter continues with some background to GIM and concepts central to the approach adopted, before introducing Fiona and the main stages and themes of the unfolding therapeutic process. Words taken from session transcripts are in italics.

FOUNDATIONAL CONCEPTS

The GIM method adopted in this context is the one pioneered by Helen Bonny (Bonny, 2002) and defined by the Association of Music and Imagery (AMI) as "a music-centered exploration of consciousness that uses specifically sequenced classical music programs to stimulate and sustain a dynamic unfolding of inner experiences" (AMI, n.d.). The individual hour and a half to two hour session is divided into four interlinked phases:

1) *Prelude:* generally verbal in nature, although drawing and other non-verbal media may be used
2) *Relaxation induction:* assisting the client to enter an altered state of consciousness (ASC) and moving to the point when the therapist provides an opening focus for the client's imagery 'journey'
3) *Music listening:* in which the client shares with the therapist the various feelings, body sensations, insights, memories, connections with the music, images, colors etc. that arise while the therapist supports with a range of verbal and non-verbal interventions aimed at holding, containing and deepening the client's inner experiences and process
4) *Postlude:* the therapist assists the client to return to the 'here and now' and to make further verbal connections between imagery and issues. Other non-verbal media may also be used (for more detailed elaborations of each phase see Abrams & Kasayaka, 2005; Bonny, 2002; Clark, 1991; Goldberg, 1995).

GIM provides a supportive and safe containing therapeutic space for the facilitating and gradual uncovering of the bereavement process (see, for example, Creagh, 2005). Listening to music in a very relaxed state with the witnessing support of the therapist provides opportunities for clients to find, at their own pace, the internal resources and strength needed to work through the shifting emotions associated with grieving. As shall be seen in Fiona's story, time is also needed for sufficient trust to occur with both the music and the therapist before there are sufficient inner resources to enable the specific loss to be addressed (for further exploration of the complex relationships transferred between music, images and therapist see Bruscia, 2002). Sometimes the music listening evokes the additional presence of inner helpers to support this unfolding process. We shall see in Fiona's story the importance of such figures as guardian angels. Support from these kinds of helpers has been reported by other therapists using GIM in grief work (Smith, 1997).

The choice of music is also crucial in this early unfolding stage. Music of a highly supportive, predictable and nurturing quality was used in the early sessions as Fiona began to connect with the feelings associated with the presenting loss. But as uncovered in these early sessions, the loss of her partner was the trigger for the gradual unraveling of a more obscured loss, that of her own childhood innocence due to a sustained history of abuse by family members. Once she had gained sufficient strength to work through some aspects of her bereavement process, she was able to bring memories of this darker material into the light of the present moment in order to re-experience these earlier losses and traumas. In this phase of the work stronger, more challenging music was used to hold and contain these complex and difficult memories and emotions.

In reviewing the case material retrospectively with my supervisor, it became *clear* that the gradual unfolding and expression of this traumatic material echoed the three-stage 'recovery' process elaborated by Herman (1992). Having established 'safety' and trust in the 'first stage' of the work, opportunities for the 'second stage' of 'remembrance and mourning' of the earlier losses arose before leading to a 'third stage' of 're-connection to ordinary life' and the making of future plans (Herman, 1992 p.155). Ventre (1994/1995) used Herman's stages to frame a 'two-year GIM process' that aided a 32-year-old woman to heal the 'wounds' from childhood periods of traumatic abuse. Later Moffitt co-published, including drawings, journal 'reflections and poetry choices' from her client, a study that incorporated aspects of Herman's stages into the recovery process from the long-lasting effects of sexual abuse from family members (Moffitt & Hall, 2004). These studies contribute to a developing literature of using GIM to address the complex issues of loss and trauma. How GIM can begin to help the abused client to acknowledge deeply buried feelings of anger, fear, sadness and resentment was discussed by Borling (1992) – and see Pickett, 1995 for a further case study example of the use of GIM to aid recovery from trauma.

The gradual accumulation of fear and anger associated with periods of abuse can lead to physical tensions kept locked within the body and the manifestation of a primitive 'freezing' response (Rothschild, 2000). This can be viewed as a means of defense, as can any resulting state of desperate 'helplessness' (Levine, 1997). There are examples of such freezing in the early parts of Fiona's narrative. There are also later moments when these deeply rooted and locked-in memories were given physical expression and release.

A review of Fiona's GIM journey provides examples of rich symbolic content existing in the liminal spaces between conscious and unconscious realms, between lightness and darkness. Romanyshyn (2007 p.27) echoes this when, referring to Jung, he notes that one of the functions of a symbol is to exist in this space between what remains hidden deep within the psyche and what is brought into the 'light' of conscious awareness. Symbols such as swans accompany Fiona at various stages throughout her journey. Other archetypal figures also occur, for example the appearance of a wise old woman, as does the exploration of younger parts of Fiona's self. A Jungian framework was used by Tasney (1993) in a GIM case study that investigated archetypes including the hero and shadow. Bringing light to illuminate the darker and more shadowy aspects of Fiona's psyche also relates to the Jungian emphasis on the union of opposites, active use of the imagination, and living through the experiencing of the images (Meadows, 2002; Ward, 2002).

THE CLIENT

Fiona was in her early fifties at the time of the referral. She had lost her partner Robert recently from cancer. She was referred to GIM to support the bereavement process but, as mentioned above and can be read in this following narrative, the loss of Robert connected to earlier expereinces of death and other traumas. Fiona's father was dead but her mother was still alive, although during the course of the sessions she was becoming increasingly unwell. Fiona worked as a volunteer carer. She was interested in art, meditation and loved nature. Although she talked of spending time with her friends, she was rather a shy and anxious person who lacked confidence.

The Opening Assessment Phase ('Taster' and Sessions 1-3)

The opening sessions of a course of therapy regularly introduce themes that permeate the entire therapeutic process. Working through the loss of her partner occupied some of this process for Fiona. But exploring this particular loss became part of a gradual unfolding of traumatic memories of child abuse with Fiona reporting that she had moments of not speaking during her childhood. Since the environment provided by her own parents was not safe she would often look for alternative mothering from her mother's sister. This pattern of seeking out different secure attachment figures has been observed in people suffering from early trauma (Körlin & Wrangsjö, 2004). Although Fiona presented with some of the features of 'Complex Post-Traumatic Stress Disorder' (Herman, 1992 pp.119-122), such as feeling guilty, she had a strong sense of self with extant coping mechanisms and defenses. This strong enough ego enabled Fiona to withstand explorations of these early memories (see Rothschild, 2000 for further psychobiological discussion of trauma and Korlin, 2002 for neuropsychological perspectives related to GIM).

Bringing light to illuminate a pathway was there from the start as the focus to the short introductory 'taster' session. Fiona felt supported during the opening two pieces of Bruscia's Pastorale[1] program: Debussy's *Prelude à l'après- midi d'un faune* and Liadov's *The Enchanted Lake* (see the Appendix A for an outline of each session). She was walking by a river with her well-trusted dog and saw two swans – *so white, pure and untouched*. She wished (not without some sadness) to be as strong, free, fearless, proud and confident as these beautiful creatures. The complex symbol of a swan points to 'the complete satisfaction of a desire' with a 'swan-song' also holding connections with death (Cirlot, 1971 p. 322). There was much beauty in this introductory session, beauty that she could smell and touch as she moved with the swans and her dog into a sunlit garden. Suddenly scared by someone jumping out, she felt protected by her dog and the swans who told her *no one will come out and hurt you*. She felt stronger, finding it hard to leave the garden.

During the next three sessions she began to trust more and to bring the light to move further away from safe pathways into denser and darker

---

[1] see Grocke (2002) for details of the music in Bonny's programs and the appendices in the same volume for details on the programs.

woods, a symbolic gradual unfolding of hidden subconscious material. The smell of Lily of the Valley reminded her of a favorite perfume on her bedroom table when a young child. She had been sent to bed for something she had not done. Too frightened to go downstairs to the bathroom she eventually was calmed to sleep at a synchronous moment with the music, being cradled and rocked during the *Shepherds' Cradle Song* from Bach's *Christmas Oratorio* (from the program Caring).

Younger and older parts of Fiona began to emerge. At the start of the second full session she recalled being frozen with fear on encountering some steers on a recent walk and the instant connections with suffocating childhood fears. Adult Fiona asked to find ways of taking care of her younger self and began to take young Fiona by the hand into the GIM journeys. During Session three an older woman, who could connect to the Jungian archetype of the wise woman, showed Fiona a beautiful, warm and sunlit house and garden. Older Fiona revealed this house (*too grand for me*) to younger Fiona. *This is what it should have been like and was taken from her. She was entitled to this.* The older Fiona became angry (another reaction to the freezing response; Levine, 1997) before this turned to *pain and sadness.... She's been in the dark for so long, she has the light now, she's so lovely, such a good person, her body's getting old.* At this integration of younger and older parts of self, Fiona seemed strong enough for the appearance of the first significant image of her dead partner. It was as if up to this point she had been gathering her personal resources, preparing the safe ground herself. Robert appeared during another musically synchronous moment, during the opening bars of Duruflé's *In Paradisum* from his *Requiem,* a piece not known to Fiona. Robert floated past wearing a long gown, appearing like a merman or fish and smiled as if to say 'Hello.' Fiona felt he had moved on and she was happy about this.

THE THERAPEUTIC PROCESS

The Loss of Robert (Session 4)

The first anniversary of Robert's death occurred near the time of the forth session. Fiona was terrified to think of Robert's bones rotting in his dark grave. She asked for the focus for the session to be at his graveside and that the music (the program Grieving) could help her to look into the grave, again using light to look into a dark place. The image of a broken skull connected with one of a broken doll in the cellar at her childhood home. She wanted to put the bones in the right order and the image kept shifting between Robert's body and her doll. She went into the nearby church to light a candle. She felt calmer. Everything was OK; the bones were all clean, white, pure and untouched (as were the earlier swans). Fiona saw a white shadowy figure, full of light. She was not alone and felt better. She too had been waiting for someone to bring her out of the dark. The light drew her between graveside and the church, the same light for Robert and for her. Robert's *spirit is in the church, in the light. The bones aren't important. They can look after themselves.* The session culminated with the appearance of four big strong angels whose *wings are like swans* (again). They were *gentle, kind and understanding* and Fiona felt that she had *known them for a long time - they're not strangers and like a nice family - mother, father, auntie, uncle* (my supervisor noted a possible connection with the four archangels). Fiona felt vibrations in her body at the reply when she asked the angels to look after Robert. The angels invited her to move on, to *go beyond the pain*. They told her: *You must trust, if you trust we will never let you down*. Fiona ended the journey by placing flowers on the grave in glorious sunlight.

The Childhood Traumas (Sessions 5 – 8)

Fiona was beginning to feel safer and more trusting of the GIM process. The mourning and some healing of Robert's memory provided a kind of catalyst to allow some of these early memories to take more shape. Glimpses had occurred from the outset with the *untouched* swans, the taking care of younger Fiona and the co-existence of the broken doll/bones in Session four. In allowing these earlier memories to surface it was as if she was beginning a grieving process for her own losses.

Stronger music used during these pivotally central sessions enabled her to explore the symbolic potential of such fearful images as:

- hiding in a smelly upstairs cupboard during one of her mother's terrifying rages
- the boarded-up fireplace and door in her bedroom
- the room where her grandmother died

- both her grandfather and her father returning home drunk in the middle of the afternoon
- the cellar where she was often thrown
- a dark and gloomy bricked-up well (glimpsed as early as Session two) that frightened and angered her parents

So many of these images were concerned with hiding, being in the dark or with something blocked up. Fiona needed to find ways of protecting and defending herself, of distancing herself from suffering and pain. During the orchestral arrangement of Bach's Passacaglia and Fugue in C minor (Session six), her guardian angel gave her the strength to look down into the well, finding life in the trapped water. Fiona began to realize her father was the weak one, controlled by her mother and who did anything to *keep the peace*. She became no longer scared of her father but began rather to pity him. Fiona began to feel freer and have more control. *The well scared them more than me. I took their fear on.*

But tragically this house held more horrors for her. She needed a lot of light and support from her ever-important guardian angel to re-visit (Session seven - Death-Rebirth) the recurring traumatic memory of discovering in the cellar the coffin of a family member who had died at a young age in childbirth. Fiona also felt as if part of her was in the coffin with the mother and child. During this journey she screamed for both the child and herself to be let out. Subsequent to this session, the following questions were explored in supervision. Was she mourning her own lost childhood? Was some of this material a creative and metaphoric fantasy all needing to be released? How did she feel at the threshold of her own adult life?

Fiona remembered how frightened she felt at the funeral, worried that perhaps the baby was not dead. Fiona created a beautiful new grave and funeral for the child and mother. Her last words of the session were: *Now there is light. She hasn't been forgotten, she's always with me, goodbye my love.* They were evoked by the final bars of Mahler's *Der Abschied* from *Das Lied von der Erde*, a farewell described by Fiona as *perfect for the funeral*. Was she symbolically saying farewell to her own childhood?

These central sessions were akin to the musical form of variations on a theme with an ever-deepening cycle of grieving, letting go and some beginning of restoration. By Session eight she had sufficient internal resources to confront the memories of the most dreadful damage done to her by family members. One constantly crippling fear was of dark buildings, church steeples and towers, holding within them symbolically very painful associations. She asked if she could use the music to face her terror of one church steeple in particular. For the focus she opted to leave her friends at the end of an enjoyable evening and moved towards the bus stop close to the dreaded steeple. After gathering strength during excerpts from Elgar's *Enigma Variations* (Positive Affect), she moved towards the steeple, terribly scared but aware that her guardian angel was with her. During the singing in Mozart's *Laudate Dominum* the angel seemed not to understand. At the start of Barber's *Adagio for Strings* the angel looked sad. As the music moved towards its intense climax there was a clear transformational matrix of working relationships: Fiona's connections to the music, the unfolding images, and to my guiding. The images unfolded thus:

> The angel can feel Fiona's pain, is hunched up, holding her stomach.
> The angel weeps.
> The angel understands and holds Fiona's hand, giving her strength.
> The angel stands up and lets go of her stomach.
> She puts her arm around Fiona.
> They look up at the steeple together (during the general pause after the loudest moment).
> Fiona realizes that the steeple represents the family abuser.
> The angel asks what is to be done with him.
> Fiona replies: *Let him go, let him flow away, take him out of the church steeple.*
> *The steeple is now just an empty, narrow passage, just stone.*
> *The steeple is a pointed ridiculous object.*

Following the Barber the *know-it-all* tenor and *self-interested* chorus in the *Sanctus* from Gounod's *St. Cecilia Mass* annoyed her. They did not understand; only her angel did. She felt stronger when the voices disappeared during the excerpt from Strauss' *Death and Transfiguration*. Here Fiona and her angel were drenched in cleansing and very healing rain.

The overwhelming dark object had lost all of its symbolic potency. As a child this fear had petrified her. She was speechless and unable to tell anyone. Now she could see the steeple for what it was - it had been cut down to size. After the session she went to look up at this steeple and at the start of the next session reported that it no longer had the same horror for her.

Releasing and Reconciliation (Sessions 9-14)

Fiona often brought objects or paintings relating to her GIM journeys to subsequent sessions, including bird feathers (relating to the swans), a drawing of one of the angels at Robert's grave, and, after the powerful work with the steeple, a painting of a black steeple now covered with glitter and white feathers. She began to talk about becoming freer, released from some of the memories and able to move on. She was aware that nobody was pulling her back, no Robert or abusive family figures.

Sessions began to oscillate (at her request) between those focused on quiet, reflective healing and restoration and those where working programs with stronger music were employed to connect again to more fearful feelings. But now there was more integration with Fiona feeling less abandoned and frightened than before.

Some of the journeys were magical in flavor, as in her very happy travel in a snowy landscape (Session nine - Quiet Music*).* A silver-clad lady took her (during Holst's *Venus*) on a ride on a carriage pulled, on this occasion, by a clean, white swan. Fiona was certainly using the music in its full liminal and transcendent capacity to enter through new portals into different spaces. Her angels began to take her to even more wonderful places, full of light and color, on one occasion *showing me a door in the cloud, a beautiful place that must be heaven...I feel like I've been here before, been a long time away but now I'm back. I know this place, this is my home, my proper real home.....I can go anywhere I want to. I feel so special.....all the pain I've suffered has dissolved...* She began to talk about wanting to help others. *I want to help other people with similar circumstances, children who've been beaten, raped, locked in the dark....I want to be their angel, to show them the light and beauty. I'm telling a little girl not to give up, she looks so sad, so alone...I've put* *some light in her heart...when she's strong one day she'll put some light in someone's heart.*

The continued releasing and reconciliatory work was exemplified by such moments as:

- Throwing all her past abusers to the bottom of the well where clear water and light dissolved them (Session eleven – Expanded Awareness)
- Gaining insight that the abusers were the scared ones
- Feeling that it was not her fault, and being sad when people continued to be angry with her
- Appreciating that she had worked hard for her *good power*
- Being thanked by Robert and letting him go, aware that he will be OK
- Realizing that she is *still needed on this earth, things I need to do*
- Restoring her childhood house to a place full of light and sunshine (Session twelve – Peak Experience) *a house to be proud of, beautiful, my house...with the clear painted white and flowers around the well*
- Tearing black clothes off her mother to reveal a sad and powerless old lady who says sorry; leading to a tender moment of forgiveness (at the end of Session twelve)
- Re-visiting the hospital room where Robert died and ritualistically saying her farewells and tidying up his personal items (Session thirteen, close to the second anniversary of his death, using the same music as in Session four, the first anniversary)
- One final visit to the dark cellar (Session fourteen – Inner Odyssey) and during the drum roll in Nielsen's 5th symphony tearing up some black plastic trash bags she had brought to the session to symbolize the remaining dark images of black objects from that horrible cellar. *Instead of it breaking me up, I'm breaking it up....no-one else will ever suffer in that place*

Years of horrible memories, frustrations and hurt were being torn up as trash and Fiona felt a new, good energy and tingling sensation in her fingers at the end of tumultuous Session fourteen. It felt as if some locked memories in the nervous system were being given an opportunity to be released on a physical level, having worked through the images, feelings and memories (Levine, 1997; Hall, 2009).

The Final Phase (Sessions 15-17)

Colleagues were noticing how Fiona was looking different and speaking out with more confidence. She was sleeping better, having fewer migraines and bad dreams. She felt better about herself and about being ready for a new relationship. The recurrent image of a swan – a *pure white swan, like an angel* - occurred in Session fifteen during Mythic Journey, a program compiled by Clark (1995). Fiona threw a list of negative thoughts into the river but was troubled that the nearby swan would become dirty with all that negativity so close. The swan gave her the strength to let go and not feel guilty. The list of negative things was also burnt and all the black ash (memories of the ash in her grandfather's fireplace) trampled underfoot. As Ravel's orchestration of Mussorgsky's *The Great Gate of Kiev* began, Fiona saw a funereal procession of ghostly black figures from the past coming towards her. She gathered strength so that the ghosts all turned back. At the climax of the music she realized that they could not touch or hurt her anymore. They were no longer a part of her. Standing on the top of a mountain she felt strong and guiltless.

At the start of her final GIM session (Session seventeen) Fiona talked of starting the work like a bird with two broken wings. One wing was the grief over Robert, which she now felt was healed; the other was the traumatic memories of her childhood abuse which were healing, but she knew would never totally disappear. However, she knew that she now had the inner resources to cope, to be independent and *to fly from this case/nest*. She talked excitedly of the free bird meeting new friends. This final session was a kind of summary of all of the GIM journeys and a reflection of her desire to bring light into darkness. She asked if the music (the program Mostly Bach) could help her move from a dark memory from a summer holiday when a young child, to being taken by her angels to a place of light and transformation. The scene was familiar: being hit and sent upstairs to her room to wait in terror for her father's return. She fell on the floor as if she had passed out. Sleep was an escape. *I just want to die. Why are people so horrible*? She saw the light bulb of her room sparkling through her tears, a comforting image. *If I wasn't crying I wouldn't see the beauty in the light bulb.* The sparkling image was like a magic fairy, strong and good. Fiona used these comforting images as a kind of refuge both at home and when she was being bullied at school. It was her means of survival, living as she said *in my own beautiful world, inside of a fishbowl, small, safe, light, so high in the sky where nobody can touch me.....it's my home.* She still needed, at times, to go that fishbowl, although everything was bigger now. Her dog was allowed in with her and *maybe one day I'll trust someone and let them peep in.*

Fiona was hoping that more people could be allowed to look into that fishbowl and begin to share more of her life with her. She did not need to keep secrets and could do so without feeling guilty. She dreamt of helping oncology patients to draw and paint. At the last review session she talked about being able to speak up more, being less overwhelmed by anxieties and past horrors. She had learnt to defend herself: she had found her voice.

CONCLUSION

During the review session we listened together to the Debussy *Prelude* as we had in the initial 'taster' session. As a focus to our joint listening, we used the image of the poppy field on the card she had left with me. The sun shone, she was with her dog, as in the 'taster', and she imagined herself as a beautiful lady wearing lovely clothes and carrying a sun umbrella. The session and our work together ended with her favorite tune – *Greensleeves* – in the arrangement by Vaughan Williams that ends the program *Quiet Music*.

REFERENCES

Abrams, B. & Kasayka, R. (2005). Music imaging for persons at the end of life. In C. Dileo & J. Loewy (Eds.), *Music Therapy at the End of Life* (pp. 159-170). Cherry Hill, NJ: Jeffrey Books.

AMI (n.d.) Association of Music and Imagery website. www.ami-bonnymethod.org. Retreived January 11th, 2009.

Bonny, H. L (2002). *Music Consciousness: The Evolution of Guided Imagery and Music* (L. Summer, Ed.). Gilsum, NH: Barcelona Publishers.

Borling, J. E. (1992). Perspectives on growth with a victim of abuse: A Guided Imagery and Music [GIM] case study. *Journal of the Association for Music and Imagery,* 1, 85-97.

Bruscia, K. E. (2002). A Psychodynamic orientation to the Bonny method. In K. E. Bruscia and D. E. Grocke (Eds.), *Guided Imagery and Music: The Bonny Method and Beyond* (pp. 225-243). Gilsum, NH: Barcelona Publishers.

Cirlot, J.E. (1971). *A Dictionary of Symbols* (2nd edition). London: Routledge & Kegan Paul.

Clark, M. (1991). Emergence of adult self in Guided Imagery and Music (GIM) therapy. In K.E. Bruscia (Ed.), *Case Studies in Music Therapy*. Phoenixville, PA: Barcelona Publishers.

Clark, M. (1995). The hero's myth in GIM Therapy. *Journal of the Association for Music and Imagery,* 4, 49-65.

Creagh, B. A. (2005). Transformative mourning: The Bonny Method of Guided Imagery and Music for widowed persons. Dissertation Abstracts International: Section B: The Sciences and Engineering. Vol. 66 (2-B).

Goldberg, F. (1995). The Bonny Method of Guided Imagery and Music. In T. Wigram, B. Saperston and R. West (Eds.), *The Art & Science of Music Therapy: A Handbook* (pp. 112-128). London, Toronto: Harwood Academic Publications.

Grocke, D. E. (2002). The Bonny Music Programs. In K. E. Bruscia and D. E. Grocke (Eds.), *Guided Imagery and Music: The Bonny Method and Beyond* (pp. 99-133). Gilsum, NH: Barcelona Publishers.

Hall, A. (2009). Personal Communication.

Herman, J. L. (1992). *Trauma and Recovery: The aftermath of violence - from domestic abuse to political terror.* New York: Basic Books.

Körlin, D. & Wrangsjö B. (2004) GIM European conference, Bulgaria. Personal communication.

Korlin, D. (2002). A neuropsychological theory of traumatic imagery in the Bonny Method of Guided Imagery and Music (BMGIM). In K.E. Bruscia & D.E. Grocke (Eds.), Guided Imagery and Music:

The Bonny Method and Beyond (pp. 379-415). Gilsum, NH: Barcelona Publishers.

Levine, P.A. (1997). *Waking the Tiger: Healing Trauma.* Berkeley, California: North Atlantic Books.

Meadows, A. (2002). Distinctions between the Bonny Method of Guided Imagery and Music (BMGIM) and other imagery techniques. In K. E. Bruscia and D. E. Grocke (Eds.), *Guided Imagery and Music: The Bonny Method and Beyond* (pp. 63-83). Gilsum, NH: Barcelona Publishers.

Moffitt, L. & Hall, A. (2004). "New grown with pleasant pain" (Keats): Recovering from sexual abuse with the use of the Bonny Method of Guided Imagery and Music and the use of poetry. *Journal of the Association for Music and Imagery,* 9, 59-77.

Pickett, E. (1995). Guided Imagery and Music: A technique for healing trauma. *Journal of the Association for Music and Imagery,* 4, 93-101.

Romanyshyn, R. D. (2007). *The Wounded Researcher: Research with Soul in Mind.* New Orleans, Louisiana: Spring Journal Books.

Rothschild, B. (2000). *The Body Remembers: The Psychobiology of Trauma and Trauma Treatment.* New York: W.W. Norton and Co.

Smith, B. (1997). Uncovering and healing hidden wounds: Using GIM to resolve complicated and disenfranchised grief. *Journal of the Association for Music and Imagery,* 5, 13-23.

Tasney, K. (1993). Beginning the healing of incest through Guided Imagery and Music: A Jungian perspective. *Journal of the Association for Music and Imagery,* 2, 35-47.

Ventre, M. (1994). Healing the wounds of childhood abuse: A Guided Imagery and Music case study. *Music Therapy Perspectives*, 12 (2), 98-103.

Ventre, M. (1995). Healing the wounds of childhood abuse: A Guided Imagery and Music case study: Errata. *Music Therapy Perspectives*, 13 (1).

Ward, K. (2002). A Jungian orientation to the Bonny Method. In K. E. Bruscia and D. E. Grocke (Eds.), *Guided Imagery and Music: The Bonny Method and Beyond* (pp. 207-224). Gilsum, NH: Barcelona Publishers.

APPENDIX A
Session Summaries

Session	Induction – Focus	GIM Programme	Some Images
Taster	Light --- path	Pastorale (part)	walk with dog, white swans
1	light --- path	Caring	perfume, bedroom
2	extra blanket --- wood	Nurturing	big and little Fiona
3	crystal --- dark wood	Explorations	wise older woman
4	breeze --- grave	Grieving	bones, church, light, four angels
5	breeze --- old trunk	Creativity I	old clothes well, Robert
6	tense/relax…well	Mostly Bach	angel, life in well, father, garden
7	light/angel…house	Death / Rebirth	cellar, coffin, new grave
8	extra blanket…bus stop	Positive Affect	church steeple
9	light…snow	Quiet Music	silver lady, white swan, flying in light
10	ball of light…into music	Sublime I	angel flight, Christmas
11	extra duvet…hill	Expanded Awareness	angel, own wings, dissolving pain
12	light…garden	Peak Experience	lamb, new house, sad mother
13	light…hospital	Grieving	re-visit hospital, sort Robert's

			things
14	angel…energy	Inner Odyssey	cellar, black trash bags
15	new breath…dockside	Mythic Journey	swan flight, burning list, letting go
16	ball of color…picture	Inner Odyssey	poppy, mother
17	warm wave…holidays	Mostly Bach	mother, punishment, tears, light, fishbowl

Acknowledgements: To 'Fiona' for giving consent to use material from her GIM sessions and to my supervisor Shelagh Layet.

Chapter Thirty

THE META-MUSICAL EXPERIENCES OF A PROFESSIONAL STRING QUARTET IN MUSIC-CENTERED PSYCHOTHERAPY

Heidi Ahonen and Colin Andrew Lee

INTRODUCTION

This chapter focuses on music-centered group psychotherapy with professional musicians, drawing together two models of music therapy: Group Analytic Music Therapy (GAMT) (Ahonen-Eerikäinen, 2007) and Aesthetic Music Therapy (AeMT) (Lee, 2003). We will describe a series of four sessions consisting of open improvisations alongside group analytic discussions. The practice of music-centered psychotherapy with musicians is a new field, focusing on the psychological and physiological stressors they encounter.

FOUNDATIONAL CONCEPTS

Music Therapy with Musicians

Performing as a professional musician can be an emotional and motivating experience. The truth, however, is that classical music is one of the five high-risk occupations among mental health threatening professions (Brodsky, 1996; Gabrielsson, 1999). Professional musicians rarely consider changing their career path even though their lives are often stressful and demanding. From early childhood through university and professional life, schedules are filled with never ending practice, competition in recitals, auditions, job opportunities, and various interpersonal conflicts or tensions among colleagues, conductor/man-agers, and others who have power over the individual musician. Because musicians often identify with their occupation (Spahn et al., 2004), this makes them vulnerable emotionally: if their performance fails, they fail as human beings. Perfectionism is a common psychological problem. Irregular working schedules and frequent traveling can affect one's relationships. It is no wonder that musicians experience both occupational and performance-related stress; they may suffer performance anxiety and also various physical injuries (e.g., hearing difficulties or lower back problems). Some develop severe health conditions such as burn-out, depression, anxiety, sleep disorders, substance abuse and various somatic problems such as stomach ache, headache and even heart disorders (Fishbein et al., 1988; Brodsky, 1996; Gabrielsson, 1999; Panasuraman & Purohit, 2000; Steptoe, 1989; Steptoe & Fidler, 1987; Jokimaki & Kivinen, 1994; Chesky & Hipple, 1997; Butler, 1995; Giga, et. al., 2002; Harper, 2002; Dews & Williams, 1989; Brandfonbrener, 1997; Hagglund, 1996; Fetter, 1993; Hamilton et al., 1995; Lehmann et al., 2007).

In light of the above, it seems that musicians can benefit from music therapy (Montello, 2002) equally to any other client group.

Aesthetic Music Therapy (AeMT)

Aesthetic Music Therapy (AeMT) (Lee, 2003) came from a need to define my developing clinical work. AeMT considers music therapy from a musicological and compositional perspective. Looking to theories of music to inform theories of therapy, AeMT can be defined as a primarily improvisational approach that views musical dialogue as its core. Interpretation of this process comes from an understanding of musical structure and how this structure is balanced within the relationship between client and therapist. The therapist must therefore be first and foremost a clinical musician. Clinical musicianship is comprised of the following components:

> 1) *Clinical Listening*: It is important that the therapist is able to hear and articulate, without bias, the sounds and music created in clinical music making through both assessment and supervision (Lee & Khare, 2001). To listen clinically is to listen analytically and dispassionately, as well as listening to the emotional and interpretive elements of the music.

2) *Applications of Aesthetics, Music Analysis and Musicology*: The therapist should have knowledge and understanding of musical theories and musicology and then know how to apply this knowledge in their clinical practice. If known and understood from this angle, musicological literature can relate directly to clinical practice and our understanding of the music therapy relationship.

3) *Musical Form and Clinical Form*: The therapist should know how musical form affects and is affected by clinical form. Looking to the musical structures of composition and improvisation and then relating them to therapeutic structures will enlighten the link between therapeutic intent and musical representation.

4) *Understanding of Seminal Works*: Western musical history provides us with a repertoire of musical greatness. By analyzing and understanding the music of seminal composers, we can add not only to the richness of our musical palette, but also to our knowledge of the human need to express through music.

5) *Therapeutic Relationship and Aesthetics*: All human beings have an aesthetic content regardless of disability, pathology or illness. AeMT believes this phenomenon is central. All clients have the ability to be great composers, and all clients have the ability to develop within a music therapy relationship that is aesthetically informed, be it beautiful or ugly.

6) *Clinical Analysis from a Composer's Perspective*: To enter improvisation with a client as a composer and therapist is an ever-shifting balance between music and therapy that is at the heart of AeMT. If the composer music therapist allows his/her knowledge of creative musical form and how musical ideas develop when composing, he/she will be able to offer clients the experience of being in a complete musical process that is both musical and therapeutically directed.

Group Analytic Music Therapy (GAMT)

"Individuals speak for the group and the group for individuals"
(Brown, 1987 p. 214, cited in Ettin, 1999 p. 172).

Group Analytic Music Therapy is an eclectic approach combining group analysis, interpersonal theories and intersubjectivity (Ahonen-Eerikäinen, 2007). As a group analytic music therapist, I am intrigued by the idea that the group can be understood from three different perspectives (Salminen, 1997; Foulkes, 1964; Ashbach & Schermer, 19894: 1) the individual in the group (the intersubjective window), 2) the group members with one another (the interpersonal window), and 3) the group-as-a-whole (the group matrix window). In real therapy situations, individual, interpersonal and group-as-a-whole processes are closely related. According to the principle of isomorphism, all group-as-a-whole processes mirror individual-level processes, and individual processes are reflected in group-as-a-whole phenomena (Ettin, 1999).

An intersubjective window focuses on clients' psychodynamic processes. The process is like any "practice of face-to-face therapy in the group circle" (Pines, 1998 p. 26). When I conduct GAMT, I am as interested in each group members' inner processes as when I practice individual therapy. I respect each group members' subjectivity, and I am interested in hearing everyone's voices.

The interpersonal window focuses on the interaction between group members and how each individual affects other members. As therapist, I observe who speaks with whom and when and what kinds of roles are present. How pairing, counteracting, splitting or joining re-creates real and imagined problems in relating in and outside the group. What kinds of power struggles are there and what kinds of nonverbal communication are occurring? Each individual has a repertoire of 'member roles' that have been *given* to him or her by other group members, and have also been received by them (Agazarian & Peters, 1981). Whenever a new person enters a group,'they must find a role from the repertoire available. That role, however, must fit them and the needs of the other members. After a while, the group-acceptable role will become a role that belongs to the individual while also being shaped to meet the needs of the group (Thompson, 1999).

While observing each individual and their reactions to each other, I also observe and treat the *group-as-a-whole.* I try to sense the group members' needs and the 'matrix' that develops from the web of interrelationships occurring in the group (Pines, 1998; Foulkes, 1999; Ettin, 1999). When group members share time, space and stories, their problems begin to transform into group dilemmas. After a while, these group dilemmas stimulate them to find more suitable personal solutions. As therapist, I maintain boundaries and search for meaning. This shapes the dynamics of communication for the individual group member.

Every group member has a rich inner language and visions. Fantasies and images, metaphors and symbols are an important part of processing. Music is an audible image, and improvisation is a metaphorical expression of inner thoughts and feelings. Group members can be seen as instruments in an orchestra. The group matrix can be anything from freezing cold to blazing hot. It is interesting how different sessions have different atmospheres. The atmosphere is a dynamic process that mirrors the different atmospheres of past experiences and the therapeutic relationship. See Appendix 1 for a detailed description of these concepts.

Music-Centered Psychotherapy in Group Work: AeMT and GAMT Combined

While GAMT is concerned more with the representation of musical experience through to verbal, conscious thought, AeMT is concerned with the musical qualities and how our understanding of the musical make-up affects the therapeutic process and/or outcome. Thus psychodynamic and music-centered therapies combine to produce a way of working that is potentially crucial when working with musicians.

Within this context, GAMT/AeMT with musicians is nondirective. Musical images take place during non-referential improvisations and are discussed. The therapy focuses on either the manifest content of the group members' music (improvisations or music itself) or the latent content (associations, feelings, images, body sensations). Music improvised in GAMT/AeMT may stay at the surface social interaction level if the therapist is not skilled in clinical musicianship (Lee, 2003). Verbal discussion may stay at the surface social interaction level if the therapist is not skilled in verbal psychotherapy. Similarly, musical dialogue may stay at the surface level if the therapist is not skilled in clinical musicianship. To integrate both skills, the therapist must guide clients to create music that is aesthetically valid and also has clear psychotherapeutic boundaries. The therapist also needs to help clients in articulating their feelings, images or other latent meanings of improvisation.

Discussion itself is not essential. It is important only if it integrates the unconscious ground and elevates these topics from the unconscious group matrix level to the conscious social interaction level. If the discussion is integrative, it can help the clients to gain an understanding of the connection between their improvised music and their current life issues, past experiences, or here-and-now situations (Ahonen-Eerikäinen, 2007).

GAMT and AeMT are two sides of the same coin. Each represents its own particular themes, both being integral to the survival of each other. It is this marriage of two similar yet disparate theories/approaches that forms the music-centered psychotherapeutic approach that is at the core of this work with professional musicians.

THE CLIENTS

The Professional String Quartet

The quartet is comprised of three males (violin 1, 2 & cello) and one female (viola). The quartet has been performing internationally for over twenty years. The current group members are in their forties. They perform works from the romantic and contemporary periods. They are a lively and energetic group who feel passionately about their work.

Therapeutic Aims

The string quartet is one of the most intimate forms of music making. Members need to be open not only to their own musical growth, but to the quartet as a whole. The main therapeutic aims that developed from our work were as follows:

1. To understand the quartet's relationships through music and how this could affect their playing on the concert platform.
2. To explore the links between, and elements of, inter-musical and inter-personal dynamics.
3. To explore individual personal dynamics and their relation to the group process.

Structure of Therapy

Each session consisted of two parts, each lasting approximately 45 minutes.
1. AeMT improvisation with Lee as therapist and Ahonen as observer.
2. GAMT verbal discussion with Ahonen as group analyst and Lee as group member.

THERAPEUTIC PROCESS

The four sessions highlight the main discussion topics of the therapeutic process. Every session was full of expectancy and excitement as the work unfolded. The transcriptions only present a part of the musical richness and dialogue as the therapeutic process danced between words and music.

Session One

Musical Description (35 minutes)
Slow dissonant intervals without pulse. Randomly placed tones creating a sense of ambivalence and openness. Animated sounds appear: Tension builds as the tempo becomes faster. Tonal, melodic lines. Slower and romantic in style. Floating sounds become faster. The music accelerates. Romantic music, consonant and precise. Rapid, atonal sounds. Intense listening that is not crowded and carefully placed. *Col legno* until Violin I begins a simple melody. The music then becomes tonal developing into a hoedown. The music becomes slower, ending with a slow romantic coda.

Someone is Missing in this Room

After the improvisation, the discussion starts on a social, interactional level, exploring various musical elements and inter-musical and interpersonal interactions. As typical in the early phase of group therapy, the members search for structure, safety and boundaries. How should they be in this new group situation? How and what should they discuss and play? The projective level activates when one of the group members says after the improvisation: "There's somebody missing in this room...." It is a new experience to play without a composer. How do they go about defining various roles? What about having a pianist (Colin) in the string quartet: Was it stimulating or disturbing? The group also explores searching for connection, hearing, the musical atmosphere and the roles impacting the music.

From a musical perspective, the improvisation was stunning. It was obvious that the quartet had connected deeply to the music, evoking an experience of the collective unconsciousness (Ahonen-Eerikäinen, 2007), in which primordial images and metaphors were activated (Jung, 1969). During the discussion, members processed these shared feelings and compared the musical experience with spirituality.

Session Two

Musical Description (7 minutes)

Cello begins with a grinding low note (D). This becomes the musical base. The tone is raw and builds in intensity, with the rest of the quartet taking the musical lead from the cello. The music builds. A slower more delicate section based on the intervals of a major 7th (D and C #) and a perfect 5th (E and A) (Piano). The music is slow and transparent. The 2nd Violin initiates a syncopated dance-like section in the style of Bartok. A short return to section II leading to a quiet and delicate ending.

I've Seen Burnout on Everybody's Faces

The discussion began on the social interaction level, investigating the musical elements. Members also investigated interpersonal connections, especially moments of synchronicity. The group discussion then begins to deepen; as the group members reflect on their busy schedules and work-related issues, they connect with feelings related to burnout.

Viola - We were talking about burnout before. I was burnt out about four years ago. I spent time thinking "how am I am going to get out of this?" I thought about other issues that impact my life: regarding sleep. It wears you down and can be depressing. I thought about ways to take care of myself. You have to do the best from where you are, to bring yourself whole to the group, to find a way to make that happen. Saying no to negative things and yes to healthy things. All of us go through moments of "I'm just hanging on." I experienced that in a dramatic way. There are still periods where I am just barely hanging on.
Heidi - Yes.
Violin II - For different reasons and solutions. Feeling burnout, coming from different sides.
Cello - Being able to re-generate yourself is something personal. You have to find it. Doing other things with other people, then you find out … you have to know what it is and then you learn.
Heidi - Learning to hear the warning signs is important. Sometimes we don't hear them. You (to Viola) said you had burnout. How did you recover? What was the key for your recovery?
Viola - At the end of the season we had a break and I regenerated. Realizing there is space in every day — there is space between. When there's too much on my plate. I see this as a group too…you feel like you're barely getting from one thing to the next. A signal to create more spaciousness. I sit at home alone. It's not meditation — it's different, but all of a sudden things start to click and settle. Part of the reason I don't sleep well is because I need time to let life be…thinking about how things are affecting me. Time to let life soak in. Realizing there are few opportunities, even if it's five minutes…not be in my office going like a crazy person. I try to be a little less crazy. It's been helpful to see the space between things.
Heidi - That makes sense.
Viola - I've seen burnout on everybody's faces.
Cello - I thought by joining a quartet it would be one way of eliminating the burnout from before (in an orchestra), but it proved to be a different burnout altogether.
Colin - You swapped it for a different kind of burnout?
Cello - It was supposed to be good.

Violin I - It's like there's no end to what you could be doing, because we're running our own business basically. We have help but...I'm always aware that we could be doing more things. We have opportunities, which is fantastic: making CD's. There are always limitations...but I've also learned to just let it happen.

Violin II - It's the nature of music. It's never satisfactory to me, so I go home after a heavy day and I think I should practice. It never stops...It can always be better. You can't say, "I'm ready." Well, I can't myself. It's sometimes an issue but I never feel like it...The pieces we have played hundreds of times on stage...I just still feel there's more to do.

Cello - That also contributes to the feeling of being overwhelmed. It doesn't matter how long you spend in the practice room, you're always going to feel dissatisfied. Even if you reach the next concert and you think "That really worked well." Then you go back in the practice room and start thinking about more things that you could do, things you could change.

Violin II - That's why being a musician is so challenging.

Heidi - It's like you're always climbing a mountain.

Four People Yielding to One Another

The quartet members end the group by investigating each other's relationships. As the quartet developed, their roles became ever more complex. Maturing within a professional musical context is essential if the group is to be elevated onto the international stage.

Viola - I remember when the quartet was younger, before Sam became the cellist. The frenetic energy we had. What Sam taught me was that I don't really need to understand everything. At times I didn't understand when Yuli [violin I] was asking; "let's explore the concept about re-birth and re-generation." I didn't understand what he was saying but then realized that in due time I would.

Violin I – We have also simplified our rehearsals. We know how to get somewhere with a piece quicker. When I first joined the group, I didn't know how to rehearse; I made a lot of mistakes. There were many irritations in those first years...it was just immaturity ...mostly my fault but...on the other hand...what were you saying?

Viola - Yuli [violin I] never listens to me is what I was saying (laughs).
Violin I - It's like letting the musical identity of the quartet be simply four people yielding to one another...rather than shellacking a conviction and trying very hard to make everyone be convinced of that idea. I feel really strongly about this. What happens if we just play and listen to each other? What evolves from that? Does that make any sense, then to have a discussion about it?
Violin II - I feel that's the only way to do it...but we know that.
Violin I - But it's not quite as intense, is it? I remember in graduate school playing chamber music with people who were strong-minded and it's just impossible. You have to be flexible to be able to feel.
Viola - That boils down to the respect that grows. We are four strong-minded people and sometimes you do sublimate...sometimes you squelch what you think. And then it might just make you pause for a moment and say, "yes, we could do it that way" and "it's possible." If somebody feels strongly and they think "it's got to be this way" or "it's here." There's a great deal of subjectivity. I like that. We play and let it have a sound and there's openness. I like it that way. We have our off days...it's not fixed. For me the last five years have been a real revelation.
Heidi - Exactly.
Viola - I've played in chamber groups for 25 years and I'm still learning.

This session helped the quartet to understand the importance of cohesion and their roles with one another. Trusting their fellow members as their relationships matured helped them to appreciate their uniqueness and the fact that they indeed function as a family.

Session Three

> Musical description (26 minutes)
> (Note: a range of percussion instruments are now made available for the quartet to play)
> The improvisation begins with a theme in E minor. The direction becomes more formed. The music is free and syncopated. A sense of rhyth-

> mic and harmonic structure becomes clear. The therapist provides a four-chord theme that acts as anchor. The quartet begins to play percussion instruments also, using mainly drums and the cymbal. The architectural tonic is D. In contrast the music takes on a quieter nature. There is a sense of sorrow and searching. It is based on minor modes that provide a sense of openness. This is balanced with a slow, lyrical section in E major. The music grows in intensity. There are sections of wild abandon balanced with more formed musical inventions. All styles are contained within a clear and expressive/energetic form. A long slow lyrical section ends the improvisation in E major.

I Felt Like Crying

After a period of playfulness explored through the improvisation, the group began talking about the emotions expressed.

> Viola - There was tension. It was cathartic.
> Cello - I endured the pain.
> Colin - There was an elevated experience when you reached a certain point.
> Viola - Yes.
> Cello - Which part was that?
> Colin - The drumming. I am not sure who was playing because I don't often look.
> Violin I - Clara [viola player] was the only one whacking the life out of the drum skin.
> Viola - It was odd, because I also felt like crying about six times, which is weird.
> Heidi - Mmmm.
> Viola - I don't know why.

Musical Euphoria

The improvisation was cathartic, and after this experience, the group members began to discuss if they had ever had similar experiences during their concerts. They then reflect this back to their improvisation, describing the improvisational experience as euphoric.

Violin I - I think what I liked, with Xavier (violin II), is the *idea of euphoria, too*. I think what we love about our profession is *those euphoric moments* that are purely musical and physical. Your reflexes are very connected to immediate signals.

C - I felt we touched on it. During the E major section especially, it felt quite euphoric, very heightened.

Musical euphoria in music therapy is at the core of the process and can affect therapeutic outcome. To be in a heightened sense of musical dialogue is beyond empirical logic and refers to the intensely creative and spiritual nature of our field. In improvisation, euphoria can take on an ever more heightened level of expression and union within a group setting. When all players become a collective musical expression, the individual voices of the group merge to find a balance that is bigger than the sum of the parts. It is this musical euphoric dialogue and union that is at the heart of music-centered practice. The musical components and pieces within the symphonic understanding of an AeMT improvisation merges with the psychotherapeutic understanding and interpretation of GAMT. Together, they allow euphoria to be experienced and understood as part of the music-centered psychotherapeutic process.

Session Four

> Musical Description (17 minutes)
>
> The music floats with the quartet exploring string configurations producing music that is nebulous and free. The music becomes tonal and overtly romantic. Quiet delicate searching. Intense listening. Faster more rhythmic music. Separate musical ideas. Faster, and more rhythmically consonant. The cymbal creates a new texture. The intervallic theme from the improvisation in session II, section two is re-introduced by the therapist as the main musical form. The improvisation takes on a feeling of the Blues leading into the Middle-Eastern mode, which concludes the improvisation quietly.

Competition

After a vivid discussion about touching music, emptiness, freedom and need of "just wanting to hear something different," the group ends up with a long dialogue about competition.

> Heidi - Is there competition between the quartet members?
> (Silence - awkward laughing)
> Violin I - In this situation of improvising?
> Heidi - No, I mean as a string quartet, and as musicians.
> Violin II - Certainly within the confines of the quartet, there's definitely competition, because we all have our own ideas, and we want our ideas to come out. On every level. Administration, to business, to music.
> Violin I - I don't feel it's all competitive.
> Violin II - I'm not saying it's necessarily a competition. I just mean there *is* competition.

It's all About Family

The interpersonal perspective opens up after an intervention from Heidi that compares the dynamics of the quartet with the dynamics of the family unit. Is the quartet nearer to the family dynamic than other chamber groups? The quartet, just like any family unit, will include competition. This may be promoted musically. The quartet, just like any family, contains roles that are given and received. Playing in the quartet includes "important" roles and "not so important" roles, along with sub-groupings, akin to sibling dynamics. Violinists are always together, while the cellist and viola player are always alone.

> Violin I - We think that the viola and cello are always alone.
> Colin - I think of the violinists as like brothers.
> Violin II - ...we're used to each other, that energy.
> Colin - Because you swap roles as well?
> Violin I - There are always two of us, but these guys [cello and viola] are always alone.

> Viola - Primo cellist and primo violist.
> Violin II - For them that's it. ...I'm the cellist ...I'm the violist ...I'm the pianist too.

Colin's comment takes the group into an in-depth discussion of their relationships with one another. Through Heidi's interventions, they come to see how their past relationships and experiences influence the ways they interact verbally and musically in the group (Ahonen-Eerikainen, 2007), and this leads to an important question: How do the quartet members deal with each other?

> Colin - In my family, I can criticize my sister or brother, but from the outside, no one is allowed to say anything bad. I felt that here. You don't want Heidi and I to think that there are problems...but inside... it must be like that? You can be mad with each other, but you won't let anybody from the outside know. Because that's the front you put on...we are a 'together' string quartet.
> Heidi - Like in any family.
> Viola - I think over the years, there's been a lot of inherent problems, especially with you guys. Like teaching, and playing...who plays first. It seems like from the outside, that our relationships have become healthier over the years. When I first joined the group, understanding how each of you talk. You are all very different players. Essentially we're all each others teachers. I look at it that way. I want to be open to what people have to say. My first instinct is: "No, it's like this" but there's a voice that says, "It could also be like that." I want to always keep that option. Except when I'm not in the right mood. I think that you guys have really developed a lot.
> Violin I - It's like a family. You're alone, and then you have a sibling, and you adjust. There's a time, but you learn how to be with one another.

Conflicts

The following intervention from Colin and Heidi helps the group recognize their conflicts. The discussion opens the door for the other group members to grasp the real topic:

> Colin - At times I really get a sense you are a family, and other times you say things, or things happen, and I realize that as our discussions continue, you're still evaluating who you are as individuals. Sometimes you really surprise me with the things you say. I think it's more in the talk. At times, I really get a sense of a close family, and other times, a family in transition.
> Viola - A family with conflicts.
> Colin - Yes, thank you, I didn't like to say that, but yes.
> Viola - I think we have our conflicts. Some difficult situations sometimes are not really resolved. They either resolve or we let them fade...then little things become touchy, or they can be...at least for me. So it can be tricky.
> Violin I - It doesn't help that it works with families in our lives.
> Colin - You have been very open, I don't think the conflicts are always negative conflicts, but they're there, aren't they?
> Heidi - (helping the group to go deeper into the issue) Do you want to speak more about that?
> Viola - About conflicts?
> Heidi - Yes, whatever you started to speak on...

The group explores their issues and how they have resolved their conflicts in the past.

Strengths and Weaknesses

This leads to another discussion in which the group compares the dynamics of a quartet and an orchestra; their roles, power struggles and games. If string quartet dynamics refers to a family unit, the orchestra dynamics refers to an extended family: no need to get along, you're playing great music, but often under horrible circumstances.

> Viola - Ultimately what the four of us should do is bring our strengths, to what we have, and we also know each other's weaknesses.
> Violin I - That was one thing I was hoping for in string quartet, that it would be an environment that was interested in each others

strengths. This is a very different environment [than an orchestra]. It has the capacity to be infinitely more supportive.
Violin II - What do you mean, praise on weakness in the orchestra?
Violin I - I mean, just the way you play, people in orchestras...the games that people play when you're actually making the music, are power struggles all the time, about who gets it right and who doesn't get it right. Who got the shift and who didn't. Just little games that people constantly play to prey on each other's weakness.
Heidi - It's like extended family.
Violin I - But it's very dysfunctional. The audition process is a prime example. All the audition process does is tests your nerves. If you've got nerves of steel, you'll win the audition, and you'll get into the band, and you might be able to deal with that dynamic of constant fighting.
Viola - Being in an orchestra, you are just a cog in a wheel, and there's something dehumanizing that sucks out my love for making music.
Violin II - That's something...there's plenty of jobs in companies you'd be in the exact same situation. You're asked to do a task, this is the task, show up to work, and do your job. The nice thing about the orchestra is there's some nice music to play at the same time.
Violin I - Part of the problem is, when music becomes, starts to feel like office work, it becomes upsetting. Sometimes there's friction, but most of the time it's a good bunch of people. If the contractor's careful, he wants a band that plays together, who gets along. At the end of the day, you make some money. It's a simple transaction. A brutal exchange of funds, it's not like a program, that's always the same people. No need to get along, you're playing great music, but often under horrible circumstances.

CONCLUSION

This work demonstrates the vital nature and connection between the aesthetic, clinical and psychodynamic processes in clinical improvisation with musicians. Words have a musical content and music can seamlessly move into the verbal dialogue. AeMT and GAMT move between each other and dance back and forth like poetic communication that is truly representative of our initial vision of combining our two voices in the ensuing work with the quartet. Metaphoric symbolic language was at the heart of this combination of music and words that we describe as the 'meta-musical.'

Every session was a process in itself while also connected to, and a part of, the previous and following improvisations and dialogue. The potency of the process culminated in discussions mostly related to the potential for burnout and conflicts among group members. Conflict and the ability to recognize when this becomes unhealthy, are normal in any family unit.

In the beginning, discussions revolved around exterior concepts, such as risk-taking and the fact that the composer was not present. The difference when working with musicians is that they need to experience skills in risk-taking and recklessness. These experiences could, in turn, influence directly their work on the concert platform. This kind of exterior outcome is specific to work with musicians. Also dealing with the conflicts within the group and their sense of family is crucial for their ongoing process and professional work. Acknowledging burn out and how they can cope with this dynamic is another essential element in working with musicians. This therapeutic fundamental is at the core of how a music-centered psychodynamic process can help professional musicians manage the difficulties they encounter as performers. These issues were explored through the improvisations, which allowed the group to look more closely and deeply at their problems. Playing (AeMT) and interpretation (GAMT) combined to produce a process that allowed them to see and reflect on the group's dynamics and develop new ways of experiencing their roles and performing skills. Transferring these concepts discussed outside the therapy situation enabled them to continue their work as professional musicians as well as explore their individual and collective responses to music.

REFERENCES

Agazarian, Y. & Peters, R. (1981). *The Visible and Invisible Group.* London: Routledge.

Ahonen-Eerikäinen, H. (2007). *Group Analytic Music Therapy.* Gilsum, NH: Barcelona Publishers.

Ashbach, C. & Schermer, V. (1994). *Object Relations, the Self, and the Group: A Conceptual Paradigm.* London: Routledge.
Brandfonbrener, A.G. (1997). Pathogenesis of medical problems of performing artists: general considerations. *Medical Problems of Performing Artists* 12, 45–50.
Brodsky, W. (1996). Music perfomance anxiety reconceptualized: A critique of current research practices and findings. *Medical Problems of Performing Artists,* 11(3), 96–116.
Butler, C.(1995). Investigating the effects of stress on the success and failure of music conservatory students. *Medical problems of Performing Artists,* 10, 24–31.
Dews, C. L. & Williams, M. S. (1989). Student musicians personality styles, stresses, and coping patterns. *Psychology of Music,* 7, 137–47.
Ettin, M. (1999). *Foundations and Applications of Group Psychotherapy.* International Library of Group Analysis, *10.* London: Jessica Kingsley Publishers.
Fetter, D. (1993). Life in the orchestra. *Maryland Medical Journal,* 42 (3), 289–292.
Fishbein, M., Middlestadt, S.E., Ottai, V., Straus, S. & Ellis, A. (1998). Medical problems among ICSOM musicians: Overview of national survey. *Medical Problems of Performing Artists,* 3, 1–8.
Fiumara, R. (1983). Analytical psychology and group analytic psychotherapy: convergences. In M. Pines (Ed.), *The Evolution of Group Analysis* (pp. 109–127). London: Routledge & Kegan Paul.
Foulkes, S. H. (1964). *Therapeutic Group Analysis.* London: George Allen & Unwin.
Gabrielsson, A. (1999). Music performance. In D. Deutch (Ed.)., *The Psychology of Music.* New York: Academic Press.
Giga, S., Faragher, B. & Cooper, C.L. (2002). *Identification of Good Practice in Stress Prevention / Management: a State of the Art Review,* University of Manchester Institute of Science and Technology, Report commissioned by the Health and Safety Executive (HSE).
Hagglund, K. (1996). A comparision of the physical and mental practice of music students in New England Conservatory and Boston

University Music School. *Medical Problems of Performing Artists,* 11, 99–107.

Hamilton, L., Kella, J. & Hamilton, W. (1995). Personality and occupational stress in elite performers. *Medical problems of Performing Artists,* 10, 86–89.

Harper, B.S. (2002). Workplace and health: A survey of classical orchestral musicians in the United Kingdom and Germany. *Medical Problems of Performing Artists,* 4, 83–92.

Jung, C. (1969). *The Archetypes and the Collective Unconscious.* Collected Works, Vol. 9. Princeton, NJ: Princeton University Press.

Kreeger, L. (Ed.) (1975). *The Large Group: Dynamics and Therapy.* London: Constable.

Kutter, P. (1982). *Basic Aspects of Psychoanalytic Group Therapy.* London: Karnac.

Lee, C. A. (2003). *The Architecture of Aesthetic Music Therapy.* Gilsum, NH: Barcelona Publishers.

Lehmann, C., Sloboda, A. & Woody. H. (2007*). Psychology for Musicians: Understanding and Acquiring the Skills.* New York: Oxford University Press.

Montello, L. (2002). *Essential Musical Intelligence: Using Music as Your Path to Healing, Creativity and Radiant Wholeness.* Wheaton, IL: Quest Books.

Panasuraman, S. & Purohit, Y. (2000). Distress and boredom among orchestral musicians: The two faces of stress. *Journal of Occupational Health Psychology,* 5, 74–83.

Pines, M. (1998). The self as a group. The group as a self. In I. N. H. Harwood and M. Pines (Eds.), *Self-Experiences in Group: Intersubjective and Self-Psychological Pathways to Human Understanding* (pp. 24–29). London: Jessica Kingsley Publishers.

Pines, M. (1998). *Circular Reflections. Selected Papers on Group Analysis and Psychoanalysis.* London: Jessica Kingsley Publishers.

Salminen, H. (1997). *Ryhmäanalyysin Perusteet.* Helsinki: SM-julkaisut.

Spahn, C., Strukely, S. & Lehmann, A. (2004). Health conditions, attitudes toward study, and attitudes toward health at the beginning of the university study: Music students in comparision with other

populations. *Medical Problems of Performing Musicians,* 19, 26–33.
Steptoe, A. & Fidler, H. (1987). Stage fright in orchestral musicians. *Psychology of Music,* 17, 3–11.
Thompson, S. (1999). *The Group Context.* London: Jessica Kingsley Publishers.
Whitaker, D. S. & Lieberman, M. A. (1964). *Psychotherapy Through the Group Process.* New York: Atherton Press.
Zinkin, L. (2000). Exchange as a therapeutic factor in group analysis. In D. Brown and L. Zinkin (Eds.), *The Psyche and the Social World* (pp. 99–117). London: Jessica Kingsley Publishers.

APPENDIX 1

Group Analytic Therapy

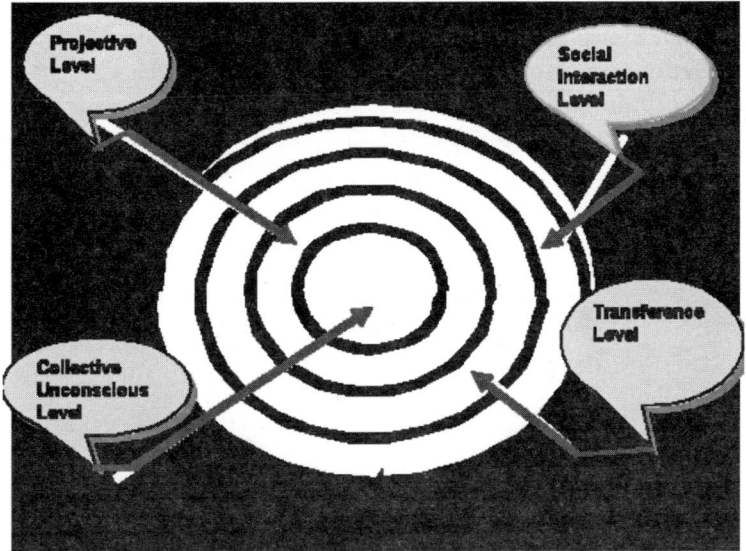

Figure 1: Group Analytic Circle

The above circle (Figure 1) introduces the conscious and unconscious levels of the group matrix (Foulkes, 1964; Fiumara, 1983; Kreeger, 1991; Salminen, 1997; Zinkin, 2000; Ettin, 1999). This conscious or unconscious communication relates to everything that happens in the group. These levels imply that the group can be discussed and understood at different levels of consciousness: both conscious and unconscious. The outer circle is *the conscious level*. It includes *the conscious level of social interactions* (Salminen, 1997; Kutter, 1982, 1983; Foulkes, 1964; Zinkin, 2000). The three inner circles are all *unconscious*. They include the *transference level* (Foulkes, 1964; Kutter, 1992; Salminen, 1997; Fiumara, 1983), the *level of projection* (Fiumara, 1983,; Salminen, 1997; Foulkes, 1964; Fiumara, 1983, 1991; Zinkin, 2000) and the *collective-unconscious level* (Salminen, 1997; Zinkin,

2000; Foulkes, 1964). The levels of the group matrix and levels of consciousness become visible in different musical images and dreams that clients experience during GAMT (Ahonen-Eerikäinen, 2007). Musical images during group matrix levels have certain characteristics. *Figure 2* and *Table 1* illustrate these characteristics in the form of *descriptive categories*.

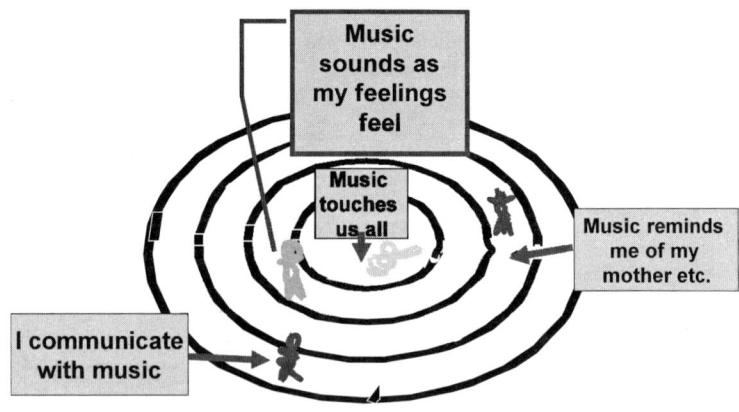

Figure 2: Characteristics of the Musical Images and the Group Matrix

Levels of the Group Matrix (Group-as-a-Whole)			
Conscious Level	Unconscious Levels		
Category I:	Category II:	Category III:	Category IV:
Level of Social Interaction	Level of Transference	Level of Projection	Level of Collective Unconscious

Characteristic of the Musical Image			
"I am able to communicate through music."	"This music reminds me of my mother." "This music sounds like my childhood home."	"This music sounds as my feelings feel." "This music sounds like me." "This music sounds like this group."	"This musical image touches us all."
Music as Transitional Object			
Musical Image as Resistance or Catharsis			
Musical Image as Communication	Musical Image as 1. Transference 2. Trauma re-construction	Musical Image as 1. Projection / Hidden Wish and Fear 2. Container 3. Self-object 4. Self-representation 5. Self-state Image	Musical Image as Transformative Group Image
Externalization–Internalization Process			

Table 1: Characteristics of the Musical Images and the Group Matrix

Chapter Thirty One

MUSIC THERAPY AND DEMENTIA: A COGNITIVE-BEHAVIORAL APPROACH

Melissa Mercadal-Brotons

INTRODUCTION

This chapter describes a music therapy intervention aimed at improving the affective state of Anne, a 68-year-old woman with a diagnosis of Alzheimer's disease. Anne attended a day care center specializing in the treatment of dementias. She participated in a total of 12 weekly group music therapy sessions. The music therapy interventions followed a cognitive-behavioral approach (Wilson, 2000), with session evaluations (sessions 1, 6, and 12) showing an increase in the rate of positive affect over time.

FOUNDATIONAL CONCEPTS

Alzheimer's disease is one of the most common and challenging diseases of our aging population (World Health Organization, 2009). Alzheimer's Disease International (2009) reports that currently there are about 30 million people in the world with dementia, with two thirds of those living in developing countries. This figure is set to increase to more than 100 million people by 2050.

Dementia primarily affects older people. Up to the age of 65, dementia develops in only about one person in 1000. The chance of having the condition rises sharply with age to one person in 20 over the age of 65. Over the age of 80, this figure increases to one person in five (Alzheimer's Disease International, 2009).

Dementia is an umbrella term for several symptoms related to a progressive decline in cognitive abilities (Alzheimer's Association, 2009), including a gradual loss of memory, problems with reasoning or judgment, disorientation, difficulty in learning, loss of language skills, and a decline in the ability to perform routine tasks. In addition, people with dementia experience changes in their personality and behavior. There are several disorders that can cause dementia, the most prevalent being Alzheimer's disease (AD). Other types of dementia include vascular dementia, mixed dementia, dementia with Lewy bodies and frontotemporal dementia (Alzheimer's Association, 2009).

Although the most salient features of dementia are the losses of cognitive abilities, there are important personality and mood changes that are also part of the disease (Hoe et al., 2009). These include physical or verbal outbursts, general emotional distress, restlessness, pacing, shredding paper or tissues, yelling, hallucinations, and delusions (Thompson et al., 2010). These symptoms vary according to the stage and type of dementia. Many individuals diagnosed with dementia find these symptoms to be the most challenging and distressing effects of the disease, since they may reduce the quality of life of the patient and disrupt the home life of family members (Schwab et al., 2009). When behavioral problems become so disruptive that the family member or other community caregiver can no longer care for the patient safely, the patient is likely to be placed in a nursing home.

In spite of the fact that there is still no cure for dementia, drug and non-drug treatments may help with both cognitive and behavioral symptoms (Kaufer, 2002). Drugs are mainly used to ameliorate some of the cognitive, behavioral and psychiatric symptoms of the dementia (Alzheimer's Association, 2009). It is recommended, though, that using a combination of pharmacological and non-pharmacological interventions that address these behavioral and psychiatric symptoms is of greater benefit than drug interventions alone (Schwab et al., 2009).

Over the last 30 years, empirical and clinical efforts to delineate and adequately meet the physical, psychological, and social needs of the elderly have grown considerably (Finnema et al., 2000). This burgeoning in research, along with clinical observation, has led to the belief that music may offer a unique component to the treatment of the elderly with dementia. Furthermore, research suggests that music therapy can be an effective treatment to ameliorate a variety of symptoms manifested in the disease process (Brotons, 2000; O'Connor et al., 2009). As such, music therapy has been an effective intervention to improve anxiety, agitation and restlessness (Gerdener, 1999; Witzke et al., 2008), depression, witdrawal, and disorientation (Ashida, 2000; Choi et al., 2008; Kydd, 2001), rapid mood changes (Götell et al., 2000); short- and long-term memory (Larkin, 2001), and language difficulties (Brotons & Koger, 2000).

Home care seems to be the choice for the majority of people with dementias in Spain, although the use of day care centers is an option that an increasing number of families are choosing (Associació de Familiar d'Alzheimer del Baix Llobregat, 2002). These day care centers face the challenge of offering appropriate programs to stimulate and treat these persons. Cognitive stimulation programs appear to be the one area that receives the highest interest from families, and the one that professionals specialized in geriatric care emphasize in the repertoire of activity programs, especially with patients in mild/moderate stages of the disease (Tárraga, 1998).

Over time, the field of music therapy has adopted different theories and philosophies, which have led to the development of different approaches and models within the profession (Bruscia, 1998). Behavioral Music Therapy is one such approach (Madsen, 1999), based on the principles of operant and classical conditioning developed by B.F. Skinner (Skinner, 1953). As behavioral practices have developed, an emphasis has also been placed on cognition, so that contemporary behavior therapy includes social and cognitive practices (Bandura, 1969). These theories assert "that man is neither internally impelled nor a passive responder to the environment, but a choosing individual engaging in reciprocal interaction with his or her environment. This approach views that behavior depends on three different but interacting regulatory processes that include: (a) external stimulus events, (b) external reinforcement, and (c) cognitive mediational processes. How an individual perceives and interprets events that occur within the environment, therefore, determines behavior" (Standley et al., 2004 p. 104). Thaut (1989) has advocated that traditional cognitive and behavioral therapies could also be complemented by methods that evoke emotions and influence mood states. Thus, within such cognitive-behavioral approaches, the affective and motivational qualities of music perception have been used to modify mood.

Behavioral Music Therapy, and its different approaches, has been applied with a variety of populations in clinical settings. In geriatrics, Ashida (2000), following the cognitive-behavioral paradigm, used music as a behavior activator (Standley et al., 2004) to prompt reminiscence in older people with dementia, demonstrating a reduction in depressive symptoms. As Standley et al. (2004) state, "cognitive-behavioral techniques are elegant solutions, very effective in alleviating the client's distress, and therefore efficient since resolution of the problem occurs in a short period of time" (p. 115). Another characteristic of this particularly well suited to dementia patients is a focus on behavior modification, as these patients no longer have the capacity to comprehend and analyse events using meta-cognition.

Thus, within this approach, techniques are used to promote specific behaviors and structure the environment so that targeted behaviors are evoked and reinforced. As identifed by Standley et al. (2004), the following therapeutic techniques are used in order to accomplish these goals:

1. *Music as a behavioral activator:* Is the use of highly motivating familiar stimuli, in this case music, to activate a client and get him/her involved in an activity.
2. *Prompting:* Is the most basic technique for aiding a client to emit a new response and is simply a cue that increases the probability of a desired response.
3. *Errorless learning:* Is a procedure to establish accurate client responses as rapidly as possible without the appearance of errors.
4. *Successive approximations:* Are behavioral elements or subsets, each of which more and more closely resembles the specified terminal behavior.
5. *Shaping:* Is systematically reinforcing each of those behaviors as they more closely approximate the desired objectives.
6. *Fading:* Is the systematic process of withdrawing cues or prompts so that behavior becomes independent and habitual.
7. *Modeling:* Involves the therapist demonstrating the action to be taught to the client, either alone or simultaneously with the client through mirroring.
8. *Positive reinforcement:* Is the contingent presentation of a stimulus that increases the future probability of the response" (pp. 108–110).

Because music was a highly reinforcing medium for Anne, and the target behaviors very clear and specific, cognitive-behavioral music therapy appeared to be a suitable approach for this client.

THE CLIENT

Anne was a 68-year-old woman with a diagnosis of probable Alzheimer's disease, in the moderate phase (two years of evolution). She had a primary school education and worked as a housewife. At the time of her music therapy, she lived with her children and extended family. Anne's family described a progressive deterioration of her mood state as a result of her husband's death, which was accompanied by complaints about her short term memory. Over time, this had an effect on her activities of daily living (ADL), whereby she required an increasing amount of assistance. Progressively, she also started showing problems with time orientation. However, Anne showed no difficulties with mobility.

Anne was referred by her neurologist to a day care center specializing in dementia patients, which she attended throughout the week. Once at the center, she received a comprehensive assessment by the neuropsychologist who learned, through family interviews, of her enjoyment of music. For this reason she was referred to music therapy and attended a one hour weekly session in a small group of five women. The aims of the weekly music therapy sessions were:

1. To maintain/improve cognitive skills, specifically in the areas of memory, language, praxis and orientation.
2. To improve the patients' mood state by actively engaging them in musical activities.

Assessment

Prior to the commencement of music therapy, Anne underwent a comprehensive series of neuropsychological tests that helped determine her cognitive functioning level. These assessments were completed one week prior to the beginning of the music therapy program (baseline), three times during treatment (at four weeks, eight weeks, and twelve weeks) and once after treatment finished (one month after the end of the intervention). In addition, all music therapy sessions were videotaped for analysis.

In addition, Anne was involved in two group music therapy assessment sessions. In these sessions, group members participated in a variety of musical activities in order for the therapist to observe their responses and preferences for specific music repertoire and activities. Singing, playing musical instruments (mainly percussion instruments), dance-movement activities, music listening, improvisation exercises and musical games were used and tested. Anne participated with encouragement. She was very quiet and would not speak spontaneously to the music therapist or to other members of the group. She would respond to questions appropriately, but needed prompts. However, it was observed that she was particularly active during singing and music activities that involved instrument playing. Improvisation, although only requiring simple responses, seemed more difficult for her to manage, as she showed the tendency to repeat what other members of the group were doing.

THE THERAPEUTIC PROCESS

The therapeutic process included a total of 12 music therapy sessions, each of 45–60 minutes duration. All sessions took place at the same time in the morning in a room familiar to the group members. Sessions were structured in the same way each week, including the following activities, along with the behavioral technique(s) associated with the activity:

The Greeting Song

Sessions always started with an opening song that was used by the therapist to greet each group member, and promote the learning of each other's names. This song involved a number of different steps (successive approximations). The first step involved each member of the group saying their name when it was their turn. Then, each group member would have to guess the name of a specific person from a given list that included three of the names of the participants (prompts). Eventually, they would have to try to remember each other's names without using any prompt (fading). In this activity, group members were required to look at the person whose name they were trying to remember. The music therapist used a high level of positive reinforcement when group members approximated the terminal behaviors: a) remembering some or all of the names of the members of the group (shaping), and b) looking at that person. This opening song would take about 10 minutes, since it was very important that attention was given to each member of the group and that each of them, individually, worked toward the desired goal.

Musical Activities

After the greeting song, group members participated in a variety of music activities based upon their interests and engagement; singing, instrument playing, music listening, musical games, and dance/movement exercises were all used (behavior activator). The order of these activities could change each day according to the activation level of the group at the beginning of the session. However, because of their difficulties with attention and concentration, it was important to introduce experiences that involved active music making. So, even when music listening was used, there was a specific task required in the listening experience. For example, during 'name the tune' group members had to listen for a specific word in the lyrics, name the singer, etc. At any point in the session, especially during listening activities, spontaneous comments made by group members were welcomed and reinforced by the music therapist.

Singing

Singing was included in all the music therapy sessions. The songs that were used were familiar Spanish popular songs from the 1940's and 50's and included boleros, pasadobles and rumbas. The music therapist always used the guitar as an accompanying instrument. As Clair (2000) clearly states, "singing is integral to the life quality of those who are in progressive dementia and their caregivers. It functions to provide islands of arousal, awareness, familiarity, comfort, community and success like nothing else can" (p. 93). Besides being fully engaging and providing a feeling of community, singing "provided experiences of the familiar that occur in a predictable structure provided by the music" (p. 95). In particular, songs were chosen according to the group members' preferences, along with specific topics that were addressed in the sessions: flowers, clothing, Spring, etc.. Thereby, special attention was given to assure that the music used was reinforcing and motivating to the group members so that it functioned as a behavioral activator. The music therapist modeled enthusiasm and engagement during all the sessions, and positive reinforcement was used in high doses to encourage participation and involvement.

Musical Games

In order to provide variety in sessions, musical games were offered as another activity. Familiar games such as bingo, crossword puzzles, and question and answer games presented in a musical context were included in some of the music therapy sessions. These games were created according to the topics and themes of the songs that were used, so that the same concepts were addressed and reinforced through different activities. Games used in sessions were structured so that interaction among the group members was required and reinforced. Besides, games can be a wonderful activity that addresses visual and auditory discrimination skills.

Instrument Playing

Another musical activity included in some of the sessions was instrument playing. Group members used simple percussion instruments to accompany singing, or while music was played in the background These instruments were experienced by group members as safe to play and usually not intimidating. Since these instruments could be played very freely, activities were often highly successful and allowed for errorless learning. This, in turn, motivated group members to try even harder to get involved.

Dance and Movement

Dance-movement activities were also included in sessions. These activities were designed to address some specific gross and fine motor skills such as arms flexion and extension, spatial concepts (up, down, right, left), and leg movements. All these exercises were accompanied by music that had a strong rhythm. The Colonel Bogey March from the movie *The Bridge on the River Kwai*, was one such example.

Closing Activity

Sessions always closed with a goodbye song that cued (prompt) the end of that day's session. Group members were encouraged to freely express how they felt during the session, to comment on some of the activities and music that they particularly enjoyed, and/or to share any thoughts or memories that the music might have evoked.

THE THERAPEUTIC PROCESS

Anne was very shy at the start of music therapy. She would not talk unless specific questions were asked of her, and verbal interactions with the other members of the group only happened when she was spoken to directly. Her answers were usually very soft. She participated in music therapy from the very first session, but only in those activities that she felt most comfortable: singing and playing instruments. However, her participation was very subtle. As her preferred songs were introduced in singing activities, Anne's involvement became more active and continuous. As the sessions progressed, it was observed that Anne's sitting posture was more open and relaxed, perhaps indicating greater comfort and security. When in the opening song, we moved from asking the name of a group member from a list of given names to the open question "What is this person's name?", her spontaneous verbalizations began to occur.

It is also important to mention that from session four onward, once the music therapy sessions finished, the group members remained in the room and continued talking and commenting on some aspects of the session or sharing memories that the music activities had brought up. Anne did not leave. She remained in the room, and became more respondent to others' comments by smiling, making eye contact, even making some comments herself.

Outcomes of Therapy

Although the therapeutic goals addressed both cognitive and affective skills, the results will focus on the affective domain. In order to understand Anne's experience of these music therapy sessions, tallies of Anne's affective behaviors were recorded at sessions 1, 6 and 12. This was done by analyzing videotapes of sessions, and counting the number of positive and negative behaviors. Positive affect was defined as positive verbalizations, spontaneous positive verbal interactions with peers and the music therapist, active participation in the music activities, smiles, and initiation of physical contact. Negative affect was defined as spontaneous negative verbalizations, physical aggression, and leaving sessions. Table 1 illustrates the percentage of Anne's positive affect for each of the three sessions evaluated. As can be observed, the mean rate of positive affect in session one was 32.4, in session six 21.9, and 38.5 in session twelve. Although the improvement was not progressive, there is clearly improvement from session 1 to session 12.

It is important to mention that these improvements seemed to be transferred to other areas and activities of the day care center. According to staff comments, Anne was much more social with the other group members: more talkative, more responsive, and also more participatory in other activities. Although music therapy is one of the therapeutic activities that is offered to the patients, music is also present at other times, specifically background music during occupational therapy or physical therapy. If the music that was played was familiar to Anne, the staff commented that she would join in singing the songs spontaneously. It appears that the function of the music as a behavioral activator not only had its effect in the music therapy sessions, but it also worked in other settings.

Table 1. Affect Mean Rate

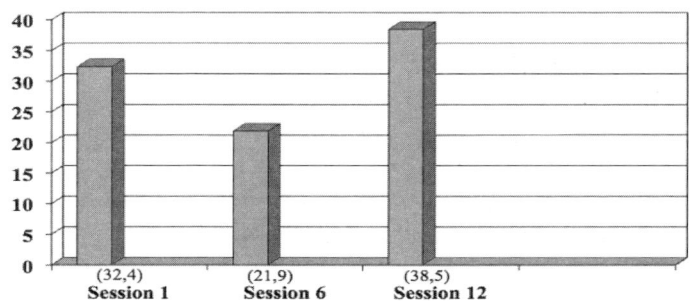

One key element of cognitive-behavioral therapy is a focus on identifying and observing behavioral indicators of cognitive or affective processes. In the case of Anne, it was very important to identify how her lack of positive affect was manifested and observed by the professionals of the center: withdrawal, lack of active participation in therapeutic activities, low rate of spontaneous interactions with peers and staff, and/or a low frequency of smiles. The next step is to operationally define positive affect, the target behavior, in order to be able to observe and document changes that may occur. After this initial phase of assessing and defining the specific behavior, it is important to introduce stimuli and contingencies in the music therapy sessions that will influence the patient into modifying the targeted behavior in the desired direction. The final step of this approach is to evaluate the results.

In this case study, the affective response(s) that we were trying to promote and increase were very specific, and it was very clear that music was highly motivating and reinforcing for Anne. This helped to work toward active engagement. The use of familiar preferred music along with activities that were adapted to Anne's functional level helped assure her success in the music activities, which in turn helped her to open up and to feel more relaxed and secure around others.

Music is an art form that people with dementia, even in advanced phases, continue to respond to and engage in. Music may become a communication channel when those afflicted can no longer use language to communicate. As such, it may be an important medium to relieve frustration, impact mood, and connect with others.

REFERENCES

Alzheimer's Association (2009). In http://www.alz.org. Retrieved April 1st, 2009.

Alzheimer's Disease International. (2009). In http://www.alz.co.uk. Retrieved April 1st, 2009.

Ashida, S. (2000). The effect of reminiscence music therapy sessions on changes in depression symptoms in elderly persons with dementia. *Journal of Music Therapy, 37*(3), 170–182.

Associació de Familiars d' Alzheimer del Baix Llobregat. (2002). *Associació de Familiars d' Alzheimer del Baix Llobregat: El malalt*

d'Alzheimer. http://www.geocities.com/HotSprings/Spat/5647/malaltia.htm.
Bandura, A. (1969). *Principles of Behavior Modification*. San Francisco: Holt, Rinehart and Winston.
Brotons, M. (2000). An overview of the music therapy literature relating to the elderly. In D. Aldridge (Ed.), *Music Therapy in Dementia Care* (pp. 33–62). London: Jessica Kingsley Publishers.
Brotons, M. & Koger, S. M. (2000). The impact of music therapy on language functioning in dementia. *Journal of Music Therapy, 37*(3), 183–195.
Brotons, M. & Pickett-Cooper, P. (1994). Preferences of Alzheimer's Disease patients for music activities: Singing, instruments, dance/movement, and composition/improvisation. *Journal of Music Therapy, 31*(3), 220–233.
Bruscia, K.E. (1998). *Defining Music Therapy* (2nd edition). Gilsum, NH: Barcelona Publishers.
Clair, A. A. (2000). An overview of the music therapy literature relating to the elderly. In D. Aldridge (Ed.), *The Importance of Singing with Elderly Patients* (pp. 81–101). London: Jessica Kingsley Publishers.
Choi, A.N., Lee, M. S. & Lim, H. J. (2008). Effects of group music intervention on depression, anxiety, and relationships in psychiatric patients: A pilot study. *Journal of Alternative and Complementary Medicine, 14*(5), 567–570.
Finnema, E., Droes, R. M., Ribbe, M. & Van Tilburg, W. (2000). The effects of emotion-oriented approaches in the care for persons suffering from dementia: A review of the literature. *International Journal of Geriatric Psychiatry, 15*(2), 141–161.
Gerdener, L. A. (1999). Individualized music intervention protocol. *Journal of Gerontological Nursing*, 25(10), 10–16.
Gotell, E, Brown, S. & Ekman, S. L. (2000). Caregiver-assisted music events in psychogeriatric care. *Journal of Psychiatric Mental Health Nursing, 7*(2), 119–125.
Hoe J., Hancock G., Livingston G., Woods B., Challis D. & Orrell M. (2009). Changes in the quality of life of people with dementia living in care homes. *Alzheimer Disease and Associated Disorders, 23*(3), 285–290.
Isaacs B. & Kenny A.T. (1973): The Set Test as an aid to detection of

dementia in old people. *British Journal of Psychiatry, 123*, 467–470.v

Kaufer, D. (2002). Treatment of neuropsychiatric symptoms in Alzheimer's Disease. *Revista de Neurología, 35*(9), 846–850.

Kydd, P. (2001). Using music therapy to help a client with Alzheimer's Disease adapt to long-term care. *American Journal of Alzheimer's Disease and Other Dementias*, 16(2), 103–108.

Larkin, M. (2001). Music tunes up memory in dementia patients. *Lancet, 357*(9249), 47.

Madsen, C. K. (1999, November). A behavioral approach to music therapy. Founding Model Address to the General Assembly, 9th World Congress of Music Therapy, Washington, DC.

O'Connor, D. W., Ames, D., Gardner, B. & King, M. (2009). Psychosocial treatment of psychological symptoms in dementia: A systematic review of reports meeting quality of standards. *International Psychogeriatrics, 21*(2), 241–251.

Olderog-Millard, K. A. & Smith, J. M. (1989). The influence of group singing on the behavior of Alzheimer's Disease patients. *Journal of Music Therapy, 26*(1), 58–70.

Schwab, W., Messinger-Rapport, B. & Franco, K. (2009). Psychiatric symptoms of dementia: Treatable but not silver bullet. *Cleveland Clinic Journal of Medicine, 76*(3), 167–174.

Scruggs, S. (1991). The effects of structured music activities versus contingent music listening with verbal prompt on wandering behavior and cognition in geriatric patients with Alzheimer's disease. Unpublished Master's thesis, Florida State University, Tallahassee.

Skinner, B. F. (1953). *Science and Human Behavior.* New York: Macmillan.

Standley, J. M., Johnson, C. M., Robb, S. L., Brownell,, M. D. & Kim, S. (2004). Behavioral approach to music therapy. In A. Darrow (Ed.), *Introduction to Approaches in Music Therapy* (pp. 103–124). Silver Spring, MD: The American Music Therapy Association, Inc.

Tàrraga, L. (1998). Terapias blandas: Programa de psicoestimulación integral. Alternativa terapéutica par alas personas con enfermedad de Alzheimer. *Revista de Neurología, 27*(1), 51–62.

Terri, L. (1994). Behavioral treatment of depression in patients with dementia. *Alzheimer's Disease and Associated Disorders, 8*, 66–74.
Thaut, M. H. (1989). Music therapy, affect modification, and therapeutic change: Towards an integrative model. *Music Therapy Perspectives, 7*, 55–62.
Thompson C., Brodaty H., Trollor J. & Sachdev P. (2010). Behavioral and psychological symptoms associated with dementia subtype and severity. *International Psychogeriatrics, 22*(2), 300–305.
Vink, A. C., Birks, J. S., Bruinsma, M. S. & Scholten, R. J. (2006). *Music therapy for people with dementia.* Cochrane Database of Systematic Reviews. Issue 3. Art. No.: CD003477. DOI: 10.1002/14651858.CD003477.pub2.
Ward, R. A. (1979). The meaning of voluntary association participation to older people. *Journal of Gerontology, 34*(3), 438–445.
Wilson, G. T. (2000). Behavior therapy. In R. Corsini and D. Wedcding (Eds.), *Current psychotherapies* (6th ed.) (pp. 205–240). Itasca, IL: F. R. Peacock.
Witzke, J., Rhone, R. A., Backhaus, D. & Shaver, N. A. (2008). How sweet the sound: Research evidence for the use of music in Alzheimer's dementia. *Journal of Gerontological Nursing, 34*(10), 45–52.
World Health Organization. (2009). Aging. In http://www.who.int/tpics/age-ing/en/. Retrieved on April 1, 2009.

Chapter Thirty Two

MUSIC AS LIFE AND LIFEGUARD: MUSIC THERAPY FOR AN OLDER ADULT WITH DEPRESSION

Ineke van Hest-de Witte, Jack Verburgt and Henk Smeijsters

INTRODUCTION

This chapter describes the case of Peter, a 60-year-old client who withdrew from life and became apathetic, anxious and depressed after his wife died. At the start of improvisational music therapy, his music sounded powerless and withdrawn. As therapy progressed, he began bringing in and sharing his music collection with other group members. This gave him the opportunity to tell others about his musical taste, which was very important to him. This also changed his musical playing, which became more dynamic and improvised as he regained energy and strength through his improvisations. In these ways, another Peter sounded himself in music.

Peter stayed with us for seven months. During music therapy sessions, it became apparent that a major cause of his depression was a grieving process that had become blocked. Peter could not deal with the loss of his wife, who had passed away a year earlier. He attended part-time treatment (three days a week) at a psychiatric clinic in Arnhem,[1] participating in group therapy intended to provide insight. Music therapy was an important part of this treatment, and his underlying issues quickly became audible and visible.

Within this context, Peter's therapy is interpreted by means of the theory of analogy (Smeijsters, 2005), which examines the relationship

---

[1] The Netherlands

between the client's music, be it composed or improvised, and his/her core self.

FOUNDATIONAL CONCEPTS

Analogy and Depression

The people in our treatment program are elderly (55 years and older) men and women with depressive symptoms related to experiences of loss, trauma and life-stage oriented problems. Many of our clients have recently stopped working. This has significant consequences, both for the individual concerned and for his/her partner. Together, they need to find new ways of "filling in the day" in order to give their lives a sense of purpose. Furthermore, our clients increasingly face the loss of social contacts, as many of their elderly friends become incapacitated or die. It is precisely this social interaction with group members who experience similar problems that can prove to be an invaluable source of support. A social network can be extremely supportive and powerful. It provides a sense of identity, empathy, solidarity and a solid basis for sharing experiences.

In the Netherlands, music therapists are rooted in the basic principles of the Dutch creative arts therapies, which are experiential and active. This means that the core of the music therapy session involves the client improvising in more or less structured ways. During a client's playing, we often hear not only his/her depressive features, but also the way in which he/she maintains the depression. The fact that Peter was depressed and extremely sad became apparent not only in his attitude and what he said; but the other group members could hear it in his playing, which made a deep impression on them.

In order to expand upon this orientation and directly address the experiences of depressed clients, Smeijsters has incorporated the concept of *analogy* into clinical practice (Smeijsters, 2005, 2006, 2008). This theory is based on the psychological and neuropsychological research of Stern (2000, 2004, 2010) and Damasio (1999). The theory of analogy describes receptive (primarily music listening and discussion) and active (primarily improvisation) music therapy by means of *vitality affects* in the core self (Stern, 2000). Vitality affects are those processes that evolve within our psyche that tell us how we experience our environment. These processes have been described by Stern (Stern, 2000) as musical phrases. As such, he suggests our psychological processes sound like music. Vitality affects are part of the *core self* that, as described by Damasio (Damasio, 1999), evokes non-cognitive, intuitive and felt forms of knowledge. Smeijsters (Smeijsters, 2005, 2006, 2008) developed these concepts, describing analogy as the felt, non-cognitive correspondence between the person's "inner musical phrases" and the musical phrases s/he hears in the music s/he wants to listen to or improvise. Music therefore makes it possible to express ourselves in a way that is very close to what we are really feeling about our environment and ourselves. Instead of describing our inner world with words and figures that are distanced from the processes we are experiencing, the musical sounds are a mirror of our core self-experiences. Within the theory of analogy, the therapeutic process is understood as a process that unfolds in music itself, and it is during this musical process that the vitality affects of the core self can be expressed, explored and changed.

Before this process is translated into words and cognitions, experience comes to sound in the music. It is not always necessary to translate these experiences into words and cognitions because an experience within the core self is "felt knowledge" that is incorporated into the psyche. But a translation into words and cognitions can help the client to make sense of these experiences in a more or less cognitive way. In the Netherlands, therefore, many music therapists also incorporate techniques of *cognitive therapy* or *insight oriented therapies* (Smeijsters, 2006). These techniques are used afterward, when the music has ended and reflection on the music experience takes place.

Although analogy focuses on the match between the musical forms and core self-experiences, it is also possible that the music can evoke *associations* and *memories* because it is sounded in a specific phase of life or context. In that case, for instance, the music reminds a person of what happened in that time period, and therapy evolves from that association.

With depressed clients, the goals of therapy are therefore twofold. First, it is important that the feelings of depression can become expressed in the music in an analogous way. In *receptive* music therapy, composed music (e.g., songs) is used to encompass musical forms that are analogous to what the client is feeling. In *active* music therapy (e.g., improvisation), the client himself plays the vitality affects of his core self and is supported by the music therapist to explore musical forms that can put his vitality affects into sound. By doing this, inner feelings that have not been well articulated can be evoked more deeply in the musical form of the improvisation. The second goal focuses on exploring positive feelings by means of composed or improvised musical forms that are analogous to these positive vitality affects.

THE CLIENTS

Group Interaction as a Representation of Analogy

Let us start by giving a brief sketch of the nature of the therapy group in which Peter became a member. When Peter's treatment started, the group had already existed for a considerable time. Peter was fortunate to join a group in which the prevailing climate was one of respect, tolerance and warmth. The group consisted of six people who met three times a week for a course of intensive treatment. The program comprised a number of different types of therapy: psycho-education, psychomotor therapy, group conversations and music therapy.

In music therapy, the focus of treatment was on the interactions within the group. That was how the client's issues became visible and audible. At the same time, the group members could also experience how they could break through their isolation and express their sorrow and pent-up feelings. In this way, analogy worked two ways. On the one hand, the depression became audible and understandable within the group interaction; on the other, the healing moments within the group acted as a sounding board for what could take place outside therapy in daily life.

Assessment Process

After a client is referred to the center, an extensive intake consultation is arranged with a psychologist or psychiatrist. During this consultation, the client's exact needs and requirements are assessed and contextualized with the client. For many clients, a series of one-to-one consultations may suffice; for others, a mixture of treatment programs may be more appropriate. Within the multi-disciplinary team, a treatment program is formulated. If the team considers that a client can benefit from insight-oriented therapy, with a focus on experiential work, the client is eligible for the treatment milieu that includes music therapy.

THE THERAPEUTIC PROCESS

It is half past two in the afternoon. The group should be arriving any moment now. It is a small group of clients, many of whom are learning to cope with grief, loss and sadness. It is an open group: every few weeks, we bid farewell to a client or welcome a new member to the group. Today, we are welcoming Peter.

A well-built man walks into the room. He keeps his eyes cast down. He extends a friendly hand. I see that he is struggling to smile. I immediately sense that I should not approach him too directly, that I should give him the time to settle into the group.

Once the group has sat down in a circle, the "moment of truth" arrives. I ask Peter to tell the group something about himself in relation to music. Casting his gaze downward (so that we can't see that he is blushing), Peter explains, in short sentences, that he loves music, but that he hasn't been able to find the inner peace he needs to enjoy music. So much has happened in his life. As he continues, we can hear that the problems Peter is experiencing are also the problems of the other group members. His story makes a huge impact. So much misery, so much sadness.

In retrospect, it was apparent that both the group members and I were intuitively inclined to treat Peter carefully, even though lots of emotions were evoked. We avoided asking too many questions. We avoided confrontation. We were conscious of his endearing shyness and did not wish to harm him, or cause him even more pain. His shyness and awkwardness also manifested themselves in his musical performances. He gently played the xylophone with his face close to the instrument, without any dynamic action. He seemed unwilling or unable to break momentary silences. Gradually, his most apparent character traits became the central theme of his music therapy treatment: "Why are you so terribly shy? Why do you appear so vulnerable? And, why do we approach you so carefully?"

Acceptance

Peter's story is heart-breaking. He was diagnosed with autism at an early age. He married later in life. His wife recently passed away after a serious illness. He lovingly cared for her for many months until she died at home. He also worried greatly about his family and how to manage without his wife. He had four children, two of secondary school age and two of primary school age. During the same period, the situation for two of his children began to deteriorate. One of the children was referred to a psychiatric clinic; the other was placed in foster care. After his wife's death, Peter found it increasingly difficult to cope with all these stressors. He was unable to manage the housework. He became increasingly withdrawn and apathetic, despite the help of family and neighbors. It was then that he was referred to our group music therapy program.

Although Peter was shy, withdrawn and anxious, he was nevertheless able to tell his story, albeit hesitantly, to the group. The group showed great understanding and acceptance of his socially withdrawn and introspective demeanour. For Peter, it was extremely important that the group acknowledged and accepted his sense of loss and desperation. But, he was (as yet) unable to express this sense of loss adequately. This, too, was accepted by the group.

Peter's improvisations during this period were sluggish and feeble. He played the xylophone, a conga drum or small rhythm instruments. He only gave a tap now and again, and his playing was without any melody or structure. He had no musical contact with the group. The group responded by also playing very softly. Everyone automatically adapted their playing to his. Gradually, Peter let the group hear more of himself, although they continued adapting their playing to his. In this way, Peter gained a place in the group. Parallel with his musical presence, he also developed his verbal presence, starting to talk more and take more initiative. He also began to take up more space in a literal sense by standing up straight rather than sitting all hunched over.

Coming out of his Shell

Although sessions included improvisations, the group also spent a lot of time listening to music, and it was through these music listening experiences that Peter was able to work through his problems. Group members brought along music that held a special place in their hearts, and a great deal of respect was shown for each other's musical tastes. Interestingly, Peter began to show a genuine interest in the musical selections of the other clients. Their musical tastes appeared to have given him a new lease on life. He also began to show his impressive knowledge of the music played by others in the group. In a similar vein, he talked enthusiastically about his own music collection. When the name Ennio Morricone[2] was mentioned, he came alive. He promised to bring along some music to the next session and talk about it. This turned out to be the beginning of a spontaneous and educational journey into the history of music.

As he became more comfortable, Peter took it upon himself to share his extensive knowledge and passion for music with the group, using a variety of themes. One theme he chose was "folksy fragments." He painstakingly prepared his presentation, writing everything down neatly, complete with suitable examples. He talked animatedly about the music he chose. He was clearly highly knowledgeable about music. Everyone was astounded. He had become a different person — someone who dared to make eye contact, smile and move effortlessly during his presentation. He enjoyed the music and loved talking about it, not because of the attention he received, but because of his passion for music. Sensing this change in his personality, the group gradually approached him less cautiously. Under the guise of "music," other group members felt able to say more, such as asking him to speak a little louder and clearer. We gradually noticed not only a change in Peter's mannerisms and speech patterns, but also in his musical performances. He was more dynamic, more daring — even daring to improvise and laugh at himself when he "hit the wrong note."

In the months that followed, he gave other presentations on themes such as *light*, *water* and *the mystery of religion*. He conscientiously prepared his presentations, but never spontaneously.

---

[2] Italian composer, well known for his film score music (e.g., "The Mission")

Blossoming

Initially, the focus of the group's attention was on Peter's taste in, and his knowledge of, music. He enthusiastically delved into his musical archive, which had remained unopened since his wife's death. His interest in and love of music had been rekindled. Gradually, the group started to focus more time and attention on different ways of listening. The group discussed "technical listening," which was Peter's preferred method when he first joined the group. He would make comments such as: "In this passage, the theme is repeated and the second violin joins in." The group also spent time in "associative listening." Here, the music evoked thoughts and images. A third concept, "emotional listening," was also discussed: What did the music "do" to an individual? What emotions and feelings did it convey? These discussions evoked a lot of emotion in Peter. Music had always played an important part in his life, and now, gradually, he began to change the way he listened. Whereas initially he concentrated on technical and aesthetic terms, he slowly began to connect music with his own emotions.

For instance, after listening to a piece of music for a brass ensemble brought along by another member, Peter played a recording of a fanfare used at his mother's funeral. While listening to this piece, he was finally able to be emotional and to show his emotions. On another occasion, he introduced the group to a piece of music that he and his wife frequently listened to during the last weeks of her life. The tears rolled freely down his cheeks. This was a touching moment for the group and for myself. I was deeply moved, yet I also sensed that we were able to support him in this moment. He readily accepted this support.

Bidding Farewell

Little by little, Peter managed to pick up the threads of his life again. He was extremely concerned about the well-being of his children. Fortunately, with the support of people in his community, he managed to cope. Within the group therapy setting, he had undergone a veritable metamorphosis. While he had not become a gregarious or extroverted man, he had certainly made his presence felt. He was not afraid to make eye contact, and he radiated confidence. He purchased a new computer and a new sound system, and continued working with his musical archive. He even drew my attention to several beautiful and unfamiliar pieces by Brahms.

As a farewell gift, Peter surprised us all with a musical lecture on "farewells," covering the gamut of classical, religious and popular music. His musical choices, with accompanying narrative, are included below:

Peter's "Farewell" Musical Lecture

A) Joseph Haydn: *Finale from (Farewell) Symphony 45* (length: 5.00)
Papa Haydn (1732-1809) served the Esterhazy Court in Eisenstadt, Germany. He composed the Farewell Symphony as a subtle protest to his employer for his gruelling touring schedule. During the last movement, one musician after the other snuffs out a candle and leaves the stage. The music dies.

B) Terry Qilkyson: *Memories are made of this* (length: 2.00)
This song became a huge hit for Dean Martin (1917–1995) in 1956. Dean Martin is one of many Italian-American artists (Perry Como, El Martino, Frank Sinatra). Also a famous movie and TV star, such as 'The Dean Martin Show.' One of his sons was killed in a plane crash in 1987.

C) John Dowland: *Now, oh now I needs must part* (length: 4.00)
The English composer Dowland (1563–1626) wrote a lot of music and songs for the lute. He spent much of his life travelling in mainland Europe. His works portray a particular type of melancholy. He called his instrumental pieces 'lachrimae,' meaning tears. This particular rendition is performed by the Anglo-German tenor Rufus Muller, best known for his performances in Messiah and St. Matthew Passion.

D) Skeeter Davis: *The end of the world* (length: 2.35)
Skeeter Davis was born in Kentucky and lived from 1931 to 2004. He was particularly known for her country and western music, but he also composed many songs. He died of lung cancer in 2004.

Don't they know it's the end of the world
Cause you don't love me anymore.

E) Johannes Brahms: *Farewell piece* (length: 3.30)
A somewhat stern character, Brahms was born in Hamburg. He lived from 1833 to 1897. Brahms was linked with Bach and Beethoven as one of the famous "3 Bs" of classical music. He had a platonic relationship with Clara Schumann for many years. Most famous for his symphonies and requiem. Many songs. The Farewell is one of 14 German folk songs:

Ich fahr dahin weil es muss sein	*I go away because it has to be*
Ich scheid mich von der Liebsten mein	*I separate from the dearest of me*
So lang ich lebe, bleib ich dein	*As long as I live, I will be yours*
Leb wohl, adieu, du Liebste mein.	*Farewell, adieu, you dearest of me.*

F) McGear: *Thank you very much* (length: 2.30)
Comedy, poetry and music trio The Scaffold, which included Paul McCartney's brother. The Scaffold are best known for their chart hit *Lily the Pink*. The song is dedicated to anything and everything: *Thank you for the birds and the bees, the family circle, love, being fat, Union Jack, nursery rhymes, Sunday times, for playing this record.*

G) Charles d'Helfer: *Introitus: Requiem* (length: 3.30)
D'Helfer is a French composer who lived in the first half of the seventeenth century. This is a reconstruction of his Requiem for the two Dukes of Lorraine. This piece comprises a composition by d'Helfer, supplemented with compositions by four other composers, including Sweelinck.

H) Wanda Jackson: *Let's have a party* (length: 2.00)
Wanda Jackson was born near Oklahoma City in 1937. She started her singing career in a church choir, before embarking on the rockabilly tour: country rock and roll. In the 1970s, she turned her attentions to more religious music. This is a sing-along song, suitable for a farewell party.

The group was very impressed by Peter's "musical lecture." Equally important, he could see in himself that his presentation expressed a certain strength and quality. He also found that he had regained his love of music and thus the strength to be part of life again. Peter's work in music therapy showed him that music could help him survive. It touched the core of his being and enabled him to find direction and meaning to his life once again. Music was "the means" in the therapy. Fittingly for Peter, it was once more an essential part of his life.

SUMMARY

Peter's work in music therapy showed how listening to and talking with others about the music that was important to him made it possible for him to regain his strength. When Peter began therapy, his music sounded weak, an expression of the inner struggles. Listening to and playing music thawed his apathy, shyness, anxiety and lack of energy. The musical pieces that were closely linked to special life events made it possible for him to feel again; not only to feel his grief, but also to feel the power to take up life again.

Active Music Therapy

When Peter began music therapy, the focus of sessions was on improvisation. As he played, we could clearly see how his music showed his shyness, hesitancy and underlying depression. He played very softly on the xylophone, without any dynamic variation. Further, he did not dare to break through silence with his sound. In the theory of *analogy,* one of the central concepts is that the client sounds himself in the music. This means that his inner forms of feelings, his *vitality affects*, are expressed in musical forms that have the same temporal contour as these inner vitality affects. This all happens in the *present moment*, as described by Stern (2004), in which the felt experience, without any distanced verbalization, is directly sounded in musical form. In Peter's case, the music sounded his depression in a very direct way.

Because of the combination of autism, the death of his wife, and problems with his children, it seemed clear that Peter had lost control of his life and therefore withdrew, becoming apathetic and anxious. The inner feeling of losing energy and strength were heard in his music in an analogous way. Peter sounded his apathy, withdrawal and anxiousness in all he played.

Receptive Music Therapy

The key to working through these problems lay in his enormous music collection. When other clients started to talk about the music they loved, Peter felt invited to do the same. His deep and enduring relationship with music allowed him to structure his musical expression, and in so doing to open up to his emotional world. Peter became very active in preparing and presenting his musical lectures, talked with more animation, made eye contact, laughed and moved freely.

As therapy unfolded, Peter began to share music that had deep emotional meaning: music associated with special events like the death of his mother and the final weeks of his wife's life. This allowed *associations* between the music and the event to develop. While listening in the present to music that sounded in the past, *memories* of the event were evoked, and by means of these memories, corresponding emotions were evoked and felt once more. However, music was more than a "cue" that triggered memories of the event. Unlike a cue, musical forms encompass temporal contours of feelings and therefore directly evoke the *vitality affects* of feelings. When listening to the music, Peter could remember the event while *at the same time* feeling the vitality affects the music was expressing.

For Peter, merely talking about the event would have been very different. This would have afforded an opportunity to re-live the event and experience related emotions. But listening to the music that sounded during the event offered the same musical forms and corresponding vitality affects. The music was able to give him the feeling he had then in the *present moment*, without any cognitive act of association. Once your feeling is back, and you recognize that you are able to feel, you can begin to work through these feelings. Feeling "in the present" allowed him to be a feeling person in the future, knowing that life could go on.

Although we can "know" and "tell" a lot about music (e.g., the composer and the performing musician), the essence of the musical experience is a process that evolves *beneath* this knowing and verbalizing. Musical forms evoke forms of feeling in a very direct way. Music is a felt, intuitive, conscious but non-cognitive way of being, processed in the *core self*. Experienced this way, music is able to do the therapeutic work without cognitive knowing and verbalization. Music is able to give life, energy and strength back.

REFERENCES

Damasio, A. (1999). *The Feeling of What Happens. Body and Emotion in the Making of Consciousness.* New York: Harcourt.

Hest-de Witte, I. van & Verburgt, J. (2008). Over leven en overleven met muziek [About living and surviving with music]. In H. Smeijsters (Ed.), *De Kunsten van Het Leven.* [The Arts of Life]. Part 2. Diemen: Veen Magazines.

Smeijsters, H. (2008). *De Kunsten van Het Leven* [The Arts of Life]. Part 1 and Part 2. Diemen: Veen Magazines.

Smeijsters, H. (2005). *Sounding the Self. Analogy in Improvisational Music Therapy.* Gilsum, NH: Barcelona Publishers.

Smeijsters, H. (Ed.) (2006). *Handboek Muziektherapie. Evidence based practice voor de behandeling van psychische stoornissen, problemen en beperkingen.* [Music Therapy Handbook. Evidence-based Practice for the Treatment of Psychic Disturbances, Problems and Limitations]. Houten: Bohn Stafleu Van Loghum.

Stern, D.N. (1995). *The Motherhood Constellation: A Unified View of Parent-Infant Therapy.* New York: Basic Books.

Stern, D.N. (2000). *The Interpersonal World of the Infant. A View from Psychoanalysis and Developmental Psychology.* New York: Basic Books.

Stern, D. (2004). *The Present Moment in Psychotherapy and Everyday Life.* New York: W.W. Norton.

Stern, D.N. (2010). *Forms of Vitality. Exploring Dynamic Experience in Psychology, the Arts, Psychotherapy, and Development.* Oxford: Oxford University Press.

Chapter Thirty Three

HOME IS WHERE THE HEART IS

Monique van Bruggen-Rufi and Annemieke Vink

INTRODUCTION

With an increase in age expectancy worldwide, dementia and other age-related illnesses are increasing in prevalence (Ferri et al, 2005). Recent estimates have suggested that over 24 million people are currently suffering from dementia worldwide, with an expected increase of 4.6 million new patients every year (WHO, 2008). In each nursing home population, an increasing number of these residents are migrants, bringing their own customs, language and music. More than ever before, people are migrating to new countries, in search of a better life. Some move by choice, but many are required to because of conflicts that force displacement (e.g., war, genocide, etc.) (U.N., 1999; 2009).

The current situation of worldwide migration has raised new demands for the care of the elderly with dementia. This has presented many care challenges, not the least being how to address their needs in music therapy. It is not unusual that bilingual residents, having developed dementia, will begin reverting back to their first language, and may even lose their "adopted" language altogether. In so doing, they may become unable to understand their own children's language, or share the language of their caretakers. As such, they can become "lost inhabitants" in nursing homes, isolated culturally and linguistically.

Music therapy is seen as one of the few approaches able to reach these clients. Singing songs of the native country and improvising on known rhythms provides a context of safety and recognition through the musical language of the clients childhood culture.

This case study will describe the experiences of Vonnie, who was born in the Dutch East Indies[1] (now Indonesia), but spent her adult life in the Netherlands. Her story resembles that of many elderly people with dementia currently living in their new, non-native country.

FOUNDATIONAL CONCEPTS

Culturally Centered Music Therapy

Music therapy has a strong positive effect on elderly people with dementia (Brotons, 2000; Vink 2000). Music therapy can decrease agitation and has a positive effect on enhancing communication and emotional well-being (Brotons, 2000; Vink, 2000). Music therapy enables the recall of life experiences and the experience of pleasant emotions. Through music, contact can be established, especially as language deteriorates during the latter stages of the dementing process. Music serves as a powerful catalyst for reminiscence, both joyful and sad (Bright, 1982). Many important life events are accompanied by music. Most of the time, these "musical memories" are stored for a longer time than the ones from the same period that were not accompanied by music (Broersen et al., 1995). If words are not recognized any longer, familiar music may provide a sense of safety and well-being, which in turn may decrease anxiety (Brotons, 2000). By making use of this quality of music to directly appeal to memories and feelings, it may be possible for an individual with dementia to come into contact once more with "lost" elements of his/her identity. For these elderly people, who are slowly losing their identities, this is very important. By offering music from the client's cultural heritage, the therapist recognizes and acknowledges the problems that the person has dealt with. In this way, the client may experience acceptance, and relevant aspects of his/her identity may be validated.

A culture-centered music therapy practice asks for a dedication and willingness to explore alternative musical forms in order to contact the

---

[1] The country was called "Dutch Indie" while it was still a Dutch colony. The inhabitants were called "Indische people" or "Indo" for short, mostly referring to a native mother and a European/Dutch father. After its independence in 1949, the country was called Indonesia. All the people who decided to stay in Indonesia were called Indonesians; the people who moved to the Netherlands were referred to as "Indische" people.

inner world of the client. For the music therapist who works with clients from different ethnic and cultural backgrounds, this means that he/she might have to readjust his/her own musical knowledge and abilities. It requires great awareness and knowledge of the role that music plays in both the personal life and culture of a client (Ruud, 1998).

If the music therapist knows the traditional songs of a given culture, the meaning of the lyrics, and is able to play them for the client, the client feels accepted and understood. Gerdner (1997, 2000) describes this need to individualize music for elderly patients with dementia, in which the music functions as a bridge between the past and the present.

Identity and Individual Repertoire

Within this larger cultural context, the client's musical preferences are like a mirror — a representation of the client. They fit the client like a "tailor-made suit" (Poismans, 2005), so that by recognizing the client's music, you recognize his/her identity. This is especially so when working with elderly migrants, war victims, refugees and asylum seekers. All these clients have one very important thing in common: they are all "rootless," in search of their identities.

Music thereby serves as a strong catalyst for reminiscing and life-review. In order to gain positive effect, the music offered to the clients will have to be individualized (Gerdner, 1997) and have specific meaning in the life of a person. Most elderly from the former Dutch East Indies have been raised with traditional Indonesian music. By offering this music, their long-term memories can be stimulated and clients can relive their childhood or adolescence in a safe way. The music needs to be carefully selected by the music therapist as it can also be associated with negative feelings, which may lead to the reliving of traumatic experiences.

For example, a music therapist once played an ethnic song for a client from an African country. He thought he had selected a very appropriate song, one that sounded very pleasant, with rich and vivid harmonies. However, he did not know that this was a song that was often used during mourning ceremonies, especially funerals. So, instead of offering his client a joyful song, the woman became very upset. The music therapist lacked cultural sensitivity by offering music that didn't fit the therapy situation.

In the case study that follows, the music therapist (the first author) drew of her knowledge and experiences of Indonesian cultural life. Born of Indonesian parents in the Netherlands, she had first-hand experience of the music, instruments and cultural traditions of the Indonesian people. Using this knowledge as a starting point, she was able to meet Vonnie within her own cultural life, acting as a bridge between her "old life" and her life in the Netherlands.

THE CLIENT

Vonnie's Cultural Background

Vonnie was an 83-year-old woman who was in the early phases of dementia (probable Alzheimer's type). She was born in the former Dutch East Indies. During the Second World War, the Indies was occupied by the Japanese (from 1942 to 1945). Japan's strategy was to liberate Indonesia from all western influences and encourage the Indonesian people to sell or destroy their Dutch belongings. After the defeat of the Japanese, Indonesian nationalists, under the leadership of Sukarno and Hatta, sought independence from their colonial administrators and declared the existence of the Republic of Indonesia. What followed was a confusing time period known as the Bersiap, in which Indonesians fought for independence from the Netherlands. For thousands of Indonesian-Dutch people, this was the beginning of a life-threatening time period. During the first year of the independence struggle, approximately 3,500 Dutch and Indonesian-Dutch lost their lives fighting against, or fleeing from, the Indonesian nationalists.

During this period of upheaval, some 300,000 men, women and children of Dutch nationality had to decide whether to become Indonesian citizens or remain Dutch nationals and travel to the Netherlands. For many Dutch citizens who were of Indonesian origin, this was a heart wrenching decision: whether to stay in Indonesia and risk their safety and financial security, or travel to a small, unknown country in Europe. For those who decided to leave, travel was long and costly, with the ever present possibility of never being able to return "home" again.

Right from the beginning, these Dutch-Indonesians did not feel welcomed when they arrived in the Netherlands. The Dutch authorities didn't know how to properly advise them on how to find adequate housing, as they had never experienced such a large migration. The Dutch people did not know anything about the cultural and historical background of these "foreigners," and were also suffering from their own traumas related to World War II, which had only just ended. These new migrants felt abandoned and isolated. They had come with insufficient clothing to manage the cold Dutch winter and lacked financial resources and adequate housing to start their new lives.

This, in short, was the historic context in which Vonnie moved to the Netherlands with her husband. Although she was then 30 years of age, she had never travelled more than a few miles outside her home village in Indonesia. Although they had no children of their own, they adopted a child of five who had lost his parents in Indonesia. They arrived together in the Netherlands, bewildered, alone and with little government support to begin rebuilding their lives.

Vonnie

When Vonnie began music therapy, she had already been widowed ten years. Her son still lived close by, but did not visit his mother on a regular basis. This caused Vonnie great grief. In recent years, Vonnie had become more and more disoriented and demonstrated symptoms of a severe cognitive disorder, which finally led to nursing home placement. After psychological evaluation, it was found that Vonnie was in the early stages of dementia. She also suffered from symptoms of depression, confusion, social isolation, hoarding behavior and delusional paranoia.

Vonnie's caregivers noticed that she tended to isolate herself on the ward, being the only person of Indonesian origin. They also felt that she tended to isolate herself because she didn't trust the people around her. She was convinced that everybody was after her belongings. She was often awake at night, suffering from confusion and anxiety. Nobody understood her Indonesian dialect, further compounding the problems she was experiencing as her dementia progressed.

THE THERAPEUTIC PROCESS

The first time that I met Vonnie she was sitting in a group with other residents in an activity room. She was sitting at the far side of the table, not participating in a conversation or engaging in any way with the others in the room. I could see that she was busy coloring a big bird. She used bright colors and was very focused. I decided to sit next to her and, without introducing myself, started to sing. I sang an old children's song from Indonesia, a song that I was almost certain she would know. The song was about a big bird, a Kakatoe, similar to the bird she was coloring. When she heard me sing the words, in her own language, she straightened her back and looked at me with a big smile on her face. She was surprised to hear a song from her past. She had never seen me before, but by singing this song, I found a way of connecting with her immediately. The song seemed to give her energy and joy.

Immediately following this, I told Vonnie who I was and I asked her to come with me. She stood up, and we walked to the music room. Once again, I told her who I was and what I do, as repetition was very important for her, especially in music. I started singing the same song again and she showed the same recognition. It was as if she felt safe right away, even though the room was foreign to her. I told her that I was from Indonesia myself, or at least my parents were, and that I would do my best to talk in her own language. She was thrilled, so much so that she started crying. Just hearing these familiar sounds again made her very happy. It had been such a long time since she last heard her native language and songs from her own cultural heritage that I could tell she trusted me right away.

In the music room, I re-created an atmosphere to remind Vonnie of Indonesia. Soft Indonesian music played on the stereo, Indonesian memorabilia lay on a table and a wide variety of Indonesian instruments were also available (bamboo percussion instruments, a bamboo flute and a ukulele). I even burned an incense stick with the scent of an Indonesian flower. By offering her authentic sounds and instruments, Vonnie was surrounded by experiences that came very close to her inner feelings. These specific sounds and visual cues made the reminiscing process easier for her.

Vonnie told me that nobody in the residence seemed to understand her or listen to her. I asked her if she knew why. She told me that she felt like "a nobody" because of her background — being "a brownie." She also told me that it was alright with her anyway because everybody was after her belongings. By recognizing and offering her music from her cultural heritage, I was able to confirm Vonnie's identity. This was especially important to her because she felt isolated culturally and was feeling the losses associated with the advancement of her dementia.

When we started to talk about her youth in Indonesia, Vonnie's eyes began to sparkle, as if this was one of the first times anyone had asked her about it. She began telling stories about her youth, and I was able to tell her that my parents were also from Indonesia, so that I had some understanding of her experiences and struggles.

When I started to play the ukulele, Vonnie began to cry again. After the song, I asked her what associations she had while listening to the music. She told me that the sounds reminded her of her mother and her youth in Indonesia. I let her talk, listening carefully, without interrupting her once. When she started talking about how she lived by a river, I started singing a song about a river back in Indonesia. Once again, she looked happy because her words and her thoughts were translated into music right away. The lyrics of the song helped connect her to her deepest memories.

As I got to know her, I saw that Vonnie still had a good memory. Each week I came and visited her, she remembered me clearly. Without hesitation she came with me. After a few weeks, I asked her if I could see her room. By doing this I hoped to find out even more about her. Vonnie was more than happy to show me her room, her pictures and her belongings. I saw a very nice painting hanging on the wall, picturing the sawas, or Indonesian rice-fields. There were mountains in the background and a volcano, tropical trees and working people. This was the same kind of painting that hung on my parent's and grandparent's walls. I also felt at home, looking at the painting. I asked her what she felt when she looked at the picture. She started crying, telling me that she longs to see her homeland again. But she recognized that she cannot anymore, as she is too sick for that. I encouraged her to keep her memories alive by talking and singing about her time there and by listening to music that takes her back. I let her know that this was exactly the reason I came to see her. She was very happy.

We looked at a lot of pictures from her family. She talked about everybody in the pictures. In the meantime, I kept strumming the ukulele or playing one of the bamboo percussion instruments. By doing so, I gave sound to her story right there in the moment. This was good for her self-confidence, and it also gave her the feeling that she was understood. After awhile, I noticed that she stopped talking, and that she was looking at me to see what I was doing. I gave her some instruments, too, and placed the ukulele in her hands. At first she started copying me, doing what I did. I challenged her to reproduce these sounds, and after she felt safe enough (which I could tell by the way she was playing), I gave her space to fill in sounds so she really felt listened to. After a while, we were engaged in a non-verbal conversation, in which I gave Vonnie all the time and space she needed to express herself musically. From this session onward, we had a lot of non-verbal, instrumental conversations like this one, each with its own character and emotional focus.

Keeping her music therapy goals in mind, I worked on several of her problems each session. One of the most important goals I addressed was Vonnie's sense of self. By recognizing her own feelings in the sound and lyrics, I sensed she felt understood. The lyrics helped her to express herself again more easily, in her native language. It seemed to me that through the music offered to her, Vonnie found herself accepted and recognized. At first she continued to think that people were stealing her belongings, but I found out from the nursing staff that this topic was not a big issue anymore. Now that she had found herself, a lot of her earlier problems no longer seemed an issue.

I kept bringing musical instruments from the East to each session, and I invited her to play along. She was initially shy, but I let her know that it was okay, and after awhile, she started playing right away, without me having to ask her to play along. In the meantime, we still sang songs from her youth. She still remembered every word of these songs, which gave her a positive and strong sense of self. After each song, I asked her what she was thinking and what the songs meant to her. Despite her decline, Vonnie couldn't stop talking about the first 30 years of her life!

The Japanese Occupation of Indonesia

After six sessions, in which I had focused primarily on positive memories, I tried to access more difficult experiences, such as the Japanese occupation of Indonesia. I knew Vonnie's background, so I could imagine what she must have been through. I didn't ask her directly about her feelings or memories, but introduced a song and told her about the story behind it. It was an old Dutch tune titled *"Zonnetje gaat van ons scheiden"* (*"The sun is saying goodbye for the day"*). This song was sung in the Japanese concentration camps by the women and children before they went to sleep. The song was about the sun that says goodbye to us all every night. The sun was symbolic for the rising sun in the Japanese flag. For them, this particular song was also a song of hope, because one day the red Japanese sun (and thus the Japanese soldiers) would also say goodbye to them. After telling her this little story behind the song, I asked her about her own memories during Japanese imprisonment.

Vonnie had been in a women's camp during the Japanese occupation. As with many of the (young) women, she was used as a "comfort woman" to entertain the Japanese soldiers. She was very ashamed to tell me this. I just responded by telling her that I understood what she had been through and that I heard what she was saying beyond the spoken words. Soft traditional music was playing in the background, and I was holding her hands while she talked and cried. After this long session, I sensed that Vonnie felt very much accepted and understood, but most important, she felt relieved.

The Past Lives with the Present

After this important session, I found out that Vonnie didn't feel ashamed talking about sex any longer. On the contrary, she couldn't stop talking about it! It was as if she was finally able to talk about something she had never been able to before. Back in her youth, sexuality was a topic that you just did not talk about. She told me that she now had a boyfriend living in the same nursing home. She told me that she did have sex with him, even though they were both rather old. I was not sure if this was true, but these conversations added a level of intimacy to our work that allowed her to be even more expressive, giving her the feeling that she could talk to me about everything, no matter what the subject was. I also made sure that the talking part of each session didn't take all our time, so after awhile, I started making music and invited her to play or sing along with me.

Talking about her boyfriend naturally led to a discussion of Vonnie's deceased husband. Although her husband died ten years ago, she still missed him a great deal. Vonnie told me about how they met and of their youth together back in Indonesia. She lovingly spoke about her marriage and of the many things she and her husband did together. Once again, traditional music showed its power within the therapeutic process. While reminiscing, I played songs from her youth. We listened to music that she and her husband danced to; music that was popular in those days. It was as if more and more memories emerged as we listened to the music together. I also brought along a lot of picture books from Indonesia, and memorabilia, to help ground and enrich these experiences.

As we continued working together, I discovered that Vonnie sometimes felt frustrated because she didn't know all the words to the different songs we sang. She even got angry at herself, which of course was not good. I assured her that it was quite all right not to remember all the lyrics by heart anymore. I told her that it was not important what words were sung, as long as the feeling and meaning of the song was expressed. From that moment on, I decided to start improvising the lyrics. I continued to use the original lyrics but also added lyrics about recent events, the weather, the nursing home, the food and her boyfriend. I also improvised about her past and stories from her youth. I challenged her to do the same, assuring her that anything she wanted to sing about was possible. I also told her that it didn't matter how she sounded, since we were the only two people who heard it!

After a few sessions getting used to this "new" method, I was surprised to see that Vonnie was actually getting better at improvising lyrics. She even started to sing about things that happened in her youth, during the Japanese occupation. Things that she had never spoken about before became songs, the lyrics developing spontaneously and creatively. Vonnie told me how much release she found in singing about her past.

Over time, Vonnie showed very good improvement in her social behavior. Every time I went to pick her up, she was sitting next to the other ladies and taking part in their conversations. She didn't seem to exclude herself any longer. The occupational therapist told me that on many occasions, Vonnie told her about her youth in Indonesia. Every time she saw me, she told the other ladies how much she enjoyed her music therapy sessions. I sometimes found her sitting at a table showing the other ladies a picture book of Indonesia.

Another Ending

After three months of work together, I had to talk to Vonnie about an upcoming ending. I told her that in a couple of weeks I wouldn't be able to visit her any longer. I told her that I was going on a long trip, and that afterward I wouldn't be working in her nursing home any more. Of course, at first she was sad to hear this, but I told her that I was so happy that she had made new friends; after all, she was no longer alone. She nodded her head and told me that she was happy about this as well.

In our last four sessions we talked about farewells. Vonnie seemed to deal with this in a very positive way. She knew that this was a goodbye, but that it didn't have to be a definitive one like moving from Indonesia for good, or losing her husband. I thought carefully about a farewell present for her — since my trip was going to be to Indonesia, I promised to bring back the ground that she was born on. I passed the little village where she was born and dug a spoonful of dirt from the ground. I brought it home with me, and after my return, I put it in a delicate silk sack. When I visited Vonnie for the last time, I give her this small present. She was very moved, not only because of its symbolism, but also because somebody had gone to the trouble of doing this especially for her.

SUMMARY

Vonnie's story is typical of many nursing home residents who were born in one country and had to move to another country because of reasons beyond their control. At a young age, people have fewer problems adjusting to their new life, to their new home. However, when they get older, and especially when they develop dementia, they have increasing difficulties adapting to their environment.

With an aging population worldwide, dementia and other age-related illnesses are increasing in prevalence. In each nursing home population, an increasing number of residents are non-native with respect to their country of residence. The current situation of worldwide migration is raising new demands for the future care provided for elderly people with dementia. How best can the needs of these patients be met through music therapy, in particular those who are migrants?

A multicultural practice asks for a devotion and willingness to explore alternative ways of being together in order to discover the client's world. It was through music that Vonnie's world opened to her, and in so doing, she was able to find a way of being in contact with the people around her, even though her own cultural background differed so greatly from those she lived with.

REFERENCES

Bright, R. (1982). *Music in Geriatric Care*. New York: Musicgrphics.

Broersen, M., de Groot, R. & Jonker, C. (1995). Muziektherapie bij Alzheimer Patienten. Enkele richtlijnen op basis van de literatuur. *Tijdschrift voor Kreatieve Therapie*, 14(1), 9–14.

Brotons, M. (2000) An overview of the music therapy literature relating to elderly people. In: Aldridge D. (Ed.), *Music Therapy in Dementia Care*. (pp. 33–62). London: Jessica Kingsley Publishers..

Brown, J. M. (2002). Towards a culturally centered music therapy practice. In C. Kenny and B. Stige (Eds.), *Contemporary Voices in Music Therapy* (pp. 83–94) Oslo: Unipub forlag.

Bruggen-Rufi, C. H. M. van (2008). Thuis west, oost best: Geïndividualiseerde, cultuurgerichte muziektherapie bij Indisch Nederlandse ouderen. *Tijdschrift voor Vaktherapie*, 2, 9–15.

Bruggen-Rufi, C. H. M. van (2006). Thuis west, oost best: geïndividualiseerde, cultuurgerichte muziektherapie bij Indisch Nederlandse ouderen. Unpublished Dissertation, Conservatory Enschede, Saxion Hogeschool, The Netherlands.

Ferri, C. P, Prince, M., Brayne, C., Brodaty, H., Fratiglioni, L., Ganguli, M., Hall, K., Hasegawa, K., Hendrie, H., Huang, Y., Jorm, A., Mathers, C., Menezes, P.R., Rimmer, E. & Scazufca, M. (2005).

Global prevalence of dementia: A Delphi consensus study. *The Lancet*, 366, 9503, 2112–2117.
Gerdner, L. A. (1997). An individualized music intervention for agitation. *Journal of the American Psychiatric Nurses Association*, 3(6), 177–184.
Gerdner, L. A. (2000). Effects of individualized versus classical "relaxation" music on the frequency of agitation in elderly persons with Alzheimer's disease and related disorders. *International Psychogeriatrics,* 12(1), 49–65.
Kenny, C. & Stige, B. (Eds.) (2002). *Contemporary Voices in Music Therapy.* Oslo: Unipub forlag.
Paradis, M. (2008). Bilingualism and neuropsychiatric disorders. *Journal of Neurolinguistics*, 21(3), 199–230.
Poismans, K. (2005). *De Muziek Werk Wijzer.* The Netherlands: ViaMuziek.
United Nations (1999). *The World at Six Billion.* http://www.un.org/esa/population/publications/sixbillion/sixbilpart1.pdf.
Ruud, E. (1998). *Music Therapy: Improvisation, Communication and Culture.* Gilsum, NH: Barcelona Publishers.
United Nations Department of Economic and Social Affairs: Population Division (2009). *Trends in International Migrant Stock: The 2008 Revision.* United Nations database, POP/DB/MIG/Stock/Rev.2008.
Vink, A. C. (2000) The problem of agitation in elderly people and the potential benefit of music therapy. In D. Aldridge (Ed.) *Music Therapy in Dementia Care* (pp. 102–18). London: Jessica Kingsley Publishers.
World Health Organization (2008) *Health, history and hard choices* http://www.who.int.

Chapter Thirty Four

SONGS OF FAITH IN END OF LIFE CARE

Russell Hilliard and Jenna Justice

INTRODUCTION

For those living with an advanced illness and a prognosis of six months or less, hospice care is often utilized for pain and symptom management (Ripamonti, 2005). Under hospice care, patients elect to forego aggressive curative treatment and opt for palliative medicine, also known as comfort care (Connor, 2009). The primary goal of this type of care is to enhance quality of life in a holistic manner (Fine, 2008). To accomplish this, hospice employs a variety of professionals to assist the patient and family. This interdisciplinary group includes physicians, nurses, nurse aides, social workers, chaplains, volunteers, bereavement counselors and adjunctive therapies (including music therapy). Hospice care can be provided in hospitals, long term care settings, private homes and in-patient hospice units (Stoddard, 1992).

Since 1995, the hospice industry has seen a dramatic increased utilization of music therapy in end of life care (Hilliard, 2005a). In part, this is due to the growth of hospice and the need for agencies to offer innovative services that set them apart within the market place. Hospice administrators have used music therapy programs within their marketing of the agency to increase the hospice census and encourage referral partners to use one agency over another, arguing that offering music therapy demonstrates the agency's commitment to quality end of life care (Hilliard, 2001, 2005a). This growth is also due to an emerging body of evidence supporting music therapy in end of life care. There are now at least seven empirical research studies in the literature that show significant differences in variables such as mood and pain, anxiety, dyspnea, comfort, relaxation, quality of life and spirituality with the treatment of music therapy in end of life care (Hilliard, 2005b). Because music therapy enhances the quality of clinical care and also provides support from a business perspective for the hospice agency, it is likely that music therapy will continue to blossom throughout the end of life care continuum.

This chapter provides a foundational framework for the utilization of music therapy in end of life care and offers a case study demonstrating the benefits of music therapy for this population. A theoretical orientation of cognitive behavioral music therapy combined with a humanistic approach are presented, and the case study provides an example of assessment, treatment planning and the achievement of therapeutic goals.

FOUNDATIONAL CONCEPTS

There are a variety of theoretical orientations guiding the practice of music therapy in patient care, and this diversity is what enriches the field and its clinicians. While some music therapists hold true to one or more theoretical orientations, others describe themselves as eclectic, pulling from multiple theories to meet patient needs (Hilliard, 2005a). Whatever the theoretical foundation of the clinician, hospice care requires therapists to uphold ethical standards interpreted by the industry to include:

- Patients' rights to autonomy. Hospice workers respect the self-determination of the patient, even though the worker may not agree with the decision.
- The experience is whatever the patient says it is. This relates to all experiences, the most prevalent of which is pain.
- Upholding non-malfeasance, the hospice worker is guided to 'do no harm' and consistently guides treatment based on the patient and family's value systems.
- The hospice worker is benevolent, always seeking to 'do good' for the patient and family.
- Hospice patients and families are richly diverse, and the hospice worker remains non-judgmental, forever seeking to understand and respect patients' beliefs, lifestyles, values, cultures and religious/spiritual practices (Hilliard, 2005a).

While the aforementioned can be descriptive of many therapeutic relationships, it is vitally important in end of life care. Most practitioners recognize the dying process as one that is entirely unique for each individual and that the grieving process is unique among and between family members. Additionally, the average length of time patients utilize hospice services varies greatly from a few days to months. Depending on the community and hospice agency, the average length of stay for a hospice patient may only be 45 days (Connor et al., 2007). Given this brief period of time to provide treatment within a therapeutic relationship, goals of care must be clearly defined.

Given that the hospice philosophy is so greatly patient centered and provides for a relatively short period of time for the provision of care, we have found cognitive behavioral music therapy (Hilliard, 2005a), combined with humanistic or person-centered therapy (Hilliard, 2005a), to be highly effective as a theoretical approach for music therapy in end of life care. This type of treatment has been tested in the literature, and the data support its use in enhancing quality of life for people diagnosed with terminal cancer in an in-home hospice program (Hilliard, 2003).

Cognitive Behavioral Therapy (CBT) was developed primarily through a merging of cognitive and behavior therapies (Simos, 2002). The common ground between the two theoretical orientations of treatment is the alleviation of symptoms and the focus on the "here and now" (Rachman, 1997). CBT evaluates how thoughts, actions and feelings work together to affect one's mood, mental health, ability to adjust, among other specific mental health needs or disorders. Specifically, CBT evaluates the patient's inner dialogue (thoughts expressed through one's inner voice), behaviors engaged that are guided by the inner dialogue or shape the inner dialogue and the emotions experienced within the thought-behavior-emotion paradigm. Because of the body of evidence supporting its efficacy in treatment, CBT has become the psychotherapy treatment of choice for mood disturbances such as anxiety and depression, sleep disturbances such as insomnia, and other mental health needs (Gould et al., 1997; Gosselin et al., 1996; Keller et al., 2000; Siversten et al., 2006). In addition to adult clients, children and adolescents respond successfully to CBT treatment for depressive disorders, anxiety and post traumatic stress disorder, among others (Kendall, 2005).

Humanistic therapies challenge the therapist to relate "as one human being to another with utter concentration and utter sincerity" (Fromm, 1964 p. 184). Client-centered therapy (also referred to as person-centered therapy), founded by Carl Rogers (1961), holds at its core the belief that each person has a natural tendency to strive to make the very best of his or her experiences. This innate motivation Rogers called *the actualizing tendency* (Rogers, 1961). Among the things we value as humans are love, affection, attention, connection, nurturance — Rogers labels these things as *positive regard* (Rogers, 1961). In the therapeutic relationship, it is important for the therapist to provide unconditional positive regard for the client and the client's situation. The following are what Rogers (1961) considers essential for success in the therapeutic relationship:

- Congruence: the therapist displays a genuine sense of care and concern and remains honest with the client.
- Empathy: the ability of the therapist to convey that the client's experiences are heard and understood through validation and reflection.
- Respect: total acceptance conveyed by the therapist for the experiences of the client.

The concepts inherent in client-centered therapy pair well with the general practices of hospice care providers. Within the end of life care community of practitioners, the concept of "meeting the patient where the patient is" parallels Roger's approach of empathy and unconditional positive regard. Respect from a Rogerian perspective is akin to the recognition of non-judgment by the hospice worker. Understanding that the patient and family are the true experts in their own care is similar to Roger's understanding of the actualizing tendency.

Combining CBT for its utilization in treating symptoms in short-term therapy with person-centered therapy for its use in providing unconditional positive regard is the basis of Cognitive Behavioral Music Therapy in hospice care. Within Cognitive Behavioral Music Therapy (CBxMT), the therapist strives to alleviate symptoms in end of life care such as anxiety, depression and insomnia in the briefest amount of time. The concept of time is of great importance at the end of life, as patients seek to optimize quality of life by alleviating symptoms to enjoy the remaining precious moments they have with their loved ones. Further, the therapist strives to provide empathy, congruence and respect while treating these symptoms, leaving the patient with a sense of validation for his or her own personal meaningfulness. Within this approach, the relationship between the therapist and patient is significantly important. Often times, patients will come to call members of the hospice team "family" because of the depth of relationship that is built during this intimate time of life. The role of the music is to treat symptoms while simultaneously affording opportunities for deeper human connectedness or communion with the patient's higher power. What follows is a case study describing how CBxMT meets the multidimensional needs of a patient diagnosed with a life-limiting illness, highlighting the central elements of this approach.

THE CLIENT

David was a 62-year-old man with a diagnosis of head and neck cancer. At the time of the music therapy assessment, David had been receiving hospice care in his home for less than one month and was receiving additional agency services from the hospice physician, registered nurse, chaplain and social worker. His physical symptoms included a visible growth on his neck (roughly the size of a golf ball), compromised speaking abilities resulting in a whispered tone, pain, productive cough of both phlegm and blood and occasional dyspnea (shortness of breath). Throughout his treatment and hospice care, David refused all medications, utilizing instead diet, prayer and vitamin supplements to combat his symptoms.

David had been married for 22 years, had no children, and was an active member of his church. Upon assessment, David reported that his spiritual journey was the most important task of his end-of-life experience, and that he wished to explore it further with the therapist. His wife reported that there had been significant changes in David's relationships in the year since his diagnosis, and that she had seen a softening in his personality, resulting in fewer disputes in their marriage and friendships.

Based on the music therapy assessment, the following treatment goals were developed:

1. Patient will experience increased spiritual support.
2. Patient will evidence increased quality of life.
3. Patient will report lowered pain perception.

Additional sessions with the patient resulted in the addition of the following treatment goal:

4. Patient will develop alternative communication skills.

THE THERAPEUTIC PROCESS

Sessions with the patient were held on either a weekly or bi-weekly basis. When the music therapist first met David, the patient was able to speak, although he was frequently interrupted by long bouts of coughing. As rapport was developed, David spent a great deal of time talking about his faith and his church experiences, commonly turning to Biblical scriptures to support his dialogue. His descriptions of his church experience during these early sessions were overwhelmingly positive. He spoke often of the important relationships he had developed at the church, and indicated that these relationships had been positive throughout his lifetime. He described his male friendships in particular as significant relationships and told stories indicating that these friendships had been longstanding and stable throughout the years.

As the sessions progressed, however, David began to disclose that his relationships had weathered difficult times, and that he held regrets about what he perceived to be his "overbearing" personality in these relationships, and his relationship with his wife. In separate dialogues with his wife, she confirmed this description of his personality. Through verbal counseling and musical validation, the music therapist explored the complexities of these relationships with David. At times, he was very forthcoming about his regrets and engaged in frank exploration of the difficult behavior patterns that he had exhibited in his relationships. He spoke of being "dominant," and rarely giving others' opinions credence or a full hearing. David cried occasionally during these difficult revelations and almost always embedded his stories with a scriptural reference that spoke to his search for positive and loving closure. At each session, the music therapist provided live music, accompanied either by guitar or keyboard. This music was almost exclusively spiritual in nature and was most frequently Christian choruses that directly utilized the scripture he discussed, or held the meaning of the scripture therein. David reported that this music felt "supportive" to him, and gave him a different way to think about the scriptures he had memorized. On occasion, the music therapist made recordings of David's favorite scripture choruses after the session for him to use during his private devotional times.

As David's illness progressed over the next several weeks, speaking became more difficult, and he began to write most of his dialogue to me and other visitors in small notebooks. His writings were vivid and detailed, and did not seem to indicate a desire to reduce communications, but rather simply find a different way to communicate. When asked about his stamina to continue to write, David seldom expressed a desire to limit this communication, and instead wrote more voluminously. In addition, his other physical symptoms also increased. He experienced greater and more regular pain levels. Utilizing the iso-principle (Hilliard, 2005a) of matching the dynamics and tempo of David's preferred music with his perceived pain level, the music therapist was able to assist him in decreasing his pain perception. His tumor began to rupture with increasing frequency, resulting in increased pain and blood loss. He reported significant weakness when walking and began limiting his trips outdoors.

It was during an increase in these negative symptoms that David expressed suicidal ideation to the music therapist. He wrote of having a gun, of not being afraid to use the gun, and of being tired of his body's breakdowns. When further pressed, together with his wife and one of his friends, David acknowledged that he didn't believe he had the "courage" to actually perform the suicide. He agreed to give the gun to his friend for safekeeping, to be returned to his wife after his death if she wished to have it. While David expressed some embarrassment during this intervention, he asked the music therapist to stay after the dialogue with his wife and his friend was complete. He then wrote a note expressing that he hadn't understood how profoundly discouraged he was, and how troubling his suicidal ideation had been to his wife and friends. He also wrote of his love and appreciation for his wife and friends, acknowledging that they had his best interests at heart. He was very moved by their caring, and by the music therapist's role in the intervention. At the closing of this session, the music therapist improvised a song expressing David's feelings of being cared for and deeply loved by his wife and friend.

Clinical Songwriting

As a result of this catharsis, the music therapist suggested to David that he work with the music therapist to find a way to communicate to his wife and friends the depth of his feelings for them, and for the roles that they have played in his life. Further counseling led David to believe that this process would also allow him to rebuild any broken parts of his relationships, and to allow him to leave a "legacy" that was more powerful than any negativity he had displayed in his friendships up to that point. He spoke of how unexpected it was to have so many male friends in his life now, when he had never had male friends throughout his life. He reported that this brought him an enormous amount of joy.

Together, the music therapist and David created a list of six friends to whom David wished to write songs. In addition to this list, he wished to write a song for his wife and a song for his church family expressing his fervent spiritual experience and hope that others may experience God as he had. For each friend, David discussed two things: 1) how that friend had impacted him, and 2) the most important thing David wanted to tell the friend. Each song had a heavily spiritual overtone, as this was David's request. His overall intent was to communicate how he wanted his life to be remembered. The themes that emerged during these discussions, subsequently painted in the songs, were:

Friend A:
    1. You were the first male in my life to say "I love you" to me.
    2. Thank you for being the one friend who called me every day of my illness.
Friend B:
    1. You led me to Jesus.
    2. We are about to meet and celebrate in eternity. (Friend had predeceased David.)
Friend C:
    1. You are a soldier for God.
    2. You taught me to be a Christian warrior.
Friend D:
    1. Your difficult times are in God's hands.
    2. You will never be alone.
Friend E:

1. You have taught me a love of nature.
   2. Thank you for being my oldest friend.
Friend F:
   1. Laughing with you has been so important to me.
   2. Though we will meet in eternity, I feel like I will miss you terribly.
Wife:
   1. Our love is a gift from God.
   2. His comfort will surround you after I am gone.
Church:
   1. You have been my family.
   2. This is my vision of heaven.

The music therapist and David spoke at length about each individual person. David discussed the difficult parts of his relationship with each, and explored not only what he wanted to "leave" for them, but also what he believed his relationship to be with them now. These were intense dialogues, utilizing a great deal of musical validation for his experiences. This musical validation was provided in the form of hymns and spiritual songs that the music therapist performed live with guitar or keyboard accompaniment. She used songbooks and lyric sheets so that David would be able to follow the lyrics as she sang. They would analyze the lyrics, drawing parallels between the messages of the songs and his own experiences and emotions. During these emotionally intense discussions, the music therapist also used music as a specific relaxation tool to combat any coughing bouts that he experienced in these sessions.

After discussing each relationship, the music therapist asked that David provide characteristics of the person for whom the song was written, and together they translated these characteristics into musical elements that would be part of the songs. For example, one song had an Irish lilt, honoring his friend's Irish heritage and love for Celtic music. Another song was written as a military march, reflecting his friend's stoicism and military countenance. The song for David's wife was written as a love song/ballad.

Upon completion of each song, the music therapist recorded the final product onto a digital minidisk recorder and burned it onto a CD. David took the lyrics for each song and put them into a document that he then printed and framed. Two of the six men were invited individually to the patient's home, where he asked the music therapist to perform his song for his friend, then proceeded to tell the friend the impetus for the song. These were heavy, tearful and powerful sessions. David reported to the music therapist that the experience was exactly what he had hoped it would be.

Some three months after they began working together, David died in his home, surrounded by his wife and friends. His wife reported that he experienced some shortness of breath as he began to weaken, but that he appeared comfortable until the end. She also spoke of his use of the recordings that had been made during his music therapy sessions, both the individual songs as well as the relaxation music that had been recorded for him, to combat any restlessness or pain during his last two days.

Legacy

After David's death, his wife asked the music therapist to sing at David's funeral. The music therapist provided the hymn that David had requested most frequently during his music therapy sessions, and then the song that he had written for his church, which described what he believed heaven was going to be like. At the reception after the service, his wife had placed all eight of David's framed songs on a table for his friends to share, and made copies of the CDs to give to each one, including the wife of the friend who had predeceased David.

CONCLUSION

Within the CBxMT theoretical framework, the music therapist provided an atmosphere of unconditional positive regard. Through this, the patient was able to express aspects of his personality that led to relationship issues he wanted to review as he approached the end of his life. The therapist's approach of congruence, empathy and respect fostered a relationship that afforded the patient an opportunity to review his life in a way that encouraged him to deepen relationships with those whom he loved. This positive regard for David allowed him to be vulnerable with the music therapist and admit his own "domineering" personality, share his spiritual beliefs, and even disclose at one point that he was experiencing suicidal ideation. Through Cognitive Behavioral Music Therapy techniques, the therapist was able to meet a variety of short-term therapeutic goals (such as pain and symptom management) with a variety of music therapy interventions. Table 1 provides a summary of these goals, along with the corresponding intervention.

Table 1: Goals Addressed and CBxMT Interventions Utilized

Goals Addressed	CBxMT Interventions
Develop therapeutic rapport; provide a sense of unconditional positive regard	Sing patient-preferred music; offer song choice; validation of song choice/music selection
Review life experiences; express emotions surrounding shared life experiences	Provide spiritual music for support and validation of meaning
Experience a sense of relationship closure	Provide song-writing opportunities
Engage in alternative communication means once verbalization was not possible due to advance disease progression	Provide alternative communication devices (e.g., notebook for writing); provide opportunities for self expression through song choices
Decrease pain perception	Iso-principle paired with patient-preferred music
Decrease suicidal ideation and gain a sense of supportive love from others	Contract with patient to maintain safety by foregoing the weapon; improvised music and lyrics about the love expressed to patient by his wife and friend
Communicate with the the patient's loved ones about his feelings for them and leave a legacy gift	Clinical songwriting; recording of songs for others to share
Bereavement support for patient's wife and friends	Singing of patient-selected songs at patient's funeral; dispersement of legacy gifts to family and friends

Quality of life is an all-encompassing concept in end of life care that includes social, emotional, physical and spiritual needs. Music therapy is highly beneficial in holistically treating the patient and his or her family, and is therefore a natural choice as a treatment option for enhancing quality of life throughout the dying process. Utilizing CBxMT techniques, the music therapist can address behaviors, physical symptoms, thoughts, emotions and relationships within a relatively brief therapeutic time. Because hospice care, by nature of its end of life treatment, is often brief in nature, CBxMT can be regarded as a viable treatment for those facing multifaceted needs at the end of life.

REFERENCES

Connor, S.R. (2009). *Hospice and Palliative Care: The Essential Guide.* New York: Routledge.

Connor, S.R., Pyenson, B., Fitch, K., Spence, C. & Iwasaki, K. (2007). Comparing hospice and non-hospice patient survival among patients who die within a three year window. *Journal of Pain and Symptom Management,* 33(3), 238–46.

Feist, J. (1990). *Theories of Personality (2nd edition).* Fort Worth: Holt, Rinehart and Winston, Inc.

Fine, P.G. (2008). *The Hospice Companion.* Oxford: Oxford University Press.

Gosselin, P., Ladouceur, R., Morin, C. M., Dugas, M. J. & Gaillargeon, L. (2006). Benzodiazepine discontinuation among adults with GAD: A randomized clinical trial of cognitive-behavioral therapy. *Journal of Consulting Clinical Psychology,* 74(5), 908–919.

Gould, R. A., Ottow, M. W., Pollack, M. H. & Yap, L. (1997). Cognitive behavioral and pharmacological treatment of generalized anxiety disorder: A preliminary meta-analysis. *Behavior Therapy,* 28(2), 285–305.

Hilliard, R. E. (2003). The effects of music therapy on the quality and length of life of people diagnosed with terminal cancer. *Journal of Music Therapy,* 40(2), 113–137.

Hilliard, R. E. (2005a). *Hospice and Palliative Care Music Therapy: A Guide to Program Development and Clinical Care.* Cherry Hill, NJ: Jeffrey Books.

Hilliard, R. E. (2005b). Music therapy in hospice and palliative care: A review of the empirical data. *Evidence-Based Complementary and Alternative Medicine*, 2(2), 173–178.

Keller, M.B., McCullough, J.P. & Klein, D.N. (2000). A comparison of nefazodone, the cognitive-behavioral analysis system of psychotherapy, and their combination in the treatment of chronic depression. *New England Journal of Medicine,* 342(20), 1462–1470.

Kendall, P.C. (2005). *Child and Adolescent Therapy: Cognitive Behavioral Procedures (3rd edition)*. New York: Guilford Press.

Rachman, S. (1997). The evolution of cognitive behavior therapy. In D. Clark, C. Fairburn and M. Gelder (Eds.) *Science and Practice of Cognitive Behavior Therapy.* Oxford: Oxford University Press.

Ripamonti,C. (2005). Prognostic factors in advance cancer patients: evidence-based clinical recommendations. *Journal of Clinical Oncology*, 23, 6240–48.

Rogers, C. (1961). *On Becoming a Person: A Therapist's View of Psycho-therapy.* London: Constable.

Simos, G. (Ed.) (2002). *Cognitive Behaviour Therapy.* Hove: Brunner-Routledge.